OXFORD WORLD'S CLASSICS

THE ESSENTIAL VICTOR HUGO

VICTOR HUGO was born in Besançon in 1802, the youngest of three sons of an officer (eventually a general), who took his family with him from posting to posting, as far as Italy and Spain. Victor's prolific literary career began with publication of poems (1822), a novel (1823), and a drama, *Cromwell* (1827), the preface of which remains a major manifesto of French Romanticism. The riot occasioned at the first performance of his drama *Hernani* (1830) established him as a leading figure among the Romantics, and *Notre-Dame* (1831) added to his prestige at home and abroad. Favoured by Louis-Philippe (1830–48), he chose exile rather than live under Napoleon III. In exile in Brussels (1851), Jersey (1853), and Guernsey (1855) he published some of his finest works, notably the satirical poems *Les Châtiments* (1853), the lyrical poems *Les Contemplations* (1856), the first series of epic poems *La Légende des siècles* (1859), and the lengthy novel *Les Misérables* (1862). Only with Napoleon III's defeat and replacement by the Third Republic did Hugo return, to be elected deputy, and later senator. His opposition to tyranny and continuing immense literary output established him as a national hero. When he died in 1885 he was honoured by interment in the Panthéon.

E. H. BLACKMORE and A. M. BLACKMORE are freelance writers and translators. Their previous Hugo translations have appeared in *Six French Poets of the Nineteenth Century* (Oxford World's Classics), *Selected Poems of Victor Hugo* (winner of the American Literary Translators' Association Prize and the Modern Language Association Scaglione Prize for Literary Translation), *The Major Epics of Victor Hugo*, and *Contemplations, Lyrics, and Dramatic Monologues by Victor Hugo*. They are currently preparing a bilingual edition of the poems of Stéphane Mallarmé for Oxford World's Classics.

OXFORD WORLD'S CLASSICS

For over 100 years Oxford World's Classics have brought readers closer to the world's great literature. Now with over 700 titles—from the 4,000-year-old myths of Mesopotamia to the twentieth century's greatest novels—the series makes available lesser-known as well as celebrated writing.

The pocket-sized hardbacks of the early years contained introductions by Virginia Woolf, T. S. Eliot, Graham Greene, and other literary figures which enriched the experience of reading. Today the series is recognized for its fine scholarship and reliability in texts that span world literature, drama and poetry, religion, philosophy and politics. Each edition includes perceptive commentary and essential background information to meet the changing needs of readers.

OXFORD WORLD'S CLASSICS

═

The Essential Victor Hugo

═

New translations with an Introduction and Notes by
E. H. *and* A. M. BLACKMORE

OXFORD
UNIVERSITY PRESS

OXFORD
UNIVERSITY PRESS

Great Clarendon Street, Oxford OX2 6DP

Oxford University Press is a department of the University of Oxford.
It furthers the University's objective of excellence in research, scholarship,
and education by publishing worldwide in

Oxford New York

Auckland Bangkok Buenos Aires Cape Town Chennai
Dar es Salaam Delhi Hong Kong Istanbul Karachi Kolkata
Kuala Lumpur Madrid Melbourne Mexico City Mumbai Nairobi
São Paulo Shanghai Taipei Tokyo Toronto

Oxford is a registered trade mark of Oxford University Press
in the UK and in certain other countries

Published in the United States
by Oxford University Press Inc., New York

British Library Cataloguing in Publication Data

Data available

Library of Congress Cataloging in Publication Data

Data available

ISBN 0–19–280363–8

1

Typeset in Ehrhardt
by RefineCatch Limited, Bungay, Suffolk
Printed in Great Britain by
Clays Ltd, St Ives plc

CONTENTS

AFTER THE EXILE I: 1870–1878

AFTER THE EXILE II: 1878–1885

INTRODUCTION

Victor-Marie Hugo was born in 1802, at Besançon, and died in 1885. During an active literary career that spanned more than sixty years, he wrote prolifically in an unparalleled variety of genres: lyrics, satires, epics, philosophical poems, epigrams, novels, history books, critical essays, travel writings, political speeches, funeral orations, diaries, letters public and private, and dramas in verse and prose.

When, late in his career, he gathered his occasional prose writings under the title *Deeds and Words* (1875–6), he divided the work into three sections: 'Before the Exile', 'During the Exile', and 'After the Exile'. The 'Exile' had been the most conspicuous public event in his eventful life. On 2 December 1851, the President of the French Republic, Louis-Napoléon Bonaparte, seized absolute power in a *coup d'état*. According to the new government's own statistics, 380 people (many of them uninvolved civilians) were killed; 26,642 were imprisoned, and 9,769 of those were deported to the notorious penal colonies in Algeria and French Guiana. Hugo, who had been one of Louis-Napoléon's most outspoken opponents, escaped into exile, first in Belgium, and then on the Channel Islands, where he remained for almost twenty years, vowing never to return to France as long as the dictator remained in power. Eventually, in September 1870, Louis-Napoléon (now the Emperor Napoléon III) was forced to abdicate as a result of France's disastrous defeat during the Franco-Prussian War; and Hugo returned to Paris in triumph.

Other, less conspicuous, upheavals also left their mark on his literary career. On 4 September 1843 his 19-year-old daughter Léopoldine drowned in a boating accident. Her unexpected death shattered him emotionally, in a way that no other experience of his long life did. In some respects he never fully recovered from it. For months he wrote almost nothing of any kind; for nearly three years he wrote no significant verse. More than thirty years later, he was still addressing the dead girl's spirit in his private diaries. And when he published his major collection of lyrical poems— *Contemplations* (1856), a kind of fictionalized diary in verse—he divided the work into two major sections, with the loss of Léopoldine at its midpoint.

Of his other life experiences, the one that most radically affected his literary output was the severe cerebrovascular stroke he suffered on 28 June 1878. His extraordinary productivity had already been waning with age; now the torrent of prose and verse virtually dried up, and during the remaining seven years of his life he wrote little.

Thus the material in the present volume is arranged in five unequal sections, separated by the death of Léopoldine in September 1843, the flight into exile in December 1851, the return from exile in September 1870, and the stroke in June 1878.

Before the Exile I: 1824–1843

Like most writers, Hugo began by imitating his predecessors; and his choice of models was significant. Some of the epigraphs to his first volume of *Odes* were drawn from the Scriptures and the Classics, especially Virgil: nothing unusual there. But the book contained almost no epigraphs from mainstream seventeenth- or eighteenth-century French literature; no Racine, for instance, and no Voltaire. Instead, there were passages from Schiller, as translated in Madame de Staël's influential eulogy of the new German Romanticism, *De l'Allemagne* (1810); from André Chénier, whose poetry broke some of the seventeenth-century rules, and whose first collected edition (posthumously published in 1819) had something of the impact in France that Gerard Manley Hopkins's had in England a century later; and from Shakespeare's *A Midsummer Night's Dream*, a work that appealed to the young French poet not only because of its adventurous and colourful imagery, but also because of its use of 'low', ignoble language (several decades later, Hugo was still relishing the fact that Shakespeare had dared to call a character 'Bottom'). The *Odes* also quoted (and addressed) the prose writer Chateaubriand, who in the early 1820s was at the height of his influence. French prose had never been as rulebound as French verse, and Chateaubriand's style was notable for a vividness, colour, and passion that went far beyond anything to be found in the poets of his generation.

In those days a writer who admired Shakespeare, Schiller, Chénier, and Chateaubriand was likely to find himself branded a

'Romantic'. Hugo tried to keep clear of partisan distinctions as long as he could. 'Today', he wrote in the preface to *New Odes* (1824), 'there are two parties in literature, just as there are in politics, and apparently the poetic war has to be no less furious and frenzied than the social one. The two camps seem keener to fight than to reach an agreement.' And he himself proposed to 'repudiate all the stock terms that these parties are hurling back and forth at each other like empty balloons—signs that signify nothing, expressions that express nothing, imprecise words that anyone can define to suit his own hatreds and prejudices'. He himself, he declared, was utterly unable to understand the alleged distinction between 'Classical' and 'Romantic' literatures. If 'Classic' was a term of praise, wasn't Shakespeare as much a Classic as Racine?

As that passage shows, he was hoping to reach a similar compromise in politics. His mother had been a committed opponent of Napoleon (indeed, she actively assisted an abortive conspiracy to overthrow him), and under her influence the young Victor Hugo had grown up as a staunch political traditionalist, a supporter of the Bourbon monarchy and a foe to the ideals of the Revolution and the Napoleonic era. But during the 1820s he became increasingly conscious that no political party had a monopoly of virtue—or of its opposite. So a poem like 'The Song of the Circus' seems to cut both ways. It can be seen as a protest against the cruelties of the late dictator; but it can be seen as a protest against the cruelties of other autocratic rulers too. If Napoleon had points of resemblance with the ancient Roman emperors, so did the Bourbon monarchs who replaced him.

In both literature and politics, however, the attempted compromise was too precarious to last. A couple of years later, in the preface to his play *Cromwell*, the 23-year-old Hugo reluctantly accepted the label that could not be detached, and identified himself with the Romantic movement. There was no longer any question of finding some middle ground between Shakespeare and Racine. Classical notions of decorum were definitively abandoned; instead, Hugo deliberately sought out subjects that would have seemed bizarre, grotesque, or tasteless in the age of Louis XIV, and he portrayed them in linguistically flamboyant, highly coloured verse that drew its imagery from the mundane and the exotic alike ('To a Traveller', written in 1826; 'Zara Bathing', written in 1828). His admirers could point to his virtuosity, his inventiveness, his sheer productivity, and his mastery of different literary genres: major works of poetry (*Orientalia*, 1829; *Autumn Leaves*, 1831), fiction (*The Last Day of a Condemned Man*, 1829; *Notre-Dame de Paris*, 1831), and drama (*Hernani*, 1830) were appearing in rapid succession. His detractors generally acknowledged the gifts but considered that they were grossly misapplied. At the first performance of *Hernani*, on 25 February 1830, there was something like a pitched battle between supporters and opponents. It may be said that the battle has never stopped. One recent critic describes Hugo, without qualification or reservation, as 'France's greatest writer'; another calls him 'a monstrous aberration in literary history'. His biographers, similarly, may be divided into Boswellian hagiolators of a humanitarian hero and Stracheyite debunkers of an Eminent Victorian. No one has yet managed to synthesize these antagonistic positions; indeed, both the eulogists and the vilifiers are arguably truer to the spirit of Hugo's work than anyone holding an intermediate position could be. His poems, plays, and novels were written to provoke extreme reactions; any sensitive account of them will register that fact.

In politics, too, Hugo became an extremist. He drifted further and further to the left, yet remained independent of any party. He welcomed the 1830 revolution that replaced an absolute monarchy with a constitutional one, and the 1848 revolution that replaced a constitutional monarchy with a republic. He denounced such institutions as slavery, capital punishment, prostitution, political censorship, and, more generally, the exploitation of any cultural group by any other: the poor by the rich, women by men, children by adults, Africans by Europeans. His religious views were equally independent. Rejecting churches and sceptics alike, he worshipped simply the God whom he saw incarnate in Jesus, the God whom he found in the writings of the prophets and apostles. During his long exile in the Channel Islands he noted the oddity of his position with relish:

To the English, I am 'shocking', 'eccentric', 'improper'. I wear my tie sloppily. I go to the corner barber for a shave—at Valladolid in the seventeenth century this would have made me seem like a Spanish grandee, on English soil in the nineteenth it makes me seem like a 'workman' (*travailleur*, the most despised person in Britain). I'm in conflict with cant;

I'm opposed to the death penalty, which isn't respectable; I say 'mister' to a lord, which is blasphemous; I'm no Catholic, no Anglican, no Lutheran, no Calvinist, no Jew, no Methodist, no Wesleyan, no Mormon; ergo, atheist. What's more, French, which is disgusting; republican, which is abominable; exiled, which is repulsive; defeated, which is infamous. To top it all off, a poet. Hence the shortage of popularity. Were it still fashionable to write of oneself in the third person, as Rousseau used to do, I'd say: 'The English have accepted Hugo in the spirit in which they rejected Byron.'[1]

By the time of *Hernani* serious problems were developing in Hugo's family life, and by the time of *Songs of the Half-Light* (1835) they were visibly affecting his work. During 1830–1 his wife had become romantically involved with his friend Sainte-Beuve (later to become famous as a literary critic); the full extent of their relationship remains unclear, but it certainly went far enough for Adèle to break off sexual relations with her husband. In the wake of this, the poet himself began a liaison with the actress Juliette Drouet, whom he met at the beginning of 1833. Nineteenth-century myth-makers glorified and aggrandized the great man's sex life (it may be said, in general, that biographers' accounts of the subject have shed more light on their own psychopathology than on Hugo's); the association with Juliette was built up into one of the great romances of history, a half-century of uninterrupted illicit passion. As usual, the truth, where it can be established, turns out to be neither as glamorous nor as scandalous as the legends. We now know that the relationship was sexual only in its earliest years; after that time Juliette was fundamentally a devoted friend and assistant rather than anything more physically intimate (her maid during the 1850s and 1860s reported that the supposed lovers hardly ever went as far as even a hug or a kiss). Moreover, as early as mid-1834 Hugo had already established a partial reconciliation with his wife. The resulting situation was rich in tensions and complications—Adèle and Juliette were not to meet for more than twenty years, though by that time they had long been living in adjacent houses—yet it must have had a fundamental stability, because it endured.

[1] Victor Hugo, *Océan*, ed. René Journet (Paris, 1989), 269–70. The word 'workman' is in English in the original.

Before the Exile II: 1843–1851

During the late 1830s a new depth and intensity became apparent in Hugo's writing; as he wrote in the preface to *Sunlight and Shadows* (1840), 'the horizon has perhaps expanded, the sky has become more azure, the tranquillity more profound'. These changes were even more noticeable in some of the poems written during 1840–3, such as 'Thérèse's Party' and 'Near Avranches' (pp. 97 and 107). But if a transformation was already occurring, the death of his daughter Léopoldine in September 1843 heightened it. On 17 November 1845 he began drafting a novel larger in scope and deeper in emotional intensity than any of its predecessors. During the second half of 1846 and 1847 he worked actively both at this novel (eventually entitled *Les Misérables*) and at a cycle of poems devoted primarily to the dead girl.

At the same time, he was becoming increasingly active in politics. In April 1845 the government of King Louis-Philippe awarded him a peerage, and on 19 March 1846 he made his first speech in the House of Peers, advocating support for the people of Poland in their struggles against Tsarist Russia. During the next couple of years, the political situation in France itself became more and more critical; in February 1848 a revolution broke out, and the monarchy was overthrown. Hugo stopped work on *Les Misérables* and, as a member of the new republican government, devoted most of his attention to politics. His concerns were characteristic. He spoke against the imposition of martial law (2 September 1848), against capital punishment (15 September 1848), against censorship of the press (11 October 1848). Over the next three years, as the main body of the Assembly became more reactionary, Hugo was increasingly associated with the left-wing minority, the radicals and reformers. On 17 June 1851, he publicly accused the Assembly's president, Louis-Napoléon Bonaparte, of plotting to seize absolute power. His speech was greeted with almost constant heckling; 'Nobody here is thinking of an empire', shouted one member of the right-wing majority. Four and a half months later, however, the predicted coup occurred. Louis-Napoléon became dictator of France, and Hugo slipped away to the Channel Islands, where he was joined by his family and friends.

During the Exile: *1851–1870*

Exile put an end to most of Hugo's non-literary activities and incited him to oppose the new regime with the only weapon he still possessed—his pen. Between January 1852 and October 1853 he produced over ten thousand lines of satirical verse dealing with Louis-Napoléon and his followers from every imaginable point of view. Much of this material was published in November 1853, at Brussels, in a volume finally entitled—after Hugo had considered and discarded almost a dozen alternatives—*Châtiments*.[2] However, it did not include all the poems written during this period; some were held back for publication later, in different contexts: 'Unity', for instance (written 2 July 1853), was eventually to appear in *Contemplations*, and 'Christ's First Encounter with the Tomb' (23 October 1852) in *The Legend of the Ages*.

In prose he was equally active. Between December 1851 and May 1852 he worked intensively on a history of France's new dictatorship; this was then set aside in favour of a shorter, more personal book, *Napoleon the Little*, which was written rapidly between 14 June and 12 July 1852 and published three weeks later. (The larger work was not completed and issued until 1877–8, when it was given the title *The History of a Crime*.) Needless to say, both *Napoleon the Little* and *Châtiments* were banned in France until the fall of Napoleon III in 1870.

In addition, exile isolated Hugo further from the dead Léopoldine. During the late 1840s he had visited her grave at Villequier every September, on the anniversary of her death; after 1851 such pilgrimages were impossible. In compensation he began trying to make contact with her in other ways, including a brief but intense foray into spiritualism. He also identified with her more closely than ever: he was now cut off from the world—dead to his former life—in one way, as she was in another. Consequently, as soon as the prose and verse satires on Louis-Napoléon were in print, he returned to the subjects that had been occupying him before the political upheavals of the late 1840s. By this time he had two major bodies of unpublished verse: the poems of 1840–3, which had been laid aside

---

[2] The title means, approximately, 'castigations' or 'chastisements', but as those words fail to carry the requisite emotional weight in our language, we have resorted to an English rendering of one of Hugo's provisional choices: *The Empire in the Pillary*.

when Léopoldine died, and the poems of 1846–8, which had been laid aside when the monarchy was overthrown. During 1854 and 1855 he added substantially to this material, and on 23 April 1856 he published much of it in a carefully shaped two-volume work entitled *Contemplations*, which rapidly became popular and remains to this day his most widely read collection of verse.

After this, the poet turned to an idea that had been interesting him for some years: a collection of 'short epics' (*petites épopées*). He worked on it during 1856–9, despite a serious disruption in 1858, when he was very ill with anthrax. A 'first series' of *The Legend of the Ages* (as the *petites épopées* were finally called), containing brilliantly incisive vignettes of human history and legend from the Garden of Eden to the Day of Judgement, was published in 1859.

After publishing the *Legend*'s first series, Hugo began work on a cycle of light, playful poems in ingeniously (at times, indeed, outrageously) rhymed quatrains, which was completed in 1865 and entitled *Songs of Street and Wood*. The little collection disconcerted many nineteenth-century readers, who had learnt to associate its author with huge, ambitious volumes on subjects of profound importance; there was a general feeling that a 63-year-old public man should not demean himself by sporting with Amaryllis in the shade. Many recent critics prize the *Songs* more highly. The amorous poems in the collection's first half are carefree but not careless. Compare, for instance, 'Nature? She's amorous everywhere . . .' (p. 321) with 'O that I could fill your deep reverie . . .' (p. 85), written to the same woman (Juliette Drouet) a quarter of a century earlier. There may be some loss of youthful passion, but there is an immense gain in the kind of intelligence known to seventeenth-century poets as 'wit': the speaker now studies the surrounding landscape more keenly, with a sharper, shrewder gaze, and when, in the final lines, he turns to his beloved, he defines his affection for her with a greater incisiveness, picking up the traditional images (lilies, doves) and weighing them carefully for accuracy while he offers them. Moreover, earthly love is here—as so often in Hugo—a kind of Socratic training for divine love, and the second half of the volume deals with issues that are not necessarily less serious than those of the *Contemplations* and the *Legend* merely because they are presented with a jauntier step.

Meanwhile, however, he had returned to the unfinished novel of

1845–8. Only about the last 20 per cent of the narrative still needed to be written; however, Hugo also drastically revised the sections drafted during the 1840s, and expanded the whole work by adding a variety of interludes—the largest and most famous being the account of Waterloo. The result, inevitably, is markedly different from his early novels: much larger, more discursive, considerably more varied in tone and style, with less sense of forward motion. The book was finally published in 1862, under the title *Les Misérables*. It provoked the usual mixed response from critics, but was an immediate success with the general public.

Hugo had published no novels since *Notre-Dame de Paris*, more than thirty years earlier, but the popularity of *Les Misérables* stimulated him to take more interest in the genre, and he entered what he called his 'prose phase', issuing three further novels—*The Toilers of the Sea* (1866), *The Laughing Man* (1869), and *Seventeen Ninety-Three* (1874)—within the space of a decade. None was as long, as eccentric, or as ambitious as *Les Misérables*, and only *The Toilers of the Sea* was generally well received by the public.

Toward the end of the exile, on 27 August 1868, Hugo's wife died in Brussels. Her body was returned to France, to be buried at Villequier beside her daughter; but Hugo himself, of course, did not accompany it past the border. By this time he had resigned himself to lifelong exile. 'No Moses ever reaches the promised land', he declared. But he was wrong.

After the Exile I: 1870–1878

Hugo's return to France, on 5 September 1870, was triumphant; but there was little joy during the months that followed. The Prussians who had captured Napoleon III reached Paris on 20 September and besieged the city for four months before it surrendered. During the ensuing turmoil, patriotic insurrection led to the establishment of a radical socialist government, which proclaimed Paris a commune on 29 March 1871. A civil war ensued; the Commune was eventually suppressed after a week of intense fighting toward the end of May, many of its leaders being killed or exiled. Hugo, however, was not actively involved in this. On 13 March 1871 his son Charles had died, and after the funeral he had gone to Brussels, largely to sort out the dead man's estate. His poems of the period, published in

1872 as *The Year of Horrors*, form a kind of verse diary in which his private sufferings and the country's public ones are interwoven. *The Year of Horrors* was his least popular collection to date; it offered its readers little variation in tone and few splashes of colour. Under the circumstances it could hardly have been otherwise.

Hugo was now guardian of Charles's two young children, Georges (born in 1868) and Jeanne (born in 1869), and he remained legally responsible for them until their mother remarried in 1877. His notebooks and sketchbooks show how much time he spent with them and how zestfully he spent it. They incited him to relive his own early life and enrich theirs, to be both child and educator, to view the world with fresh, untutored eyes that are unaware of (or unconstrained by) adult rules and conventions. Again the experience gradually generated a body of verse, which was finally issued in 1877 as *The Art of Being a Grandfather*. Its popularity was as inevitable as the unpopularity of *The Year of Horrors*, but it is far more than the standard 'children's book' that might have been expected. It contains some of Hugo's most inventive, adventurous poetry, and reworks many of his favourite themes in unexpectedly subtle and creative ways. A 'new series' of *The Legend of the Ages* was published in the same year.

After his return from exile he was also active in politics, though in limited ways. In 1876 he was elected to the French Senate, where his major concern was to obtain an amnesty for all those who had taken part in the 1871 Commune. But the wounds were still fresh, and the amnesty was granted only at the third attempt, in 1880.

After the Exile II: 1878–1885

After his 1878 stroke, Hugo never regained his former literary productivity. Yet the general public saw no evidence of this. There was such a backlog of unpublished material in his files that 'new' works could be released as frequently as ever: *Religions and Religion* in 1880, *The Four Winds of the Spirit* in 1881, a 'final volume' of *The Legend of the Ages* in 1883. Each of these collections contained some verse dating from the 1850s, and some from the 1870s.

When Hugo died in 1885, much of his work still remained in manuscript. His literary executors (primarily his long-term associate Paul Meurice) published most of it in the years between his death and the centenary of his birth (1902). Excerpts from his diaries were issued in two series (1887 and 1900) under the title *Things Seen*, which Hugo himself had applied to some of his observations from real life. The epic *God* appeared in 1891. Shorter poems were collected in *The Whole Lyre* (1888–97) and *Last Gleanings* (1902), and travel writings in *Alps and Pyrenees* (1890). By 1902 the bulk of the poetry was in print, but significant quantities of non-fiction prose were not issued until after 1950. Even today some material, especially from Hugo's diaries and notebooks, still awaits publication.

NOTE ON THE TEXT AND TRANSLATION

Hugo was one of the most prolific writers of his age (or any age); therefore, an *Essential Hugo* must contain only a representative, not a comprehensive, selection of his essence. The present volume attempts to cover as many facets of his literary output as possible, while devoting most space to the most widely admired works— particularly *Notre-Dame de Paris*, *Les Misérables*, and *Les Contemplations*. The arrangement is approximately chronological, but not rigorously so. Many sections of *Les Misérables* were written during the 1840s and substantially revised during the 1860s; in such cases, our placement merely indicates the date when the *bulk* of the chosen excerpt was composed. Moreover, we have broadly grouped the material into successive blocks of verse and prose, so that the reader will not be forced to alternate too frequently between bilingual pages and English-only pages.

It should be noted that the collections entitled *Things Seen, The Whole Lyre*, *Alps and Pyrenees*, and *Last Gleanings* were prepared not by Hugo but by his posthumous editors. Following the convention usual in Hugo studies, numbers that refer to sections, chapters, or poems in the printed volumes are given in roman numerals (e.g. *Les Misérables*, II. i. vii), whereas the numbers customarily assigned to Hugo's manuscripts are given in arabic numerals (e.g. MS 106/518b).

Hugo had definite ideas about translation,[1] and we have of course tried to conform to his wishes. He wanted a rendering to imitate the content, mood, and style of its source as closely as the character of the target language would allow—but he also emphasized that a translator must be sensitive to the natural constraints imposed by both the target language and its underlying culture. For instance, modern English does not readily tolerate apostrophes ('O Liberty ...') and historic present tenses ('Napoleon asks him ...'); on Hugo's own principles, we have sometimes been forced to adjust these.

Hugo's prose is strikingly different from his verse—even though

[1] Marie-Claire Pasquier, 'Hugo et la traduction', *Romantisme*, 106 (1999), 21–30.

the same vibrantly individual voice can be heard in both—and requires different strategies in translation. If his prose and verse accounts of the same subject are set side by side, it will be found that the prose relies much more on eyecatching typographical mannerisms (e.g. single-sentence paragraphs) and mind-catching syntactic mannerisms (e.g. verbless sentences). It also uses colloquialisms much more extensively (the supreme example being Cambronne's famous *merde*). In fact, it appears quirky. It is not much like the prose of any of Hugo's contemporaries, and it was not used as a model by any of his great successors, who preferred to base their styles on those of Sand, Stendhal, and Balzac. Hugo's verse looks and feels much more 'normal': its typographical layout and syntatic structure are essentially those common to the majority of nineteenth-century French poets, from Lamartine and Baudelaire to Verlaine and Mallarmé. Both in verse and in prose, his work tended to become more flexible as its author developed; *The Toilers of the Sea* is written in a distinctly more relaxed style than the Preface to *Cromwell*, and *The Art of Being a Grandfather* than *Odes and Ballads*. We have tried to reflect these differences in our renderings.

Judith Luna of Oxford University Press and the Press's anonymous pre-publication reader have contributed significantly to the choice of material for the anthology. To Dr and Mrs H. J. Blackmore and Drs Warner and Erica Quarles de Quarles we are indebted in many ways that no acknowledgement could adequately summarize.

SELECT BIBLIOGRAPHY

Complete Editions

Œuvres complètes, 46 vols. (Paris, 1880–5). The *ne varietur* edition.

Œuvres inédites, 16 vols. (Paris, 1886–1902). Prepared by Hugo's literary executors (principally Paul Meurice).

Œuvres complètes, 45 vols. (Paris, 1904–52). The Imprimerie nationale edition, under the supervision of, successively, Paul Meurice, Gustav Simon, and Cécile Daubray.

Œuvres complètes, ed. Jean Massin, 18 vols. (Paris, 1967–71).

Œuvres complètes, gen. ed. Jacques Seebacher and Guy Rosa, 15 vols. (Paris, 1985–90).

Individual Works: Verse

Les Orientales, ed. Elisabeth Barineau, 2 vols. (Paris, 1952–4).

Les Châtiments, ed. Paul Berret, 2 vols. (Paris, 1932).

Les Contemplations, ed. Joseph Vianey, 3 vols. (Paris, 1922).

—— ed. Léon Cellier (Paris, 1969).

Les Deux Trouvailles de Gallus, ed. John J. Janc (New York, 1983). Book II of *Les Quatre Vents de l'esprit*.

La Légende des siècles, ed. Paul Berret, 6 vols. (Paris, 1920–7).

Contribution aux études sur Victor Hugo 2: Le Texte de La Fin de Satan, ed. René Journet and Guy Robert (Paris, 1979).

Dieu: L'Océan d'en haut, ed. René Journet and Guy Robert (Paris, 1960).

Dieu: Le Seuil du gouffre, ed. René Journet and Guy Robert (Paris, 1961).

Dieu (fragments), ed. René Journet and Guy Robert, 3 vols. (Paris, 1969).

Individual Works: Prose

Le Préface de Cromwell, ed. Maurice Souriau (Paris, 1897).

Notre-Dame de Paris, ed. Jacques Seebacher, and *Les Travailleurs de la mer*, ed. Yves Gohin (Paris, 1975).

Claude Gueux, ed. Paul Savary-Casard (Paris, 1956).

Littérature et philosophie mêlées, ed. A. R. W. James, 2 vols. (Paris, 1976).

Les Misérables, ed. Maurice Allem (Paris, 1951).

—— ed. Marius-François Guyard, 2 vols. (Paris, 1957).

Quatrevingt-treize, ed. Jean Boudout (Paris, 1957).

Journal de ce que j'apprends chaque jour, ed. René Journet and Guy Robert (Paris, 1965).

Correspondance familiale et écrits intimes, 1802–1839, ed. Jean Gaudon, Sheila Gaudon, and Bernard Leuillot, 2 vols. (Paris, 1985–91).

Correspondance Victor Hugo-Pierre-Jules Hetzel, ed. Sheila Gaudon (Paris, 1979).

Lettres à Juliette Drouet and *Le Livre de l'anniversaire*, ed. Jean Gaudon, 2nd edn. (Paris, 2001).

Individual Works: Drama

Hernani, ed. John J. Janc (Lanham, Md, 2001).

Hernani, dir. Raymond Rouleau (Paris, 1975). Videorecording.

Ruy Blas, ed. Anne Ubersfeld, 2 vols. (Paris, 1971–2).

Ruy Blas, dir. Raymond Rouleau (Paris, 1971). Videorecording.

Théâtre en liberté, ed. Arnaud Laster (Paris, 2002).

Torquemada, ed. John J. Janc (Lanham, Md, 1989).

Torquemada, dir. Jean Kerschbron (Paris, 1976). Videorecording.

Textual Studies

Journet, René, and Guy Robert, *Autour des Contemplations* (Paris, 1955).

—— *Le Manuscrit des Contemplations* (Paris, 1956).

—— *Des Feuilles d'automne aux Rayons et les ombres* (Paris, 1957).

—— *Notes sur les Contemplations* (Paris, 1958).

—— *Le Manuscrit des Misérables* (Paris, 1962).

—— *Notes sur Les Chansons des rues et des bois* (Paris, 1973).

Biographical Studies

Victor Hugo raconté par un témoin de sa vie, 2 vols. (Paris, 1863). By Hugo's wife (Adèle I). The original draft, *Victor Hugo raconté par Adèle Hugo*, ed. Anne Ubersfeld and Guy Rosa (Paris, 1985), should also be consulted.

Hugo, Adèle, *Le Journal d'Adèle Hugo*, ed. Frances Vernor Guille and Jean-Marc Hovasse, 4 vols. (Paris, 1968–2002). The diary of Hugo's daughter (Adèle II).

Hugo, Georges, *Mon Grand-Père* (Paris, 1902). By Hugo's grandson.

Drouet, Juliette, *Mille et une lettres d'amour à Victor Hugo*, ed. Paul Souchon (Paris, 1951).

—— *Lettres à Victor Hugo*, ed. Evelyn Blewer, 2nd edn. (Paris, 2001).

Barrère, Jean-Bertrand, *Victor Hugo: L'Homme et l'œuvre* (Paris, 1949).

Besson, André, *Victor Hugo: Vie d'un géant* (Paris, 2001).

Decaux, Alain, *Victor Hugo* (Paris, 1984).

Gallo, Marc, *Victor Hugo*, 2 vols. (Paris, 2002).

Gaudon, Jean, *Victor Hugo 1802–1885* (Paris, 2002).

Hovasse, Jean-Marc, *Victor Hugo 1: Avant l'exil* (Paris, 2001).

Juin, Herbert, *Victor Hugo*, 3 vols. (Paris, 1980–6).

Maurois, André, *Olympio ou la vie de Victor Hugo* (Paris, 1954).

Novarino, Albine, *Victor Hugo et Juliette Drouet* (Paris, 2001).

Richardson, Joanna, *Victor Hugo* (London, 1967).

Robb, Graham, *Victor Hugo* (London, 1997).

Stapfer, Paul, *Victor Hugo à Guernsey* (Paris, 1905).

Critical Studies

Affron, Charles, *A Stage for Poets: Studies in the Theatre of Hugo and Musset* (Princeton, 1971).

Albouy, Pierre, *La Création mythologique chez Victor Hugo* (Paris, 1963).

—— *Mythographies* (Paris, 1976).

Barrère, Jean-Bertrand, *La Fantaisie de Victor Hugo*, 3 vols. (Paris, 1949–60).

Bénichou, Paul, *Les Mages romantiques* (Paris, 1988).

Bishop, Michael, *Nineteenth-Century French Poetry* (New York, 1993).

Brombert, Victor, *Victor Hugo et le roman visionnaire* (Paris, 1985).

Butor, Michel, *Répertoire II* (Paris, 1964).

Cellier, Léon, *L'Épopée humanitaire et les grands mythes romantiques* (Paris, 1973).

Chahine, Samia, *La Dramaturgie de Victor Hugo* (Paris, 1971).

Charles, David, *La Pensée technique dans l'œuvre de Victor Hugo* (Paris, 1997).

Chenet-Faugeras, Françoise, *Les Misérables ou L'Espace sans fond* (Paris, 1995).

Denommé, Robert T., *Nineteenth-Century French Romantic Poets* (Carbondale, Ill., 1969).

Frey, John A., *Les Contemplations of Victor Hugo* (Charlottesville, Va, 1988).

Friedemann, Joë, *Victor Hugo, un temps pour rire* (Saint-Genough, 2002).

Gaudon, Jean, *Le Temps de la contemplation* (Paris, 1969).

—— *Victor Hugo et le théâtre*, 2nd edn. (Paris, 1985).

Gély, Claude, *Victor Hugo: Poète de l'intimité* (Paris, 1969).

Glauser, Alfred, *Hugo et la poésie pure* (Geneva, 1957).

—— *La Poétique de Hugo* (Paris, 1978).

Grant, R. B., *The Perilous Quest* (New York, 1968).

Greenberg, Wendy, *The Power of Rhetoric: Hugo's Metaphor and Poetics* (New York, 1985).

Grossman, Kathryn, *The Early Novels of Victor Hugo* (Geneva, 1986).

Halsall, Albert W., *Victor Hugo et l'art de convaincre* (Montreal, 1995).

Houston, John Porter, *Victor Hugo*, 2nd edn. (Boston, 1988).

Hunt, Herbert J., *The Epic in Nineteenth-Century France* (Oxford, 1941).

Ireson, J. C., *Victor Hugo: A Companion to His Poetry* (Oxford, 1997).

Jeanneney, Jean-Noël, *Victor Hugo et la république* (Paris, 2002).

Kirsch, F. P., *Probleme der Romanstruktur bei Victor Hugo* (Vienna, 1973).

Laforgue, Pierre, *Gavroche, etudes sur Les Misérables* (Paris, 1994).

Lejeune, Philippe, *L'Ombre et la lumière dans Les Contemplations* (Paris, 1969).

Levaillant, Maurice, *La Crise mystique de Victor Hugo* (Paris, 1954).

Maillon, Jean, *Victor Hugo et l'art architectural* (Paris, 1962).

Meschonnic, Henri, *Écrire Hugo* (Paris, 1977).

—— *Hugo, la poésie contre le maintien de l'ordre* (Paris, 2002).

Moreau, Pierre, *Les Contemplations de Victor Hugo* (Paris, 1962).

Nash, Suzanne, *Les Contemplations of Victor Hugo* (Princeton, 1976).

Peyre, Henri, *Victor Hugo: Poetry and Philosophy* (Tuscaloosa, Al, 1980).

Piroué, Georges, *Victor Hugo romancier* (Paris, 1964).

Porter, Laurence M., *Victor Hugo* (New York, 1999).

Rétat, Claude, *X ou le divin dans la poésie de Victor Hugo à partir de l'exil* (Paris, 1999).

—— *La Légende des siècles de Victor Hugo* (Paris, 2001).

Roman, Myriam, *Victor Hugo et le roman philosophique* (Paris, 1999).

—— and Marie-Christine Bellosta, *Les Misérables, roman pensif* (Paris, 1995).

Savey-Casard, Paul, *Le Crime et la peine dans l'œuvre de Victor Hugo* (Paris, 1956).

Seebacher, Jacques, *Victor Hugo ou le calcul des profondeurs* (Paris, 1993).

Swinburne, Algernon Charles, *A Study of Victor Hugo* (London, 1886).

Ubersfeld, Anne, *Le Roi et le bouffon: Étude sur le théâtre de Hugo*, 2nd edn. (Paris, 2001).

Ward, Patricia A., *The Medievalism of Victor Hugo* (University Park, Pa, 1975).

Further Reading in Oxford World's Classics

Balzac, Honoré de, *Cousin Bette*, trans. Sylvia Raphael (Oxford, 1998).

Baudelaire, Charles, *The Flowers of Evil*, ed. and trans. James McGowan (Oxford, 1993).

Hugo, Victor, *Notre-Dame de Paris*, trans. Alban Krailsheimer (Oxford, 1993).

Six French Poets of the Nineteenth Century: Lamartine, Hugo, Baudelaire, Verlaine, Rimbaud, Mallarmé, ed. E. H. and A. M. Blackmore (Oxford, 2000).

Verlaine, Paul, *Selected Poems*, ed. and trans. Martin Sorrell (Oxford, 1999).

A CHRONOLOGY OF VICTOR HUGO

1789	French Revolution.
1793	Death of Louis XVI.
1799	Napoleon Bonaparte seizes absolute power as First Consul.
1802	26 February: birth of Victor-Marie Hugo, the youngest son of Léopold and Sophie Hugo, at Besançon.
1811	April: on their way to Spain (where Léopold is a general in the Napoleonic army), Sophie and her children stay for a month at Bayonne.
1812	29 October: Hugo's godfather, General Victor Lahorie, is executed for conspiring against Napoleon.
1814	14 April: Napoleon abdicates and is exiled to Elba; the Bourbon monarchy is restored, and Louis XVIII becomes king.
1815	1 March: Napoleon returns to France from Elba. Louis XVIII flees to Belgium.
	18 June: battle of Waterloo. Napoleon is exiled to Saint Helena; Louis XVIII is restored to the throne.
1821	5 May: death of Napoleon.
	27 June: death of Hugo's mother Sophie.
1822	8 June: publication of Hugo's first volume of verse, *Odes and Other Poems* (*Odes et poésies diverses*).
	12 October: Hugo marries Adèle Foucher ('Adèle I').
1823	8 February: publication of *Han of Iceland* (*Han d'Islande*, novel).
1824	13 May: publication of *New Odes* (*Nouvelles Odes*, verse).
	28 August: birth of Hugo's daughter Léopoldine.
	16 September: death of Louis XVIII; Charles X becomes king.
1826	February: publication of *Bug-Jargal* (novel).
	2 November: birth of Hugo's son Charles.
	November: publication of *Odes and Ballads* (*Odes et ballades*, verse), first edition.
1827	5 December: publication of *Cromwell* (drama), with its famous Preface.
1828	30 January: death of Hugo's father Léopold.
	August: publication of *Odes and Ballads* (*Odes et ballades*), revised and enlarged edition.
	21 October: birth of Hugo's son Victor ('François-Victor').

1829	19 January: publication of *Orientalia* (*Orientales*, verse).
	3 February: publication of *The Last Day of a Condemned Man* (*Le Dernier Jour d'un condamné*, novel).
1830	23 February: first performance of *Hernani* (drama).
	27–9 July: the July Revolution. Charles X is exiled; Louis-Philippe becomes king under a new, relatively more democratic constitution.
	28 July: birth of Hugo's daughter Adèle ('Adèle II').
1831	16 March: publication of *Notre-Dame de Paris* (novel).
	1 December: publication of *Autumn Leaves* (*Les Feuilles d'automne*, verse).
1832	22 November: first performance of *Le Roi s'amuse* (drama), which is promptly banned as being politically subversive.
1833	2–3 January: Hugo meets Juliette Drouet.
	2 February: first performance of *Lucrezia Borgia* (*Lucrèce Borgia*, drama), with Juliette in a minor role.
	6 November: first performance of *Mary Tudor* (*Marie Tudor*, drama), with Juliette in a supporting role.
1834	19 March: publication of *A Blend of Literature and Philosophy* (*Littérature et philosophie mêlées*, essays and journals).
1835	27 October: publication of *Songs of the Half-Light* (*Les Chants du crépuscule*, verse).
1837	26 June: publication of *Inner Voices* (*Les Voix intérieures*, verse).
1838	8 November: first performance of *Ruy Blas* (drama).
1840	16 May: publication of *Sunlight and Shadows* (*Les Rayons et les ombres*, verse).
1841	7 January: Hugo is elected to the Académie française.
1842	28 January: publication of *The Rhine* (*Le Rhin*, travel book).
1843	15 February: Hugo's daughter Léopoldine marries Charles Vacquerie.
	7 March: first performance of *Les Burgraves* (drama).
	18 July–12 September: Hugo travels to the Pyrenees.
	4 September: Léopoldine and her husband are drowned in a boating accident at Villequier.
1845	13 April: Hugo is appointed a Peer of France.
	17 November: Hugo begins to write the novel that will ultimately become *Les Misérables*.
1848	22–4 February: the February Revolution. Louis-Philippe abdicates; the Second Republic is established.
	4 June: Hugo is elected to the National Assembly.
	10 December: Louis-Napoléon Bonaparte is elected president of the Republic.

1850   21 August: funeral of Balzac, at which Hugo delivers a
                speech.

1851   2 December: Louis-Napoléon seizes absolute power. Hugo
                is exiled and flees to Belgium.

1852   August: Hugo and his family move to Jersey.

                5 August: publication of *Napoleon the Little* (*Napoléon le
                petit*, political pamphlet).

                2 December: Louis-Napoléon is proclaimed emperor as
                Napoleon III.

1853   23 November: publication of *The Empire in the Pillory*
                (*Châtiments*, verse).

1855   31 October: Hugo and his family move to Guernsey.

1856   23 April: publication of *Contemplations* (*Les Contemplations*,
                verse), mainly written 1838–43 and 1846–55.

1858–65   publication of François-Victor's translation of the works of
                Shakespeare.

1859   26 September: publication of the First Series of *The Legend
                of the Ages* (*La Légende des siècles*, verse), mainly written
                1846–59.

1862   30 March–30 June: publication of *Les Misérables* (novel),
                written 1845–8 and 1860–2.

1864   14 April: publication of *William Shakespeare* (literary
                criticism).

1865   17 October: Charles Hugo marries Alice Lehaene.

                25 October: publication of *Songs of Street and Wood*
                (*Les Chansons des rues et des bois*, verse), written 1859 and
                1865.

1866   12 March: publication of *The Toilers of the Sea* (*Les
                Travailleurs de la mer*, novel).

1868   16 August: birth of Charles's son Georges.

                27 August: death of Adèle I.

1869   19 April–8 May: publication of *The Laughing Man*
                (*L'Homme qui rit*, novel).

                29 September: birth of Charles's daughter Jeanne.

1870   19 July: Napoleon III declares war on Prussia.

                2 September: defeat of the French army at Sedan; Napoleon
                III is taken prisoner.

                4 September: the Third Republic is proclaimed; Hugo
                returns to Paris.

1871   13 March: death of Charles. Hugo is appointed guardian of
                Georges and Jeanne.

                18 March–28 May: the Paris Commune, ending in a week of

street fighting and summary executions. Hugo is in Brussels 21 March–30 May, initially to deal with Charles's estate.

1872   20 April: publication of *The Year of Horrors* (*L'Année terrible*, verse).

1873   26 December: death of François-Victor.

1874   20 February: publication of *Seventeen Ninety-Three* (*Quatrevingt-treize*, novel).

1875–6   May 1875–July 1876: publication of *Deeds and Words* (*Actes et paroles*, political writings and speeches), in three volumes.

1877   26 February: publication of the New Series of *The Legend of the Ages* (*La Légende des siècles*, verse), mainly written 1853–62 and 1869–77.

    12 May: publication of *The Art of Being a Grandfather* (*L'Art d'être grand-père*, verse), mainly written 1870–7.

1877–8   October 1877–March 1878: publication of *History of a Crime* (*Histoire d'un crime*, political history), written 1851–2 and 1877–8.

1878   29 April: publication of *The Pope* (*Le Pape*, verse), mainly written 1874–7.

    28 June: Hugo suffers a serious cerebrovascular stroke.

1879   28 February: publication of *The Supreme Compassion* (*La Pitié suprème*, verse), written 1857–8.

1880   April: publication of *Religions and Religion* (*Religions et religion*, verse), mainly written 1856 and 1870.

    24 October: publication of *The Donkey* (*L'Âne*, verse), written 1857–8.

1881   31 May: publication of *The Four Winds of the Spirit* (*Les Quatre Vents de l'esprit*, verse), mainly written 1846–60 and 1870–5.

1882   26 May: publication of *Torquemada* (drama), written 1869.

1883   11 May: death of Juliette Drouet.

    9 June: publication of the Last Volume of *The Legend of the Ages* (*La Légende des siècles*, verse), written 1847–57 and 1870–6.

    September: publication of the definitive edition of *The Legend of the Ages*.

    6 October: publication of *The Channel Islands* (*L'Archipel de la Manche*, essay), written 1865 as the prologue to *The Toilers of the Sea*.

1885   22 May: death of Victor Hugo.

1886   publication of *The End of Satan* (*La Fin de Satan*, verse),

BEFORE THE EXILE I: 1824–1843

from *Odes et ballades*

Le Chant du cirque

César, empereur magnanime,
Le monde, à te plaire unanime,
A tes fêtes doit concourir!
Éternel héritier d'Auguste,
Salut! prince immortel et juste,   5
César! sois salué par ceux qui vont mourir!

Seul entre tous les rois, César aux dieux de Rome
Peut en libations offrir le sang de l'homme.
A nos solennités nous invitons la Mort.
De monstres pour nos jeux nous dépeuplons le monde;   10
Nous mêlons dans le cirque, où fume un sang immonde,
Les tigres d'Hyrcanie aux barbariens du Nord.

Des colosses d'airain, des vases de porphyre,
Des ancres, des drapeaux que gonfle le zéphyre,
Parent du chant fatal les murs éblouissants;   15
Les parfums chargent l'air d'un odorant nuage,
Car le peuple romain aime que le carnage
Exhale ses vapeurs parmi des flots d'encens.

Des portes tout à coup les gonds d'acier gémissent.
La foule entre en froissant les grilles qui frémissent.   20
Les panthères dans l'ombre ont tressailli d'effroi,
Et, poussant mille cris qu'un long bruit accompagne,
Comme un fleuve épandu de montagne en montagne,
De degrés en degrés roule le peuple-roi.

Les deux chaises d'ivoire ont reçu les édiles.   25
L'hippopotame informe et les noirs crocodiles
Nagent autour du cirque en un large canal;

from *Odes and Ballads*

The Song of the Circus

Magnanimous Caesar, emperor,
Immortal ruler, just and true,
Augustus'* heir for evermore,
The world unites to honour you,
And gathers at the pleasures you supply;
Hail, Caesar, hail from those about to die!*

No king but Caesar, among all the nations,
May give the gods such human blood-libations;
Death is made welcome at our grave pursuits.
We rob the world of monsters for our sport;
Into the blood-steeped circus we have brought
Hyrcanian tigers and Hibernian brutes.*

Porphyry jars, colossi made of bronze,
Anchors, and breeze-inflated gonfalons
Adorn the gay and death-resounding walls;
Perfumes infuse the air with fragrant clouds—
Such a delight it is, to Roman crowds,
When scents of carnage blend with incense palls!

The gates groan suddenly on metal hinges;
In runs the mob; the jostled lattice cringes,
While panthers in the darkness quake with fear;
The people-king emits a motley shriek,
And, as a river spills from peak to peak,
Hordes scatter through the place from tier to tier.

Two ivory chairs receive the Aediles,* while
Foul hippopotamus and crocodile
Swim round the circus in a huge canal;

Dans leurs cages de fer les cinq cents lions grondent;
Les vestales en chœur, dont les chants se répondent,
Apportent l'autel chaste et le feu virginal.   30

L'œil ardent, le sein nu, l'impure courtisane
Près du foyer sacré pose un trépied profane.
On voile de cyprès l'autel des Suppliants.
A travers leur cortège et de rois et d'esclaves,
Les sénateurs, vêtus d'augustes laticlaves,   35
Dans la foule, de loin, comptent tous leurs clients.

Chaque vierge est assise auprès d'une matrone.
A la voix des tribuns, on voit autour du trône
Les soldats du prétoire en cercle se ranger;
Les prêtres de Cybèle entonnent la louange;   40
Et, sur de vils tréteaux, les histrions du Gange
Chantent, en attendant ceux qui vont s'égorger.

Les voilà!...—Tout le peuple applaudit et menace
Ces captifs, que César d'un bras puissant ramasse
Des temples de Manès aux antres d'Irmensul.   45
Ils entrent tour à tour, et le licteur les nomme;
Vil troupeau, que la mort garde aux plaisirs de Rome,
Et que d'un fer brûlant a marqué le Consul.

On découvre en leurs rangs, à leur tête penchée,
Des Juifs, traînant partout une honte cachée;   50
Plus loin, d'altiers Gaulois que nul péril n'abat;
Et d'infâmes Chrétiens, qui, dépouillés d'armures,
Refusant aux bourreaux leurs chants ou leurs murmures,
Vont souffrir sans orgueil et mourir sans combat.

Bientôt, quand rugiront les bêtes échappées,   55
Les murs, tout hérissés de piques et d'épées,
Livreront cette proie entière à leur fureur.—
Du trône de César la pourpre orne le faîte,
Afin qu'un jour plus doux, durant l'ardente fête,
Flatte les yeux divins du clément empereur.   60

In iron pens five hundred lions roar.
The Vestals,* in an antiphonic corps,
Bring virgin fire to the chaste pedestal.

Bright-eyed bare-breasted harlots with no shame
Set profane tripods by the sacred flame.
The Suppliants' Altar bears a cypress shroud.
Senators draped in glorious purple gowns
And flanked by their attendant kings and clowns
Mark, far away, their clients in the crowd.

Every young maiden keeps a matron near.
See! at the tribunes' summons, there appear
Praetorian soldiers, who surround the throne;
Gangeans* sing in the cheap actors' quarter,
And wait for those who will be led to slaughter;
Priests of Cybele* solemnly intone.

There they are!...—All the plebs applaud and jeer
These slaves, whom Caesar's mighty arm brought here
From Irminsul's or Mani's* holy land.
They pass, and lictors name them one by one—
A vile herd kept by Death for Roman fun,
And branded with the Consul's* iron brand.

We see among them Jews with heads held low,
Dragging their dark shame everywhere they go;
Proud Gauls* whom danger never mortified;
Base Christians who, despising all defence,
Uttering neither pleas nor reverence,
Die without fighting, perish without pride.

The beasts are loosed, and bellow; very soon,
Within these walls pike-tipped and spear-bestrewn,
Their prey has been delivered to their cries.
Caesar sits on a purple-shrouded height,
So that, during the heat, a milder light
May please the clement ruler's sacred eyes.

César, empereur magnanime,
Le monde, à te plaire unanime,
A tes fêtes doit concourir!
Éternel héritier d'Auguste,
Salut! prince immortel et juste,   65
César! sois salué par ceux qui vont mourir!

A un passant

Au soleil couchant,
Toi qui vas cherchant
        Fortune,
Prends garde de choir;
La terre, le soir,
        Est brune.

Maint voleur te suit;
La chose est, la nuit,
        Commune.
Les dames des bois
Nous gardent parfois
        Rancune.

L'océan trompeur
Couvre de vapeur
        La dune.
Vois; à l'horizon,
Aucune maison!
        Aucune!

Elles vont errer;
Crains d'en rencontrer
        Quelqu'une.
Les lutins de l'air
Vont danser au clair
        De lune.

La Chanson du fou

Voyageur qui, la nuit, sur le pavé sonore
De ton chien inquiet passes accompagné,
Après le jour brûlant, pourquoi marcher encore?
Où mènes-tu si tard ton cheval résigné?

La nuit!—Ne crains-tu pas d'entrevoir la stature   5
Du brigand dont un sabre a chargé la ceinture,
Ou qu'un de ces vieux loups, près des routes rôdants,
Qui du fer des coursiers méprisent l'étincelle,
D'un bond brusque et soudain s'attachant à ta selle,
Ne mêle à ton sang noir l'écume de ses dents?   10

Ne crains-tu pas surtout qu'un follet à cette heure
N'allonge sous tes pas le chemin qui te leurre,
Et ne te fasse, hélas! ainsi qu'aux anciens jours,

Magnanimous Caesar, emperor,
Immortal ruler, just and true,
Augustus' heir for evermore,
The world unites to honour you,
And gathers at the pleasures you supply;
Hail, Caesar, hail from those about to die!

To a Traveller

The last sunlight dies.
Are you seeking some prize?
    Then hark!
Beware of your doom!
The earth in the gloom
    Is dark.

The sly sea arrays
The dune in a haz-
    y pall;
Along the horizon
No house to set eyes on
    At all!

Thieves slink after you—
At nightfall they do
    Act thus.
The forest nymphs might
Be showing their spite
    For us.

Don't meet them—take care!
They flit here and there
    In flight.
The imps of the air
Whirl round in the fair
    Moonlight.

Mad Song*

You traveller, while the night streets echo on and on
And your timorous dog accompanies your course,
Why must you journey when the fiery day has gone?
Where do you ride so late on your submissive horse?

Have you no fear that, in the dark, you may be faced
By some tall brigand with a sabre at his waist?
Or that along the road a sly old wolf may scud,
And, scorning the bright sparks struck from your horse's feet,
May with a single bound dislodge you from your seat
And sink its foaming teeth quickly in your dark blood?

Or, worse, that some will-o'-the-wisp, at this hour, may
Allure your footsteps on a far-extending way
As in the olden days, alas! till you are led

Rêvant quelque logis dont la vitre scintille
Et le faisan doré par l'âtre qui pétille,   15
Marcher vers des clartés qui reculent toujours?

Crains d'aborder la plaine où le sabbat s'assemble,
Où les démons hurlants viennent danser ensemble;
Ces murs maudits par Dieu, par Satan profanés,
Ce magique château dont l'enfer sait l'histoire,   20
Et qui, désert le jour, quand tombe la nuit noire,
Enflamme ses vitraux dans l'ombre illuminés!

Voyageur isolé, qui t'éloignes si vite,
De ton chien inquiet la nuit accompagné,
Après le jour brûlant, quand le repos t'invite,   25
Où mènes-tu si tard ton cheval résigné?

from *Les Orientales*

Sara la baigneuse

Sara, belle d'indolence,
    Se balance
Dans un hamac, au-dessus
Du bassin d'une fontaine
    Toute pleine   5
D'eau puisée à l'Illysus;

Et la frêle escarpolette
    Se reflète
Dans le transparent miroir,
Avec la baigneuse blanche   10
    Qui se penche,
Qui se penche pour se voir.

Chaque fois que la nacelle,
    Qui chancelle,
Passe à fleur d'eau dans son vol,   15

Toward some fancied house where glass and pheasant glint,
Tinged with the flickering fireside's shimmering golden tint,
Although the gleams of light keep vanishing ahead?

Have you no fear that witches meet on the expanse
Where howling demons flock to join the sabbath-dance
In halls that God has cursed, which Satan now degrades?
The history of that magic tower is known to hell;
It lay deserted all the day, but when night fell
Its windowpanes lit up and glimmered through the shades!

You lonely night-time traveller, scurrying quickly on
While your timorous dog accompanies your course,
When sleep is calling you, when fiery day has gone,
Where do you ride so late on your submissive horse?

from *Orientalia*

Zara Bathing

Zara, lovely lazy thing,
    Starts to swing
While her hammock's cords support her
Just above a fountain-spring
    Billowing
Full of the Illysus'* water.

And the frail swing can be seen
    In the sheen
Of the water's clear tableau,
With the lovely bather who
    Leans to view,
Leans to view herself below.

As her cradle skims the air
    Here and there
On its flight within a speck

On voit sur l'eau qui s'agite
    Sortir vite
Son beau pied et son beau col.

Elle bat d'un pied timide
    L'onde humide   20
Où tremble un mouvant tableau,
Fait rougir son pied d'albâtre,
    Et, folâtre,
Rit de la fraîcheur de l'eau.

Reste ici caché, demeure;   25
    Dans une heure,
D'un œil ardent tu verras
Sortir du bain l'ingénue,
    Toute nue,
Croisant ses mains sur ses bras.   30

Car c'est un astre qui brille
    Qu'une fille
Qui sort d'un bain au flot clair,
Cherche s'il ne vient personne,
    Et frissonne,   35
Toute mouillée au grand air.

Elle est là, sous la feuillée,
    Éveillée
Au moindre bruit de malheur;
Et rouge, pour une mouche   40
    Qui la touche,
Comme une grenade en fleur.

On voit tout ce que dérobe
    Voile ou robe;
Dans ses yeux d'azur en feu,   45
Son regard que rien ne voile
    Est l'étoile
Qui brille au fond d'un ciel bleu.

Of the brim, the troubled stream
      Shows a gleam
Of her pretty foot and neck.

When she dabs her timid toes,
      All the flow's
Lucid pictures writhe and fold,
And her pale foot flushes red;
      Empty-head,
She laughs at the liquid's cold.

Wait: keep hidden! By and by
      Your keen eye
Will observe her artless charms:
After bathing, she'll be viewed
      Wholly nude,
With her hands across her arms.

When a girl steps from her bath,
      Scans the path
For men coming, quakes with fright,
Dripping water everywhere
      In the air—
Isn't it a dazzling sight!

There she is, beneath the trees,
      Quick to seize
Every sound of harm she can: at
Every midge's lightest tread,
      She turns red
As a ripening pomegranate.

You see all that gown or cape
      Ever drape;
And the flame in her blue eyes
Flares with an unclouded gaze,
      Like the blaze
Of a star in azure skies.

L'eau sur son corps qu'elle essuie
    Roule en pluie,   50
Comme sur un peuplier;
Comme si, gouttes à gouttes,
    Tombaient toutes
Les perles de son collier.

Mais Sara la nonchalante   55
    Est bien lente
A finir ses doux ébats;
Toujours elle se balance
    En silence,
Et va murmurant tout bas: 60

«Oh! si j'étais capitane,
    Ou sultane,
Je prendrais des bains ambrés,
Dans un bain de marbre jaune,
    Près d'un trône,   65
Entre deux griffons dorés!

«J'aurais le hamac de soie
    Qui se ploie
Sous le corps prêt à pâmer;
J'aurais la molle ottomane   70
    Dont émane
Un parfum qui fait aimer.

«Je pourrais folâtrer nue,
    Sous la nue,
Dans le ruisseau du jardin,   75
Sans craindre de voir dans l'ombre
    Du bois sombre
Deux yeux s'allumer soudain.

«Il faudrait risquer sa tête
    Inquiète,   80
Et tout braver pour me voir,

Water swishes off her form
  Like a storm
Raining on a poplar tree;
As if pearls have come undone
  One by one
From her strings of jewellery.

Zara, though, rocks to and fro,
  Very slow
To end her delightful play,
Nonchalantly murmuring
  On her swing
In a surreptitious way:

'If I were a capitana
  Or sultana,
I would bathe in amber balm
In a bath of yellow stone
  By a throne
With gold griffins* on each arm!

For my hammock, silken thread
  Would be spread
Underneath limbs all-but-spent,
With a tender ottoman
  Shedding an
Amorous alluring scent.

Naked I could romp and run
  In the sun
By my garden's flowing stream,
With no fear that, through the shade
  Of some glade,
Suddenly two eyes might gleam.

Men would have to risk their all—
  Heads would fall
If they tried to get a view,

Le sabre nu de l'heiduque,
        Et l'eunuque
Aux dents blanches, au front noir!

«Puis, je pourrais, sans qu'on presse   85
        Ma paresse,
Laisser avec mes habits
Traîner sur les larges dalles
        Mes sandales
De drap brodé de rubis.»   90

Ainsi se parle en princesse,
        Et sans cesse
Se balance avec amour,
La jeune fille rieuse,
        Oublieuse   95
Des promptes ailes du jour.

L'eau, du pied de la baigneuse
        Peu soigneuse,
Rejaillit sur le gazon,
Sur sa chemise plissée,   100
        Balancée
Aux branches d'un vert buisson.

Et cependant des campagnes
        Ses compagnes
Prennent toutes le chemin.   105
Voici leur troupe frivole
        Qui s'envole
En se tenant par la main.

Chacune, en chantant comme elle,
        Passe, et mêle   110
Ce reproche à sa chanson:
—Oh! la paresseuse fille
        Qui s'habille
Si tard un jour de moisson!

Braving the slave's javelin
    And the grin
Of the black-browed eunuch too!

Then I'd be as much at ease
    As I please;
I'd let all the clothes I choose
Strew the flagstones everywhere,
    With my pair
Of plush ruby-studded shoes.'

So the little libertine
    Plays the queen
As incessantly she swings—
Swings, and amorously coquettes,
    And forgets
That the day has fleeting wings.

Water, from the careless beat
    Of her feet,
Splashes round the garden now,
On the folds of her chemise
    In the trees
Hanging from a leafy bough.

Yet her friends are coming back
    Down the track
Leading from the countryside.
See! here is their flippant band,
    Hand in hand,
Flitting past with an airy glide.

All the members of the throng
    Ape her song
As they pass along the way:
'Lazy creature! I protest,
    She gets dressed
Mighty late, on harvest day!'

from *Cromwell*

Preface

The drama that you are about to read has no real claim to the public's attention or good will. It won't attract the interest of political partisans, since it hasn't had the advantage of an official censorship ban; it won't elicit the literary sympathies of discerning readers, since it hasn't even had the honour of being formally rejected by an infallible theatre committee.*

Consequently, it presents itself for inspection like the wretch in the Scriptures, 'alone and poor and naked' (*solus, pauper, nudus**).

The author hesitated to clutter his play with notes and prefatory material. Readers don't generally pay much attention to such things. They are more interested in a writer's talent than his opinions; and whether a work is good or bad, they don't particularly care about the ideas behind it or the attitude that moulded it. When you walk through the rooms of a building, you seldom visit its cellars; when you eat the fruit of a tree, you don't give much thought to its roots.

Besides, notes and prefaces are sometimes an easy way to increase the weight of a book and enhance (at least in appearance) its importance. Strategies of the same kind are used by army generals, who make their ranks look more impressive by putting even the baggage carts in the front line. While the critics pounce on the preface and the scholars on the notes, the work itself may escape their notice and slip past their crossfire without a scratch, as an army gets out of a bad situation while its vanguard and rearguard do all the fighting.

Whatever may be said in their favour, those factors haven't influenced the present author. This volume didn't need to be padded out; it's too big already. Furthermore, the author doesn't know why, but his prefaces, though frank and unpretentious, have always driven critics to attack him* rather than support him. Instead of being his true and faithful shields, his prefaces have been strange costumes drawing attention to the soldier who wears them and bringing all the fire on his head in the heat of battle, while they themselves are never put to the test—a nasty trick.

No, the author has been influenced by other considerations. He felt that, though you may seldom visit a building's cellars for your own amusement, it isn't always a bad idea to examine its foundations. So, once again, he will expose himself to the wrath of the magazines by issuing a preface. *Che sera, sera*.* He has never been particularly concerned about the fate of his works; the literary question 'What will people think?' has never greatly frightened him. In the heated debate that has brought theatres and schools, public and Académie* into conflict, it may be interesting to hear the voice of a lone 'apprentice' of nature and truth, who withdrew early from the literary world because he loves literature. What does he have to offer? Good intentions rather than 'good taste', conviction rather than talent, study rather than knowledge.

Furthermore, he'll confine himself to general issues of art, rather than turning them into a highway for his own work; he doesn't claim to be writing a defence of anyone or an indictment of anyone. The important question isn't whether his book is attacked or supported; he, more than anyone, recognizes that! Nor are personal squabbles much to his taste. Duelling egos are always a sorry sight. Therefore, he protests in advance against any such interpretation of his ideas or application of his words, saying with the Spanish storyteller:*

> If you take personally what I've said,
> May you eat it with your daily bread!

In fact, several leading champions of 'sound literary doctrine' have already done him the honour of throwing down the gauntlet to him, a simple and unseen spectator of this curious fray, in the depths of his obscurity. He won't be fool enough to pick it up. Here, in the following pages, are the arguments that he could use against them; here are his sling and his stone; but other people may, if they choose, hurl them at the heads of the Classical Goliaths.*

Having said that, let's move on.

Let's start with a fact: the earth hasn't always been occupied by a single kind of civilization, or (to use a more precise, though more wide-ranging, term) a single society. The human race as a whole has grown, developed, matured as each one of us does individually. It has been a child, it has been an adult; now we're seeing it in its venerable old age. Before the time that we moderns call 'ancient', there existed another era, which antiquity called 'fabulous', but which might more accurately be called 'primitive'. Here, then, we have three successive major phases of civilization, from its beginnings to the present day. Now, poetry always arises out of society; and so, by considering the character of the latter, we can try to distinguish the nature of the former, during each of the three great epochs of world history: primitive times, ancient times, and modern times.

In primitive times, when man first woke in a newborn world, poetry woke with him.* He was faced with marvels, which dazzled and enchanted him, and so his first utterance was simply a hymn. He was still so close to God that his every thought was an ecstasy, his every dream a vision. He opened his heart and sang as naturally as he breathed. His lyre had only three strings—God, the soul, the creation—but this threefold mystery enfolded everything, this threefold concept included everything. The earth was still virtually deserted. There were families rather than nations; fathers rather than kings. Each tribe lived peacefully; no property, no law, no jostling, no warfare. Everything was there for everyone. Society was communal, without anything to constrain the individual man, who led a pastoral, nomadic life of the kind that occurs at the dawn of every civilization. Such a life encourages solitary contemplations and fanciful dreams. He drifted and wandered. His way of thinking, like his way of living, might be compared to a cloud changing shape and direction in response to every wind that blows. There you have the first man, the first poet. He was young, he was lyrical. His only form of religion was prayer; his only form of poetry was the ode.

This poem, this ode of the primitive times, was the Book of Genesis.*

Little by little, however, the world outgrew its first youth. Every realm expanded; the family became a tribe, the tribe a nation. Each of these groups of people gathered around a common centre, and kingdoms appeared. The nomadic impulse was replaced by the social impulse. Camps gave way to cities, tents to palaces, arks to temples. The leaders of these embryonic states were still shepherds, but shepherds of people; their shepherds' staffs were already starting to look like sceptres. Everything became settled and fixed. Religion assumed a form; prayer was dictated by rituals, worship by dogmas. Thus priest and king shared the fatherhood of their people; a theocratic society replaced a patriarchal one.

At the same time, the nations began to pack the earth too closely. They inconvenienced each other, they jostled against each other; as a result, empires clashed—warfare (see the *Iliad*). Some displaced others; as a result, tribes travelled—migration (see the *Odyssey*). Poetry reflected these great events; it moved from ideas to things. It sang of ages, peoples, empires. It became epic; it gave birth to Homer.*

Homer, in fact, dominates ancient society. In such a society, everything is simple, everything is epic. Poetry is religion, religion is law. The virginity of the world's first phase is followed by the chastity of the second. From individual morality to social custom, everything is stamped with a kind of solemn gravity. Only one aspect of nomadic life has been preserved: respect for the stranger, the traveller. The family has a fatherland, which is the centre of everything; there is a cult of the hearth, and a cult of the sepulchre.

I repeat: such a civilization must necessarily express itself in an epic way. Its epics may take various forms, but they will retain that essential character. Pindar is priestly rather than patriarchal, epic rather than lyric. This second age of the world does inevitably have its annalists, but in vain do they strive to gather traditions and reckon ages; chronology can't drive away poetry; history remains epic. Herodotus* is another Homer.

But the epic tendency is most striking of all in the ancient Greek tragedies. It walks onto the stage without any reduction of its immense and inordinate proportions. Its characters are still heroes, demigods, gods; its driving forces are still dreams, oracles, dooms; its scenes are still musterings, funerals, battles. What the rhapsodists* sang, the actors declaim; that's the only difference.

To take the point further. When the whole action and setting of the epic poem were transferred bodily to the stage, the chorus took over what was left. The chorus commented on the tragedy, encouraged the heroes, summoned and sent away the daylight, narrated, mourned, rejoiced, sometimes added the scenery, explained the moral of the story, flattered the audience. Now, what is this chorus, this bizarre character placed between spectacle and spectator? Isn't it simply the poet completing his epic?

The ancients' theatres, like their dramas, were grandiose, pontifical, epic. They could hold thirty thousand spectators; performances took place in the open air, in broad daylight, and lasted all day. The actors lifted up their voices, masked their features, heightened their size; they made themselves into giants, like their roles. The stage was huge. It could stand for either the interior or exterior of a temple, a palace, a camp, a city. Immense spectacles were presented on it. To cite a few examples from memory: Prometheus on the mountain; Antigone on the heights of a citadel, looking for her brother Polyneices in the enemy army (*The Phoenician Women*);* Evadne flinging herself from the top of a cliff into the flames where the body of Capaneus was burning (Euripides' *Suppliant Women*); a ship visibly coming into port, and unloading fifty princesses with their retinue (Aeschylus' *Suppliant Women*). Every aspect of it—its architecture, its poetry—was monumental. The ancient world knew nothing more solemn or majestic; its religion and its history merged into its drama. Its leading actors were priests; its dramas were religious ceremonies, national festivities.

One last point, to finish our portrait of the epic character of those times: in its content, as in its form, tragedy simply repeated epic. All the ancient tragedians took their material from Homer. The same myths, the same catastrophes, the same heroes. They all drew from the Homeric river. Everything was the *Iliad* and the *Odyssey*. Like Achilles dragging the body of Hector, Greek tragedy kept circling around Troy.*

Yet the age of the epic was drawing to its close. Like the civilization it depicted, that type of poetry revolved around itself and wore itself out as it did so. Rome copied Greece, Virgil* imitated Homer; and epic poetry, apparently wanting to die with suitable dignity, perished in that last act of childbirth.

It was high time. A new era was about to begin, for the world and poetry alike.

A spiritual religion* replaced material, external paganism; it crept to the very heart of the ancient world, killed it, and planted the seed of modern civilization within the corpse of the civilization that had decayed. This religion was complete, because it was true; it established morality securely between its teachings and its rites. First of all, it taught man that he has two lives: one transient, the other eternal; one earthly, the other heavenly. It showed him that he, like his destiny, is twofold; within him there are an animal and a mind, a soul and a body—that he is, in short, the point of intersection, the link connecting the two chains of beings that encompass all creation:

material beings and immaterial beings, the former rising from stones to people, the latter rising from people to God.

Some of these truths may have been suspected by a few sages of the ancient world, but their full, radiant, large-scale revelation came with the Gospel. The pagan schools of thought had been groping in the dark, grasping at falsehoods and truths alike in their random wanderings. At times some philosophers shed light on the things around them, but it was a dim light that lit only one side and intensified the darkness on the other. Hence all the fantastic inventions of ancient philosophy. Nothing but the strong, steady, even light of God's wisdom could replace all those flickering gleams of human wisdom. Pythagoras, Epicurus, Socrates, Plato* were candles; Christ is daylight.

Moreover, the ancient theogony* had been utterly material. Instead of distinguishing spirit and body, as Christianity does, it bestowed shapes and faces on everything, even concepts and mental faculties. It treated everything as visible, tangible, physical. Its gods required a cloud to veil them from sight. They drank, ate, slept. They were wounded, and their blood was shed; they were lamed, and they went around limping ever after. That religion had full gods and partial gods. Its thunder was beaten on an anvil from (among other ingredients) three streaks of rain twisted together (*tres imbris torti radios*). Its Jupiter held the world by a golden chain; its sun rode in a four-horse chariot; its hell was a chasm with an opening geographically marked on the map; its heaven was a mountain.*

Thus paganism, which moulded all its creations from the same clay, belittled divinity and aggrandized humanity. Homer's heroes were almost the same size as his gods. Ajax defied Jupiter. Achilles was the equal of Mars.* But as we have just seen, Christianity drew a sharp distinction between spirit and matter. It fixed a great gulf between soul and body, an abyss between the human race and God.

To complete the picture we have started to draw, we should note that the arrival of Christianity coincided with—and caused—the development of a new feeling in the human mind, a feeling unknown to the ancients and remarkably prominent in modern times, something more than solemnity and less than misery: melancholy. And, after all, how could the human heart, which had previously been numbed by purely hieratic and sacerdotal rituals, fail to awaken and become conscious of some unforeseen faculty stirring within it, at the breath of a religion that was human because it was divine, a religion that made the rich man's treasure the poor man's prayer, a religion of equality, freedom, and charity? How could the human heart fail to see everything in a new light, now that the Gospel had shown it the soul beyond the senses, and eternity behind life?

At the same time, moreover, there was such a profound revolution in the world that a similar revolution in the human mind became inevitable. Before that time, regal catastrophes had rarely reached the very heart of the population; only kings had fallen, only rulers had vanished. Lightning had blasted only the heights, and, as we have already pointed out, events had seemed to unfold with epic solemnity. In the ancient world, each individual occupied a very lowly position; the only disasters that could affect him were those that occurred in his own family. Thus he scarcely knew any misfortune apart from domestic troubles. National upheavals almost never disrupted his personal life. But as soon as a Christian society was established, the old order was shaken to its foundations. Everything was uprooted. There were repeated clashes and conflicts; some nations were hurled into the light, others into the darkness, under the impact of the events that were destroying the old Europe and rebuilding it in a new way. There was so much hubbub and tumult in the world that some of it inevitably reached the very heart of the people. It was more than an echo, it was a repercussion. Man, retreating into himself when his superiors were shaken, began to pity the human race, and to reflect on life's bitter ironies. This feeling, which had been a sense of despair for the pagan Cato,* was transformed by Christianity into melancholy.

In that era, the spirit of enquiry and curiosity was born. The great upheavals of the age were also great spectacles, notable revolutions. Here was the North rushing against the South, the Roman world changing shape, the final death agonies of a whole world. As soon as that world was dead, vast clouds of orators, grammarians, sophists, settled like flies on its gigantic corpse. They could be seen and heard buzzing and seething in that den of putrefaction. It was open to all investigators, all commentators, all debaters. Every member, every muscle, every fibre of the colossal fallen body was pulled and pushed in every possible direction. Those anatomists of thought must have been overjoyed at the prospect of conducting even their earliest experiments in dissection on such a grand scale, with a whole dead society as their first guinea pig.

Thus we find the spirit of melancholy and meditation and the demon of analysis and controversy appearing together—virtually arm in arm. Longinus marks one end of this transitional age, Augustine* marks the other. We mustn't eye the period too scornfully; it was the seedbed of everything that has come to fruition since, and (allow me to use a banal but expressive image) its second-rate writers made it a dunghill to fertilize the future harvest. The Middle Ages were grown from the Byzantine empire.

So there we have a new religion and a new society; on that dual basis, inevitably a new kind of poetry would develop. In ancient times—if I may draw attention to something that the reader will already have deduced from the preceding pages—in ancient times, the Muse had been purely epic, and, in keeping with the old polytheism and the old philosophy, she had seen nature only from one side; when she imitated the world around her, she firmly rejected from art anything that didn't correspond to a particular type of beauty. That type was, at first, magnificent; but, as with anything that has been systematized, it ultimately became unrealistic, trite, and conventional. Christianity has led poetry to the truth. Like it, the modern Muse must look at things more loftily, and more broadly. She must feel that not everything in creation is 'beautiful' in human terms, that there is ugliness alongside beauty, deformity next door to gracefulness, grotesquerie just on the other side of sublimity, evil with goodness, darkness with light. She must wonder whether an artist's limited, relative logic is preferable to the infinite, absolute logic of the Creator; whether a human being has the right to correct God; whether Nature is made more beautiful by being mutilated; whether (so to speak) it is Art's job to cut up humanity, life, creation; whether anything can move better when its muscles and supports have been taken away; whether, in short, something is more harmonious when it is less complete. Then, keeping in view both the sublime and the ridiculous, influenced by the spirit of Christian melancholy and philosophic evaluation just mentioned, poetry must make a great, decisive step forward, a step that must change the whole face of the intellectual world like the shock of an earthquake. Poetry must resolve to do what Nature does: to mingle (though not to confound) darkness with light, the sublime with the ridiculous—

in other words, body with soul, animal with spirit, since poetry and religion always have the same point of departure. Everything hangs together.

So a new concept, a principle unfamiliar to the ancient world, is introduced into poetry; and therefore a new form of art develops. (Add an extra component to an entity, and you change the whole entity.) The new concept is the grotesque; the new art-form is comedy.

This is a point that needs to be stressed, because, in my view, it's the crucial factor, the fundamental difference between modern art and ancient art, current art and extinct art, or (to use less precise but more familiar words*) 'Romantic' literature and 'Classical' literature.

'Aha!' cry the people who have 'seen this coming' for some time, 'now we've got you! we've caught you red-handed! So you're saying that the *ugly* ought to be imitated, the *grotesque* ought to be a component of art! [1] But where does that leave elegance—good taste—

---

[1] Yes, of course; yes again; still yes! This is the place to thank a famous foreign writer,* who has kindly given some attention to the author of this book. May I show my esteem and gratitude by pointing out an error he seems to have made? The honourable critic has 'noted' (this is the exact word he uses) a declaration made by the author in the preface to another work: 'There is neither "Classical" nor "Romantic", but, in literature as in everything else, only two categories: good and bad, beautiful and ugly, true and false.' There wasn't any need to study that profession of faith so solemnly. The author never has deviated from it, and never will. It can be reconciled readily enough with 'the *ugly* ought to be imitated, the *grotesque* ought to be a component of art'. The two statements aren't contradictory. The distinction between beauty and ugliness in art doesn't correspond exactly to that in nature. In the arts, only the execution of a work can make anything beautiful or ugly. When faithfully and poetically transposed into the domain of art, something that is distorted, horrible, and hideous becomes beautiful, admirable, and sublime—without losing any of its monstrous quality; on the other hand, when the most beautiful things in the world are falsely and systematically arranged in an artificial composition, they become ridiculous, absurd, hybrid, *ugly*. Callot's orgies, Salvator Rosa's *Temptation* with its extraordinary devil, his *Battle* with all its ghastly figures of death and carnage, Bonifacio's *Triboulet*, Murillo's fleabitten beggar, and the carvings in which Benvenuto Cellini makes fun of such hideous figures in arabesques and acanthuses, are ugly things from the standpoint of nature, beautiful things from that of art; while nothing is 'uglier' than all the Greek and Roman profiles, the patchwork ideal beauty emitted by the second-rate school of David* with its fluffy purplish colouring. Job and Philoctetes, with their purulent festering sores, are beautiful; Campistron's* kings and queens are mighty ugly in their purple robes and under their tinsel crowns. In art, anything done well is beautiful, anything done badly is ugly. The author had already made his position clear by relating this distinction to those between 'true and false' and 'good and bad'. Moreover, in art as in nature, grotesquerie is a single component, not the ultimate goal. What is merely grotesque isn't complete [*Hugo's note*].

and so on? Don't you understand that Art ought to improve on Nature? that things have to be ennobled? that you have to pick and choose what you do? Did our predecessors ever put ugly and grotesque things into their works? Did they ever mingle comedy and tragedy? Consider the writers of the ancient world, sir! And what's more, Aristotle. And what's more, Boileau. And what's more, La Harpe.* Honestly now!'

These are, no doubt, significant arguments (their most notable merit being their originality). But I don't have any obligation to answer them. I'm not erecting any system here—God preserve us from systems! I'm simply stating a fact. I'm writing history, not criticism. Like it or not, this is the way things are.

To return to the point, then, let's try to show that this fertile union of the grotesque with the sublime has been the origin of the modern spirit—so complex, so varied in form, so infinite in its creations (in striking contrast to the uniform simplicity of the ancient spirit); this must be our point of departure, if we are to describe the real and radical difference between the two systems.

Not that comedy and grotesquerie were absolutely unknown to the ancients. How could they have been? Nothing comes from nothing; the seeds of the new era always exist within the old one. As far back as the *Iliad*, Thersites and Vulcan were providing comedy among men and gods respectively. Greek tragedy was too true to nature and too original to shun comedy altogether. Consider—to cite a couple of examples that happen to spring to mind—the scene between Menelaus and the palace doorkeeper in Act I of *Helen*, or the scene with the Phrygian in Act IV of *Orestes*. The Tritons, the Satyrs, and the Cyclopes are grotesques; the Sirens, the Furies, the Fates, and the Harpies are grotesques; Polyphemus is a tragic grotesque; Silenus* is a comic grotesque.

But in those days that aspect of art was still recognizably in its infancy. It was constrained, indeed crushed, by the dominant artform of the period—the epic. The grotesquerie of ancient art is timid, always trying to hide its face. You feel that it isn't on its home territory, because it doesn't behave quite naturally. It disguises itself as much as it can. The Satyrs, Tritons, and Sirens are scarcely misshapen. The Fates and Harpies are hideous because of their attributes rather than their characters; the Furies are beautiful, and are called Eumenides*—'the Gentle Ones' or 'the Kindly Ones'.

Other grotesque figures are veiled with grandeur or divinity. Polyphemus is a giant; Midas is a king; Silenus is a god.

So comedy can pass almost unnoticed in the great epic scheme of ancient art. Next to the Olympians' chariots, what is Thespis' cart? Alongside the Homeric giants, Aeschylus, Sophocles, and Euripides, what are Aristophanes and Plautus?[1]* Homer sweeps them away with him, as Hercules carried away the pygmies concealed in his lionskin.*

In the minds of modern writers, by contrast, grotesquerie plays a highly important part. It pervades their whole thinking; it generates deformity and horror on one side, comedy and clowning on the other. It surrounds religion with thousands of original superstitions, poetry with countless picturesque fantasies. It sows earth, air, water, and fire with the myriads of intermediate beings that appear, teeming with life, in the popular traditions of the Middle Ages; it sets the Witches' Sabbath dancing in the dark, it gives Satan horns and cloven hoofs and the wings of a bat.* Sometimes it casts into Christendom's hell the hideous figures conjured up by the austere genius of Dante and Milton, sometimes the absurd creatures among which Callot, that burlesque Michelangelo, finds amusement. When it turns from the ideal world to the real one, it unleashes countless parodies of human foibles. Its fancy creates Scaramouches and Crispinos and Harlequins—grinning silhouettes of mankind, types utterly unknown to solemn antiquity, even though they arose in Classical Italy. And it sets Sganarelle gambolling around Don Juan, and Mephistopheles around Faust*—painting the same work in colours imagined now by the south, now by the north.[2]

---

[1] These two names are joined, but not confused, here. Aristophanes stands incomparably higher than Plautus; Aristophanes has a place among the ancient poets, as Diogenes has among the ancient philosophers.

It's obvious why Terence isn't mentioned in this passage alongside the two popular comic writers of the ancient world. Terence is the drawing-room poet of the Scipios,* an elegant and charming engraver whose hand obliterates the uncouth old comedy of the ancient Romans [*Hugo's note*].

[2] This great drama of human damnation dominates the whole medieval imagination. Mister Punch carried off by the devil to the great amusement of street crowds is merely a trifling and popular manifestation. When you compare the twin comedies *Don Juan* and *Faust*, the really remarkable point is that Don Juan is a materialist, Faust a spiritualist. The former has tasted all forms of pleasure, the latter all forms of learning. Both have attacked the tree of good and evil; one has stolen the fruits, the other has dug up the roots. The former is damned for the sake of enjoyment, the latter for the sake of knowledge. One is an aristocrat, the other a philosopher. Don Juan is the body, Faust the mind. The two plays are complementary [*Hugo's note*].

And how free, how frank, its allure is! How boldly it displays all the bizarre forms so timidly swaddled and shrouded by the previous era! When an ancient poet had to provide lame Vulcan with companions, he tried to conceal their deformity by building them on a colossal scale. The modern spirit retains this myth of subterranean blacksmiths, but gives them a radically different and much more remarkable character: it turns giants into dwarfs, Cyclopes into gnomes. With similar originality, it replaces the rather banal Lernaean hydra with the various local dragons of our own legends: the gargoyle of Rouen, the *graouillio* of Metz, the *chairsallée* of Troyes, the *drée* of Montlhéry, the *tarasco* of Tarascon—monsters very diverse in shape, and with an additional attraction in their uncouth names. All these creations have an inherently vigorous, profound character from which the ancient world apparently tended to flinch. The Greek Eumenides are decidedly less horrible, and therefore decidedly less real, than the witches of *Macbeth*. Pluto* isn't the devil.

In my view, a most original book could be written about the use of the grotesque in art. Such a book could show what powerful effects modern artists have drawn from that fruitful type, which is still attacked by conservative critics today. Our theme may shortly lead us to note a few aspects of this vast topic, but at present, I'll merely say that, both as a means of contrast and as a goal alongside the sublime, I find the grotesque as rewarding as any source of artistic inspiration that Nature could possibly supply. Rubens,* no doubt, thought so; he loved to introduce some hideous court dwarf into coronation scenes, glittering ceremonies, displays of royal pomp. The universal beauty that ancient artists solemnly spread over everything did have its monotonous side; a single tone, endlessly reiterated, can become tiring after a while. It's hard to produce much variety when one sublimity follows another—and we do need an occasional rest from everything, even from beauty. Now, the grotesque may act as a pause, a contrast, a point of departure from which we can approach what is beautiful with fresher and keener powers of perception. A salamander can set off a water-sprite; a gnome can embellish a sylph.

Another valid point could also be made. Contact with the grotesque has made the sublime purer, greater, indeed more sublime than it was in ancient times. Inevitably so. When art is internally consistent, it produces all its effects much more tellingly. If Homer's

Elysium lacks most of the ethereal harmony and angelic beauty of Milton's Eden, it's because the latter has a far more terrible hell beneath it than the pagan Tartarus. Do you think Beatrice and Francesca da Rimini would seem as enchanting in the hands of a poet who didn't lock us in the Tower of Famine and force us to share Ugolino's revolting meal? Dante would have less charm if he had less strength. Are plump Naiads, sturdy Tritons, and libertine Zephyrs as diaphanously graceful as our sylphs and water-sprites? The modern imagination has sent vampires, ogres, *aulnes*,[1] *psylli*, ghouls, *brucolaques*, *aspioles*,* prowling fearsomely through the graveyard— and isn't that why it can also give its fairies a far more bodiless, ethereal character than the pagan nymphs? The Venus of ancient times was, no doubt, beautiful and admirable; but why do Jean Goujon's* figures possess such a curious dainty delicate grace, such an obscure impression of vitality and grandeur? Isn't that due to the proximity of rough, vigorous medieval sculptures?

If these necessary digressions (which could be pursued much further) haven't distracted the reader from my train of thought, he'll certainly have recognized by now how much the grotesque, that seed of comedy, must have grown and thrived when transported by the modern Muse into a more favourable soil than that of paganism and the epic. In fact, nowadays there has to be a distinction within humanity and creation. In the new form of poetry, the grotesque will stand for the bestial side of man, whereas the sublime will present the human soul in its new state, refined by Christian morality, with all contaminants and impurities removed. The sublime will possess all kinds of elegance, grace, beauty; in the course of time, it will inevitably be able to create a Juliet, a Desdemona, an Ophelia. The grotesque will possess all kinds of inadequacy, ugliness, incongruity; it will be assigned all the passions, vices, crimes; it will be lecherous, grovelling, gluttonous, stingy, treacherous, quarrelsome, hypocritical; it will be now Iago, now Tartuffe, now Basilio; now Polonius, now Harpagon, now Bartolo; now Falstaff, now Scapin, now Figaro.* There is only one type of beauty; there are myriad types of ugliness. Why? Because beauty (to put it in human terms) is form considered

---

[1] The superstitions behind the German ballad *Erlking** (in French, *Le Roi des aulnes*) aren't related to alder trees, as people commonly imagine. The *aulnes* (late Latin *alcunae*) are a group of sprites who play a role in Hungarian legends [*Hugo's note*].

only in its simplest aspect, its most perfect symmetry, its most absolute harmony with the way we ourselves are designed. Consequently, its overall effect, though always complete, is always limited, just as we ourselves are. What we call ugliness, on the other hand, is a detail of a vast pattern that extends beyond our comprehension, and harmonizes not with humanity but with the whole of creation. That's why it always appears to us in new, incomplete shapes.

It's interesting to trace the emergence and development of the grotesque during the modern era. First of all there's an influx, an invasion, an irruption—a river bursting its banks. At its origin, it runs through the dying Latin literature; it tinges Persius, Petronius, Juvenal, and leaves behind the *Golden Ass* of Apuleius.* After that, it flows out into the imaginations of the new races who are making a new Europe. It floods through their storytellers and chroniclers and novelists. You can see it spread from south to north. It dallies with the dreams of the Teutonic nations, and at the same time, it quickens the impressive Spanish *romanceros*—the *Iliad* of chivalry—with the breath of life. To choose one example, in the *Romance of the Rose* it depicts a solemn ceremony, the election of a king, in these terms:

> They chose a villain of the hugest kind,
> The biggest-boned they could possibly find.*

Above all, it stamps its character on the marvellous architecture that held pride of place among the arts during the Middle Ages. It brands its mark on cathedrals' brows; it frames its hells and purgatories in ogive doorways, and sets them burning in stained glass windows; it unleashes its demons and monsters around capitals, along friezes, on eaves. It sprawls in countless shapes on the wooden façades of the houses, the stone façades of castles, the marble façades of palaces. From art it moves to lifestyle; while it offers comic *graciosos* for the people to applaud, it also supplies kings with court jesters. (Later, in the age of etiquette, it will present us with the spectacle of Scarron on the very edge of Louis XIV's bed.) In the meantime it inspires the science of heraldry, and draws hieroglyphic feudal symbols on the knights' shields. From lifestyle it passes into law; thousands of bizarre customs bear witness to its effect on the institutions of the Middle Ages. Just as it had set wine-spattered Thespis skipping in his cart, it dances with the law-clerks on the famous marble table that was used for both popular farces and royal banquets. Finally, having gained acceptance in art, lifestyle, and law, it enters the church itself. We can see it ordaining curious ceremonies in every Catholic town—strange processions in which all sorts of superstitions march side by side with religion: sublimity flanked by all kinds of grotesquerie. In a nutshell, its verve, its vitality, its creativity, were so great, at this literary dawn, that its very first ray of light cast three comic Homers across the threshold of modern poetry:[1] Ariosto in Italy, Cervantes in Spain, Rabelais* in France.

No need to stress further the influence of grotesquerie on the third age of civilization. Every aspect of the so-called 'Romantic' era illustrates its intimate creative alliance with beauty. Even the most naïve popular legends sometimes depict this mystery of modern art with remarkable intuitive skill. The ancient world couldn't have devised *Beauty and the Beast*.*

Indeed, in the literature of the epoch we've just been discussing, the grotesque actually predominates over the sublime. But that's a passing fever, an initial passion for novelty, a first flood that soon begins to subside. Beauty quickly regains its rightful place and function—not to exclude the other principle, but to control it. From that time on, grotesquerie must be content with a corner of the composition in Murillo's royal frescoes and Veronese's* sacred paintings; it must be content to be a component of the two remarkable *Last Judgements* in which art can take such pride: Michelangelo's scene of rapture and horror that enriches the Vatican, and Rubens's fearful human souls hurled down from the vaults of Antwerp Cathedral. The time has come: the two principles are held in balance. A man, a poet-king (*poeta soverano*, as Dante says of Homer),* is going to reconcile everything. The two rival spirits unite their fires, and the result is Shakespeare.

This brings us to the great poetic master of modern times. Shakespeare is Drama; and drama is the characteristic art-form of the third era of poetry, the literature of the present day. Drama unites the grotesque and the sublime, the terrible and the ridiculous, the tragic and the comic.

---

[1] The remarkable expression 'comic Homer' was coined by Monsieur Charles Nodier to describe Rabelais; I ask his pardon for broadening it to include Cervantes and Ariosto [*Hugo's note*].

To summarize briefly what we have seen so far, there have been three ages of poetry, each corresponding to a phase of society: ode, epic, and drama. Primitive times were lyric, ancient times were epic, modern times are dramatic. The ode sings of eternity, the epic commemorates history, the drama portrays life.[1] The first type of poetry is naïve, the second type is simple, the third is realistic. Rhapsodists marked the transition from lyric to epic; novelists, similarly, mark the transition from epic to drama. Historians arose during the second era, chroniclers and critics during the third. The characters of odes are colossi—Adam, Cain, Noah; those of epics are giants—Achilles, Atreus, Orestes; those of dramas are men—Hamlet, Macbeth, Othello.* Odes draw their life from the ideal, epics from the grandiose, dramas from the real. And finally, the three types of poetry flow from three sources: the Bible, Homer, and Shakespeare.

Such, then (I am merely making an observation), have been the distinctive features of thought during the different phases of human society. Those have been its three faces—the faces of youth, adulthood, and old age. Whether you look at one particular literature, or all literatures together, you will reach the same conclusion: lyric poets come before epic poets, epic poets before dramatic poets. In France, Malherbe before Chapelain, Chapelain before Corneille. In ancient Greece, Orpheus before Homer, Homer before Aeschylus. In the Book of primitive times, Genesis before Kings, Kings before Job.* Or, to return to the great ladder of worldwide poetry that we have just traversed, the Bible before the *Iliad*, the *Iliad* before Shakespeare.

At first, society sings its dreams; then it tells its deeds; finally it depicts its thoughts. That, incidentally, is why drama, uniting the most opposed characteristics, can be both profound and pellucid, both philosophical and picturesque, at the same time.

It follows, moreover, that everything in nature and life goes

---

[1] 'But drama, too, depicts human history', it will be said. So it does; but as *life*, not as *history*. Drama leaves the historian to deal with the exact sequence of general facts, the order of dates, the great mass movements, the battles, the conquests, the divisions of empire, the whole exterior of history. It takes the interior. The things that historians ignore or despise—details of costume, lifestyle, personal appearance, the underside of events—in a word, life—are its property. When these little things are taken up by a great hand (*prensa manu magna*), drama can appear immense and be immense as a whole; but we mustn't look for pure history in drama (even 'historical' drama). It writes legends, not facts. It chronicles, but it isn't chronological [*Hugo's note*].

through the same three phases—lyric, epic, and dramatic—because everything is born, lives, and dies. It would be absurd to link the imagination's flights of fancy with logic's unemotional deductions; otherwise, a poet might say, for instance, that sunrise is a hymn, midday a dazzling epic, sunset a sombre drama—a struggle between day and night, life and death. But that would be poetry, perhaps lunacy; and 'what does it prove?'*

Let's confine ourselves to the points stated above; and let's complete them with an important additional observation. I haven't tried to assign the three phases of poetry to exclusive realms; I've merely noted their predominant characteristics. As we saw a moment ago, the Bible, that sacred monument of lyricism, contains an embryonic epic, the book of Kings, and an embryonic drama, the book of Job. Throughout the Homeric epics you can discern a remnant of lyric poetry and a beginning of dramatic poetry. The epic is the point at which ode and drama intersect. Everything exists in everything; but each thing has a generative element, to which all the other elements are subordinate, and which gives the whole work its distinctive character.

Drama is complete poetry. It is the development of both ode and epic; it summarizes and epitomizes them, while they contain merely the seeds of it. The man who said 'the French have no head for epics'* said something clever and true; and if he'd gone so far as to say 'the moderns', his statement would have been wise as well as witty. All the same, there is undeniably something of the epic spirit in the amazing *Athalie*, which is so lofty, so simply sublime, that the age of kings wasn't able to appreciate it. Clearly, too, Shakespeare's cycle of chronicle plays has a prominent epic side. Lyric poetry is even more congenial to drama; it never clashes with it; it conforms to all its fancies, it readily adjusts to all its aspects—now sublime, as in Ariel, now grotesque, as in Caliban. Our age is outstandingly lyric precisely because it is pre-eminently dramatic. Beginning and end have many points in common; sunset resembles sunrise, an old man is twice a child. But that second childhood is different from the first; it is as sad as the other was happy. So also with lyric poetry. At the dawn of the human race it was dazzling and visionary; at the decline it reappears, sombre and reflective. The Bible opens with the smiling Genesis, and closes with the ominous Revelation.* Modern odes are still inspired, but they are no longer ignorant. They meditate rather than contemplate; their reveries are melancholic. The offspring of that Muse show that she has been coupling with drama.

To illustrate the ideas I've been presenting, I might compare primitive lyric poetry to a peaceful lake, which reflects the sky's clouds and stars; the epic is a river flowing out of it, reflecting on the way its banks, forests, fields and cities, and emptying into the sea of drama. Like the lake, drama reflects the sky; like the river, it reflects its banks; but it alone has tempests and chasms.

All modern poetry, therefore, tends toward drama. *Paradise Lost* is primarily a drama, only secondarily an epic. Its author, we know, first imagined it in dramatic terms,* and its readers still tend to remember it in such terms: the old dramatic framework of Milton's epic structure is still conspicuous. When Dante finished his remarkable *Inferno* and shut its gates, and needed only to find a name for his work, his genius instinctively showed him that his multifarious poem was an emanation of drama rather than epic; and on the first page of the great masterpiece his bronze pen wrote the words *Divina Commedia*.

Thus it will be seen that the only two modern poets who can be ranked with Shakespeare support his position. Like him, they colour all modern poetry with drama; like him, they mingle grotesquerie and sublimity; and, instead of standing apart from the vast literary edifice that rests on Shakespeare, they act to some extent as twin buttresses of the structure in which he is the central pillar or the capstone.

Let's now summarize some of the above points, which need additional stress. We've reached our goal; now it must become our point of departure.

When Christianity first said to mankind: 'You are dual; you are made up of two entities, one perishable, the other immortal—one fleshly, the other ethereal—one enslaved to passions and appetites, the other borne on wings of zeal and fancy—one constantly bent toward its mother Earth, the other forever drawn toward its homeland Heaven'—on that very day, drama was created. Isn't that simply the perennial contrast, the perpetual conflict between two opposed principles that are always in existence, fighting for possession of man, from the cradle to the grave?

The poetry that has sprung from Christianity, the poetry of our era, is therefore dramatic. Drama is characterized by realism; realism arises from a natural combination of two elements, the sublime and the grotesque, which intersect in drama just as they do in life and in the created universe. True poetry, complete poetry, consists of a harmony of opposites. Furthermore—it's time to state this explicitly, and here above all, the apparent exceptions confirm the rule—everything that exists in Nature exists in Art.

When we try, from this standpoint, to evaluate our puny conventional rules and disentangle all the scholastic labyrinths and sort out all the petty aesthetic problems so laboriously constructed by the critics of the last two centuries, it's remarkable how quickly the question of the modern theatre resolves itself. The Lilliput Militia have been trying to tie down our sleeping drama with spiderwebs; but its slightest movement will break them.*

When, therefore, thoughtless pedants (the two words aren't mutually exclusive) claim that art should never imitate deformity, ugliness, and grotesquerie, the answer is that grotesquerie is comedy—and comedy manifestly does fall within the realm of art. Tartuffe isn't beautiful, Pourceaugnac* isn't noble; but Pourceaugnac and Tartuffe are excellent artistic creations.

If, driven back from that position to their second line of defence, they deny that grotesquerie and comedy may be allied with sublimity and tragedy, they need to be shown that the former represents the bestial side of humanity, the latter the soul, in the poetry of Christian races. If these two rootstocks of art are systematically segregated, if their branches are prevented from mingling, their only fruits will be abstract vices and absurdities on one side, and abstract concepts of crime, heroism, and virtue on the other. Thus isolated and left to its own devices, each of the two types will go its own way, one on the right hand and one on the left—and reality will remain between them, untouched.[1] After such abstractions, therefore, something still needs to be depicted—namely mankind; after such comedies and tragedies, something still needs to be produced—namely drama.

---

[1] Why is Molière so much more true than our tragic writers? And, to go further, why is he almost always true? Because, even though his era's prejudices imprison him short of pathos and tragedy, he still blends his grotesques with scenes of great sublimity, which complete the humanity of his plays. Because, also, comedy is much closer to nature than tragedy. Molière's characters do weep from time to time; but we can easily imagine plays in which the characters were constantly laughing or being laughed at, and yet remained natural. Yet can we imagine any situation—however terrible and restricted it might be—in which not only did the principal actors refrain from smiling (even with sarcasm or irony), but no human being, from prince to attendant, ever had a moment of

In drama (as we can at least envisage it, even if we can't create it) everything is interdependent and interrelated, just as it is in real life. Body and soul both have their parts to play in it; people and events are set in motion by that twofold agency, and pass across the stage, now clownish, now dreadful—and now both clownish and dreadful at one and the same time. 'Put him to death, and now let's go to dinner!' says the judge. The Roman senate deliberates on the case of Domitian's turbot. Socrates, while drinking hemlock and discoursing about the immortal soul and the one true deity, breaks off to say that a cock should be sacrificed to Aesculapius. Queen Elizabeth curses and talks Latin. Richelieu defers to the Capuchin Father Joseph, and Louis XI to his barber, Master Olivier-the-Devil. Cromwell declares, 'I have Parliament in my bag and the King in my pocket', or spatters with ink the smiling face of the regicide who brings him Charles I's death warrant—using the very hand with which he signed it. Caesar in his triumphal chariot is afraid of falling.* Yes, people of genius, however great they may be, always carry within them a bestial side which mocks their intellectual prowess. That is what makes them human—and dramatic. 'There is only one step from the sublime to the ridiculous', Napoleon used to say when he was convicted of being human. That flash of lightning from a fiery soul illuminates both art and history; that cry of anguish summarizes both drama and life.

It's notable that contrasts of all such kinds can be found within poets themselves, considered as human beings. As they meditate on existence, highlighting its bitter irony, heaping sarcasm and mockery on our frailties, these people who make us laugh so heartily become intensely sad. They are Heraclitus as well as Democritus.* Beaumarchais was morose, Molière gloomy, Shakespeare melancholy.

The grotesque, then, is one of drama's supreme beauties. It isn't merely useful, it's often necessary. Sometimes it appears in homogeneous lumps, in complete characters: Dandin, Prusias, Trissotin,

laughter or human nature? Finally, Molière is more true than our tragic writers because he makes use of the new principle, the modern principle—the dramatic principle—the principle of grotesquerie and comedy—whereas they waste their powers and abilities returning to the ancient epic circle. That circle is closed; an old, worn-out mould, from which no truth appropriate to our own day can emerge, because it doesn't have the form of modern society [*Hugo's note*].

Brid'oison, Juliet's nurse; sometimes tinged with terror: Richard III, Bégears, Tartuffe, Mephistopheles; sometimes even shrouded in grace and refinement: Figaro, Osric, Mercutio, Don Juan.* It touches everything, because just as the lowliest often have their moments of sublimity, the loftiest frequently pay their mite to triviality and absurdity. On stage, therefore, though it may be intangible and imperceptible, it is ever present—even when silent or eclipsed. It prevents monotony. It pours now laughter, now horror into tragedy. It confronts Romeo with the apothecary, Macbeth with the three witches, Hamlet with the gravediggers. At times, indeed, as in the dialogue between King Lear and his fool, it can blend its howling voice with the darkest, most sublime, most thoughtful music of the soul—and without creating any sense of discord when it does so.

That is what Shakespeare alone was capable of doing—in his own unique way, which neither should nor could be imitated. He, the god of the theatre, seems to encompass, like a trinity, the three distinctive geniuses of our own stage: Corneille, Molière, Beaumarchais.

See how soon arbitrary distinctions of genre collapse in the presence of common sense and good taste! It's just as easy to dispose of the alleged law of the two unities.* (I say two rather than three unities, because the unity of action or overall effect—the only true, well-established unity—has long been left out of the dispute.)

Both in our own country and elsewhere, illustrious present-day writers have already attacked (in practice, as well as in theory) this fundamental rule of the pseudo-Aristotelian law code. And the battle was bound to be a short one. The beams of the old scholastic hovel were so worm-eaten that they broke under the very first assault.

It's curious that the creatures of habit claim to base their 'law of the two unities' on realism, when reality is exactly what kills it. Could anything be less realistic than the vestibule—the peristyle— the antechamber—the nondescript place where our tragedies smugly unfold, where, in succession and for no apparent reason, the conspirators come to utter tirades against the tyrant and the tyrant comes to utter tirades against the conspirators? Perhaps they are thinking of the line from the *Eclogues*: 'Let's sing in alternating verses; the Muses love alternation.'*

Where has anyone ever seen such a vestibule or peristyle? What could be less realistic? (I won't say 'less truthful'; scholastics set little value on truth.) As a result, everything that is too distinctive, too intimate, too localized, to happen in an antechamber or a street—in other words, everything that makes up the real drama—has to happen offstage. In effect, all we see on stage are the elbows of the action; its hands are somewhere else. Instead of scenes we have narrations, instead of tableaux descriptions. Solemn-faced personages stand between the drama and us, like ancient choruses; they come and tell us what is happening in the temple, in the palace, in the public square, until we're often tempted to cry out: 'Really? Well then, take us there! That'd be nice to see; we'd get some real entertainment then!' To which no doubt they'd reply: 'Maybe it would entertain or interest you, but that's beside the point; we have to preserve the dignity of our French Melpomene.'* There you have it!

'But', I'll be told, 'the law that you're rejecting was borrowed from Greek theatre.' Well, just how similar was Greek drama to ours? And in any case, we've already seen that the vast size of the ancient stage often allowed it to encompass a whole region, so that the poet could take the action at whim from one part of the theatre to another, as the story required—virtually as if there had been a modern change of scenery. An odd contradiction! The Greek theatre, enslaved to a political and religious purpose, was still freer than ours, which aims merely to entertain and (perhaps) instruct the audience. The former submitted only to laws that were appropriate for it; the latter assiduously follows rules that are quite alien to its nature. One is art, the other is artifice.

Today we're beginning to understand that correct localization is one of the first principles of realism. The characters who talk and act aren't the only ones who stamp a faithful imprint of the action on the spectator's mind. The place where a certain catastrophe occurs becomes a dreadful, inescapable witness of it; and the absence of that silent character would leave the greatest historical scenes incomplete. What poet would dare to murder Rizzio anywhere other than in Mary Stuart's bedroom, or stab Henri IV anywhere other than in the Rue de la Ferronnerie cluttered with tubs and carriages, or burn Joan of Arc anywhere other than in the marketplace at Rouen, or behead the Duc de Guise anywhere other than in the Château de Blois where his own ambition had summoned large numbers of supporters, or decapitate Charles I and Louis XVI anywhere other than within sight of Whitehall and the Tuileries,* where their ominous scaffolds seemed to mirror their palaces?

The unity of time is just as insubstantial. It's as absurd to imprison the action forcibly within twenty-four hours as within a vestibule. Every plot has its own appropriate timespan, just as it has its own distinctive place. Why administer the same dose of time to every kind of events? Why use the same measuring instrument in all cases? We'd laugh at a cobbler who wanted to put the same size of shoe on everyone's feet. If we cross the unity of time and the unity of place like the bars of a cage, and bring pedantically into it (courtesy of Aristotle) all the deeds, nations, and individuals that Providence lavishes on a vast scale in reality, we'll mutilate people and facts, and make history wince. To go further: the whole thing will die on the operating table. That's why the doctrinaire mutilators usually achieve the results they do: everything that was alive in the history books is dead on the tragic stage. And that's why, in most cases, the cage of the unities encloses only a skeleton.

What's more, if two hours can represent twenty-four, then four hours should logically be able to encompass forty-eight. Thus the unity of time wouldn't be the same in Shakespeare's case as in Corneille's. Mercy on us!

Such, however, are the cheap tricks that mediocrity, envy, and conventionalism have been playing on genius for the past two centuries. That's what has cramped the flight of our greatest poets; their wings have been clipped with the scissors of the unities. And in place of the eagle feathers lopped from Corneille and Racine, what have we been given? Campistron.

Someone might possibly argue: 'If the scenery is changed too often, the spectator grows tired and confused, and his attention span is overloaded. Repeated shifts from place to place, and time to time, could also demand elaborate explanations that bore him. And we need to beware of leaving gaps in the action that prevent the drama's parts from holding closely together, which could also disturb the spectator because he doesn't know what might take place in those empty spaces....' But those are precisely the challenges of the art. They're the specific difficulties inherent in a given subject, and can't be solved by any all-purpose rule. They have to be overcome by genius, not evaded by some 'art of poetry'.

One final point, drawn from the very bowels of art, will be enough to show that the law of the two unities is an absurdity. There is a third unity, the unity of action—the only one that is universally accepted, because it's based on a fact: the fact that the human eye and mind can grasp only one thing at a time. This unity is as necessary as the others are superfluous. It gives the drama its characteristic viewpoint; and for that very reason, it excludes the other two unities. There can no more be three unities in a drama than three horizons in a painting. We must be careful, however, not to confuse unity of action with simplicity of action. Overall unity can be entirely consistent with subplots that contribute to the main action. The parts merely need to be skilfully subordinated to the whole; they need to point constantly toward the central action and be grouped around it at different stages, or rather on different planes. Overall unity is the drama's law of perspective.

'But', the intellectual customs officers will exclaim, 'great geniuses have submitted to these rules that you're rejecting!' Why, so they have, unfortunately! What would they have done, those gifted people, if they'd been allowed to go their own way? At least they didn't accept your chains without a fight. Consider how Pierre Corneille, harassed at the very outset over his wonderful *Cid*, struggles under the weight of Mairet and Claveret and d'Aubignac and Scudéry—how he denounces these men to posterity for their violence! They 'whitewash themselves with Aristotle', he says. Consider how he is told (I'm quoting the very language of the era): 'Thy Youth must be instructed before it teacheth; which, if thou art not a Scaliger or a Heinsius, passeth all suffrance!' At which point Corneille rebels and asks if they want to him to stoop 'lower euen than Claueret'! This makes Scudéry, in lofty indignation, remind 'the thrice worthy Authour of the *Cid* . . . of the modestie with which Tasso, that greatest man of his age, did defend the noblest of his Workes, against the cruellest and most uniust Censure that euer was or, perhaps, euer will be made. Monsieur Corneille', he adds, 'sheweth well by his Answers, that he is as far from the moderation as from the merit of that excellent Authour.' The 'youth' so 'justly' and 'gently censured' still dares to resist; then Scudéry returns to the attack; he calls the 'Eminent Academy' to his aid: 'O MY IUDGES, pronounce a iudgement worthie of your Renowne, which shall teache all Europe that *Le Cid* is farre from being the master-peece of the greatest man in Frãce, but much rather, the least iudicious worke of Monsieur Corneille himselfe. Ye owe this, both for your owne glorie in particular, and also for that of oure whole Nation; for

Strangers who behold this fine master-peece, after having had Tassos and Guarinis in their owne midst, shall beleeve our greatest Masters to be little more than Apprentices.'

That instructive little passage encapsulates the immemorial strategy of envious routine in the presence of rising talent. The same thing is still happening in our own day, supplementing (to take one example) Lord Byron's earliest efforts with a remarkable page of criticism. Scudéry gives us the gist of the method: the previous works of a man of genius always better than the new ones, showing that he's going down rather than up (*Mélite* and *La Galerie du Palais* ranked above *Le Cid*); the names of the dead perpetually thrown in the teeth of the living (Corneille stoned with Tasso and Guarini— Guarini!—just as, later, Racine will be stoned with Corneille, Voltaire with Racine, and any rising author of the present day with Corneille and Racine and Voltaire). The technique, as you can see, is well worn, but it must be good, because it's still in use. And yet the great man, poor devil, struggled on. Scudéry, the bully boy of this tragicomedy, is now driven to extreme measures. Here we can admire the way in which he mercilessly deploys his classic artillery to abuse and maltreat his opponent. He 'shows' the author of the *Cid* 'what Episodes shoulde be, according to Aristotle, who teacheth it in the tenthe and sixteenthe Chapters of his *Poetics*'; he shoots Corneille down using the same Aristotle 'in the eleventhe Chapter of his *Arte of Poetry*, wherein the *Cid* will be found condemn'd' and Plato 'in the tenthe Booke of his *Republique*' and Marcelin 'in the twenty-seuenthe Booke, as may be seene' and 'the tragedies of Niobe and Jephthah' and 'the *Ajax* of Sophocles' and 'Heinsius, *The Constitution of Tragedy*, in the sixt Chapter; and Scaliger the Sonne, in his poems' and, finally, by 'the Canonists and Iurisconsults'. The former arguments had been addressed to the Académie; this one went to the cardinal. Needle him first, then club him. A judge was needed to settle the question. Chapelain passed judgement. Thus Corneille found himself condemned, the lion was muzzled, or, in the language of the day, the 'crow' was 'plucked'. Now here's the sad side of this grotesque drama. Having been thus crushed at the very outset, this utterly modern genius, raised on Spain and the Middle Ages, was forced to be untrue to himself and retreat into antiquity. So he supplied us with a Castilian Rome, impressive no doubt in its own way, but—except perhaps in the *Nicomède** so savagely ridiculed last century for its boldness and naturalness—we never meet either the real Rome or the real Corneille.

Racine experienced the same troubles, but didn't offer the same resistance. Neither his abilities nor his character had the lofty austerity of Corneille's. He bowed in silence, and abandoned his delightful elegy *Esther* and his magnificent epic *Athalie* to an age that scorned them. This shows that if he hadn't been so paralysed by the prejudices of his day, if he hadn't been so often stunned by the Classical numbfish, he wouldn't have deleted Locusta from his play about Narcissus and Nero, and, above all, wouldn't have left offstage the splendid banquet scene with Seneca's pupil poisoning Britannicus in the cup of reconciliation.* But can we ask a bird to fly in a vacuum? How many excellent things we have lost because of the 'people of taste', from Scudéry to La Harpe! You could make a very fine work from everything that their dry breath has blasted before its time. All the same, our great poets did still manage to express their genius despite all these obstacles. People often failed to lock them up inside rules and dogmas. Like the Hebrew giant,* they simply carried their prison gates away with them onto the mountain.

Nevertheless, people keep saying, and no doubt will keep saying for some time yet: 'Follow the rules! Imitate the great examples! The great examples were created by the rules!' Now just a moment! There are two kinds of 'great examples' under consideration here: those that were created by the rules, and those from which the rules were derived in the first place. Which kind would a genius produce? It's never pleasant to have any contact with pedants—but wouldn't it be a thousand times better to teach them than to be taught by them? Then there's the question of imitation. Can a reflection match a light source? Can a planet constantly moving in the same circle match the central star that generates it? Virgil, with all his poetry, is merely a moon of Homer.

And whom are we supposed to imitate? The ancients? We've just seen that their theatre was quite different from ours. In any case, Voltaire, who wouldn't accept Shakespeare,* wouldn't accept the Greeks either. Let him tell us why: 'The Greeks attempted spectacles that we find equally disgusting. Hippolytus, brained by his fall, enumerates his wounds and utters pitiful howls. Philoctetes collapses under his sufferings; dark blood flows from his wound. Oedipus, covered in blood (and it is still dripping from the eyes he has just torn out), rails against gods and mortals alike. Clytemnestra is heard shrieking while her own son butchers her and Electra cries out on stage: "Strike her down, don't pity her, she didn't pity our father." Prometheus is nailed through the stomach and arms to a rock. The Furies howl inarticulately in response to the bloody ghost of Clytemnestra. . . . Art was in its infancy in the days of Aeschylus—just as it was in London in the days of Shakespeare.'* Then are we to imitate the moderns? What! Imitate imitations? Spare us!

'But', it will be retorted again, 'judging from your notion of art, you seem to expect nothing but great poets—you seem to depend entirely on genius!' Well, art doesn't depend on mediocrity. Art offers no advice to mediocrity; it knows nothing of mediocrity; in art's eyes, mediocrity doesn't exist. Art provides wings, not crutches. Alas! D'Aubignac followed the rules. Campistron imitated the great examples. What has that to do with art? Art never builds its palace for ants. Art lets them make their own anthill, and never cares whether they construct their parody of that palace on its own foundations.

Critics of the scholastic school put their poets in a curious position. On the one hand, they keep shouting at them: 'Imitate the great examples!' On the other hand, they habitually maintain that those same examples are 'inimitable'. Now, what happens if their workers, by sheer hard work, do manage to drum up some pallid copy, some colourless replica of the masters? The ungrateful critics look at the new rehash and begin crying out either: 'That isn't like anything else!' or else: 'That's just like everything else!' And, by a process of reasoning specifically tailored to the purpose, each formula expresses an adverse judgement.

Let's speak out boldly. The time has come. It would be strange if freedom, like light, nowadays penetrated everything except the things that are intrinsically freest of all—the things of the mind. Let's take the axe to theories, parties, and systems. Let's knock down the old plasterwork that is masking the façade of art. There are no rules or models; or rather, there are no laws apart from (*a*) the general laws of nature, which affect the whole of art, and (*b*) the special laws that apply to each individual composition, which arise from the specific requirements of its subject. The former are eternal, intrinsic, and universal; the latter are variable, extrinsic, and apply only in one particular case. The former are the framework on which the house is built; the latter are the scaffolding that helps to build it, which needs to be done afresh for each new edifice. In short, the former are drama's skeleton, the latter are its clothing. And they can't be found in any 'art of poetry'. Richelet* hasn't a hint of them. An artist of genius, by intuition rather than instruction, draws the former from the general order of things, the latter from the individual character of the subject he is handling in each particular work; not like a chemist, who lights his burner, fans his fire, heats his crucible, analyses and decomposes; but like a bee, which flies on golden wings, alights on every flower, and draws honey from it without the calyx losing any of its brilliance or the corolla any of its perfume.

A poet, I must emphasize, can learn only from nature, truth, and his own inspiration (which is itself a part of truth and nature).

> When I have to write a comedy,
> I lock its laws with a sixfold key,

says Lope de Vega.* To lock laws, indeed, 'a sixfold key' is scarcely enough. A poet must above all beware of copying anyone—whether Molière or Shakespeare, Corneille or Schiller.[1] If a writer of genuine talent could abandon his true nature to that extent, set aside his own originality, turn himself into someone else, and play Sosie,* he'd lose everything. He'd be a god turning himself into a slave. We must draw our water from the fountainhead. All the trees of the forest—so diverse in shape, fruit, and foliage—are generated by the same soil-bound moisture. Writers of the most varied genius are fertilized and nourished by the same nature. The true poet is a tree who can be

---

[1] Nor will art make great progress by adapting novels (even Walter Scott's) for the stage. It may be all right to do that once or twice, especially if the transposers have other, more substantial merits; but in the end it will only replace one kind of imitation by another.

Another point. When I say that we shouldn't copy Shakespeare or Schiller, I'm talking about the bungling imitators who try to find rules where those poets relied only on genius, and copy their form without their spirit, their bark without their sap. I'm not talking about translations done skilfully by genuine poets. Madame Tastu has translated several scenes of Shakespeare excellently. At this very moment, Monsieur Émile Deschamps* is reproducing *Romeo and Juliet* on our stage, with such dexterity that he makes the whole of Shakespeare flow through his lines, as he has already made the whole of Horace do. That, clearly, is itself artistic, poetic work, a task that doesn't exclude either originality or life or creativity [*Hugo's note*].

buffeted by every wind and watered by every dew, and whose fruits
are his works, produced as the old storytellers used to produce their
stories. Why rely on a master or cling to a model? Better, far better,
to be a bramble or thistle, nourished in the same soil as the cedars
and palm trees, than to be a patch of fungus or lichen on the trunks
of those mighty trees. Brambles live, fungus vegetates. And however
tall the cedars and palm trees may be, you won't grow tall yourself
by drawing on their sap. A giant's parasite must be, even at best, a
dwarf. For all their gigantic size, oaks can support and nourish
nothing more than mistletoe.

Did some of our poets manage to be great even when they were
imitating someone else? If so, though they may have been using
ancient models, they were often listening to nature and their own
genius all the same; they were, in a sense, still themselves. Make no
mistake about that! Their branches may have been clinging to the
tree alongside them, but their roots must have been delving into the
soil of art. Then along came the subsidiary imitators, who had no
roots in the ground and no genius in their soul, and were necessarily
confined to imitation. As Charles Nodier says, 'school of Athens',
'school of Alexandria'. A flood of mediocrity arose, and the land
swarmed with textbooks of poetry, so obstructive to talent, so useful
to mediocrity. People declared that everything had been done;
God wasn't allowed to create new Molières and Corneilles. Memory
replaced imagination—it was made a sovereign rule, and embodied
in aphorisms. 'To imagine', says La Harpe in his naïvely confident
way, 'is fundamentally only to remember.'

Back to Nature, then! Nature and truth.—And here let's see that
the new ideas, instead of destroying art, merely set it on a more solid
and more secure foundation. Note, in this context, that there's an
impenetrable boundary between artistic reality and natural reality.
It's folly to confuse them, as some rather backward partisans of
'Romanticism' do. Artistic truth can never be, as some people claim,
absolute reality. Art can't present us with that. Suppose one of these
unthinking advocates of absolute nature—nature as seen outside
art—is faced with a performance of a Romantic play, such as *Le Cid*.
'What's this?' he says at the very outset; 'the Cid is talking verse!
It isn't *natural* to talk in verse.' 'Well then, how should he talk?' 'In
prose.' 'Have it your own way.' A moment later he adds, if he's
logical: 'Why, the Cid is talking French!' 'Well?' 'Well, he'd *naturally*

talk his own language; he'd have to talk Spanish.' 'I don't see why; but once again, have it your own way.'—You think that would be all? Indeed it wouldn't. Before the sixth Castilian sentence had been spoken, he'd be obliged to get up and ask if the Cid who was talking was the real Cid, the flesh-and-blood Cid. 'What right has this actor, Pierre or Jacques, to call himself the Cid? That's *false*.' Nothing would stop him from subsequently demanding the sun instead of floodlights, and *real* trees and houses instead of deceitful scenery. Once you set out on that path, logic has got you by the throat, and you're no longer able to stop.

If we want to escape absurdity, then, we have to recognize that art and nature have quite different domains. Nature and art are two distinct things; otherwise, one or other of them wouldn't exist. As well as an ideal side, art has a down-to-earth practical side. Whatever it does, it remains within a framework of syntax and prosody, Vaugelas and Richelet.* Its most fanciful creations have their forms, their methods of execution, a whole mechanism to set in motion. For genius, these are instruments; for mediocrity, tools.

Other writers have, I believe, already made the point: drama is a mirror reflecting nature. But if the mirror is an ordinary mirror, a single plane surface, it will show only flat, lifeless images, faithful but inanimate. Simple reflection, we know, causes a reduction in light and colour. Thus drama needs to be a concentrating mirror, which gathers and condenses the coloured light-rays instead of diluting them, and which turns glow into light, light into flame. Only then can drama be called artistic.

The theatre is a focal point. Everything that exists in the world, history, life, and humanity can and should be reflected there—but reflected under the magic wand of art. Art leafs through the ages, it leafs through nature, it questions the chronicles, it strives to reproduce factual reality (especially the reality of customs and characters, which are far less open to question than deeds),[1] to replace what the

---

[1] It's surprising to find the following lines in Monsieur Goethe's writings: 'Strictly speaking, there are no historical characters in poetry; when the poet wants to depict the world he has invented, he merely honours certain people whom he has met in history by borrowing their names and assigning them to creatures of his own invention' (*Art and Antiquity*). You can see where this doctrine would lead, if taken seriously—straight to falsehood and fantasy. It must have seemed true to the illustrious poet at one time, since he let it slip; fortunately, though, he doesn't practise it. He certainly wouldn't draw a Muhammad like a Werther, or a Napoleon like a Faust* [*Hugo's note*].

annalists excised, reconstruct their source materials, detect their omissions and remedy them, fill their gaps with historically appropriate fantasies, gather what they left scattered, get the human marionettes moving under the strings of Providence, drape everything in a form that is both natural and poetic, and give it the true, vibrant life that gives birth to illusion, the glitter of reality that dazzles spectators (and the poet himself first of all, since a true poet is in earnest). The artistic goal, then, is almost divine: to resurrect history or create poetry.

It's a fine, impressive thing to see a drama unfolding on such lines—a drama in which art is developing nature, a drama in which the action moves smoothly and surely to its conclusion, without constraints or digressions; a drama in which the poet has fully achieved art's multiple purpose, opening a double horizon before the spectators' eyes, illuminating human beings both internally and externally—externally through their conversations and actions, internally through their asides and monologues—and thus interweaving the drama of life and the drama of conscience in a single composition.

For a work of this kind, clearly, a poet must choose not what is beautiful, but what is *characteristic*. This isn't a matter of what people nowadays call 'adding local colour', i.e. touching up an otherwise utterly false and conventional composition with a few garish afterthoughts. 'Local colour' shouldn't be on the surface of the drama but in its depths, at the very heart of the work, and extending out from there naturally, intrinsically, evenly, to every corner of the drama, like sap rising from the roots to the topmost leaves on a tree. A drama should be radically impregnated with the flavour of its age, which should be embedded in its very air— perceptible only on the way in and out, when there is a change of period and atmosphere. A certain amount of effort, a certain amount of hard work is needed to achieve that; so much the better. It's a good thing for the paths of art to be blocked with brambles that deter everyone except the strong-willed from entering. And such effort, driven by intense inspiration, will protect drama from a fatal vice— the vice of being *commonplace*. The commonplace is the failing of all short-sighted short-winded poets. When seen from the perspective of the theatre, every figure must be reduced to its most striking, most individual, most exact feature. Even vulgarity and triviality must have their own distinct accents. Nothing should be rejected. A true poet, like God, is present in all parts of his work at the same time. Genius is a press stamping the royal effigy on copper coins and gold pieces alike.

There's no doubt in my mind—and this will show unprejudiced readers yet again that I'm far from wanting to deform art—there's no doubt in my mind that verse is one of the best ways to preserve drama from the scourge noted in the previous paragraph, and one of the most powerful barriers against the irruption of the *commonplace*, which, like democracy, is constantly flooding into people's minds. I believe that the literary world of the young—a world already rich in writers and writings—has fallen into an error that I may perhaps be allowed to point out, an error all too readily justified by the extra-ordinary aberrations of the old school. The new century is still in the growing phase, when it can easily be straightened.

Not long ago a curious school of dramatic poetry developed—a late outgrowth from the old Classical trunk, or, better still, an excrescence or polyp of the kind that develop in old age and are much less a proof of life than a sign of decomposition. I think the master and originator of this school was the poet who marked the transition from the eighteenth century to the nineteenth, the expert in description and circumlocution, the Delille who (so we're told) boasted at the end of his life, in a sort of Homeric catalogue,* that he had 'made' twelve camels, four dogs, three horses (including Job's), six tigers, two cats, a chess game, a billiard game, a backgammon game, a game of draughts, several winters, numerous summers, even more springs, fifty sunsets, and so many sunrises that he'd altogether lost count of them.

Now, Delille went over to tragedy. He (not Racine, in heaven's name!) is the father of the so-called school of elegance and good taste that has been flourishing lately. This school doesn't think of tragedy as (for instance) our good friend Will Shakespeare did, as a source of emotions of every possible kind, but rather as a set of easy-to-solve incidental descriptive puzzles. Far from rejecting the 'low' and trivial aspects of life as the true French Classical school used to do, this Muse eagerly seeks them out and collects them. Grotesquerie, which had been ostracized as bad company by the tragedies of Louis XIV's day, can't be left in peace by this damsel. 'It must be described'— that is, 'ennobled'! Scenes in the guardhouse, rebellions, fish markets, prisons, taverns, Henri IV's famous 'chicken in the pot', are all grist to her mill. She pounces on them, she cleans up the old rascal and stitches her glitter and tinsel onto his knaveries: 'a purple rag is sewn on'.* Evidently she wants to raise all this dramatic rabble to the peerage; and her Honours Lists consist entirely of poetic orations.

This Muse must be a remarkable prude. She is accustomed to the caresses of circumlocution. Plain speech is sometimes too rough for her; it shocks her. To talk naturally wouldn't suit her dignity. She blue-pencils old Corneille's blunt sayings:

> '*A herd of men ruined by debt* and crime!'
> 'Ximena, *who'd have thought it*?' 'Rodrigo, *who'd have said so*?'
> 'When their Flaminius *bought* Hannibal.'
> 'Don't force me to *fall out with* the republic!'

His 'Steady, sir!' still niggles at her. And it took lots of 'my lords' and 'my ladies' for her to forgive Racine his so monosyllabic 'dogs' and the Claudius so shamelessly 'put in Agrippina's bed'.*

This 'Melpomene', as she calls herself, would shudder at the thought of touching a history book. She leaves it to the costume designer to determine in what era her dramas are set. In her eyes, history is bad form and bad taste. For instance, it's intolerable to have kings and queens swearing. They must be elevated from their royal dignity to tragic dignity. She promoted Henri IV in just such a way; the king of the people, cleaned up by Monsieur Legouvé, found his *'sbodikins** driven out of the royal mouth by a pair of fine sentences, so that, like the girl in the fairy tale, he was forced to drop from the said mouth nothing but pearls, rubies, and sapphires (all false, to tell the truth).

Nothing, really, is more *commonplace* than conventional elegance and nobility of that kind. There's nothing devised, imagined, or invented, in such a style. Merely things that can be seen anywhere— rhetoric, inflation, cliché, school-prize poetry, exercises in Latin verse. Borrowed ideas clad in cheap finery. The poets of this school are elegant in the same sense as stage monarchs; they can go to labelled storeroom boxes and be ever confident of finding all-purpose hand-me-down pinchbeck crowns and robes there. Such poets may not thumb the Bible, but they do have a big book of their own—the rhyming dictionary. That's their source of poetry, their 'fountain of waters'.*

In the midst of all this, nature and truth obviously have to fend for themselves as best they can. Only by sheer chance could any scraps of them survive this maelstrom of false art, false style, and false poetry. That's where some of our most distinguished reformers have gone astray. They have been annoyed by the stiffness and pomp and pomposity of this so-called dramatic poetry, and they've decided that our poetic language is incompatible with nature and truth. Verse has bored them so often that they have condemned it without a fair hearing, and have concluded, perhaps a little hastily, that drama ought to be written in prose.

This is a mistake. Falsity is indeed king over both the style and the content of some French tragedies, but we shouldn't blame the verse for that; we should blame the versifiers. We should condemn the people who have used the form, not the form itself; the workers, not the tools.

If we want to see how readily and freely our poetry can express anything that is true, perhaps we should study much of Corneille's verse and all of Molière's, rather than Racine's. Racine, the divine poet, is elegiac, lyrical, epic; Molière is dramatic. It's time to vindicate his excellent style from critics stuffed with the bad taste of last century, and declare plainly that Molière stands at the very summit of our theatre, not only as a poet, but also as a writer. 'He really has two hands.'

With Molière, the verse hugs the idea close, absorbs it into itself, compresses it and develops it, shapes it into something slimmer, stricter, more complete—gives us, so to speak, the very essence of it. Verse is the visible form of thought. That's why it is especially suited to the stage. Written in a certain way, it highlights things that would otherwise have seemed ordinary and insignificant. It strengthens and refines the fabric of style. It's the knot that stops the thread from slipping, the belt that holds the garment in place and gives it its pleats. What, therefore, could nature and truth lose by being presented in verse? What do they lose in the poetry of Molière? (Let our prosaists answer that question themselves!) If I may be allowed yet another pedestrian image, does wine stop being wine when it's in a bottle?

Supposing I had the right to state what style should be used for drama, I'd choose a free, straightforward, faithful kind of verse that dared to say everything without prudery or affectation; a kind of verse that moved naturally between comedy and tragedy, sublimity and grotesquerie; down-to-earth and poetic in turn, always artistic and inspired, profound and startling, broad and true; varying its caesuras* skilfully in order to disguise the monotony of the standard verse line; running the sense over from line to line, rather than clogging it with inversions; faithful to rhyme, that slave-queen who is the supreme elegance of our poetry and generates its metre; inexhaustibly varied in phrasing, inexplicably graceful in design; assuming a thousand shapes, like Proteus,* without changing its nature or personality; shunning oratory; relaxed in dialogue; hiding always behind the characters; striving above all to be appropriate (when it does happen to be 'beautiful', being so without any pre-meditation, and without appearing to be conscious of the fact);[1] lyric, epic, dramatic, as appropriate; encompassing the whole poetic scale from the heights to the depths, from the loftiest to the basest concepts, from the silliest to the most solemn, from the most con-crete to the most abstract, without ever going beyond the limits of stage dialogue; the kind of verse, in short that a man would write if some fairy gave him the soul of Corneille and the brain of Molière. I do think that such verse would be 'just as good as prose'.

Poetry of that kind would have nothing in common with the corpse we autopsied a few moments ago. The distinction can be presented easily if I may be allowed to borrow an epigram made by a perceptive man to whom I am personally indebted: the other kind of poetry was descriptive, this kind would be picturesque.

To repeat a crucial point: in the theatre, verse ought to abandon all self-centredness, obtrusiveness, and coquetry. In such a context, verse is merely a form, and a form that must accept everything; it can't impose anything on the drama—on the contrary, it must receive everything from the drama and simply transmit it to the audience: French, Latin, legal documents, royal oaths, popular catchwords, comedy, tragedy, laughter, tears, prose, and poetry. Woe

---

[1] The author of the present play was talking about it one day with Talma,* and explaining some of his ideas about dramatic style to the great actor. (This conversation should be recorded at some later time, when the author can no longer be suspected of trying to bolster his works or sayings with authority figures.) 'Yes indeed!' exclaimed Talma, interrupting him brusquely; 'that's what I'm so tired of telling them: No fine lines!' 'No fine lines!'—that wise precept came from the instinct of a genius. 'Fine lines' are indeed the death of fine plays [*Hugo's note*].

to the poet if his lines turn up their noses at anything! But this form is made of bronze; the thought is embedded in its metre; a drama composed of it is indestructible; it sticks more readily in an actor's mind, warns him if he adds or omits anything, prevents him from altering his role and putting himself in the author's place; it makes every word sacred, and ensures that the poet's utterances will long remain in his listeners' memories. Concepts become more incisive and more brilliant when they are tempered in verse. They are iron transformed to steel.

Prose clearly doesn't have those abilities. It's inevitably much more timid than verse. It necessarily robs drama of all lyric or epic poetry, restricting it to the conversational and the pedestrian. Its wings are far less broad. Moreover, it's much easier to write; mediocrity is thoroughly at home in it, and it would quickly clutter art with abortions and embryos, despite a few notable works such as those that have recently appeared.

Another group of reformers favours dramas written in both verse and prose, like Shakespeare's. This method has some advantages. Still, it can lead to incongruity at the transitions from one form to the other; a fabric is much stronger when it is homogeneous. In any case, the question of whether dramas should be written in prose or verse, or both, is really a mere detail. A work's stature should be determined not by its form but by its intrinsic value. In questions of this kind, there is only one answer; there is only one weight that can turn the scales of art—genius.

All things considered, the most important ability for any dramatist, whether prose-writer or verse-writer, is accuracy. Not the superficial accuracy for which the descriptive school was famous or infamous, making Lhomond's Latin grammar and Restaut's French grammar into the two wings of their Pegasus, but a profound, substantial, commonsense accuracy, based on a feel for idiom that goes right down to the etymological roots; free at all times, because it is sure of its ground and is always working in accordance with the nature of the language. It keeps grammar on a tight rein (whereas Lady Grammar kept the descriptive school's accuracy in leading-strings); it can dare, risk, create, invent its own style; it has the right to do so. Whatever certain thoughtless people (including, notably, the writer of these lines) may have said, the French language isn't 'fixed' and never will be fixed. No language is ever fixed. The human spirit is constantly changing, indeed advancing—taking its languages with it. That's the way things are. When the body changes, how can the clothes remain unaltered? Nineteenth-century French can no more be eighteenth-century French than the latter could be seventeenth-century French, or seventeenth-century French sixteenth-century. Montaigne's language is no longer Rabelais's; Pascal's* is no longer Montaigne's; Montesquieu's is no longer Pascal's. Considered on its own, each of these four languages is excellent, because it's original. Every era has its own ideas, and it must also have the right words for those ideas. Languages are like the sea, constantly flowing. At certain times they leave one shore of the world of thought and overrun another. Everything thus abandoned by their tide dries up and disappears. That's how ideas fade and words pass away. As with everything else, so with human speech: each era adds something and takes away something. It's fated; nothing can be done about it. So it's vain to try to petrify the mobile facial features of our speech in some prescribed form. It's vain for today's literary Joshuas* to order language to stop; neither language nor the sun will stop nowadays. The day when they become 'fixed', they're dead. That's why the French of a certain present-day school is a dead language.

Those, roughly speaking (though a fuller exposition would be needed to complete the picture), are this author's *current* ideas about drama. Not that he has the pretension to offer his own attempt at drama as a manifestation of those ideas; on the contrary, to put it crudely, the ideas are much more likely to have arisen from the attempt. No doubt it would be very convenient (and rather more astute) to ground the book on its preface and use each of them to defend the other. But he prefers less craft and more honesty. There-fore, let him be the first to acknowledge that this preface has only the most tenuous of connections with the play itself. At first, out of sheer laziness, he intended to publish the work on its own—'the devil without horns', as Iriarte* used to say. But after he had duly finished his work, some friends (probably not very wise ones) persuaded him to call himself to a reckoning—to map out in a preface the poetic journey he had just made, with an account of the things (good or bad) that he had brought back and the new aspects of art's domain that he had seen. No doubt people will take advantage of this admission to criticize him, as a German reviewer has already done, for constructing 'a theory of poetry to suit his poems'. Never mind. He set out with the intention of destroying rather than devising theories of poetry. And after all, which is better: constructing a theory of poetry to suit poems, or constructing poems to suit a theory of poetry? But, let it be said again, he has neither the talent to create a system of ideas nor the pretention to establish one. 'Systems', Voltaire wittily remarked, 'are like rats; they slip through twenty holes and then find that they can't fit through a couple of others.'* So the labour would have been futile, as well as beyond the author's powers. Instead, he has argued for artistic freedom, in opposition to the despotism of systems, laws, and rule-books. He's in the habit of following his poetic subject matter wherever it leads him, and forming a new scheme every time he writes a new composition. He shuns artistic dogmatism above all things. God preserve him from joining the ranks of the writers, Romantic or Classical, who write works 'according to their system' and are doomed never to envisage any form of art except one—who are always trying to 'prove' something and follow laws other than those of their own nature and temperament. In the eyes of art, the artificial work of such people—whatever talent they may display in other respects— simply doesn't exist. It's theory, not poetry.*

from *Things Seen*

Joanny

7 March [1830], midnight

Hernani has been playing at the Théâtre français* since 28 February. It brings in five thousand francs every time. Every night the audience hisses every line; it's a rare uproar—the pit boos, the boxes burst out laughing. The actors are upset and hostile; most of them sneer at the things they have to say. The press has been virtually unanimous; every morning it keeps ridiculing the play and the playwright. If I go into a reading room, I can't pick up a newspaper without reading 'as silly as *Hernani*', 'as preposterous as *Hernani*', 'as foolish, false, bloated, pretentious, extravagant, and nonsensical as *Hernani*'. If

I go to the theatre during a performance, I keep seeing, in every corridor where I venture, spectators leaving their box and slamming the door in annoyance.

Mademoiselle Mars plays her role fairly and faithfully, but makes fun of it, even in my presence. Michelot plays his responsibly and makes fun of it behind my back. There isn't a stagehand, an extra, a lamplighter who doesn't point the finger at me.

Today, at his invitation, I had dinner with Joanny.* Joanny is playing Ruy Gomez. He lives at 1 Rue du Jardinet with his nephew, a young seminarist. The dinner was serious and friendly. A few journalists were there (including Madame Dorval's husband, Monsieur Merle*). After dinner, Joanny, who has the finest possible head of white hair, rose, lifted his glass, and turned toward me. I was on his right. Here, without a syllable altered, is what he said to me (I've just come home, and I'm writing it down word for word):

'Monsieur Victor Hugo, the now-forgotten old man who played the role of Don Diego in *The Cid* two hundred years ago was no more filled with admiration and respect for the great Corneille* than the old man who plays Don Ruy Gomez today is for you.'

from *A Blend of Literature and Philosophy*

from Journal of the Ideas and Opinions of a Revolutionary of 1830

August

After July 1830* we need the thing 'republic' and the word 'monarchy'.

The present day belongs to the kings; the future belongs to the peoples.

Many good things are tottering and trembling after the sudden shock that has just taken place. Men of art, in particular, are utterly stunned, and are scurrying in all directions after their scattered theories. They needn't worry. Once this earthquake is over, I'm quite sure we'll find our edifice of poetry still standing and all the stronger for the shocks it has faced. We too are concerned with freedom; this too is a revolution. It will go safely hand in hand with its sister the political one. Revolutions, like wolves, don't eat one another.

September

My old Royalist/Catholic faith of 1820 has been tumbling down bit by bit for ten years before age and experience. Something of it still remains within my mind, but it's merely a religious and poetic ruin. I turn aside now and then to view it with respect, but I no longer go and pray there.

The concept of God and the concept of kingship are two distinct things and ought to remain so. The monarchy of Louis XIV* conflated them—with results detrimental to both earthly and spiritual harmony. That royalism led to a kind of political mysticism or monarchist fetishism, some sort of cult of the king's person; its temple was a palace, its priests were the Gentlemen of the Privy Chamber, its ten commandments were the rules of etiquette. Hence all the fictions known as 'divine right', 'legitimate authority', 'grace of God'.* Such things are the antithesis of the true divine right, which is justice; the true legitimate authority, which is the intellect; the true grace of God, which is reason. This courtiers' religion put nothing less than the shirt of a man in place of the banner of the church.

Revolutions are wonderful improvisers. A bit dishevelled sometimes.

There are some people who think themselves very advanced and have never got any further than 1688. Yet we left 1789* behind us a long time ago.

In the current condition of Europe, every country has its own slave, every realm is dragging its own ball and chain. Turkey has Greece, Russia has Poland, Sweden has Norway, Prussia has the Grand Duchy of Posen, Austria has Lombardy, Sardinia has Piedmont, England has Ireland, France has Corsica, Holland has Belgium. So there's a nation of slaves alongside every nation of masters; a country in an unnatural state alongside every country in the natural state. A shoddily built edifice; half marble, half rubble.

October

The spirit of God, like the sun, is constantly shedding all of its light. The spirit of man is like the pale moon, which has its phases, its disappearances and reappearances, its bright patches and dark patches, its fullness and its invisibility, which derives all its light from the sun's rays and yet sometimes dares to block them out.

All that is going on in the realm of politics at the moment is a mere bridge of boats. It's good enough to get us from one bank to the other. But it has no foundation in the river of ideas flowing under-neath—the river that lately swept away the old stone bridge of the Bourbon monarchy.*

A poor tribute to a man if you say that his political opinions haven't changed for forty years. That means that he has never had a day's experience or reflection or fluctuation of thought in response to events. It's like praising a lake for being stagnant or a tree for being dead; it's like preferring an oyster to an eagle. No, in matters of opinion everything is subject to variation; nothing is absolute in matters of politics, except the inner morality of those matters. And that morality is a question of conscience, not of opinion. A man can change his opinion honourably, as long as he doesn't change his conscience. Whether forward or backward, movement is fundamentally vital, human, social.

What is shameful is to change your opinion because it's in your interest to do so, whether it's loot or promotion that impels you to shift from the white flag to the tricolour or vice versa.

Equality in the sight of the law is equality in the sight of God translated into the language of politics. Every constitution ought to be a version of the Gospel.

November

Some great things are not the work of an individual, but of a nation. The pyramids of Egypt are anonymous; so is the July Revolution.*

December

9 December 1830: Benjamin Constant,* who died yesterday, was one of the few men who polish, brighten, and sharpen the common ideas

of their day—which are the people's weapons, and splinter the army's. Only revolutions can cast such men into society. It takes a volcano to make pumice.

A single day has brought news of the deaths of Goethe, Benjamin Constant, and Pius VIII.* Three popes' corpses.

There are rocks that don't stop a river; events simply flow past human obstructions without being turned from their course.

Final Pages (Undated)*

France is always a fashion-setter in Europe.

The Scriptures report that there was a king* who lived for seven years as a wild beast in the woods, then resumed his human form. The same thing sometimes happens to a nation. It too spends seven years as a fierce animal, then becomes human again. These metamorphoses are called revolutions.

The nation, like the king, gains wisdom from the experience.

A curious parallelism in the destinies of ancient and modern Rome! After a senate that made gods, a conclave that makes saints.*

Great men are the coefficients of their age.

As with the sun, so with a great man. He never seems finer to us than when he's close to the ground—at his rise, and at his setting.

You mustn't look at everything in life through the prism of poetry. It's like the ingenious lenses that enlarge objects. They show you the heavenly spheres in all their brilliance and splendour; but lower the same lenses to the earth, and all you can see are vague shapes—gigantic, yes, but faint and blurry.

Providence is thrifty with her great men. She doesn't lavish or squander them. She sends them out and takes them back at the right moment, and never puts them in charge of anything that isn't fit for them. When she wants a petty job done, she assigns it to petty hands; she uses only mean tools to shift blood and filth. So Mirabeau departs before the Reign of Terror, Napoleon doesn't arrive until it's over. Between the two giants, a hive of nasty little men, guillotines, massacres, executions by drowning, 1793. And for 1793, Robespierre* will do; he's good enough for that.

I've heard eminent men of the present day—politicians, writers, scientists, etc.—complain about envy, hatred, slander, etc. They were wrong. That's the rule; it's an honour. Notable people undergo such trials. Hatred hunts them down everywhere. In its eyes, nothing is sacred. The public stage exposes Shakespeare and Molière to it all the more; prison doesn't keep it away from Christopher Columbus; the cloister doesn't spare Saint Bernard from it, or the throne Napoleon.* For a gifted person there's only one true refuge on earth: the grave.

from *Notre-Dame de Paris*

Notre-Dame

No doubt she's still a sublime and majestic edifice, the cathedral of Notre-Dame de Paris. But however much of her beauty she may have retained with age, it's hard to avoid groaning, it's hard to avoid growing angry at the countless degradations and mutilations that have been inflicted on this venerable monument by time and humanity, without any respect for either Charlemagne (who laid the first stone) or Philippe Auguste* (who laid the last).

Beside every wrinkle on the face of this ancient queen of French cathedrals, you'll find a scar. *Tempus edax, homo edacior.** Which I'd be inclined to translate: 'Time is blind, humanity is stupid.'

If we had the chance to examine with the reader every individual trace of destruction imprinted on this ancient church, we'd see that time's share has been far less than humanity's—especially artistic humanity's. I'm forced to use the term 'artistic humanity' because of certain people who, during the last two centuries, have called themselves architects.

To cite only a few outstanding examples, there can surely be few finer pages in architecture than the façade, where the three recessed ogive* doorways, the serrated and embroidered array of twenty-eight royal niches, the great central rose window with its two side windows (like deacon and subdeacon on either side of a priest), the high slender gallery of trefoiled arches bearing a heavy platform on delicate little columns, and finally the two massive dark towers with slate eaves—harmonious parts, rising one above the other in five gigantic storeys, of a magnificent whole—unfold before the viewer successively but simultaneously, massed and unconfused. Their countless details of statuary, sculpture, and carving contribute immensely to the tranquil grandeur of the work as a whole—a huge symphony in stone, as it were; the colossal achievement of a man and a people, an entity both unified and complex, like her sisters the *Iliad* and the *romanceros*;* the mighty result of everything an era could contribute (on every stone the worker's imagination, disciplined by the artist's genius, catches your eye in hundreds of ways); in short, a kind of human creation, as powerful and prolific as the divine creation whose two characteristics—variety and eternity—she seems to have stolen.

And what we're saying about the façade would have to be said about the whole church; and what we're saying about the cathedral church of Paris would have to be said about every church of medieval Christendom. In this self-created, logical, well-proportioned art, everything hangs together. Measure one toe, and you measure the whole giant.

Let's consider the façade of Notre-Dame as it appears to us today, when we go reverently to admire this cathedral so mighty and solemn and (according to its chroniclers)* terrifying—'striking terror into the beholders by its sheer massiveness'.

Three crucial things are now missing from that façade: (*a*) the flight of eleven steps that used to raise it above ground level; (*b*) the bottom row of statues that occupied the niches in the three doorways; and (*c*) the upper row of the twenty-eight earliest kings of France, from Childebert* to Philippe Auguste (with 'imperial apples' in their hands), which filled the first-storey gallery.

The flight of steps? Time obliterated that, by slowly and inevitably raising the ground level of the City. But while it caused the eleven steps that once enhanced the building's majestic stature to be swallowed up one after another by the rising tide of Paris's pavements, time may have given the church more than it has taken away. Time, after all, has spread across its façade the sombre antiquarian tinge that makes a monument's old age its era of greatest beauty.

But who knocked down the two rows of statues? Who emptied the niches? Who cut that new, bastard ogive right in the middle of the central doorway? Who had the audacity to place there, alongside Biscornette's arabesques, that stodgy, tasteless wooden door carved in Louis XV* style? Humanity—architects, the artists of today.

And if we go inside the building, who knocked down its colossal Saint Christopher—as famous among statues as the Grand Hall of the Palace was among halls, or the spire of Strasbourg among steeples? And the myriads of statues that used to inhabit every space between the columns of its nave and choir—kneeling, standing, horsed, men, women, children, kings, bishops, soldiers, in stone, marble, gold, silver, bronze, even wax—who swept them away so brutally? Not time.

And who replaced the old Gothic altar, and the shrines and reliquaries that cluttered it so splendidly, with a ponderous marble sarcophagus bearing angels' heads and clouds, which looks like some spare oddment from Val-de-Grâce or the Invalides? Who was fool enough to load that ponderous stone anachronism down on Hercandus' Carolingian pavement? Wasn't it Louis XIV—in fulfilment of a vow made by Louis XIII?*

And who put those chilly white windows in place of the deep-tinted stained glass that made our fathers' eyes hesitate in wonder between the rose window above the great doorway and the ogives of the chancel? And what would a sixteenth-century succentor say if he could see the lovely yellow distemper daubed all over the cathedral by our archiepiscopal vandals? He'd recall that the public executioner used the same colour to smear 'infamous' buildings; he'd remember the Hôtel du Petit-Bourbon, likewise plastered with yellow after its Constable's* treason ('a yellow moreover so well fashioned and so meritorious', says Sauval,* 'that the passage of more than a century hath not yet made it lose its hue'). He'd think the holy place had been defiled; and he'd flee.

And if we climb on top of the cathedral, without being stopped by countless barbarities of every kind on the way, what have they done with the pretty little spire that used to stand right above the crossing? It, as frail and daring as its neighbour (likewise destroyed) on the Sainte-Chapelle, used to pierce even further into the heavens than the slender sharp-pointed sonorous fenestrated towers. An architect of taste (1787) amputated it and thought the wound could be covered well enough with a big lead sticking-plaster that looks like the lid of a saucepan.

That's how the wonderful art of the Middle Ages has been treated almost everywhere—especially in France. Across its ruins you find three kinds of damage, each at a different depth: (*a*) time, which has eroded the surface imperceptibly in some places and rusted it all over; (*b*) political and religious revolutions, which, being inherently blind and hot-tempered, have dashed against it in a frenzy, ripped away its rich attire of sculptures and reliefs, shattered its rose windows, snapped off its necklaces of arabesques and figurines, and uprooted its statues (in some cases because of their mitres, in others because of their crowns); and (*c*) changes of fashion, ever more stupid and preposterous, which have succeeded one another in the inevitable decline of architecture, from the chaotic though magnificent aberrations of the 'Renaissance' onward. Fashions have wreaked more havoc than revolutions. They have cut into the quick, they have got at the very bone structure of the art, they have hewn, hacked, disrupted, murdered the edifice, in both form and symbolism, in both logic and beauty. And then they've remade it— which neither time nor revolutions ever had the hide to attempt. In the name of 'good taste', they've brazenly festooned the wounds in the Gothic architecture with their own wretched ephemeral trinkets, their marble ribbons, their metal pompoms, a veritable leprosy of ovoli, volutes, backdrops, draperies, garlands, fringes, stone flames, bronze clouds, sated cupids, bloated cherubs, which began to eat away the face of Art in Catherine de Médicis's oratory, and two centuries later, in Madame du Barry's* boudoir, caused it to drop dead with horrible grimaces and convulsions.

In summary, then, Gothic architecture is now disfigured by three kinds of damage. The wrinkles and warts on its skin are the work of time; the marks of violence, brutal injuries, contusions, and fractures are the work of revolutions—from Luther to Mirabeau. The mutilations, amputations, dislocations of its limbs, and 'restorations' are the Greek, Roman, and barbarian work of professors who followed the precepts of Vitruvius and Vignola.* The magnificent art produced by the Vandals has been killed by the academies. Centuries and revolutions at least devastated impartially and majestically; but they were supplemented by a swarm of school-bred architects, committed and authorized and accredited, who debased with the discernment and selectivity of bad taste, replacing Gothic filigree with Louis XV chicory to the greater glory of the Parthenon.* This is the ass who gave a kick at the dying lion. It's the old moribund oak tree being capped with stings, bites, and nibbles from grubs.

How far we've come since the days of Robert Cenalis. He drew a comparison between Notre-Dame de Paris and the famous Temple of Diana at Ephesus, 'so praised by the pagans of antiquity', which had bestowed immortality on Herostratus;* and he judged the Gallic cathedral 'more excellent in length, breadth, height, and construction'!

All the same, Notre-Dame de Paris isn't what could be called a complete, definite, classifiable monument. It's no longer a Romanesque church, it's not yet a Gothic one. It isn't a typical building. Unlike the Abbey of Tournus, it doesn't have the solemn, massive physique, the broad, circular vaulting, the icy bareness, the majestic simplicity of buildings based on the round arch. Unlike Bourges Cathedral,* it isn't the magnificent, light, multiform, ornate, spiky, flowery product of the ogive. You can't classify it among the ancient tribe of churches that are sombre, mysterious, low-set, as if crushed by the round arch; virtually Egyptian, but for their ceilings; utterly hieroglyphic, utterly sacerdotal, utterly symbolic, teeming with more zigzags and lozenges than flowers, more flowers than animals, more animals than people; the work of a bishop rather than an architect; the first transformation of the art (imbued through and through with theocratic military discipline) that had sprung up during the Byzantine Empire and ended in the days of William the Conqueror. Nor can you place our cathedral in the tribe of tall, airy churches, rich in stained glass and sculpture; pointed in shape and bold in stance; communal and comradely as political monuments, free and fanciful and undisciplined as works of art; a second transformation of architecture—from the hieroglyphic, immutable, and sacerdotal, to the artistic, progressive, and popular—which began with the return from the Crusades and ended in the time of Louis XI. Notre-Dame de Paris isn't of pure Roman stock like the former group, nor of pure Arab stock like the latter.

It's a building of the transitional period. The Saxon architect was just finishing the first pillars of the nave, when the ogive came back from the Crusades and throned itself like a conqueror on broad Romanesque capitals that had been designed to bear only round arches. From that time on, the ogive was in command, and it constructed the rest of the church. At first, however, it was shy and inexperienced, broad and spreading and unadventurous—not yet daring to soar up in spires and lancets, as it was later to do in so many wonderful cathedrals. It seemed to feel the presence of the heavy Romanesque pillars nearby.

Still, buildings of the transitional period between Romanesque and Gothic repay examination just as much as the pure types. They express a particular kind of art that would otherwise have been lost: a grafting of the ogive onto the round arch.

Notre-Dame de Paris is a particularly interesting example of this. Every side, every stone of the venerable monument is a page not only of our country's history, but also of the history of science and art. So—to mention only some of the main points—the little Porte-Rouge achieves almost the ultimate in fifteenth-century Gothic delicacy, yet the nave pillars, with their bulk and solidity, go all the way back to the Carolingian abbey of Saint-Germain-des-Prés. You'd think the door and the pillars were separated by six centuries. Even the hermetics see the symbolism of the great doorway as a satisfying résumé of their science, which was so fully and hieroglyphically embodied in the church of Saint-Jacques-de-la-Boucherie.* So Romanesque abbey, philosophical church, Gothic art, Saxon art, heavy round pillars reminiscent of Gregory VII, hermetic symbolism of the kind that made Nicolas Flamel* a forerunner of Luther, papal unity, schism, Saint-Germain-des-Prés, Saint-Jacques-de-la-Boucherie, are all fused and combined and amalgamated in Notre-Dame. This central, seminal church is a sort of chimera among the old churches of Paris: it has the head of one, the limbs of a second, the rump of a third—bits and pieces of all of them.

To the artist, antiquary, or historian, I repeat, hybrid constructions like this aren't the least interesting ones. They show how primitive a thing architecture is; like the Cyclopean ruins,* Egyptian pyramids, and gigantic Hindu pagodas, they demonstrate that architecture's greatest achievements are collective rather than individual creations—the child of a whole nation in travail, not the inspiration of some man of genius; the deposit left behind by a nation; the accumulated detritus of the ages; the residue from successive evaporations of human society; in short, a rock formation of one kind or another. Every wave of time deposits its alluvium, every race lays down its stratum, every individual contributes his pebble to the monument. So it is with beavers and bees; so it is also with people. Babel, the great emblem of architecture, is a beehive.

Great buildings, like great mountains, are the work of centuries. Art often undergoes a transformation while they are in progress: 'the works are broken off in suspense';* and they calmly go on in accordance with the transformation. The new style takes the monument as it stands, adds an encrustation on its surface, assimilates it to itself, develops it in whatever way it wants, and, if possible, completes it. The thing is done painlessly, effortlessly, smoothly, in keeping with the peaceful laws of nature. A graft is made, the sap begins to flow, the plant recovers. These successive weldings of different styles at different levels on a single monument surely contain matter enough for massive tomes—in many cases, for a universal history of the human race. The man, the artist, the individual are erased from these great anonymous masses of stone; they contain only a sum and summary of the human mind. Time is the architect, the whole nation the builder.

To speak only of European Christian architecture—that younger sister of the great stone structures in the Orient—it looks like a huge rock formation in three well-defined zones, superimposed one on top of the other: Romanesque, Gothic, and Renaissance (which I'd prefer to call Graeco-Roman). The Romanesque[1] stratum, the oldest and deepest, is occupied by the round arch, which reappears at the top of Greek columns in the most recent, uppermost stratum, the Renaissance. Between the two comes the ogive. Buildings that belong solely to one of those three layers—Jumièges Abbey, Rheims Cathedral, Sainte-Croix at Orléans—are perfectly distinct, consistent, and coherent. But at their edges the three zones mingle and blend, like colours in the solar spectrum. Result: complex monuments, buildings of nuance and transition. One of them may have Romanesque feet, a Gothic midriff, and a Graeco-Roman head—simply because it took six hundred years to build. That variety is rare. (The keep at Étampes is one example.) But monuments in two strata are more common: Notre-Dame de Paris (which is basically an ogival building, but with its earliest pillars grounded

---

[1] According to place, type, and climate, this is also called Lombard, Saxon, and Byzantine. The four terms are four matching sister architectures, each with its own distinctive character, but all derived from the same principle: the round arch.

> Tho' various features did the sisters grace,
> A sister's likeness was in ev'ry face* [*Hugo's note*].

in the Romanesque zone where Saint-Denis's doorway and Saint-Germain-des-Prés's nave are embedded); the lovely half-Gothic chapter house at Bocherville (which is in the Romanesque stratum up to the waist); Rouen Cathedral* (which would be wholly Gothic if the tip of its central spire didn't penetrate into the Renaissance zone).[1]

Still, all these nuances and distinctions are merely surface differences. Art has simply changed its skin. The basic structure of the Christian church hasn't been affected. It still has the same inner design, the same logical arrangement of its parts. However the surface of a cathedral may be carved and ornamented, underneath you will always find—at least in embryonic, rudimentary form—the Roman basilica. Its ground plan eternally follows the same law. There are invariably two naves that intersect in the shape of a cross, the upper end of which is rounded into an apse and forms the choir; there are always side aisles for chapels and internal processions—lateral walkways linked with the nave by the bays. Beyond that, the number of chapels, doorways, steeples, spires can be varied endlessly, in whatever ways the age, the nation, and the state of the art may fancy. Once the needs of worship have been met satisfactorily, Architecture can do as she pleases. Statues, stained glass windows, rose windows, arabesques, denticulations, capitals, bas-reliefs—she can combine all these inventions according to whatever logarithm suits her. Hence the prodigious external variousness of these buildings that contain so much order and unity at the centre. A tree's trunk is fixed; its foliage is subject to caprice.

An Impartial Peep at the Magistrates of Old

In the year of our Lord 1482 he was a very lucky man, the noble Robert d'Estouteville, knight, Sieur of Beyne, Baron of Yvri and Saint-Andry in la Marche, Councillor and Chamberlain to the King, and Keeper of the Provostry in Paris. It was now almost seventeen years since he'd received from the king (on 7 November 1465, in the

---

[1] This, being wooden, was precisely the part of the spire destroyed by lightning in 1823 [*Hugo's note*].

year of the comet)*[1] his fine post as provost of Paris, which was regarded as an honour rather than an office—'a dignity', says Joannes Loemnoeus, 'which is accompanied by no small political power, together with many rights and prerogatives'.* In 1482 that was a most remarkable thing—a gentleman holding the king's commission with letters of appointment that dated all the way back to the time when Louis XI's illegitimate daughter was married to the Bastard of Bourbon! On the same day when Robert d'Estouteville had replaced Jacques de Villiers as Provost of Paris, Master Jean Duvet had replaced Messire Hélye de Thorrettes as First President of the High Court, Jean Jouvenel des ursins had supplanted Pierre de Morvilliers as Chancellor of France, and Regnault des Dormans had displaced Pierre Puy as Master of Requests in Ordinary to the King's Household. And on how many different heads had the aforesaid presidency, chancellorship, and mastership fallen since Robert d'Estouteville got the provostship of Paris! It had been 'granted to his keeping', the letters of appointment said; and truly he had kept it well. He'd clung to it, incorporated himself in it, identified himself with it. So well, in fact, that he'd escaped Louis XI's mania for change—that monarch being a suspicious, querulous, industrious king, intent on keeping his power supple by means of frequent appointments and dismissals. What's more, the gallant knight had even secured the reversion of the office for his son; and for the past two years the name of the noble Jacques d'Estouteville, Esquire, had figured alongside his own at the head of the provostry register. Truly a rare and notable honour! Granted, Robert d'Estouteville was a fine soldier, who had loyally raised his banner against the League of Public Welfare, and had presented to the queen a most wonderful stag made from preserves, on the day when she entered Paris in 14—. Also, he was a good friend of Messire Tristan l'Hermite,* Provost-Marshal of the King's Household.

So Messire Robert's existence was a very cosy and contented one. Pretty good salary, for a start—linked, and hung (like extra bunches of grapes on his vine), with the revenue from the provostry's civil and criminal registries, plus the revenue (civil and criminal) from the lower courts of the Châtelet, not to mention a bit of toll from the

---

[1] This is the comet that will reappear in 1835. Pope Callistus, the uncle of Alexander VI, ordered public prayers to be said against it [*Hugo's note*].

Mantes and Corbeil bridges, and the profits from the tax on Parisian blacksmiths' iron, and from firewood and salt inspections. Add to that the pleasure of riding around town and outclassing the half-red, half-tan robes of the municipal magistrates and centurions with a show of his fine military uniform (which you can still admire today carved on his tomb in Valmont Abbey, in Normandy) and his war helmet (which had been dented badly at Montlhéry).* And on top of that, was it nothing to have supreme authority over the sergeants of the *douzaine*, the Châtelet's porter and its watchmen and its jailer and its two auditors (the *auditores Castellati*), the commissioners of the sixteen districts, the four hereditary sergeants, the hundred and twenty mounted sergeants, the hundred and twenty catchpole sergeants, and the captain of the watch with his watch, under-watch, rear-watch, and counter-watch? Was it nothing to exercise justice at every level, with the right to turn, hang, and draw—to say nothing of the initial (*in prima instantia*, as the charters put it) petty jurisdiction over the viscounty of Paris with its glorious supplement of seven noble bailiwicks? Can you imagine anything more pleasant than passing sentence and judgement—as Messire Robert d'Estouteville did every day—in the Grand Châtelet, beneath Philippe Auguste's broad, flattened ogives? And going every evening—as he habitually did—to the pretty house in the Rue Galilée, within the precincts of the Palais Royal, which he held by virtue of his wife, Madame Ambroise de Loré, and relaxing there after the stress of sending some poor devil to spend *his* night in 'that little Cell in the Rue de l'Escorcherie, which the Provosts and Municipal Magistrates of Paris were wont to make their Prison; the which hath eleven feet in length, seven feet and four inches in breadth, and eleven feet in heighth'?*

And Messire Robert d'Estouteville didn't have only his own judicial authority as provost and viscount of Paris; he also had a share, as onlooker and partaker, in the King's high justice. Any head of even the least distinction passed through his hands before it fell to the public executioner. He was the man who had brought Monsieur de Nemours from the Bastille Saint-Antoine to Les Halles and Monsieur de Saint-Pol to the Grève, despite the latter's clamours and complaints—much to the delight of Monsieur the Provost, who was no great lover of Monsieur the Constable.*

That's more than enough, no doubt, to make your life happy and illustrious, and to earn you an honourable page in the interesting history of Paris provosts, where we learn that Oudard de Villeneuve had a house in the Rue des Boucheries, that Guillaume de Hangest bought Greater and Lesser Savoy, that Guillaume Thiboust gave his houses in the Rue Clopin to the nuns of Sainte-Geneviève, that Hugues Aubriot lived at the Hôtel du Porc-Épic, and other items of domestic information.

Still, in spite of all these reasons for taking life calmly and contentedly, Messire Robert d'Estouteville woke up on the morning of 7 January 1482 in a surly mood and a murderous temper. Why? He himself couldn't have explained it. Because the sky was grey, perhaps? Because the buckle of his old Montlhéry swordbelt had been done up too tight, and was squashing his provostical paunch in too military a fashion? Because he'd seen some base scoundrels going along the street beneath his window and making fun of him—a posse of four, with no shirts under their doublets and no crowns to their hats, clutching wallets and bottles? Or did he have some vague premonition of the three hundred and seventy *livres* sixteen sous eight deniers that the future King Charles VIII* was going to deduct next year from the provost's income? My readers can take their pick. Personally, I'd be inclined to think that he was in a bad mood simply because he was in a bad mood.

Besides, it was the day after a holiday; and that's a bad day for anyone, especially the magistrate responsible for cleaning up all the filth, literal and metaphorical, left behind by a holiday in Paris. What's more, he was due to sit in judgement at the Grand Châtelet. Now, I've noticed that judges generally arrange things so that the days when they hold a sitting are also the days when they're in a bad mood. This ensures that they always have somebody on whom they can comfortably vent their feelings, in the name of the king and law and justice.

Nevertheless, the hearing had started without him. As usual, his civil, criminal, and personal deputies were doing his work for him; and ever since eight a.m. several dozen male and female townspeople had been crammed and congested in a dark corner of the Châtelet's lower court, between a sturdy oak barrier and the wall, where they blissfully watched the lively and varied spectacle of civil and criminal justice being dispensed—a bit chaotically, and quite haphazardly—

by Master Florian Barbedienne, Deputy Provost and Auditor to the Châtelet.

The room was small, low, and vaulted. At the back stood a table covered with fleurs-de-lis, and a big carved-oak armchair, which was empty—it was the Provost's. On the left was a stool for the auditor, Master Florian. Below sat the Clerk of Court, scribbling busily. Opposite them were the people; and in front of the door and table were numerous provost sergeants in purple camlet tunics with white crosses. Two sergeants from the Parloir-aux-Bourgeois, in their All Saints' Day jackets (half red, half blue), stood on guard before a low, closed door, which you could see at the back behind the table. From a solitary ogive window set deep in the massive wall, a pallid ray of January light lit up two bizarre figures: the fanciful stone demon carved as a *cul-de-lampe* on the keystone of the vault, and the judge sitting at the back of the room above the fleurs-de-lis.

Just imagine Master Florian Barbedienne, Auditor to the Châtelet, propped on his elbows at the Provost's table between two piles of legal documents, his feet on the skirts of his plain brown robe, his face framed in white lambswool (from which his eyebrows also seemed to have been cut), ruddy, recalcitrant, blinking, bearing majestically fat, fleshy jowls that met beneath his chin.

Now, the auditor was deaf. Not much of a defect for an auditor. All the same, Master Florian dispensed justice most fittingly, and with no appeal allowed. What really matters is that a judge should *appear* to listen; and the venerable auditor fulfilled this requirement (the only one necessary for good justice) all the better because no sound could distract his attention.

Incidentally, the audience contained a merciless critic of his deeds and gestures, in the shape of our friend Jehan Frollo du Moulin, the young student of the previous day, a rambler whom you could be sure to meet anywhere in Paris except at the feet of his teachers.

'Well, well,' he whispered to his companion, Robin Poussepain, who was chuckling alongside him while he gave a running commentary on the various scenes that unfolded in front of their eyes, 'there's Jehanneton du Buisson, the pretty daughter of that lazy dog at the Marché-Neuf.* My word, the old fellow's convicted her! His eyes can't be any better than his ears. Fifteen sous four *deniers parisis*, for wearing two sets of rosary beads! That's a bit steep. The letter of the law is cruel.* Now who's this? Robin Chief-de-Ville, hauberk

maker! For having been received into the said trade and admitted
master of it? That's his entrance fee. Oho, two gentlemen in this
rogues' gallery! Aiglet de Soins, Hutin de Mailly. Two esquires,
corpus Christi! Aha, they've been playing dice. We'll see our rector
here sooner or later. Fined a hundred *livres parisis*, payable to the
king! Old Barbedienne won't hear of moderation—he's too deaf! If
that's going to stop me gambling—gambling night and day, and
living and dying a gambler, and betting my soul on top of my shirt—
then I'm my brother the archdeacon! Holy Virgin, what a lot of girls!
One after another, the little lambs! Ambroise Lécuyère! Isabeau la
Paynette! Bérarde Gironin! Good Lord, I know 'em all! Fine 'em,
fine 'em! That'll teach you to wear gold belts! Ten *sols parisis*, you
little flirts! Just look at the old pigface of a judge—deaf and brainless! O you numbskull Florian! O you dumbcluck Barbedienne! This
is all meat and drink to him! He gulps down the plaintiffs, he gulps
down the lawsuits, he chews and chomps and stuffs himself till he's
got a bellyful! Fines, lost property, taxes, expenses, costs (strictly
legit.), salaries, damages and interests, fire and brimstone and jail
and prison, stocks with costs, they're just Christmas cake with icing
on top to him! Just look at the pig! Hullo—great, here's another
amorous lassie! Thibaud la Thibaude, no less! For leaving the Rue
Glatigny! Now who's this lad? Gieffroy Mabonne, crossbowman.
Took the name of Our Father in vain. Fine 'em both, Thibaude and
Gieffroy, fine the pair of 'em! Why, the old deaf adder! He's got the
two cases mixed up, for sure. Ten to one he's fining the tart for
swearing and the soldier for lovemaking! Hullo hullo, Robin Poussepain, what are they going to bring in now? What a lot of sergeants!
By Jove, they've called in every last hound of the pack! They must
have bagged the big one this time. A wild boar. So it is, Robin, so it
is—and a beauty! By Hercules, it's our prince from yesterday, our
Pope of Fools, our bellringer, our one-eyed hunchback and gargoyle!
It's Quasimodo!'

Sure enough, it was none other.

It was Quasimodo—roped, bound, trussed, pinioned, and under
heavy guard. The squad of sergeants surrounding him was supported
by the captain of the watch in person, with the arms of France
embroidered on his breast and those of the city on his back. Yet
there was nothing about Quasimodo—apart from his deformity—to
justify this array of halberds and harquebuses. He was silent, calm,

and sullen. Every now and then his one eye surreptitiously glared at the ropes around him; that was all.

He looked around too, with the same expression, but so lifelessly and lethargically that the women merely pointed at him and laughed.

Meanwhile, Master Florian, the auditor, was leafing attentively through the dossier of charges against Quasimodo, which the clerk had handed to him. His quick survey finished, he seemed to ponder for a moment. He always took this precaution before proceeding with an interrogation; as a result, he knew in advance the names, titles, and crimes of the accused, and was able to make predictable retorts to the predictable answers—so that he could pick his way through the twists and turns of the interrogation without making his deafness too obvious. The case dossier was to him what a guide dog is to a blind man. If some irrelevant remark or unintelligible question did happen to reveal his infirmity, some people set it down to his profundity, others to his stupidity. Either way, magistratic honour was preserved; it's much better for a judge to be thought profound or stupid than deaf. So he took great pains to hide his deafness from the public, and usually he succeeded so well that he even began to deceive himself. Which is easier than you might think, incidentally. Hunchbacks always go around with their heads high, stammerers always make speeches, deaf people always talk in a whisper. He himself thought that his hearing was, at the utmost, a bit recalcitrant. That was his one concession to public opinion, in his moments of self-criticism and self-examination.

Therefore, he brooded on Quasimodo's case for a while, and then threw back his head and narrowed his eyes, to make himself seem more impartial and authoritative—the result being that he became blind as well as deaf. Two attributes without which no judge can be perfect. And in that magisterial attitude he began the interrogation.

'Your name?'

Now here was a situation that hadn't been 'foreseen by the law': one deaf man having to interrogate another.

Quasimodo had no notion that he had been asked a question. He kept staring at the judge and didn't answer. The judge was deaf and had no notion that the accused was also deaf. He thought that the fellow had answered, as almost every defendant does, and so, with his mindless mechanical self-assurance, he went on:

'Good. Your age?'

Quasimodo didn't reply to that question either. The judge thought it had been answered, and continued:

'Now then, your occupation?'

The same silence as before. The audience, meanwhile, had begun to whisper and exchange looks.

'That will do,' went on the imperturbable auditor, assuming that the defendant had completed his third reply. 'You are accused before us first, of causing a nocturnal disturbance; secondly, of an act of bodily violence against a woman of loose conduct, prejudicial to the wellbeing of a harlot; thirdly, of insubordination and disloyalty toward the archers of our master the king's ordinance. Let us hear your defence on all these points... Clerk, have you written down what the accused has said so far?'

At this luckless question a roar of laughter went up from clerks and general public alike. It was so vigorous, so wild, so infectious, and so universal, that even the two deaf men noticed it. Quasimodo turned around, hunching his shoulders scornfully. Master Florian was equally surprised. He imagined that the spectators' laughter had been prompted by some impertinent reply from the defendant, and that the shrug of the shoulders was a visible sign of this; so he said to him angrily:

'That remark of yours deserves the gallows, you scoundrel! Do you know who you're speaking to?'

This outburst was hardly the thing to halt the general hilarity. It struck everyone as so inept and incongruous that the gales of laughter spread even to the sergeants from the Parloir-aux-Bourgeois, those knaves of spades whose stupidity was part of their uniform. Quasimodo alone remained solemn, for the good reason that he couldn't understand anything that was happening around him. The judge, becoming more and more annoyed, felt obliged to proceed in the same manner, in the hope that this would strike terror into the defendant and therefore impress the general public.

'So then, you arch-pervert and arch-pillager, you've got the nerve to be disrespectful toward the Auditor of the Châtelet, the magistrate appointed to police the people of Paris, responsible for investigation of crime, vice, and misconduct, supervision of trade, prevention of monopoly, upkeep of roads, prevention of recycled poultry, game, and wildfowl, inspection of firewood and other kinds of wood, eradication of sewage from the city and contagious diseases from the air—in short, constant attention to the public good, without any payment or any desire for payment! Do you realize that I am Florian Barbedienne, the Provost's personal deputy, and what's more, commissioner, investigator, comptroller, and examiner, with equal powers in provostry, bailiwick, conservancy, and presidial matters?'

When one deaf man talks to another, there's no reason why he should ever stop. Lord knows when and where Master Florian would have reached land in this full-sail voyage across the high seas of eloquence, if the low door at the back hadn't suddenly opened and admitted the Provost in person.

Master Florian didn't break off when he entered, but spun round on his heels and abruptly aimed at the Provost the harangue with which he had just been blasting Quasimodo.

'My lord,' he said, 'I request whatever penalty it may please you to impose on the accused here present, for flagrant exorbitant contempt of court.'

And he sat down again, puffing and panting, wiping away the big drops of sweat that were falling from his face like tears and drenching the outspread parchments in front of him. Messire Robert d'Estouteville furrowed his brows and gestured so imperiously and emphatically at Quasimodo that the deaf man partly realized he was being told to pay attention.

The Provost said to him sternly, 'What did you do to bring you here, you scoundrel?'

The poor devil imagined that the Provost had asked for his name, so he broke his customary silence and, in a hoarse, guttural voice, replied: 'Quasimodo.'

This reply tallied so little with the question that renewed gales of laughter broke out, and Messire Robert, reddening with anger, exclaimed: 'Are you making fun of me too, you rascal?'

'Bellringer at Notre-Dame', replied Quasimodo, thinking he had to tell the judge who he was.

'Bellringer!' echoed the Provost. As we've said, he had woken in a bad mood that morning, and he had no need of these odd replies to fan the flames of his rage. 'Bellringer! I'll get them to ring the chimes on your back with a horsewhip through every street in Paris. Do you understand, you rogue?'

'If you want to know how old I am,' said Quasimodo, 'I think I'll be twenty next Martinmas.'

This was the final straw. The Provost lost his temper altogether.

'So, you wretch, you're making fun of the Provostship! Catchpole sergeants, take this fellow to the Grève pillory, flog him, and turn him round for an hour. He'll pay for this, by God! And I'll have this sentence publicly cried, with four sworn trumpeters in attendance, through all seven castellanies in the viscounty of Paris.'

The clerk immediately began to draw up the sentence.

'Guts Almighty, that's a fine sort of sentence!' shouted the young student Jehan Frollo du Moulin from his corner.

The Provost swung round and, with his eyes blazing, glared once more at Quasimodo. 'I do believe the scoundrel said "Guts Almighty!" Clerk, add a fine of twelve *deniers parisis* for swearing, half of which will go to the fabric fund at Saint-Eustache. I am *particularly* devoted to Saint Eustachius.'*

Very soon the sentence was drawn up. Its drift was short and simple; President Thibaut Baillet and King's Advocate Roger Barme* hadn't yet reshaped the common law of the provostry and viscounty of Paris. Those two jurisconsults hadn't yet clogged it with the lofty thicket of legal jots and tittles which they planted there at the beginning of the sixteenth century. Everything was plain, practical, pertinent. It went straight to the point; there were no undergrowths and no byways; you could see the wheel, gallows, or pillory at the end of every path. At least you knew where you were going.

The clerk gave the sentence to the Provost, who stamped it with his seal and left to continue on his rounds through the various courtrooms, in a state of mind that must have filled every gaol in Paris that day. Jehan Frollo and Robin Poussepain were laughing up their sleeves. Quasimodo was eyeing the whole scene with an indifferent, bewildered expression.

But just as it was Master Florian Barbedienne's turn to read over the sentence and sign it, the clerk began to feel some pity for the poor fellow who had been condemned. In the hope of mitigating the sentence, he came as close to the auditor's ear as he could, pointed at Quasimodo, and said: 'He's deaf.'

He was hoping that this bond of infirmity might rouse Master Florian's interest and act in favour of the convicted man. But for one thing, we've already seen that Master Florian didn't like his deafness to be noticed. And for another, he was so hard of hearing that he didn't catch a syllable of the clerk's statement; but he wanted to give the appearance of having heard, and so he answered: 'Oho, that's a different matter. I didn't know that. In that case, one hour extra in the pillory.'

And he signed the thus-modified sentence.

'A good job, too', said Robin Poussepain, who had a grudge against Quasimodo. 'That'll teach him to treat people so roughly.'

from *Les Feuilles d'automne*

Ce qu'on entend sur la montagne

Avez-vous quelquefois, calme et silencieux,
Monté sur la montagne, en présence des cieux?
Était-ce aux bords du Sund? aux côtes de Bretagne?
Aviez-vous l'océan au pied de la montagne?
Et là, penché sur l'onde et sur l'immensité,   5
Calme et silencieux, avez-vous écouté?

Voici ce qu'on entend.—Du moins un jour qu'en rêve
Ma pensée abattit son vol sur une grève,
Et, du sommet d'un mont plongeant au gouffre amer
Vit d'un côté la terre et de l'autre la mer,   10
J'écoutai, j'entendis, et jamais voix pareille
Ne sortit d'une bouche et n'émut une oreille.

Ce fut d'abord un bruit large, immense, confus,
Plus vague que le vent dans les arbres touffus,
Plein d'accords éclatants, de suaves murmures,   15
Doux comme un chant du soir, fort comme un choc d'armures
Quand la sourde mêlée étreint les escadrons
Et souffle, furieuse, aux bouches des clairons.

C'était une musique ineffable et profonde,
Qui, fluide, oscillait sans cesse autour du monde,   20
Et dans les vastes cieux, par ses flots rajeunis,
Roulait élargissant ses orbes infinis
Jusqu'au fond où son flux s'allait perdre dans l'ombre
Avec le temps, l'espace et la forme et le nombre.
Comme une autre atmosphère épars et débordé,   25
L'hymne éternel couvrait tout le globe inondé.
Le monde, enveloppé dans cette symphonie,
Comme il vogue dans l'air, voguait dans l'harmonie.

from *Autumn Leaves*

Heard on the Mountain

Have you, silently, calmly, scaled the height
Of some tall mountain, in the heavens' sight?
Was it beside the Sound?* in Brittany?
Below that mountain, did you face the sea?
And, bent above the waves and boundless air,
Silently, calmly, did you listen there?

Then you heard this—at least, my thoughts one day
Alighted on the margin of a bay
Where a peak swept into the salty tide,
And saw the land and ocean on each side.
I heard, I listened. Never did I hear
Anything like it leave a mouth, or stir an ear!

First came a vast sound, vaguer than a breeze
Passing confusedly through leafy trees,
Full of soft murmurs and imposing chords,
Sweet as night music, strong as clashing swords
When armies meet in some muffled affray
That stirs the trumpets' furious mouths to bray.

It was a deep, ineffable harmony
Quivering round the world incessantly,
And rolling countless spheres still further on
Through the vast skies till the whole tide had gone,
Driven by new waves, in the distant shade
Where time and space and shape and number fade.
Like some new atmosphere spread and unfurled,
That timeless hymn covered the flooded world.
The globe, wrapped in its music everywhere,
Floated through harmony as through the air.

Et pensif, j'écoutais ces harpes de l'éther,
Perdu dans cette voix comme dans une mer.   30

Bientôt je distinguai, confuses et voilées,
Deux voix dans cette voix l'une à l'autre mêlées,
De la terre et des mers s'épanchant jusqu'au ciel,
Qui chantaient à la fois le chant universel;
Et je les distinguai dans la rumeur profonde,   35
Comme on voit deux courants qui se croisent sous l'onde.

L'une venait des mers; chant de gloire! hymne heureux!
C'était la voix des flots qui se parlaient entre eux.
L'autre, qui s'élevait de la terre où nous sommes,
Était triste; c'était le murmure des hommes.   40
Et dans ce grand concert, qui chantait jour et nuit,
Chaque onde avait sa voix et chaque homme son bruit.

Or, comme je l'ai dit, l'océan magnifique
Épandait une voix joyeuse et pacifique,
Chantait comme la harpe aux temples de Sion,   45
Et louait la beauté de la création.
Sa clameur, qu'emportaient la brise et la rafale,
Incessamment vers Dieu montait plus triomphale,
Et chacun de ses flots, que Dieu seul peut dompter,
Quand l'autre avait fini, se levait pour chanter.   50
Comme ce grand lion dont Daniel fut l'hôte,
L'océan par moments abaissait sa voix haute,
Et moi je croyais voir, vers le couchant en feu,
Sous sa crinière d'or passer la main de Dieu.

Cependant, à côté de l'auguste fanfare,   55
L'autre voix, comme un cri de coursier qui s'effare,
Comme le gond rouillé d'une porte d'enfer,
Comme l'archet d'airain sur la lyre de fer,
Grinçait; et pleurs, et cris, l'injure, l'anathème,
Refus du viatique et refus du baptême,   60
Et malédiction, et blasphème, et clameur,
Dans le flot tournoyant de l'humaine rumeur,
Passaient, comme le soir on voit dans les vallées

And then, lost in that voice as in a sea,
I listened to those strange harps thoughtfully.

Within the sound, after a while, two blurred
And intermingled voices could be heard;
The seas and lands in a united throng
Shed to the skies their universal song;
I could distinguish them in that deep sound,
As, in the ocean depths, two currents may be found.

One came, a glorious hymn, from the sea's flow—
The speech of billows passing to and fro;
The other, from the earth, our dwelling place,
Rose sadly—the groan of the human race;
In that great concert singing night and day
Every man had his voice, and each wave said its say.

Now, as I said before, the mighty sea
Uttered its voice gladly and peacefully,
Sang like a harp in Zion's* congregation,
And praised the beauty of the whole creation.
Its noise, swept by the gales and tempests, soared
In ever-greater triumph to the Lord;
When one wave, which the Lord alone can quell,
Ended, the next one rose and sang as well.
At times the ocean's mighty roars would cease
Like some great lion leaving Daniel's* soul in peace,
And, in the fiery dusk, I seemed to ascertain
The Lord's hand passing through its golden mane.

Beside that fanfare, though, the other sound
Groaned like hell's rusty hinges turning round,
Like the neighing of frightened stallions,
Like a steel lyre struck by a bow of bronze;
And tears and cries, cursing and commination,
Refusal of baptism and salvation,
Everything that condemns, blights, and destroys,
Passed in that whirling flood of human noise,
As, when the sun has set, black birds of night

De noirs oiseaux de nuit qui s'en vont par volées.
Qu'était-ce que ce bruit dont mille échos vibraient?   65
Hélas! c'était la terre et l'homme qui pleuraient.

Frères! de ces deux voix étranges, inouïes,
Sans cesse renaissant, sans cesse évanouies,
Qu'écoute l'Éternel durant l'éternité,
L'une disait: NATURE! et l'autre: HUMANITÉ!   70

Alors je méditai; car mon esprit fidèle,
Hélas! n'avait jamais déployé plus grande aile;
Dans mon ombre jamais n'avait lui tant de jour;
Et je rêvai longtemps, contemplant tour à tour,
Après l'abîme obscur que me cachait la lame,   75
L'autre abîme sans fond qui s'ouvrait dans mon âme.
Et je me demandai pourquoi l'on est ici,
Quel peut être après tout le but de tout ceci,
Que fait l'âme, lequel vaut mieux d'être ou de vivre,
Et pourquoi le Seigneur, qui seul lit à son livre,   80
Mêle éternellement dans un fatal hymen
Le chant de la nature au cri du genre humain?

«Quelquefois, sous les plis des nuages trompeurs . . .»

Quelquefois, sous les plis des nuages trompeurs,
Loin dans l'air, à travers les brèches des vapeurs
　　Par le vent du soir remuées,
Derrière les derniers brouillards, plus loin encor,
Apparaissent soudain les mille étages d'or   5
　　D'un édifice de nuées;

Et l'œil épouvanté, par delà tous nos cieux,
Sur une île de l'air au vol audacieux,
　　Dans l'éther libre aventurée,
L'œil croit voir jusqu'au ciel monter, monter toujours,   10
Avec ses escaliers, ses ponts, ses grandes tours,
　　Quelque Babel démesurée.

Are seen leaving the glades in teeming flight.
What was this sound, where myriad echoes twined?
Ah! it was weeping earth and humankind!

My friends, one of these two strange mystifying
Voices, ever reborn, and ever dying,
Which the Eternal* hears eternally,
Said: 'NATURE!' and one said: 'HUMANITY!'

I pondered then; my soul had never tried,
I must confess, to spread its wings so wide;
Never, within my gloom, had such light shone;
And for a long time I reflected on
The dark abyss veiled by the ocean's roll
And the vast chasm gaping in my soul.
Why are we here, then? I began to ask;
What can it all mean? What is the soul's task?
Living, or simply being—which is better?
And why does God, who alone reads his letter,
For ever wed in one fatal embrace
The song of Nature and the sobbing of our race?

'Sometimes, beneath the clouds' deceptive twists . . .'

Sometimes, beneath the clouds' deceptive twists,
Far away in the air, through fissured mists
    That the late breeze has ploughed,
Behind the last haze suddenly there soars,
With its more distant thousand golden floors,
        An edifice of cloud.

Beyond the heavens we know, our dazzled sight
Seems to glimpse a bold island taking flight
    Bravely in the free air,
On which some monstrous Babel's* turrets rise,
Rise constantly, up to the highest skies,
        With many a spire and bridge and stair!

from *Les Chants du crépuscule*

Sur le bal de l'Hôtel de Ville

Ainsi l'Hôtel de Ville illumine son faîte.
Le prince et les flambeaux, tout y brille, et la fête
Ce soir va resplendir sur ce comble éclairé,
Comme l'idée au front du poëte sacré.
Mais cette fête, amis, n'est pas une pensée.   5
Ce n'est pas d'un banquet que la France est pressée,
Et ce n'est pas un bal qu'il faut, en vérité,
A ce tas de douleurs qu'on nomme la cité!

Puissants! nous ferions mieux de panser quelque plaie
Dont le sage rêveur à cette heure s'effraie,   10
D'étayer l'escalier qui d'en bas monte en haut,
D'agrandir l'atelier, d'amoindrir l'échafaud,
De songer aux enfants qui sont sans pain dans l'ombre,
De rendre un paradis au pauvre impie et sombre,
Que d'allumer un lustre et de tenir la nuit   15
Quelques fous éveillés autour d'un peu de bruit!

O reines de nos toits, femmes chastes et saintes,
Fleurs qui de nos maisons perfumez les enceintes,
Vous à qui le bonheur conseille la vertu,
Vous qui contre le mal n'avez pas combattu,   20
A qui jamais la faim, empoisonneuse infâme,
N'a dit: Vends-moi ton corps,—c'est-à-dire votre âme!
Vous dont le cœur de joie et d'innocence est plein,
Dont la pudeur a plus d'enveloppes de lin
Que n'en avait Isis, la déesse voilée,   25
Cette fête est pour vous comme une aube étoilée!
Vous riez d'y courir tandis qu'on souffre ailleurs!
C'est que votre belle âme ignore les douleurs;
Le hasard vous posa dans la sphère suprême;

from *Songs of the Half-Light*

A Ball at the Hôtel de Ville

The Hôtel de Ville's roof is shining bright;
From prince to torches, all things glitter now;
Revels will light that pinnacle tonight
Like inspiration on a poet's brow!
But, friends, that party is no inspiration.
Banquets are hardly vital to our nation;
Nor does it need a dance, this mass of pity
  And suffering that we call the city!

No! Let our lords and ladies strive to heal
The wounds today that shuddering sages feel—
Build up the stairs that lead to loftier scenes,
Improve the workshops and reduce the guillotines,
Think about homeless children starving, and
Lead godless poor men to the Promised Land—
Rather than setting chandeliers alight
So a few noisy fools can stay awake all night!

You wives, domestic queens, chaste, virtuous,
Flowers who scent our strong-walled homes for us,
Whose good luck always kept you pure within,
Who never had to struggle against sin—
No Hunger offered you her poisoned bowl,
Saying: 'Sell me your body... and your soul';
Your inmost depths are innocent and hale;
Your shame is shrouded in a thicker veil
Than Isis,* the veiled goddess, ever knew—
This ball is like a starry dawn to you!
While you frolic here, people bleed elsewhere;
Your pretty souls are simply unaware
Of pain; Luck set you on the utmost height;

Vous vivez, vous brillez, vous ne voyez pas même,   30
Tant vos yeux éblouis de rayons sont noyés,
Ce qu'au-dessous de vous dans l'ombre on foule aux pieds!

Oui, c'est ainsi.—Le prince, et le riche, et le monde
Cherche à vous réjouir, vous pour qui tout abonde.
Vous avez la beauté, vous avez l'ornement;   35
La fête vous enivre à son bourdonnement,
Et, comme à la lumière un papillon de soie,
Vous volez à la porte ouverte qui flamboie!
Vous allez à ce bal, et vous ne songez pas
Que parmi ces passants amassés sur vos pas,   40
En foule émerveillés des chars et des livrées,
D'autres femmes sont là, non moins que vous parées,
Qu'on farde et qu'on expose à vendre au carrefour;
Spectres où saigne encor la place de l'amour;
Comme vous pour le bal, belles et demi-nues;   45
Pour vous voir au passage, hélas! exprès venues,
Voilant leur deuil affreux d'un sourire moqueur,
Les fleurs au front, la boue aux pieds, la haine au cœur!

«Oh! pour remplir de moi ta rêveuse pensée . . .»

Oh! pour remplir de moi ta rêveuse pensée,
Tandis que tu m'attends, par la marche lassée,
Sous l'arbre au bord du lac, loin des yeux importuns,
Tandis que sous tes pieds l'odorante vallée,
Toute pleine de brume au soleil envolée,   5
Fume comme un beau vase où brûlent des parfums;

Que tout ce que je vois, les coteaux et les plaines,
Les doux buissons de fleurs aux charmantes haleines,
      La vitre au vif éclair,
Le pré vert, le sentier qui se noue aux villages,   10
Et le ravin profond débordant de feuillages
      Comme d'ondes la mer,

You live, you shine; you never even mark,
Your eyes being so blinded by the light,
The trampled hordes beneath you in the dark!

So it goes.—Socialite, rich man, and king
Strive to delight you, who have everything.
You possess loveliness, trinkets, and toys;
Parties enrapture you with their gay noise,
So to this blazing open door you came
Like silken butterflies drawn to a flame!
You thronged this ballroom, without one reflection
That, through the crowds who flocked in your direction,
Dazed by the coats and carriages on view,
Were other women no less jewelled than you,
Made up and sold off in the public street,
Ghosts ever bleeding from love's very seat.
Just to see you in passing they have queued,
Like you in your ballgowns, pretty, half nude,
Masking their sorrows with a smile ice-cold—
Floral-faced, filthy-footed, bitter-souled!

'O that I could fill your deep reverie . . .'

O that I could fill your deep reverie
While, wearied by your walk, you wait for me
Under the lakeside tree, far from unwelcome eyes,
While the whole fragrant vale, whose mists retreat
Before the sunlight, steams beneath your feet
Like a sublime vase from which smouldering perfumes rise!

May everything you see—the hillside and the plain,
The vivid gleam that flashes from the window pane,
The flowering shrubs with their sweet smell,
The verdant pastureland, the little path that weaves
From town to town, the deep ravine that brims with leaves
As the sea does with swell—

Que le bois, le jardin, la maison, la nuée,
Dont midi ronge au loin l'ombre diminuée,
Que tous les points confus qu'on voit là-bas trembler,   15
Que la branche aux fruits mûrs, que la feuille séchée,
Que l'automne, déjà par septembre ébauchée,
Que tout ce qu'on entend ramper, marcher, voler,

Que ce réseau d'objets qui t'entoure et te presse,
Et dont l'arbre amoureux qui sur ton front se dresse   20
     Est le premier chaînon,
Herbe et feuille, onde et terre, ombre, lumière et flamme,
Que tout prenne une voix, que tout devienne une âme,
     Et te dise mon nom!

«Les autres en tout sens laissent aller leur vie . . .»

Les autres en tout sens laissent aller leur vie,
Leur âme, leur désir, leur instinct, leur envie.
Tout marche en eux au gré des choses qui viendront,
L'action sans l'idée et le pied sans le front.
Ils suivent au hasard le projet ou le rêve,   5
Toute porte qui s'ouvre ou tout vent qui s'élève.
Le présent les absorbe en sa brièveté.
Ils ne seront jamais et n'ont jamais été;
Ils sont, et voilà tout. Leur esprit flotte et doute.
Ils vont, le voyageur ne tient pas à la route,   10
Et tout s'efface en eux à mesure, l'ennui
Par la joie, oui par non, hier par aujourd'hui.
Ils vivent jour à jour et pensée à pensée.
Aucune règle au fond de leurs vœux n'est tracée;
Nul accord ne les tient dans ses proportions.   15
Quand ils pensent une heure, au gré des passions,
Rien de lointain ne vient de derrière leur vie
Retentir dans l'idée à cette heure suivie;
Et pour leur cœur terni l'amour est sans douleurs,
Le passé sans racine et l'avenir sans fleurs.   20

May the garden, the house, the woodland bowers,
The cloud whose shadow the noon light devours,
The branch whose fruits are ripe, the foliage that is dry—
    May all the faint dots quivering over there,
    The autumn these September days prepare,
Everything that you hear slither or stalk or fly—

May this whole web that throngs you here, that grips you now,
Whose first strand is the loving tree above your brow,
    May the shadow, the light, the flame,
The soil, the stream, the grassblade and the leafy bole—
May all these things assume a voice, become a soul,
        And name my name!

'The rest of them drift any way at all . . .'

The rest of them drift any way at all,
Wherever whim and wish and impulse call.
Their thoughtless actions and their brainless feet
Are swung and swayed by everything they meet.
Haphazardly they follow to and fro
All doors that open and all winds that blow.
The present grips them in its brevity.
They never were, and never will they be;
They merely are. Their spirits doubt and stray,
They travel without keeping to the way,
And all things cancel out for them—distress
And pleasure, past and present, no and yes.
They live from day to day, from thought to thought.
Their hopes have no design of any sort;
Their life has no harmonious balance in it.
If passion sets them thinking for a minute,
Nothing more deep or distant echoes through
The notion they must instantly pursue;
Love, in their wornout hearts, has no dark hours,
Yesterday has no roots, tomorrow has no flowers.

Mais vous qui répandez tant de jour sur mon âme,
Vous qui depuis douze ans, tour à tour ange et femme,
Me soutenant là-haut ou m'aidant ici-bas,
M'avez pris sous votre aile ou calmé dans vos bras;
Vous qui, mettant toujours le cœur dans la parole,   25
Rendez visible aux yeux, comme un vivant symbole,
Le calme intérieur par la paix du dehors,
La douceur de l'esprit par la santé du corps,
La bonté par la joie, et, comme les dieux même,
La suprême vertu par la beauté suprême;   30
Vous, mon phare, mon but, mon pôle, mon aimant!
Tandis que nous flottons à tout événement,
Vous savez que toute âme a sa règle auprès d'elle;
Tout en vous est serein, rayonnant et fidèle,
Vous ne dérangez pas le tout harmonieux,   35
Et vous êtes ici comme une sphère aux cieux.
Rien ne se heurte en vous; tout se tient avec grâce;
Votre âme en souriant à votre esprit s'enlace,
Votre vie, où les pleurs se mêlent quelquefois,
Secrète comme un nid qui gémit dans les bois,   40
Comme un flot lent et sourd qui coule sur des mousses,
Est un concert charmant des choses les plus douces.
Bonté, vertu, beauté, frais sourire, œil de feu,
Toute votre nature est un hymne vers Dieu.
Il semble, en vous voyant si parfaite et si belle,   45
Qu'une pure musique, égale et solennelle,
De tous vos mouvements se dégage en marchant.
Les autres sont des bruits; vous, vous êtes un chant!

from *Les Rayons et les ombres*

Sur un homme populaire

O peuple! sous ce crâne où rien n'a pénétré,
Sous l'auguste sourcil morose et vénéré
    Du tribun et du cénobite,

But you shed so much daylight in my heart;
Year by year, angel-woman, you impart
Your help with heavenly or earthly things,
Soothing me in your arms or with your wings,
Putting your soul in every word you say.
You, like a symbol sprung to life, display
Inner tranquillity through outward peace,
Spiritual bliss through bodily release,
Goodness through happiness; like gods, you drape
The finest virtue in the fairest shape.
You are my beacon, magnet, prize, and pole;
Loyalty, light, and calmness fill your soul;
And while we drift about on every tide,
You know that human hearts have their own guide.
You never mar the heavenly concord; here
Among us, you are a celestial sphere!
Within you, nothing clashes; all is grace;
Your radiant spirit and your mind embrace;
Shy as a nest that murmurs in the trees,
Your life, though it has had its tragedies,
Like a slow stream rippling through mosses, brings
A lovely harmony of sweetest things.
Bright-eyed and smiling, virtue in accord
With beauty, your whole nature hymns the Lord.
Watching you walk, so perfect and so fair,
Music seems to flow from you everywhere,
Grave and harmonious, as you move along.
The rest of them are noises. You? You are a song!

from *Sunlight and Shadows*

A Popular Man

Within this never-penetrated skull,
Beneath these august brows, revered and dull
    With duty and devotion—

Sous ce front dont un jour les révolutions
Feront en l'entr'ouvrant sortir les visions,   5
          Une pensée affreuse habite.

Dans l'Inde ainsi parfois le passant curieux
Contemple avec respect un mont mystérieux,
          Cime des nuages touchée,
Rêve et croit respirer, sans approcher trop près,   10
Dans ces rocs, dans ces eaux, dans ces mornes forêts,
          Une divinité cachée.

L'intérieur du mont en pagode est sculpté.
Puis vient enfin le jour de la solennité.
          On brise la porte murée.   15
Le peuple accourt poussant des cris tumultueux;—
L'idole alors, fœtus aveugle et monstrueux,
          Sort de la montagne éventrée.

«Puits de l'Inde! tombeaux! monuments constellés! . . .»

Puits de l'Inde! tombeaux! monuments constellés!
Vous dont l'intérieur n'offre aux regards troublés
Qu'un amas tournoyant de marches et de rampes,
Froids cachots, corridors où rayonnent des lampes,
Poutres où l'araignée a tendu ses longs fils,   5
Blocs ébauchant partout de sinistres profils,
Toits de granit, troués comme une frêle toile,
Par où l'œil voit briller quelque profonde étoile,
Et des chaos de murs, de chambres, de paliers,
Où s'écroule au hasard un gouffre d'escaliers!   10
Cryptes qui remplissez d'horreur religieuse
Votre voûte sans fin, morne et prodigieuse!
Cavernes où l'esprit n'ose aller trop avant!
Devant vos profondeurs j'ai pâli bien souvent
Comme sur un abîme ou sur une fournaise,   15
Effrayantes Babels que rêvait Piranèse!

This head that revolutions soon will split,
And all its visions will escape from it—
      There dwells a dreadful notion.

So curious Indian travellers may seek
With reverence some immense mysterious peak,
      Some mount whose crest is clouded,
And think they breathe from far off, in their dreams,
Among these gloomy woods and rocks and streams,
      A deity enshrouded.

The mountain has a sculptured shrine inside.
The great day comes; the door is opened wide;
      In rushes the transported
Multitude, with a wild ecstatic shriek—
Then out of the eviscerated peak
      The blind and monstrous idol is aborted.

'Indian caverns! tombs! monumental arrays . . .'

Indian caverns! tombs! monumental arrays
Whose inside, to the troubled eye, displays
Only a swirling mass of steps and flights,
Cold dungeons, corridors lit by gleaming lights,
Beams where the spider weaves its long-drawn threads,
Crags casting silhouettes of sinister heads,
Granite roofs holed like flimsy webbing, where
Some glimmering star is glimpsed deep in the air,
Whole chaoses of landings, chambers, walls,
Through which a crumbling stepwise chasm falls!
Whose domes, prodigious, dismal, and immense,
Steep the whole crypt in dreadful reverence!
Where the mind dares not penetrate too deep!
Ghastly Babels of Piranesi's* sleep!
Often I have turned pale at such a scene,
As at a furnace or a vast ravine!

Entrez si vous l'osez!
                    Sur le pavé dormant
Les ombres des arceaux se croisent tristement;
La dalle par endroits, pliant sous les décombres,
S'entr'ouvre pour laisser passer des degrés sombres   20
Qui fouillent, vis de pierre, un souterrain sans fond;
D'autres montent là-haut et crèvent le plafond.
Où vont-ils? Dieu le sait. Du creux d'une arche vide
Une eau qui tombe envoie une lueur livide.
Une voûte au front vert s'égoutte dans un puits.   25
Dans l'ombre un lourd monceau de roches sans appuis
S'arrête retenu par des ronces grimpantes;
Une corde qui pend d'un amas de charpentes
S'offre, mystérieuse, à la main du passant.
Dans un caveau, penché sur un livre, et lisant,   30
Un vieillard surhumain, sous le roc qui surplombe,
Semble vivre oublié par la mort dans sa tombe.
Des sphinx, des bœufs d'airain, sur l'étrave accroupis,
Ont fait des chapiteaux aux piliers décrépits;
L'aspic à l'œil de braise, agitant ses paupières,   35
Passe sa tête plate aux crevasses des pierres.
Tout chancelle et fléchit sous les toits entr'ouverts.
Le mur suinte, et l'on voit fourmiller à travers
De grands feuillages roux, sortant d'entre les marbres,
Des monstres qu'on prendrait pour des racines d'arbres.   40
Partout, sur les parois du morne monument,
Quelque chose d'affreux rampe confusément;
Et celui qui parcourt ce dédale difforme,
Comme s'il était pris par un polype énorme,
Sur son front effaré, sous son pied hasardeux,   45
Sent vivre et remuer l'édifice hideux!

Aux heures où l'esprit, dont l'œil partout se pose,
Cherche à voir dans la nuit le fond de toute chose,
Dans ces lieux effrayants mon regard se perdit.
Bien souvent je les ai contemplés, et j'ai dit: 50

—O rêves de granit! grottes visionnaires!
Cryptes! palais! tombeaux, pleins de vagues tonnerres!

If you dare, enter!
                    On the slumbering ground
Shadows of doleful vaults are interwound;
Flagstones sink beneath debris here and there,
And part to make room for some dusky stair,
Some stone spiral that plumbs the bottomless pit
Or soars and cleaves the ceiling opposite.
Where does it lead? God knows. Streams plunge below
A hollow arch, and shed a livid glow.
A green-browed vault drips into a deep crypt.
A heavy pile of fallen rocks is gripped
Tightly within the dark by climbing brambles;
A mysterious cord, hung from a shambles
Of timberwork, brushes the wanderer's hand.
Stooped at a book, striving to understand,
An ancient demigod in the rocky gloom
Lives on, forgotten by death, inside his tomb.
Sphinxes, bronze oxen, squat upon the prows
Of battered colonnades, and cap their brows;
A burning-eyed flickering viper passes
His flat head through the mineral crevasses.
All things totter beneath the gaping eaves.
The walls are oozing; through huge russet leaves,
Emerging from the marble slabs, one sees
Writhing monsters that seem like roots of trees.
A dreadful Something indistinctly crawls
On all parts of the monument's bleak walls;
Whoever wanders this misshapen maze,
As if snared in some giant polyp's rays,
Feels the whole structure's grim heart live and beat
Above his pale brow, under his rash feet!

At the hours when the mind's all-searching sight
Struggles to fathom all things in the night,
In those dread realms my gaze would lose its way,
And, pondering them, often I would say:

'Ah, dreams of granite! visionary caves!
Crannies filled with dim thunder! mansions! graves!

Vous êtes moins brumeux, moins noirs, moins ignorés,
Vous êtes moins profonds et moins désespérés
Que le destin, cet antre habité par nos craintes,   55
Où l'âme entend, perdue en d'affreux labyrinthes,
Au fond, à travers l'ombre, avec mille bruits sourds,
Dans un gouffre inconnu tomber le flot des jours!—

L'Ombre

Il lui disait:—Vos chants sont tristes. Qu'avez-vous?
Ange inquiet, quels pleurs mouillent vos yeux si doux?
Pourquoi, pauvre âme tendre, inclinée et fidèle,
Comme un jonc que le vent a ployé d'un coup d'aile,
Pencher votre beau front assombri par instants?   5
Il faut vous réjouir, car voici le printemps,
Avril, saison dorée, où, parmi les zéphires,
Les parfums, les chansons, les baisers, les sourires,
Et les charmants propos qu'on dit à demi-voix,
L'amour revient aux cœurs comme la feuille aux bois!—   10

Elle lui répondit de sa voix grave et douce:
—Ami, vous êtes fort. Sûr du Dieu qui vous pousse,
L'œil fixé sur un but, vous marchez droit et fier,
Sans la peur de demain, sans le souci d'hier,
Et rien ne peut trembler, pour votre âme ravie,   15
La belle vision qui vous cache la vie.
Mais moi, je pleure!—Morne, attachée à vos pas,
Atteinte à tous ces coups que vous ne sentez pas,
Cœur fait, moins l'espérance, à l'image du vôtre,
Je souffre dans ce monde et vous chantez dans l'autre.   20
Tout m'attriste, avenir que je vois à faux jour,
Aigreur de la raison qui querelle l'amour,
Et l'âcre jalousie alors qu'une autre femme
Veut tirer de vos yeux un regard de votre âme,
Et le sort qui nous frappe et qui n'est jamais las.   25
Plus le soleil reluit, plus je suis sombre, hélas!
Vous allez, moi je suis; vous marchez, moi je tremble,
Et tandis que, formant mille projets ensemble,

You are less dark, less misty, less malign,
Less deep, less unexplored, less saturnine
Than fate—that cavern peopled by our fears,
Where, lost in dreadful labyrinths, the soul hears
The flood of days fall with a muffled echoing sound
Into some unknown chasm underground!'

The Shadow

He said: 'Your songs are sad, my angel—why?
And your eyes are so gentle—must they cry?
Poor tender faithful restless soul, bent low
    As a reed bends when stormwinds blow,
Why should you darken and abase your brow?
I want to please you—it is springtime now,
April, the golden month when, through the breeze,
The scents and kisses, smiles and melodies
    And lovely whispered pleas,
Love returns to our hearts like leaves to trees.'

In her grave gentle voice, then, she replied:
'Dear, you are strong; you trust in God your guide,
Fix your eyes on a goal, and walk straight on,
Heedless of what will come or what is gone;
To your rapt spirit, nothing can undo
The lovely vision veiling life for you.
But I must weep. Dejected, at your heel,
Hurt by all of the blows you never feel,
Lacking your hope, yet made to your design—
While you sing in your world, I mourn in mine.
All things depress me: futures I half see,
Thoughts that condemn my love so bitterly,
Jealous pangs that some other woman may
Snatch a glance from your very soul one day,
And Fate, which never fails to strike us down.
The more the sun shines, then, the more I frown.
You go, I follow; you move on, I quake;
And while, among the thousand plans you make,

Vous semblez ignorer, passant robuste et doux,
Tous les angles que fait le monde autour de nous,   30
Je me traîne après vous, pauvre femme blessée.
D'un corps resté debout l'ombre est parfois brisée. —

from *Les Contemplations*

La Fête chez Thérèse

La chose fut exquise et fort bien ordonnée.
C'était au mois d'avril, et dans une journée
Si douce, qu'on eût dit qu'amour l'eût faite exprès.
Thérèse la duchesse à qui je donnerais,
Si j'étais roi, Paris, si j'étais Dieu, le monde,   5
Quand elle ne serait que Thérèse la blonde,
Cette belle Thérèse, aux yeux de diamant,
Nous avait conviés dans son jardin charmant.

On était peu nombreux. Le choix faisait la fête.
Nous étions tous ensemble et chacun tête à tête.   10
Des couples pas à pas erraient de tous côtés.
C'étaient les fiers seigneurs et les rares beautés,
Les Amyntas rêvant auprès des Léonores,
Les marquises riant avec les monsignores;
Et l'on voyait rôder dans les grands escaliers   15
Un nain qui dérobait leur bourse aux cavaliers.

A midi, le spectacle avec la mélodie.
Pourquoi jouer Plautus la nuit? La comédie
Est une belle fille et rit mieux au grand jour.
Or on avait bâti, comme un temple d'amour,   20
Près d'un bassin dans l'ombre habité par un cygne,
Un théâtre en treillage où grimpait une vigne,
Un cintre à claire-voie en anse de panier,
Cage verte où sifflait un bouvreuil prisonnier,
Couvrait toute la scène, et sur leurs gorges blanches   25

You, strong kind traveller, never seem to know
What strife confronts us everywhere we go,
I trail behind you, female, bruised and spent.
The straightest object's shadow may be bent.'

from *Contemplations*

Thérèse's Party

It was an exquisite thing, and extremely well managed.
It was in April, and the day was so mild that
You would have sworn that Cupid* had made it on purpose.
Thérèse the duchess—to whom I should give all of Paris,*
Were I the king, and the world itself, were I the Lord God,
If she was simply Thérèse and had only her blonde hair—
Lovely Thérèse, with her diamond eyes, had in-
Vited us to her delectable garden.

Not a great number—the party was made by selection;
So there we were, all together, and everyone intimate.
Couples were roaming hither and thither on all sides.
Haughty patricians were flanked by exceptional beauties,
Amintas were pining for neighbouring Leonoras,*
Marquises giggled with Monsignors; and
On the great stairways, you could see a dwarf lurking
And filching the gentlemen's purses.

Midday: a show with some music.
Why play Plautus* at night? Comedy, being a
Pretty girl, laughs all the better by daylight.
Now, a kind of Temple of Love, a trellis
Stage with a vine entwining it, had been erected
Next to a pool in the shade which a swan was haunting.
There was a latticework arch, a verdant
Cage for a singing and captive bullfinch,
Over the set; and the actresses felt the shadows of

Les actrices sentaient errer l'ombre des branches.
On entendait au loin de magiques accords;
Et, tout en haut, sortant de la frise à mi-corps,
Pour attirer la foule aux lazzis qu'il répète,
Le blanc Pulcinella sonnait de la trompette.   30
Deux faunes soutenaient le manteau d'Arlequin;
Trivelin leur riait au nez comme un faquin.
Parmi les ornements sculptés dans le treillage,
Colombine dormait dans un gros coquillage,
Et, quand elle montrait son sein et ses bras nus,   35
On eût cru voir la conque, et l'on eût dit Vénus.

Le seigneur Pantalon, dans une niche, à droite,
Vendait des limons doux sur une table étroite,
Et criait par instants:—Seigneurs, l'homme est divin.
Dieu n'avait fait que l'eau, mais l'homme a fait le vin.—   40
Scaramouche en un coin harcelait de sa batte
Le tragique Alcantor, suivi du triste Arbate;
Crispin, vêtu de noir, jouait de l'éventail;
Perché, jambe pendante, au sommet du portail,
Carlino se penchait, écoutant les aubades,   45
Et son pied ébauchait de rêveuses gambades.

Le soleil tenait lieu de lustre; la saison
Avait brodé de fleurs un immense gazon,
Vert tapis déroulé sous maint groupe folâtre.
Rangés des deux côtés de l'agreste théâtre,   50
Les vrais arbres du parc, les sorbiers, les lilas,
Les ébéniers qu'avril charge de falbalas,
De leur séve embaumée exhalant les délices,
Semblaient se divertir à faire les coulisses,
Et, pour nous voir, ouvrant leurs fleurs comme des yeux,   55
Joignaient aux violons leur murmure joyeux;
Si bien qu'à ce concert gracieux et classique,
La nature mêlait un peu de sa musique.

Tout nous charmait, les bois, le jour serein, l'air pur,
Les femmes tout amour et le ciel tout azur.   60

Branches brushing their fair white bosoms.
Far in the distance you could hear magical harmonies;
While at the top, jutting waist-deep out of the frieze, was a
Pale Punchinello blowing a trumpet, at-
Tracting the crowds to the jibes he repeated.
Fauns on each side propped up the proscenium;
Trivelin laughed in their face like a scoundrel.
Columbine slept in a huge ornamental
Cockleshell carved in the trellis;
Had she been baring her breasts and her arms, you
Would have thought there was the scallop, and there was Venus.*

In a niche, off to the right, Signor Pantaloon was
Selling sweet citrons on a small table,
Now and then shouting: 'Gentlemen, Man is divine!
God has only made water, but Man has made wine!'
And in a corner, Scaramouche plagued with his slapstick
Tragic Alcantor, with tearful Arbates* behind him.
Black-costumed Crispino toyed with a fan; Carlino—
Poised, legs dangling, over the top of the portico—
Leant and listened to serenades, with his
Feet tracing fanciful capers.

The sun stood in for a chandelier; the time of year had be-
Dizened the whole lawn with blossoms;
Many a frolicsome group sat on its carpet of greenery.
Ranged on both sides of the rustic theatre,
Rowans and lilacs, the real trees of the pleasure-ground,
Ebonies burdened by April with frills and flounces,
Shed the delights of their fragrant sap,
Seemed to enjoy creating a glimpse of life backstage,
Opened their flowers to watch us like eyes, and
Mingled their pleasant rustle among the violins;
So to these elegant classical harmonies
Nature was adding a touch of *her* music.

Everything pleased us, the woods, the clear air, the fine weather,
The girls all romance, and the heavens all radiance.

Pour la pièce, elle était fort bonne, quoique ancienne.
C'était, nonchalamment assis sur l'avant-scène,
Pierrot qui haranguait dans un grave entretien
Un singe timbalier à cheval sur un chien.

Rien de plus. C'était simple et beau.—Par intervalles   65
Le singe faisait rage et cognait ses timbales;
Puis Pierrot répliquait.—Écoutait qui voulait.
L'un faisait apporter des glaces au valet;
L'autre, galant drapé d'une cape fantasque,
Parlait bas à sa dame en lui nouant son masque;   70
Trois marquis attablés chantaient une chanson.
Thérèse était assise à l'ombre d'un buisson,
Les roses pâlissaient à côté de sa joue,
Et, la voyant si belle, un paon faisait la roue.

Moi, j'écoutais pensif un profane couplet   75
Que fredonnait dans l'ombre un abbé violet.

La nuit vint; tout se tut; les flambeaux s'éteignirent;
Dans les bois assombris les sources se plaignirent;
Le rossignol, caché dans son nid ténébreux,
Chanta comme un poëte et comme un amoureux.   80
Chacun se dispersa sous les profonds feuillages;
Les folles en riant entraînèrent les sages;
L'amante s'en alla dans l'ombre avec l'amant;
Et, troublés comme on l'est en songe, vaguement,
Ils sentaient par degrés se mêler à leur âme,   85
A leurs discours secrets, à leurs regards de flamme,
A leur cœur, à leurs sens, à leur molle raison,
Le clair de lune bleu qui baignait l'horizon.

Quia pulvis es

Ceux-ci partent, ceux-là demeurent.
Sous le sombre aquilon, dont les mille voix pleurent,
Poussière et genre humain, tout s'envole à la fois.

As for the play, it was pretty good, although old-fashioned.
It was about Pierrot, who sat informally
Down at the footlights, and solemnly lectured a
Simian drummer who rode on a puppy.

Nothing else happened. It was artistic and simple.
Sometimes the monkey rapped at his drums in a temper;
Then Pierrot answered him back.—You could listen if
   you wanted.
Someone was sending a valet away for some ices;
Somebody else, a gallant all festooned in a fantastic cape, was
Whispering to his fair lady and tying her mask on;
Three marquis in a party were singing a chorus.
Thérèse was sitting under a bush, in its shadow.
Next to her cheeks, the roses went pale; and a
Peacock, seeing how pretty she was, spread its feathers.

I was just pondering, listening to an irreverent ditty
Lilted away in the shade by a violet abbé.

Night came, everything quietened; out went the torches;
In the now-darkening woods, the fountains were sobbing;
A nightingale, hidden within his shadowy nest,
Sang like a poet or lover.
Everyone straggled away into the depths of the foliage;
Lady friend vanished into the night with her gentleman;
Giggling featherbrains went by with sages in tow. And,
Dimly perturbed as you are in a dream, they could
Slowly feel, merging into their souls and their secret
Chatter and passionate glances,
Into their hearts and their senses and rudderless
Minds, the blue moonlight that bathed the horizon.

For Dust Thou Art

Some are passing on, others are remaining.
Before the myriad-voiced ever-complaining
Dark wind, all of us, dust or human, flee.

Hélas! le même vent souffle, en l'ombre où nous sommes,
    Sur toutes les têtes des hommes,   5
    Sur toutes les feuilles des bois.

    Ceux qui restent à ceux qui passent
Disent:—Infortunés! déjà vos fronts s'effacent.
Quoi! vous n'entendez plus la parole et le bruit!
Quoi! vous ne verrez plus ni le ciel ni les arbres!   10
    Vous allez dormir sous les marbres!
    Vous allez tomber dans la nuit!—

    Ceux qui passent à ceux qui restent
Disent:—Vous n'avez rien à vous! vos pleurs l'attestent.
Pour vous, gloire et bonheur sont des mots décevants.   15
Dieu donne aux morts les biens réels, les vrais royaumes.
    Vivants! vous êtes des fantômes.
    C'est nous qui sommes les vivants!

Écrit sur la plinthe d'un bas-relief antique

La musique est dans tout. Un hymne sort du monde.
Rumeur de la galère aux flancs lavés par l'onde,
Bruits de villes, pitié de la sœur pour la sœur,
Passion des amants jeunes et beaux, douceur
Des vieux époux usés ensemble par la vie,   5
Fanfare de la plaine émaillée et ravie,
Mots échangés le soir sur les seuils fraternels,
Sombre tressaillement des chênes éternels,
Vous êtes l'harmonie et la musique même!
Vous êtes les soupirs qui font le chant suprême!   10

Pour notre âme, les jours, la vie et les saisons,
Les songes de nos cœurs, les plis des horizons,
L'aube et ses pleurs, le soir et ses grands incendies,
Flottent dans un réseau de vagues mélodies.
Une voix dans les champs nous parle, une autre voix   15
Dit à l'homme autre chose et chante dans les bois.
Par moment, un troupeau bêle, une cloche tinte.

The same gale, in our gloom, has buffeted
    The hairs on every head,
    The leaves on every tree.

Those who remain tell those who have passed on:
'Soon, luckless souls, your memory will be gone.
From now on, you will hear no sound at all;
You will no longer see the trees and sky;
    Into the darkness you will fall;
    Beneath the gravestones you will lie!'

Those who have passed on tell those who remain:
'Your tears show there is nothing you retain!
Your bliss and glory are deceptive boasts;
The dead, by God's will, truly reign and thrive;
    You living souls are merely ghosts;
    We are the ones who are alive!'

Written on the Plinth of an Ancient Bas-Relief

From the world a hymn rises: there is music in all things.
    The sound of the galley's side splashed by the waves;
The city's din; sister consoling sister;
    The tenderness of an old married pair,
Both lifeworn now; the passion of young lovers;
    The fanfares of the dazzling dazzled fields;
The words that pass at dusk between fraternal households;
    The sombre trembling of the timeless oaks—
Yes, they are harmony—are indeed music—
    Are the sighs that compose the crowning song!

To us, days, life, the seasons, our hearts' reveries,
    The pleats on the horizon, evening with
Its far-flung bonfires, daybreak with its weepings,
    Drift in a web of half-heard melody.
One voice, in the fields, talks to us; another
    Says something else—it sings within the woods.
Now and then a flock bleats, or else a bell tolls.

Quand par l'ombre, la nuit, la colline est atteinte,
De toutes parts on voit danser et resplendir,
Dans le ciel étoilé du zénith au nadir,   20
Dans la voix des oiseaux, dans le cri des cigales,
Le groupe éblouissant des notes inégales.
Toujours avec notre âme un doux bruit s'accoupla;
La nature nous dit: Chante! Et c'est pour cela
Qu'un statuaire ancien sculpta sur cette pierre   25
Un pâtre sur sa flûte abaissant sa paupière.

«L'enfant, voyant l'aïeule à filer occupée . . .»

L'enfant, voyant l'aïeule à filer occupée,
Veut faire une quenouille à sa grande poupée.
L'aïeule s'assoupit un peu; c'est le moment.
L'enfant vient par derrière, et tire doucement
Un brin de la quenouille où le fuseau tournoie,   5
Puis s'enfuit triomphante, emportant avec joie
La belle laine d'or que le safran jaunit,
Autant qu'en pourrait prendre un oiseau pour son nid.

from *Dernière Gerbe*

«La vie, ô gentilhomme, est une comédie . . .»

La vie, ô gentilhomme, est une comédie
Étrange, folle, gaie, effroyable, hardie,
Taillée au vieux patron des pièces du vieux temps,
Avec des spadassins, avec des capitans.
La morale en est sombre et cependant fort saine.   5
Tout s'y tient. La vertu, dès la première scène,
Tombe dans une trappe, et la richesse en sort;
Chacun pousse son cri pour se plaindre du sort,
Le savant brait, le roi rugit, le manant beugle;
Le mariage est borgne et l'amour est aveugle,   10

At nightfall, when the hills are gripped by gloom,
A brilliant syncopated composition
    Can be seen dancing, gleaming, everywhere,
Throughout the star-strewn sky—from zenith down to nadir—
    Throughout the bird-calls and the cricket-cries.
Music has always mated with man's spirit;
    Nature urges us 'Sing!' And that is why
An ancient sculptor carved on this stone block a shepherd
    Intent, with his eyes lowered, on his flute.

'The child saw Grandma busy spinning . . .'

The child saw Grandma busy spinning, and
Thought her big doll should have a distaff too.
Grandma dozed off—the moment was at hand.
The child crept up behind, and softly drew
A wisp away, right where the spindle rolled;
Then she fled, clutching with triumphant zest
The pretty fleece that saffron coloured gold—
Just as much as a bird might gather for its nest.

from *Last Gleanings*

'Life, dear sir, is a comedy . . .'

Life, dear sir, is a comedy—wild, daring,
Witty, extravagant, and overbearing,
Done in the style of old-time melodrama,
With thugs in capes and officers in armour.
The moral is severe, but strong and clean.
It's all coherent. In the opening scene
Virtue falls down the trap, and Wealth comes out.
Scholars bleat, peasants moo, and monarchs shout;
Everyone wails and thinks his fate unkind.
Matrimony is one-eyed, Love is blind,

La justice est boiteuse et l'honneur est manchot;
L'enfer, dont on voit luire en un coin le réchaud
Qui jette au front du riche un reflet écarlate,
De toutes les vertus a fait des culs-de-jatte;
Le bravo quête un duel, l'amoureux un duo;   15
L'eunuque—c'est l'envie—enrage, crie: «Ah! oh!»
Et jette à tout sultan des regards effroyables;
Toutes les passions, qui sont autant de diables,
Ont leur rôle, tantôt dolent, tantôt pompeux.
C'est beau! Figure-toi la pièce, si tu peux;   20
Elle a le cœur humain pour scène, et pour parterre
Elle a le genre humain.

                          A la fin du mystère,
Le rideau tombe. On siffle.—Absurde! tout est mal!
On demande l'auteur et l'acteur principal.
Le riche veut ravoir son argent. Cris, tapage.   25
—L'auteur! l'auteur! nommez l'auteur! à bas l'ouvrage!...
Alors, apparaissant devant la rampe en feu,
Satan fait trois saluts, et dit: «L'auteur, c'est Dieu.»

from *Les Quatre Vents de l'esprit*

Près d'Avranches

La nuit morne tombait sur la morne étendue.

Le vent du soir soufflait, et, d'une aile éperdue,
Faisait fuir, à travers les écueils de granit,
Quelques voiles au port, quelques oiseaux au nid.

Triste jusqu'à la mort je contemplais ce monde.   5
Oh! que la mer est vaste et que l'âme est profonde!
Saint-Michel surgissait, seul sur les flots amers,
Chéops de l'occident, pyramide des mers.

Honour has lost its right arm, Justice limps.
In one corner Hell's gas stove gives a glimpse
Of the rich fellow lit with scarlet ripples.
It turns all of the virtues into cripples.
Bullies seek duels, lovers seek duets;
The eunuch (who is Envy) howls and frets
And gives every last sultan nasty looks.
All of the passions—all of them are crooks—
Play their parts, whining or Olympian.*
It's great! Imagine the play if you can:
Onstage the human heart, and in the pit
The human race.

              Then, at the end of it,
The curtain falls. Boos. 'Lousy, every bit!'
Calls for the author and the leading man.
The rich chap wants his money back. Howls, jeers.
'Down with the work! Who wrote it? Name the clod!'...
At the footlights, in fire, Satan appears.
He bows three times and says: 'The author's God.'

from *The Four Winds of the Spirit*

Near Avranches

Across the grim expanse the grim night fell.

The dusk wind stirred, and started to dispel
Desperately, past granite crags and crests,
Sailing ships to their ports, birds to their nests.

I, deadly sad, watched everything around.
Seas are so vast, and souls are so profound!
Through the waves rose Saint-Michel,* solitary
Western Cheops*—a pyramid at sea.

Je songeais à l'Égypte aux plis infranchissables,
A la grande isolée éternelle des sables,   10
Noire tente des rois, ce tas d'ombres qui dort
Dans le camp immobile et sombre de la mort.

Hélas! dans ces déserts qu'emplit d'un souffle immense
Dieu, seul dans sa colère et seul dans sa clémence,
Ce que l'homme a dressé debout sur l'horizon,   15
Là-bas, c'est le sépulcre, ici, c'est la prison.

I thought how, ever shrouded, Egypt stands
Alone eternally among the sands,
A black tent for the kings, those shades abed
In the immobile dark camp of the dead.

Among these wastes where the Lord's breath, alone
In anger and in clemency, has blown,
What has man raised above the earth's frontier?
A sepulchre there, and a prison here!

from *Things Seen*

Talleyrand

In the Rue Saint-Florentin there's a palace and a sewer. The palace is in an opulent, impressive, lugubrious style of architecture. For a long time it was called 'Hôtel de l'Infantado'; today, on the façade above the main doorway, you see the words 'Hôtel Talleyrand'. During the forty years that he lived here, the last resident in this palace may never have given the sewer a single glance. He was a curious, imposing, important character; his name was Charles-Maurice de Périgord; he was an aristocrat like Machiavelli, a priest like Gondi; he was unfrocked like Fouché, witty like Voltaire,* and lame like the devil. You might say that everything in him was equally lame— his aristocratic origin, which he had placed at the service of the Republic; his priestliness, which he had dragged over the parade ground and dumped in the gutter; his marriage, which he had shattered with dozens of scandals and a voluntary separation; his intellect, which he had debased and dishonoured. Yet this man did have a kind of greatness.

He united the splendours of the two successive regimes: he was a prince of the old kingdom of France and a prince of the French Empire. For thirty years, he had virtually controlled Europe from the depths of his palace and the depths of his mind. He had allowed the French Revolution to slap him on the back, and he had smiled— ironically, to be sure, but the Revolution hadn't noticed that. He had met and known and studied and fathomed and influenced and transformed and probed and mocked and inspired all the men of his time, all the ideas of his day. There had been moments in his life when he had held in his hand the four or five crucial threads that moved the civilized world, and when Napoleon I, Emperor of the French, King of Italy, Protector of the Confederation of the Rhine, Mediator of the Swiss Confederacy, had been his puppet. That was the game he had played. After the July Revolution,* after the fall of the old race whose high chamberlain he was, he found himself still on his feet. He told the 1830 folk sitting bare-armed on a heap of old paving stones, 'Make me your ambassador!'

He had heard Mirabeau's last confession and Thiers's* first state secret. He used to say that he was a great poet, that he had composed a trilogy in three acts: Act I, *The Empire of Bonaparte*; Act II, *The House of Bourbon*; Act III, *The House of Orléans*. He had done all that in his palace; in the said palace, like a spider in its web, he had lured and caught heroes, thinkers, geniuses, conquerors, kings, princes, emperors, Bonaparte, Sieyès, Madame de Staël, Chateaubriand, Benjamin Constant, Alexander of Russia, Wilhelm of Prussia, Francis of Austria, Louis XVIII, Louis-Philippe,* all the glittering gleaming flies that have been buzzing through the history of these last forty years, one after another. The whole sparkling swarm of insects had been fascinated by this man's penetrating eye, and had passed in succession through this sombre doorway with the words HÔTEL TALLEYRAND inscribed on its architrave.

Well, the day before yesterday—the man died.

Doctors came and embalmed the body. To do so, they removed the bowels from the abdomen and the brain from the skull, Egyptian style. After the job was done and the Prince de Talleyrand had been turned into a mummy and the mummy had been nailed inside a coffin lined with white satin, they went away. The brain—the brain that had thought so many things, inspired so many men, erected so many schemes, led two revolutions, deceived twenty kings, encompassed the whole world—they left on a table. When the doctors had gone, a servant came in. He saw what they had left. Hello! They've forgotten this. What's to be done with it? He remembered that there was a sewer in the street; he went out and dropped the brain into the sewer.

That was how it all ended.

from *Alps and Pyrenees*

Bayonne

26 July [1843]

I wasn't able to enter Bayonne unemotionally. Bayonne is one of my childhood memories. I came to Bayonne when I was very young,

seven or eight years old, around 1811 or 1812, in the days of the
great wars. My father was doing his job as one of the Emperor's
soldiers in Spain; he was holding in check two provinces that had
been incited to rebel by El Empecinado:* Avila, Guadalajara, and the
whole Tagus valley. On her way to join him, my mother stopped at
Bayonne to wait for an escort—because if you wanted to travel from
Bayonne to Madrid in those days, you had to be accompanied by
three thousand men and preceded by four cannon. Some day I'll
write up that trip; it has its points of interest, if only as historical
documentation. My mother had brought along my two brothers
Abel and Eugène and myself—I was the youngest of the three. As I
recall, the day after our arrival at Bayonne some kind of tubby signor
overadorned with ornaments and jabbering Italian presented himself
at my mother's. We children watched him enter through a glass
door; to us he seemed like a street mountebank. He was the director
of the Bayonne theatre. He had come to ask my mother to take a box
at his theatre. My mother hired a box for a month. (That was about
how long we were due to stay in Bayonne.) The hiring of this box
made us leap for joy. We children had previously entered the theatre
only once a year; our only dramatic memory was Molière's *Comtesse
d'Escarbagnas*; and now we were to go to a play every night for a
whole month! That very evening we kept pestering our mother—
who yielded to us, as mothers always do, and took us to the theatre.
The ticket collector installed us in a magnificent box draped with
hangings of red calico adorned with saffron rosettes. They were
playing *The Ruins of Babylon*,* a famous melodrama that was
immensely popular all over France in those days. It was glorious, at
least in Bayonne. Apricot knights and Arabs arrayed from head to
foot in chain mail kept rushing onstage all the time and annihilating
each other to the accompaniment of horrendous prose, amid pasteboard ruins full of caltrops and wolf traps. Caliph Harun and Giafar
the eunuch were there. We were in ecstasy. Next evening we pestered
our mother again, and again she yielded. There we were at the
playhouse, in our rosetted box—What were they going to play? We
were on tenterhooks. The curtain went up. Enter Giafar. They were
playing *The Ruins of Babylon*. That didn't bother us in the least. We
were glad to see that fine work again, and once again it entertained
us very much. The next day my mother was wonderful, as always,
and we went back to the theatre. They were playing *The Ruins of*

Babylon. We watched the play again with pleasure, though we would have preferred some other ruins. Surely on the fourth day the play would have to be changed; we went there—my mother let us have our own way, and accompanied us with a smile. They were playing *The Ruins of Babylon*. That time we fell asleep. On the fifth day we sent Bertrand, my mother's footman, to see the poster. They were playing *The Ruins of Babylon*. We begged our mother not to take us. On the sixth day they were playing *The Ruins of Babylon* again. This went on for the whole month. One fine day the poster changed. That day we left town.

That memory is what made me speak somewhere of 'Chance, the tease who sports with children'.

Anyhow, but for *The Ruins of Babylon*, my recollections of that month at Bayonne are pleasant ones. By the water's edge, beneath the trees, there was a lovely promenade where we used to stroll every evening. On the way we'd thumb our noses at the theatre, which roused in us a kind of boredom mingled with dread, and where we'd never again set foot. We used to sit on a bench and watch the ships and listen to our mother—that noble and pious woman who is now merely an image in my memory, but who will continue to shine within my soul and upon my life until the day I die.

The house where we were staying was delightful. I can remember my bedroom window with its lovely hanging clusters of ripe maize. Throughout the whole long month we never had a moment's bore-dom—*The Ruins of Babylon* always excepted. One day we went to see a ship of the line anchored at the mouth of the Adour. An English squadron had been pursuing it; after a battle lasting several hours it had taken refuge here, and the English were holding it blockaded. I can still see that splendid vessel, as clearly as if it were before my eyes at this very moment. She lay a quarter of a league offshore, lit by a brilliant shaft of sunlight, resting proudly on the waves with all her sails taken in. To me there seemed something indescribably ominous about her, because she had just come from the firing line and might perhaps be on the point of going back into it.

Our house abutted onto the fortifications. There, on the slopes of green turf, among guns turned with their touch-holes to the grass and mortars upside down with their mouths against the ground, we used to go and play from dawn onwards. In the evenings, the three of us—Abel, poor Eugène, and myself—used to gather around our mother and besmear the saucers of a watercolour paint box in our efforts to surpass each other in illuminating the engravings of an old copy of the Arabian *Nights* as barbarously as possible. That copy had been given to me by General Lahorie,* my godfather, who perished on the Grenelle plain a few months later.

Eugène and I used to buy from the town's little boys all the goldfinches and greenfinches that they could bring us. We used to put these poor birds in wicker cages. When one cage was full, we'd buy another for them. In this way we filled five cages. When we had to leave, we set all those pretty birds free. That was both joyous and heartrending for us.

My mother was renting the house from one of the townspeople— a widow, I think. The widow herself lived in a pavilion near our house. She had a daughter fourteen or fifteen years old. Thirty years later my memory has lost no detail of that girl's angelic form. I can see her now. She was slim and blonde, and seemed very tall to me. She had a sweet, faraway look, the Virgilian features that you imagine in Amaryllis or Galatea* fleeing toward the willows. Her neck was exquisitely poised and beautifully pure; her hands were small, her arms fair and her elbows slightly reddened (due to her age—a circumstance which I, at *my* age, still didn't know). She usually wore a tea-coloured madras kerchief with a green border, tightly drawn down from the crown of her head to the nape of her neck, so that her brow was exposed and only half her hair was covered. I don't remember what dress she used to wear.

That pretty child used to come and play with us. Sometimes Abel and Eugène, my elders (who were bigger and more serious than I, and 'acted the man', as my mother used to say), would go off to watch the firing practice on the ramparts, or else would go upstairs to study Sobrino and look through Cormon.* Then I would be alone, I'd feel boredom coming on, what was I going to do? Then she'd call me and say, 'Come here and I'll read you something.' In the court-yard a few steps led up to a door with a big rusty bolt that I can still see, a round bolt with a handle like a pig's tail, the kind that you sometimes find in old cellars. She used to go and sit on those steps. I'd stand behind her and lean back against the door. She'd read to me from some book—I forget what—open on her lap. Overhead we'd have a brilliant sky and a glorious sun that pierced the lime trees with light and transformed the green leaves into gold leaves. A warm breeze came through the chinks in the old door and caressed our faces. She'd bend over her book and read aloud. While she was reading, I wouldn't listen to the sense of her words, I'd listen to the sound of her voice. Sometimes I'd lower my eyes; my glance would light on her half-open shawl, and, with a sense of confusion mingled with strange fascination, I'd see her fair round bosom gently rising and falling in the dark, dimly gilded by a shaft of warm sunshine. Now and then, at those times, she'd suddenly raise her big blue eyes and say, 'Well, Victor, aren't you listening?'

I'd be utterly disconcerted, I'd blush and tremble and pretend to toy with the big bolt.

I never made any move to kiss her. She was the one who would call me and say, 'Come and give me a kiss.' On the day when we left, I had two great sorrows: parting with her and setting my birds free.

Well, my friend, what did this mean? What did I, little as I was, feel in the presence of that big beautiful innocent girl? In those days I didn't know. I've often thought of it since. I've continued to recall Bayonne as a bright-hued happy place. It's the home of my very first romantic memory. A time of innocence—already sweetly troubled, though! It's the place where, in the darkest recesses of my soul, I saw the first rays of indescribable light breaking, the sacred dawn of love.

Wouldn't you say, my friend, that such a memory is a bond—a bond that can never be broken?

Strange that two creatures can be linked for life by this bond, and yet never feel any need for each other, never seek each other out, remain strangers to each other, without even knowing each other! The bond that binds me to that dear child has never been broken, yet its strands have been cut. Almost as soon as I arrived in Bayonne I went around the town's ramparts, hunting for the house, the door, the bolt—I found nothing, or at least recognized nothing. Where is she? What is she doing? Is she dead? Is she still alive? If she is still alive, no doubt she is married, she has children. She may be widowed and growing old in her turn. How can beauty depart and yet the woman remain? Is the woman of today really the same creature as the young girl of yesteryear? Maybe I have just met her? Maybe she is the commonplace woman from whom I asked the way just a moment ago, and who watched me vanish like a stranger? There's such bitter sadness in all this. So then, we're merely shadows. We pass each other by, and we disappear like puffs of smoke in the deep blue sky of eternity. People are in space what hours are in time. When they have struck, they vanish. Where does our youth go? Where, alas, does our childhood go? Where is the pretty girl of 1812? Where is the child I was then? We made contact in those days, and now maybe we are still in contact—and there is a chasm between us. Memory, that bridge of the past, has broken down between the two of us. She wouldn't know my face, and I wouldn't recognize the sound of her voice. She no longer knows my name, and I don't know hers.

BEFORE THE EXILE II: 1843–1851

from *Things Seen*

King Louis-Philippe

August 1844

Last month the king went to Dreux. It was the anniversary of the death of the Duc d'Orléans.* The king had chosen that day to rearrange the coffins of his relatives in the family vault.

Among them was a coffin containing all the bones of princes of the House of Orléans which the Duchesse d'Orléans, the king's mother, had been able to collect after the French Revolution, when they had been violated and scattered. The coffin was in a separate vault, and had recently been smashed by the fall of an arch. Debris from the arch—stones and plaster—was mingled with the bones.

The king had the coffin brought to him and opened. He was alone in the vault apart from the chaplain and two aides-de-camp. Another coffin had been made—one that was larger and less fragile. The king himself took the bones of his ancestors out of the damaged coffin one by one, with his own hands, and laid them carefully in the new coffin. He wouldn't allow anyone else to touch them. At intervals he counted the skulls and said: 'This is the Duc de Penthièvre. This is the Comte de Beaujolais.'* Then, to the best of his ability, he did as much as he could to complete each group of bones.

This ceremony lasted from nine a.m. to seven p.m., without the king taking any rest or any nourishment.

Villemain

Dictated by me*
3 December 1845

In the early days of December 1845, I remember I went to see Villemain; it was the third, I think. I hadn't seen him since 3 July—exactly five months earlier. During the last days of December 1844 Villemain had been stricken with the cruel malady that put an end to his political career.

It was cold, the weather was dismal, I was gloomy myself; just the time to go and comfort someone. So I called on Villemain. He was then living in the rooms provided for the life secretary of the Académie française, on the second floor of the staircase on the right, at the rear of the Institute's* second courtyard. I ascended the staircase; I rang the bell at the door on the right, nobody came; I rang the doorbell a second time; the door opened. There was Villemain himself.

He was pale, untidy, clad in a long black frock-coat buttoned at the top with one solitary button, his grey hair dishevelled. He eyed me gloomily and said without smiling, 'Oh, it's you; hello.'

Then he added, 'I'm all alone, I don't know where my servants are, come in.' He led me through a long corridor into a room, and from there into his bedroom. The whole place is dismal, and feels a bit like an attic in a convent. The bedroom was lit by two windows facing the courtyard; its only furnishings were a mahogany bed with no curtains or counterpane, a sheet of white paper carelessly dropped on the bed, a few horsehair chairs, a chest of drawers between the two windows, and a desk covered with papers, books, newspapers, and opened letters. Virtually all the letters were on letterhead paper with such titles as 'House of Peers', 'Institute of France', 'Council of State', 'Journal of Scholarship', etc. On the mantelpiece, the current *Moniteur*,* a few letters, and a few books, including Monsieur de Lacretelle's *History of the Consulate and the Empire*,* which had just appeared.

Beside the bed was a child's cot with mahogany rails and a green counterpane. On the wall opposite the bed, three framed pictures: a lithograph of Villemain and oil paintings of his two oldest girls, reasonably good likenesses. On the mantelpiece an out-of-order clock showing the wrong time; in the fireplace a fire that had just about gone out.

Villemain sat me down and took hold of my hands. He looked rather distraught, but kind and serious. He asked me what I'd been doing this summer, told me he'd been on a journey, mentioned (in some cases affectionately, in others mistrustfully) a few friends that we have in common. Then he seemed to settle down, and for a quarter of an hour he talked about literary things in a most intelligent way—lucid, simple, elegant, thoughtful, though still sad and never smiling at all.

Suddenly he looked me straight in the eye and said:

'There's something painful in my mind. I'm in trouble. I'm worried about some upsetting things. If you only realized what conspiracies are going on against me!'

'Villemain,' I said, 'please don't fret.'

'No,' he rejoined, 'it's really dreadful.' After a pause he added, as if to himself: 'They started by separating me from my wife, I loved her, I still love her, she had something in her mind; that could have made her imagine fantastic things. But what's much more certain is that they've succeeded in making her hate me. And then they separated me from her, and after that, they separated me from my children. The poor little girls, they're lovely creatures, you've seen them, they're my pride and joy. Well, I daren't go and see them, and when I do see them, I just make sure that they're getting along all right and they're bright and happy and healthy, and I'm afraid to give them even a kiss on the forehead. Good Lord, if I touched them, that might be the cause of some harm coming to them. How do I know what schemes these people might be plotting? So they've separated me from my wife; they've separated me from my children, now I'm all alone!'

After a pause he went on:

'No, I'm not alone! I'm not even alone! I've got enemies. They're everywhere—here, outside, around me, even in my home. You see, my friend, I made a mistake. I shouldn't have gone into politics. To succeed there, to be strong and steadfast, I would have needed two kinds of support: internal support from happiness, and external support from—someone.' (Presumably he meant the king.) 'I missed out on those kinds of support. Both of them. I plunged so recklessly into a world of hate. I was naked and unarmed; they pounced on me. Now I'm done with everything.'

Then suddenly looking at me with a sort of anguish:

'My friend, whatever people say to you, whatever they tell you, whatever allegations they make about me, please, my friend, please promise me that you won't believe any of the slanders. It's just that they're so wicked. Yet my life is very gloomy, but it's absolutely blameless. If you only knew the things they make up, you can't imagine. Oh, they're such horrible things! It's enough to drive a man out of his senses. If I didn't have my little girls I'd kill myself. You know what they say? Oh, I won't even repeat it!' A bit later he said to me: 'They say freemasons climb through that window at night and sleep with me.'

I burst out laughing. 'And you're upset by that? Why, it's just stupid; it's ridiculous!'

'Oh,' he said, 'this is on the second floor, but they're so underhand, they put big ladders against the wall at night to make people believe it. And when I think how these things, these filthy things, they're whispered in a corner and they're believed all over the place, and nobody stands up for me! People just put on a mask, either a mask of coldness or a mask of falseness. Victor Hugo, promise me that you won't believe any of the slanders.' He stood up, I was deeply touched, I said all the kind and friendly things I could to calm him. He went on:

'Oh, all this atrocious hate! See, this is how it started. Whenever I left home, they'd arrange things so that everything I saw looked ominous, I met only men buttoned up to the chin, people dressed in red, bizarre costumes, women dressed half in black half in violet who kept looking at me and shouting for joy, and hearses of little children everywhere with other children following them, some in black and some in white. You'll tell me, "But those things are only premonitions, sensible people don't worry about premonitions." Lord in heaven, I know that well enough; it isn't the premonitions that are frightening me, it's the thought that they hate me so much that they went to all this trouble to get together so many depressing sights all around me. If a man hates me enough to surround me with flying crows all the time, it isn't the crows that worry me, it's the hatred.'

Here I interrupted him again. 'You've got enemies,' I told him, 'but remember, you've got friends too.' Quickly he pulled his hands away from mine.

'Look here,' he said, 'listen carefully to what I'm going to tell you, Victor Hugo, and you'll see what's on my mind. You'll know how much I'm suffering and how far my enemies have managed to shake all my confidence and rob me of all hope. I no longer have any idea where I've got to, or what anyone wants from me. Look here, you, for instance, you're as noble a man as anyone, you come from rebels' blood, military blood, I'll go further, I'll say warriors' blood. Every fibre of you is true and honest. You don't need anything or anyone. I've known you for twenty-eight years and I've never seen you do anything that wasn't fine and honourable. Well now, this will show you what a wretched state I'm in. In my heart of hearts I'm not sure that you haven't been sent here by my enemies to spy on me.'

He was in such distress that I couldn't but feel sorry for him. I took his hand again. He gave me a haggard glance.

'Villemain,' I said, 'doubt that the sky is blue, but don't doubt that the man talking to you now is a true friend of yours.'

'Forgive me,' he replied, 'please forgive me, oh, I know that perfectly well, I know I've been talking nonsense, you've never let me down, though you must have had cause to complain about me sometimes. But I've got so many enemies! If you only knew! This building is full of them. They're everywhere, hidden, invisible, they plague me, I can feel their ears listening to me, I can feel their eyes looking at me. It's a dreadful thing to live like this!'

At this very moment, by one of the strange coincidences that happen from time to time as if on purpose, a little door hidden in the wainscotting near the fireplace suddenly blew open. Hearing the noise, he swung round. 'What's that?' He went to the door, it opened onto a little corridor. He looked down the corridor.

'Is there anyone there?' he asked.

There was no answer.

'It's the wind', I told him.

He came back to me, put his finger on his lips, eyed me steadily, and whispered in an indescribable tone of terror,

'Oh, no!'

Then he remained motionless and silent for a few moments, with his finger on his lips, like someone listening; his eyes were half turned toward the door (he had left it open). I felt it was time to have a proper talk with him. I sat him down again, I took his hand. 'Listen to me, Villemain,' I said, 'you have your enemies, many enemies, I admit—'

He interrupted me. His face lit up with a gleam of melancholy joy.

'Ah,' he said, 'you at least admit it, you do! All these silly fools keep telling me that I haven't any enemies and I'm just imagining.'

'Yes indeed,' I went on, 'you do have your enemies, but who hasn't? Guizot has enemies, Thiers has enemies, Lamartine* has enemies. Look at me—haven't I been fighting for twenty years? Haven't I been hated, torn in pieces, double-crossed, betrayed, hooted at, booed, mocked, insulted, slandered, for the last twenty years? Haven't my books been parodied and my actions travestied? I too am plagued and spied on, I too have traps set for me, I've even been caught in them; who knows whether I wasn't followed this very day when I went from my home to yours? But why should I care about any of that? I just treat it with disdain. One of the hardest and most important things in life is learning to treat things with disdain. Disdain can protect, it can crush; it's a breastplate and a club. You've got enemies? Why, that's the story of every man who has done a great deed or come up with a new idea. It's the thundercloud around everything that shines. Fame will attract enemies just as light will attract insects. Don't fret about it. Treat it with disdain. Keep your mind calm, just as you keep your life clean. Don't give your enemies the satisfaction of thinking that they're hurting you and upsetting you. Be happy and cheerful and disdainful and strong.'

He shook his head sadly. 'That's easy for you to say, Victor Hugo! But I'm a weak creature. Oh, I know myself through and through. I know my own limitations. I can write with a bit of talent, but I know just how far it extends; I can think with a bit of clarity, but I know just how far *that* extends. I get tired easily. I'm short-winded. I'm fragile, hesitant, wavering. I haven't achieved everything that I could have achieved. In the realms of thought I don't have the necessary creativity. In the realm of action I don't have the necessary fighting power. Strength—that's the thing I'm lacking! And disdain is a form of strength.'

He remained lost in thought for a moment; then he added, with a smile this time, 'All the same, you've done me some good, you've calmed me down, I don't feel so bad. Peace of mind is contagious. Oh, if I could only manage to handle my enemies the way you handle yours!'

At this point the door opened, two people came in, a Monsieur Fortroul I think and a nephew of Villemain's. I stood up.

'You're going away already?' he asked me.

He led me along the corridor to the staircase.

There he said to me:

'I trust you, my friend.'

'Well then,' I said, 'I told you to treat your enemies with disdain. Do it. But you've got two enemies that need to be dealt with and eliminated. They're isolation and brooding. Isolation causes unhappiness, and brooding causes worry. Don't stay on your own, and don't brood about things. Get out, go out, get moving, get some of the outside air into your thoughts, take a few good strong breaths, visit your friends, come around and see me.'

'Yes, but would you be willing to see me?' he asked.

'I'd be delighted.'

'When?'

'Every evening, if you want.'

He hesitated, then said:

'Well, all right, I'll come. I really ought to see you often. You've done me good. See you soon.'

He hesitated again, then added: 'But what if I don't come?'

'Then I'll come and see you', I told him.

I shook hands with him and went downstairs.

As I reached the bottom and was about to go out into the court-yard, I heard his voice saying:

'I'll see you soon, won't I?'*

I looked up. He had come down one flight of stairs, and was saying goodbye with a gentle smile.

from *Les Misérables*

A Righteous Man

i. Monsieur Myriel

In 1815 Monsieur Charles-François-Bienvenu Myriel was bishop of Digne.* He had held that position since 1806, and was now about seventy-five years old.

In the hope of leaving no stone unturned, it may be useful to mention here some of the rumours and bits of gossip about him that were going around when he first came to the diocese—even though they have nothing to do with the essence of our story. The things that are said (justly or unjustly) about a man often have as much bearing on his life, and especially on his destiny, as the things that he does. Monsieur Myriel was the son of a judge in the High Court of Aix—a member of the legal aristocracy. It was said that his father, expecting him to inherit that office, had arranged a marriage for him very early in life, when he was about eighteen or twenty, according to a custom common in prominent legal families. In spite of this marriage, Charles Myriel had been the subject of a lot of gossip, so it was said. Though rather short, he was handsome, elegant, graceful, and witty. His early years were entirely devoted to worldly affairs and romance. Then came the French Revolution. Things happened quickly; the ancient legal families were pursued, hunted down, decimated, and scattered. At the very outset of the Revolution, Monsieur Charles Myriel emigrated to Italy. There his wife died of tuberculosis, which had long afflicted her. They had never had any children. What was the next phase in Monsieur Myriel's destiny? Did the collapse of the old French way of life, the downfall of his own family, and the tragic events of 1793*—possibly even more harrowing for exiles who watched them from a distance and magnified them through their own fears—rouse in his mind ideas of renunciation and solitude? In the midst of the frivolities and flirtations that filled his existence, was he suddenly touched by the kind of terrible and mysterious blow that can strike a man to the heart and transform him more than any public disaster affecting his life or property? Nobody could tell; the only definite item of information was that, when he came back from Italy, he was a priest.

In 1804 Monsieur Myriel was curé of Brignolles. He was already old, and he lived in profound seclusion.

Around the time of Napoleon's coronation,* some little piece of parish business (no one now remembers what it was) took him to Paris. On behalf of his parishioners he went to see various influential people, including Cardinal Fesch.* One day the worthy little curé happened to be waiting in the cardinal's antechamber when the Emperor passed through it to visit his uncle. Napoleon noticed the old man eyeing him with a certain curiosity; he turned round and said brusquely:

'Why are you looking at me like that, my good man?'

'Sire,' replied Monsieur Myriel, 'you're looking at a good man, and I'm looking at a great one. Both of us may benefit from the experience.'

That very evening the Emperor asked the cardinal the curé's name, and some time later, Monsieur Myriel found to his surprise that he had been appointed bishop of Digne.

Still, just how much truth was there in the various tales about Monsieur Myriel's early life? No one could really tell. Very few families had known the Myriels before the Revolution.

Monsieur Myriel had to endure the fate of any newcomer in a small town where there are many tongues wagging but hardly any brains thinking. Even though he was a bishop—indeed, precisely because he was a bishop—he still had to endure it. But after all, the gossip linked with his name may have been merely gossip; rumours, words, talk or even less than talk—*palabres*, in the colourful language of the South.

However that may be, all the tales that initially filled small-town conversation—and small-mind conversation—were utterly forgotten by the time he had lived in Digne for nine years as the local bishop. Nobody would have dared to talk about them or even remember them.

Monsieur Myriel had come to Digne accompanied by his sister, Mademoiselle Baptistine, an old maid ten years younger than himself.

Their only servant was a woman about the same age as Mademoiselle Baptistine; her name was Madame Magloire. Previously she had been simply 'the curé's servant'; now she acquired the double title of Mademoiselle's maid and Monseigneur's housekeeper.

Mademoiselle Baptistine was tall, pale, lean, and gentle; she was the living embodiment of the word 'respectable' (a woman can't, it seems, be 'venerable' unless she has been a mother). She had never been pretty. Her whole life had been devoted to pious works, which had eventually shrouded her in a kind of whiteness and radiance; and as she grew old she acquired what might be called the beauty of goodness. What had been thinness in her youth became transparency in her age; and through that diaphanous veil her angelic character became visible. She was more a spirit than a virgin. She seemed to be made of shadow; scarcely enough body to belong to either sex; a few atoms of matter that contained a gleam of light; large, always downcast eyes; a mere pretext for a soul to remain on earth.

Madame Magloire was a little white-haired plump old woman, always busy and always breathless—partly because of her constant activity, and partly because of asthma.

When Monsieur Myriel arrived, he was installed in his episcopal mansion with all the honours laid down in the imperial decrees (which ranked a bishop immediately below a field marshal). The mayor and the presiding judge were the first to visit him, while he himself first visited the general and the prefect.

Once the installation was over, the town waited to see its bishop at work.

ii. Monsieur Myriel Becomes Monseigneur Bienvenu

The Digne episcopal mansion was next to the hospital.

The mansion was a large, tasteful stone edifice that had been built early in the eighteenth century by Monseigneur Henri Pujet, Abbé of Simore and Professor of Theology at the University of Paris, who had become bishop of Digne in 1712. It was a truly palatial residence. Everything had an air of grandeur—the bishop's own apartments, the reception rooms, the bedrooms, the courtyard (very wide, with arcades in the old Florentine style), the gardens planted with magnificent trees. The dining room was a long, opulent gallery on the ground floor, opening onto the garden. There, on 29 July 1714, Monseigneur Henri Pujet had given a ceremonial dinner for Messeigneurs Charles Brulant de Genlis (Prince Archbishop of Embrun), Antoine de Mesgrigny (Capuchin and Bishop of Grasse), Philippe de Vendôme (Grand Prior of France and Abbé of Saint Honoré de Lérins), François de Berton de Grillon (Lord Bishop of Vence), César de Sabran de Forcalquier (Lord Bishop of Glandève), and Jean Soanen (Priest of the Oratory, Preacher in Ordinary to the King, and Lord Bishop of Senez).* Portraits of these seven reverend individuals now adorned the room, and the memorable date '29 July 1714' was inscribed in letters of gold on a white marble tablet there.

The hospital was a lowly, narrow single-storey building with a small garden.

Three days after his arrival, the bishop visited the hospital. When the visit was over, he asked the hospital superintendent to come back with him to the mansion.

'Tell me, Superintendent, how many patients do you have at the moment?' he asked.

'Twenty-six, Monseigneur.'

'Yes, I counted them', said the bishop.

'The beds are very close together', the superintendent added.

'Yes, I noticed that.'

'The wards are only the size of ordinary rooms; air doesn't circulate through them very well.'

'Yes, that was my own impression.'

'And when we do get any sunshine, the garden is rather too small to hold the convalescents.'

'Yes, that's exactly what I was thinking.'

'When there's an epidemic—we had typhus this year, miliary fever two years ago, sometimes a hundred patients—we don't know what to do.'

'Yes, that had occurred to me, too.'

'Still, it's only to be expected, isn't it, Monseigneur?' said the superintendent; 'one has to accept these things.'

The conversation was taking place in the ground-floor dining hall.

The bishop remained silent for a moment; then he turned suddenly to the hospital superintendent.

'Tell me, sir,' he said, 'how many beds do you think this room would hold?'

'What!' exclaimed the superintendent, stupefied; 'Your Lordship's dining room?'

The bishop was running his eyes round the room, apparently judging distances and making calculations.

'It'd hold a good twenty beds', he said as if to himself; then, raising his voice, he added: 'Look here, Superintendent, let me put an idea to you. Obviously there's something wrong. There are twenty-six of you over there in five or six small rooms; there are three of us here, and we've got space enough for sixty. You see, it's all wrong. You're in my house and I'm in yours. You should let me have mine back. This is the place where you should be.'

Next day the twenty-six paupers were installed in the bishop's mansion and the bishop moved to the hospital.

Monsieur Myriel didn't have any property of his own; his family had been ruined by the Revolution. His sister had an annuity—five hundred francs a year—which had been enough for their personal needs when he was a curate. As bishop, Monsieur Myriel received a government stipend of fifteen thousand francs. On the day when he moved to the hospital, he settled once and for all how this money was to be used, in the following way (we are copying a note written in his own hand):

Household Budget

For the small seminary	1,500 francs
Mission congregation	100 francs
The Lazarists of Montdidier	100 francs
Seminary of Foreign Missions, Paris	200 francs
Congregation of the Saint-Esprit	150 francs
Religious establishments in the Holy Land	100 francs
Societies for Mothers	300 francs
Ditto at Arles, extra	50 francs
For improving prisons	400 francs
For relief and release of prisoners	500 francs
Aid for fathers imprisoned for debt	1,000 francs
To supplement the salaries of poor schoolteachers in the diocese	2,000 francs
Public granary in the Hautes-Alpes	100 francs
Ladies' Associations at Digne, Manosque, and Sisteron, to educate poor girls	1,500 francs
For the poor	6,000 francs
My personal expenses	1,000 francs
Total	15,000 francs

During his whole time as bishop of Digne, Monsieur Myriel hardly ever departed from this plan. He called it (as we've seen) his 'household budget', and declared that it had been 'settled'.

Mademoiselle Baptistine submitted absolutely to this scheme. The pious woman regarded his lordship as both her brother and her bishop, her friend in the flesh and her superior in the church. She loved and revered him, and that was that. If he spoke, she deferred; if he acted, she assisted. Only their servant, Madame Magloire, grumbled a bit. The bishop, as you'll have noticed, had retained a mere thousand francs for himself; adding Mademoiselle Baptistine's income, that made fifteen hundred francs a year.* On those fifteen hundred francs the two old women and the old man lived.

And whenever a village curé came to Digne, the bishop always found means to entertain him hospitably—thanks to Madame Magloire's strict economies and Mademoiselle Baptistine's sensible administration.

One day—he'd been at Digne about three months—the bishop said:

'I have all this money, yet I'm still so short of funds!'

'I should think so!' exclaimed Madame Magloire. 'Monseigneur hasn't even asked the department for the allowance to cover his carriage expenses in town and on trips around the diocese. All the bishops used to get it in the old days.'

'Why, you're absolutely right, Madame Magloire!' said the bishop. He made out his application.

Some time later, the local council, having duly considered the matter, voted him an annual sum of three thousand francs, designated 'Bishop's allowance for carriage expenses and cost of pastoral journeys'.

This caused a great deal of outcry among the townsfolk. As a result, an imperial senator, a fomer member of the Council of Five Hundred who had supported Napoleon's seizure of power in 1799* and now held an important senatorial seat near Digne, wrote an angry little confidential note to the Minister of Religious Practices, Monsieur Bigot de Préameneu. Here are some of its actual lines:

' "Carriage expenses"—in a town of less than four thousand people! Why? "Cost of journeys"! In the first place, what good do the journeys do? And in the second place, how do you travel by carriage in mountainous country like this? There aren't any roads. Everyone travels on horseback. Even the bridge over the Durance at Château-Arnoux can scarcely take an oxcart. These priests are all the same—greedy and stingy. This one played the Good Samaritan at the start, but now he's acting just like all the others—he has to have his carriage and post-chaise. He has to live in luxury like all the old-time bishops. Priestcraft all over! Dear Comte, things will never go right till the Emperor rids us of all these Holy Joes. To hell with the Pope!' (Relations with Rome were a little strained at the time.)* 'Give me Caesar any day, that's my motto.' And so on.

Madame Magloire, by contrast, was delighted with the situation. 'Good,' she told Mademoiselle Baptistine, 'Monseigneur kept thinking of others at first, but now he's learnt that he's got to think of himself in the end. He's fixed up all his charities. Now we've got three thousand francs just for us. And about time!'

That very evening, the bishop wrote and gave his sister the following note:

Carriage and Travel Expenses

Meat broth for hospital patients	1,500 francs
Society for Mothers at Arles	250 francs
Society for Mothers at Draguignan	250 francs
Foundlings	500 francs
Orphans	500 francs
Total	3,000 francs

That was Monsieur Myriel's budget.

As for the standard episcopal needs—marriage licences, dispensations, baptisms, sermons, church and chapel consecrations, weddings, etc.—the bishop funded them by collecting from the rich, which he did all the more zealously since he was passing the money on to the poor.

Donations of money soon began to pour in. Haves and Have-Nots kept knocking on Monsieur Myriel's door; as soon as somebody came to give alms, somebody else came to receive it. Within a year the bishop had become a universal treasurer of benevolence and reliever of suffering. Considerable sums of money passed through his hands; but nothing could make him change his way of life or add the smallest luxury to his requirements.

Far from it. You might say that everything was given away before it was received, because there's always more wretchedness at the bottom than kindness at the top. It was like water poured out on desert ground; no matter how much money he received, he never had enough. So he plundered from himself.

It was customary for a bishop to head his decrees and pastoral letters with all his Christian names. As a result, the poor of the district had seen their new bishop's full array of names and had picked out, with instinctive affection, the one that meant something to them. They always called him Monseigneur Bienvenu ['Welcome']. I shall follow their example, when appropriate, and give him the same name. Besides, he liked to be called that. 'It's a name I like', he said; 'the Bienvenu counteracts the Monseigneur.'

I don't necessarily expect you to believe the portrait I'm sketching; but I do say that it's a reasonable likeness.*

The Fall

i. The Evening after a Day's Walk

One day at the beginning of October 1815, a man travelling on foot entered the town of Digne about an hour after sunset. The few locals who happened to be at their doors or windows eyed the traveller uneasily. It would have been hard to find a more disreputable-looking fellow. He was a stocky, solidly built man of medium height, in the prime of life; his age might have been, perhaps, about forty-six to forty-eight.* A low leather cap partly hid his face, which was weatherbeaten and very sweaty. The hair of his chest could be seen through a coarse yellow shirt fastened by a small metal clasp at the neck. He wore a scarf twisted like a rope, rough shabby blue trousers faded at one knee and frayed at the other, and a ragged old grey jacket with a green patch sewn onto one elbow with twine. On his back was a brand-new soldier's knapsack, very full and buckled tight; he was carrying a huge gnarled stick in his hand; his stockingless feet were in hobnailed boots. His hair was cut short, but his beard was long.

Sweat, dust, his walk, and the day's heat had given him a peculiarly squalid, worse-for-wear look.

His head had been shaved, but was now stubbly; evidently his hair had been cut some days ago and was starting to grow back.

Nobody knew him. Presumably he was just passing through. Where had he come from? Somewhere in the south—the coast, perhaps; he was entering Digne by the very road that the Emperor Napoleon had used seven months earlier, on his way from Cannes to Paris.* The fellow must have been walking all day. He looked very tired. In the ancient town (on the lower slopes of the modern one) some women had seen him stop at the end of the Boulevard Gassendi, beneath the trees, and drink at the drinking-fountain there. He must have been decidedly thirsty, because some children who were following him saw him stop again a couple of hundred paces further on, and drink at the fountain in the marketplace.

When he came to the corner of the Rue Poichevert he turned left, went to the Town Hall, and entered it. Fifteen minutes later he came out again. There was a gendarme sitting near the doorway, on the

stone bench where General Drouot* had stood on 4 March to read
the Golfe Jouan Proclamation to the frightened populace. The man
raised his cap respectfully to the gendarme.

The gendarme gave no reply, but looked closely at the man, kept
watching him for some time afterwards, and then went inside the
building.

In those days Digne had a fine inn that bore the sign 'Croix-de-
Colbas'. The innkeeper was a certain Jacquin Labarre; he was highly
regarded in the town because he was related to another Labarre, a
former guide who kept the Trois-Dauphins Inn at Grenoble. At
the time when the Emperor landed, there had been many rumours
about the Trois-Dauphins Inn. General Bertrand, disguised as a
carter, was supposed to have called at the place frequently in January,
handing out decorations to the soldiers and fistfuls of coins to the
citizens. The truth is that the Emperor had refused to stay at the
Prefecture when he came to Grenoble; he had thanked the Prefect
politely but said: 'I'm going to see a fine old fellow I know.' And he had
gone to the Trois-Dauphins Inn. The glory of the Trois-Dauphins
Labarre was reflected across twenty-five leagues onto the Crois-de-
Colbas Labarre. In the town they called him 'the cousin of the one at
Grenoble'.

The man went to this inn—it was the best in the region—and
entered it through the kitchen, which opened directly onto the street.
All the stoves were alight, and a big fire was burning brightly in the
hearth. The innkeeper, who doubled as the cook, was scurrying
busily from fire to saucepan, preparing a fine meal for some wagoners
who could be heard laughing and chattering rowdily in the next
room. As any traveller can testify, nobody dines more heartily than
wagoners. A plump marmot was turning on a long spit in front of the
fire, with grouse and white partridges beside it; two big carp from
Lake Lauzet and a trout from Lake Alloz were cooking on the stoves.

The host heard the door open and someone enter; without looking
up from his work, he said:

'What will Monsieur have?'

'Food and a bed', said the man.

'Easily done', said the host; but then he turned his head, looked
the traveller up and down, and added: 'if you can pay.'

The man produced a big leather purse from his jacket pocket and
replied:

'I've got money.'

'In that case', said the host, 'I'm at your service.'

The man put the purse back in his pocket, took off his knapsack, and put it down next to the door; then, with the stick still in his hand, he sat down on a low stool by the fire. Digne is in the mountains. It gets cold there after sunset in October.

But the host, as he moved back and forth, continued to study the traveller.

'Is it long till dinner-time?' asked the latter.

'Not very', said the host.

While the newcomer was warming himself with his back turned, the worthy innkeeper Jacquin Labarre took a pencil out of his pocket and tore a corner off a sheet of old newspaper that was lying on a little table by the window. He scrawled a line or two in the printless area, folded it, and handed the bit of paper, unsealed, to a boy who seemed to be a combination of lackey and assistant chef. The innkeeper whispered a few words to the boy, who then scampered away in the direction of the Town Hall.

The traveller saw nothing of this.

'Is it long till dinner-time?' he asked again.

'Not very', said the host.

The boy returned with the bit of paper. The host unfolded it hastily, as if he had been anxious for an answer. He read it, apparently with some care, then shook his head and pondered for a moment. Finally he moved toward the traveller, who seemed to be preoccupied with thoughts of a not very pleasant kind.

'I'm afraid we can't have you here, Monsieur', he said.

The man half rose from his seat.

'Why not?' he asked. 'Are you scared I won't pay? You want me to pay in advance? I've got money, I tell you.'

'It isn't that.'

'Well what is it, then?'

'You've got money—'

'That's right', said the man.

'—but I haven't any rooms left', said the host.

'Then put me in the stable', the man replied coolly.

'I can't do that.'

'Why not?'

'There's only room for the horses.'

'Well then,' the man pursued, 'a corner of the hayloft, a bit of straw—we can fix it up after dinner.'

'I can't offer you dinner.'

He uttered the statement in a firm, steady voice, and the stranger seemed to take it very seriously. He got up.

'But look here, I'm starving to death. I've been walking ever since sunrise. I've come a good twelve leagues. I can pay the money, and I want to eat.'

'There's nothing available', said the host.

The man burst out laughing and swung round toward the fireplace and the stoves.

'Nothing! What's all that, then?'

'That's all reserved.'

'Who reserved it?'

'The wagoners.'

'How many of them are there?'

'Twelve.'

'There's enough food here for twenty.'

'They ordered the lot of it, and they paid in advance.'

The man sat down again and said, without raising his voice:

'I'm at an inn, I'm hungry, and I'm going to stay.'

The innkeeper leant over him and said in a tone that startled him: 'Get out.'

The traveller was bent over at the time, poking some coals into the fire with the metal ferrule on his stick. He turned sharply and opened his mouth to reply; but the host stared hard at him and said, keeping his voice down: 'Look, let's cut the talk. You want me to tell you who you are? Your name is Jean Valjean. And you want me to tell you *what* you are? I had my suspicions when I saw you come in here. I sent a note to the Town Council, and this is the answer I got. Can you read?'

With those words, he held out the opened piece of paper that had just been from Inn to Town Hall and back again. The man gave it a brief glance. There was a moment's silence, and then the innkeeper went on:

'I like to be polite with everyone. Now, off you go.'

The man lowered his head, picked up his knapsack, and went out.

He took the main street. He went straight ahead, walking at random, keeping close to the houses. He seemed sad and humiliated.

He never looked back. If he had, he would have seen the Croix-de-Colbas innkeeper standing in his doorway, talking excitedly to a group of guests and passers-by, and pointing at him; and from their looks of fear and antagonism, he would have known that his arrival would soon be the talk of the whole town.

But he saw none of it. Downtrodden people don't look back. They know only too well that bad luck is dogging their heels.

For a while he went along in the same way, walking randomly down unknown streets, and, as happens in a time of suffering, forgetful of his own weariness. Then, quite suddenly, he felt a pang of hunger. Night was falling. He looked around for a lodging of some kind.

The town's decent inn was closed to him; he was now looking for some third-rate tavern or cheap cellar.

And, indeed, there was a light coming from the end of the street; against the pale evening sky he could see a burning pine branch slung from an iron bracket. He went towards it.

Sure enough, it was a tavern. The one in the Rue de Chaffaut.

The traveller stopped for a moment and looked through the window into the tavern's low-ceilinged hall, lit by a small lamp on a table and a big fire in the fireplace. A few men were drinking there. The host was warming himself by the fire. An iron pot hung from a hook was simmering in the heat of the flames.

This tavern is also an inn of sorts; you can enter it through two doors—one from the street, the other from a small court containing a large dungheap.

The stranger didn't dare to enter by the street door. He slipped into the courtyard, stopped again, then timidly raised the latch and pushed the door open.

'Who's there?' asked the host.

'I want some food and a bed.'

'Fine. Food and a bed can be got here.'

He went in. All the drinkers turned around and watched him for a while, as he took off his knapsack. The lamp was lighting him from one side, the fire from the other.

The host said to him: 'Come in and warm yourself up at that fire over there, my friend. Supper's cooking in the pot.'

He went over to the fire and sat down, stretching out his weary legs in front of it. There was a good smell coming from the pot. His face—as much of it as could be seen under his low cap—took on a vaguely contented look, without losing the poignancy that comes from prolonged suffering.

It was a strong, sad, lively face, and a curiously ambivalent one; it looked humble at first sight, but after a while it came to seem stern. The eyes glimmered with light beneath the brows, like fire in a thicket.

But one of the men at the table was a fishmonger who had put his horse in Labarre's stable before coming to the Rue de Chaffaut tavern. It so happened that he'd met the suspicious-looking stranger travelling between Bras d'Asse and—I forget the name of the place, I think it's Escoublon—that very morning. The man, who seemed very tired even then, had asked to be taken up behind him, on the horse's crupper; but the fishmonger's only reply had been to quicken his pace. More recently—half an hour ago—the fishmonger had been a member of the Croix-de-Colbas throng gathered around Jacquin Labarre, and had told them about his unpleasant morning encounter. Now he signalled surreptitiously to the tavern-keeper. The tavern-keeper went over to him. They exchanged a few quiet words. The traveller was again lost in thought.

The tavern-keeper returned to the fireside, grabbed the man firmly by the shoulder, and said to him:

'You're not staying here.'

The stranger turned round and said quietly:

'Oh—you know, do you?'

'Yes.'

'They turned me out of the other inn.'

'Well, you're being kicked out of this one too.'

'Where am I supposed to go?'

'Not here, anyway.'

The man picked up his knapsack and stick, and went away.

Some children—they had followed him from the Croix-de-Colbas and seemed to be waiting for him—threw stones at him as he came out. He turned back angrily and threatened them with his stick; the children scattered like a flight of birds.

He came to the prison. There was an iron bell-chain hanging by the door. He rang the bell.

A peephole opened.

'Excuse me, jailer', he said, politely taking off his cap, 'but would you mind opening up and letting me stay here overnight?'

A voice replied:

'This isn't a hotel, it's a prison. Go and get yourself arrested. Then we'll open up all right.'

The peephole closed again.

He went down a narrow street where there were lots of gardens. Some of them were fenced only by hedges, so that the street had a cheery look. Among these gardens and hedges he noticed a little single-storey house with a lighted window. He looked through the window, just as he'd done when he came to the tavern. Inside was a big whitewashed room with a cradle in one corner, a bed with India-print calico drapes, a few wooden chairs, and a double-barrelled shotgun on the wall. A table was laid in the middle of the room. A brass lamp lit its coarse white linen tablecloth; its wine-filled pewter jug shone like silver, and its brown tureen was steaming. Sitting at the table was a man about forty years old, with a pleasant, honest face; he was bouncing a small child on his knees. Next to him was a very young woman nursing another child. The father was laughing, the child was laughing, the mother was smiling.

The traveller lingered thoughtfully for a moment before this restful domestic scene. What was going through his mind? Only he himself could have said. Very likely he imagined that this lively home might be hospitable—that he might possibly find some kindliness where he saw so much happiness.

He tapped very faintly on the window pane.

Nobody heard him.

He tapped again.

He heard the woman say: 'I think there's someone knocking.'

'Nonsense', said her husband.

He tapped a third time.

The husband got up, took the lamp, and opened the door.

He was a tall man, half peasant, half craftsman. He wore a big leather apron that passed over his left shoulder; a hammer, a red handkerchief, a powderhorn, and all sorts of other things were held in place by its belt, which made a kind of pocket in it. He carried his head high; his shirt was open and folded back, revealing a pale bull-like neck. He had prominent eyes, thick eyebrows, immense black sideburns, and a lantern jaw, topped off by an indefinable air of being thoroughly at home.

'Sorry to trouble you, sir', said the traveller. 'If I pay for it, could you please give me a plate of soup and a corner of your garden shed to sleep in? Could you? If I pay for it?'

'Who are you?' asked the master of the house.

The man replied: 'I've come from Puy-Moisson. I've been walking all day. I've come a good twelve leagues. Could you? If I pay for it?'

'Well,' said the peasant, 'I wouldn't turn away any decent man that could pay for it. But why didn't you go to the inn?'

'They haven't got any rooms left.'

'Rubbish! Can't be right. It isn't market day, and there isn't any fair in town. Did you try Labarre?'

'Yes.'

'Well?'

'I don't know', said the traveller uncomfortably; 'he wouldn't take me.'

'Did you try Thingummy's in the Rue de Chaffaut?'

The stranger became even more uncomfortable. He stammered:

'He wouldn't take me either.'

A look of suspicion came over the peasant's face. He eyed the newcomer up and down, and suddenly exclaimed nervously:

'Are you the man—?'

He glanced at the newcomer again, took three steps backward, put the lamp on the table and got down the shotgun.

But at the words 'Are you the man—?', the woman had jumped up, gathering her children in her arms, and rushed behind her husband, her breast still bare and her eyes wide. She stared at the stranger in horror and muttered: '*Tso-maraude.*'[1]

All this happened far more quickly than it can be described. The master of the house examined 'the man' for a few moments as if he were a viper, then moved back to the door and said:

'Get out of here!'

'Please,' said the man, 'just a glass of water.'

'Just a shot of lead!' said the peasant.

Then he slammed the door shut, and the man outside could hear two heavy bolts sliding. A moment later the shutters were fastened, and there was the sound of an iron bar being moved into position.

---

[1] 'Cat on the prowl', in French Alpine dialect [*Hugo's note*].

The night was steadily darkening. There was a cold Alpine wind blowing. By the last traces of daylight the stranger could glimpse some kind of shed, apparently made of turf, in one of the gardens facing the street. He scrambled briskly over a wooden fence and found himself inside the garden. He moved toward the shed. It had a very low, narrow entrance and looked like the kind of rough road-side shelter put up by road workers. He took for granted that it was indeed such a shelter. He was suffering from cold and hunger. He could bear the hunger, and here at least was some protection from the cold. Now, sheds of this kind are not usually occupied at night. He lay flat on his belly and crawled inside. The hut was warm, and there was a pretty good bed of straw. For a moment he simply lay on that bed; he was so tired he couldn't move. Then the knapsack on his back began to bother him, and anyhow, he could use it as a pillow; so he began to unbuckle the straps. Just at that moment there was some kind of ferocious growling sound. He looked up. The head of an enormous bulldog was silhouetted against the entrance to the shed.

It was a dog-kennel.

Well, he himself was strong and fearsome too. He clutched his stick, used his knapsack as a shield, and got out of the hut as best he could—though this didn't exactly reduce the holes in his already tattered garments.

He also got out of the garden, but did so facing backwards; out of respect for the bulldog, he had to use his stick in the way known to fencers as *la rose couverte*.

With some difficulty he went back over the fence and found himself in the street again, alone, homeless, roofless, shelterless, driven away from even the straw in a wretched dog-kennel. Then he dropped, rather than sat, on a stone; and, so we're told, someone who happened to be passing heard him cry out: 'I'm not even a dog!'

Soon he got up and started to walk again. In the hope of finding some tree or haystack where he could shelter, he left the town.

He went along for some time with his head bowed. Eventually, when he thought he was far away from all human habitation, he did raise his eyes and look around. He was in a field; in front of him a low stubble-covered hillock of the kind that are left behind after harvest and look like shaved heads.

The horizon was very black, not only with the darkness of the night, but also with some extremely low-lying cloud that actually seemed to be resting on the hillock and rising from it to cover the whole sky. However, the moon was about to rise, and there were still some hints of twilight high above, so that the clouds made a kind of pallid vault in the heavens and faintly illuminated the earth.

The earth, therefore, was more brightly lit than the heavens; this gave it a peculiarly sinister look, and the meagre stunted hillock loomed dim and faint against the shadowy horizon. The whole scene was hideous, wretched, desolate, and drab. Nothing in the field or on the hillock—apart from one writhing, shuddering misshapen tree a few steps away from the traveller.

He didn't, of course, have any of the sensitive intellectual and spiritual faculties that respond to the mysteries of nature; but that particular sky and hill and plain and tree were somehow so profoundly desolate that, after a moment's motionless contemplation, he turned abruptly away and resumed his walk. There are times when nature herself seems an enemy.

He retraced his steps. The gates of Digne were now shut. During the Wars of Religion* Digne had faced sieges, and in 1815 it was still surrounded by old square-turreted walls, which have since been demolished. He passed through a gap in the walls and re-entered the town.

It might have been about eight p.m. Since he didn't know any of the streets, once again he simply walked at random.

His journey led him to the Prefecture, then to the seminary. He crossed the cathedral square and shook his fist at the church.

There's a printing shop on the corner of the square. That's where the proclamations from the Emperor and Imperial Guard to the French army were first printed; they were brought here from the island of Elba, after Napoleon himself had dictated them.

The man was utterly worn out and had lost all hope. He lay down on the stone bench just in front of the shop.

At that moment, an old woman was coming out of the church. She saw him stretched out in the dark. 'What are you doing there, sir?' she asked.

He replied in a rough, angry voice: 'My good woman, you can see perfectly well what I'm doing. I'm going to bed.'

The good woman (she did indeed deserve that description) was the Marquise de R——.

'On that bench?' she asked.

'For nineteen years I've had a wooden mattress', said the man; 'tonight I've got a stone one.'

'You've been a soldier?'

'That's right, my good woman; a soldier.'

'Why don't you go to the inn?'

'I haven't got any money.'

'I'm sorry', said Madame de R——; 'there are only four sous in my purse.'

'I'll take them anyway.'

The man took the four sous. Madame de R—— continued: 'You won't be able to stay at an inn if that's all you've got. Still, have you really tried? You can't possibly spend the whole night here. You must be cold, and hungry. Someone should have taken you in out of simple kindness.'

'I've knocked on every door.'

'Well, what happened?'

'They all turned me away.'

The 'good woman' touched the man's sleeve and pointed across the square to a little house beside the bishop's mansion.

'You've knocked on every door?' she asked.

'Yes.'

'Have you knocked on that one?'

'No.'

'Go and knock on it.'

ii. A Word of Caution to the Wise

That evening, after his usual walk around the town, the Bishop of Digne stayed up fairly late in his room. He was busy with a large work (never completed, unfortunately) on the subject of Duty. He was carefully scrutinizing everything that the Fathers and Doctors of the Church said about this important topic. His book was divided into two parts: (1) universal duties; (2) individual duties that depend on each person's particular situation. The universal duties are the main ones. There are four of them, listed in the Gospel according to Matthew: duties toward God (Matt. 6); duties toward oneself (Matt. 5: 29, 30); duties toward one's neighbour (Matt. 7: 12); duties toward the created world (Matt. 6: 20, 25). As for the more specific duties, the bishop found them discussed elsewhere: duties for rulers and their subjects, in the Letter to the Romans; for magistrates, wives, mothers, and young men, in the writings of Peter; for husbands, fathers, children, and servants, in the Letter to the Ephesians; for believers, in the Letter to the Hebrews; for virgins, in the Letter to the Corinthians.* He was carefully combining all these instructions into a harmonious whole, which he hoped to offer humanity.

By eight p.m. he was still at work, writing rather awkwardly on small slips of paper with a big book open on his knees, when Madame Magloire entered as usual to take the silverware out of the cupboard by the bed. A moment later the bishop, guessing that the table was laid and that his sister might be waiting for him, closed his book, got up from his work, and went into the dining room.

The dining room was a rectangular room with a fireplace, a door opening (as we've said) directly onto the street, and a window facing the garden.

Sure enough, Madame Magloire had just finished laying the table.

While she attended to the plates, she was chatting with Mademoiselle Baptistine.

There was a lamp on the table; the table was near the fireplace. A pretty good fire was burning.

It isn't hard to imagine these two women, both over sixty: Madame Magloire small, plump, lively; Mademoiselle Baptistine gentle, slim, frail, a little taller than her brother, and wearing a plum-coloured silk dress—she had bought it in Paris in 1806,* when that colour was the latest fashion, and had never parted with it. To use the popular idioms that say more in a word than a writer can in a whole page, Madame Magloire 'looked like a peasant', and Mademoiselle Baptistine 'looked every inch a lady'. Madame Magloire was wearing a fluted white cap, a gold cross at her neck (the only bit of feminine jewellery in the house), a very white kerchief above a black homespun dress with short loose sleeves, a green-and-red-check calico apron tied at the waist with a green ribbon, and a matching stomacher pinned up in front by two pins; she had thick shoes and yellow stockings of the kind worn in Marseilles. Mademoiselle Baptistine's dress had the 1806-style high waist, straight skirt, puffed sleeves, tabs, and buttons. She hid her grey hair under the kind of curly wig known as *à l'enfant*. Madame Magloire looked shrewd, quick-witted, and kindly; the corners of her mouth were uneven, and the upper lip jutted out beyond the lower, giving her a somewhat stubborn, imperious expression. As long as Monseigneur remained silent, she would talk to him quite matter-of-factly, with a combination of respect and familiarity; but the moment he began to speak, she deferred to him without question, just as Mademoiselle did. We've seen that already. Mademoiselle Baptistine hardly spoke at all. She simply tried to be obedient and helpful. Even in her youth she had never been pretty; she had prominent big blue eyes and a long pinched nose; but as we said earlier, her whole face, her whole being, radiated a goodness that can't be put into words. She had been marked out for meekness from the very cradle; but the three virtues that enrich the soul—faith, hope, and love—had gradually raised her meekness into holiness. Nature had merely made her a lamb; religion had made her into an angel. The poor holy woman—her memory is long gone now!

In later life, Mademoiselle Baptistine often told the story of what happened at the bishop's house that evening—so often that there are people still living who know the tiniest details of the tale by heart.

At the moment when the bishop came into the room, Madame Magloire was talking rather volubly. She was talking to 'Mademoiselle' about one of her favourite topics, one that was quite familiar to the bishop. It was the subject of locking the front door.

Apparently Madame Magloire had heard some rumours here and there while she had been out shopping for the evening meal. An ugly-looking prowler was said to be on the loose; a suspicious-looking vagabond had turned up, he must still be somewhere around, and there could be nasty business in store for anyone who stayed out late that night. What's more, the police force was in pretty bad shape, because the Prefect and the Mayor were at loggerheads and were keen to make trouble for each other if they could. So any sensible person would have to do his own policing and look after his own safety. So everyone ought to shut his house tight and bolt and bar everything *and lock the front door properly*.

Madame Magloire laid particular stress on these last words; but the bishop had come from his own room, which was rather cold, and he was now sitting by the fire, warming himself and thinking of other things. In fact, he didn't hear a word of what Madame Magloire had just been saying. She repeated it. Then Mademoiselle Baptistine, wanting to please Madame Magloire without displeasing her brother, ventured to say timidly:

'Did you hear what Madame Magloire was saying, brother?'

'More or less,' said the bishop; 'some of it.' Then he turned his chair halfway round, put his hands on his knees, and looked at the old servant. His good-humoured friendly face was lit from below by the firelight. 'Well now, what's the matter? Are we in any serious danger?'

Then Madame Magloire told the whole tale over again, no doubt exaggerating it a bit. There seemed to be some kind of dangerous beggar in town—a tramp, a gypsy. He'd tried to get lodgings with Jacquin Labarre, who had turned him away. He'd been seen coming into town along the Boulevard Gassendi and prowling the streets in the dark. A pillage-and-noose man with a dreadful-looking face.

'Is that so?' said the bishop.

This little show of interest encouraged Madame Magloire; she deduced from it that the bishop was actually starting to get worried. So she went on triumphantly:

'Yes, Monseigneur. That's what he's like. There's going to be some trouble in town tonight. Everyone says so. And on top of that, the police force is in such bad shape' (useful repetition). 'Here we are in the mountains, and after dark we don't even have street lights! You go out, and it's black as pitch! Well, Monseigneur, what I say is—and Mademoiselle there says just the same as me—'

'Me!' the sister interrupted. 'I'm not saying anything. My brother will do whatever is the right thing to do.'

Madame Magloire went on, as if the protest had not even been uttered:

'What we say is, this house isn't safe at all; and if Monseigneur will let me, I'll go and tell Paulin Musebois' (the locksmith) 'to come and put the old bolts back in the door; we've got them right here, it wouldn't take him more than a minute. What I say is, we need to have locks, Monseigneur, even if it's only for this one night; because what I say is, there's nothing worse than a door that's only latched and can be opened from outside by anyone that happens to come along; and on top of that, Monseigneur always keeps telling people to come in, even in the middle of the night, good heavens, they don't even need to ask first—'

At that moment there was a violent knock on the door.

'Come in', said the bishop.

iii. The Heroism of Unquestioning Obedience*

The door opened.

It opened quite wide, briskly, as if someone had pushed it boldly and resolutely.

A man came in.

We already know him. He was the traveller we lately saw wandering around looking for shelter.

He came in, took a step forward, and stopped, leaving the door open behind him. His knapsack was on his back, and his stick was in his hand. He had a tough, hard, weary, defiant look in his eyes. The firelight illuminated him. He was a horrible, ominous sight.

Madame Magloire didn't even have the strength to scream. She just stood there trembling, her mouth open.

Mademoiselle Baptistine turned around, saw the new arrival, and half rose in fear; then she slowly turned back to see what her brother was doing, and her face resumed all its usual placid serenity.

The bishop was looking at the man quite calmly.

He was just opening his mouth to speak—no doubt to ask the stranger what he wanted. But the man leant on his stick with both hands, surveyed the old man and the women one by one, and, without waiting for the bishop to speak, said loudly:

'Now listen here. I'm Jean Valjean, that's my name. I'm an ex-convict. I've done nineteen years in jail. I was let out four days ago, and I'm going to Pontarlier. I've walked from Toulon in four days. I've done a good twelve leagues today on foot. Tonight, when I got to this part of the country, I went to an inn, and they turned me away because of my yellow ticket-of-leave* that I showed the Town Council like I'm supposed to do. I went to another inn. They told me to get lost. First one place, then the other. Nobody wanted anything to do with me. I went to the jail, and the jailer wouldn't let me in. I went into a dog-kennel. The dog bit me and drove me out just like he was human. You'd think he must have known who I was. I went out into the fields so I could sleep under the stars. Well, there weren't any stars. I thought it's going to rain, and there's no God in heaven to stop the rain falling, so I went back into town to see if I could find a doorway to sleep in. I was lying on a block of stone in the square. Some nice woman pointed at your house and told me 'Go and knock there.' Well, I've knocked. What kind of place is this? Are you an inn? I've got money. I've been saving. Hundred and nine francs fifteen sous that I got working for nineteen years in jail. I'll pay all right—I don't mind, I've got the money. I'm dead tired, walking for twelve leagues, I'm starving. Can I stay here please?'

'Madame Magloire,' said the bishop, 'please lay an extra place.'

The man took three steps toward the lamp on the table. 'Hang on a moment,' he said, as if he hadn't understood the situation, 'that isn't how it is. Didn't you listen to what I said? I'm a convict. A jailbird. I'm just out of jail.' He drew a big yellow sheet of paper from his pocket, and unfolded it. 'There's my ticket. Yellow, see? That gets me kicked out of everywhere I go. Want to read it? I can read, I can. I learnt in jail. They've got classes there if you want to learn. Look, there's what they put on the ticket: "Jean Valjean, released convict, born at"—you don't want to know all that stuff— "nineteen years in prison. Five years for burglary. Fourteen years for attempting to escape four times. Highly dangerous." There you are! Everyone keeps kicking me out. You want to take me in? Is this place an inn? Can you give me some food and a bed? Have you got a stable?'

'Madame Magloire,' said the bishop, 'please put some clean sheets on the bed in the alcove.'

We've already seen how obedient these two women were.

Madame Magloire went off to carry out her instructions.

The bishop turned to the man.

'Please sit down and warm yourself at the fire, sir. We'll be having supper in a minute, and we'll get your bed ready for you while you eat.'

This time the man did understand. His face lost its sullen, menacing look and assumed an extraordinary expression of mingled stupefaction, disbelief, and delight. He began to babble like a madman.

'Really? What, you're going to let me stay? You're not going to kick me out—a convict! You called me "sir"—you didn't talk down at me. "Get lost, dog" is what they always say to me. I really thought you'd turn me out too. So I just told you right away who I am. That's a good lady that told me to come here! I'm going to get some food! and a bed! A real bed with a mattress and sheets on it, like everyone else! Nineteen years I've never slept in a real bed. You really going to let me stay? You're proper decent people here! I've got money, too.

I'll pay really good. And excuse me, sir, but what's your name? I'll pay anything you want. You're a good man, you are. You're an innkeeper, aren't you?'

'I'm a priest,' said the bishop, 'and I live here.'

'A priest!' the man exclaimed. 'Oh well, you're a good sort of man for a priest! You won't want me to pay then, will you? You're the curé, right? the curé of that big church next door? Hey, that's right. I'm a real idiot, aren't I! I never noticed your hat.'

As he spoke, he put his knapsack and stick in a corner, returned his ticket-of-leave to his pocket, and sat down. Mademoiselle Baptistine was looking at him in a kindly way. He went on:

'You're a real human being, Father. You don't treat people like dirt. A good priest is a mighty good thing. So, I won't need to pay you then, right?'

'No', said the bishop; 'keep your money. How much do you have? Didn't you say you had a hundred and nine francs?'

'And fifteen sous', added the man.

'A hundred and nine francs fifteen sous. And how long did it take you to earn that?'

'Nineteen years.'

'Nineteen years!'

The bishop emitted a deep sigh.

'I've still got all my money', the man went on. 'In four days I've only spent twenty-five sous I earned when I helped unload carts in Grasse. We had a chaplain in the jail—I'm telling you that because you're a priest yourself. And one day I even saw a bishop. Monseigneur, they called him. He was the bishop of La Majore, at Marseilles. He's the big priest that's over all the other priests. But you already know all that—sorry, I'm putting it badly, but for someone like me, it's miles away! You know—for people like us. He said Mass right there in the jail, on an altar, he had a kind of gold pointy thing on his head. It was the middle of the day, it was shining in the sunlight. We were all lined up in rows. On three sides. With the guns pointed at us ready to fire. We couldn't see very good. He was speaking, but he was too far back, we couldn't hear him. Anyhow, that's what a bishop is.'

While he was speaking, the bishop went to the door, which was still wide open, and closed it.

Madame Magloire came back. She set another place at the table.

'Madame Magloire,' said the bishop, 'please put it as close to the fire as you can.' He turned to his guest and said: 'The wind gets very biting at night in the Alps. You must be cold, sir?'

Every time he said the word 'sir' in his mild, serious, welcoming voice, the man's face lit up. 'Sir' to a convict was like a glass of water to a castaway on the *Medusa* raft.* Disgrace thirsts for respect.

'This lamp isn't giving us much light', said the bishop.

Madame Magloire understood him. She got the two silver candle-sticks from the mantelpiece in Monseigneur's bedroom, lit them, and put them on the dining-room table.

'You're very good to me, Father', said the man. 'You didn't treat me like dirt. You let me stay in your home. You've lit your candles for me. And I never hid from you where I come from or what kind of problems I've got.'

The bishop, sitting beside him, touched the back of his hand gently and said: 'You didn't have to tell me who you were. This isn't my house, it's Jesus Christ's. It doesn't ask who someone may be, but what troubles he may have. You're in need; you're hungry and thirsty; so you're welcome here. Now, don't start thanking me and telling me that I've let you stay in my home. This place isn't any man's home, unless he's in need of help. So you see it's more your home than mine, even though you're just passing by. Everything here is yours. Why should I need to know your name? Besides, I knew it even before you told me.'

The man opened his eyes in astonishment.

'Really? You already knew what my name was?'

'Yes', replied the bishop; 'your name is Brother.'

'Look here, Father,' said the man, 'I was feeling awful hungry when I came here, but you've treated me so good that I hardly know what I'm feeling any more. It's all gone away.'

The bishop looked at him and said:

'You must have been through a great deal.'

'Oh, well—convict uniform, ball and chain, plank to sleep on, heat, cold, hard labour, chain gang, floggings. Double chains for nothing. Solitary if you let out a single word. Even when you're sick in bed, you're still chained up. Look at the dogs—even the dogs are better off than that! Nineteen years! I'm forty-six. And now a yellow ticket! That's how it goes.'

'Yes', the bishop replied; 'you've come from an unhappy place. But listen, there's more joy in heaven over the tears of one sinner who repents than over the white robes of a hundred righteous. If you've come out of that sorry place feeling angry and hateful, you'll deserve to be treated with compassion; but if you've come out with feelings of goodwill, kindness, and peace, you'll be superior to any of us.'

Meanwhile Madame Magloire had served up the meal. Clear soup, oil, bread, and salt; a bit of bacon, a little mutton, some figs, a fresh cheese, and a big loaf of rye bread. In addition, she had taken the liberty of supplementing the bishop's normal diet with a bottle of old Mauves wine.

The bishop's face instantly assumed the cheerful expression characteristic of people who are hospitable by nature. 'Mealtime!' he announced blithely. As usual when there was a guest, he placed the man on his right. Mademoiselle Baptistine, who was perfectly calm and entirely at her ease, sat on his left.

The bishop gave thanks, then, as he customarily did, served the soup himself. The man began to eat voraciously.

Suddenly the bishop said: 'I do believe there's something missing from the table.'

Madame Magloire had, in fact, laid places only for the three people present. But when the bishop had a dinner guest, all six of the silver services were usually laid out on the table in an innocent display of elegance. This added a childlike touch of luxury to the kindly but austere household, and dignified its poverty.

Madame Magloire understood what he meant; she went out without a word. A moment later the three extra places requested by the bishop had been neatly laid opposite the three diners, and were glittering on the tablecloth.

iv. A Brief Guide to the Pontarlier Cheese Industry*

To give some idea of the things that happened during the meal, we couldn't improve on a passage in a letter from Mademoiselle Baptistine to her childhood friend* Madame de Boischevron. Here the conversation between convict and bishop is related with naïve minuteness.

. . . The man kept eating greedily all the time without paying any attention to anyone. Just as if he was starving. But then, after the soup, he said:

'This is all much too good for me, Father, but I ought to tell you that those wagoners—who wouldn't let me eat with them—get much better meals than you do.'

Just between you and me, when I heard him say that, I was rather shocked. Then my brother said:

'Well, they get more tired than I do.'

'It isn't that', said the man; 'it's that they've got more money. You're quite poor—I can see that plain enough. Maybe you're not even a curé. Are you even a curé? My word, if the Lord God had any justice, you'd be a curé all right.'

'The Lord God has more than justice', said my brother.

Then a moment later he said:

'Monsieur Valjean, you said you were going to Pontarlier?'

'Yes—and I've got no choice how I get there.'

At least I think that's what he said. Then he went on:

'I've got to be going by sunrise tomorrow. It's a tough journey. Maybe the nights are cold, but the days are hot.'

'You're going to a nice part of the country', said my brother. 'In the Revolution—my family was ruined—at first I went to Franche-Comté where it was safer, and I stayed there for a while, working with my own hands. I was willing enough, and I found plenty to keep me occupied—it was all there for the picking. They have paper mills, tanneries, breweries, oil refineries, big clockmaking firms, steelworks, copper works, at least twenty iron foundries—the four at Lods, Châtillon, Audincourt, and Beure are very large places—'

I think those are the towns my brother named, but I might be wrong. Then he broke off and said to me:

'We'd have some relatives in that part of the country, wouldn't we, sister?'

And I said:

'We used to have. One of them was Monsieur de Lucenet, who was Captain of the Gates at Pontarlier before the Revolution.'

'Yes,' said my brother, 'but in 1793 nobody had any relatives; all we had was our own hands. Well, I worked. In the Pontarlier region—where you're going, Monsieur Valjean—they have a very patriarchal, very charming industry (isn't that so, sister?). It's cheesemaking. They call their dairies *fruitières*.'

My brother kept plying the man with food, and all the time he was describing the Pontarlier *fruitières* in great detail—how there were two kinds of them—the 'big farms' belonging to wealthy people, where there are forty or fifty cows producing seven or eight thousand cheeses each summer, and the 'associated *fruitières*' belonging to poor people, the peasants living in the foothills, who put all their cows together and share the produce. They hire a cheesemaker (they call him a *grurin*)—he takes the milk from the associated farmers three times a day and records the quantities in a double register—cheesemaking starts towards the end of April—the cheesemakers take their cows up into the mountains around the middle of June.

Meanwhile the man was starting to feel better because of the food. My brother gave him some of the good Mauves wine that he doesn't drink himself because he says it's too expensive. My brother was telling him all this information in his ordinary relaxed cheerful way—you know how he is—and every now and then turning politely to me as well, while he spoke. He kept coming back to the good position that a *grurin* has—as though he was wanting the man to see that it would be a secure position for him, though without telling him so too directly and pointedly. One thing especially I noticed. This man was just the way I've told you. Well, apart from saying a few words about Jesus when he first came in, my brother didn't make any remarks during the whole meal or the whole evening that might remind the man what sort of man he himself was, or show him what sort of man my brother was. And it would have been such a wonderful opportunity to preach a little sermon and explain that he was a bishop and make a big impression on the convict. If someone else had got hold of this poor man, he might have seized the chance to feed his soul as well as his body and give him a proper rebuke along with some good advice and morality—or else a bit of sympathy along with an exhortation to behave better in the future. But my brother never even asked him where he came from or what his past life had been. Because his past life would have included his crime, and my brother seemed to keep away from anything that could bring up that topic. So much so that, at one stage, when my brother was talking about the Pontarlier mountain people and their 'enjoyable work close to heaven' and how they are 'happy because they're innocent', he broke off suddenly in case the word 'innocent', which had just slipped out, might hurt the man's feelings. Thinking it over, I do feel I can understand what must have been in my brother's mind—he would have been thinking that this man Jean Valjean was already suffering quite enough inwardly and the best thing was to distract him from it and give him the feeling, even if only for a moment, that he was just a human being like anyone else. And so he kept treating him in this perfectly ordinary way. Well now, isn't that what charity really means? Isn't that something like the true gospel—the sort of tact that doesn't sermonize or moralize or make any pointed allusions? When someone has a painful wound, isn't it kindest to avoid touching it in any way? So I fancy that's what my brother was privately thinking. Still, I must say that, if he *was* thinking that, he never showed it—even to me. From start to finish he was just the same as on any other evening—he dined with Jean Valjean in exactly the same way that he would have dined with the provost, Monsieur Gédéon, or the parish curé.

Then near the end, while we were having the dessert, there was a knock on the door—it was poor Madame Gerbaud carrying her baby. My brother gave the child a kiss on the forehead, and borrowed fifteen sous that I happened to have with me, and gave them to Madame Gerbaud. Well, while this was happening the man didn't pay any real attention to it—he was looking all tired out and wasn't talking any more. Then the old woman left and my brother said prayers. And then he turned to the man and said to him: 'You must be well and truly ready for bed.' Madame Magloire promptly cleared the table. Then I realized that we ought to retire so that the traveller could get some sleep. So we both went upstairs, but a moment later I sent Madame Magloire down to put a Black Forest buckskin rug from my room on the man's bed. The nights are icy cold, and it keeps things warm. It's a bit old, unfortunately—all the hair is falling off. My brother bought it when he was in Germany, at Totlingen, near the source of the Danube, along with the little ivory-handle knife I use at meals.

And then Madame Magloire came back right away and we said our prayers in the room where we hang out the washing. And then we both went to our rooms without saying anything else.

v. Peace and Quiet

After saying goodnight to his sister, Monseigneur Bienvenu picked up one of the silver candlesticks from the table and gave the other to his guest, saying:

'Let me show you to your room, sir.'

The man followed him.

As I said earlier, the house was so arranged that you could only enter or leave the alcove in the oratory by passing through the bishop's bedroom.

While they were going through that room, Madame Magloire happened to be putting away the silver in the bedside cupboard—that being her final task each evening before she retired to bed.

The bishop ushered his guest into the alcove. The bed was newly made, with clean white sheets. The man put the candlestick on a small table.

'Now then, sleep well', said the bishop. 'Tomorrow morning, before you set out, we'll give you a cup of warm milk from our cows.'

'Thank you, Father', said the man.

But as soon as he uttered those words of peace, suddenly, quite without warning, he did something strange—something that would certainly have terrified the two good women, if they had been there to see it. To this very day it's hard to account for it. What drove him to do it? Was he trying to give a warning—or a threat? Or was he guided simply by some instinctive impulse, which even he himself couldn't have explained? He swung round abruptly, faced the old man, folded his arms, glared at his host, and exclaimed in a harsh voice:

'Well, well! So you're letting me stay in your own house, and right next door to you!'

He stopped himself and added, with a rather sinister laugh:

'Have you really thought what you're doing? Who says I don't go around murdering people?'

The bishop glanced upwards and replied:

'Oh, that's the Lord's business.'

Then, moving his lips like someone praying or talking to himself, he solemnly raised two fingers of his right hand and blessed the man—who didn't stoop to receive it. Then, without turning his head or looking back, he withdrew to his own room.

When the alcove was occupied, a massive serge curtain was drawn across the oratory to screen the altar. On his way out, the bishop knelt in front of this curtain and said a short prayer.

A few moments later he was out in the garden, walking around and pondering, with his spirit and soul immersed in contemplation of the eternal mysteries revealed by God in the night to eyes that remain open.

As for the man, he was so worn out that he didn't even make use of the good white sheets. He blew out the candle with his nostrils, as convicts do, and then dropped on top of the bed fully clothed. A moment later he was sleeping soundly.

When the bishop returned from the garden into his room, midnight was striking.

Soon afterwards, the whole house was asleep.

vi. Jean Valjean

Some time in the middle of the night, Jean Valjean awoke.

Jean Valjean came from a poor family of peasants in the Brie region. As a child he had never been taught to read. When he reached manhood, he had started work as a pruner at Faverolles. His mother's name Jeanne Mathieu, his father was called Jean Valjean or Vlajean, probably a nickname—a contraction of *Voilà Jean*.*

Like most people with affectionate natures, Jean Valjean was thoughtful but not melancholy. Still, on the whole he was somewhat immature and unremarkable, at least outwardly. He had lost both his parents while he was still very young. His mother had died of a poorly treated milk fever.* His father, who was also a pruner, had been killed by a fall from a tree. Jean Valjean's only remaining relative was an older sister, a widow with seven children, girls and boys. He had been brought up by that sister; she had housed and fed him as long as her husband was alive. Her husband had died. The oldest of her seven children had been eight years old, the youngest was one. Jean Valjean had just turned twenty-four. Taking the father's place in the family, he supported the sister who had brought him up. This happened quite naturally, as if it were simply a duty, but he still did it with a touch of surliness. That was how his youth was spent, in hard, poorly paid work. Nobody in the region ever knew him to have a 'girlfriend'.* He never had the time to be in love.

He came home tired in the evening and ate his supper without a word. During the meal his sister, Madame Jeanne, often took the best things out of his bowl—a bit of meat, a slice of bacon, the heart of a cabbage—and gave them to one or other of her children. He kept on eating, with his head bent over the table—virtually in the soup—and his long hair falling over the dish and hiding his eyes. He simply let it happen; he didn't even seem to see it. Not far from the Valjeans' cottage at Faverolles, just across the lane, there was a farmer's wife called Marie-Claude. The Valjean children, being perpetually hungry, would sometimes borrow a jug of milk from Marie-Claude in their mother's name, and drink it behind a hedge or in some alley corner, snatching the jug so greedily from each other that the girls spilt it on their aprons and bibs. If their mother had known of these escapades she would have punished the delinquents severely. But Jean Valjean, gruff and grumpy though he was, always paid Marie-Claude for the milk; and the children went unpunished.

In the pruning season he earned twenty-four sous a day; when that was over, he hired himself out as a reaper, a manual labourer, or a cattleman. He did what he could. His sister worked too—but how could anyone manage with seven young children? They were a sad little band, with poverty closing in on them more and more tightly. Then came a particularly severe winter. Jean was out of work. The family didn't have any bread—literally. With seven children.

One Sunday night, Maubert Isabeau, the baker in the Place de l'Église at Faverolles, was just getting ready for bed when he heard a loud crash coming from the barred window of his shop. He got there in time to see an arm reaching through a hole in the glass. The arm grabbed a loaf of bread and made off with it. Isabeau rushed out; the thief was running away at top speed; Isabeau chased him and caught him. The thief had thrown the loaf away, but his arm was still bleeding. He was Jean Valjean.

That happened in 1795. Jean Valjean stood trial before the tribunal of that period on charges of 'burglary at night in an inhabited house'. He had a gun which he used for more practical purposes than marksmanship—he was something of a poacher, which told against him. There's an understandable prejudice against poachers. Poachers, like smugglers, are just about brigands. Still, we should note in passing that there's an immense gulf between such men and the dreadful killers in the towns. Poachers ply their trade in the woods, smugglers in the mountains or at sea. Towns make men cruel because they make them corrupt. Mountains, seas, forests, make men savage; they bring out the wildness in their nature, but don't generally destroy their humanity.

Jean Valjean was found guilty. The terms of the penal code* were explicit. Sometimes, terribly, our civilization punishes a crime in a way that ruins the criminal's life. It's a fateful thing when society sits back and consigns an intelligent creature to irrevocable perdition. Jean Valjean was sentenced to five years' hard labour.

On 22 April 1796 Paris heard news of a victory at Montenotte. The victory had been won by the general commanding the French army in Italy; his name was given by the Directory (in a message dated 2 Floréal, Year IV,* and addressed to the Five Hundred) as 'Buona-Parte'. The same day a big prison gang was chained together in the Bicêtre jail. Jean Valjean was part of it. A former jailer, now nearly ninety years old, can still clearly recall the poor wretch who was chained at the end of the fourth row in the north corner of the yard. He was sitting on the ground, just like all the others. He seemed to have no awareness of his situation—except that it was horrible. And, probably, he felt that it was worse than he deserved. (These, of course, being merely the naïve ideas of a poverty-stricken man who knew absolutely nothing.) He kept weeping while the iron collar was being riveted around his neck with heavy hammer-blows. The tears stifled him—prevented him from saying anything except, now and then, 'I used to be a tree-pruner at Faverolles.' Then, still sobbing, he raised and lowered his right arm seven times, as if touching seven successive heads at different heights, to show that whatever he'd done had been done to feed and clothe seven little children.

He was taken to Toulon. He got there after a journey of twenty-seven days on a cart with his neck chained. At Toulon he was dressed in a red uniform. His whole past life, even his name, was wiped out; he was no longer Jean Valjean, he was Number 24601. What happened to his sister? What happened to the seven children? Who cared? What happens to the leaves on a growing tree when its trunk is cut down?

It's the same old story. With no support, no guidance, no shelter left, those poor little creatures—made by God himself—were simply set adrift. Who knows where they went? Each one may have taken a different path, vanishing gradually into the cold fog that engulfs all solitary destinies, in the dismal gloom where so many unfortunate souls disappear as the human race walks grimly on. They left the region. The steeple on what had been their village church forgot them; the hedgerows in what had been their fields forgot them; and after some years in jail, Jean Valjean himself forgot them. Where his heart had been wounded, a scar had developed. That's all. In all the time he was at Toulon, only once did he hear anything of his sister. This was, I think, near the end of his fourth year in prison. I can't remember exactly how the news reached him. Someone who had known them back home had seen his sister. She was now in Paris. She was living in a wretched street near Saint-Sulpice—the Rue du Gindre. Only one of the children—the youngest, a little boy—was still with her. Where were the six others? Even she herself may not have known. Every morning she went to a printing shop, 3 Rue du Sabot, where she worked as a folder and bookbinder. She had to be there at six a.m.—well before daybreak, in winter. In the same building there was a school, to which she took her little boy (he was seven years old). But she went into the printing shop at six, and the school didn't open till seven, so the child had to wait in the courtyard for an hour till the school opened; in winter this was an hour of darkness, in the open air. The child wasn't allowed into the shop; he was a nuisance, they said. Every morning, passing workmen could see this poor little thing sitting on the pavement half asleep—or, quite often, slumped on his basket in the dark, altogether asleep. When it was raining, an old woman, the doorkeeper, would take pity on him and bring him into her little room, which contained only a straw mattress, a spinning wheel, and two wooden chairs; and the lad would sleep there in a corner, nestling against the cat to keep warm. At seven o'clock the school opened and in he went. That's what Jean Valjean was told. One day he was given that information, a momentary flash of light, like a window suddenly opening for an instant on the fate of the creatures he had loved, and then everything shut again; he heard nothing more about them—ever. Nothing more from them ever reached him; he never saw them again, he never came across them again; and the rest of this unhappy tale will contain no further glimpse of them.

Towards the end of that fourth year, Jean Valjean got his turn to escape. His fellow prisoners helped him, as they usually do in such dismal places. He got away. For two days he wandered across the countryside and was free—if you're free when you're being tracked down; when you're looking around constantly; when you're jumping at the slightest sound; when you're frightened of everything—men passing, dogs barking, horses galloping, clocks striking the hour, chimneys emitting smoke, daytime because things can be seen, night-time because they can't, roads, paths, bushes, and sleep itself. On the evening of the second day he was caught. He hadn't eaten or slept for thirty-six hours. The maritime tribunal sentenced him to a further three years for this offence—making eight years in all. In the sixth year, he got another turn to escape; he made use of it, but couldn't manage to get out of the jail. He'd been missing at roll-call. The alarm gun was fired, and at night the watch found him hiding beneath the keel of a boat under construction; when the guards grabbed him, he struggled against them. Escape and resisting arrest. Under the provisions of the special code, these crimes were punished by an additional five years' imprisonment, two of them in double chains. Thirteen years. In the tenth year his turn came up again, and he tried again. He had no better luck this time. Three years for the new attempt. Sixteen years. Finally—I think it was during the thirteenth year—he made one last attempt and was caught after only four hours away. He got three years for those four hours. Nineteen years. In October 1815 he was released; he'd gone in in 1796, for breaking a pane of glass and taking a loaf of bread.

A brief parenthesis at this point. In the present author's writings on the penal question and damnation by law, this is the second time that the theft of a loaf of bread has led to the ruin of a man's life. Claude Gueux* stole a loaf of bread; Jean Valjean stole a loaf of bread. In London, according to English statistics, hunger is the immediate cause of four-fifths of all thefts.

Jean Valjean had gone into the prison sobbing and trembling; he came out unemotional. He'd been in despair when he entered; he was merely grim when he left.

What had happened inside the man's soul?

vii. Despair Seen from Within

Let's try to answer that question.

It's vital for society to look at such things, because society has created them in the first place.

He was, as we've said, an ignorant man, but he wasn't stupid. Light was innately shining inside him. Misfortunes also enlighten, in their own way, and they had added to the illumination within his mind. Lashings, chains, solitary confinement, daily wear and tear, the burning prison sun, and the convict's plank bed, had driven him to examine his own conscience and ponder.

He put the whole situation on trial.

First of all he sat in judgement on himself.

He could see that he wasn't an innocent man who was being punished unjustly. He admitted that he'd done something drastic, reprehensible. Perhaps, if he'd asked for the loaf of bread, it wouldn't have been denied him; and anyhow, it would have been better to wait, either for kindness or for work. Can you wait when you're starving, it might be objected—but that argument isn't unanswerable. In the first place, very few people literally starve to death; and in the second place, whether it's a blessing or a curse, human beings are so designed that they can stand long, hard suffering, both morally and physically, before they die of any cause. He should have been patient, then. That would have been better— even for the poor little children. He, frail wretched fellow, had done foolishly when he tried to grab the whole of society by the throat and fancied that he could get out of his troubles by stealing. The way that leads to disgrace is always a bad way out of trouble. In short, he'd been wrong.

But then he started to ask himself:

Was he the only person who had been wrong, in that disastrous chain of events? For one thing, wasn't it a serious matter if he, a hard-working, industrious man, couldn't find any work and couldn't get any bread? And for another thing, once the crime had been committed and confessed, hadn't the penalty been rather cruel— unnecessarily so? Hadn't the law's punishment been worse than the criminal's crime? Hadn't there been too much weight on one side of the balance—the expiatory side—with the result that the offence had been reversed rather than removed: the guilty man's crime had been replaced by a crime of oppression, the criminal had been turned into a victim, and society now owed him a debt rather than the other way round; so that justice was ultimately on the side of the very person who had violated justice? Hadn't the situation been aggravated by the additional penalties imposed for his successive attempts to escape? And hadn't his punishment finally become a sort of assault committed by a stronger body on a weaker body—a crime committed by society against the individual—a crime that happened again every day and lasted for nineteen years?

Does human society have any right to force its own members to suffer from its thoughtless negligence or premeditated callousness? Does it have any right to trap the poorer classes for ever between a lack—lack of work—and an excess—excess of punishment? If, simply by chance, some of its members have been less endowed with wealth than others, isn't it a monstrous thing that society should treat them in such a way? Aren't they precisely the ones who deserve to be treated with the greatest kindness?

He asked himself these questions and answered them, and sat in judgement on society and sentenced it.

He sentenced it to his hatred.

He held it responsible for the things he was suffering; and he decided that he wouldn't feel the slightest compunction if, some day, he was given the chance to call it to account. He told himself that the wrongs now being inflicted on him were out of proportion to the wrongs he had done. In short, he concluded that though it may not have been, strictly speaking, unfair to punish him, it was certainly wicked.

It may be foolish and silly to get angry; it may be wrong; but when a person feels outraged, there's some reason at the bottom of it somewhere. And Jean Valjean did feel outraged.

In addition, human society had never done him anything but evil. She had shown him only the cruel face she turns toward those she wants to strike down—the face she calls 'Justice'. Whenever men had touched him, it had been to hurt him. Every time he had come into contact with them, it had been a blow. Never since childhood had he been given a friendly word or a kindly glance by anyone except his mother and his sister. As suffering followed suffering, he came to the conclusion that life was a war—a war in which he was one of the losers. His only weapon was hatred. He resolved to sharpen it in prison and take it away with him when he left.

Some rather ignorant monks in Toulon ran a school for the prisoners, and taught the bare essentials to any of the wretches who were willing to listen. Well, he was among those who were willing. At the age of 40, he went to school and learnt to read and write and count. He felt that by strengthening his brains, he could strengthen his hatred. In some situations, education and enlightenment can actually aggravate evil.

Not only did he sit in judgement on society for creating his misfortunes, but also, sad to say, he sat in judgement on Providence for creating that society.

Providence, too, he condemned.

So, during those nineteen years of torment and slavery, this human being rose and fell at the same time. Light entered him from one side, and darkness entered him from the other.

As we've seen, Jean Valjean wasn't innately bad. He was still basically good when he reached the jail. In that place he condemned society—and could feel himself becoming wicked; in that place he also condemned Providence—and could feel himself becoming irreligious.

At this point it's difficult to avoid a brief observation.

Can human nature ever be utterly transformed by such means— inwardly and outwardly? God made man good;* can he be made wicked by man? Can the human soul be totally reshaped by circumstances, and turn bad when its destiny is bad? Can the human heart become warped, permanently blighted, permanently damaged, under the impact of a stress that is too severe for it—like a vertebral column under a roof that is too low for it? Doesn't every human soul—and, in particular, didn't Jean Valjean's soul—contain an initial spark, an element of the divine, which remains incorruptible in this world and immortal in the next? Can't goodness nurture and kindle and ignite it, and make it burst into flame and blaze bright? And can evil ever wholly extinguish it?

Serious, difficult questions; but if any physiologist had been at Toulon during a rest period (which Jean Valjean used as a reflection period) and had seen that serious, silent, sullen, thoughtful convict—cast out by the law, and damned by civilization—sitting with his arms folded on the bar of some windlass, the end of his chain stuffed into his pocket so that it wouldn't drag, while he stared angrily at the human race and grimly at the heavens—then the physiologist might well have denied (and denied without hesitation) that Jean Valjean's soul contained any such spark.

Indeed—and we won't dispute this—scientific observers wouldn't have been able to find any solution for this man's problems. They might have pitied him for his law-caused sickness, but they wouldn't have attempted to treat it; they would have turned away from the sight of the chasms within his soul, and, like Dante at the gates of hell,* they would have wiped out of his life the word that God's finger nevertheless does write on the brow of every human being—*Hope!*

Was Jean Valjean's state of mind as clear to the man himself as I've tried to make it to my readers during the above discussion? Did Jean Valjean have any precise idea of the various components of his moral degradation—either while they were taking shape, or afterwards? Had this rough, illiterate man really noticed the successive ideas that had led him up and down, step by step, till he reached the dismal realm that formed the inner landscape of his mind for so many years? Was he aware of everything that had happened inside him, and everything that was now stirring there? I wouldn't presume to say so; indeed, I don't believe so. Jean Valjean was so ignorant that his thoughts must have remained very vague, even after all his troubles. At times he wouldn't have been clear about his own feelings. Jean Valjean was in the dark; he was suffering in the dark; he was hating in the dark; you might say that he hated whatever was ahead of him. He was living constantly in the shadows, groping about like a blind man, like a dreamer. Yet at times, quite suddenly, either from within himself or from outside, a rush of anger came over him, an overflow from his sufferings, a sudden bright flash of lightning that lit up his entire soul and fleetingly revealed everywhere around him, in a hideous glow of light, the dreadful precipices and dismal panoramas of his fate.

After the flash of lightning had passed, night fell again—and where was he? He no longer had any idea.

Punishments of such a kind—punishments that are predominantly merciless, and therefore brutalizing—characteristically turn a man, bit by bit, by a process of mindless transformation, into a wild animal. Sometimes a ferocious animal. The law can have that strange effect when it operates on a human soul, as Jean Valjean's repetitive, stubborn attempts to escape demonstrate. Utterly useless and foolish though those attempts were, Jean Valjean would have kept repeating them as often as he had the chance, without thinking for a moment what the result would be, or what his past experiences had been. He escaped simply on impulse, like a wolf who finds its cage open. Instinct told him: 'Get away!' Reason would have said: 'Stay!' But in the presence of so intense a temptation, reason vanished, and only instinct remained. It was a purely animal reaction. And when he was recaptured, the further punishments inflicted on him merely made him more savage than ever.

One point we mustn't overlook: he was physically stronger than any other inmate of the jail. When it came to hard labour—hauling up a cable, or turning a windlass—Jean Valjean was the equal of four ordinary men. Sometimes he'd lift immense weights on his back and hold them there, doing the work of the instrument now known as a 'jack' (formerly called an *orgueil*—which, by the way, is how the Rue Montorgueil, near Les Halles in Paris, got its name). His fellow prisoners called him Jean-the-Jack. On one occasion, when the balcony of the Toulon Town Hall was being repaired, one of its supports (Puget's marvellous caryatids)* tottered and was on the point of falling. Jean Valjean, who happened to be there, held it up with his shoulder until the workmen had time to reach it.

His agility was even greater than his strength. Some convicts are constantly dreaming of escape, and eventually unite strength and skill in what is really a specialist discipline. They become muscle specialists. Such prisoners, perpetually envious of the birds and the flies, practise a mysterious daily ritual of weight science. Scaling perpendicular walls, and finding footholds where the surface hardly seemed to have the merest dint, became child's play to Jean Valjean. Given the angle of a wall, he would use the pressure of his back and thighs to hoist himself up three storeys as if by magic, with his elbows and heels braced against the rough surface of the stone. Sometimes, by such methods, he even reached the prison roof.

He didn't say much, and he didn't laugh. It took some particularly intense emotion to get a grim convict's laugh out of him. This happened once or twice a year—and sounded like an echo of the devil's laughter. Outwardly he seemed to be forever brooding on something terrible.

And he was.

His thoughts were the thoughts of a crushed mind and an unfinished soul, and therefore they were frail; but he dimly felt that something monstrous was burdening him. He was crawling through a realm of pallid, ill-defined twilight; and every time he turned his head and tried to look up, he could discern, with mingled rage and terror, a dreadful mass of entities, laws, prejudices, people, and actions piling up, building up, rising up above him with horrible ramparts as far as the eye could see. He couldn't make out its contours, he was stunned by its immensity. It was simply the colossal pyramid known to us as civilization. Here and there within this teeming, shapeless mass he could make out, sometimes nearby, sometimes far away on inaccessible heights, some composition, some detail brilliantly lit up—here a warder with his truncheon, here a gendarme with his sword, over there a mitred archbishop, and at the very top, in a kind of sunburst, the Emperor crowned and resplendent. It seemed to him that these distant glories, instead of dispelling his darkness, made it all the blacker and more dismal. And all these things—laws, prejudices, deeds, people, entities—came and went above him, impelled with the strange and complex motion that God imposes on civilization. They walked right over him, they trampled him down, with extraordinarily serene cruelty and extraordinarily relentless indifference. Human beings who have been rejected by the law—ill-starred souls who have fallen as low as misfortune can push them and are lost in a limbo so low that they are no longer visible—can feel their heads crushed beneath the whole weight of society, so formidable to those who are outcasts and so terrible to those who are downtrodden.

That was Jean Valjean's situation when he pondered—and so what thoughts could he possibly have?

If a millet seed underneath a millstone could think, no doubt it would think what Jean Valjean did.

All these things—realities teeming with wraiths, fantasies teeming with realities—had ultimately produced an almost indescribable mental state deep inside him.

Now and then he'd pause in the midst of his prison work. He'd start to think. His mind, more mature yet also more troubled than it used to be, would grow rebellious. Everything that had happened to him would seem absurd; everything that was now surrounding him would seem impossible. 'It's just a dream', he'd tell himself. He'd look at the warder standing only a few steps away; the warder would look like a mere phantom to him—and suddenly the phantom would start beating him with its truncheon.

The visible world, the world of nature, hardly existed for him. It would almost be true to say that Jean Valjean had no sun, no fine summer days, no clear skies, no cool April dawns. His soul was lit, day after day, by some faint glimmer through a vent-hole.

Finally, let's sum up what we've just been saying—as much of it as can be summed up and expressed in concrete terms. We'll simply observe that, thanks to nineteen years of prison training, Jean Valjean the harmless tree-pruner of Faverolles and dangerous criminal of Toulon became capable of doing wrong in two different ways: first, a sudden unpremeditated type of wrongdoing, utterly thoughtless, utterly instinctive, a kind of retaliation for the misfortunes he had suffered; and secondly, a serious, deliberate type of wrongdoing, carefully thought out and premeditated with all the false ideas that such misfortunes can breed. As happens with people of a certain character, his plans went through three successive stages: reasoning, decision-making, and stubborn perseverance. Habitual resentment, bitter-mindedness, and a deep sense of the injuries he had suffered, motivated him to act even against good, innocent, or righteous people—if any such creatures really did exist. All his thoughts started and ended with hatred for human laws. And unless its growth is arrested by some providential incident, such a hatred will in time become a hatred of society, then a hatred of the human race, then a hatred of all creation, which will express itself in an unfocused, incessant, vicious urge to hurt any living creature of any kind whatever.—You can see that the ticket-of-leave wasn't altogether wrong when it characterized Jean Valjean as 'highly dangerous'.

Year by year, this human soul had withered more and more— slowly, but fatally. Dried-up hearts have dry eyes. When he left prison, he hadn't shed a tear for nineteen years.

ix. New Troubles

When the time came for Jean Valjean to leave prison, and he heard the strange words 'You are free', his situation seemed implausible, unreal; a ray of brilliant light, the true light of the living, shot through him. But this radiance quickly faded. Jean Valjean had been dazzled by the idea of freedom. He had believed in a new life. Soon, very soon, he discovered what kind of freedom comes with a yellow ticket attached to it.

And on top of that, there were many other bitter disappointments.

He'd calculated that his savings during his stay in prison amounted to one hundred and seventy-one francs. True, he'd forgotten to allow for the compulsory rest on Sundays and holidays, which subtracted about twenty-four francs during the nineteen years. But even apart from that point, his savings had been reduced by various local regulations to a total of one hundred and nine francs fifteen sous, and that was the amount counted out to him when he left.

He didn't understand any of this, and thought he'd been cheated—to put it bluntly, robbed.

The day after his release, he saw some men unloading bales outside an orange-blossom perfumery in Grasse. He offered his services. The job was urgent, so he was taken on. He set to work. He was clever, strong, and skilful; he did his best; the boss seemed to be satisfied. While he was working away, a gendarme came past, noticed him, and asked to see his papers. He had to produce the yellow ticket. Then he went back to work. Some time earlier, he'd asked one of the workers how much they earned at this job; and he'd been told, 'Thirty sous a day.' That evening he went to the boss and asked for his wages, since he had to leave next morning. The boss handed him twenty-five sous without a word of explanation. He protested. The reply was: 'That's good enough for the likes of you.' He kept on. The boss looked him between the eyes and said: 'Don't go getting yourself jugged!'[1]

Once again he felt he'd been robbed.

Society—the government—had robbed him on a grand scale by reducing his savings. Now an individual had followed suit and robbed him on a small scale.

Release isn't deliverance. You can leave your jail behind, but not your sentence.

That's what had happened to him in Grasse. We've already seen what kind of welcome he got in Digne.

x. He Wakes Up

So, as the cathedral clock was striking two, Jean Valjean woke up.

What woke him was the fact that the bed was too comfortable. For nearly twenty years he hadn't slept in a bed, and although

---

[1] Imprisoned [*Hugo's note*].

he was still dressed, the sensation was too novel not to disturb his sleep.

He'd been asleep for over four hours. He no longer felt tired. He was used to relatively short spells of sleep.

He opened his eyes and gazed briefly at the darkness around him; then he shut them again and tried to get back to sleep.

When you've had a day disrupted with many different sensations, when your mind is preoccupied, you can fall asleep once but not a second time. Sleep comes more easily than it comes back. That's how it now was with Jean Valjean. He couldn't get back to sleep, and he began to think.

It was one of those times when the mind is full of disturbing ideas. His mind kept drifting vaguely to and fro. Old memories and recent memories floated there in a jumbled mass and mingled chaotically, changing shape, enlarging out of all proportion, then suddenly vanishing as if in a muddy, turbulent stream. Many different thoughts came to him, but one of them kept reappearing and driving out the others. We'll state it at once: he'd noticed the six sets of silver and the big ladle that Madame Magloire had put on the table.

Those six sets of silver obsessed him.—They were right there.—Only a few steps away.—The old servant had put them in a little cupboard near the head of the bed in the next room.—He'd been passing through that room at the time, on the way to his current room.—He'd taken good note of that cupboard.—On the right, as you came in from the dining room.—They were huge.—And antique silverwork.—Along with the big ladle, they should fetch at least two hundred francs.—Twice as much as he'd been able to earn in nineteen years.—Mind you, he would have earned more if 'the government' hadn't 'robbed' him.

His mind wavered back and forth for a whole hour, going through something of a struggle. The clock struck three. He opened his eyes again, abruptly sat up, put out an arm, and groped around for the knapsack that he'd tossed into a corner of the alcove. Then he swung out his legs and put his feet on the ground, and found himself seated on the edge of his bed, almost without knowing how he'd got there.

For a while he remained there, thinking. His position would have looked rather sinister to anyone who happened to see him there in the shadows—the only creature awake in the sleeping house.

Suddenly he bent down, took off his shoes, and put them very quietly on the mat beside the bed. Then he stopped moving and resumed his pensive stance.

During that dreadful meditation, the ideas we've just described kept stirring up his brain, coming and going and returning incessantly, pressing down on him like a weight. And then—without knowing why, and with the mechanical insistence that happens when the mind is reflecting—he started to think also about a convict named Brevet (he'd known him in jail) whose trousers were held up only by a single strip of knitted cotton. The pattern on that cotton kept coming back to his mind.

He remained in the same position, and might have stayed like that till daybreak, if the clock hadn't struck—marking the quarter- or the half-hour. That sound seemed to tell him: 'Get moving!'

He stood up, hesitated a moment longer, and listened. The entire house was silent. Then he walked straight ahead, very cautiously, toward the window, which was dimly visible. The night wasn't very dark; there was a full moon, across which large windblown clouds were scudding. This created alternating patches of light and darkness outside—eclipses and illuminations; indoors it created a kind of twilight, enough for you to see where you were going. The clouds made it an intermittent twilight, like the light that falls through a cellar window when pedestrians walk to and fro beyond it. Jean Valjean reached the window and examined it. It wasn't barred; it opened onto the garden; and, in accordance with local custom, it was fastened only by a small latch. He opened it—but instantly closed it again, as a stiff, cold breeze swept into the room. He eyed the garden with the intent gaze of someone studying a scene rather than looking at it. The garden was surrounded by a fairly low white wall—an easy thing to climb over. Beyond, in the background, he could make out a number of treetops spaced at regular intervals, showing that the wall separated the garden from some kind of avenue or lane lined with trees.

Having looked the place over, he swung round with the air of someone who has made a decision. He walked into the alcove, took his knapsack, opened it, searched through it, and took out something, which he put on the bed. He stuffed his shoes into one of his pockets, closed the knapsack, tossed it onto his back, and put on his cap, pulling it down almost over his eyes. He groped for his stick and put it in a corner near the window. Then he came back to the bed and coolly picked up the object he had left on it. It looked like a short iron bar with one sharp, pointed end, like a spear.

In the gloom, it would have been hard to recognize the purpose of this piece of iron. Might it have been a lever? Might it have been a bludgeon?

By daylight you would have seen that it was simply a miner's spike. In those days, convicts were sometimes put to work quarrying stone from the hills around Toulon, and it wasn't unusual for them to have mining tools in their possession. Miners' spikes are made of solid iron with a pointed lower end to be driven into the rock.

He picked up the spike in his right hand, held his breath, and tiptoed toward the door of the next room (which, as we know, was the bishop's). When he got to the door, he found it ajar. The bishop hadn't even closed it.

xi. His Next Move

Jean Valjean listened. Not a sound.

He gave the door a push.

He pushed it with the tip of one finger, very lightly, with the tense, stealthy, surreptitious motion of a cat trying to get indoors.

The door yielded to his push and moved a little, silently, imperceptibly, widening the opening a fraction.

He waited a moment, then pushed the door again, more firmly.

It continued to yield in silence. Now the opening was large enough to let him through. But a small table stood close beside the door at an awkward angle, blocking the entrance.

Jean Valjean saw the problem. Whatever the cost, the opening had to be enlarged still further.

He took the plunge and pushed the door a third time, harder than before. This time one of the hinges, which needed oiling, let out a long raucous squeak in the darkness.

Jean Valjean shuddered. To him, it sounded as clear and awesome as the last trumpet on the Day of Judgement.

For a few moments his mind elaborated the sound fantastically, almost as if the hinge had suddenly sprung to life and become a terrible animate creature barking like a dog to warn the whole world and rouse everyone who was asleep.

He halted, trembling, distraught, and sank back onto his heels. He could hear the arteries of his temples beating like hammers in a forge, and his breath seemed to be making a sound like wind leaving a cavern. He was positive that the ghastly din made by that angry hinge must have shaken up the whole house like an earthquake. At his touch the door had sounded the alarm as loudly as it could; the old man was going to jump out of bed, the two old women were going to scream, people were going to come running to help; in a quarter of an hour the whole town would be abuzz and the gendarmes would be on the move. For a moment he thought he was lost.

He stayed right where he was, petrified like the proverbial pillar of salt. He didn't dare to move a muscle.

Several minutes slipped by. The door was wide open. He ventured a glance into the room. Nothing had stirred. He listened. Not a rustle in the house. The sound of the rusty hinge hadn't woken anyone.

That initial danger was over; but he was still in a state of fearful turmoil. All the same, he didn't back down. Even when he thought he was lost, he hadn't backed down. And now his one thought was to get the thing over as fast as possible. He took a step into the room.

The room was perfectly tranquil. Here and there, faint, indistinct shapes could be made out—by daylight, they were papers strewn across a table, open folios, volumes piled on a stool, an armchair with clothes on it, a prie-dieu; but at the moment, they were merely dark crannies and lighter patches. Jean Valjean moved forward cautiously, making sure he didn't bump into the furniture. In the depths of the room he could hear the calm, steady breathing of the sleeping bishop.

Suddenly he stopped. He was right next to the bed. He'd reached it sooner than he expected.

Sometimes Nature blends her scenes and designs with our actions, showing a solemn, intelligent aptness when she does so—as if she wanted us to reflect. For nearly half an hour a huge mass of cloud had been covering the sky. But just when Jean Valjean stopped beside the bed, the cloud mass broke up, as if on purpose; a long ray of moonlight suddenly fell through the high window and lit the bishop's pallid face. He was sleeping peacefully in his bed. Because of the cold Alpine night he was almost fully dressed, in a brown woollen garment with wrist-length sleeves. His head lay back on the pillow in a negligent attitude of repose; over the bedside dangled his hand with its episcopal ring—the hand that had done so many good deeds and pious acts. His whole face was glowing with a vague look of contentment, hope, and beatitude. It was something more than a smile—almost a radiance. On his brow lay an indescribable reflection from some unseen source of light. Righteous souls contemplate a mysterious heaven in their sleep.

A shaft of light from that heaven had fallen on the bishop.

Yet it was also a glowing transparency—because that heaven was within him. It was his conscience.

And when the moonlight overlay (so to speak) that inner radiance, there seemed to be a halo around the sleeping bishop. It was mild, however; it was veiled in inexpressible twilight. The moon in the heavens, the slumbering universe, the unstirring garden, the still house, the time, the moment, the silence, added something unutterable, something curiously solemn, to the wise man's venerable repose, so that a kind of serene and majestic aureole shrouded his white hair and his shut eyes, his face replete with hope and trust, his elderly head and his childish sleep.

There was something almost divine within this man, something unconsciously noble.

As for Jean Valjean, he stood there in the shadows with the iron bar in his hand, unmoving, terrified by the sight of the luminous old man. He had never seen anything like it. The man's assurance bewildered him. Surely the moral universe contains no more remarkable sight than this—a restless, tormented conscience, on the brink of a crime, faced with the slumber of a righteous soul.

He was dimly, but intensely, conscious that such a slumber—in such isolation, and in the presence of someone like himself—had something sublime about it.

Nobody, not even he himself, could have said what was going on inside him. To have any idea of it, you would need to imagine the utmost violence juxtaposed with the utmost gentleness. Nothing definite could have been seen in his face. It had a kind of stunned, haggard look. He was looking at—*that*. Nothing more. But what was he thinking? No one could have guessed. It was plain enough that he was deeply moved—thrown off balance. But by what kind of emotion?

He couldn't take his eyes off the old man. The only thing clearly apparent in his posture and appearance was a state of curious uncertainty. He seemed to be wavering between two chasms—one that would lead to destruction, and one that would lead to salvation. He seemed on the point of smashing the man's skull—or else kissing his hand.

After a short while, his left hand slowly rose to his head, and he took off his cap. Then the hand moved down again, just as slowly, and Jean Valjean resumed his contemplations—cap in left hand, bludgeon in right hand, hair bristling on his brutish head.

Under that dreadful gaze the bishop continued to sleep with the utmost tranquillity.

Over the fireplace, a ray of moonlight dimly illuminated a crucifix, which seemed to stretch out its arms toward both of them, blessing one and forgiving the other.

Suddenly Jean Valjean put his cap back on his head and, without looking at the bishop, walked quickly alongside the bed to the cupboard faintly visible near the bedhead. He raised the iron spike as if to force the lock, but the key was already there. He opened the door. The very first thing he saw was the basket of silverware. He took it; moved across the room with long, negligent strides, regardless of the noise; reached the door; re-entered the oratory, opened the window, picked up his stick, clambered over the windowsill, tipped the silver into his knapsack, threw away the basket, crossed the garden, leaped over the wall like a tiger, and ran away.

xii. The Bishop Goes to Work

Next morning, at sunrise, Monseigneur Bienvenu was out walking in his garden. Madame Magloire came running to him in a state of great distress.

'Monseigneur, Monseigneur,' she cried, 'the silverware basket—does Your Lordship know where it is?'

'Yes', said the bishop.

'Thank the Lord!' she declared. 'I couldn't make out what had become of it.'

The bishop had just retrieved the basket from one of the flower-beds. He passed it to Madame Magloire.

'Here it is.'

'Why, there's nothing inside it!' she said. 'Where's the silver?'

'Oh!' said the bishop. 'So it's the silver you're thinking about, is it? Well, I don't know where that is.'

'Good heavens, it's been stolen! That man last night—he stole it!'

Madame Magloire was an active old woman. Within a moment, in her sprightly way, she had rushed to the oratory, gone into the alcove, and returned to the bishop. The bishop was stooped in mourning over a cochlearia from Les Guillons,* which had been crushed by the basket when it fell into the flowerbed. At Madame Magloire's cry, he stood up.

'Monseigneur, the man's gone! The silver's been stolen!'

As she uttered this exclamation, she noticed a corner of the garden where there were signs that the wall had been climbed, and a stone had been dislodged from the coping.

'Look, that's where he went! He climbed out into Cochefilet Lane! Oh, what a villain! He's stolen our silver!'

The bishop was silent for a moment. Then he looked up at Madame Magloire with a serious expression in his eyes, and said gently:

'Well, in the first place, did the silver belong to us?'

Madame Magloire was dumbfounded. There was another silence; then the bishop went on:

'It was wrong of me, Madame Magloire, to keep that silver back for so long. It really belonged to the poor. And who was that man? Obviously he was one of the poor.'

'Lord in heaven!' returned Madame Magloire. 'I'm not thinking about myself or Mademoiselle. It doesn't matter to us. I'm thinking about Your Lordship. What is Your Lordship going to eat with now?'

The bishop looked at her in astonishment.

'But surely there's some pewter, isn't there?'

Madame Magloire shrugged her shoulders.

'Pewter smells.'

'Well, what about iron?'

Madame Magloire grimaced expressively.

'Iron has a taste.'

'Well, wood, then', said the bishop.

A few moments later he was breakfasting at the very table where

Jean Valjean had been sitting the night before. During the meal, he cheerily observed to his sister (who didn't say anything) and Madame Magloire (who merely muttered under her breath) that nobody needs spoons and forks, even wooden ones, to dip a piece of bread into a bowl of milk.

'Just imagine!' declared Madame Magloire to herself, while she scurried to and fro; 'taking in such a man as that! and giving him a berth for the night right next to you! Well, it's a mercy he didn't do anything worse than stealing! Lord above! I get the shudders just thinking about it!'

Just as the brother and sister were on the point of rising from the table, there was a knock at the door.

'Come in', said the bishop.

The door opened. An odd and dangerous-looking group of people appeared on the threshold. Three men were gripping a fourth by the collar. The three men were gendarmes; the fourth was Jean Valjean.

An officer was standing by the door; he seemed to be in charge of the group. He entered the room and, with a military salute, advanced toward the bishop.

'Monseigneur—' he said.

Jean Valjean had been looking glum and downcast; but at that word he raised his head in stupefaction.

'Monseigneur!' he muttered. 'So that isn't the curé, then?'

'Quiet!' said one of the gendarmes. 'That's his lordship the bishop.'

Meanwhile Monseigneur Bienvenu was moving toward them as quickly as his age allowed.

'Oh, there you are!' he exclaimed, looking at Jean Valjean. 'I'm very glad to see you. But look here—I gave you the candlesticks too. They're silver like the other things, and you could easily get two hundred francs for them. Why didn't you take them with the rest of your silverware?'

Jean Valjean opened his eyes wide, and looked at the venerable bishop with an expression beyond the power of any human language to describe.

'Then this fellow was telling the truth, Monseigneur?' said the officer. 'We came across him. The way he was moving, he seemed to be making a getaway. We arrested him on suspicion. He had all this silver—'

'And he told you', the bishop interrupted with a smile, 'that he'd been given it by a nice old priest at whose house he'd spent the night? I can see just how it was. And so you brought him back here, did you? Well, it was just a misunderstanding.'

'In that case', said the officer, 'I suppose we can let him go.'

'Of course you can', replied the bishop.

The gendarmes released Jean Valjean. He shrank back.

'Are you really letting me go?' he asked. He was mumbling indistinctly, like a man talking in his sleep.

'We're letting you go all right', said one of the gendarmes. 'What's the matter? Don't you understand?'

'Before you go, my friend,' the bishop added, 'here are your candlesticks. Go on, take them.'

He went to the mantelpiece, took the two silver candlesticks, and handed them to Jean Valjean. The two women didn't venture a word, look, or gesture to stop him. They simply watched it happen.

Jean Valjean was trembling all over. He took the candlesticks mechanically, with a dazed look.

'Now then,' said the bishop, 'go in peace. And by the way, my friend, next time you come here, there's no need to go through the garden. You can always get in and out through the front door. It's only on a latch, day and night.'

Then he turned to the gendarmes.

'Thank you, gentlemen, you can go now.'

The gendarmes withdrew.

Jean Valjean looked like a man about to faint.

The bishop moved closer to him, and said quietly:

'Don't forget—don't ever forget—that you've promised me to use this silver to turn yourself into an honest man.'

Jean Valjean couldn't recall having made any promise at all. He stood there speechless. The bishop had uttered the words quite emphatically. He went on, in a rather solemn way:

'Brother Jean Valjean, you no longer belong to evil, but to good. What I'm doing is buying your soul. I'm taking it away from black thoughts and the spirit of perdition, and I'm giving it to God.'

from *Things Seen*

The Living Pictures

During autumn 1846 there was a show that created an immense sensation in Paris. It consisted of naked women, draped only in pink tights and a gauze skirt, performing tableaux that were known as 'Living Pictures', with a few men to link the groups. This went on at the Porte-Saint-Martin* and the Circus. I was curious to go along one evening and see them at close range. I went into the Porte-Saint-Martin theatre, where, incidentally, *Lucrezia Borgia* was about to be revived. Villemont, the stage manager (a shabby-looking intelligent lad), said to me, 'I'll let you into the gynaeceum.' He led me into a space behind the backcloth, lit by battens and numerous side-lights. There were about twenty men coming and going, working or watching—authors, actors, firemen, lampmen, stagehands, etc.— and, in the midst of these men, seven or eight stark naked women coming and going likewise, with the utmost simplicity and tranquillity. The pink silk tights that covered them from the feet to the neck were so thin and transparent that you could see not only the toes, the navel, the nipples, but also the veins and the colour of every mark on the skin in every part of the body. Toward the pelvis, however, the tights were thicker and you could make out only the shape. The men who assisted them were dressed similarly. All these people were English. Every few minutes the curtain parted and they performed a tableau. For that purpose, they were placed and arranged in motionless poses on a large wooden disc, which revolved on a pivot. A fourteen-year-old boy, who lay underneath on a mattress, was enough to work the disc. The men and women were rigged out in bits of gauze or merino that were very ugly from a distance and very squalid at close range. They were pink statues. When the disc had completed one revolution and shown the statues from all angles to the spectators huddled in the dark auditorium, the curtain closed, another tableau was arranged, and a moment later the whole thing started again.

Two of the women were very pretty. One of them looked like Madame Rey, who played the queen in *Ruy Blas** in 1840. She was the one who represented Venus. She was physically very striking. Another was more than pretty, she was beautiful and stately. You'd never see anything more magnificent than her sad dark eyes, her scornful mouth, her ravishing yet haughty smile. I think her name was Maria. In a scene depicting a slave market, she had all the imperious despair and stoic dejection of a queen sold stark naked in the street to the first taker. Her tights, split at the hip, allowed a glimpse of her firm white flesh. By the way, all of them were poor girls from London. All of them had filthy fingernails.

Backstage, they shared a laugh readily with stagehands and writers alike, uttering broken French and arranging all sorts of dreadful cheap finery on their lovely faces. They wore the peaceful smile of either perfect innocence or utter corruption.

The Princes

The Duc de Montpensier greets all passers-by gracefully and pleasantly. The Duc d'Aumale greets them as little as he can; at Neuilly,* they say that he doesn't want to mess his hair; he merely lifts the brim of his hat. The Duc de Nemours does it neither as enthusiastically as Monsieur de Montpensier nor as grudgingly as Monsieur d'Aumale. Furthermore, women say that when he greets them he looks at them 'in an embarrassing way'.

The Palais royal has been used for the princes' frolics and secret escapades before marriage. It has a little door with a female doorkeeper appointed specifically for that purpose. One of my wife's former chambermaids, named Mélanie Rolland, used to serve under that woman, who is a kind of madam. Until his marriage, Monsieur de Montpensier had Madame Beausire of the Opéra as his mistress. She is a pretty woman, and married. The husband got wind of the business. He began spying on his wife. One day, Madame Beausire arrived at the Palais royal all of a quiver. She rushed upstairs. A man ascended behind her, so close that he could hear the rustle of her evening gown. It was her husband, a surly kind of fellow who wasn't living with her and whom she never saw. 'Save me!' said Madame Beausire to the doorkeeper, and went up to the next floor. 'Where are you going, sir?' asked the doorkeeper. 'I want to know', said the husband boldly, 'where that woman who has just gone upstairs is going.' 'I don't know what you're talking about.' 'Well, I *do* know, and I want to see that woman.' 'I'll call the sentry and get you put behind bars.' 'I'll call the police superintendent and get my wife arrested.'

The quarrel grew more and more heated. The prince was very much afraid; he could hear Monsieur Beausire's breathing on the staircase. At that moment, Mélanie, who was in a recess, had an idea. She put her head out of a window and said to the doorkeeper, 'Look here, Madame, please send that man away; I don't know him at all, and he's followed me all the way here!' At the sound of her voice the husband was stunned. He looked at her, thought he'd made a mistake, and went away absolutely satisfied, after offering thousands of apologies.

Mélanie is married to a soldier whose release from the army Monsieur de Montpensier arranged. She is now Madame Marty and works as a corset-maker. She lives at 8 Rue des Orties, on the mezzanine floor.

I might add that Monsieur de Montpensier was very much in love with Madame Beausire. Last October, the night before he left for Madrid to marry the Infanta,* he spent the night with Madame Beausire in his little room at the Palais royal. Both of them wept as they parted. Since then, he has never set eyes on her. Madame Beausire made many attempts to get in touch with him; she went to Mélanie and asked her to carry letters to him. Mélanie undertook the task, went to the Tuileries,* and delivered the letters. But one day the prince's valet told her not to come back any more and to tell Madame Beausire that she was refused admittance at the Tuileries. Poor woman, poor girls, playthings of the princes' youthful caprices! Wretched indeed if they aren't in love, more wretched still if they are!

from *Les Contemplations*

Paroles dans l'ombre

Elle disait: C'est vrai, j'ai tort de vouloir mieux;
Les heures sont ainsi très doucement passées;
Vous êtes là; mes yeux ne quittent pas vos yeux
Où je regarde aller et venir vos pensées.

Vous voir est un bonheur; je ne l'ai pas complet.   5
Sans doute c'est encor bien charmant de la sorte.
Je veille, car je sais tout ce qui vous déplaît,
A ce que nul fâcheux ne vienne ouvrir la porte;

Je me fais bien petite en mon coin près de vous,
Vous êtes mon lion, je suis votre colombe;   10
J'entends de vos papiers le bruit paisible et doux;
Je ramasse parfois votre plume qui tombe;

Sans doute je vous ai, sans doute je vous voi.
La pensée est un vin dont les rêveurs sont ivres,
Je le sais; mais pourtant je veux qu'on songe à moi.   15
Quand vous êtes ainsi tout un soir dans vos livres,

Sans relever la tête et sans me dire un mot,
Une ombre reste au fond de mon cœur qui vous aime;
Et, pour que je vous voie entièrement, il faut
Me regarder un peu de temps en temps vous-même.   20

Un Soir que je regardais le ciel

Elle me dit, un soir, en souriant:
—Ami, pourquoi contemplez-vous sans cesse
Le jour qui fuit, ou l'ombre qui s'abaisse,

from *Contemplations*

Uttered in the Shadows

She said: 'I shouldn't long for more, I know;
Time passes very pleasantly just so;
You're there; I never turn my eyes from yours,
Where I can watch your thoughts flit to and fro.

To see you is a blessing; it's still more
Delightful when it's incomplete, I'm sure.
I know what bothers you, so I keep guard
And never let a nuisance through the door.

I stay near, in my corner, very small;
Your papers murmur their calm gentle call;
You are my lion, I'm your turtledove;
I pick your pen up if you let it fall.

No doubt I have you, and I see you, too.
The wine of thought makes dreamers drunk, it's true;
All the same, I do want to be remembered.
When you keep to your books the whole night through,

And never lift your head or speak to me,
A shadow falls across my constancy;
For me to see you fully, you do need
To look at me sometimes, if only fleetingly.'

While Looking at the Heavens One Evening

She said to me one evening, with a smile:
'Why are you contemplating all this while
The golden star that climbs the eastern knoll,

Ou l'astre d'or qui monte à l'orient?
Que font vos yeux là-haut? je les réclame.　　　　5
Quittez le ciel; regardez dans mon âme!

Dans ce ciel vaste, ombre où vous vous plaisez,
Où vos regards démesurés vont lire,
Qu'apprendrez-vous qui vaille mon sourire?
Qu'apprendras-tu qui vaille nos baisers?　　　　10
Oh! de mon cœur lève les chastes voiles.
Si tu savais comme il est pleine d'étoiles!

Que de soleils! Vois-tu, quand nous aimons,
Tout est en nous un radieux spectacle.
Le dévouement, rayonnant sur l'obstacle,　　　　15
Vaut bien Vénus qui brille sur les monts.
Le vaste azur n'est rien, je te l'atteste.
Le ciel que j'ai dans l'âme est plus céleste!

C'est beau de voir un astre s'allumer.
Le monde est plein de merveilleuses choses.　　　　20
Douce est l'aurore et douces sont les roses.
Rien n'est si doux que le charme d'aimer!
La clarté vraie et la meilleure flamme,
C'est le rayon qui va de l'âme à l'âme!

L'amour vaut mieux, au fond des antres frais,　　　　25
Que ces soleils qu'on ignore et qu'on nomme.
Dieu mit, sachant ce qui convient à l'homme,
Le ciel bien loin et la femme tout près.
Il dit à ceux qui scrutent l'azur sombre:
Vivez! aimez! le reste, c'est mon ombre!　　　　30

Aimons! c'est tout. Et Dieu le veut ainsi.
Laisse ton ciel que de froids rayons dorent!
Tu trouveras dans deux yeux qui t'adorent
Plus de beauté, plus de lumière aussi.
Aimer, c'est voir, sentir, rêver, comprendre.　　　　35
L'esprit plus grand s'ajoute au cœur plus tendre.

The passing daylight, the descending black?
Why are your eyes aloft? I want them back!
Let the sky be, and look into my soul!

You love the dark, you read it avidly,
And yet, compared to a few smiles from me,
What is the whole vast heaven teaching you?
Or compared to the kisses we impart!
Come, and lift up the chaste veils of my heart!
How many stars it has, if you but knew!

How many suns! When we are lovers—why,
Everything in us is a radiant sky!
Fidelity shining through good and ill
Is well worth Venus gleaming on the heights.
I swear there's nothing in these azure nights:
The heavens in my soul are heavenlier still!

Oh, it's a fine thing to watch stars appear:
The world is full of wonders far and near.
A rose, a dawn, is lovely on the whole—
Yet nothing is as lovely as romance!
The truest flame, the clearest radiance,
That is the light that springs from soul to soul!

Love is more, in the valleys here below,
Than stars that people name and never know.
The Lord sees what is good for man: he made
The heavens far away, woman close by.
He says to those who scan the gloomy sky:
"Come, live and love! The rest is but my shade!"

Why, love is everything—so say God's laws;
Then put aside that ice-gilt sky of yours!
You'll find, within two eyes that care for you,
More beauty—yes, more light as well—is gleaming!
Loving is seeing, feeling, knowing, dreaming;
The softest heart—the noblest spirit, too.

Viens, bien-aimé! n'entends-tu pas toujours
Dans nos transports une harmonie étrange?
Autour de nous la nature se change
En une lyre et chante nos amours!   40
Viens! aimons-nous! errons sur la pelouse.
Ne songe plus au ciel! j'en suis jalouse!—

Ma bien-aimée ainsi tout bas parlait,
Avec son front posé sur sa main blanche,
Et l'œil rêveur d'un ange qui se penche,   45
Et sa voix grave, et cet air qui me plaît;
Belle et tranquille, et de me voir charmée,
Ainsi tout bas parlait ma bien-aimée.

Nos cœurs battaient; l'extase m'étouffait;
Les fleurs du soir entr'ouvraient leurs corolles...—   50
Qu'avez-vous fait, arbres, de nos paroles?
De nos soupirs, rochers, qu'avez-vous fait?
C'est un destin bien triste que le nôtre,
Puisqu'un tel jour s'envole comme un autre!

O souvenir! trésor dans l'ombre accru!   55
Sombre horizon des anciennes pensées!
Chère lueur des choses éclipsées!
Rayonnement du passé disparu!
Comme du seuil et du dehors d'un temple,
L'œil de l'esprit en rêvant vous contemple!   60

Quand les beaux jours font place aux jours amers,
De tout bonheur il faut quitter l'idée;
Quand l'espérance est tout à fait vidée,
Laissons tomber la coupe au fonde des mers.
L'oubli! l'oubli! c'est l'onde où tout se noie;   65
C'est la mer sombre où l'on jette sa joie.

My love, when we are in our ecstasy,
Don't you sense some mysterious harmony?
Around us Nature becomes lyre, and sings
About our love—she's utterly reborn!
Come and be lovers—roam out on the lawn.
Forget the stars! I'm jealous of the things!'

So my love spoke—spoke very softly, and
Rested her forehead on her lovely hand.
With a rapt gaze—an angel bending low—
In her enchanting way, tranquil and fair,
Delighted simply because I was there,
Softly, in solemn tones, my love spoke so.

Our hearts were beating; passion stifled me;
Petals were parting in the twilit flowers...
Where are the sighs and longings we expressed?
Have they been snatched away by rock and tree?
Indeed, what a sad destiny is ours,
When such a day can pass like all the rest!

Memory! treasure gathered in the night!
Sombre horizon of our recollection,
Illumination of things lost from sight,
Enlightenment of the now-vanished past!
Far from the temple, outside and outcast,
The spirit's eye still looks in your direction.

When sweet day has made way for bitter day,
All further thought of pleasure must be lost.
When hope is utterly abandoned, down
Into the sea-depths must the cup be tossed.
Oblivion is the wave where all things drown,
The dark gulf where our joys are cast away.

«Oh! je fus comme fou dans le premier moment . . .»

Oh! je fus comme fou dans le premier moment,
Hélas! et je pleurai trois jours amèrement.
Vous tous à qui Dieu prit votre chère espérance,
Pères, mères, dont l'âme a souffert ma souffrance,
Tout ce que j'éprouvais, l'avez-vous éprouvé?   5
Je voulais me briser le front sur le pavé;
Puis je me révoltais, et, par moments, terrible,
Je fixais mes regards sur cette chose horrible,
Et je n'y croyais pas, et je m'écriais: Non!
Est-ce que Dieu permet de ces malheurs sans nom   10
Qui font que dans le cœur le désespoir se lève?—
Il me semblait que tout n'était qu'un affreux rêve,
Qu'elle ne pouvait pas m'avoir ainsi quitté,
Que je l'entendais rire en la chambre à côté,
Que c'était impossible enfin qu'elle fût morte,   15
Et que j'allais la voir entrer par cette porte!

Oh! que de fois j'ai dit: Silence! elle a parlé!
Tenez! voici le bruit de sa main sur la clé!
Attendez! elle vient! Laissez-moi, que j'écoute!
Car elle est quelque part dans la maison sans doute!   20

«Pendant que le marin . . .»

Pendant que le marin, qui calcule et qui doute,
Demande son chemin aux constellations;
Pendant que le berger, l'œil plein de visions,
Cherche au milieu des bois son étoile et son route;
Pendant que l'astronome, inondé des rayons,   5

Pèse un globe à travers des millions de lieues,
Moi, je cherche autre chose en ce ciel vaste et pur.
Mais que ce saphir sombre est un abîme obscur!
On ne peut distinguer, la nuit, les robes bleues
Des anges frissonnants qui glissent dans l'azur.   10

'At first, oh! I was like a maniac . . .'

At first, oh! I was like a maniac,
For three days I wept bitterly!*
You parents who have suffered like me,
Whose dearest hope the Lord has taken back,
Have you felt what I felt? Have you found what I found?
I wanted to gash my head against the ground;
Then I rebelled, and sometimes, shuddering,
Stared at the dreadful thing
And cried out, disbelieving: 'No!
Could God ever allow such nameless woe
And make the human heart despair?' It seemed
Nothing more than a nightmare I had dreamed;
She couldn't possibly have left me so,
I could hear her laughing in the next room, close beside,
She couldn't possibly have died,
I was going to see her walk in through that very door!

'Quiet! that was her voice!' I often cried;
'Yes—that's her hand on the doorlatch—there!
She's on her way! Just let me listen! She's sure-
Ly in the house somewhere!'

'While mariners, who estimate and doubt . . .'

While mariners, who estimate and doubt,
Ask constellations for their path at night—
While shepherds, when strange visions fill their sight,
Search in the woods their star and their way out—
And while astronomers immersed in light

Measure some globe immense leagues distant—I
Seek something else within this vast pure sky.
But its dark sapphire is a dim ravine!
In the gloom, as the shimmering angels fly
The azure, their blue robes cannot be seen.

Veni, vidi, vixi

J'ai bien assez vécu, puisque dans mes douleurs
Je marche, sans trouver de bras qui me secourent,
Puisque je ris à peine aux enfants qui m'entourent,
Puisque je ne suis plus réjoui par les fleurs;

Puisqu'au printemps, quand Dieu met la nature en fête, 5
J'assiste, esprit sans joie, à ce splendide amour;
Puisque je suis à l'heure où l'homme fuit le jour,
Hélas! et sent de tout la tristesse secrète;

Puisque l'espoir serein dans mon âme est vaincu;
Puisqu'en cette saison des parfums et des roses, 10
O ma fille! j'aspire à l'ombre où tu reposes,
Puisque mon cœur est mort, j'ai bien assez vécu.

Je n'ai pas refusé ma tâche sur la terre.
Mon sillon? Le voilà. Ma gerbe? La voici.
J'ai vécu souriant, toujours plus adouci, 15
Debout, mais incliné du côté du mystère.

J'ai fait ce que j'ai pu; j'ai servi, j'ai veillé,
Et j'ai vu bien souvent qu'on riait de ma peine.
Je me suis étonné d'être un objet de haine,
Ayant beaucoup souffert et beaucoup travaillé. 20

Dans ce bagne terrestre où ne s'ouvre aucune aile,
Sans me plaindre, saignant, et tombant sur les mains,
Morne, épuisé, raillé par les forçats humains,
J'ai porté mon chaînon de la chaîne éternelle.

Maintenant, mon regard ne s'ouvre qu'à demi; 25
Je ne me tourne plus même quand on me nomme;
Je suis plein de stupeur et d'ennui, comme un homme
Qui se lève avant l'aube et qui n'a pas dormi.

Veni, Vidi, Vixi

Yes, I have lived enough: since in my grief
I walk, and find no arm to comfort me;
Flowers themselves afford me no relief;
I scarcely smile in children's company;

Since in the spring, when God makes Nature play,
I see its passion, yet no joy it brings;
Since it is time for me to shun the day,
And sense the hidden sadness of all things;

Since, in this hour of flower-scent and rose,
Every calm hope within has had rebuff,
And I long, child, for the shade where you repose;
My heart is dead—yes, I have lived enough.

No duty on the earth have I reviled.
There is my furrow; and my harvest, here.
I lived—ever more peaceably—and smiled;
I stood—yet stooped when mysteries were near.

I did what I could do—now watch, now wait;
Yet very often people mocked my woe.
Curious indeed that I evoked such hate,
Seeing I suffered and I laboured so!

Here in this wingless earthly prison yard
I bled, fell headlong, and did not complain.
Scorned by my fellow convicts, sad and scarred,
I bore my link in the eternal chain.

My eyes now scarcely open half their span,
Nor do I even turn when now addressed.
I am stunned, I am wearied—like a man
Who rose before the dawn and had no rest.

Je ne daigne plus même, en ma sombre paresse,
Répondre à l'envieux dont la bouche me nuit.   30
O Seigneur! ouvrez-moi les portes de la nuit,
Afin que je m'en aille et que je disparaisse!

«Demain, dès l'aube, à l'heure où blanchit la campagne . . .»

Demain, dès l'aube, à l'heure où blanchit la campagne,
Je partirai. Vois-tu, je sais que tu m'attends.
J'irai par la forêt, j'irai par la montagne.
Je ne puis demeurer loin de toi plus longtemps.

Je marcherai les yeux fixés sur mes pensées,   5
Sans rien voir au dehors, sans entendre aucun bruit,
Seul, inconnu, le dos courbé, les mains croisées,
Triste, et le jour pour moi sera comme la nuit.

Je ne regarderai ni l'or du soir qui tombe,
Ni les voiles au loin descendant vers Harfleur,   10
Et quand j'arriverai, je mettrai sur ta tombe
Un bouquet de houx vert et de bruyère en fleur.

I don't so much as deign, in my dark plight,
To answer what the envious may say.
Open to me, O God, the gates of night,*
So that I may depart and pass away!

'Tomorrow, when the fields grow light . . .'

Tomorrow, when the fields grow light, I'll go.
    You're waiting for me there, I know.
I'll cross the woods, I'll cross the mountains too.
    No longer can I keep from you.

As I walk I'll see nothing but my mind,
    I'll hear no sounds of any kind,
Back bowed, hands clasped, sad, unknown, solitary,
    And day will be like night to me.

I won't notice the gold at end of day
Or the sails off to Harfleur far away;
And when I reach the place, I'll drape your tomb
    With holly sprays and heath in bloom.

from *Things Seen*

At the Académie française

17 [December 1846]

Today (Thursday) at the Académie I was lecturing Dupin senior* on the subject of Balzac.* He interrupted me:

'Damn it all, you want Balzac to get into the Académie right away at the very first go, just like that! You keep citing precedents, but they don't prove a thing.' (I'd cited Messieurs Flourens, Patin, Saint-Marc Girardin, Polé, Brifaut.)* 'Just imagine! Balzac in the Académie right away! You haven't thought it through. Can't be done. No, there's one thing you're forgetting: he deserves it!'

14 [January 1847]

Today Alfred de Vigny* and I spoiled the election at the Académie. Empis was being proposed on one side, Victor Leclerc on the other. We didn't want either of them. We put in blank ballot papers. There were thirty-four voters—majority: eighteen votes. Five successive ballots were held. Monsieur Empis got as far as fifteen votes, Monsieur Victor Leclerc* as far as sixteen. At various stages votes were cast for Messieurs Émile Deschamps, Lamennais, Alfred de Musset, and Béranger.* With our two votes we could have settled the election. We held firm. It had to be postponed, and they've put it off till next month.

At the first ballot, when the two blank ballot papers were announced, Monsieur Flourens said: 'There's two votes thrown away.' I replied: 'Thrown away? No, invested sensibly!' I hope to make one of the parties come to an agreement with us, since we hold the balance of power, and nominate Balzac or Dumas in exchange for our votes. That's how I got Alfred de Vigny nominated two years ago.

11 January [1849], Académie

We're electing Chateaubriand's successor.*

I set out in good time for the Académie. The appointed time was midday.

As I was crossing the courtyard of the Louvre, there was a crowd gathered round the shapeless pedestal that used to bear the Duc d'Orléans's statue. In February the following words had been painted on both sides of the pedestal:

TO THE CITIZENS OF PARIS

WHO DIED FOR LIBERTY

on 22, 23, and 24 February*

FROM THE GRATEFUL REPUBLIC

Well, now the side of the inscription facing the Rue Croix-des-Petits-Champs had collapsed into rubble on the steps of the monument. Who had done that? As I went by, I heard a workman saying 'It was the rain.' And an old woman coming from the direction of Saint-Germain-l'Auxerrois replied: 'No; it was the heavens.'

Anyhow, I cross the Pont des Arts and there I am at the Institute.* According to the clock, it's a quarter past twelve. Latecomers are hurrying in.

It's pouring with rain. The politicians are arriving in carriages, the literary folk on foot, soiled and sodden like the dogs in Ronsard or the poets in Boileau. Classicists are coughing their way up the staircase. Various groups of academicians in the great hall—Monsieur Cousin with Monsieur Saint-Marc-Girardin, Monsieur Mérimée with Monsieur de Rémusat, Monsieur Pasquier with Monsieur Molé. Monsieur Dupaty* accosts me, declaring that he thinks about everything just the way I do, and takes advantage of my smile to read me some poetry. The old academicians take off their greatcoats and the young (fifty-five-year-old) ones their overcoats. They put their umbrellas in the corners of the room, shake hands, sign the attendance book, and enquire about what La Fontaine* used to call 'remuneration'. No payment yet for the month of December. Will the Treasury pay up? Monsieur Pingard, in breeches and black stockings, bows and declares gracefully, 'No, I'm sorry to say!' The Académie smells bankruptcy in the air and makes a face.

I enter the little hall and take my place. Monsieur de Sainte-Aulaire says hello and sits down nearby. Monsieur de Barante button-holes me. Monsieur de Feletz, my right-hand neighbour, tells me his grudges against Monsieur de Falloux. Empis and Pongerville whisper in my ear, 'Balzac, eh?' Reply: 'You bet!' Monsieur Pasquier comes to my bench. We have a chat. He complains about his eyes. There's a call for silence. Monsieur Villemain* reads the minutes.

The Académie is all spread out around the green cloth. 'Green cloth' is the term for some narrow little tables arranged in squares, with T-shaped extension leaves facing inwards, and draped in heavy green cloth.

The previous election comes into my head. It was about a year ago. That was when Monsieur Vatout was elected. Monsieur de Chateaubriand, who was already ill, wasn't at that session; I had a long talk with Monsieur Guizot; Monsieur de Lamartine* arrived after the voting had begun, and his vote decided the election. Now Monsieur de Chateaubriand is dead, Monsieur Guizot is in exile, Monsieur de Lamartine is fallen from power. The monarchy and the immortal whom we created—Monsieur Vatout—both had time to die between the two elections.

There are thirty-one academicians, arranged in the following order (starting from the right of the desk):

Right to left: Ségur, Ampère, Vitet, Rémusat, Mérimée, Lamartine, Baour, Tissot, Empis, Dupaty, Scribe, Flourens, Pongerville, Hugo, Feletz, Brifaut, Sainte-Aulaire, Barante, Mérimée, Lebrun, Mignet, Patin, Saint-Marc Girardin, Pasquier, Dupin senior, Tocqueville, Thiers, Cousin.

At the desk: Villemain, Viennet (chairman), Ancelot* (secretary).

At the start Monsieur Villemain read the candidates' letters— there are only two of them: Monsieur de Balzac and Monsieur de Noailles.* Monsieur de Balzac's letter recalls his titles and his 'visits'; there are a few murmurs at the statement: 'I withdrew when Monsieur Hugo was nominated by Monsieur Nodier.'* The Duc de Noailles's letter contains this grammatical blunder: 'I wish to be appointed as *successor to the chair* that Monsieur de Chateaubriand used to occupy.' It is noticed that Balzac says 'the Vicomte de Chateaubriand' whereas the Duc de Noailles says 'Monsieur de Chateaubriand'.

The regulations having been read, the academicians take the old oath that they haven't promised their votes to anyone. Monsieur de Ségur is the first to be asked. When Monsieur Viennet, the chairman, asks him: 'Have you promised your vote to anyone?' he answers: 'No more than you have.' Monsieur Thiers takes the oath with a smile on his face; you'd think it was a political promise.

It's a quarter to one.

We proceed to the poll. But before we do, just what is the poll? Every time an election is held, each academician finds some little trimmed and prepared squares of paper in front of him when he sits down at his place, and on the desk he sees what are known as 'the urns'. They are indeed urns; two tinplate things painted the colour of mahogany. You can't help ascribing these objects to the days of the Empire, when the 'dry style' was in fashion. Nothing could be more drab, more ponderous, more downtrodden, more angular, more podgy, more ugly than those vote-containers, ghastly moulds that have emitted all the academicians for the past forty years. When the chairman has said the sacrosanct words 'Gentlemen, we shall proceed to the poll', Monsieur Pingard magisterially picks up one of the two urns and passes it around in front of the academicians, each one drops his scrap of paper into the hideous casserole dish, and when 'the ballot is complete', Pingard goes and empties the whole lot onto the desk. The chairman counts the votes and they are tallied up.

One time I dropped into the urn the following little rhyme:

> I won't cast any vote at all,
> Because good taste and talent fall
> A prey to envy in these jugs;
> Nothing is drawn from them but mugs.

Monsieur de Noailles got twenty-five votes, Balzac four; there were two informals—one blank, the other inscribed 'A man of letters, and no more dukes if possible!' When it was read, Monsieur Brifaut cried out: 'There aren't any dukes here!' The inscription—a pretty foolish one—came from Viennet. I voted for Balzac, as did Empis, Pongerville, and Lamartine.

Then I went to the National Assembly. As I arrived, I met Berryer,* who gave me his hand. I told him, 'You could have got us out of our difficulty.' Berryer retorted, 'You needed a very talented man to replace Chateaubriand, and there's none at hand.' 'Oh yes there is!' I replied, shaking his.

Académie française, 19 March 1850

The prose competition is being judged. Here's how:

Monsieur de Barante is reading a pamphlet. Monsieur Mérimée is writing. Messieurs Salvandy* and Vitet are having a loud chat.

Messieurs Guizot and Pasquier are having a quiet chat. Monsieur de Ségur is holding a newspaper. Messieurs Mignet, Lebrun, and Saint-Aulaire are laughing at some joke or other that Monsieur Viennet has made. Monsieur Scribe is drawing with his pen on a wooden paperknife. Monsieur Flourens is just arriving and taking off his overcoat. Messieurs Patin, de Vigny, Pongerville, and Empis are looking at the ceiling or the carpet. Monsieur Villemain is reading the manuscript and complaining about the sunlight coming in through the window opposite him. Monsieur de Noailles is engrossed in some kind of calendar that he's holding half open. Monsieur Tissot is sleeping. As for me, I'm writing this. The other academicians are absent.

(The subject of the competition is In Praise of Madame de Staël.)*

12 September 1850

Today, Thursday 12 September 1850, while the Académie was at work on the Dictionary,* this illustration of the word 'increase' [*accroître*] was suggested—taken from Madame de Staël:

'Poverty increases ignorance, and ignorance increases poverty.'

Three objections were instantly raised:

1. Antithetical.
2. Modern writer.
3. Dangerous thing to say.

The Académie rejected the example.

The Death of Balzac

On 18 August 1850, my wife, who had been to see Madame de Balzac* during the day, told me that Monsieur de Balzac was dying. I hurried to his home.

Monsieur de Balzac had been suffering from cardiac hypertrophy for eighteen months. After the February Revolution* he had gone to Russia, where he had married. I met him in the street a few days before his departure; he was already complaining, and his breath was wheezy. In May 1850 he came back to France, married, rich, and dying. By that time his legs were already swollen. Four doctors were consulted and listened to his heart. One of them, Monsieur Louis, told me on 6 July: 'He has less than six weeks to live.' He had the same disease as Frédéric Soulié.*

On 18 August, my uncle, General Louis Hugo,* was dining with me. As soon as we rose from the table, I left him and took a cab to 14 Avenue Fortunée, Beaujon,* which was where Monsieur de Balzac was living. He had bought what remained of Monsieur de Beaujon's home, a few lower rooms that happened to have escaped demolition; he had furnished those hovels luxuriously and turned them into a delightful little house, with a carriage gate opening onto the Avenue Fortunée. The only garden was a long narrow courtyard, its paving stones intercut here and there with flowerbeds.

I rang the bell. The moonlight was partly veiled by clouds. The street was empty. Nobody came. I rang again. The door opened. A maid appeared with a candle.

'What do you want, Monsieur?' she asked.

She was in tears.

I mentioned my name. I was shown into the drawing room on the ground floor, where David's* huge marble bust of Balzac stood on a console table opposite the fireplace. In the centre of the room, a candle was burning on an opulent table with six exquisitely gilded statuettes for legs.

Another woman, also in tears, came and told me:

'He's dying. Madame has gone back to her own room. The doctors gave up all hope of him yesterday. There's a sore on his left leg. It's gangrene. The doctors don't know what they're doing. They said Monsieur's dropsy was a thick dropsy, an infiltration, that's what they called it, and the skin and the flesh were like fat, and it couldn't be drained. Well, last month, when he was going to bed, Monsieur bumped into some of the ornamental furniture and gashed his skin, and all the water that was in his body ran out. The doctors said "Fancy that!"—it amazed them—and since then they've been draining it the same way. "Imitating Nature", they called it. But now an abscess has developed on his leg. Monsieur Roux was the one who operated on it. Yesterday they took off the bandages. Instead of having any pus on it, the wound was dry, red, and burning. Then they said "He's beyond help" and they haven't been back since. We've gone to four or five of them, but it's no use. They all said: "Nothing can be done." It's been a bad night.

This morning, at nine o'clock, Monsieur couldn't speak any more. Madame sent for a priest. The priest came and gave Monsieur the last rites. Monsieur did make a sign to show he understood. An hour later, he shook hands with his sister, Madame de Surville. He's had a rattle in his throat since twelve o'clock, and he can't see anything any more. He won't last out the night. If you like, Monsieur, I'll go and get Monsieur de Surville—he hasn't gone to bed yet.'

The woman left me. I waited a few minutes. The candle hardly lit the room's splendid furnishings and fine paintings by Pourbus and Holbein.* The marble bust stood out dimly in the gloom, like the ghost of the man who was about to die. A cadaverous smell filled the whole house.

Monsieur de Surville came in and confirmed everything that the maid had said. I asked to see Monsieur de Balzac.

We went along a passage, climbed a staircase carpeted in red and lined with works of art—vases, statues, pictures, enamels on console tables—then another passage, and I could see an open door. I heard a loud, ominous rattling sound.

I was in Balzac's bedroom.

There was a bed in the middle of the room. A mahogany bed with straps and bars at its head and foot for moving the sick man. In this bed lay Monsieur de Balzac, his head propped up on a pile of pillows supplemented with red damask cushions from the room's sofa. His face was purple, almost black, and leaned to the right; his beard was unkempt, his hair grey and close-cut, his eyes open and fixed. I was looking at him in profile, and from that perspective he looked like Napoleon.

An old woman, the nurse, was standing at one side of the bed, and a manservant at the other. Behind the head of the bed, a candle was burning on a table; another was on a chest of drawers by the door. There was a silver vase on the night table.

The man and woman remained silent, with a kind of terror, and listened to the death rattle of the dying man.

A picture of a young, pinkish, smiling man was hanging near the fireplace. The candle behind the bed cast a brilliant light on it.

An unbearable smell was coming from the bed. I lifted the counterpane and took Balzac's hand. It was very clammy. I pressed it. He didn't respond to the pressure.

This was the very room in which I had called on him a month earlier. He had been cheerful, optimistic, with no doubts that he would get better; he had chuckled as he showed me his swelling.

We had talked a long time and argued about politics. He accused me of 'rabble-rousing'. He was a royalist. He asked me: 'How could you shed so lightly the title Peer of France?* Only King of France would be finer!'

He also told me: 'I've got Monsieur de Beaujon's house, except for the garden, but including the gallery that overlooks the little street-corner church. A door on my staircase opens into the church. One turn of the key, and I'm at Mass. That gallery means more to me than the garden.'

When I was leaving him, he led me back as far as the staircase, walking with difficulty; he showed me the door, and then called out to his wife: 'Make sure you show Hugo all my pictures.'

The nurse said to me: 'He'll die just about daybreak.'

I went back downstairs, carrying that livid face in my mind; on the way through the drawing room, again I found the motionless, passionless, aloof, vaguely radiant bust, and I compared death with immortality.

When I arrived back home—it was a Sunday—I found several people waiting for me, including Riza Bey the Turkish chargé d'affaires, Navarrete the Spanish poet, and Count Arrivabene* the Italian exile. I said to them: 'Gentlemen, Europe is about to lose a great spirit.'

He died during the night. He was fifty-one years old.

He was buried on the Wednesday.

He was laid first in the Beaujon chapel, having been taken through that door whose mere key was more precious to him than all the paradisiac gardens of the erstwhile farmer-general.*

On the day of his death Giraud* drew his portrait. They wanted to take a death mask of him, but couldn't; he decomposed too quickly. The morning after his death, the modellers came but found his face deformed and his nose fallen on his cheek. He was placed in an oak coffin lined with lead.

The service was held at Saint-Philippe-du-Roule. There, by that coffin, I reflected that this was the very place where my second daughter had been christened; I hadn't seen the church since that day. In our recollections, death makes contact with birth.

Baroche,* the Minister of the Interior, came to the funeral. He sat beside me in church, facing the bier, and spoke to me now and then.

'He was a notable man', he said.

'He was a genius', I replied.

The procession went through Paris and along the boulevards to the Père Lachaise cemetery. Spots of rain were falling as we left the church and as we reached the cemetery. It was one of those days when heaven seems to shed a few tears.

I walked at the head of the coffin, on the right, holding one of the silver tassels of the pall; Alexandre Dumas* being on the other side.

When we came to the grave, which was high up on the hillside, there was a huge crowd; the way was rough and narrow, the horses had trouble pulling the hearse upward—it kept rolling back down again. I was cornered between a wheel and a tomb—I was very nearly crushed. Some spectators who were standing on the tomb lifted me up by the shoulders, and set me alongside them.

We made the whole journey on foot.

The coffin was lowered into the grave; Charles Nodier and Casimir Delavigne* lay nearby. The priest uttered the last prayer, and I said a few words.

While I was speaking, the sun was setting. I could see the whole of Paris in the distance, shrouded in the glorious haze of the setting sun. A few clods slid into the grave almost at my feet, and I was interrupted by the dull thud of that earth dropping onto the coffin.

from *Deeds and Words*

Balzac's Funeral

21 August 1850

Ladies and gentlemen,

The man who has just been placed in this grave was among those who are mourned by the general public. Today, every kind of pretence has vanished. The people in the public gaze nowadays are not kings but thinkers, and when one of those thinkers disappears, the whole country shudders. When a man of talent dies, at the present day, the people grieve; and when a man of genius dies, the entire nation grieves.

Ladies and gentlemen, Balzac's name will be part of the light that our era will leave behind it.

Monsieur de Balzac belonged to the mighty generation of nineteenth-century writers who arose after Napoleon, just as the famous seventeenth-century constellation arose after Richelieu*—as if there is some natural law in the development of civilization, which requires those who rule by the sword to be followed by those who rule by the mind.

Monsieur de Balzac stood out even among the greatest and the noblest. This isn't the place for a full discussion of his sovereign brilliance. All his books make up a single book, a book that is living and radiant and profound, where the whole of our present-day civilization can be seen coming and going and passing and moving, with something fearful and terrible in its reality; a marvellous book, which the poet called a comedy, and which he might have called a history, which adopts every form and every style, which surpasses Tacitus and encompasses Suetonius, which crosses Beaumarchais and goes as far as Rabelais;* a book which is both observed and imagined; which lavishes in abundance what is real, intimate, bourgeois, trivial, physical, and which sometimes strips away every kind of reality with a huge, abrupt gesture, to reveal a sudden glimpse of the darkest and most tragic ideality.

Without realizing it, whether he liked it or not, whether he wanted it or not, the author of that vast strange work belonged to the great tribe of revolutionary writers. Balzac goes straight to the point. He grapples bodily with modern society. He tears something—an illusion, a hope, a howl, or a mask—from everyone. He delves into vice, he dissects passion. He searches and plumbs the depths of humanity, the soul, the heart, the bowels, the brain, the abyss that lies within each one of us. And, because he is temperamentally free and healthy—because he is one of the present-day thinkers who have seen revolution at close range and therefore have a deeper grasp of human destiny and the ways of providence—Balzac emerges serene and smiling from studies of the formidable kind that made Molière melancholy and Rousseau* misanthropic.

That is what he did in our midst. That is the body of work he has left us—a body of work that is lofty and solid, a strong flight of granite steps, a monument!—a body of work on the heights, from which his fame will continue to shine with the passage of time. Great people make their own pedestal; the future supplies the statue.

His death has struck Paris dumb. Some months ago he came back to France. Conscious that he was dying, he wanted to see his homeland again, like a man turning back to kiss his mother goodbye before setting out on a great journey.

He had a short life, but a full one—a life full of works rather than days.

Alas! this strong and never-tiring worker, this philosopher, this thinker, this poet, this genius, lived in our midst the life of storms and struggles, quarrels and conflicts, common to all great men in every age. Today, here he is—at peace. He is leaving behind disputes and jealousies. At the same time he is entering into glory and into the tomb. From now on he will shine, far above the clouds that hang over our own heads, among the stars of the nation!

Is there anyone here today who doesn't feel inclined to envy him?

Ladies and gentlemen, whatever sorrow we may personally feel in the presence of such a loss, we must learn to accept these disasters. We must accept them in all their poignancy and severity. Perhaps, in an era like ours, it may sometimes be a good thing, a necessary thing, for the death of a great man to rouse a flutter of religious feeling in minds overwhelmed with doubt and scepticism. Providence knows what it is doing, when it forces people to face the supreme mystery in this way, and meditate on death, which is both the great equalizer and the great liberator.

Providence knows what it is doing, because this is the supreme kind of teaching. Everyone must think stern and serious thoughts, when a great soul makes its majestic entry into the next life, when a genius who has soared above the multitude so long, on visible wings, suddenly unfurls new and invisible wings, and vanishes all at once into the unknown.

No—it isn't the unknown! No—as I've said before, on another day of grief, and as I'll never tire of repeating, it isn't darkness, it's light! It isn't the end, it's the beginning! It isn't non-existence, it's eternity! I ask everyone who can hear me, isn't that the truth? A grave like this is a demonstration of immortality; in the presence of some illustrious deaths, we feel more clearly the divine destiny of the spirits that pass across the earth in order to suffer and grow pure—the spirits that we call human—and we recognize that someone who has been a genius during his life cannot fail to be a soul after his death!

from *Things Seen*

Pius IX and Louis Bonaparte

April 1850

Pope Pius IX is simple, mild-mannered, timid, fearful, slow-moving, negligent of his person. He usually goes around with two or three days' growth of beard, which gives him a disreputable appearance. Like Charles X, he emits more smiles than words. You'd think he was a country curé. Alongside him, the red-stockinged Antonelli,* with his diplomat's eyes and secret agent's eyebrows, looks like a bodyguard appointed to mind the poor fellow.

Just at present, Pius IX is spending his time writing a book on the mystery of the Immaculate Conception.*

And here's what the President of the French Republic is doing at the same time.

Every day at two o'clock, Louis Bonaparte goes into the Bois de Boulogne* in a two-horse open carriage. Another two-horse carriage, a service vehicle, follows him. That makes four horses. He reaches a roundabout where he finds two horses held by two footmen on horseback. That makes eight horses. Virtually at the same time, there arrives at the same roundabout a good-looking English blonde, Miss Howard,* also in a two-horse open carriage and followed by two servants on horseback. That makes twelve horses. The president and Miss Howard get out of their carriages, mount their horses, and ride off into the woods. They caper about for an hour or two, depending on the weather. Then they dismount at a pavilion which is noted for the good English 'grog' dispensed there. They partake of the said grog. Meanwhile the two carriages have arrived at the pavilion. Once the grog has been drunk, the president and Miss Howard depart amid the throng of regulars that attend them almost all the time. He kisses the good-looking blonde's hand, helps her into her carriage, gets into his own, and both of them resume their way to the Élysée.*

Each day he spends part of the morning playing Guess-who-touched-you with the same Miss Howard, Lady Douglas, Princess Mathilde, and the Marquise de Contades.*

So, the immaculate conception of the Holy Virgin, grog with a pretty Englishwoman—those are the things that occupy Pius IX in Rome and Louis Bonaparte in Paris. Those are the things that fill two brains on which the fate of Europe is hanging.

from *Deeds and Words*

Proposed Grant to Monsieur Bonaparte

6 February 1851

In January 1851, immediately after receiving a motion of no confidence, Monsieur Louis Bonaparte held out his hand to the assembly that had just slapped it, and asked for three million francs. A princely grant indeed. The Assembly debated his request, first in committees, then in a public sitting. The public discussion lasted only one day and contained little of note. The committee discussions, which were held on 6 February, had provoked much public interest, and when the issue reached the light of day, it had in effect been exhausted by that preliminary debate.

In the twelfth committee especially, the debate had been long and intense. It lasted for two and a half hours, though by that time the public session had already commenced. Many other members of the Assembly gathered at the committee room's large frosted glass doors and listened from outside to this battle. The successive speakers were Messieurs Léon Faucher, Sainte-Beuve (who had drafted the motion of no confidence), Michel (de Bourges), and Victor Hugo.

Monsieur Combarel de Leyval opened the debate; Monsieur Léon Faucher and, later in the discussion, Monsieur Bineau,* both of whom were former ministers of Bonaparte, strongly advocated the proposed grant. Monsieur Léon Faucher's impassioned speech brought Monsieur Victor Hugo into the debate.

*

Monsieur Léon Faucher's words are forcing me to speak. I'll have very little to say. I have no desire to be appointed a member of the commission; I'm still not well enough to take the floor, and I had no intention of making a speech, even here.

In my opinion, the Assembly made one mistake when it approved the first grant* ten months ago; if it approved the new grant today, it would be making a second and more serious mistake.

I'm considering not only the national interest, the burden on the public, the need to lighten the budget rather than adding to it; I'm considering also the true interests of the Assembly, I'm considering the interests of the executive power itself, and I believe that from all these points of view—narrow and broad alike—it would be a great mistake to approve what is now being asked of you.

As a matter of fact, sirs, the relationship between the two powers has developed in unexpected ways since the first grant was approved. Then we were at peace, now we are at war. A major conflict has arisen.

This conflict—according to the very people who are most actively supporting the executive power—this conflict is causing disorder, trouble, disturbance, and everyone's interests are suffering from it; this conflict has virtually developed into a national calamity.

Now, sirs, let's examine this conflict. What's behind it? The first grant.

Yes, without that grant, you wouldn't have had the travels, the harangues, the army parades, the non-commissioned officers hobnobbing with generals at parties, Satory, the Place du Havre, the Tenth of December Society, the cries of 'Long live the Emperor!', and the fisticuffs. You wouldn't have had all those Praetorian attempts* to make the republic's future look like an empire. No money, no empire.

You wouldn't have had all those strange doings, which have so deeply disturbed the nation, and which have inevitably put the legislative power on the alert and provoked a motion of no confidence from the so-called coalition—a coalition which is really a mere juxtaposition.

Remember that motion, sirs; the facts were brought to your attention, you evaluated them conscientiously, and you solemnly declared your lack of confidence.

The legislative power expressing a lack of confidence in the executive power!

Now, how did the executive power—which is, after all, your subordinate—how did it receive that warning from the sovereign Assembly?

It took absolutely no notice of it. It wiped your motion out of existence. It approved the cabinet that you had declared to be suspect. A stand that has worsened the conflict and increased your lack of confidence.

And what is the executive power doing now?

It's turning to you and asking you for the means to finish what it started. It's saying to you, 'You have no confidence in me. Very well! Pay up anyhow, I'm going to keep behaving the same way.'

The executive power is scarcely considering its own dignity, sirs, when it presents you with such a request at such a time. You need to consider yours, and refuse.

Monsieur Faucher talked about the fact that the nation voted Monsieur Bonaparte into office. But were his remarks right? I myself, who am speaking to you now, voted for Monsieur Bonaparte. I, in my own sphere of action, supported his election. So I have the right to say a few words about the attitude of the people who acted as I did, and about my own personal attitude too. Well, no, we didn't vote for a Napoleon because he was a Napoleon; we voted for a man who had matured in a political prison and had written some notable books in support of the underprivileged classes.* As a matter of fact, we voted for him because we were confronted with so many would-be monarchists, and we thought it would be helpful to have a prince who relinquished his titles and was appointed by the country to act as president of the republic.

And notice one other point. This prince—since people keep reminding us of his title—was a revolutionary prince, a member of an upstart dynasty, a prince who had risen from the Revolution, and who was an affirmation rather than a negation of that revolution. That's why we appointed him. Within the political prisoner, there was a thinker; within the prince, there was a democrat. We had some hopes of him.

Our hopes were disappointed; what we expected from him, we expected in vain. The prince has done everything he was capable of doing, and he keeps doing it—asking for grants at the same time.

Anyone else, in his place, couldn't do that, wouldn't do it, wouldn't dare to do it. Let's suppose General Changarnier was in power. Probably he'd adopt much the same political policy as Monsieur Bonaparte, but he wouldn't dream of coming and asking you for two million francs on top of one million two hundred thousand—for the very simple reason that, being a mere commoner before his appointment, he really wouldn't have any idea what to do with such a bankroll. Monsieur Changarnier wouldn't need to have people shouting 'Long live the Emperor!' around him. So it's the prince, and only the prince, who needs two million francs. The first Napoleon himself, when he was in a similar position, was content with five hundred thousand—and he used the money, not to put himself into debt, but to pay, very nobly, the debts of his generals.

Let's put an end to these regrettable habits; let's say, as we vote, 'That's enough!'

Who reopened this debate? Did you? Did we? We've just been told that the revival of this discussion was an act of bad citizenship. Well, if it was, should the rebuke be addressed to us? Oh no! The bad citizen, if there is one, isn't within the Assembly.

Let me finish with this point. When the majority voted for the first grant, they didn't know what was behind it.

Now you do know. To vote for it then was merely unwise; to vote for it now would be aiding and abetting.

Look here, you advocates of law and order. Do you really want law and order? Then accept the republic. Accept it, accept it in all good faith without cavil or question. No more princes, no more dynasties, no more unconstitutional ambitions; I won't say no more schemes, but I will say no more daydreams. When no one has any more daydreams, everyone will settle down. Do you think the best way to soothe worriers and pacify thinkers is to go around all the time, saying aloud 'It can't possibly last' and *sotto voce* 'Let's prepare something else'? Let's put an end to it, sirs. All these princely doings, these grants wretchedly begged and regrettably spent, these hopes that will lead to who knows what, these aspirations for a future dictatorship—which would mean a future revolution—such things are lawless and disorderly. Let's accept the republic. You can't have law and order without permanence.

As we know, the Assembly rejected the proposed grant.

from *Toute la lyre*

Post-scriptum

....

Tu me dis: Finis donc ton livre des *Misères*.

Ami, pour achever ce vaste manuscrit,
Il me faut avant tout ma liberté d'esprit.
Quand un monde se meut dans le cerveau d'un homme,
Il ne peut pas songer aux Jésuites, à Rome,   5
A Monsieur Bonaparte, à Faucher, à Molé.
Rends-moi l'espace immense et le ciel étoilé!
Rends-moi la solitude et la forêt muette!
Hélas! on ne peut être en même temps poëte
Qui s'envole et tribun coudoyant Changarnier,   10
Aigle dans l'idéal et vautour au charnier.

from *The Whole Lyre*

Postscript

....

'Go on,' you say, 'finish your book *Misères*.'*

Before completing works of that vast sort,
My friend, I need some liberty of thought.
When a whole world stirs in the human heart,
You can't reflect on Monsieur Bonaparte,
The Jesuits, Rome, Faucher, or Molé.*
Give me the silent woods, the Milky Way,
Solitude, and the far-flung starry night!
How can you be both poet in full flight
And tribune swallowing what some Nosy Parker* says,
Eagle in the ideal and vulture among carcasses?

DURING THE EXILE: 1851–1870

from *History of a Crime*

Paris Sleeps; the Doorbell Rings

On 2 December 1851, Representative Versigny,* of the Haute-Saône, was asleep in his home at 4 Rue Léonie, Paris. He was deeply asleep; he'd been working for much of the night. Versigny was a young man of thirty-two, with a gentle face, a fair complexion, a bold spirit, and an interest in social and economic studies. During the first part of the night he'd been reading and annotating a book by Bastiat;* then, leaving the book open on the table, he'd fallen asleep. Suddenly there was a sharp ring at the bell, and he woke with a start. He sat up. Day was just breaking. It was about seven a.m.

He couldn't imagine why anyone should be visiting him so early; he thought someone had rung the wrong doorbell. He lay down again and was drifting back to sleep when a second ring, still more insistent than the first, properly roused him. He got up in his nightshirt and went to the door.

Michel de Bourges and Théodore Bac* came in. Michel de Bourges was a neighbour of Versigny; he lived at 16 Rue de Milan.

Both Michel and Théodore Bac were pale, and seemed much disturbed.

'Versigny,' said Michel, 'put your clothes on right away. Baune* has just been arrested.'

'What!' exclaimed Versigny. 'Is this the Mauguin* business all over again?'

'It's bigger than that', said Michel. 'Baune's wife and daughter came to my place half an hour ago. They woke me up. Baune was arrested in bed at six this morning.'

'What's the meaning of it?' asked Versigny.

The bell rang again.

'That's going to tell us, I expect', replied Michel de Bourges.

Versigny went to the door. It was Representative Pierre Lefranc.* And he did have the solution to the puzzle.

'You know what's happening?' he said.

'Yes', said Michel; 'Baune is in jail.'

'The Republic's in jail', said Pierre Lefranc. 'Have you seen the posters?'

'No.'

Pierre Lefranc told them that the walls were now covered with posters; inquisitive bystanders were crowding around to read them. He'd gone up to one at the corner of his street. The coup had fallen.

'The coup?' Michel exclaimed. 'You mean the crime!'

Pierre Lefranc went on to say that there were three different posters—a decree and two proclamations. All three were on white paper, and they were pasted close together.

The decree was in very big print.

Then Laissac* came in. He was a former Constituent; like Michel de Bourges, he lived in the neighbourhood (4 Cité Gaillard). He brought the same news and told of other arrests during the night.

There wasn't a minute to lose.

They went to tell Yvan,* the Secretary of the Assembly, who had been appointed by the left; he lived in the Rue Boursault.

There had to be a meeting. The republican Representatives who were still free had to be warned and summoned immediately. Versigny said, 'I'm going to find Victor Hugo.'

It was eight a.m. I was awake; I was working in bed. My servant came in and told me rather apprehensively:

'There's a Representative of the People outside, sir. He wishes to speak with you.'

'Who is it?'

'Monsieur Versigny.'

'Show him in.'

Versigny came in and told me the situation. I sprang out of bed.

He told me about the planned meeting at Laissac's home.

'Go and tell some of the other Representatives, quickly', I said.

He left me.

How Dark the Crime Was

Versigny had just left me.

While I was hurriedly dressing, a man I trusted came in. He was a poor out-of-work cabinet-maker called Girard—a woodcarver, and not at all illiterate—and I'd given him shelter in a room of my house. He came in from the street. He was trembling.

'Well, what are people saying?' I asked him.

'It's chaos', Girard replied. 'The thing has been done in such a way that nobody realizes what it is. Working men just read the posters and go off to their work without uttering a word. There isn't one in a hundred who says anything about it. And then it's only "Fine!" I'll tell you the way they look at it. "The law of 31 May has been abolished." "Fine!" "Universal suffrage has been re-established." "Good!" "The reactionary majority has been expelled." "Wonderful!" "Thiers has been arrested." "Perfect!" "Changarnier* has been placed in custody." "Bravo!" There are yes-men planted around every poster. Fred Flunkey explains the *coup d'état* to Joe Blow. Joe Blow swallows it hook, line, and sinker. Fact is, in my opinion, people are just going along with it.'

'Let them', I said.

'But what are you going to do, Monsieur Hugo?' Girard asked me.

I took my scarf of office from a cupboard and showed it to him.

He understood.

We shook hands.

As he was on the way out, Colonel Carini came in.

Carini is a brave man. He had commanded the cavalry under Mieroslawski* during the Sicilian revolt; he has told the story of that noble rebellion in a few poignant and deeply felt pages. Carini is one of the Italians who love France as we French love Italy. In the present age, every man with a soul has two homelands—ancient Rome and modern Paris.

'Thank God you're still free', said Carini.

He went on:

'The coup has been carried out in a pretty high-handed way. The Assembly is surrounded. I've just come from there. The Place de la Révolution, the quays, the Tuileries, the boulevards—they're all crawling with troops. All the soldiers have been supplied with packs. The batteries have been set up. If there's any fighting, it will be dreadful.'

'There will be fighting', I answered.

Then, with a smile, I went on: 'You've proved that colonels can write like poets; now the poets have to show that they can fight like colonels.'

I went into my wife's room. She hadn't heard the news, and was calmly reading the paper in bed.

I had taken five hundred francs in gold. I put on my wife's bed a box containing nine hundred francs—all the rest of the cash I had—and I told her what was happening.

She turned pale, and said: 'What are you going to do?'

'My duty.'

She kissed me, and said only two words:

'Do it.'

from *Napoleon the Little*

Biography

Charles-Louis-Napoléon Bonaparte was born in Paris on 20 April 1808. He's the son of Hortense de Beauharnais, whom the Emperor had married to Louis-Napoléon, King of Holland. In 1831 Louis Bonaparte was involved in the insurrections in Italy (during which his older brother was killed); he was trying to overthrow the papacy. On 30 October 1836, at Strasbourg, he tried to overthrow King Louis-Philippe.* He failed; and, having been pardoned by the king, he set out for America, leaving his accomplices behind to face trial. On 11 November he wrote: 'The king, *in his mercy*, has ordered me to be sent to America.' He declared that he was 'deeply moved by the king's *generosity*', and added: 'Certainly all of us were guilty of taking up arms against the government, but *I was the guiltiest of all.*' He ended the letter in this way: 'I behaved *criminally* toward the government; the government has behaved *generously* toward me.'[1]

He returned from America to Switzerland, and was made a captain of artillery at Berne and a burgher of Salenstein in Thurgau. In view of the various diplomatic complications caused by his presence there, he was careful to avoid describing himself as either

---

[1] Letter read to the Court of Assizes by the lawyer Pasquin—who, after reading it, declared, 'Among Louis-Napoléon's many faults, at least we needn't count ingratitude!' [*Hugo's note*].

French or Swiss. To reassure the French government, he restricted himself (in a letter of 20 August 1838) to a statement that he was living 'almost alone' in the house 'where my mother died', and that it was his 'firm intention' to 'remain at peace'. On 6 August 1840, in a parody of the famous landing at Cannes,* he landed at Boulogne wearing the traditional little hat[1] and accompanied by a gilt eagle on the top of a banner, a live eagle in a cage, a bevy of proclamations, and sixty lackeys, cooks, and stableboys disguised as French soldiers—in uniforms bought at the public markets, with buttons of the 42nd Regiment made in London. He threw money to bystanders in the streets of Boulogne, brandished his hat on the point of a sword, shouted out 'Long live the Emperor!' himself, fired a shot at an officer[2] (which hit a common soldier, knocking out three of his teeth), and fled. He was caught, and five hundred thousand francs in gold and banknotes were found on him.[3] Attorney General Frank Carré told him before the full Court of Peers: 'You practised bribery and tried to corrupt soldiers with money for treasonable purposes.'

The peers sentenced him to life imprisonment. He was locked up at Ham.* There his mind appeared to ripen and grow introspective; he wrote and published some books* tinged with the spirit of democracy and faith in progress (in spite of a certain ignorance of France and the contemporary situation): *The Abolition of Poverty*, *An Analysis of the Sugar Question*, and *Napoleonic Ideas*, in which he made the Emperor into a 'humanitarian'. In a work entitled *Fragments of History*, he wrote: 'I am a citizen first, a Bonaparte second.' In 1832, in his book *Political Dreams*, he had already called himself a 'republican'.

After six years of captivity he escaped from Ham disguised as a mason, and took refuge in England. Then came the February Revolution of 1848.* He hailed the Republic, took his seat as Representative of the People in the Constituent Assembly, and said, in an address to the Assembly on 21 September, 'I shall devote my whole life to strengthening the Republic.' He published a manifesto, which may be summarized in two lines: liberty, progress, democracy,

---

[1] Court of Peers, *The Attack of 6 August 1840*, p. 140; testimony of Grenadier Geoffroy [*Hugo's note*].

[2] Captain Col-Puygellier, who had told him: 'You're a traitor and a conspirator' [*Hugo's note*].

[3] Court of Peers, testimony of Mayor Adam of Boulogne [*Hugo's note*].

amnesty, abolition of all decrees of banishment and exile. He was elected president of the Republic by 5,500,000 votes, solemnly swore on 20 December 1848 to uphold the Constitution, and on 2 December 1851, broke it. In the interim he had suppressed the Roman Republic and restored (in 1849) the very papacy he had attempted to overthrow in 1831. Furthermore, he had taken some dubious part in the shady transaction known as the 'Gold Ingot Lottery';* in the weeks before the *coup d'état* this moneybag had become transparent, and a hand resembling his could be seen within it.

On 2 December and the following days, he, the Executive Power, attacked the Legislative Power, arrested the inviolable Representatives,* dispelled the Assembly, dissolved the State Council, expelled the High Court of Justice, suppressed the laws, took twenty-five million francs from the bank, gorged the army with gold, riddled Paris with gunfire, terrorized the country, strewed the streets with corpses, and shed rivers of blood. Since then he has exiled eighty-four Representatives of the People, robbed the Princes of Orléans of the property that belonged to their father Louis-Philippe (to whom he owed his own life), decreed despotism in fifty-eight articles under the name of a constitution, employed the army to do his dirty work, throttled the Republic, used the sword of France to gag Liberty, jobbed in railway shares, rifled the people's pockets, balanced the budget by a categorical decree, deported 10,000 democrats to Africa and Cayenne, exiled 40,000 republicans to Belgium, Spain, Piedmont, Switzerland, and England, and brought anguish to every heart and a blush to every brow.

Louis Bonaparte thinks he's ascending a throne. What he doesn't realize is that he's ascending a scaffold.

5 April 1852

Here's what was seen at the Tuileries* on 5 April 1852.

Toward eight p.m., the anteroom began to fill with solemn, majestic men in red robes, who spoke in a low voice and held gold-trimmed black velvet caps in their hands; most of them were white-haired. They were the presidents and councillors of the Supreme Court of Appeal, the presiding judges of the Courts of

Appeal, and the attorney generals—all the legal bigwigs of France. And in that anteroom they stayed. An aide-de-camp ushered them in and left them there. A quarter of an hour went by, then half an hour, then an hour; they strolled up and down, back and forth, talking to one another, looking at their watches, waiting for a bell to ring. At the end of an hour they noticed that they didn't even have any chairs to sit on. One of them, Monsieur Troplong,* went into another anteroom, where the servants were, and complained. They brought him a chair. At last a folding door opened, and they passed higgledy-piggledy into a drawing room. A man in a black coat was standing there with his back to the fireplace. Why had the men in red robes come to see this man in the black coat? They were going to swear allegiance to him. He was Monsieur Bonaparte.

He gave a nod of the head, and they all knelt down on the floor, as was fit and proper. A few steps in front of Monsieur Bonaparte stood his chancellor, Monsieur Abbatucci,* once a liberal deputy, and now minister of *coup d'état* justice. Proceedings were begun. Monsieur Abbatucci delivered a discourse, and Monsieur Bonaparte made a speech. Looking at the carpet, the prince uttered a few drawling disdainful words about his 'legitimate rights'. After which, the magistrates took the oath. One after another, they raised their hand and swore. During this, Monsieur Bonaparte faced the other way and chatted with the throng of aides around him. When it was all over, he turned his back on them altogether, and they went away, shaking their heads, shamed and humiliated—not because they'd done a contemptible thing, but because they hadn't been given any chairs in the anteroom.

On the way out, the following dialogue was heard.

'Well, that oath had to be taken', said one of them.

'It has to be kept, too', replied another.

'Just like the lord of the house does', added a third.

All this is mere squalor; so let's move on. Among the presiding judges who swore allegiance to Louis Bonaparte were a certain number of ex-peers of France, who, when they were peers, had sentenced Louis Bonaparte to life imprisonment. But why look so far back? Let's keep moving on; here's something better. Among these magistrates were seven—Hardouin, Moreau, Pataille, Cauchy, Delapalme, Grandet, Quénaut—who had formed the High Court of Justice until 2 December. The first—Hardouin—had been its president, the last two its deputies, the other four its judges. Under the 1848 Constitution, these men had received, and accepted, a mandate in the following terms:

'ARTICLE 68. Any measure taken by the President of the Republic to dissolve or prorogue the National Assembly, or to obstruct it in the exercise of its duties, is a crime of high treason.

'Under penalty of forfeiting their office, the judges of the High Court shall immediately meet together and convoke juries in some specified place to put the President and his accomplices on trial. They themselves shall appoint magistrates to fill the functions of the public ministry.'

On 2 December, when they were faced with the blatant outrage, they had indeed begun such a trial, and had appointed an attorney general, Monsieur Renouard, who accepted the task of prosecuting Louis Bonaparte for the crime of high treason. So we can add Renouard to the seven others. On 5 April, all eight of them were in Louis Bonaparte's anteroom. What they did there we've just seen.

Here you can't help pausing for a moment.

There are some unpleasant thoughts that have to be faced; there are some cesspools of degradation that have to be plumbed.

Look at this man. No one knows exactly where he was born—in a shack or hovel or slum of some kind—or who his parents were—his birth was an accident, a misfortune. He came out of the dirt and dropped into the mud. He had a father and mother only to the extent that was necessary for him to be born at all. After which, he was deprived of everything. He crawled around as well as he could. He grew up barefooted, bareheaded, dressed in rags, without any idea why he was alive. He can't read. He doesn't know that there are laws over him; he hardly even knows that there's a sky. He has no home, no roof, no family, no faith, no book. He's a blind soul. His mind has never been opened; minds open only in the light, just as flowers open only in the daytime, and he's in the dark. He has to eat, though. Society has made him a brute beast, and hunger has made him a wild beast. He lays in wait for travellers at the edge of a wood, and robs them of their money. He's caught and sent to prison. Fine.

Now look at this other man. He isn't wearing red livery, he's wearing red robes. He believes in God, reads Nicole,* is a Jansenist and a zealot, goes to confession, and dispenses consecrated wafers of bread. He's what is known as well born. He doesn't want for anything and never *has* wanted for anything. When he was a child, his family lavished everything on him—nurture, education, advice, Greek and Latin, tutors. He's a solemn, conscientious character. So he gets made a magistrate. Society has seen this man spending his time in meditation on all the great writings, sacred and secular—in the study of law, in the practice of religion, in the contemplation of right and wrong—and society has entrusted to his keeping its most important and venerable possession, the lawcode. It has appointed him to judge and punish treason. It has said to him: 'A day may come, an hour may arrive, when the nation's earthly ruler will trample law and justice underfoot; then you, being the man of Right, shall rise up with your rod and strike down the man of Might.' For that reason, in the expectation of that ultimate perilous day, society has heaped honours on him and clothed him in purple and ermine. The day does indeed come, the special, solemn hour, the great moment of duty; the man in the red robe begins to stammer out the words of the law; and suddenly he discovers that justice isn't prevailing—that treason is in the ascendant. And then this man who has spent his whole life imbuing his mind with the pure and holy light of justice— this man who is nothing if not hostile to the triumph of evil—this learned man, this conscientious man, this pious man, this judge who has been entrusted with the keeping of the law and, in a sense, the conscience of humanity—turns toward the successful perjurer, and with the very same lips, the very same voice that would have sentenced the traitor to the galleys if the fellow had been defeated, he says, 'My lord, I swear allegiance to you!'

Take a pair of scales, put the judge in one side and the criminal in the other, and tell me which side goes down.

The Littleness of the Master

Don't worry; History has him in her clutches.

Still, if Monsieur Bonaparte's ego is flattered by the fact that he's in the grip of history, if he happens to have any illusions about his stature as a political villain (and it really does look as though he has), he should abandon them.

He mustn't think that he'll be able to reach the level of history's greatest bandits just because he has piled horror on horror. Here and there, in some pages of this book, we've compared him to such people; but perhaps that's been a mistake. No; he's committed great crimes, but he himself remains petty. He'll never be anything more than the man who throttled liberty in the dark; he'll never be anything more than the man who intoxicated the army—not with glory, as Napoleon I did, but with liquor. He'll never be anything more than the pygmy tyrant of a giant nation. From top to toe, the fellow isn't cut out for greatness—not even in vice. As a dictator he's a clown; as an emperor he'll be simply absurd. That'll be the finish of him. The human race will just shrug their shoulders at him; that'll be his fate. Does this mean that he won't suffer any serious punishment? Not at all. Scorn doesn't mitigate anger; he'll be hideous, and he'll still be ludicrous. That's all. History can laugh and blast at the same time.

Not even the most intense indignation can raise him beyond that point. Great thinkers delight in attacking great despots, and sometimes even exaggerate their greatness slightly in order to make them worthy of their fury. But what can history do with this particular chap?

All a historian can do is drag him forward to posterity by the scruff of his neck.

After the man has been stripped of his success, after the pedestal has been removed and the dust has settled, after all the tinsel and glitter and the big sharp sword have been taken away and the poor little skeleton is left naked and shivering—who can imagine anything more wretched and pitiful?

History does have her tigers. Historians, the immortal zoo-keepers, exhibit this imperial menagerie to the nations. The mighty lion-tamer Tacitus alone caught and caged eight or ten such tigers in the iron bars of his prose. Look at them: they're stunning and superb; indeed, the black marks on their skin add to their beauty. Here's Nimrod the hunter of men; here's Busiris the tyrant of Egypt; here's Phalaris, who roasted people alive in his bronze bull so as to make the bull bellow; here's Ahasuerus, who scalped the seven Maccabees and then had them burnt alive; here's Nero, the arsonist of Rome, who covered Christians with wax and pitch and lit them as torches; here's Tiberius, the fellow of Capri; here's Domitian; here's Caracalla; here's Heliogabalus; there's Commodus, who had the further horrible distinction of being

Marcus Aurelius's son; those are the tsars; those are the sultans; those are the popes (note the Borgia tiger among them); there's Philip who was called the Good, as the Furies were called the Eumenides; there's Richard III, sinister and deformed; there's Henry VIII, with his fat face and his fat paunch, who ripped up one of his five wives and killed two others; there's Christian II, the Nero of the North; there's Philip II,* the Satan of the South. Fearsome things, aren't they? Listen to them roar; study them one by one. Historians bring these fierce and terrible creatures to you, drag them to the front of their cages, open their jaws, show you their teeth, show you their claws; you may well say about each of them, 'Now that's a right royal tiger, that is.' And indeed they've been caught on every throne on earth. History parades them through the ages; she keeps them alive and takes good care of them. They're her property, those tigers. She doesn't put them in the same cage with jackals. She keeps such filthy creatures apart, in a separate place.

Monsieur Bonaparte, like Claudius and Ferdinand VII of Spain and Ferdinand II* of Naples, will be in the hyena cage.

He's a bit of a bandit, but more of a small-time crook. You can never forget that he's the poor wage-slave prince who lived by his wits in England. His current prosperity and splendour and majesty don't affect that; his purple cloak is trailing over hobnailed boots. Napoleon the Little, no more and no less. The title of this book is an apt one.

The shabbiness of his vices undermines the greatness of his crimes. That's only to be expected. Pedro the Cruel slaughtered, but he didn't pilfer; Henry VIII assassinated, but he didn't swindle; Tamerlane crushed children under his horses' hoofs, much as Monsieur Bonaparte butchered old men and women on the streets of Paris, but he didn't tell lies. Here's what the Arab historian says: 'Timur Beg, Sahibqaran (lord of the world and the age, lord of the planets in conjunction), was born at Kesh in 1336. He murdered a hundred thousand captives. When he was besieging Siwas,* the inhabitants tried to appease him by sending him a thousand little children crying "Allah! Allah!" and bearing the Qur'an on their heads. He had the sacred books respectfully removed, and then crushed the children under the hooves of his horses. He used seventy thousand human heads, together with cement, stone, and brick, to build towers at Harat, Sabzawar, Takrit, Aleppo, and Baghdad. He hated lies. Whenever he gave his word, you could rely on it.'

Monsieur Bonaparte doesn't measure up to that. He hasn't the dignity that the great Eastern and Western despots blended with their ferocity. He hasn't the stature to be a Caesar. If you want to put up a good show and look like all the illustrious executioners who have tortured the human race for the last four thousand years, you mustn't be a cross between a minor lieutenant-general and a Champs-Élysées mountebank; you mustn't have done a stint as a London bobby; you mustn't have faced the full Court of Peers with downcast eyes and wiped Monsieur Magnan's stinging denunciations off your brow; you mustn't have been called a pick-pocket by the English newspapers; you mustn't have been threatened with Clichy* jail; in short, you mustn't have been a mere skunk.

Dear Monsieur Louis-Napoléon, you're aiming high, you've got plenty of ambition, but you do need to be told the truth. What do you expect us to do? It's all very well for you to abolish the French parliament and fulfil, in your own style, Caligula's 'I wish the human race had only one head, so that I could chop it off at a single stroke'; it's all very well for you to banish republicans by the thousand as Philip III expelled Moors and Torquemada hunted down Jews; it's all very well for you to have Pedro the Cruel's forts and Khayr ad-Din's galleys and Ezzelino's dungeons and Michel Le Tellier's gun-point persecutions; it's all very well for you to perjure yourself like Ludovico Sforza; it's all very well for you to butcher and massacre wholesale like Charles IX*—it's all very well for you to make us remember those names whenever we think of yours; you're nothing more than a clod. Nobody can become a monster just by wishing it.

from *Things Seen*

Writing to France

Today, 17 March [1853], I wrote to Jules Janin, at Paris. For the letter to reach him in spite of the honourable Mr Bonaparte's police, here's what had to be done: I posted a letter to Monsieur Savoye, Member of the Assembly in exile, 52 Milton Street, Dorset Square, London. Inside the envelope there was a letter addressed to 'Monsieur Flaubert, Croisset, near Rouen', which Monsieur Savoye was asked to post. Inside that envelope there was a third letter addressed to Madame Louise Colet, 90 Rue de Sèvres, Paris, which Monsieur Flaubert was asked to post. Inside the envelope addressed to Madame Colet was the letter to Janin, 20 Rue Vaugirard.

Charles II

Jersey, 29 May 1853

Just now I saw some carts decorated with oak branches going past on the road in front of my house. I went up to one of the drivers and asked him: 'Why is your horse wearing those oak branches?' He replied, in a Jersey accent: 'There was a king that hid in an oak tree once on 29 May, it's 29 May today, and we're putting oak on our carriages.' And off he went.

Then I remembered that Charles II hid in the branches of an oak after being defeated by Cromwell at the battle of Worcester, on 29 May 1651.* Nine years later the aforesaid Charles II came to the throne, erected gibbets and scaffolds, chopped off numerous heads, sold Dunkirk to Louis XIV, corrupted Parliament, had England crushed by Holland in the great four-day naval battle between 1 and 4 June 1666; bastards pullulated around his bed, and his whole reign, except for the bloodshed, was one long orgy. He was as weak as Louis XIII, as dissipated as Louis XV, and as cruel as Louis XI.* And today, two hundred years later, a nation still remembers the fellow without hating him. O the stubbornness of this old Anglo-Norman race! How solidly built prejudices are! And how Chinese the English are!

from *Les Châtiments*

«France! à l'heure où tu te prosternes . . .»

France! à l'heure où tu te prosternes,
Le pied d'un tyran sur ton front,
La voix sortira des cavernes;
Les enchaînés tressailleront.

Le banni, debout sur la grève,   5
Contemplant l'étoile et le flot,
Comme ceux qu'on entend en rêve,
Parlera dans l'ombre tout haut;

Et ses paroles qui menacent,
Ses paroles dont l'éclair luit,   10
Seront comme des mains qui passent
Tenant des glaives dans la nuit.

Elles feront frémir les marbres
Et les monts que brunit le soir;
Et les chevelures des arbres   15
Frissonneront sous le ciel noir;

Elles seront l'airain qui sonne,
Le cri qui chasse les corbeaux,
Le souffle inconnu dont frissonne
Le brin d'herbe sur les tombeaux;   20

Elles crieront: Honte aux infâmes,
Aux oppresseurs, aux meurtriers!
Elles appelleront les âmes
Comme on appelle des guerriers!

from *The Empire in the Pillory*

'When, France, you are mere prostrate slaves . . .'

When, France, you are mere prostrate slaves
    Crushed by the ravager,
A voice will come out of the caves;
    All those in chains will stir.

The exile, standing by the sea,
    Surveying star and stream,
Will call through the obscurity
    Like a voice in a dream,

And utter warnings and alarms
    That flash with dazzling light;
His words will be like passing arms
    Brandishing swords at night.

Mountains and monuments will quake,
    Hearing those words go by;
The leaves on all the trees will shake
    Beneath the evening sky.

They will be blasts of trumpet, cries
    That make the ravens flee,
An unknown breath that terrifies
    Grass in the cemetery.

To the vile they will cry out: 'Shame!'—
    To thieves and murderers—
And they will call the souls by name
    As one calls warriors!

Sur les races qui se transforment,   25
Sombre orage, elles planeront;
Et si ceux qui vivent s'endorment,
Ceux qui sont morts s'éveilleront.

«C'est la nuit; la nuit noire, assoupie et profonde . . .»

C'est la nuit; la nuit noire, assoupie et profonde;
L'ombre immense élargit ses ailes sur le monde.
Dans vos joyeux palais gardés par le canon,
Dans vos lits de velours, de damas, de linon,
Sous vos chauds couvre-pieds de martres zibelines,   5
Sous le nuage blanc des molles mousselines,
Derrière vos rideaux qui cachent sous leurs plis
Toutes les voluptés avec tous les oublis,
Aux sons d'une fanfare amoureuse et lointaine,
Tandis qu'une veilleuse, en tremblant, ose à peine   10
Éclairer le plafond de pourpre et de lampas,
Vous, duc de Saint-Arnaud, vous, comte de Maupas,
Vous, sénateurs, préfets, généraux, juges, princes,
Toi, César, qu'à genoux adorent tes provinces,
Toi qui rêvas l'empire et le réalisas,   15
Dormez, maîtres...—Voici le jour. Debout, forçats!

Apothéose

Méditons! Il est bon que l'esprit se repaisse
De ces spectacles-là. L'on n'était qu'une espèce
De perroquet ayant un grand nom pour perchoir;
Pauvre diable de prince, usant son habit noir,
Auquel mil huit cent quinze avait coupé les vivres.   5
On n'avait pas dix sous, on emprunte cinq livres.
Maintenant, remarquons l'échelle, s'il vous plaît.
De l'écu de cinq francs on s'élève au billet
Signé Garat; bravo! puis du billet de banque
On grimpe au million, rapide saltimbanque;   10

Their sombre thunderstorm will sweep
    Across the hordes, and break;
And if those who are living sleep,
    Those who are dead will wake!

'Night—dark night, deep, and full of drowsy things . . .'

Night—dark night, deep, and full of drowsy things;
Across the world the vast gloom spreads its wings.
In your palatial cannon-flanked retreats,
Within your velvet, damask, linen sheets,
Warm in the sable quilts that swathe your bed,
With soft white clouds of muslin overhead,
Behind your curtains, whose obscure folds screen
Everything ignominious and obscene,
To the sound of remote romantic airs,
And while a quivering night light hardly dares
To light the silk-and-purple-hung tableau,
You, Comte de Maupas, Duc de Saint-Arnaud,*
You, general, judge, prefect, senator,
And you, tyrant whom prostrate realms adore
(You dreamed of empire and you got your prize),
Sleep well, you lords...—Dawn breaks. Convicts, arise!

Apotheosis

Come, let's reflect—it's good to let the mind
Dwell on such scenes. The chap was just some kind
Of parrot, with a great name as his perch;
1815* had left him in the lurch,
Poor devil, black prince in a threadbare coat;
He lacked ten cents, and borrowed a pound note.
Now, please watch the ascent: from one five-franc
Piece, he climbs up to an official bank
Note signed by Garat;* bravo! then, with paper
Money, he grabs a million—a neat caper!

Le million gobé fait mordre au milliard.
On arrive au lingot en partant du liard.
Puis carrosses, palais, bals, festins, opulence;
On s'attable au pouvoir et l'on mange la France.
C'est ainsi qu'un filou devient homme d'état.   15

Qu'a-t-il fait? Un délit? Fi donc! un attentat;
Un grand acte, un massacre, un admirable crime
Auquel la haute cour prête serment. L'abîme
Se referme en poussant un grognement bourru.
La Révolution sous terre a disparu   20
En laissant derrière elle une senteur de soufre.
Romieu montre la trappe et dit: Voyez le gouffre!
Vivat Mascarillus! roulement de tambours.
On tient sous le bâton parqués dans les faubourgs
Les ouvriers ainsi que des noirs dans leurs cases;   25
Paris sur ses pavés voit neiger les ukases;
La Seine devient glace autant que la Néva.
Quant au maître, il triomphe; il se promène, va
De préfet au préfet, vole de maire en maire,
Orné du deux décembre et du dix-huit brumaire,   30
Bombardé de bouquets, voituré dans des chars,
Laid, joyeux, salué par des chœurs de mouchards.
Puis il rentre empereur au Louvre, il parodie
Napoléon, il lit l'histoire, il étudie
L'honneur et la vertu dans Alexandre six;   35
Il s'installe au palais du spectre Médicis;
Il quitte par moments sa pourpre ou sa casaque,
Flâne autour du bassin en pantalon cosaque,
Et riant, et semant les miettes sur ses pas,
Donne aux poissons le pain que les proscrits n'ont pas.   40
La caserne l'adore, on le bénit au prône;
L'Europe est sous ses pieds et tremble sous son trône.
Il règne par la mitre et par le hausse-col.
Ce trône a trois degrés, parjure, meurtre et vol.

O Carrare! ô Paros! ô marbres pentéliques!   45
O tous les vieux héros des vieilles républiques!
O tous les dictateurs de l'empire latin!

He gulps that down, then wants it thousandfold;
So half a farthing leads to solid gold.
Next, coaches, parties, balls, extravagance;
He feeds on Power and devours all France.
That's how a sneak thief gets a government place.

What's he done? an offence? Bah! a disgrace.
A slaughter, a great deed, a glorious crime,
With the Supreme Court backing him. The slime
Closes again, with a glum gurgling sound,
And Revolution vanishes underground;
A stench of sulphur rises up from it.
'That's hell!' says Romieu,* pointing to the pit.
By threats of flogging, labourers, like blacks,
Are kept tight in their suburbs or their shacks.
Let the drums roll—long live our king Joe Blow!*
Ukases drop on Paris streets like snow,
And the Seine, like the Neva, freezes over.*
The boss? He's at his ease, living in clover,
Strolling among the prefects, flitting among the mayors,
Adorned with all the *coups d'état* he wears,
Chariot-drawn, bombarded with bouquets,
Smug, ugly, hailed by hordes of popinjays.
Then, turned to emperor, he gets engrossed
In history; home with the Medici ghost,*
He bases his idea of all that's holy on
Alexander the Sixth,* and spoofs Napoleon.
Doffing his purple or his stripes, he moons
Around the lake in Cossack pantaloons,
And, chuckling, strewing crumbs at every tread,
Gives the fish what the exiles don't have—bread.
To honour him, troops cheer and priests intone;
Europe is at his feet, and writhes beneath his throne,
Which has three steps: lies, murders, robberies.
Brass hats and mitres are his deputies.

Carrara! Paros! Attic marbles!* Bold
Heroes from brave democracies of old!
And you dictators of the Roman state!

Le moment est venu d'admirer le destin.
Voici qu'un nouveau dieu monte au fronton du temple.
Regarde, peuple, et toi, froide histoire, contemple.   50
Tandis que nous, martyrs du droit, nous expions,
Avec les Périclès, avec les Scipions,
Sur les frises où sont les victoires aptères,
Au milieu des césars traînés par des panthères,
Vêtus de pourpre et ceints du laurier souverain,   55
Parmi les aigles d'or et les louves d'airain,
Comme un astre apparaît parmi ses satellites,
Voici qu'à la hauteur des empereurs stylites,
Entre Auguste à l'œil calme et Trajan au front pur,
Resplendit, immobile en l'éternel azur,   60
Sur vous, ô panthéons, sur vous, ô propylées,
Robert Macaire avec ses bottes éculées!

L'Homme a ri

«M. Victor Hugo vient de publier à Bruxelles un livre qui a pour
titre: *Napoléon le petit*, et qui renferme les calomnies les plus
odieuses contre le prince-président.

«On raconte qu'un des jours de la semaine dernière un fonction-
naire apporta ce libelle à Saint-Cloud. Lorsque Louis Napoléon
le vit, il le prit, l'examina un instant avec le sourire du mépris
sur les lèvres; puis, s'addressant aux personnes qui l'entouraient,
il dit, en leur montrant le pamphlet: ‹Voyez, messieurs, voici
Napoléon le petit, par Victor Hugo le grand.›»

(*Journaux élyséens*, août 1852.)

Ah! tu finiras bien par hurler, misérable!
Encor tout haletant de ton crime exécrable,
Dans ton triomphe abject, si lugubre et si prompt,
Je t'ai saisi. J'ai mis l'écriteau sur ton front;
Et maintenant la foule accourt et te bafoue.   5
Toi, tandis qu'au poteau le châtiment te cloue,
Que le carcan te force à lever le menton,
Tandis que, de ta veste arrachant le bouton,
L'histoire à mes côtés met à nu ton épaule,

It's time to marvel at the deeds of Fate:
A new god rises on the temple—see,
O plebs! behold, O frigid history!
While we, martyred for justice, undergo
The doom of Pericles and Scipio,*
There shines, immobile in the timeless blue,
Like a star seen among its retinue,
Tall as the pillared emperors on high,
Near Trajan's clear brow and Augustus'* steady eye,
On the propylaea and pantheons,
Between eagles of gold and wolves of bronze,
On the friezes where Wingless Victories stand,
Among the Caesars in their sovereign band
Purple-clad, laurelled, drawn by feline brutes—
    Sweeney Todd* in his hobnailed boots!

The Man Has Laughed

'Monsieur Victor Hugo has just published at Brussels a book called *Napoleon the Little*, containing the most detestable calumnies against the Prince-President.
'We are told that one day last week an official brought this libel to Saint-Cloud. When Louis-Napoléon saw it, he took it, examined it briefly with a scornful smile, then turned to those around him and said, showing them the pamphlet: "See, gentlemen, here is *Napoleon the Little*, by Victor Hugo the Great." '

(Elysian newspapers, August 1852)

Ah, you wretch, you'll be wailing in due time!
Still panting from your execrable crime—
In all your abject glory, slick and base—
I caught you, stuck the placard on your face;
And now the mob runs up and jeers at you.
While, at the stake, Punishment nails you through,
With iron fetters straightening your chin,
History beside me strips you to the skin,
Tears off your jacket, bares your shoulderblade.

Tu dis: je ne sens rien! et tu nous railles, drôle!   10
Ton rire sur mon nom gaîment vient écumer;
Mais je tiens le fer rouge et vois ta chair fumer.

Les Commissions mixtes

Ils sont assis dans l'ombre et disent: nous jugeons.
Ils peuplent d'innocents les geôles, les donjons,
        Et les pontons, nefs abhorrées,
Qui flottent au soleil, sombres comme le soir,
Tandis que le reflet des mers sur leur flanc noir   5
        Frissonne en écailles dorées.

Pour avoir sous son chaume abrité des proscrits,
Ce vieillard est au bagne, et l'on entend ses cris.
        A Cayenne, à Bone, aux galères,
Quiconque a combattu cet escroc du scrutin   10
Qui, traître, après avoir crocheté le destin,
        Filouta les droits populaires!

Ils ont frappé l'ami des lois; ils ont flétri
La femme qui portait du pain à son mari,
        Le fils qui défendait son père;   15
Le droit? on l'a banni; l'honneur? on l'exila.
Cette justice-là sort de ces juges-là,
        Comme des tombeaux la vipère.

Le Chasseur noir

        —Qu'es-tu, passant? Le bois est sombre,
        Les corbeaux volent en grand nombre,
                Il va pleuvoir.
        —Je suis celui qui va dans l'ombre,
                Le chasseur noir!   5

'I feel nothing!' you smirk, you wretched jade;
You mock my name, you have your little joke;
And yet my red-hot brand is making your flesh smoke.

The Joint Commissions

'We're judges'—so they say, perched in the gloom,
Sending innocent victims to their doom,
Filling up dungeons and abhorrent jails
And prison-hulks that drift as dark as night
While wavetops glint beside them in the light,
    Reflecting golden scales.

An old man shelters exiles in his shed;
Send him to prison—let him howl instead!
If you struggle against this Thief of Polls,
This renegade who picked the lock of Fate
And filched the people's rights, off with you straight
    To foreign hulks and holes!*

They batter down the friend of law; they beat
The girl who dared to bring her husband meat,
The boy who tried to set his father free.
Duty and truth are banished in their wake.
Such justice slithers from them, as a snake
    Slinks from a cemetery.

The Black Hunter

'Traveller, what's wrong? The woods are black,
The crows fly in a teeming pack,
    Rainstorms are coming.'
'I travel down a sombre track;
    I'm the Black Hunter.'

Les feuilles des bois, du vent remuées,
      Sifflent... on dirait
Qu'un sabbat nocturne emplit de huées
      Toute la forêt;
Dans une clairière au sein des nuées,   10
      La lune apparaît.

Chasse le daim, chasse la biche,
Chasse dans les bois, cours dans la friche,
      Voici le soir.
Chasse le czar, chasse l'Autriche,   15
      O chasseur noir!

Les feuilles des bois—

     Souffle en ton cor, boucle ta guêtre,
     Chasse les cerfs qui viennent paître
         Près du manoir.
     Chasse le roi, chasse le prêtre,   20
         O chasseur noir!

Les feuilles des bois—

     Il tonne, il pleut, c'est le déluge.
     Le renard fuit, pas de refuge
         Et pas d'espoir!
     Chasse l'espion, chasse le juge,   25
         O chasseur noir!

Les feuilles des bois—

     Tous les démons de saint Antoine
     Bondissent dans la folle avoine
         Sans t'émouvoir;
     Chasse l'abbé, chasse le moine,   30
         O chasseur noir!

Les feuilles des bois—

Leafy trees, which the wind has bowed,
　　Rustle... the woods have been
Filled with a midnight sabbath crowd,
　　Witches who cry and keen;
Within a clearing, through the cloud,
　　　　The moon is seen!

Hunt where the hinds and roebucks are,
Through woods and waste lands near and far;
　　The night has fallen.
Hunt down the Austrians and the Tsar,
　　　　Black Hunter!

Leafy trees...

Come, set your horn-calls echoing,
Buckle your boots, drive foraging
　　Deer from the manor.
Hunt down the priest, hunt down the king,
　　　　Black Hunter!

Leafy trees...

Rain, thunder; floods are rising high;
Without a hope the foxes fly,
　　There is no shelter!
Hunt down the judge, hunt down the spy,
　　　　Black Hunter!

Leafy trees...

All Saint Anthony's* demons pass
With leaps and bounds through the wild grass,
　　But cannot shake you;
Hunt down the monks of every class,
　　　　Black Hunter!

Leafy trees...

Chasse les ours! ta meute jappe.
Que pas un sanglier n'échappe!
    Fais ton devoir!
Chasse César, chasse le pape,   35
    O chasseur noir!

Les feuilles des bois—

    Le loup de ton sentier s'écarte.
Que ta meute à sa suite parte!
    Cours! fais-le choir!
Chasse le brigand Bonaparte,   40
    O chasseur noir!

Les feuilles des bois, du vent remuées,
    Tombent... on dirait
Que le sabbat sombre aux rauques huées
    A fui la forêt;   45
Le clair chant du coq perce les nuées;
    Ciel! l'aube apparaît!

    Tout reprend sa force première.
Tu redeviens la France altière
    Si belle à voir,   50
L'ange blanc vêtu de lumière,
    O chasseur noir!

Les feuilles des bois, du vent remuées,
    Tombent... on dirait
Que le sabbat sombre aux rauques huées   55
    A fui la forêt;
Le clair chant du coq perce les nuées;
    Ciel! l'aube apparaît!

«C'était en juin, j'étais à Bruxelles . . .»

C'était en juin, j'étais à Bruxelles; on me dit:
Savez-vous ce que fait maintenant ce bandit?
Et l'on me raconta le meurtre juridique,

Hunt down the bears! Your pack-hounds roar!
No, never spare a single boar!
    Go, do your duty!
Hunt down the pope and emperor,
       Black Hunter!

Leafy trees...

Seeing you, off the wolves all dart!
Follow them, hounds, as they depart;
    Drive them off quickly!
Hunt down the brigand Bonaparte,
       Black Hunter!

From the trees which the wind has bowed
    The leaves fall... it is clear
That the dark witches shrieking loud
    Are fleeing the frontier;
The cock's bright crow pierces the cloud;
      The dawn is here!

All things regain their previous might;
Proud France, so lovely to the sight,
    Is what she once was,
The white archangel clothed with light,
       Black Hunter!

From the trees which the wind has bowed
    The leaves fall... it is clear
That the dark witches shrieking loud
    Are fleeing the frontier;
The cock's bright crow pierces the cloud;
      The dawn is here!

'I was in Brussels; it was June...'

I was in Brussels; it was June. Said they,
'Can you guess what the thug has done today?'
I heard of legal murders everywhere,

Charlet assassiné sur la place publique,
Cirasse, Cuisinier, tous ces infortunés   5
Que cet homme au supplice a lui-même traînés
Et qu'il a de ses mains liés sur la bascule.
O sauveur, ô héros, vainqueur de crépuscule,
César! Dieu fait sortir de terre les moissons,
La vigne, l'eau courante abreuvant les buissons,   10
Les fruits vermeils, la rose où l'abeille butine,
Les chênes, les lauriers, et toi la guillotine.

Prince qu'aucun de ceux qui lui donnent leur voix
Ne voudrait rencontrer le soir au coin d'un bois!

J'avais le front brûlant; je sortis par la ville.   15
Tout m'y parut plein d'ombre et de guerre civile;
Les passants me semblaient des spectres effarés;
Je m'enfuis dans les champs paisibles et dorés;
O contre-coups du crime au fond de l'âme humaine!
La nature ne put me calmer. L'air, la plaine,   20
Les fleurs, tout m'irritait; je frémissais devant
Ce monde où je sentais ce scélérat vivant.
Sans pouvoir m'apaiser, je fis plus d'une lieue.
Le soir triste monta sous la coupole bleue;
Linceul frissonnant, l'ombre autour de moi s'accrut;   25
Tout à coup la nuit vient, et la lune apparut
Sanglante, et dans les cieux, de deuil enveloppée,
Je regardai rouler cette tête coupée.

Ultima verba

La conscience humaine est morte; dans l'orgie,
Sur elle il s'accroupit; ce cadavre lui plaît;
Par moment, gai, vainqueur, la prunelle rougie,
Il se retourne et donne à la morte un soufflet.

La prostitution du juge est la ressource.   5
Les prêtres font frémir l'honnête homme éperdu;
Dans le champ du potier ils déterrent la bourse,
Sibour revend le Dieu que Judas a vendu.

Of Charlet butchered in the public square,
Cirasse, Cuisinier,* all the wretches whom
This man in person dragged off to their doom,
Tying them with his own hands to the mark.
Ah, saviour, hero, conqueror of dark,
Caesar! God brings forth crops and bright-hued fruits,
Vines, oak trees, streams that nourish fresh young shoots,
Roses in which the honeybees can glean,
Laurels; and you bring forth the guillotine.

No one who voted him his plebiscite*
Would care to meet him in the woods at night!

My brow was burning; through the town I went.
It seemed all civil war and discontent;
The passers-by looked like scared ghosts to me.
I fled into the fields, golden and free,
Counterpoising the crimes of human brains!
But nature failed to calm me. Breezes, plains,
Flowers, all bothered me; I shuddered at
The world in which I felt that living rat.
I walked for miles, and yet I felt no peace.
Under the blue, gloom started to increase;
The dusk, a shuddering gravecloth, deepened; soon
Night fell; up came the bloodstained moon
And, in the skies with mourning robes outspread,
I watched the rolling of that severed head.

The Last Word

The conscience of humanity has died;
He debauches her corpse, he loves it so;
At times, jaunty, triumphant, and red-eyed,
He beats the poor dead thing with one more blow.

Whores are the judges' favourite pursuit.
The priests make any sane man's blood run cold;
They dig the Potter's Field to get its loot,
Sibour* resells the God that Judas sold.

Ils disent:—César règne, et le Dieu des armées
L'a fait son élu. Peuple, obéis! tu le dois.—   10
Pendant qu'ils vont chantant, tenant leurs mains fermées,
On voit le sequin d'or qui passe entre leurs doigts.

Oh! tant qu'on le verra trôner, ce gueux, ce prince,
Par le pape béni, monarque malandrin,
Dans une main le sceptre et dans l'autre la pince,   15
Charlemagne taillé par Satan dans Mandrin;

Tant qu'il se vautrera, broyant dans ses mâchoires
Le serment, la vertu, l'honneur religieux;
Ivre, affreux, vomissant sa honte sur nos gloires;
Tant qu'on verra cela sous le soleil des cieux;   20

Quand même grandirait l'abjection publique
A ce point d'adorer l'exécrable trompeur;
Quand même l'Angleterre et même l'Amérique
Diraient à l'exilé:—Va-t-en! nous avons peur!

Quand même nous serions comme la feuille morte,   25
Quand, pour plaire à César, on nous renîrait tous;
Quand le proscrit devrait s'enfuir de porte en porte,
Aux hommes déchiré comme un haillon aux clous;

Quand le désert, où Dieu contre l'homme proteste,
Bannirait les bannis, chasserait les chassés,   30
Quand même, infâme aussi, lâche comme le reste,
Le tombeau jetterait dehors les trépassés;

Je ne fléchirai pas! Sans plainte dans la bouche,
Calme, le deuil au cœur, dédaignant le troupeau,
Je vous embrasserai dans mon exil farouche,   35
Patrie, ô mon autel! liberté, mon drapeau!

Mes nobles compagnons, je garde votre culte;
Bannis, la république est là qui nous unit.
J'attacherai la gloire à tout ce qu'on insulte;
Je jetterai l'opprobre à tout ce qu'on bénit!   40

'Caesar is king—he is the Lord's elect',
They tell us; 'plebs, obey him! it's the law!'
And while they chant, tight-fisted, circumspect,
You see gold sequins slip from paw to paw.

Ah! while this wretch, this bandit autocrat
With the Pope's blessing, lords it as he likes,
Sceptre in this hand, jemmy-bar in that,
Charlemagne shrunk by Satan to Bill Sikes,*

While he keeps wallowing, crunching in his jaws
Piety, oaths, and honour, one by one,
Vomiting his drunk filth on our great cause;
While that keeps happening under heaven's sun;

If people sink to such vile wretchedness
That they adore this sneaking renegade;
If even the UK and the US
Tell the exiles: 'Get out! we're too afraid!'

If we, for Caesar's sake, are shunned by all,
Blown away like dead leaves before the gales;
If outlaws have to slink from wall to wall,
Torn from humanity like rags from nails;

If deserts, which are God's rebuke to men,
Banish the banished, oppress the oppressed;
If graves themselves spurn the dead citizen,
And prove as base and timorous as the rest;

I shall not flinch! Scorning the vulgar herd,
Calm, sorrowful, through exile and mischance
I shall embrace without one bitter word
My banner Freedom and my altar France!

Yes, fellow exiles, I still keep your cult—
The Republic unites us nonetheless.
I shall praise everything that they insult,
I shall condemn everything that they bless.

Je serai, sous le sac de cendre qui me couvre,
La voix qui dit: malheur! la bouche qui dit: non!
Tandis que tes valets te montreront ton Louvre,
Moi, je te montrerai, césar, ton cabanon.

Devant les trahisons et les têtes courbées,   45
Je croiserai les bras, indigné, mais serein.
Sombre fidélité pour les choses tombées,
Sois ma force et ma joie et mon pilier d'airain!

Oui, tant qu'il sera là, qu'on cède ou qu'on persiste,
O France! France aimée et qu'on pleure toujours,   50
Je ne reverrai pas ta terre douce et triste,
Tombeaux de mes aïeux et nid de mes amours!

Je ne reverrai pas ta rive qui nous tente,
France! hors le devoir, hélas! j'oublîrai tout.
Parmi les éprouvés je planterai ma tente;   55
Je resterai proscrit, voulant rester debout.

J'accepte l'âpre exil, n'eût-il ni fin ni terme,
Sans chercher à savoir et sans considérer
Si quelqu'un a plié qu'on aurait cru plus ferme,
Et si plusieurs s'en vont qui devraient demeurer.   60

Si l'on n'est plus que mille, eh bien, j'en suis! Si même
Ils ne sont plus que cent, je brave encor Sylla;
S'il en demeure dix, je serai le dixième;
Et s'il n'en reste qu'un, je serai celui-là!

from *Les Contemplations*

Les Oiseaux

Je rêvais dans un grand cimetière désert.
De mon âme et des morts j'écoutais le concert,

In my sackcloth and ashes, I shall be
The voice and tongue that vilify and rebel.
While Caesar's slaves show him his majesty,
Why! I shall show him to his padded cell.

Despite each traitor and each downcast head,
I shall stand firm, arms crossed, severe but calm.
May solemn faithfulness to what is dead
Be my bronze pillar, my support, my psalm!

Whatever people may succumb or stand,
While he remains in sad beloved France
I never can return to that fair land,
Grave of my fathers, nest of my romance!

I can't return to its enticing shore;
Among the sufferers I must pitch my tent.
Duty must fill my mind, and nothing more;
To stand firm, I must stay in banishment.

Harsh exile I accept, however long,
Without enquiring, without being swayed
By the weakness of some who had seemed strong,
The departure of some who should have stayed.

Only a thousand left? I'm with them, then!
Were there a hundred, still I'd brave the Hun;*
I'd be the tenth, if there were only ten;
If there were only one, I'd be that one.

from *Contemplations*

The Birds

I was pondering in a vast and deserted graveyard,
Listening to my soul and the dead singing in harmony

Parmi les fleurs de l'herbe et les croix de la tombe.
Dieu veut que ce qui naît sorte de ce qui tombe.
Et l'ombre m'emplissait.

                   Autour de moi, nombreux,   5
Gais, sans avoir souci de mon front ténébreux,
Dans ce champ, lit fatal de la sieste dernière,
Des moineaux francs faisaient l'école buissonnière.
C'était l'éternité que taquine l'instant.
Ils allaient et venaient, chantant, volant, sautant,   10
Égratinant la mort de leurs griffes pointues,
Lissant leur bec au nez lugubre des statues,
Becquetant les tombeaux, ces grains mystérieux.
Je pris ces tapageurs ailés au sérieux;
Je criai:—Paix aux morts! vous êtes des harpies.   15
—Nous sommes des moineaux, me dirent ces impies.
—Silence! allez-vous-en! repris-je, peu clément.
Ils s'enfuirent; j'étais le plus fort. Seulement,
Un d'eux resta derrière, et, pour toute musique,
Dressa la queue, et dit:—Quel est ce vieux   20
    classique?

Comme ils s'en allaient tous, furieux, maugréant,
Criant, et regardant de travers le géant,
Un houx noir qui songeait près d'une tombe, un sage,
M'arrêta brusquement par la manche au passage,
Et me dit:—Ces oiseaux sont dans leur fonction.   25
Laisse-les. Nous avons besoin de ce rayon.
Dieu les envoie. Ils font vivre le cimetière.
Homme, ils sont la gaîté de la nature entière.
Ils prennent son murmure au ruisseau, sa clarté
A l'astre, son sourire au matin enchanté;   30
Partout où rit un sage, ils lui prennent sa joie,
Et nous l'apportent; l'ombre en les voyant flamboie;
Ils emplissent leurs becs des cris des écoliers;
A travers l'homme et l'herbe et l'onde et les halliers,
Ils vont pillant la joie en l'univers immense.   35
Ils ont cette raison qui te semble démence.

Among the flowers in the grass and the crosses upon the tombstones.
Such is the Lord's will: birth is constantly springing from downfall.
Shadows were filling me.

                    Round about me, teeming and chirpy,
Quite unconcerned by the gloom on my forehead,
There in that field, that fatal bed of the final siesta,
Various bold little sparrows were playing the truant—
Transience thumbing its nose at all of eternity.
They were hither-and-thithering, flitting and skipping and singing,
Scratching at death with their sharp little clawtips,
Scraping their beaks on the statues' lugubrious noses,
Pecking at those mysterious seeds known as gravestones.
Well, I took the feathery rioters seriously;
'Let the dead rest in peace!' I cried; 'you're such harpies!'
'Nonsense; we're sparrows', replied the blasphemous creatures.
'Quiet! Be off', I replied, not very politely.
Off they all flew—I had the muscle power. Only
One stayed behind and, as its sole melody,
Hitched up its tail and asked: 'Just who is this old-fashioned
    classicist?'

As they all fled, furious and fuming,
Yelling, and eyeing the giant distinctly askance, a
Sage, a dark holly bush daydreaming close to a tombstone,
Suddenly caught me in passing, clutched at my sleeve and
Told me: 'Those birds are simply doing their job here.
Leave them alone. We all need a bit of their sunlight.
They come from the Lord, and add life to the graveyard.
Yes, you human; they contain all Nature's gaiety,
They draw babblings from brooks and radiance from stars and
Smiles from the rapturous sunrise;
Wherever a sage is chuckling, they borrow his laughter
And bring it to us; the gloom brightens up at the sight of them.
Stuffing their beaks with the rumpus of schoolboys,
Pillaging bliss from all parts of the universe,
Where people and grasses and waters and thickets are,
They have good sense of a kind that you think sheer lunacy.

Ils ont pitié de nous qui loin d'eux languissons;
Et, lorsqu'ils sont bien pleins de jeux et de chansons,
D'églogues, de baisers, de tous les commérages
Que les nids en avril font sous les verts ombrages,   40
Ils accourent, joyeux, charmants, légers, bruyants,
Nous jeter tout cela dans nos trous effrayants,
Et viennent, des palais, des bois, de la chaumière,
Vider dans notre nuit toute cette lumière!
Quand mai nous les ramène, ô songeur, nous disons: 45
Les voilà! tout s'émeut, pierres, tertres,
       gazons;
Le moindre arbrisseau parle, et l'herbe est en extase;
Le saule pleureur chante en achevant sa phrase;
Ils confessent les ifs devenus babillards;
Ils jasent de la vie avec les corbillards;   50
Des linceuls trop pompeux ils décrochent l'agrafe;
Ils se moquent du marbre; ils savent l'orthographe;
Et, moi qui suis ici le vieux chardon boudeur
Devant qui le mensonge étale sa laideur
Et ne se gêne pas, me traitant comme un hôte,   55
Je trouve juste, ami, qu'en lisant à voix haute
L'épitaphe où le mort est toujours bon et
       beau,
Ils fassent éclater de rire le tombeau.

Unité

Par-dessus l'horizon aux collines brunies,
Le soleil, cette fleur des splendeurs infinies,
Se penchait sur la terre à l'heure du couchant;
Une humble marguerite, éclose au bord d'un champ,
Sur un mur gris, croulant parmi l'avoine folle,   5
Blanche, épanouissait sa candide auréole;
Et la petite fleur, par-dessus le vieux mur,
Regardait fixement dans l'éternel azur
Le grand astre épanchant sa lumière immortelle.
—Et moi, j'ai des rayons aussi! lui disait-elle.   10

They take pity on us, who are languishing far from them;
When they are brimming with playtime and song,
Idylls and kisses and all the sly gossip that birdnests
Utter in April in shady green coverts,
Then they come flocking from mansions and forests and cottages,
Rowdy and joyous and charming and frolicsome,
Shedding the whole of that light on our dreadful deep burrows,
Pouring the lot of it into our darkness!
Dreamer, whenever May brings them back to us,
We cry out: "There they are!" Everything—mounds, lawns,
    gravestones—gets ex-
Cited; the tiniest shrubs start talking, the grass is ecstatic;
Willows stop weeping and burst into song. They
Hear the confessions of newly prattlesome yew trees,
Chat about life with the hearses, and unpick the
Overly grandiose graveclothes.
Oh, they know how to read; they make fun of marble; and
I—the aged curmudgeonly thornbush
In whose presence a lie always feels quite at home and
Spreads out its unashamed ugliness everywhere—
I find it fit and proper, my friend, that after
Reading the epitaph, where the deceased is always so righteous and
    fair,
They make the very sepulchre burst with laughter.'

Unity

Above the hillsides growing overcast,
The sun, that blossom of the glorious Vast,
Was leaning earthwards at the twilight hour.
On a grey crumbling wall, a lowly flower
In the wild grass proceeded to unroll
        Its innocent white aureole.
The little daisy on the old wall there
Gazed at the great star in the timeless air
Shedding eternal luminosity.
        'Ah yes, I have rays too!' said she.

Halte en marchant

Une brume couvrait l'horizon; maintenant
Voici le clair midi qui surgit rayonnant;
Le brouillard se dissout en perles sur les branches,
Et brille, diamant, au collier des pervenches.
Le vent souffle à travers les arbres sur les toits   5
Du hameau noir cachant ses chaumes dans les bois,
Et l'on voit tressaillir, épars dans les ramées,
Le vague arrachement des tremblantes fumées;
Un ruisseau court dans l'herbe entre deux hauts talus
Sous l'agitation des saules chevelus;   10
Un orme, un hêtre, anciens du vallon, arbres frères
Qui se donnent la main des deux rives contraires,
Semblent, sous le ciel bleu, dire: A la bonne foi;
L'oiseau chante son chant plein d'amour et d'effroi
Et du frémissement des feuilles et des ailes;   15
L'étang luit sous le vol des feuilles et des ailes;
Un bouge est là, montrant dans la sauge et le thym
Un vieux saint souriant parmi des brocs d'étain,
Avec tant de rayons et de fleurs sur la berge,
Que c'est peut-être un temple ou peut-être une auberge.   20
Que notre bouche ait soif, ou que ce soit le cœur,
Gloire au Dieu bon qui tend la coupe au voyageur!
Nous entrons.—Qu'avez-vous?—Des œufs frais, de l'eau fraîche.
On croît voir l'humble toit effondré d'une crèche.
A la source du pré, qu'abrite un vert rideau,   25
Une enfant blonde alla remplir sa jarre d'eau,
Joyeuse, et soulevant son jupon de futaine.
Pendant qu'elle plongeait sa cruche à la fontaine,
L'eau semblait admirer, gazouillant doucement,
Cette belle petite aux yeux de firmament.   30

Et moi, près du grand lit drapé de vieilles serges,
Pensif, je regardais un Christ battu de verges.

Wayside Pause

The skyline had been veiled in mist, but now
Midday emerges, bright and beaming;
The fog dissolves in pearls on every bough;
On all the periwinkles diamond necklaces are gleaming;
Among the woods, above the roofs, a breeze
Stirs the dark hamlet hidden in the trees;
A faint uprooted strand of smoke now billows
Tremulously across that leafy realm;
A brook runs through the grass, between high banks,
Beneath the wavering and tousled willows;
The valley's elders, brother trees, an elm
And beech, shake hands across its opposite flanks,
And murmur 'How d'ye do?' under the bright blue skies.
A songbird sings
Of love and fear and trembling leaves and wings;
A pool is glistening underneath green damselflies.
There, peeking through the sage and thyme, a cottage lies,
An old saint* smiling among pitchers made of tin;
So many flowers and light-rays deck its brink
That it could be a temple—or an inn.
Praise to the Lord who offers travellers drink,
Whether your mouth is thirsty, or your soul!
In we go. 'What have you got?' 'Fresh eggs, fresh water.'
It looks no roomier than a cubbyhole.
A blonde-haired daughter,
Joyously hitching up her fustian skirt,
Goes to draw water from the field's green-girt
Spring. While she fills her jug, the fountainhead
Murmurs, it seems, with an admiring glance
At this pretty girl eyed like the expanse.

Meanwhile, beside the big old serge-draped bed,
I ponder a Christ being buffeted.*

Eh! qu'importe l'outrage aux martyrs éclatants,
Affront de tous les lieux, crachat de tous les temps,
Vaine clameur d'aveugle, éternelle huée   35
Où la foule toujours s'est follement ruée!

Plus tard, le vagabond flagellé devient Dieu;
Ce front noir et saignant semble fait de ciel bleu,
Et, dans l'ombre, éclairant palais, temple, masure,
Le crucifix blanchit et Jésus-Christ s'azure.   40
La foule un jour suivra vos pas; allez, saignez,
Souffrez, penseurs, des pleurs de vos bourreaux baignés!
Le deuil sacre les saints, les sages, les génies;
La tremblante auréole éclôt aux gémonies,
Et sur ce vil marais flotte, lueur du ciel,   45
Du cloaque de sang feu follet éternel.

Toujours au même but le même sort ramène.
Il est, au plus profond de notre histoire humaine,
Une sorte de gouffre où viennent tour à tour
Tomber tous ceux qui sont de la vie et du jour.   50
Les bons, les purs, les grands, les divins, les célèbres,
Flambeaux échevelés au souffle des ténèbres.
Là se sont engloutis les Dantes disparus,
Socrate, Scipion, Milton, Thomas Morus,
Eschyle, ayant aux mains des palmes frissonnantes.   55
Nuit d'où l'on voit sortir leurs mémoires planantes!
Car ils ne sont complets qu'après qu'ils sont déchus.
De l'exil d'Aristide au bûcher de Jean Huss,
Le genre humain pensif—c'est ainsi que nous sommes—
Rêve ébloui devant l'abîme des grands hommes.   60
Ils sont, telle est la loi des hauts destins penchant,
Tes semblables, soleil! leur gloire est leur couchant;
Et, fier Niagara dont le flot gronde et lutte,
Tes pareils; ce qu'ils ont de plus beau, c'est leur chute.

Un de ceux qui liaient Jésus-Christ au poteau   65
Et qui sur son dos nu jetaient un vil manteau,
Arracha de ce front tranquille une poignée
De cheveux qu'inondait la sueur résignée,

Did dazzling martyrs care when they faced shame
And all the ages' spittle and all the nations' blame
And the vain blind howl, the eternal cry
That always rose where the mob madly trod?

That flogged vagabond, later, became God.
His bloodstained dark brow seems like azure sky;
Christ, in the gloom, glows blue, and the cross white,
Lighting slum, temple, palace, with its light.
Bleed, suffer, sages, bathed in your oppressors' tears!
The mob one day will follow where you go.
Mourning sanctifies thinkers, saints, and seers;
The Gemonies* release a quivering glow;
On that vile swamp, an age-old heavenly gleam,
The will-o'-the-wisp of the bloodstained sewer, drifts downstream.

The same fate always leads to the same place:
Deep in the history of the human race
Is an abyss, where, in succession, all
Those who belong to life and light must fall,
The good, the great, the famous, and the fair,
Those torch-flames ruffled when the shadows blow;
The vanished Dantes have been swallowed there,
Aeschylus, palm-branch quivering in hand,
Socrates, Milton, More, and Scipio.*
Out of that night their soaring memories flow!
Only after their fall are they complete.
Thoughtful (our race *is* thoughtful) people stand
Amazed before the chasm of the great,
From Aristides' exile to John Huss's* brand.
They, by the sovereign will of Fate,
Are like the sun whose glory is its setting,
Or proud Niagara with its howling, fretting
Torrent: their finest hour is their defeat.

When Christ was crucified, one of the pack
Who tossed a cheap cloak onto his bare back
Ripped from his brow a handful of hair, wet
With tranquil sweat.

Et dit: Je vais montrer à Caïphe cela!
Et, crispant son poing noir, cet homme s'en alla;   70
La nuit était venue et la rue était sombre;
L'homme marchait; soudain, il s'arrêta dans l'ombre,
Stupéfait, pâle, et comme en proie aux visions,
Frémissant;—il avait dans la main des rayons.

«Je lisais. Que lisais-je? Oh! le vieux livre austère . . .»

Je lisais. Que lisais-je? Oh! le vieux livre austère,
Le poëme éternel!—La Bible?—Non, la terre.
Platon, tous les matins, quand revit le ciel bleu,
Lisait les vers d'Homère, et moi, les fleurs de Dieu.
J'épelle les buissons, les brins d'herbe, les sources;   5
Et je n'ai pas besoin d'emporter dans mes courses
Mon livre sous mon bras, car je l'ai sous mes pieds.
Je m'en vais devant moi dans les lieux non frayés,
Et j'étudie à fond le texte, et je me penche,
Cherchant à déchiffrer la corolle et la branche.   10
Donc, courbé,—c'est ainsi qu'en marchant je traduis
La lumière en idée, en syllabes les bruits,—
J'étais en train de lire un champ, page fleurie,
Je fus interrompu dans cette rêverie;
Un doux martinet noir avec un ventre blanc   15
Me parlait; il disait:—O pauvre homme, tremblant
Entre le doute morne et la foi qui délivre,
Je t'approuve, il est bon de lire dans ce livre.
Lis toujours, lis sans cesse, ô penseur agité,
Et que les champs profonds t'emplissent de clarté!   20
Il est sain de toujours feuilleter la nature,
Car c'est la grande lettre et la grande écriture;
Car la terre, cantique où nous nous abîmons,
A pour versets les bois et pour strophes les monts.
Lis. Il n'est rien dans tout ce que peut sonder l'homme   25
Qui, bien questionné par l'âme, ne se nomme.
Médite. Tout est plein de jour, même la nuit;
Et tout ce qui travaille, éclaire, aime ou détruit,

'I'll show Caiaphas* this!' he said.
And, clenching his dark fist, away he sped.
The street was sombre; night had come;
He walked on, in the gloom, then suddenly stopped, struck dumb,
Pallid, as if oppressed by visions, and
Shuddered—there were light-rays in his hand.

'I was reading. Reading what? The timeless poem . . .'

I was reading. Reading what? The timeless poem,
    The stern old book. The Bible? No, the earth.
When blue skies were reborn each morning, Plato
    Used to read Homer's lines; I read God's flowers.*
I spell out bushes, grass blades, springs of water;
    And while I stroll around, I never need
To hold my book under my arm; it's underfoot.
    Off I go, heading for untrodden realms;
I stoop, study the text in depth, attempt to
    Decipher all the petals and the boughs.
So, bowed down—that's the way I walk, translating
    Light into thought, sounds into syllables—
I was reading a field, a flowering page, when
    I was disrupted in my reverie;
A gentle black white-bellied martlet
    Spoke to me, saying: 'Well done, you poor man
Wavering between lugubrious doubt and saving faith!
    It's good to read that book. Keep reading it,
Read it incessantly, you troubled thinker;
    May those profound fields fill your soul with light!
It's healthy to keep turning nature's pages,
    The vast letter inscribed on the vast scale,
The earth, that canticle in which we plunge ourselves—
    Its versicles are woods, its stanzas peaks!
Read on. Anything that a man can fathom
    Will state its name when questioned by the soul.
Reflect. All things—yes, even night—are full of daylight,
    All things that glimmer, toil, love, or destroy

A des rayons: la roue au dur moyen, l'étoile,
La fleur, et l'araignée au centre de sa toile.   30
Rends-toi compte de Dieu. Comprendre, c'est aimer.
Les plaines où le ciel aide l'herbe à germer,
L'eau, les prés, sont autant de phrases où le sage
Voit serpenter des sens qu'il saisit en passage.
Marche au vrai. Le réel, c'est le juste, vois-tu;   35
Et voir la vérité, c'est trouver la vertu.
Bien lire l'univers, c'est bien lire la vie.
Le monde est l'œuvre où rien ne ment et ne dévie,
Et dont les mots sacrés répandent de l'encens.
L'homme injuste est celui qui fait des contre-sens.   40
Oui, la création tout entière, les choses,
Les êtres, les rapports, les éléments, les causes,
Rameaux dont le ciel clair perce le réseau noir,
L'arabesque des bois sur les cuivres du soir,
La bête, le rocher, l'épi d'or, l'aile peinte,   45
Tout cet ensemble obscur, végétation sainte,
Compose en se croisant ce chiffre énorme: DIEU.
L'éternel est écrit dans ce qui dure peu;
Toute l'immensité, sombre, bleue, étoilée,
Traverse l'humble fleur, du penseur contemplée;   50
On voit les champs, mais c'est de Dieu qu'on s'éblouit.
Le lys que tu comprends en toi s'épanouit.
Les roses que tu lis s'ajoutent à ton âme.
Les fleurs chastes, d'où sort une invisible flamme,
Sont les conseils que Dieu sème sur le chemin;   55
C'est l'âme qui les doit cueillir, et non la main.
Ainsi tu fais; aussi l'aube est sur ton front sombre,
Aussi tu deviens bon, juste et sage; et dans l'ombre
Tu reprends la candeur sublime du berceau.—
Je répondis:—Hélas! tu te trompes, oiseau,   60
Ma chair, faite de cendre, à chaque instant succombe;
Mon âme ne sera blanche que dans la tombe;
Car l'homme, quoi qu'il fasse, est aveugle ou méchant.—
Et je continuai la lecture du champ.

Have rays: the star, the wheel with its strong axle,
　　The flower, the spider centred in its web.
Take note of God. Understanding is loving.
　　The plains where the sky helps the grass to sprout,
The streams, the meadows, are all sentences; a wise man
　　Sees sense meander there, and fleetingly
Grasps it. Walk toward truth—reality is justice;
　　See what is true, and you'll find what is good.
If you read the world well, you'll read life well.
　　Creation is a work that never lies
Or strays; its sacred words are shedding fragrance.
　　Unrighteous people misinterpret it.
Yes: heaven and earth and all things in them, entities,
　　Creatures, relations, causes, elements,
Branches with bright sky showing through their black mesh,
　　Forest arabesques against evening's bronze,
The whole dark mass of holy vegetation,
　　Animals, rocks, golden wheat, painted wings,
Enlarges into this enormous cipher: GOD—
　　The timeless written in the transient.
The whole blue sombre starry Vast traverses
　　One humble flower which thinkers contemplate;
You see the fields, but what is dazzling you is God.
　　The lilies that you grasp blossom within you;
The roses that you read contribute to your soul.
　　The pure flowers that emit an unseen fire
Are counsels planted by God on the wayside;
　　A soul, and not a hand, must gather them.
When you do that, dawn breaks across your dark brow;
　　You become good, wise, righteous; in the gloom
You regain the sublime innocence of your cradle.'
　　'Ah, little bird, you're wrong there!' I replied;
'My flesh is dust—is vanquished every moment;
　　My soul will be white only when I've died.
Man, whatever he does, is blind or evil.'
　　And I went on reading the countryside.

Le Mendiant

Un pauvre homme passait dans le givre et le vent.
Je cognai sur ma vitre; il s'arrêta devant
Ma porte, que j'ouvris d'une façon civile.
Les ânes revenaient du marché de la ville,
Portant les paysans accroupis sur leurs bâts.   5
C'était le vieux qui vit dans une niche au bas
De la montée, et rêve, attendant, solitaire,
Un rayon du ciel triste, un liard de la terre,
Tendant les mains pour l'homme et les joignant pour Dieu.
Je lui criai:—Venez vous réchauffer un peu.   10
Comment vous nommez-vous?—Il me dit:—Je me nomme
Le pauvre.—Je lui pris la main:—Entrez, brave homme.—
Et je lui fis donner une jatte de lait.
Le vieillard grelottait de froid; il me parlait,
Et je lui répondais, pensif et sans l'entendre.   15
—Vos habits sont mouillés, dis-je, il faut les étendre
Devant la cheminée.—Il s'approcha du feu.
Son manteau, tout mangé des vers, et jadis bleu,
Étalé largement sur la chaude fournaise,
Piqué de mille trous par la lueur de braise,   20
Couvrait l'âtre, et semblait un ciel noir étoilé.
Et, pendant qu'il séchait ce haillon désolé
D'où ruisselait la pluie et l'eau des fondrières,
Je songeais que cet homme était pleine de prières,
Et je regardais, sourd à ce que nous disions,   25
Sa bure où je voyais des constellations.

Mugitusque boum

Mugissement des bœufs, au temps du doux Virgile,
Comme aujourd'hui, le soir, quand fuit la nuit agile,
Ou, le matin, quand l'aube aux champs extasiés
Verse à flots la rosée et le jour, vous disiez:
Mûrissez, blés mouvants! prés, emplissez-vous d'herbes!   5
Que la terre, agitant son panache de gerbes,

The Beggar

In the frost, in the gale, a poor man was going past.
I rapped on the window pane; he paused in front of
My door, which I opened politely.
Donkeys were coming back saddled from the marketplace
With country folk perched on them.
He lives, this old man, in some humble dog's retreat
At the foot of the hill, quite alone, hoping
For a cold sunbeam from heaven, or half a farthing from earth,
With hands spread out to man or clasped to God.
'Come and warm up', I bellowed; 'what is your name?'
He said, 'I am the
Poor.' I took his hand. 'Come in, sir', I told him.
I got him a bowl of milk.
He was shivering with cold, the old fellow; he talked and
I answered without hearing, my thoughts elsewhere.
'Your clothes are all wet', I said; 'you should hang them in front of
The fireplace.' He moved closer to the fire.
His cloak, moth-eaten, and formerly blue,
Slung right across the warm blaze,
Riddled with thousands of holes by the light of the flames,
Shrouded the hearth, and looked like a black starry sky.
Then, while he dried those wretched tatters
Dripping with rain and ditch water,
I thought how this man was utterly steeped in prayer;
Deaf to what we were saying, I
Gazed at the cloth, in which I could see constellations.

Lowing of Oxen

Those lowing oxen, in the days of gentle Virgil*—
    At dusk, when agile night came rushing through,
Or at dawn, when the sun poured floods of dew and daylight
    On ravished fields—declared, just as ours do:
'Ripen, you flowing wheat, and fill with grass, you meadows!
    And may the land, stirring its plumes of grain,

Chante dans l'onde d'or d'une riche moisson!
Vis, bête; vis, caillou; vis, homme; vis, buisson!
A l'heure où le soleil se couche, où l'herbe est pleine
Des grands fantômes noirs des arbres de la plaine   10
Jusqu'aux lointains coteaux rampant et grandissant,
Quand le brun laboureur des collines descend
Et retourne à son toit d'où sort une fumée,
Que la soif de revoir sa femme bien-aimée
Et l'enfant qu'en ses bras hier il réchauffait,   15
Que ce désir, croissant à chaque pas qu'il fait,
Imite dans son cœur l'allongement de l'ombre!
Êtres! choses! vivez! sans peur, sans deuil, sans nombre!
Que tout s'épanouisse en sourire vermeil!
Que l'homme ait le repas et le bœuf le sommeil!   20
Vivez! croissez! semez le grain à l'aventure!
Qu'on sente frissonner dans toute la nature,
Sous la feuille des nids, au seuil blanc des maisons,
Dans l'obscur tremblement des profonds horizons,
Un vaste emportement d'aimer, dans l'herbe verte,   25
Dans l'antre, dans l'étang, dans la clairière ouverte,
D'aimer sans fin, d'aimer toujours, d'aimer encor,
Sous la sérénité des sombres astres d'or!
Faites tressaillir l'air, le flot, l'aile, la bouche,
O palpitations du grand amour farouche!   30
Qu'on sente le baiser de l'être illimité!
Et paix, vertu, bonheur, espérance, bonté,
O fruits divins, tomber des branches éternelles!—

Ainsi vous parliez, voix, grandes voix solennelles;
Et Virgile écoutait comme j'écoute, et l'eau   35
Voyait passer le cygne auguste, et le bouleau
Le vent, et le rocher l'écume, et le ciel sombre
L'homme...—O nature! abîme! immensité de l'ombre!

Apparition

Je vis un ange blanc qui passait sur ma tête;
Son vol éblouissant apaisait la tempête,
Et faisait taire au loin la mer pleine de bruit.

Sing in the dark about the gold of a rich harvest!
    Stones, men, plants, beasts—be alive! On the plain,
At the hour when the sun is bedding down, when dusky
    Phantoms of trees are filling the terrain
Up to the distant writhing, growing mountains,
    When the brown ploughman leaves the hillsides for
His own roof, out of which a trail of smoke is rising*—
    May the desire to see his wife once more,
And the beloved child he warmed in his arms yesterday—
    May that thirst, at his every step, progress
Within his heart, like the progressing darkness!
    Be alive, all things! fearless, sorrowless,
Numberless! let them all spread in a smile of brilliance!
    May people have repose, and oxen sleep!
Be alive! increase! sow your seed at random!
    In the dim tremblings of the distant deep,
Among the nests, on the white thresholds of the houses,
    In the green grass, in clearing, cave, and spring,
Throughout the whole of nature, may a far-flung
    Embrace of love be felt, all quivering,
Beneath the calm of the dark golden constellations—
    Endless love, constant love, ever complete.
You mighty, untamed love, set all winds and waves pulsing,
    Set all wings and mouths pulsing with your beat!
Let them feel the unbounded I AM's kisses!
    And, all you everlasting branches, shed
Your sacred fruits—peace, virtue, joy, hope, kindness!'

    So those great voices, solemn voices, said;
And Virgil heard them just as I do; and the water
    Saw the majestic swan go past,
The birch the wind, the rock the spray, and the night sky
    Man... Nature! you abyss! so dark, so vast!

Apparition

    I saw an angel passing overhead;
    Its dazzling flight-path quieted
    The storm, and stilled the distant ocean's roll.

—Qu'est-ce que tu viens faire, ange, dans cette nuit?
Lui dis-je.—Il répondit:—Je viens prendre ton âme.   5
Et j'eus peur, car je vis que c'était une femme;
Et je lui dis, tremblant et lui tendant les bras:
—Que me restera-t-il? car tu t'envoleras.—
Il ne répondit pas; le ciel que l'ombre assiège
S'éteignait...—Si tu prends mon âme, m'écriai-je,   10
Où l'emporteras-tu? montre-moi dans quel lieu.
Il se taisait toujours.—O passant du ciel bleu,
Es-tu la mort? lui dis-je, ou bien es-tu la vie?—
Et la nuit augmentait sur mon âme ravie,
Et l'ange devint noir, et dit:—Je suis l'amour.   15
Mais son front sombre était plus charmant que le jour,
Et je voyais, dans l'ombre où brillaient ses prunelles,
Les astres à travers les plumes de ses ailes.

Cérigo

I

Tout homme qui viellit est ce roc solitaire
Et triste, Cérigo, qui fut jadis Cythère,
Cythère aux nids charmants, Cythère aux myrtes verts,
La conque de Cypris sacrée au sein des mers.
La vie auguste, goutte à goutte, heure par heure,   5
S'épand sur ce qui passe et sur ce qui demeure;
Là-bas, la Grèce brille agonisante, et l'œil
S'emplit en la voyant de lumière et de deuil;
La terre luit; la nue est de l'encens qui fume;
Des vols d'oiseaux de mer se mêlent à l'écume;   10
L'azur frissonne; l'eau palpite; et les rumeurs
Sortent des vents, des flots, des barques, des rameurs;
Au loin court quelque voile hellène ou candidote.
Cythère est là, lugubre, épuisée, idiote,
Tête de mort du rêve amour, et crâne nu   15
Du plaisir, ce chanteur masqué, spectre inconnu.
C'est toi? qu'as-tu fait de ta blanche tunique?
Cache ta gorge impure et ta laideur cynique,

'Angel, why have you come tonight?' I said.
It answered: 'I have come to take your soul.'
I shuddered—it was female,* I could see.
Then, spreading my arms timidly,
I asked: 'What will be left after you've fled?'
It gave no answer; and the gloom-ringed sky
Dimmed... 'If you take my soul,' I began to cry,
'Where will you take it? answer me!'
Still it was silent. 'Heavenly passer-by,'
I asked it, 'are you Death?—or Life?' Above
My spellbound soul, the sunlight died away;
The angel, turning black, said: 'I am Love.'
Yet its dark brow was lovelier than day;
Its eyes, within the gloom, were radiant things,
And I could see the stars against the feathers of its wings.

Cerigo

I

Every man who is growing old is here: a
Sad lonely rock, Cerigo, once Cythera
With lovely nests and verdant myrtle trees,
The Cyprian's sacred shell* in distant seas.
Drop by drop, hour by hour, Life, in her splendour, rains
Down on what vanishes and what remains;
Here, glittering Greece is dying, and the sight
Fills your gaze with both misery and light;
Clouds smoke with incense; earth is all ablaze;
Flights of marine birds merge with ocean sprays;
Water and blue sky quiver; murmurs slip
From every wind and wave, sailor and ship.
Here lies Cythera, dismal, spent, and dull—
The death's head of the dream Love, the bare skull
Of Pleasure, that masked singer, that strange ghost.
Boats, Greek or Cretan, scurry past her coast.
Where are you, soul? Where are you, star?* Confess!
Is that you? If so, where is your white dress?

O sirène ridée et dont l'hymne s'est tu!
Où donc êtes-vous, âme? étoile, où donc es-tu?   20
L'île qu'on adorait de Lemnos à Lépante,
Où se tordait d'amour la chimère rampante,
Où la brise baisait les arbres fremissants,
Où l'ombre disait: J'aime! où l'herbe avait des sens,
Qu'en a-t-on fait? Où donc sont-ils, où donc sont-elles,   25
Eux, les olympiens, elles, les immortelles?
Où donc est Mars? où donc Éros? où donc Psyché?
Où donc le doux oiseau bonheur, effarouché?
Qu'en as-tu fait, rocher, et qu'as-tu fait des roses?
Qu'as-tu fait des chansons dans les soupirs écloses,   30
Des danses, des gazons, des bois mélodieux,
De l'ombre que faisait le passage des dieux?
Plus d'autels; ô passé! splendeurs évanouies!
Plus de vierges au seuil des antres éblouies;
Plus d'abeilles buvant la rosée et le thym.   35
Mais toujours le ciel bleu. C'est-à-dire, ô destin!
Sur l'homme, jeune ou vieux, harmonie ou souffrance,
Toujours la même mort et la même espérance.
Cérigo, qu'as-tu fait de Cythère? Nuit! deuil!
L'éden s'est éclipsé, laissant à nu l'écueil.   40
O naufragée, hélas! c'est donc là que tu tombes!
Les hiboux même ont peur de l'île des colombes.
Ile, ô toi qu'on cherchait, ô toi que nous fuyons,
O spectre des baisers, masure des rayons,
Tu t'appelles oubli! tu meurs, sombre captive!   45
Et, tandis qu'abritant quelque yole furtive,
Ton cap, où rayonnaient les temples fabuleux,
Voit passer à son ombre et sur les grands flots bleus
Le pirate qui guette ou le pêcheur d'éponges
Qui rôde, à l'horizon Vénus fuit dans les songes.   50

II

Vénus! que parles-tu de Vénus? elle est là.
Lève les yeux. Le jour où Dieu la dévoila
Pour la première fois dans l'aube universelle,
Elle ne brillait pas plus qu'elle n'étincelle.

Veil your lewd breast and cynic ugliness,
You wrinkled siren* who has lost her canto!
The isle revered from Lemnos to Lepanto,*
Where crawled the cockatrice of amorous bliss,
Where the breeze gave the trembling trees a kiss,
Where shadows loved, where grass was sensitive,
Where is it? And the gods who used to live,
The nymphs and the Olympians,* where are they?
Have Cupid, Mars, and Psyche* gone away?
Where is the timid gentle bird Repose?
Where on this rock are they—and every rose,
And dances, and harmonious woods, and grass,
And the shade where the gods once used to pass,
And all the songs that blossomed out of sighs?
No shrine is left—how the past's glory dies!—
No honeybee sipping the thyme and dew;
No dazzled virgin at some cavern rendezvous.
And yet, O Destiny, the sky is always blue!
Above man, young or old, in bliss or gloom,
Hangs always the same hope and the same doom.
Where is Cythera, Cerigo? Despair!
Eden has vanished, leaving the rock bare.
Castaway, that is where you must be laid!
The isle of doves* makes even owls afraid.
The isle we used to seek, which now we shun,
Grim captive, dies!—is called Oblivion!
A ghost of kisses, and a slum of light!
And—while, protecting fragile skiffs, its height,
Where fabled sanctuaries once used to glow,
Sees stealthy pirates or sponge-divers go
Past in its shade across the high blue seas—
On the horizon, Venus fades into fantasies!

II

Venus! Why mourn for Venus? She is there!
Look higher! When the Lord God laid her bare*
For the first time in the dawn's vast array,
She shone no brighter than she shines today.

Si tu veux voir l'étoile, homme, lève les yeux.   55
L'île des mers s'éteint, mais non l'île des cieux;
Les astres sont vivants et ne sont pas des choses
Qui s'effeuillent, un soir d'été, comme les roses.
Oui, meurs, plaisir; mais vis, amour! O vision,
Flambeau, nid de l'azur dont l'ange est l'alcyon,   60
Beauté de l'âme humaine et de l'âme divine,
Amour, l'adolescent dans l'ombre te devine,
O splendeur! et tu fais le vieillard lumineux.
Chacun de tes rayons tient un homme en ses nœuds.
Oh! vivez et brillez dans la brume qui tremble,   65
Hymens mystérieux, cœurs vieillissant ensemble,
Malheurs de l'un par l'autre avec joie adoptés,
Dévouement, sacrifice, austères voluptés,
Car vous êtes l'amour, la lueur éternelle,
L'astre sacré que voit l'âme, sainte prunelle,   70
Le phare de toute heure, et, sur l'horizon noir,
L'étoile du matin et l'étoile du soir!
Ce monde inférieur, où tout rampe et s'altère,
A ce qui disparaît et s'efface, Cythère,
Le jardin qui se change en rocher aux flancs nus;   75
La terre a Cérigo, mais le ciel a Vénus.

«O strophe du poëte, autrefois dans les fleurs . . .»

O strophe du poëte, autrefois dans les fleurs,
Jetant mille baisers à leurs mille couleurs,
Tu jouais, et d'avril tu pillais la corbeille;
Papillon pour la rose et pour la ruche abeille,
Tu semais de l'amour et tu faisais du miel;   5
Ton âme bleue était presque mêlée au ciel;
Ta robe était d'azur et ton œil de lumière;
Tu criais aux chansons, tes sœurs: Venez! Chaumière,
Hameau, ruisseau, forêt, tout chante. L'aube a lui!—
Et, douce, tu courais et tu riais. Mais lui,   10
Le sévère habitant de la blême caverne
Qu'en haut le jour blanchit, qu'en bas rougit l'averne,

To see that star, people, lift up your eyes;
The seas have lost their isle, but not the skies;
A star remains alive, and never throws
Its petals off some evening like a rose.
Pleasure dies, yes; but love, that dream, lives on,
That blue nest guarded by the halcyon,*
That flame, gracing divine and human hearts.
A young lad glimpses her in dim-lit parts,
Glorious! and with her aid an old man shines.
In every one of her rays a person twines.
You ageing couples wedded with strange rites,
Devotion, sacrifice, austere delights,
Joyfully sharing in each other's woe,
Ah! live on through the quaking mists, and glow,
For you are love—light that can never die,
The star seen by the soul, that sacred eye,
The constant lighthouse, and, in darkness far
Away, the morning star and evening star!*
Our earth has what must fade and disappear—a
Garden transformed to a bare rock, Cythera,
Where everything writhes and becomes uncleanness—
Earth has Cerigo, yes; but heaven has Venus.

'The poet's verse-form used to pillage April's basket . . .'

The poet's verse-form used to pillage April's basket
    And play among the blossoms formerly.
She strewed a thousand kisses on their thousand colours;
    A butterfly to roses, and a bee
To beehives, she would sow love and make honey;
    Her blue soul almost blended with the sky;
Her eye was light, her skirt was azure. 'All things—
    Streams, hamlets, woods—are singing!' she would cry
To her sisters the songs; 'come here; the dawn has broken!'
    She skipped and laughed, the sweet thing. One day, though,
The stern inhabitant of the pale cavern whitened
    By day above, reddened by hell below,

Le poëte qu'ont fait avant l'heure vieillard
La douleur dans la vie et le drame dans l'art,
Lui, le chercheur du gouffre obscur, le chasseur d'ombres,　15
Il a levé la tête un jour hors des décombres,
Et t'a saisie au vol dans l'herbe et dans les blés,
Et, malgré tes effrois et tes cris redoublés,
Toute en pleurs, il t'a prise à l'idylle joyeuse;
Il t'a ravie aux champs, à la source, à l'yeuse,　20
Aux amours dans les bois près des nids palpitants;
Et maintenant, captive et reine en même temps,
Prisonnière au plus noir de son âme profonde,
Parmi les visions qui flottent comme l'onde,
Sous son crâne à la fois céleste et souterrain,　25
Assise, et t'accoudant sur un trône d'airain,
Voyant dans ta mémoire, ainsi qu'une ombre vaine,
Fuir l'éblouissement du jour et de la plaine,
Par le maître gardée, et, calme et sans espoir,
Tandis que, près de toi, les drames, groupe noir,　30
Des sombres passions feuillettent le registre,
Tu rêves dans sa nuit, Proserpine sinistre.

Éclaircie

L'océan resplendit sous sa vaste nuée.
L'onde, de son combat sans fin exténuée,
S'assoupit, et, laissant l'écueil se reposer,
Fait de toute la rive un immense baiser.
On dirait qu'en tous lieux en même temps, la vie　5
Dissout le mal, le deuil, l'hiver, la nuit, l'envie,
Et que le mort couché dit au vivant debout:
Aime! et qu'une âme obscure, épanouie en tout,
Avance doucement sa bouche vers nos lèvres.
L'être, éteignant dans l'ombre et l'extase ses fièvres,　10
Ouvrant ses flancs, ses seins, ses yeux, ses cœurs épars,
Dans ses pores profonds reçoit de toutes parts
La pénétration de la sève sacrée.
La grande paix d'en haut vient comme une marée.

The poet whom life's sufferings and art's dramas
 Had aged before his time,
The seeker of the dim abyss, the shadow-hunter,
 Raised his head from the slime
And seized her flitting through the grass and wheatfields.
 Despite her desperate cries and shuddering,
He caught her, weeping, in her pleasant dalliance—
 Stole her away from field and oak and spring
And love affairs among the throbbing nests within the forest.
 Now, captive and yet queen,
A prisoner in his deep soul's darkest regions,
 Among the drifting wavelike visions seen
Within his skull, celestial and subterranean,
 She sits, slumped on a brazen throne,
Placidly, hopelessly, well guarded by her master,
 Recalling the bright plains and days all flown
Away like flimsy shadows. While black throngs of dramas
 Are leafing through the inventory
Of sombre passions, in his darkness
 She sits and dreams—a sinister Persephone.

The Weather Clears

Beneath its mass of clouds, the sea shines bright.
Its waves, worn out by their incessant fight,
Subside, giving the reef some breathing-space,
And turn the shore into one vast embrace.
So, everywhere at once, life seems to quell
Misery, evil, winter, night, and hell;
A soul within all things, outspread, unknown,
Tenderly offers her lips to our own.
The bedded corpse cries 'Love!' to those still living;
Life slakes its thirst in gloom and rapture, giving
Its various breasts and eyes, its heart and lap,
So that its pores receive on every side
The penetration of the sacred sap.*
Peace comes down from the heavens like a tide.

Le brin d'herbe palpite aux fentes du pavé; 15
Et l'âme a chaud. On sent que le nid est couvé.
L'infini semble plein d'un frisson de feuillée.
On croit être à cette heure où la terre éveillée
Entend le bruit que fait l'ouverture du jour,
Le premier pas du vent, du travail, de l'amour, 20
De l'homme, et le verrou de la porte sonore,
Et le hennissement du blanc cheval aurore.
Le moineau d'un coup d'aile, ainsi qu'un fol esprit,
Vient taquiner le flot monstrueux qui sourit;
L'air joue avec la mouche, et l'écume avec l'aigle; 25
Le grave laboureur fait ses sillons et règle
La page où s'écrira le poëme des blés;
Des pêcheurs sont là-bas sous un pampre attablés;
L'horizon semble un rêve éblouissant où nage
L'écaille de la mer, la plume du nuage, 30
Car l'océan est hydre et le nuage oiseau.
Une lueur, rayon vague, part du berceau
Qu'une femme balance au seuil d'une chaumière,
Dore les champs, les fleurs, l'onde et devient lumière
En touchant un tombeau qui dort près du clocher. 35
Le jour plonge au plus noir du gouffre, et va chercher
L'ombre, et la baise au front sous l'eau sombre et hagarde.
Tout est doux, calme, heureux, apaisé; Dieu regarde.

«O gouffre! l'âme plonge . . .»

O gouffre! l'âme plonge et rapporte le doute.
Nous entendons sur nous les heures, goutte à goutte,
    Tomber comme l'eau sur les plombs;
L'homme est brumeux, le monde est noir, le ciel est sombre;
Les formes de la nuit vont et viennent dans l'ombre; 5
    Et nous, pâles, nous contemplons.

Nous contemplons l'obscur, l'inconnu, l'invisible.
Nous sondons le réel, l'idéal, le possible,
    L'être, spectre toujours présent.

Grass-blades in every crack are palpitating;
Spirits are warm, and nests are incubating.
Infinity seems full of rustling leaves,
As when, at dawn, the wakened earth perceives
The sound of daybreak, the first stir of air
And work and love and mankind everywhere,
The doorbolt being resonantly drawn,
And the proud neighing of the white horse Dawn.
A sparrow on the wing, like a mad elf,
Teases the smiling monstrous sea itself;
Spray plays with eagles, and wind plays with flies.
The earnest ploughman rules his pages, plies
His furrows, writes the poem of the wheat;
Fishermen sit in some vine-draped retreat;
And the horizon seems a dazzling dream
Where feather-cloud and scaly ocean-stream
Swim (for the sea is serpent, the cloud bird).
A luminescence, a vague gleam, is stirred
Where some girl rocks a cradle at her door;
It gilds the countryside, the flowers, the shore,
And grows bright on a grave at church asleep.
Day sinks, and kisses Gloom in the black deep
Beneath those waves so wild and woebegone.
All is calm, soft, content; the Lord is looking on.

'The soul dives in the chasm . . .'

The soul dives in the chasm—and brings back Doubt.
We can hear, drop by drop, hours trickling out
    Like rain on tin roofs over us;
The world is black, man foggy, heaven stark,
And shapes of night are passing through the dark;
      We ponder, pale and dubious.

We ponder the unknown, the dim, the real,
The unseen, the uncertain, the ideal,
     And life, that ever-present shade.

Nous regardons trembler l'ombre indéterminée.   10
Nous sommes accoudés sur notre destinée,
    L'œil fixe et l'esprit frémissant.

Nous épions des bruits dans ces vides funèbres;
Nous écoutons le souffle, errant dans les ténèbres,
    Dont frissonne l'obscurité;   15
Et, par moments, perdus dans les nuits insondables,
Nous voyons s'éclairer des lueurs formidables
    La vitre de l'éternité.

from *Les Quatre Vents de l'esprit*

Tourmente

Oh! comme tout devient terrible sur la mer!
Ces noirs chanteurs chantant sans cesse le même air,
    Les flots, dressent leur blanche crête;
Et la nuée accourt soufflant sur l'eau qui fuit
Toute l'horreur du gouffre et tout ce que la nuit   5
    Contient de haine et de tempête;

Et voici l'ouragan qui monte en mugissant
Avec un grincement de chaîne, et qui descend,
    Et qui remonte dans la brume,
Et moi, plus frissonnant que l'air dans mon manteau,   10
Je dis:—Seigneur! Seigneur! qu'est-ce que le marteau
    Fait à cette heure sur l'enclume?

Dieu! quels événements d'airain, quels rois de fer,
Quels colosses armés des glaives de l'enfer,
    Quels géants à l'horrible forme,   15
Vont sortir de votre ombre, et qu'allons-nous donc voir?—
Ainsi je rêve au bruit que fait sous le ciel noir
    Le soufflet de la forge énorme.

We watch the shudderings of the occult gloom.
We bend over and gaze down at our doom,
　　Eye fixed and soul afraid.

We spy on noises in the dismal Vast;
We hear breeze in the shadows drifting past
　　That stirs the dark; and, fleetingly,
Lost in the deep unfathomable night,
We glimpse, lit up by some great flare of light,
　　The glass pane of Eternity.

from *The Four Winds of the Spirit*

Storm

How terrible it all is now, that sea!
The black swell, which sings one song ceaselessly,
　　Is tossing its white crest;
The clouds fling at the waves, as they rush past,
The gulf's full horror—all the hate and blast
　　That Night ever possessed;

And see! the stormwind rises with a roar
Of chains, and plunges, and sweeps up once more
　　Into the foggy air.
Trembling more than my windblown cloak, I say:
'What is your hammer fashioning today,
　　Lord, on your anvil there?

What bronze occurrences, what iron kings
Brandishing swords from hell, what giant things
　　Are going to meet our eyes?
What monstrous shapes, Lord, will your gloom disgorge?'
Thus I ponder the din of that vast forge
　　Beneath the dismal skies.

from *Dieu*

from *Le Seuil du gouffre*

UNE AUTRE VOIX

Ah! c'est l'obscurité, c'est la source profonde
Que ton œil veut scruter, que veut fouiller ta sonde,
O songeur dont la nuit hérisse les cheveux!
Ah! c'est l'énigme Dieu qui t'occupe! Tu veux
Aller au fond! tu veux voir clair dans la nuée!   5
Vider l'ombre! Il te faut, pauvre âme exténuée,
Cette science-là...

          Voyons, tente; entreprends;
Avec les papyrus, les missels, les korans,
Les bibles que les sphinx portaient sur leurs poitrines,
Rebâtis la charpente informe des doctrines;   10
Des croyances de l'homme écrasé sous le faix
Échafaude l'amas redoutable, et refais
Un édifice avec ces poutres mal unies
Qu'on nomme vérités, dogmes, théogonies;
Restaure, démolis, fonde. Fais des essais.   15
Remets le vieux bahut debout sur ses vieux ais;
Crois comme Jean Climaque et Jean Catéchumène;
Ou taille un meuble neuf dans la science humaine
Pour y mettre sous clef l'ombre et l'éternité.
Questionne l'autel d'Horus ou d'Astarté,   20
Ou les temples payens peu salués des sages,
Ayant des noirs corbeaux nichés dans leurs bossages,
Ou le blême Irmensul debout sur le menhir;
Creuse dans le passé, creuse dans l'avenir;
Regarde fixement le Temps noir qui feuillette   25
L'homme et la vie avec son pouce de squelette;
Épelle l'univers que l'inconnu créa,
Texte dont chaque monde est un alinéa;
Chiffre et déchiffre; éprouve, interprète, proclame;

from *God*

from *The Threshold of the Abyss*

ANOTHER VOICE

Oh! so your plummet wants to sound,* your eye
Wants to survey the source's depths, the dimness!
Dreamer whose hair is bristling at the dark,
The mystery God obsesses you! You want
To reach the core—see clear into the cloud—
Empty the gloom! You poor gaunt soul, you need
To know that!—

                Very well, try it, attempt it;
Rebuild the shapeless skeleton of doctrine
With missals, korans, and papyri, and
The bibles borne on sphinxes' breasts;*
Stack up that fearsome mass
Of overburdened human creeds; remake
An edifice with those ill-fitting boards
Known as truths, dogmas, and theogonies;*
Restore, demolish, lay foundations. Venture.
Put the old hut back on its old planks; trust
In John Climacus or John Catechumenus;*
Or carve a new stone out of human knowledge
To make a jail for darkness and eternity.
Consult Astarte's altar, or else Horus's,*
Or pagan shrines rarely revered by wise men
With black crows set deep in their bosses, or
The pallid Irminsul* fixed on a menhir;
Tunnel into the past, into the future;
Stare at black Time who probes life and humanity
With his skeletal thumb;
Spell out that text whose lines are different worlds,
The universe created by the Unknown;
Cipher, decipher, test, translate, proclaim;

Confronte ce que l'homme a d'ombre dans son âme   30
Avec ce que le ciel a d'âme dans sa nuit;
Relance Olympe ermite au fond de son réduit;
Interroge le ver sur la toile qu'il file;
Montre et vois; fais la pâque ainsi que Théophile
Le quatorzième jour de la lune de Mars;   35
Visite Ammon; tiens tête aux colosses camards;
Conteste, affirme, nie, attends; dis ton rosaire;
Sens la terre trembler sous toi comme Césaire;
Prêche avant d'être prêtre ainsi que Bellarmin;
Exprime en ton cerveau tout le savoir humain;   40
Fais-toi de tout comprendre une étrange prouesse;
Vois venir au-devant l'un de l'autre Boëce
Et saint Denis, chacun sa tête dans sa main;
De la même façon fais le même chemin;
Hante les profondeurs dont Pythagore est pâle;   45
Commente Onuphre, Adon, Glareanus de Bâle;
Sois druide, fakir, bonze, magicien;
Installe, si tu veux, sur le modèle ancien,
Au-dessus des brouillards de l'erreur chimérique,
Une sagesse avec entablement dorique;   50
Sois le médiateur des aveugles; Volta
Dément Clairaut; Cyrille au front de Golgotha
Voit dans l'ombre une croix haute de quinze stades;
Bossuet de Calvin tance les incartades;
L'évêque Archelaüs poursuit l'errant Manès;   55
Hildebrand dit: Moi seul. Luther dit: Herr omnes.
Ce qu'adore Pascal, Diderot le diffame;
Reuchlin dit: Vos trois rois, conte de bonne femme!
—D'où viennent-ils? demande Arouet à Calmet;
De l'Inde ou de l'Afrique? Et Paracelse met   60
Trois pégases de flamme aux ordres des trois mages;
Salomon sculpte l'arche; Huss brise les images;
Pélage veut la lutte; Augustin veut la foi;
Interviens; crée un centre, une règle, une loi;   65
Trouve l'axe commun des doctrines contraires;
A force de raison rends les raisonneurs frères;
Amalgame Épicure avec Ézéchiel;
Pour ceux-ci, l'univers n'a que l'enfer pour ciel;

Compare the gloom inside man's soul
With the soul inside heaven's night;
Resuscitate Olympius* the monk
In the depths of his cell; question the silkworm
About its weaving; show, see; like Theophilus,*
Fix Easter on day fourteen of the March moon;
Brave the pug-nosed colossi; visit Ammon;*
Dispute, affirm, deny, wait; tell your beads;
Feel the earth quake beneath you, like Caesarius;
Preach, like Bellarmine,* before ordination;
Unite all human learning in your brain;
Perform the curious feat of knowing everything;
See Denis meet Boethius,* each with his
Head in his hand; travel that way yourself;
Haunt the depths where Pythagoras turns pale;
Annotate Ado and Onofrio
And Glareanus of Basle;*
Be druid, fakir, bonze,* magician; set up
A wisdom with Doric entablature*
On the old pattern, if you like, above
Mists of chimeric error; be
A mediator for the sightless. Volta
Contradicts Clairaut; in the dark, at Golgotha,
Cyril sees a cross fifteen stadia high;
Bossuet attacks Calvin's errors; Bishop
Archelaus hunts down the fleeing Mani;
'I ALONE', Gregory says; Luther, 'HERR OMNES.'
What Pascal honours, Diderot defames;
'Your three kings—a fine fairy tale!' cries Reuchlin.
Voltaire asks Calmet where they came from—'Africa
Or India?'—while Paracelsus puts
Three blazing Pegasi at their disposal.
Solomon carves the ark; Huss smashes images;
Pelagius wants works, Augustine grace.*
Step in: create a law, a rule, a centre,
Find common points in contradictory doctrines;
Reconcile reasoners by reasoning;
Fuse Epicurus with Ezekiel.*
Some people say the only heaven is hell—

C'est le cachot du mal dont vous êtes les proies;
Pour ceux-là, c'est le lieu des fêtes et des joies;   70
Les uns vivent chantant: tout est plaisir et jeu!
D'autres lisent le livre à la lueur du feu.
Mets d'accord ce zénith et ce nadir des sages.
Fais pour ton œil, penché sur les faits, sur les âges,
Une lentille avec tout ce que l'homme apprit;   75
Cherche; dis-toi:—Je vais faire dans mon esprit
Converger la clarté pour la changer en flamme,
Condenser Dieu sur moi pour allumer mon âme.—
Fouille Alcuin, saint Thomas, Gorgias Léontin,
Le ménologe grec, le rituel latin;   80
Va de Thèbe Heptapyle à Thèbe Hécatompyle;
Éblouis-toi d'énigme et d'effroi la pupille;
Écris et lis; sois gond du portail; sois flambeau;
Sois cardinal avec Sadolet èt Bembo;
Va-t'en dans le désert manger des sauterelles   85
Comme Jean qui de l'ombre écoutait les querelles;
Fais une enquête; prends des informations
Près des vents, près des flots où sont les alcyons;
Cueille chaque chimère et chaque schisme; laisse
Novatus pour Eustathe, Arius pour Mélèce;   90
Va des juifs aux parsis, va des esprits aux corps,
De la ronde des dieux à la ronde des morts,
De la danse morphasme à la danse macabre.
Veille; allume ta lampe au sombre candélabre
Que tiennent, près du trône où Septentrion luit,   95
Persée et Sirius, ces nègres de la nuit.
Interpelle le germe et la cendre; rédige
Un interrogatoire en forme de prodige;
Écoute pétiller le feu dans l'encensoir;
Écoute le cri sourd de la foudre, et, le soir,   100
Dans le campo santo le bruit que fait la pioche;
Parle à Domnus premier, évêque d'Antioche;
Et sur l'irrémissible et sur le véniel
Consulte Cassien, Scaliger, Torniel;
Sois le voyant; pareil aux tremblants aruspices,   105
Va regarder, la nuit, l'horreur des précipices;
Que tout gouffre pour toi soit un sinistre aimant;

A prison for the sin that holds you captive;
Others call it a place of joy and feasting.
Some live for pleasure, singing 'Fun is everything!'
While others read the book by fiery gleams.
Harmonize wisdom's zenith and its nadir.
Shape human scholarship into a lens
When you peer down at facts and ages; seek;
Decide to focus light within your mind
And make a flame—to condense God himself
And so illuminate your soul. Search Alcuin,
Gorgias Leontinus and Aquinas*
And Greek menologies* and Latin liturgies,
Thebes with a hundred gates and Thebes with seven;*
Dazzle your eyes with mystery and terror;
Write and read; be a door-hinge, or a torch;
Like Sadolet or Bembo,* be a cardinal;
Go and eat locusts in the wilderness,
Like John,* who heard the dark disputing; make
Inquiries; gather information where
Halcyons* are, close to the waves and winds;
Collect each fantasy, each schism; leave
Novatus for Eustathius, Arius for
Meletius; from Rabbis turn to Parsees,*
From souls to bodies, from morphastic dances*
And divine dances to the dance of death.
Stay awake; light your lamp from the dark candlestick
Held by night's negroes Sirius and Perseus
Near the throne where Septentrion* is shining.
Question seeds, question cinders, and draw up
A cross-examination based on miracle;
Then listen to fire spluttering in the censer,
To thunder's muffled roaring, and, at nightfall,
To the pick in the burial ground. Consult
Domnus the First, bishop of Antioch,
Scaliger, Cassian, and Tornielli,*
Become a seer—like trembling haruspices,*
Watch the grim precipices after dark;
Treat every chasm as a dreadful loadstone;

Observe, spectateur des deux gouffres, comment
L'homme entre dans la mort et l'astre dans l'éclipse;
Lègue aux vierges ta plume ainsi que Juste Lipse;   110
Attends dans l'infini, leur morne promenoir,
Zénon, le sage fou, Gerbert, le pape noir;
Prie, évoque, bénis, sacre, exorcise, adjure;
Accoude-toi sur l'être obscur; fais la gageure
De l'énigme, du sphinx, du gouffre, de demain,   115
D'hier, de l'avenir; jauge, la toise en main,
Le ciel par kilomètre ou bien par centiare;
Drape-toi d'un suaire ou coiffe une tiare;
Tâte dans le cercueil l'affreux nœud gordien;
Prends-toi pour unité, fais-toi méridien;   120
Ajoute ta raison, ton but, ta conjecture
Et ta pensée ainsi qu'un faîte à la nature;
Mets sur cette Chéops le pyramidion;
Sois un convertisseur comme Spiridion;
Sois un avertisseur comme le coq sonore;   125
Monte sur le cheval terrible de Lénore,
Ayant pour t'éclairer le feu de ses naseaux,
Et la clarté qu'auront les spectres sur leurs os;
Superpose et bâtis comme une tour solide
Wiclef, Leibniz, le diacre Ambroise, Basilide,   130
Swedenborg, Lyranus, Rupert, Abulensis,
Cardan, sous l'escarboucle inexprimable assis,
Photin, Cassiodore, Alcidamas, Eusèbe,
Potamon d'Héraclée et Paphnuce de Thèbe,
Tous les docteurs, vrais, faux, grands, petits, inconnus,   135
Connus, depuis Sophron jusqu'à Théotechnus,
Les devins, les savants, Paris, Rome, Épidaure,
Les poëtes sereins, ces frères de l'aurore
Faits de la même pourpre et dorés du même or,
La congrégation des pères de saint Maur,   140
La grâce, le péché, l'oraison impétrante,
Les vingt-cinq sessions du concile de Trente,
Les feuillets sibyllins tombés on ne sait d'où,
Le livre turc, le livre hébreu, le livre indou,
Passe les jours, les nuits; deviens blanc dans les rêves;   145
Sois Jérome; oui, sois Jean rôdant le long des grèves;

Observe the two abysses—see how people
Pass into death, and stars into eclipse;
Like Lipsius, bequeath your pen to virgins;
Wait for the mad sage Zeno and the black pope
Gerbert* in their dark gallery, the infinite;
Pray, invocate, bless, curse, adjure, and exorcise;
Kneel down on dim existence; challenge yesterday,
Tomorrow, time to come, the pit, the mystery,
The sphinx; rod in hand, measure heaven
In centiaires* or kilometres; wear
A shroud or a tiara; probe the coffin's
Grim Gordian knot; regard yourself as unity,
Make yourself the meridian; add your own
Reasoning, thinking, schemes, and speculations
To Nature, like a pinnacle, and cap
That Cheops with a pyramidion;*
Win converts like Spiridion;* cry warnings
Like the resounding cock;
Ride on Lenore's ghastly horse,*
With the flame of its nostrils and the glowing
Of ghostly bones to light your way;
Superimpose, build solid as a tower,
Wycliffe, Leibnitz, Ambrose, Basilides,
Swedenborg, Lyra, Rupert, Abulensis,
Cardano underneath the mystic carbuncle,
Alcidamas, Eusebius, Photinus, Cassiodorus,
Potamon of Heraclea, Paphnutius of Thebes,
All the church fathers, true, false, great, small, unknown,
Known, from Sophronius to Theotechnus,*
Soothsayers, scholars, Paris, Epidaurus,*
Rome, and dawn's brothers the calm poets, formed
Of the dawn's purple, gilded with the dawn's gold;
Grace, trespass, impetrating prayer;*
The Congregation of Saint-Maur, the Council
Of Trent* (twenty-five sessions),
Sibylline Leaves* dropped from some unknown source,
Turkish books, Hebrew books, and Hindu books.
Spend days and nights; grow white-haired pondering;
Become Jerome, or John roaming the shores;

Sois Dante pour penser et sois Newton pour voir;
Sois Origène, Euler, Platon… Veux-tu savoir
Ce que tu construiras sur Dieu?—De la fumée.

Oui, combine l'Égypte, et Delphe, et l'Idumée;   150
Cherche le sens des mots: Zéus, Vichnou, Mithra;
Fouille le zodiaque obscur de Denderah;
Espère où Nicomaque et Thalès désespèrent;
Reprends les chiffres noirs où d'autres se trompèrent;
Reprends-les tous, reprends ceux où tu te trompas;   155
Tous les cercles que peut contenir ton compas,
Trace-les; songe; parle aux arbres; fais-leur signe;
Compte, compte, recompte; additionne, aligne,
Devant l'impénétrable et devant le fatal,
Devant ce qui n'a pas de nombre et de total,   160
Tous tes zéros, anneaux du rideau de la tombe;
Le sépulcre, c'est là que toujours on retombe,
Se dresse devant toi, regarde tes travaux,
Bons, mauvais, inexacts, exacts, anciens, nouveaux!
Et ce tas de calculs que ta pensée anime,   165
Et te jette ce cri, le seul mot de l'abîme
Qu'il sache, et le seul nom qu'il se connaisse: Après?

Question que se font dans l'ombre les cyprès.

UNE AUTRE VOIX

As-tu vu les penseurs s'en aller dans les cieux?
Les as-tu vus partir, hautains, séditieux,
Jetant dans l'inconnu leur voix terrifiante,
Espérant abuser de la nuit confiante,
Méditant des larcins prodigieux, rêvant   5
D'aller toujours plus loin et toujours plus avant,
Se proposant d'atteindre à la source première,
Au centre, au but; de prendre ou l'ombre ou la lumière
Ou l'être, et de saisir le météore au vol,
Emportés comme Élie, ailés comme saint Paul,   10
Et de trouver le fond, dût-on faire le vide,
Dût-on escalader le mystère livide,

Become Dante to think, Newton to see;
Be Plato, Euler, Origen...* What will you
Produce concerning God?—Nothing but vapour.

Yes; combine Egypt, Delphi, Idumaea;*
Search for the meaning of 'Zeus', 'Mithra', 'Vishnu';*
Examine the strange zodiac of Dendera;*
Hope where Nicomachus despaired—and Thales;*
Review the dark signs that deceive your colleagues,
Even those that deceived yourself;
Trace all the circles that your compass can;
Reflect; speak to the trees, or signal to them;
Count, count, and count again;
Before what has no number and no total—
The fathomless, the fatal—add up, line up
All of your zeros, which are the grave's curtain-rings;
The tomb—the point to which all always fall—
Rises in front of you, watches your labours,
Good, bad, old, new, exact, inexact—all
The computations quickened by your mind—
And shouts at you the only name it knows,
The one word the abyss has taught it: 'So?'

Cypresses ask each other that question in the dark.

ANOTHER VOICE

Have you seen thinkers set off for the heavens?*
Have you watched them depart, haughty, seditious,
Hurling their fierce words at the unknown—hoping
To take advantage of the trusting night,
Plotting prodigious crimes, dreaming to go
Still further, still beyond, hoping to reach
The primal fountainhead, the goal, the centre—
Trying to catch the meteors in flight,
To grasp light, darkness, or existence—something,
Carried off like Elijah, winged like Paul,*
To find the core, even if all must be emptied,
Even if pallid mystery must be scaled,

L'obscurité, les cieux brumeux, les cieux vermeils,
Avec effraction d'azurs et de soleils?
Les as-tu vus, fuyants, blanche robe du prêtre,   15
Bras levés du devin, décroître et disparaître
Dans la profondeur sourde où tout s'évanouit?
Parle! et les as-tu vus devenir de la nuit?
Es-tu resté tremblant, cherchant leur trace vague?
Puis, regardant l'éther, les ténèbres, le vague,   20
Passant les jours, les nuits, seul debout sur sa tour,
O songeur, as-tu vu ces hommes au retour?
Les as-tu vus de l'ombre énorme redescendre?
Et toi, l'obscur veilleur vêtu du sac de cendre,
Te dressant au-devant de leur vol éperdu,   25
Leur as-tu dit: Eh bien?—Et qu'ont-ils répondu,
Ces noirs navigateurs sans navire et sans voiles?
Et qu'ont-ils rapporté, ces oiseleurs d'étoiles?

Ils n'ont rien rapporté que des fronts sans couleur,
Où rien n'avait grandi, si ce n'est leur pâleur.   30

Tous sont hagards après cette aventure étrange;
Songeur! tous ont, empreints au front, des ongles d'ange,
Tous ont dans le regard comme un songe qui fuit,
Tous ont l'air monstrueux en sortant de la nuit!
On en voit quelques-uns dont l'âme saigne et souffre,   35
Portant de toutes parts les morsures du gouffre.

UNE AUTRE VOIX

Les monts sont vieux; cent fois et cent fois séculaires,
Muets, drapés de nuit sous leurs manteaux polaires,
Leur âge monstrueux épouvante l'esprit;
Sur leur front ténébreux tout un monde est écrit;
L'âpre neige des jours a neigé sur leur tête;   5
Le temps est un morceau de leur masse; leur faîte,
De loin morne profil qui s'efface de près,
Livre au vent une barbe épaisse de forêts;
Ils ont vu tous les deuils, toutes les défaillances,
Toutes les morts passer autour de leurs silences;   10

Obscurity, misty or scarlet heavens,
Or azure skies and suns have to be burgled?
And have you seen them fleeing—the white priest-robes,
The soothsayers' raised arms—shrinking, diminishing
Into the silent depths where all things vanish?
Speak! Have you seen them turning into night?
Were you left trembling, searching for vague traces?
Then, when you watched wave, space, and shadow, spending
Days and nights on your tower alone—O dreamer,
Did you see them come back then? Did you see them
Redescend from the vast dark? And if so,
Did you, watching in sackcloth and ashes dimly
Before their desperate flight—did you call out to them?
What did they answer, those dark navigators
Shipless and sailless? What did they bring back,
Those birdcatchers of stars?

                      They brought back nothing;
Nothing but colourless brows, in no way greater
Except perhaps in pallor.

After their strange adventure, all were haggard;
Their brows had all been stamped by angels' claws;
All bore within their eyes some fleeting dream,
And all seemed monstrous, when they left the dark!
Some can be seen whose souls still bleed and suffer,
Riddled throughout with tooth-marks from the chasm.

ANOTHER VOICE

Old are the mountains;* hundred hundred times
Centennial, silent, draped in night beneath
Their polar mantles; their stupendous age
Frightens the soul; on their dark brows a whole
World is inscribed; the bitter snow of days
Has snowed down on their heads; time is chipped from their rock;
Their ridges—melancholy profiles, vanishing
Nearby—raise to the wind thick beards of trees;
They have seen every sorrow, every failure,
Every cadaver passing through their silences;

Ils ont vu s'écrouler des astres dans le puits
De l'horreur infinie et sourde; ils ont, depuis
Bien des millions d'ans, la lassitude d'être;
Eh bien, sur leurs noirs flancs décrépits, le vent traître,
L'orage furieux, l'éclair fauve, ce ver   15
Qui serpente dans l'ombre immense de l'hiver,
L'ouragan qui, farouche, aux grands sommets essuie
Sa chevelure d'air, de tempête et de pluie,
L'aquilon qui revient quand on croit qu'il s'enfuit,
La grêle, et l'avalanche, et la tombe, et le bruit,   20
Toutes les visions des affreuses nuées,
La tourmente et ses chocs, la bise et ses huées,
S'acharnent, et ne font, sous leurs dais de brouillards,
Pas même remuer ces effrayants vieillards.

Sois comme eux. Si tu vas dans l'espace terrible,   25
Ne chancelle pas, homme; et garde un calme horrible.

from *L'Aigle*

Qu'es-tu? Réponds.

        Sais-tu le but, l'objet, la loi?   1421
Sais-tu pourquoi le taon mord la vache, pourquoi
L'oiseau mange la mouche et le ver le concombre?
Dis, où sont les poumons du vent? Connais-tu l'ombre?
Es-tu dans le secret? Et, quand il a tonné,   1425
Sais-tu ce qu'on a dit? As-tu questionné
Les flots, quand vers l'écueil que bat leur inclémence
Ils viennent, commentant dans leur rumeur immense
Les actes inconnus de l'onde et de la nuit?
L'univers est un texte obscur; l'as-tu traduit?   1430
Qu'est-ce que nous voulaient les aurores enfuies?
Pourquoi le larmoiement formidable des pluies?
Comment l'arbre tient-il dans le pépin du fruit?
As-tu questionné le Gibel et son bruit,
L'Atlas et son semoun, l'Alpe et son avalanche?   1435
Connais-tu la Jungfrau, la grande vierge blanche?

They have seen stars collapse into the well
Of infinite mute horror; they have wearied,
For many million years, of their existence;
Now, on their dark decrepit flanks, wild storm,
Treacherous gale, brute thunderbolt—a worm
Wriggling its way through the vast gloom of winter—
The savage hurricane, wiping its locks
Of wind and rain and tempest on their great peaks;
North wind, returning when it seems to flee;
Avalanche, hail, blast, whirlwind, all the visions
Of dreadful clouds, tempest and impact, blizzard
And howling, break relentlessly about them;
Yet, underneath their canopy of mist,
Never once do these elders even budge.

Human, be as they are; if you cross terrible
Space, never slip; preserve a dreadful calmness.

from *The Eagle*

'What are you? Tell me!

                    Do you know the end,
The goal, the law? And do you know why gadflies
Bite cows, why birds eat flies, and worms cucumbers?
Where are the wind's lungs? Do you know the shadow?
Speak! Are you in the secret? When it thunders,*
Do you know what it says? Have you questioned sea-waves
When they come cruelly breaking on a reef,
Commenting with a roar on the unknown
Deeds of the surge and night? The universe
Is an obscure text: well, have you translated it?
What did the fled dawns want with us? And why
The mighty tears of rain? How is a tree
Contained inside a pip? Have you consulted
The sound of Jebel, the simoon of Atlas,
The Alpine avalanche? Do you know Jungfrau,*
The great white maid? Has she revealed to you

T'a-t-elle dit le fond de la virginité?
As-tu rempli ta cruche au puits éternité,
Et ta stupidité puise-t-elle à l'abîme?
Parle, ton ignorance, homme, est-elle la dîme   1440
Que tu viens prélever, précédé du corbeau,
Sur la science étrange et morne du tombeau,
Brume où se sont perdus tant de mages célèbres?
T'es-tu penché pour boire à même les ténèbres?
Et t'es-tu redressé sur le vide où tu vas,   1445
Recrachant ta gorgée et criant: Dieu n'est pas!

En est-il ainsi, brute? En ce cas, je m'afflige
De te voir. C'est Dieu seul qui règne et vit, te dis-je!
Et Dieu seul qui survit. Fais-tu le froid, le chaud,
La nuit, l'aube? Est-ce toi qui fais hurler là-haut   1450
L'orage maniaque, et toi qui le fais taire?
Es-tu le personnage immense du mystère?
Prouve-le-moi. Voyons, homme. Quand le torrent,
Cet ouvrier terrible, inquiet, dévorant,
Sciant les rocs, traînant les terres aux campagnes,   1455
Se met à décharner dans l'ombre les montagnes,
Empêche-le donc! Dis à l'océan: A bas!
Est-ce toi qui, prenant les lions, les courbas
Si bien qu'on ne sait plus dans leurs fuites funèbres
Si ce sont des lions ou si ce sont des zèbres!   1460
Es-tu de ceux qui vont dans l'inconnu sans voir,
Qui se heurtent la nuit à l'immense mur noir,
Et qui, battant l'obstacle avec leurs sombres ailes,
Glissent sans fin le long des parois éternelles?
Sors-tu de quelque grotte affreuse, aux âpres flancs,   1465
Où ton œil est resté fixe quatre mille ans,
Comme Satan dans l'ombre où Dieu le fit descendre?
As-tu l'esprit qu'avait la payenne Cassandre
Lorsqu'elle allait voyant d'avance Ajax brigand,
Comptant les grands palais en flamme et distinguant   1470
Dans la profonde nuit le glaive nu d'Égisthe?
Parle. Es-tu plein du gouffre? Es-tu le trismégiste?
Marches-tu de plain-pied avec les cieux, disant
Aux douze heures: Venez me parler, à présent

The essence of virginity? Have you
Filled your jar at the well Eternity;
Does your stupidity draw from the Abyss?
Speak. Is your ignorance the tithe you come
To levy, with the raven as your precursor,
On the strange gloomy knowledge of the grave,
That fog where so many wise men have lost themselves?
Have you bent down to drink the very darkness?
And did you rise from your void destination,
Spit out your mouthful, and cry: "There's no God"?

Is that so, brute? If so, I am sorry to see you.
God alone lives and reigns; and God alone
Remains, I tell you. Do you create cold,
Heat, darkness, dawn? Do you send manic storms
Howling upon the heights—and do you silence them?
Are you the great character of the mystery?
Prove it. Come, human: when the torrent, that
Terrible workman, restless and voracious,
Scything the rocks, sweeping earth through the countryside,
Sets out to flay the mountains in the dark—then
Stop the thing! still the waves!* Do you subdue
Lions—dismay and scatter them till no one
Can tell if they are truly lions or zebras?
Are you one of those who pass sightlessly
Through the unknown, who fling themselves by night
At the vast wall, who, beating their dark wings
Against the blockage, prowl the timeless barriers
For ever? Do you come from some rough grotto
Where your eyes have been fixed for four millennia,
Like Satan's in the blackness where God cast him?*
Do you possess the spirit of heathen Cassandra
When she foresaw Ajax the brigand, counted
The mighty palaces aflame, discerned
In the deep nights the drawn sword of Aegisthus?*
Speak. Are you filled with the abyss—thrice-greatest,*
And strolling on a level with the heavens,
Telling the twelve hours: "Now that you're on earth,

Que vous voilà sur terre, ayant en vous chacune   1475
La gaîté du soleil ou l'horreur de la lune?
As-tu vécu parmi les bêtes dans les bois,
Le tigre t'indiquant la source, et disant: Bois!
Et, lorsque tu songeais la face contre terre,
Un ange, qu'adoraient le lynx et la panthère,   1480
T'a-t-il jeté, de l'ombre écartant les rideaux,
Quelque effrayant manteau d'étoiles sur ton dos?
Pour parler de la sorte, es-tu celui qui lie
Et qui délie? As-tu le double esprit d'Élie?
Qu'es-tu? Dis-moi ton nom. Les prophètes jadis,   1485
A l'heure où, sur les monts par la brume engourdis,
La large lune d'or surgissait comme un dôme,
Faisant sur l'horizon des gestes de fantôme,
Dialoguaient avec les vents, et grands, et seuls,
Ils secouaient les nuits ainsi que des linceuls;   1490
Car le désert, prenant de graves attitudes,
Jadis parlait à l'homme, et l'homme aux solitudes;
La mer ouvrant son gouffre et l'aigle ouvrant son bec
Entendaient les devins, dans Endor, dans Balbeck,
Faire des questions aux ténèbres, et l'ombre   1495
Donner aux noirs devins l'explication sombre.
Es-tu de ceux-là? Non! Tu serais le dernier
Que tu ne serais pas si fou de le nier.

Serais-tu par hasard, ô parleur dérisoire,
Un des grands mécontents de l'immensité noire?   1500
Trouves-tu que les cieux sacrés vont de travers?
Peut-être étais-tu là quand Dieu fit l'univers?
Et sans doute, en ce cas, ta peine fut cruelle
De voir que ce maçon n'avait pas de truelle
Et qu'il bâtissait l'ombre et l'azur et le ciel,   1505
Et l'être collectif et l'être partiel,
Et l'étendue où fuit le pâle météore,
Qu'il bâtissait le temps, qu'il bâtissait l'aurore,
Qu'il bâtissait le jour que l'aube épanouit,
Les vastes firmaments bleus jusque dans la nuit,   1510
Et les dômes profonds où vole la tempête,
Sans monter à l'échelle, une auge sur la tête!

Holding the moon's horror or the sun's happiness,
Come here and chat with me"? Or have you lived with
The forest animals—the tiger, showing you
The stream, and saying "Drink!"—and, when you dreamed
Face to the ground, did some angel revered
By lynx and panther cast a fearful mantle
Of stars across your back, to part night's curtains?
Likewise, are you the one who binds and looses?
Have you the double spirit of Elijah?*
What are you? Name yourself. Once, at the hour
When the great golden moon rose like a dome
Over the fog-numbed mountains, in the distance
Prophets made phantom gestures, held discussions
With winds, and, great and solitary, shook
The nights like shrouds; for deserts, once, spoke solemnly
To men, and men to deserts; eagles opened
Their beaks, and seas their gulfs, and listened to
Endor's and Baalbek's black diviners* questioning
The dark—which gave them sombre answers. Are you
One of those? No! If you were least of all, you
Would never make so foolish a denial.

Might you be, O derisive talker, one of
The great malcontents of the dark immensity?
Do you think the sacred heavens are askew?
You were there, maybe, when God made the universe?
In which case, no doubt, you were most aggrieved
To see the mason working with no trowel—
Building shadow and heaven,
Azure and partial and collective being
And the expanse where pallid meteors flee—
Fashioning time, dawn, daybreak, skies whose blue
Extends into the night, and immense vaults
Blasted by storm—without
Climbing a ladder, mortar on his head!

Es-tu quelque être à qui la clarté dit: Va-t-en!
Sorti du grand flanc sombre et triste de Satan?
Non! tu n'es qu'un passant frêle et vain.

        Je convie   1515
Ton esprit à songer que Dieu seul est la vie;
Tout le reste est la mort; et je l'affirme, en toi,
A l'homme, ce buveur de la coupe d'effroi,
Ce pâle choisisseur de redoutables routes,
Cet aveugle qui guette et ce sourd aux écoutes!   1520

from the *reliquat* of *Dieu*

«Quelle idée as-tu donc de la mort, vain penseur? . . .»

Quelle idée as-tu donc de la mort, vain penseur?
Devant l'obscurité, la brume, la noirceur,
La tombe au fond du sort et la mort infaillible,
Tu frémis; car ce monde est un temple terrible.
L'affreux fourmillement des fosses te fait peur;   5
A travers sa malsaine et fétide vapeur,
Le tombeau, s'il fallait que tu l'approfondisses,
T'apparaîtrait ainsi qu'un gouffre d'immondices,
Plein d'êtres beaux jadis, lugubres maintenant,
Au lieu de la prunelle et de l'œil rayonnant   10
N'ayant sous leur sourcil qu'un horrible cratère,
D'où sortent leurs regards devenus vers de terre.
Non. Le cercueil n'est pas, homme, ce que tu crois.
La mort, sous le plafond des tombeaux noirs et froids,
C'est la mystérieuse et lumineuse offrande.   15
Ce n'est pas seulement pour l'âme qu'elle est grande,
Mais pour la chair, poids vil sur la terre gisant.
La tombe, astre central, vers qui tout redescend,
Jetant un rayon double à la double frontière,
Transfigure l'esprit, transforme la matière.   20
La mort, qui n'est pour toi qu'un spectre monstrueux,
Saisit l'être et le tord entre ses doigts noueux,

Are you some thing that Light has told to vanish,
Shed from the great sad sombre flanks of Satan?
No, a mere fleeting vapour!

                              God alone
Is life; all other things are death; I say so
To you and all mankind, who drink the cup
Of fear, who pallidly choose dreadful paths,
Who blindly spy, and deafly listen!'

from the *reliquat* of *God*

'What do you think of death, you vain philosopher? . . .'

'What do you think of death, you vain philosopher?
Faced with obscurity, darkness, and doubt,
Fate ending in the grave, death inescapable,
You shudder—this world is a dreadful temple!
The ghastly horde of graves is terrifying;
And if you had to plumb the sepulchre,
Beyond its foul and foetid vapour you would find
A seeming chasm of filth
Filled with creatures once lovely yet now dismal,
With mere craters instead of gleaming eyes
Beneath their brows, and shedding worms
Instead of glances.
No, mortal; coffins are never what you think.
Beneath the vaults of dark and icy tombs,
Death is the strange and luminous offering.
It benefits not only soul
But body, that vile weight prone in the ground.
The grave, the central star where all things fall,
Shedding a dual light on its dual frontier,
Transfigures mind and transforms matter. Death,
Which seems to you merely a monstrous spectre,
Seizes the creature, twists it in its gnarled claws,

Et, comme une laveuse agenouillée au fleuve,
Blanchit les os, les corps, la chair de l'esprit veuve,
La guenille animale et le haillon humain,   25
Dans un ruissellement de lumière sans fin.
C'est dans de la splendeur que tout se décompose.
La mort, c'est l'unité qui reprend toute chose.
Oh! cette obscure mort dont Dieu sait le secret,
Quel éblouissement elle te jetterait,   30
Si, comme nous dont l'œil voit l'aspect véritable,
Tu pouvais, dans l'espace étrange et redoutable,
Voir, partout à la fois, à toute heure, en tous lieux,
En roses sur la terre, en phosphores aux cieux,
En fleurs, en fruits, en sève, en parfum, en aurore,   35
La pourriture énorme et magnifique éclore!

«Le fond de l'être est clos par un nuage obscur . . .»

Le fond de l'être est clos par un nuage obscur,
Traversé de lueurs, aux prodiges semblable,
Voile de l'insondable et de l'incalculable,
Sans limite, sans fin, sans contour, sans milieu;
C'est ce nuage noir que l'homme appelle Dieu.   5
Un lugubre aquilon qui souffle en ce mystère,
Et qui vient par moments jusque sur votre terre
Des chercheurs inquiets éteindre les flambeaux,
A ce sombre nuage arrache des lambeaux;
Et ces lambeaux, épars sous les nocturnes dômes,   10
Flottent dans l'ombre avec des formes de fantômes;
Et Jupiter chassé par le vent, et Vénus,
Moloch, Mithra, Brahma, Cybèle aux huit seins nus,
Odin, Isis, des sphynx de Thèbes saluée,
Sont les vagues flocons de l'énorme nuée.   15

Oui, ces spectres, de feux rougis, d'aube dorés,
Ces aspects vains, voilà ce que vous adorez;
Oui, vos religions naissent de ces passages
De vents et de brouillards dans l'esprit de vos sages;
Oui, ces arrachements du nuage sacré,   20

And, like a washerwoman at the riverside,
Whitens the widowed spirit's flesh, the bones
And bodies, bestial rags and human tatters,
In an unending stream of light.
All things decompose into splendour; death
Is unity retrieving everything.
How it would dazzle you, this obscure death
Whose secret the Lord knows,
If you, like we whose eyes behold the truth,
Could see throughout the strange and fearful realms
Of space, everywhere, all at once, together,
The roses on earth, the glimmers in heaven,
The flowers, fruit, sap, scent, and break of day
Born from that vast magnificent decay!'

'The depths of the I AM are swathed in cloud . . .'

'The depths of the I AM are swathed in cloud
Traversed by gleams like prodigies, a veil
Of the incalculable and unfathomable,
Limitless, endless, with no midst or outline;
And this dark cloud, humanity calls "God".
A gloomy north wind whistling through the mystery,
And sometimes coming down as far as earth
To quench the lamps of restless seekers, tears
The sombre cloud to pieces; and those pieces,
Scattered about through the nocturnal vaults,
Are drifting in the shadow—phantom shapes:
Jupiter driven by the wind, and Venus,
And Molech, Mithra, Brahma, Odin, Isis,
Thebes' honoured sphinxes, eight-breasted Cybele,*
Are indistinct wisps torn from the vast cloud mass.

Yes: all these ghosts, fire-reddened, sunrise-gilded,
Vain apparitions, these are what you worship;
And thus are your religions born—from passings
Of wind and fog in the minds of your wise men;
These fragments scrambled from the sacred cloud—

Ces fragments monstrueux du grand Tout ignoré,
Qui dans le crépuscule errent, et se déforment,
Sinistres, sur le front des hommes qui s'endorment,
Ces haillons d'infini, vus des pâles mortels,
Sont rêves dans vos nuits et dieux sur vos autels.   25

from *La Légende des siècles*

Le Sacre de la femme

I

L'aurore apparaissait; quelle aurore? Un abîme
D'éblouissement, vaste, insondable, sublime;
Une ardente lueur de paix et de bonté.
C'était aux premiers temps du globe; et la clarté
Brillait sereine au front du ciel inaccessible,   5
Étant tout ce que Dieu peut avoir du visible;
Tout s'illuminait, l'ombre et le brouillard obscur;
Des avalanches d'or s'écroulaient dans l'azur;
Le jour en flamme, au fond de la terre ravie,
Embrasait les lointains splendides de la vie;   10
Les horizons, pleins d'ombre et de rocs chevelus
Et d'arbres effrayants que l'homme ne voit plus,
Luisaient, comme le songe et comme le vertige,
Dans une profondeur d'éclair et de prodige;
L'éden pudique et nu s'éveillait mollement;   15
Les oiseaux gazouillaient un hymne si charmant,
Si frais, si gracieux, si suave et si tendre,
Que les anges distraits se penchaient pour l'entendre,
Le seul rugissement du tigre était plus doux;
Les halliers où l'agneau paissait avec les loups,   20
Les mers où l'hydre aimait l'alcyon, et les plaines
Où les ours et les daims confondaient leurs haleines,
Hésitaient, dans le chœur des concerts infinis,
Entre le cri de l'antre et la chanson des nids.

These monstrous scraps of the great unknown All,
Which roam the twilight, and which twist themselves
Sinisterly on the brows of sleepers—these
Rags of the vast, seen by pale mortals, are
Dreams in your nights, deities on your altars.'

from *The Legend of the Ages*

The Consecration of Woman

I

Dawn was breaking. What dawn? An abyss
Of brilliance, fathomless, immense, sublime;
A blazing glow of kindliness and bliss.
Now, this was in the planet's earliest time;
On heaven's far-off brow, light shone serene;
It was all of the Lord that could be seen.
Even the mist and shade were shining too;
Avalanches of gold fell through the blue;
Deep in the ravished world, the burning day
Kindled the glories of life far away;
Horizons steeped in gloom, with fearsome trees
And tufted rocks no longer seen, were gleaming
Like dizziness, like dreaming,
In deeps of lightnings and of prodigies;
Eden was softly waking, naked, chaste.
The birds warbled a hymn in such good taste,
So graceful and so tender and so clear,
That it distracted angels, who leant down to hear.
The tiger's very roar had milder strains;
The groves where lamb and wolf both grazed, the seas
Where sea-serpent loved halcyon,* the plains
Where bear's and deer's breath mingled in the breeze,
All wavered, in this endless psalming throng,
Between the cavern's cry and the nest's song.

La prière semblait à la clarté mêlée;   25
Et sur cette nature encore immaculée
Qui du verbe éternel avait gardé l'accent,
Sur ce monde céleste, angélique, innocent,
Le matin, murmurant une sainte parole,
Souriait, et l'aurore était une auréole.   30
Tout avait la figure intègre du bonheur;
Pas de bouche d'où vint un souffle empoissonneur;
Pas un être qui n'eût sa majesté première;
Tout ce que l'infini peut jeter de lumière
Éclatait pêle-mêle à la fois dans les airs;   35
Le vent jouait avec cette gerbe d'éclairs
Dans le tourbillon libre et fuyant des nuées;
L'enfer balbutiait quelques vagues huées
Qui s'évanouissaient dans le grand cri joyeux
Des eaux, des monts, des bois, de la terre et des cieux.   40
Les vents et les rayons semaient de tels délires
Que les forêts vibraient comme de grandes lyres;
De l'ombre à la clarté, de la base au sommet,
Une fraternité vénérable germait;
L'astre était sans orgueil et le ver sans envie;   45
On s'adorait d'un bout à l'autre de la vie;
Une harmonie égale à la clarté, versant
Une extase divine au globe adolescent,
Semblait sortir du cœur mystérieux du monde;
L'herbe en était émue, et le nuage, et l'onde,   50
Et même le rocher qui songe et qui se tait;
L'arbre, tout pénétré de lumière, chantait;
Chaque fleur, échangeant son souffle et sa pensée
Avec le ciel serein d'où tombe la rosée,
Recevait une perle et donnait un parfum;   55
L'Être resplendissait, Un dans Tout, Tout dans Un;
Le paradis brillait sous les sombres ramures
De la vie ivre d'ombre et pleine de murmures,
Et la lumière était faite de vérité;
Et tout avait la grâce, ayant la pureté.   60
Tout était flamme, hymen, bonheur, douceur, clémence,
Tant ces immenses jours avaient une aube immense!

Prayer seemed to merge with light;
Throughout this realm in which no sin occurred,
Which still preserved the accents of the timeless Word,
Throughout this world, angelic, pure, and bright,
The morning murmured holy things and smiled,
And the dawn was an aureole.
The face of happiness still remained whole;
No breath was tainted or defiled;
No creature lacked its primal majesty.
All the light that the Boundless ever casts
Burst through the air promiscuously;
The wind toyed with that sheaf of lightning-blasts
In a free, fleeing whirl of cloud.
From base to summit, and from gloom to glow,
A sense of brotherhood began to grow;
Worms were not envious, stars were not proud;
Life was in love from shore to shore.
Hell stammered a few faintish cries
Lost in the glad and mighty roar
Of mountains, streams, and woods, of earth and skies.
Sunshine and wind sowed such delight, that the entire
Forestland was vibrating like a massive lyre.
Rising, it seemed, from earth's mysterious core,
A harmony that matched the light unfurled
Divine ecstasy on the ripening world;
It stirred the grass, the cloud, the sea,
Even the rock silently pondering;
Trees, steeped in light, began to sing;
The flowers exchanged breath and philosophy
With the clear heavens from which dewdrops fall,
Received a pearl and gave a scent;
Jehovah shone, All in One, One in All.*
Eden, beneath dark boughs, was radiant
With life ravished by shade and rich in sound;
Its light was formed from truth; all things around
Were gracious, for all things were innocent;
All things were flame, bliss, marriage, mercy, praise,
Dawn was so glorious in those glorious days!

II

Ineffable lever du premier rayon d'or,
Du jour éclairant tout sans rien savoir encor!
O matin des matins! amour! joie effrénée   65
De commencer le temps, l'heure, le mois, année!
Ouverture du monde! instant prodigieux!
La nuit se dissolvait dans les énormes cieux
Où rien ne tremble, où rien ne pleure, où rien ne souffre;
Autant que le chaos la lumière était gouffre;   70
Dieu se manifestait dans sa calme grandeur,
Certitude pour l'âme et pour les yeux splendeur;
De faîte en faîte, au ciel et sur terre, et dans toutes
Les épaisseurs de l'être aux innombrables voûtes,
On voyait l'évidence adorable éclater;   75
Le monde s'ébauchait; tout semblait méditer;
Les types primitifs, offrant dans leur mélange
Presque la brute informe et rude et presque l'ange,
Surgissaient, orageux, gigantesques, touffus;
On sentait tressaillir sous leurs groupes confus   80
La terre, inépuisable et suprême matrice;
La création sainte, à son tour créatrice,
Modelait vaguement des aspects merveilleux,
Faisait sortir l'essaim des êtres fabuleux
Tantôt des bois, tantôt des mers, tantôt des nues,   85
Et proposait à Dieu des formes inconnues
Que le temps, moissonneur pensif, plus tard changea;
On sentait sourdre, et vivre, et végéter déjà
Tous les arbres futurs, pins, érables, yeuses,
Dans des verdissements de feuilles monstrueuses;   90
Une sorte de vie excessive gonflait
La mamelle du monde au mystérieux lait;
Tout semblait presque hors de la mesure éclore;
Comme si la nature, en étant proche encore,
Eût pris, pour ses essais sur la terre et les eaux,   95
Une difformité splendide au noir chaos.

Les divins paradis, pleins d'une étrange séve,
Semblent au fond des temps reluire dans le rêve,

II

The golden first ray rising—indescribably;
Day lighting all things, knowing, as yet, nothing!
Morning of mornings! love! the utter joy of
Beginning time—the hour, the month, the year!
The opening of the world—a wondrous moment!
Night was melting away in the vast skies
Where nothing quavered, wept, or suffered; light was
A chasm matching chaos;
God was revealing himself in his calm glory,
Certainty to the soul and splendour to the eyes;
From peak to peak, in heaven and on earth,
Throughout creation's countless massive vaults,
Blazed forth the testimony that elicits adoration.
The world was being prepared. Everything seemed
To ponder; primal forms* that mingled something
Like rough-hewn brute with something else like angel
Arose, tempestuous, gigantic, shaggy;
The earth's supreme and never-emptied womb
Seemed to be quivering under their vague hordes.
Sacred creation was itself creative,
And shaped miraculous shapes, shed a swarm
Of fabled creatures through woods, seas, and clouds,
Offering to the Lord God unknown forms
Which time, that thoughtful reaper, would transfigure;
Already every future tree—oak, maple,
Pine—seemed to be sprouting, living, vegetating
Within those green things with their monstrous foliage.
An overflow of life was swelling
The world's breast, which bore secret milk; all things
Seemed to unfold almost unboundedly;
As if, being still close to dark-hued chaos,
Nature had drawn from it a glorious formlessness
For her attempts, whether on land or sea.

These sacred paradises, teeming with mysterious sap,
Seem to glow once more in the depths of time, in reverie;

Et, pour nos yeux obscurs, sans idéal, sans foi,
Leur extase aujourd'hui serait presque l'effroi;   100
Mais qu'importe à l'abîme, à l'âme universelle
Qui dépense un soleil au lieu d'une étincelle,
Et qui, pour y pouvoir poser l'ange azuré,
Fait croître jusqu'aux cieux l'éden démesuré!

Jours inouïs! le bien, le beau, le vrai, le juste,   105
Coulaient dans le torrent, frissonnaient dans l'arbuste;
L'aquilon louait Dieu de sagesse vêtu;
L'arbre était bon; la fleur était une vertu;
C'est trop peu d'être blanc, le lys était candide;
Rien n'avait de souillure et rien n'avait de ride;   110
Jours purs! rien ne saignait sous l'ongle et sous la dent;
La bête heureuse était l'innocence rôdant;
Le mal n'avait encor rien mis de son mystère
Dans le serpent, dans l'aigle altier, dans la panthère,
Le précipice ouvert dans l'animal sacré   115
N'avait pas d'ombre, étant jusqu'au fond éclairé;
La montagne était jeune et la vague était vierge;
Le globe, hors des mers dont le flot le submerge,
Sortait beau, magnifique, aimant, fier, triomphant,
Et rien n'était petit quoique tout fût enfant;   120
La terre avait, parmi ses hymnes d'innocence,
Un étourdissement de séve et de croissance;
L'instinct fécond faisait rêver l'instinct vivant;
Et, répandu partout, sur les eaux, dans le vent,
L'amour épars flottait comme un parfum s'exhale;   125
La nature riait, naïve et colossale;
L'espace vagissait ainsi qu'un nouveau-né.
L'aube était le regard du soleil étonné.

III

Or, ce jour-là, c'était le plus beau qu'eût encore
Versé sur l'univers la radieuse aurore;   130
Le même séraphique et saint frémissement
Unissait l'algue à l'onde et l'être à l'élément;
L'éther plus pur luisait dans les cieux plus sublimes;
Les souffles abondaient plus profonds sur les cimes;

To our dim faithless and ideal-less eyes
Their rapture would be almost terrifying.
But what is that to the abyss, the universal
Soul, which squanders suns like sparks, and raises
A towering Eden to the skies
So that the azured seraphim may walk there!

Amazing days! Truth, goodness, justice, beauty,
Flowed in the streams and rippled through the bushes;
The north winds, robed in wisdom, praised the Lord.
Flowers were virtues, trees were bountiful,
Lilies were innocent, not merely white;
Nothing was sullied, nothing wrinkled—days
Of purity! no tooth or claw shed blood.
Beasts were content—were innocence at large;
The mystery of evil never touched
Snakes, panthers, lofty eagles;
The gaping chasm in each sacred animal
Was quite unshadowed, was clear to its depths;
Mountains were young, and waves were virginal;
The globe rose out of its immersing seas
Glorious, lovely, loving, proud, triumphant.
Nothing was little, though all things were children;
Singing untainted psalms, the earth was dazed
With sap and growth; the instinct to live pondered
The instinct to be fertile;
And, spread out everywhere, in winds, in waters,
Love drifted as a fragrance might have done;
The innocent colossus Nature smiled,
And Space was crying like a newborn child.
Dawn was the gaze of the astonished sun.

III

This was the fairest day that radiant dawn could yet disperse
Across the universe;
A single holy and seraphic shimmer went
Through weed and wave, creature and element.
Space gleamed in finer skies with greater purity;
The breezes on the peaks seemed keener, fathomless;

Les feuillages avaient de plus doux mouvements;   135
Et les rayons tombaient caressants et charmants
Sur un frais vallon vert, où, débordant d'extase,
Adorant ce grand ciel que la lumière embrase,
Heureux d'être, joyeux d'aimer, ivres de voir,
Dans l'ombre, au bord d'un lac, vertigineux miroir,   140
Étaient assis, les pieds effleurés par la lame,
Le premier homme auprès de la première femme.

L'époux priait, ayant l'épouse à son côté.

IV

Ève offrait au ciel bleu la sainte nudité,
Ève blonde admirait l'aube, sa sœur vermeille.   145

Chair de la femme! argile idéale! ô merveille!
O pénétration sublime de l'esprit
Dans le limon que l'Être ineffable pétrit!
Matière où l'âme brille à travers son suaire!
Boue où l'on voit les doigts du divin statuaire!   150
Fange auguste appelant le baiser et le cœur,
Si sainte, qu'on ne sait, tant l'amour est vainqueur,
Tant l'âme est vers ce lit mystérieux poussée,
Si cette volupté n'est pas une pensée,
Et qu'on ne peut, à l'heure où les sens sont en feu,   155
Étreindre la beauté sans croire embrasser Dieu!

Ève laissait errer ses yeux sur la nature.

Et, sous les verts palmiers à la haute stature,
Autour d'Ève, au-dessus de sa tête, l'œillet
Semblait songer, le bleu lotus se recueillait,   160
Le frais myosotis se souvenait; les roses
Cherchaient ses pieds avec leurs lèvres demi-closes;
Un souffle fraternel sortait du lys vermeil;
Comme si ce doux être eût été leur pareil,
Comme si de ces fleurs, ayant toutes une âme,   165
La plus belle s'était épanouie en femme.

The foliage stirred with greater tenderness.
Light-rays were coming down sweetly, caressingly,
Into a cool green glade
Where, overflowing with ecstasy,
Worshipping this great sky aflame with glow,
Content to be, delighted to love, entranced to see,
By a lake's dizzying mirror in the shade,
Their feet brushed by the water's flow,
The first man sat by the first woman's side.

And the bridegroom was praying with the bride.

IV

Eve offered the blue heavens holy nakedness;
She, being blonde, admired her rosy sister Dawn.

Woman's flesh—the ideal clay! a miracle!
Spirit sublimely penetrating
The dust which the I AM has moulded!
Matter where, through its shroud, the soul is gleaming!
Mire with the fingerprints of the divine sculptor!
Majestic soil inciting kisses and devotion,
Something so sacred that its bliss seems an ideal—
That, when your senses are aflame, you feel yourself
Embracing God while you are holding beauty,
Since love is so imperious, since your soul
Is driven so intensely toward this mysterious bed!

Eve let her eyes drift over the creation.

And, underneath the tall green palm trees,
Around her, the carnations and blue lotuses
And cool forget-me-nots seemed to be pondering,
Dreaming, recalling; roses with half-closed
Lips sought her feet,
And rose-tipped lilies shed a kindred scent—
As if this gentle creature was their sister;
As if, among these blooms, each with its soul,
The loveliest had blossomed into woman.

V

Pourtant, jusqu'à ce jour, c'était Adam, l'élu
Qui dans le ciel sacré le premier avait lu,
C'était le Marié tranquille et fort, que l'ombre
Et la lumière, et l'aube, et les astres sans nombre,   170
Et les bêtes des bois, et les fleurs du ravin
Suivaient ou vénéraient comme l'aîné divin,
Comme le front ayant la lueur la plus haute;
Et, quand tous deux, la main dans la main, côte à côte,
Erraient dans la clarté de l'éden radieux,   175
La nature sans fond, sous ses millions d'yeux,
A travers les rochers, les rameaux, l'onde et l'herbe,
Couvait, avec amour pour le couple superbe,
Avec plus de respect pour l'homme, être complet,
Ève qui regardait, Adam qui contemplait.   180
Mais, ce jour-là, ces yeux innombrables qu'entr'ouvre
L'infini sous les plis du voile qui le couvre,
S'attachaient sur l'épouse et non pas sur l'époux,
Comme si, dans ce jour religieux et doux
Béni parmi les jours et parmi les aurores,   185
Aux nids ailés perdus sous les branches sonores,
Au nuage, aux ruisseaux, aux frissonnants essaims,
Aux bêtes, aux cailloux, à tous ces êtres saints
Que de mots ténébreux la terre aujourd'hui nomme,
La femme eût apparu plus auguste que l'homme!   190

VI

Pourquoi ce choix? pourquoi cet attendrissement
Immense du profond et divin firmament?
Pourquoi tout l'univers penché sur une tête?
Pourquoi l'aube donnant à la femme une fête?
Pourquoi ces chants? Pourquoi ces palpitations   195
Des flots dans plus de joie et dans plus de rayons?
Pourquoi partout l'ivresse et la hâte d'éclore,
Et les antres heureux de s'ouvrir à l'aurore,
Et plus d'encens sur terre et plus de flamme aux cieux?

Le beau couple innocent songeait silencieux.   200

V

Until now, Adam—the elect who first surveyed
The sacred skies, the Bridegroom, calm and strong,
The divine Elder—was the one whom shade
And light and sunrise and the countless starry throng,
Beasts in the wood and blossoms in the glade,
Always followed or venerated;
He, of all creatures, was the most illuminated;
And when they both, side by side, hand in hand,
Roamed through the light of Eden's radiant land,
Fathomless Nature, with her eyes strewn everywhere
In rock and bough, grass-blade and spring,
Gazed lovingly upon the glorious pair—
Eve looking, Adam pondering—
But honoured the man, the complete Being, more.
Yet now, within the veils that hide
The Vastness, countless eyes seemed to adore
Not the groom, but the bride,
As though, to feathered nests lost in the echoing trees,
To clouds, brooks, beasts, clods, swarms of shimmering bees,
To the entire array
Of sacred things which Earth now names in a dark way,
On that religious gentle day
Most blessed of all days and dawns since time began,
The woman seemed more noble than the man.

VI

Why was she chosen? Why had such compassion
Come from the vast and sacred firmament?
Why was the whole universe now bending
Over a single head? Why should the dawn
Be celebrating woman? Why the songs,
Why the waves pulsing with more radiance and more happiness?
Why rapture everywhere, an urge to blossom,
Caverns eager to open to the dawn,
More fragrance on the earth, and more flame in the heavens?

The lovely innocent pair were pondering in silence.

VII

Cependant la tendresse inexprimable et douce
De l'astre, du vallon, du lac, du brin de mousse,
Tressaillait plus profonde à chaque instant autour
D'Ève, que saluait du haut des cieux le jour;
Le regard qui sortait des choses et des êtres,   205
Des flots bénis, des bois sacrés, des arbres prêtres,
Se fixait, plus pensif de moment en moment,
Sur cette femme au front vénérable et charmant;
Un long rayon d'amour lui venait des abîmes,
De l'ombre, de l'azur, des profondeurs, des cimes,   210
De la fleur, de l'oiseau chantant, du roc muet.

Et, pâle, Ève sentit que son flanc remuait.

Booz Endormi

Booz s'était couché de fatigue accablé;
Il avait tout le jour travaillé dans son aire;
Puis avait fait son lit à sa place ordinaire;
Booz dormait auprès des boisseaux pleins de blé.

Ce vieillard possédait des champs de blés et d'orge;   5
Il était, quoique riche, à la justice enclin;
Il n'avait pas de fange en l'eau de son moulin,
Il n'avait pas d'enfer dans le feu de sa forge.

Sa barbe était d'argent comme un ruisseau d'avril.
Sa gerbe n'était point avare ni haineuse;   10
Quand il voyait passer quelque pauvre glaneuse:
—Laissez tomber exprès des épis, disait-il.

Cet homme marchait pur loin des sentiers obliques,
Vêtu de probité candide et de lin blanc;
Et, toujours du côté des pauvres ruisselant,   15
Ses sacs de grains semblaient des fontaines publiques.

VII

Yet the strange tenderness that seemed to leave
Star and lake, mossy shoot and valley, all
Quivered more and more deeply around Eve,
Whom daylight hailed from heaven's pinnacle;
The gaze that rose from creatures, entities,
Holy waves, sacred woods, and priestly trees,
Growing ever more pensive, settled now
In reverence round this woman's lovely brow.
A long ray of love reached her from the heights,
The deeps, the chasms, the blue skies, the nights,
From flower and silent rock and singing bird.

And, paling, Eve felt something in her womb that stirred.*

Boaz Asleep

Boaz was sleeping, overworn and wearied;
He'd worked hard on his threshing-floor all day,
Then made his bed in the same place as ever;
With wheatbags all around him, there he lay.

The old man owned paddocks of wheat and barley;
Rich he was, but he strove to be fair as well.
The water in his mill was never filthy,
Nor was the furnace in his forge a hell.

His beard was silvered like a stream in April;
He farmed without greed or hostility;
When he saw some poor woman go past gleaning*
He'd say, 'Drop a few ears deliberately.'

He walked straight forward, far from crooked dealings,
Clothed in white linen and plain honest law;
His sacks of grain seemed to be public fountains
Spilling out constantly toward the poor.

Booz était bon maître et fidèle parent;
Il était généreux, quoiqu'il fût économe;
Les femmes regardaient Booz plus qu'un jeune homme,
Car le jeune homme est beau, mais le vieillard est grand. 20

Le vieillard, qui revient vers la source première,
Entre aux jours éternels et sort des jours changeants;
Et l'on voit de la flamme aux yeux des jeunes gens,
Mais dans l'œil du vieillard on voit de la lumière.

*

Donc, Booz dans la nuit dormait parmi les siens; 25
Près des meules, qu'on eût prises pour des décombres,
Les moissonneurs couchés faisaient des groupes sombres;
Et ceci se passait dans des temps très anciens.

Les tribus d'Israël avaient pour chef un juge;
La terre, où l'homme errait sous la tente, inquiet 30
Des empreintes de pieds de géants qu'il voyait,
Était encor mouillée et molle du déluge.

*

Comme dormait Jacob, comme dormait Judith,
Booz, les yeux fermés, gisait sous la feuillée;
Or, la porte du ciel s'étant entre-bâillée 35
Au-dessus de sa tête, un songe en descendit.

Et ce songe était tel, que Booz vit un chêne
Qui, sorti de son ventre, allait jusqu'au ciel bleu;
Une race y montait comme une longue chaîne;
Un roi chantait en bas, en haut mourait un dieu. 40

Et Booz murmurait avec la voix de l'âme:
«Comment se pourrait-il que de moi ceci vînt?
Le chiffre de mes ans a passé quatrevingt,
Et je n'ai pas de fils, et je n'ai plus de femme.

Boaz was a good relative and master,
Frugal and generous at the same time;
Women took note of him more than of young men—
Young men are handsome, old men are sublime.

Old men return toward the source, toward days
That last forever and do not take flight;
You may see fire within the eyes of young men,
But in the eyes of old men you see light.

*

So Boaz slept at night among his people.
The harvesters lay strewn in dark arrays
Among the millstones that arose like ruins.
Now this occurred in very ancient days;

A judge was leader* of the tribes of Israel;
The earth was still moist from the Deluge, and
Tent-dwelling nomads roamed across it, trembling
When they saw giant footprints on the land.

*

Thus Boaz slept like Jacob or like Judith,*
Beneath the trees, with eyes closed. Overhead
The door of heaven slowly began to open,
And through that open door a dream was shed.

This was the dream: he saw an oak tree spring
From his loins to the heavens; a long chain
Of people were ascending it; a king
Sang at the base, on high a god* was slain.

Then, speaking in his spirit, Boaz said:
'But how could I bring such a thing to life?
Why, I have numbered more than eighty years;
I have no child, and I have lost my wife.

«Voilà longtemps que celle avec qui j'ai dormi,   45
O Seigneur! a quitté ma couche pour la vôtre;
Et nous sommes encor tout mêlés l'un à l'autre,
Elle à demi vivante et moi mort à demi.

«Une race naîtrait de moi! Comment le croire?
Comment se pourrait-il que j'eusse des enfants?   50
Quand on est jeune, on a des matins triomphants,
Le jour sort de la nuit comme d'une victoire;

«Mais, vieux, on tremble ainsi qu'à l'hiver le bouleau;
Je suis veuf, je suis seul, et sur moi le soir tombe,
Et je courbe, ô mon Dieu! mon âme vers la tombe,   55
Comme un bœuf ayant soif penche son front vers l'eau.»

Ainsi parlait Booz dans le rêve et l'extase,
Tournant vers Dieu ses yeux par le sommeil noyés;
Le cèdre ne sent pas une rose à sa base,
Et lui ne sentait pas une femme à ses pieds.   60

* * *

Pendant qu'il sommeillait, Ruth, une moabite,
S'était couchée aux pieds de Booz, le sein nu,
Espérant on ne sait quel rayon inconnu,
Quand viendrait du réveil la lumière subite.

Booz ne savait point qu'une femme était là,   65
Et Ruth ne savait point ce que Dieu voulait d'elle.
Un frais parfum sortait des touffes d'asphodèle;
Les souffles de la nuit flottaient sur Galgala.

L'ombre était nuptiale, auguste et solennelle;
Les anges y volaient sans doute obscurément,   70
Car on voyait passer dans la nuit, par moment,
Quelque chose de bleu qui paraissait une aile.

Long ago she with whom I used to sleep
Left my side, Lord, and went to yours instead;
And she and I are intermingled still,
For she is half alive, and I half dead.

A whole race born from me! Can it be true?
Shall I have children now? How could that be?
When we are young, our sunrise blazes bright,
Day rises from the dark victoriously;

But as we age, we sway like winter trees;
I am alone, widowed, on evening's brink,
And, Lord, my soul bends down toward the grave,
As thirsty oxen bend their brows to drink.'

So he spoke, sleeping, turning eyes replete
With dream and rapture to God's dwelling-place.
Cedars do not feel roses at their base;
He did not feel a woman at his feet.

*

While he was sleeping, Ruth, a Moabite,*
Lay at his feet, lay with her breast exposed
Hoping that some strange dawn would be disclosed
When they awakened in the morning light.

Boaz knew nothing of the woman there,
Neither could Ruth tell what God planned for her.
Cool scents rose from the asphodel, and were
Wafted on Gilgal* by the evening air.

The gloom was nuptial, solemn, conquering;
Angels were surely flying through the dark;
In the shadows, at times, you saw the mark
Of some blue shape that seemed to be a wing.

La respiration de Booz qui dormait,
Se mêlait au bruit sourd des ruisseaux sur la mousse.
On était dans le mois où la nature est douce,   75
Les collines ayant des lys sur leur sommet.

Ruth songeait et Booz dormait; l'herbe était noire;
Les grelots des troupeaux palpitaient vaguement;
Une immense bonté tombait du firmament;
C'était l'heure tranquille où les lions vont boire.   80

Tout reposait dans Ur et dans Jérimadeth;
Les astres émaillaient le ciel profond et sombre;
Le croissant fin et clair parmi ces fleurs d'ombre
Brillait à l'occident, et Ruth se demandait,

Immobile, ouvrant l'œil à moitié sous ses voiles,   85
Quel dieu, quel moissonneur de l'éternel été
Avait, en s'en allant, négligemment jeté
Cette faucille d'or dans le champ des étoiles.

Première Rencontre du Christ avec le tombeau

En ce temps-là, Jésus était dans la Judée;
Il avait délivré la femme possédée,
Rendu l'ouïe aux sourds et guéri les lépreux;
Les prêtres l'épiaient et parlaient bas entre eux.
Comme il s'en retournait vers la ville bénie,   5
Lazare, homme de bien, mourait à Béthanie.
Marthe et Marie étaient ses sœurs; Marie, un jour,
Pour laver les pieds nus du maître plein d'amour,
Avait été chercher son parfum le plus rare.
Or, Jésus aimait Marthe et Marie et Lazare.   10
Quelqu'un lui dit: Lazare est mort.

                            Le lendemain,
Comme le peuple était venu sur son chemin,
Il expliquait la loi, les livres, les symboles,
Et, comme Élie et Job, parlait par paraboles.

Boaz's breathing, as he lay at rest,
Merged with the muffled sound of streams on moss.
It was the month when lilies bloom across
The hills, and Nature's mood is tenderest.

Down from the sky abundant blessings sank;
Grass darkened, bells were heard on distant sheep;
Ruth meditated, Boaz lay asleep;
It was the calm hour when the lions drank.

Ur and Jerimadeth* felt harmony;
Stars were adorning heaven's sombre height;
A slim bright crescent lit those flowers of night.
Far to the west; Ruth, gazing tranquilly

With drowsy eyes which her veils half concealed,
Wondered what careless god, as he went past
Reaping the summer endlessly, had cast
That golden sickle in the starry field.

Christ's First Encounter with the Tomb

In those days, Christ was in Judaea; he
Had freed the demon-possessed woman,
Made the deaf hear, and healed the lepers;
The priests kept watch on him, whispering together.
As he returned toward the holy city,
A righteous man, Lazarus, died at Bethany.
Martha and Mary were his sisters; Mary,
One day, had sought out her most precious ointment
To wash the feet of the all-loving Lord.
Now, Jesus loved Martha, Mary, and Lazarus.
And someone told him: 'Lazarus is dead.'

Next day, as the crowds met him on the way,
He taught the law, the scriptures, and the mysteries;
He, like Job and Elijah,* spoke in parables:
'Those who follow me will be like the angels.

Il disait:—Qui me suit, aux anges est pareil.   15
Quand un homme a marché tout le jour au soleil
Dans un chemin sans puits et sans hôtellerie,
S'il ne croit pas, quand vient le soir, il pleure, il crie;
Il est las; sur la terre il tombe haletant.
S'il croit en moi, qu'il prie, il peut au même instant   20
Continuer sa route avec des forces triples.—
Puis il s'interrompit, et dit à ses disciples:
—Lazare, notre ami, dort; je vais l'éveiller.—
Eux dirent:—Nous irons, maître, où tu veux aller.—
Or, de Jérusalem, où Salomon mit l'arche,   25
Pour gagner Béthanie, il faut trois jours de marche.
Jésus partit. Durant cette route souvent,
Tandis qu'il marchait seul et pensif en avant,
Son vêtement parut blanc comme la lumière.

Quand Jésus arriva, Marthe vint la première,   30
Et, tombant à ses pieds, s'écria tout d'abord:
—Si nous t'avions eu, maître, il ne serait pas mort.
Puis reprit en pleurant:—Mais il a rendu l'âme.
Tu viens trop tard. Jésus lui dit:—Qu'en sais-tu, femme?
Le moissonneur est seul maître de la moisson.   35

Marie était restée assise à la maison.

Marthe lui cria:—Viens, le maître te réclame.
Elle vint. Jésus dit:—Pourquoi pleures-tu, femme?
Et Marthe à genoux lui dit:—Toi seul es fort.
Si nous t'avions eu, maître, il ne serait pas mort.   40
Jésus reprit:—Je suis la lumière et la vie.
Heureux celui qui voit ma trace et l'a suivie!
Qui croit en moi vivra, fût-il mort et gisant.—
Et Thomas, appelé Didyme, était présent.
Et le seigneur, dont Jean et Pierre suivaient l'ombre,   45
Dit aux juifs accourus pour le voir en grand nombre:
—Où donc l'avez-vous mis?—Ils répondirent: Vois,
Lui montrant de la main, dans un champ, près d'un bois,
A côté d'un torrent qui dans les pierres coule,
Un sépulcre.

When a man travels in the sun all day
With no well and no shelter, then at evening,
If he has no faith, he is weary; he
Weeps and groans, and falls panting to the ground.
If he believes in me and prays, immediately
He will resume his way with tripled strength.'*
Then, pausing, he told his disciples: 'Lazarus
Our friend is sleeping; I shall go to wake him.'
They said, 'Lord, we will go wherever you choose.'
Jerusalem, where Solomon* set the ark,
Is three days' journey off from Bethany.*
Jesus set out. Often, along the way,
While he went forward, solitary and thoughtful,
His garments would seem white, as if with light.

When Jesus came, Martha went out first, fell at
His feet, and cried: 'Lord, if you had been here,
Then he would not have died.' She added, weeping:
'But he has given up the ghost; you are too late.'
'Woman, how do you know?' said Jesus;
'The harvester alone is Lord of harvest.'

Mary still sat within the house.

Martha told her, 'The Lord is calling for you.'
She went. Jesus said, 'Why are you weeping, woman?'
Kneeling down, Mary said, 'Lord, you alone are strong;
If you had been here, he would not be dead.'
Jesus replied, 'I am the light and life;
Blessed are those who see my way and follow it!
He that believes in me will live,
Even if he is dead and buried.' (Thomas,*
Called Didymus, was present.) The Lord said
To the crowd of Jews who had come to see him,
While John and Peter followed in his shadow:
'Where have you laid him?' 'See', they answered, pointing
To a tomb in a meadow, near a wood,
Beside a stream that ran among the stones.

Et Jésus pleura.

                  Sur quoi la foule   50
Se prit à s'écrier:—Voyez comme il l'aimait!
Lui qui chasse, dit-on, Satan et le soumet,
Eût-il, s'il était Dieu, comme on nous le rapporte,
Laissé mourir quelqu'un qu'il aimait de la sorte?

Or, Marthe conduisit au sépulcre Jésus.   55
Il vint. On avait mis une pierre dessus.
—Je crois en vous, dit Marthe, ainsi que Jean et Pierre;
Mais voilà quatre jours qu'il est sous cette pierre.

Et Jésus dit:—Tais-toi, femme, car c'est le lieu
Où tu vas, si tu crois, voir la gloire de Dieu.—   60
Puis il reprit:—Il faut que cette pierre tombe.—
La pierre ôtée, on vit le dedans de la tombe.

Jésus leva les yeux au ciel et marcha seul
Vers cette ombre où le mort gisait dans son linceul,
Pareil au sac d'argent qu'enfouit un avare.   65
Et, se penchant, il dit à haute voix: Lazare!

Alors le mort sortit du sépulcre; ses pieds
Des bandes du linceul étaient encor liés;
Il se dressa debout le long de la muraille;
Jésus dit:—Déliez cet homme, et qu'il s'en aille.—   70
Ceux qui virent cela crurent en Jésus-Christ.

Or, les prêtres, selon qu'au livre il est écrit,
S'assemblèrent, troublés, chez le préteur de Rome;
Sachant que Christ avait ressuscité cet homme,
Et que tous avaient vu le sépulcre s'ouvrir,   75
Ils dirent:—Il est temps de le faire mourir.

Jesus wept.

       Then the multitudes exclaimed,
'See how he loved him! He is said to cast out
Satan and bind him; now, if he were God,
As we are told, would he have let his friend die?'

Martha led Jesus to the tomb. He went.
A stone was laid against it. Martha said,
'Lord, I believe in you, like John and Peter;
But he has been beneath that stone four days.'

And Jesus said, 'Be silent, woman; if you
Believe, in this place you will see God's glory.'
Then he said: 'Take away the stone.' When it
Was lifted, they could see inside the tomb.

Raising his eyes to heaven, Jesus went alone
Into the darkness where the dead man lay
In his shroud, like a miser's buried moneybag.
Stooping, he cried out with a loud voice, 'Lazarus!'

Then the dead man came from the tomb, his feet
Still bound with wrappings. He stood against the wall.
'Unbind him', Jesus said, 'and let him go.'
Those who saw it believed in Jesus Christ.

Now, the priests—it is written in the book—
Were troubled; they met with the Roman governor.
Knowing that Christ had raised this man,
That everyone had seen the opening of the tomb,
They said, 'It is time he was put to death.'

from *Les Chansons des rues et des bois*

O Hyménée!

Pancrace entre au lit de Lucinde;
Et l'heureux hymen est bâclé
Quand un maire a mis le coq d'Inde
Avec la fauvette sous clé.

Un docteur tout noir d'encre passe   5
Avec Cyllanire à son bras;
Un bouc mène au bal une grâce;
L'aurore épouse le fatras.

C'est la vieille histoire éternelle;
Faune et Flore; on pourrait, hélas,   10
Presque dire: A quoi bon la belle?
Si la bête n'existait pas.

Dans un vase une clématite,
Qui tremble, et dont l'avril est court!
Je trouve la fleur bien petite,   15
Et je trouve le pot bien lourd.

Que Philistine est adorable,
Et que Philistin est hideux!
L'épaule blanche à l'affreux râble
S'appuie, en murmurant: Nous deux!   20

Le capricieux des ténèbres,
Cupidon compose, ô destin!
De toutes ces choses funèbres
Son éclat de rire enfantin.

Fatal amour! charmant, morose,   25
Taquin, il prend le mal au mot;
D'autant plus sombre qu'il est rose,
D'autant plus dieu qu'il est marmot!

from *Songs of Street and Wood*

Connubial Bliss

Pancrace enters Lucinda's bed;
And when the mayor puts turkey cock
And lovely warbler under lock
And key, the happy pair is wed.

Along an inkstained pedant ambles
In Cyllanira's sweet embraces;
He-goats go dancing with the Graces;*
The sunrise dallies with the shambles.

A tale old as the world, at least—
Flora and Faun;* we'd feel a duty,
Perhaps, to ask: 'What use is Beauty?'
If there did not exist the Beast.

A clematis blooms in a jar;
She quakes; her springtime soon must fall!
I find the blossom oh-so-small;
I find the pot too coarse by far.

O how atrocious is Goliath!
O how attractive is Delilah!*
So fair a torso, on so vile a
Carcass! 'Just thou and I!' she sigheth...

And so, O Fate! these sordid stupid
Compounds of dissonance and gloom are
Coupled to suit the infant humour
Of that small Imp of Darkness Cupid.*

Thus fatal Eros, charming, wild,
Wreaks havoc at the slightest wink—
The grubbier for being pink,
The godlier for being a child.

«La nature est pleine d'amour . . .»

La nature est pleine d'amour,
Jeanne, autour de nos humbles joies;
Et les fleurs semblent tour à tour
Se dresser pour que tu les voies.

Vive Angélique! à bas Orgon!   5
L'hiver, qu'insultent nos huées,
Recule, et son profil bougon
Va s'effaçant dans les nuées.

La sérénité de nos cœurs,
Où chantent les bonheurs sans nombre,   10
Complète, en ces doux mois vainqueurs,
L'évanouissement de l'ombre.

Juin couvre de fleurs les sommets,
Et dit partout les mêmes choses;
Mais est-ce qu'on se plaint jamais   15
De la prolixité des roses?

L'hirondelle, sur ton front pur,
Vient si près de tes yeux fidèles,
Qu'on pourrait compter dans l'azur
Toutes les plumes de ses ailes.   20

Ta grâce est un rayon charmant;
Ta jeunesse, enfantine encore,
Éclaire le bleu firmament,
Et renvoie au ciel de l'aurore.

De sa ressemblence avec toi   25
Le lys pur sourit dans sa gloire;
Ton âme est une urne de foi
Où la colombe voudrait boire.

'Nature? she's amorous everywhere . . .'

Nature? she's amorous everywhere,
Jeanne, round about our lowly pleasures;
The flowers in turn expose their treasures
Simply so you can see them there.

Down with the stooge! Cheer the soubrette!*
Winter, whose act was roundly hissed,
Backs off—vanishes in the mist,
Hiding his grumpy silhouette.

During these lovely conquering days,
Our coupled hearts serenely sing
With countless raptures, finishing
The dissolution of the greys.

In floral coverings June encloses
The peaks; unvaried is her strain—
But then, does anyone complain
Of repetition among roses?

Your forehead's chaste allurement brings
Swallows so near your steadfast eye
That we could number in the sky
Every last feather of their wings.

Your elegance is a ray of light;
Your freshness—childlike still, newborn—
Restores to heaven's expanse its dawn,
And makes the blue above us bright.

Lilies see their relationship
To you, and smile with modest pride;
From the devotion cupped inside
Your soul, the very doves could sip.

De la femme au ciel

L'âme a des étapes profondes.
On se laisse d'abord charmer,
Puis convaincre. Ce sont deux mondes.
Comprendre est au delà d'aimer.

Aimer, comprendre: c'est la faîte.   5
Le Cœur, cet oiseau du vallon,
Sur le premier degré s'arrête;
L'Esprit vole à l'autre échelon.

A l'amant succède l'archange;
Le baiser, puis le firmament;   10
Le point d'obscurité se change
En un point de rayonnement.

Mets de l'amour sur cette terre
Dans les vains brins d'herbe flottants,
Cette herbe devient, ô mystère!   15
Le nid sombre au fond du printemps.

Ajoute, en écartant son voile,
De la lumière au nid béni,
Et le nid deviendra l'étoile
Dans la forêt de l'infini.   20

Une Alcôve au soleil levant

L'humble chambre a l'air de sourire;
Un bouquet orne un vieux bahut;
Cet intérieur ferait dire
Aux prêtres: Paix! aux femmes: Chut!

From Woman to Heaven

The soul goes through successive planes.
Things fascinate, then satisfy.
Knowledge is far off, love nearby;
The two are different domains.

Love, know—and then you reach the top.
The spirit rises to the heights;
The heart's a bird of lower sites—
At the first stage it tends to stop.

Kissing leads to the heavens' expanse;
Lovers turn into seraphim;
The very point that once was dim
Becomes a source of radiance.

When love is shed across earth's breast
Through flimsy blades of waving grass,
A mystery then comes to pass—
Those blades become a springtime nest.

Now, take the veil away from it,
And light the nest thus sanctified—
Then it becomes a star inside
The forests of the infinite.

An Alcove in the Sunrise

Flowers are gracing an old sill;
The humble room seems like a smile;
Women would whisper: 'Quiet!' while
Bishops would say: 'Be still!'

Au fond une alcôve se creuse.   5
Personne. On n'entre ni ne sort.
Surveillance mystérieuse!
L'aube regarde: un enfant dort.

Une petite en ce coin sombre
Était là dans un berceau blanc,   10
Ayant je ne sais quoi dans l'ombre
De confiant et de tremblant.

Elle étreignait dans sa main calme
Un grelot d'argent qui penchait;
L'innocence au ciel tient la palme   15
Et sur la terre le hochet.

Comme elle sommeille! Elle ignore
Le bien, le mal, le cœur, les sens.
Son rêve est un sentier d'aurore
Dont les anges sont les passants.   20

Son bras, par instants, sans secousse,
Se déplace, charmant et pur;
Sa respiration est douce
Comme une mouche dans l'azur.

Le regard de l'aube la couvre;   25
Rien n'est auguste et triomphant
Comme cet œil de Dieu qui s'ouvre
Sur les yeux fermés de l'enfant.

Pendant une maladie

On dit que je suis fort malade,
Ami; j'ai déjà l'œil terni;
Je sens la sinistre accolade
Du squelette de l'infini.

A sunken alcove at the rear.
No one has come, no one has gone.
Mysterious vigil! Dawn looks on:
A child is sleeping here.

A white cot lies in this dark nook;
In it a little girl is laid.
She seems to have, amid the shade,
A tremulous trusting look.

Her fingers placidly deploy
A silver bell, dangling and calm;
In heaven, innocence holds a palm,
And on the earth, a toy.

And how she sleeps! quite unaware
Of soul or senses, wrong or right!
Her dreams are paths of dawning light;
Angels are passing there.

At times a movement flutters through
Her unflurried enchanting limbs;
Her breathing lightly drifts and swims
Like a fly in the blue.

In the gaze of the dawn she lies.
No grander or more glorious thing
Than that Eye of God, opening
Over the child's shut eyes!

During an Illness

Friends, I am very sick, they say;
My eyesight is already gone;
I feel the Infinite's skeleton
Embrace me in its grisly way.

Sitôt levé, je me recouche;   5
Et je suis comme si j'avais
De la terre au fond de la bouche;
Je trouve le souffle mauvais.

Comme une voile entrant au havre,
Je frissonne; mes pas sont lents,   10
J'ai froid; la forme du cadavre,
Morne, apparaît sous mes draps blancs.

Mes mains sont en vain réchauffées;
Ma chair comme la neige fond;
Je sens sur mon front des bouffées   15
De quelque chose de profond;

Est-ce le vent de l'ombre obscure?
Ce vent qui sur Jésus passa!
Est-ce le grand Rien d'Épicure,   20
Ou le grand Tout de Spinosa?

Les médecins s'en vont moroses;
On parle bas autour de moi,
Et tout penche, et même les choses
Ont l'attitude de l'effroi.

Perdu! voilà ce qu'on murmure.   25
Tout mon corps vacille, et je sens
Se déclouer la sombre armure
De ma raison et de mes sens.

Je vois l'immense instant suprême
Dans les ténèbres arriver.   30
L'astre pâle au fond du ciel blême
Dessine son vague lever.

L'heure réelle, ou décevante,
Dresse son front mystérieux.
Ne crois pas que je m'épouvante;   35
J'ai toujours été curieux.

I rise, but go straight back to bed;
I seem to feel a clod of dung
At the very back of my tongue,
So filthy is the breath I shed.

I keep shuddering like a sail
In harbour; grim cadaverous shapes
Appear beneath my clean white drapes;
I feel cold, and my footsteps trail.

In vain I try to warm my hand;
My flesh is melting like the snow.
Over my face gusts come and go
From some wind hard to understand;

Is it a blast that Jesus knows—a
Gale from the shadows that obscure us?
The great Nothing of Epicurus,*
Or else the great All of Spinoza?*

The doctors go away dismayed;
Around me there are whisperings;
Everyone droops—inanimate things
Themselves appear to be afraid.

'Past hope!' everyone softly wails.
My body wavers, and I find
The solemn armour of my mind
And senses starts to lose its nails.

I see, within the gloom, arise
The final and momentous time.
Its pallid star begins to climb
Faintly, far off, in livid skies.

The Hour—real or calamitous—
Raises its mystifying brow.
Well, I'm not worried, anyhow;
I always *have* been curious.

Mon âme se change en prunelle;
Ma raison sonde Dieu voilé;
Je tâte la porte éternelle,
Et j'essaie à la nuit ma clé.   40

C'est Dieu que le fossoyeur creuse;
Mourir, c'est l'heure de savoir;
Je dis à la mort: Vieille ouvreuse,
Je viens voir le spectacle noir.

My thoughts delve the veiled Deity;
My spirit turns into an eye.
I test the age-old door, and try
To open Midnight with my key.

When people die, why, then they know;
God is in the gravedigger's trench.
I tell Death: 'Old box-office wench,
I'm here to watch the great black show.'

from *Les Misérables*

Waterloo

i. Seen on the Road from Nivelles

One fine May morning last year (1861), a traveller—the author of
this story*—was going from Nivelles toward La Hulpe. He was on
foot. He was following a wide paved road lined with trees; it
undulated across a succession of hills, which raised and dropped
it like great ocean waves. He had already passed Lillois and Bois-
Seigneur-Isaac. To the west he could see the slate-roofed steeple
of Braine-l'Alleud, shaped like an upturned vase. He had just left
behind a wooded knoll and a crossroad with a kind of worm-eaten
signpost inscribed 'Former Tollgate No. 4', beside which was
a tavern fronted by the sign 'The Four Winds. Échabeau, private
café.'

An eighth of a league past this tavern, he went down into a little
valley, where a stream was running under a bridge built into the
road's embankment. A clump of scattered (but very green) trees
filled one side of the valley, spread out on the other side into
meadows, and finally straggled off in graceful disarray toward
Braine-l'Alleud.

On the right, beside the road, was an inn with a four-wheeled
farm-cart in front of the door, a big bundle of hop-stakes, a plough, a
pile of dry brushwood near a quickset hedge, some lime smouldering
in a square lime-pit, and a ladder lying beside an old barn with straw
mangers. A young girl was hoeing a field, where a big yellow poster
(probably for a travelling show at some village fair) was fluttering
in the breeze. At the corner of the house a flotilla of ducks was
navigating a pond; nearby, a rough gravel footpath vanished into the
scrub. The traveller followed it.

The path led him alongside a fifteenth-century wall topped by a
steep gable of criss-crossed brickwork. After a hundred paces
or so, he found himself facing a big arched stone doorway with
square pillars in the solemn Louis XV style, bordered by two flat
medallions. A stern façade towered over the entrance; a wall jutted

out perpendicular to the façade and virtually made contact with the doorway, flanking it sharply at right angles. In front, on the grass, lay three harrows, with all the flowers of May poking higgledy-piggledy through them. The entrance was shut. It was closed by a dilapidated double door adorned with a rusty old knocker.

It was delightfully sunny; the branches stirred with the gentle Maytime rustling that seems to be caused rather by birds' nests than by wind. One fine little fellow of a bird, probably amorous, was singing passionately in a big tree.

The traveller stooped to examine a fairly broad circular hole, like the concave inner surface of a globe, low in the stone of the left jamb. Just at that moment the doors swung open, and a country woman came out.

She saw the traveller and noticed that he was looking at the hole.

'A French cannon ball did that', she said.

Then she added:

'See that hole higher up, in the door near that nail? That was done by a big Biscay gun. It didn't get through the wood.'

'What's the name of this place?' asked the traveller.

'Hougoumont', said the woman.

The traveller stood up. He went away a few steps and looked over the hedges. On the horizon, through the trees, he could see a kind of hillock, and far away, on the hillock, something that looked at that distance like a lion.*

He was on the battlefield at Waterloo.

ii. Hougoumont

Hougoumont—it was a fateful place: the first sign of hindrance; the first obstacle enountered at Waterloo by Europe's great lumberjack Napoleon; the first knot in the timber that met his axe.

It used to be a château; now it's only a farm. To students of history, Hougoumont is *Hugomons*. The manor house had been built by Hugo lord of Somerel, the man who endowed the sixth chaplaincy in Villers Abbey.

The traveller pushed open the door, brushed past an old carriage under the porch, and entered the courtyard.

Inside the yard, the first thing that caught his eye was a sixteenth-century doorway; everything around it had fallen down, and it remained there like an arch. Ruins often come to look monumental. Near the arch was a wall pierced by another doorway, one with Henri IV keystones; orchard trees could be seen beyond it. Near it, a rubbish dump, some spades and shovels, a few carts, an old well equipped with flagstone and iron pulley, a frisky colt, a strutting turkey, a chapel capped by a little belfry, a pear tree in bloom on a lattice against the chapel wall—this was the courtyard that Napoleon had dreamed of conquering. If he'd been able to capture this patch of earth, it might have given him the whole world. Now some hens were pecking in its dust. A growling noise could be heard; it came from a big snarling dog—a replacement for the English.

The English had done impressive deeds here. In this place, four companies of Guards under Cooke had held their ground for seven hours against a furious army onslaught.

When you look at it on the map, laid out geometrically with its buildings and yard, Hougoumont is a kind of irregular rectangle with one corner cut off. At that corner stands the south gate, protected by—and yet within point-blank range of—its wall. Hougoumont has two gates: the château gate to the south, and the farm gate to the north. Napoleon sent his brother Jérôme against Hougoumont; Guilleminot's, Foy's, and Bachelu's divisions were hurled against it; virtually the whole of Reille's corps was used against it—and failed; Kellermann's bullets were spent against that heroic wall. Bauduin's brigade couldn't penetrate it from the north, and Soye's brigade could only assault it from the south, without capturing it.

The farm buildings border the courtyard on the south. The French broke down the north gate, and smashed it; a piece of it— four planks nailed to two cross-pieces—now dangles from the wall. You can still see the battle scars on it.

The north gateway has been patched to replace the panel hanging from the wall. It stands, partly open, at the lower end of the yard. It's embedded in a wall made of stone below and brickwork above, which blocks off the northern side of the courtyard. It's an ordinary farm-cart gateway, the sort you find on any small farm: a broad double gate of rustic planks; beyond, meadows. The struggle at this entrance was particularly intense. All kinds of bloodstained hand-prints could be seen on the gateposts for a long time afterwards. This was the place where Bauduin was killed.

The blast of battle is still present in this courtyard; you can still see its horrors; the violence of the conflict has been fossilized here; there's life here, there's death here; it happened only yesterday. The walls are still in their final throes, the stones are falling, the breaches are howling, the holes are gaping wounds; the trees hang down and shudder, and seem to be trying to get away.

In 1815 the courtyard was more built up than it is today. Structures that have now been torn down formed simple jutting fortifications there, with square corners and angular crannies.

The English barricaded themselves inside it; the French broke in but couldn't hold their position. Beside the chapel stands one wing of the château, battered, you could almost say gutted: the sole remaining relic of the Hougoumont manor house. The château acted as a castle keep, the chapel as a fort. The combatants slaughtered each other there. From everywhere—from behind walls, from the tops of barns, from the depths of cellars, through casements and air vents and gaps between stones—snipers shot at the French, who gathered bundles of sticks and set fire to buildings and men alike: gunshots were answered with flames.

Through the iron-barred windows in the ruined wing, you can glimpse the broken-down rooms of a brick mansion; the English Guards lay in ambush there. The spiral staircase, now holed from top to bottom, looks like a broken snail shell. It went up two floors; the English, besieged on it and crammed onto the upper steps, cut away the lower ones. They were broad blue stone slabs; they're still heaped among the nettles. A dozen inaccessible steps still cling to the wall; the topmost has a picture of a trident carved on it. They're solidly fixed in their sockets; all the rest of the staircase looks like a toothless jawbone. Two old trees stand there; one is dead, the other is damaged at the base but still manages to put out new foliage every April. Since 1815 it has started to grow up through the staircase.

People massacred each other in the chapel. Its interior, now at peace once more, is a strange place. Mass has never been said there since the carnage. Yet the altar is still there, a rough wooden altar backed by rough stone. Four whitewashed walls, a door opposite the altar, two little arched windows, a big wooden crucifix over the door, a square vent blocked with straw above the crucifix, an old shattered window-frame on the ground at one side—that's the chapel. A fifteenth-century wooden statue of Saint Anne is nailed near the altar; the head of the Infant Jesus was blown off by a bullet. The French controlled the chapel for a while, but were dislodged, and set fire to it. The little building filled with flames; it became a furnace; the door burned down, the floor burned away, the wooden Christ didn't burn. The fire devoured its feet—nowadays you can see only their charred stumps—then stopped. A miracle, say the locals. The beheaded Infant Jesus wasn't so fortunate.

The walls are covered with inscriptions. The name 'Henquinez' can be read near the feet of the Christ. So can others: 'Conde de Rio Maïor'. 'Marques y Marquesa de Almagro (Habana)'. There are French names with furious exclamation marks. The wall was whitewashed anew in 1849. The nations had been hurling insults at each other on it.

A corpse with an axe in its hand was found by the chapel door. That corpse had been Sub-Lieutenant Legros.

When you go out of the chapel you see a well on your left. There are two in the courtyard. Why doesn't this one have a bucket and pulley, you ask. Because nobody draws water from it any more. Why doesn't anybody draw water from it any more? Because it's full of skeletons.

The last person to draw water from it was a man named Guillaume Van Kylsom. He was a peasant who lived in Hougoumont; he was a gardener there. His family fled on 18 June 1815 and hid in the woods.

The forest around Villers Abbey sheltered luckless stragglers of this kind for several days and nights. Even today, a few recognizable traces—old burned tree trunks, for instance—show the location of their wretched cowering camps deep in the thickets.

Guillaume Van Kylsom remained at Hougoumont 'to look after the château' and hid in a cellar in terror. The English found him there. They dragged him from his hiding place and beat him with the flat of their sabres to make him obey them. They were thirsty; Guillaume brought them water to drink. He drew it from this well. For many of them, it was their last mouthful. The well from which so many of the dead had drunk was doomed to die itself.

After the engagement, there was an urgent need to bury the bodies. Death has her own special way of tarnishing victory; in the hour of glory, she brings plague. Typhus complements triumph. The well was deep, they made it into a sepulchre. Three hundred corpses were thrown into it. Perhaps rather too hastily. Were all of them dead? Legend says no. The night after the burial, faint voices were allegedly heard calling from the well.

This well stands on its own in the middle of the courtyard. Three half-stone half-brick walls, shaped like a square turret and turned back like the leaves of a screen, surround it on three sides. The fourth side is open. That's where the water used to be drawn. On the back wall is a kind of shapeless bull's eye, perhaps a shell hole. This turret used to have a roof; only its beams now remain. The iron brace on the right-hand wall is shaped like a cross. You lean down over the well, and your gaze vanishes in a deep brick cylinder full of accumulated shadows. The bottom of the surrounding walls is shrouded in nettles on all sides.

This well isn't fronted by one of the large blue flagstones that pave the approaches to wells in all parts of Belgium. Here, the blue flagstone is replaced by a crossbar with five or six misshapen wooden stumps, knotty and stiff like gigantic bones. It no longer has any bucket or chain or pulley; but it still has its stone overflow-trough. Rainwater piles up in it; now and then a bird from the neighbouring forest comes to drink from it, and flies off again.

Among these ruins one house, the farmhouse, is still inhabited. Its door opens onto the courtyard. The door has a pretty Gothic lock plate and, beside it, a cloverleaf-shaped iron handle, hanging downwards. Lieutenant Wilda of the Hanoverians tried to take shelter in the farmhouse; at the very moment when he took hold of this handle, a French sapper struck off his hand with an axeblow.

The former gardener Van Kylsom died long ago. He was the grandfather of the family now living in the house. A grey-haired woman tells you: 'I was there. I was three years old. My sister, who was older, was scared; she was crying. They took us into the woods. I was in my mother's arms. They put their ears against the ground to listen. I kept mimicking the cannons; I kept going *boom boom*.'

As I said, one of the courtyard gates, the left-hand one, leads to the orchard.

The orchard is a ghastly place.

It's divided into three parts—you could almost say three acts. The first part is a garden, the second is the orchard, the third is a wood. The whole trio is enclosed by a hedge on the left, a wall on the right, a wall at the back, and the farm and château buildings in front. The

right wall is brick, the back wall is stone. You enter the garden
first. It has a downward slope; it's planted with gooseberry bushes,
overgrown with weeds, and closed off by a formal terrace of hewn
stone, with double-curved columns. It used to be an upper-class
garden in the old pre-Le Nôtre* French style; today it's just ruins and
brambles. The pillars are capped with spheres like stone cannon
balls. Forty-three columns are still standing; the rest are lying in
the grass. Nearly all of them have been damaged by gunshots. One
broken column is slumped on its pedestal like a broken leg.

The garden is lower than the orchard. Six men of the First Light
Infantry got into it and weren't able to get out again. Caught
and cornered like bears in a pit, they took on two companies of
Hanoverians; one of the companies was armed with carbines. The
Hanoverians were ranged along the balustrade, firing from above.
The infantrymen returned fire from below, six brave men against
two hundred, with no other shelter than the gooseberry bushes; it
took them a quarter of an hour to die.

You go up a few steps, and pass from the garden into the orchard
proper. Here, within these few square metres, fifteen hundred men
fell in less than an hour. The wall seems ready to start fighting again.
The thirty-eight loopholes made by the English at various levels are
still there. In front of the sixteenth lie two English granite gravestones. The loopholes are only in the south wall; the main assault
came from that side. This wall is hidden from the outside by a big
quickset hedge; the French came in, thought they had only the
hedge to deal with, crossed it, and found the wall—both obstacle and
ambush—with the English Guards behind it and the thirty-eight
loopholes all firing at once, a hail of gunshots small and great; and so
Soye's brigade was broken. That was how Waterloo began.

And yet the orchard was taken. There weren't any ladders, so the
French clawed up the wall with their fingernails. Hand-to-hand
fighting went on under the trees. All the grass was soaked in blood. A
whole battalion from Nassau, seven hundred men, was mown down
in this place. The outside of the wall, which bore the full brunt of
Kellermann's two batteries, is riddled with grapeshot.

Like all orchards, this one responds to the month of May. It has its
daisies and buttercups, the grass grows long, farm horses graze on it,
clotheslines are slung between the trees, forcing visitors to bend their
heads; you walk across this teeming wilderness and catch your foot

on molehills. Amid the grass you notice a fallen, uprooted mossy tree trunk. Major Blackman lay against it when he was dying. The German General Duplat, who came from a French family exiled by the revocation of the Edict of Nantes,* fell beneath a large tree nearby. Next to it droops an unhealthy old apple tree that is being treated with a bandage of straw and clay. Nearly all the apple trees are dying of old age. Not one of them has escaped some gunshot or cannon shot. This orchard is full of dead trees' skeletons. Crows fly into the branches, the woods beyond are full of violets.

Bauduin killed, Foy wounded, fire, slaughter, carnage, a furiously mingled stream of French and English and German blood, a well crammed with corpses, whole regiments from Nassau and Brunswick wiped out, Duplat killed, Blackman killed, the English Guards cut to pieces, twenty of Reille's forty French battalions decimated, three thousand men bayoneted, butchered, slaughtered, shot, burned to death, on this little farmstead at Hougoumont, just so that nowadays some country bumpkin can say to the visitor: 'If you like, Monsieur, I'll tell you all about Waterloo; three francs, please!'

iii. 18 June 1815

Let's go back (this is one of the storyteller's privileges) to the year 1815, shortly before the events described in the first part of this book.

If it hadn't rained in the night of 17–18 June 1815, the future of Europe would have been different. A few extra drops of water were enough to swing the scales against Napoleon. Providence needed only a bit of rain to make Waterloo put an end to Austerlitz;* an unseasonable mass of cloud crossing the sky was enough to destroy a world.

The battle of Waterloo (this is what gave Blücher time to arrive) couldn't start till half past eleven. Why not? Because the ground was too wet. It had to dry out a bit before the artillery could manoeuvre.

Napoleon was an artillery officer, and it showed. The extraordinary commander was founded on the man who said in his report to the Directory about Abu Qir:* 'Some of our shots killed six men.' All his battle plans were tailored to suit projectiles. For him, the key to victory was artillery fire focused on a particular point. He treated the enemy general's strategy as a citadel, and he pounded it till it gave way. He overwhelmed the weak points with grapeshot; he ravelled and unravelled battles with cannon fire. There was a dash of the marksman in his genius. Penetrating battle squares, pulverizing regiments, breaking through lines, disrupting and scattering formations—for him, that was the heart of the matter: battering, battering, battering constantly—and he relied on cannon balls to do it. A formidable approach; and that approach, plus his genius, had made this sombre prizefighter in the military arena invincible for fifteen years.

On 18 June 1815 he relied more than ever on artillery, because the numbers were in his favour. Wellington had only 159 big guns; Napoleon had 240.

Suppose the ground had been dry and the artillery able to move. The battle would have started at six a.m. Everything would have been done and won by two p.m.—three hours before the Prussians altered the situation.

How much of the defeat was Napoleon's fault? When should you blame the pilot for a shipwreck?

Was Napoleon's obvious physical decline associated, at this time, with some kind of mental deterioration? Had twenty years of warfare worn down the sword as well as the scabbard, the soul as well as the body? Was a veteran becoming all too evident within the commander? In short, was this man of genius now in eclipse, as many notable historians have maintained? Was he growing frantic in his efforts to hide his weaknesses from himself? Was he starting to waver under the buffets of fortune? Was he starting not to care about dangers (a serious fault in a general)? Do the great worldly men whom we may call giants of action become short-sighted at a certain age? Senility has no hold on imaginative genius; Dantes and Michelangelos improve with age; do Hannibals* and Bonapartes deteriorate? Had Napoleon lost his instinct for victory? Was he no longer able to see problems, detect traps, sense the cliffs crumbling around an abyss? Had he lost the knack of recognizing fatal blunders? In the past he had always known the road to victory, he had always pointed it out with a sovereign gesture from the height of his fiery chariot; did he now have some grim mental aberration that drove him to lead his teeming armies over the precipice? Had he finally gone mad, at the age of forty-six? Had destiny's titanic coachman become an utter danger to life and limb?

I don't think so.

His battle plan was, everyone agrees, masterly. March straight at the centre of the Allied lines, pierce the enemy's ranks, divide them in two, drive the British half toward Hal and the Prussian half toward Tongres, separate Wellington from Blücher, carry Mont Saint-Jean, seize Brussels, hurl the Germans into the Rhine and the English into the sea. This battle, for Napoleon, involved all that. After which, he'd see what he'd do next.

I'm not, of course, writing a history of Waterloo in this book. One of the key scenes in our drama depends on this battle, but its history isn't our concern. In any case, such history has been told, and told superbly, from one standpoint by Napoleon, and from another by a whole glittering constellation of historians—Walter Scott, Lamartine, Vaulabelle, Charras, Quinet, Thiers.* We'll leave the historians to their labours; I'm simply a distant witness, a traveller wandering over the plain, an observer studying this landscape steeped in human flesh, and very likely mistaking appearances for realities. I'm not qualified to grapple scientifically with a mass of facts that must surely be tainted by fancy; I don't have either the military experience or the strategic knowledge to construct any theories. At Waterloo, in my view, both commanders were at the mercy of a series of chance events. And when a case involves that mysterious defendant Destiny, I pass judgement much as any ordinary plain-minded person would do.

iv. A

If you want to get the Battle of Waterloo clear in your mind, just imagine a capital letter A drawn on the ground. The A's left leg is the road from Nivelles, its right leg is the road from Genappe, its crossbar is the sunken road from Ohain to Braine-l'Alleud. Its apex is Mont Saint-Jean—that's where Wellington is; its left foot is Hougoumont—that's where Reille and Jérôme Bonaparte are; its right foot is La Belle Alliance—that's where Napoleon is. Just below the point where the A's crossbar intersects with its right leg is La Haye Sainte. The midpoint of the crossbar is exactly where the battle's last word was spoken. That's where the lion has been placed, an unwitting symbol* of the final heroism of the Imperial Guard.

The triangle at the top of the A, between the two legs and the crossbar, is the Mont Saint-Jean plateau. The entire battle revolved around the struggle for that plateau.

The wings of the two armies spread out right and left from the Genappe and Nivelles roads; d'Erlon faced Picton, and Reille faced Hill.

Beyond the A's apex, beyond the Mont Saint-Jean plateau, is the forest of Soignes.

As for the plain itself, imagine a huge area of undulating ground. Each undulation commands a view of the next; they rise toward Mont Saint-Jean, and end there in the forest.

Two hostile armies on a battlefield are like two wrestlers. Their bodies are locked together. Each one is trying to throw the other. They clutch at everything; a thicket is used as a pivot, the angle of a wall as a prop; a regiment may lose its footing for lack of a little hut at its back; a depression in the plain, a patch of uneven ground, a convenient crossroad, a copse, a ravine, may catch the heel of the colossus Army and stop it from falling back. Whoever leaves the field is beaten. Hence the leader involved needs to examine the smallest clump of trees and understand the slightest variation in the landscape.

Both generals had made a careful study of the Mont Saint-Jean plain (now known as the plain of Waterloo). Wellington, with shrewd foresight, had examined it the previous year, already considering it as a possible major battlefield. On this particular terrain, and for this particular clash, Wellington was favourably situated, Napoleon unfavourably; the English army occupied higher ground than the French.

To sketch a picture of Napoleon on horseback, spyglass in hand, on the heights of Rossomme at sunrise on 18 June 1815, would be almost superfluous. No need to show it; everyone has seen it already. The calm profile under the little College of Brienne cocked hat, the green tunic, the white facings hiding the decorations, the grey over-coat hiding the epaulettes, the streak of red sash under the waistcoat, the leather breeches, the white horse draped in purple velvet with a crowned *N* and an eagle at each corner, the cavalry boots over silk stockings, the silver spurs, the Marengo* sword—the whole shape of the last emperor is alive in everyone's imagination, whether they praise him or condemn him.

Every side of that shape has been in the light for a long time now. It was affected by the passage of befogging legends, which most heroes generate, and which always veil the truth for a while. But now daylight and history are here.

History's light is merciless. Although it's luminous, and precisely because it's luminous, it has a strange, divine ability to cast shadows where radiance had previously been visible. It creates two contrasted images from a single man; one image attacks and punishes the other, and the darkness of the despot struggles against the brilliance of the military commander. So the world ultimately comes to see things more accurately. The rape of Babylon degrades Alexander, the enslavement of Rome degrades Caesar, the slaughter of Jerusalem degrades Titus.* At the heels of a tyrant comes tyranny. Woe to the man who is followed by a patch of shadow in his own shape!

v. The *Quid Obscurum** of Warfare

Everyone is familiar with the early stages of the battle—its blurred, dubious, hesitant beginning, ominous to both sides, but particularly to the English.

It had been raining all night; the ground was soggy from the downpour; here and there pools of water lay like washbasins in the hollows on the plain. In some places, the wagons' wheels sank up to the axles; mud dripped from the horses' bellies; movement of any kind would have been impossible, especially in the valleys toward Papelotte, but for the fact that wheat and rye were flattened by all the advancing vehicles, filling the ruts and acting like straw beneath the wheels.

The engagement began late. As we've said, Napoleon customarily kept all the artillery in his own grip, like a pistol to be aimed now at one point of the battle, now at another; he wanted to wait till the field batteries could move fast and freely, and that couldn't be achieved till the sun came out and dried the ground. But the sun didn't come out. This wasn't the battle of Austerlitz. When the first gun was fired, General Colville, on the English side, looked at his watch and observed that the time was eleven thirty-five.

The French left wing on Hougoumont began the battle furiously, perhaps more furiously than the Emperor would have wished. Simultaneously, Napoleon attacked the centre by hurling Quiot's brigade against La Haye Sainte, and Ney advanced the French right wing against the English left wing, which took its stand near Papelotte.

The attack on Hougoumont was partly a feint, the plan being to lure Wellington in that direction and make him concentrate on the French left wing. It would have succeeded—but for the determination with which the four companies of English Guards and Perponcher's brave Belgian detachment held their position. Wellington, therefore, instead of having to mass his forces at that point, could simply send four extra companies of Guards and a battalion of Brunswickers as reinforcements.

The French right-wing headlong attack on Papelotte was meant to overwhelm the English left, cut the road to Brussels, prevent any possible Prussian arrival, carry Mont Saint-Jean, and force Wellington back first to Hougoumont, then to Braine-l'Alleud, then to Hal. Nothing could have been more straightforward. Except in a few minor respects, this attack was successful. Papelotte was indeed taken; La Haye Sainte was indeed carried.

One small point worth noting. The English infantry, especially Kempt's brigade, contained a large number of new recruits. Faced with our own formidable infantry, the young soldiers did very bravely; despite their inexperience, they came out of the affair like heroes. They were particularly good as sharpshooters. As a sharpshooter, a soldier is left more or less to his own devices; he becomes, in effect, his own general; and these recruits fought rather independently and rather passionately, like Frenchmen. The novice infantrymen showed a certain amount of enthusiasm. Wellington didn't approve.

After La Haye Sainte had been captured, the battle hung in the balance.

From noon to four o'clock that day, there was a cloudy period; the middle phase of the battle seems relatively obscure, tainted by the sombreness of the conflict. Everything was twilit. You can glimpse immense fluctuations through the mist, a whirling mirage, old-fashioned—and now almost forgotten—trappings of war, fiery busbies, fluttering sabre-belts, crossed shoulder-straps, grenade pouches, hussars' dolmans, crinkled red boots, heavy shakos festooned with fringe, virtually black Brunswick infantry side by side with scarlet English infantry, English soldiers with big white circular pads for epaulettes, Hanoverian light horsemen with copper-banded oblong leather helmets and plumes of red horsehair, Scots with bare knees and plaid kilts, our own grenadiers with big white gaiters— pictures rather than battle lines, calling for a Salvator Rosa rather than a Gribeauval.*

There's a certain storminess about any battle. *Quid obscurum, quid divinum.* In this chaos, every historian tends to pick out whichever patterns he likes best. Whatever combination of leaders may be involved, the actual clash of the massed armies has repercussions that can't be predicted; the two commanders' plans interact and distort each other. One part of the battlefield consumes more soldiers than another, just as soils soak up more or less water depending on their porosity. You have to pour more soldiers into such a place than you wanted. An unforeseen expense. The line of battle winds and wavers like a thread; streams of blood are shed regardless of logic; the army fronts undulate like ocean waves, with retreating and advancing regiments as the bays and headlands. And all these rocks are moving constantly in relation to each other; where there was infantry, artillery appears; where there was artillery, up rides the cavalry; battalions are simply clouds of smoke. Something was over there; now look for it, it's gone; the lighting keeps changing; dark ripples keep advancing and retreating; a sort of wind from the grave keeps blowing these tragic multitudes back and forth, amassing and dispersing them. What is a battle? An oscillation. A motionless mathematical diagram can illustrate a moment, but not a day. To depict a battle, you need the kind of master painter who has chaos in his brush; Rembrandt would be more useful than Van der Meulen. Van der Meulen's exact representation of midday would be utterly wrong by three o'clock. You can't rely on geometry; only a hurricane contains the truth. That's why Folard is able to contradict Polybius.* I should add that there invariably comes a time when the battle degenerates into hand-to-hand combat, becomes specific, and shatters into innumerable minute details. Such things, to borrow Napoleon's own expression, 'belong to the biographies of the various regiments, not the history of the army'. In such situations, a historian obviously has the right to summarize. Even at best, he can merely seize on the main outlines of the conflict. No narrator, however conscientious he may be, has the power to fix once and for all the shape of the horrible cloud known as a battle.

That's true of any great army encounter; but it's particularly applicable to Waterloo.

Yet, at a certain time in the afternoon, the battle did take on a definite shape.

vi. Four p.m.

By about four o'clock, the English army was in a very difficult situation. Hill had been commanding the right wing, Picton the left wing, and the Prince of Orange the centre. The Prince of Orange, in desperation, kept calling out bravely to his Dutch and Belgian troops: 'Nassau! Brunswick! never retreat!' Hill was failing, and had just fallen back on Wellington. General Picton was dead; the French had shot him through the head at the very moment when the English had taken the colours of the French 105th regiment. From Wellington's perspective the battle had two key points, Hougoumont and La Haye Sainte. Hougoumont was still holding out, but it was in flames; La Haye Sainte had fallen. Of the German battalion that had been defending it, only forty-two men were still alive; all but five of the officers had been killed or taken prisoner. Three thousand soldiers had been slaughtered in that farmhouse. A sergeant in the English Guards, the best boxer in England, who had been regarded by his comrades as invincible, had been killed by a little French drummer-boy. Baring had been driven out, Alten put to the sword. The colours of several regiments had been lost, including one from Alten's division and one from the Luneburg battalion; it had been carried by a prince of the Deux-Ponts family. The Scots Greys had been wiped out; Ponsonby's heavy dragoons had been cut to pieces—that valiant cavalry brigade had given way before Bro's lancers and Travers's cuirassiers. Only six hundred of its twelve hundred horse remained; two of its three lieutenant-colonels were on the ground—Hamilton wounded, Mater killed. Ponsonby had fallen, struck down by seven sabre-thrusts. Gordon was dead, Marsh was dead. Two divisions, the fifth and the sixth, had been annihilated.

With Hougoumont giving way and La Haye Sainte taken, only one crucial point remained: the centre. That was still holding firm. Wellington reinforced it. He called in Hill from Merbe-Braine and Chassé from Braine-l'Alleud.

The centre of the English army was in a strong position, slightly concave, very close-packed and very compact. It was occupying the Mont Saint-Jean plateau, with the village behind it and the slope (fairly steep in those days) in front. At its back was a sturdy stone house—a sixteenth-century edifice so solid that gunfire ricocheted off it and didn't pierce it; it stood at the crossroads and was officially, at the time, the property of Nivelles. All round the plateau, the English had cut back the hedges, made embrasures in the hawthorns, propped up cannons on pairs of branches, and hacked loopholes in the bushes. Their artillery was lurking in ambush beneath the shrubbery. No doubt this Carthaginian-style trickery is a legitimate method of warfare; in war it's permissible to lay traps. The work was done so well that Haxo, who had been sent by the Emperor at nine a.m. to reconnoitre the enemy batteries, didn't see any of it; he went back to Napoleon and told him that there was nothing in the way except for two barricades blocking the roads to Nivelles and Genappe. The crops are tallest at that time of year; on the verge of the plateau, a whole battalion of Kempt's brigade, the 95th, was lying in the full-grown wheat, armed with carbines.

Thus placed, and thus protected, the centre of the Anglo-Dutch army was in an excellent situation.

The weak point of its position was the forest of Soignes, which in those days lay right next to the battlefield and was interrupted by the Groenendael and Boitsfort marshes. An army couldn't retreat into it without breaking up; the regiments would instantly have been separated, and the artillery would have been lost in the swamps. Many military men believed (though others certainly didn't) that any such retreat would have turned into utter panic.

Wellington reinforced the centre with one of Chassé's brigades taken from the right wing and one of Wincke's taken from the left, in addition to Clinton's division. He supplemented his English troops (Halkett's regiments, Mitchell's brigade, Maitland's Guards) with support from the Brunswick infantry, the Nassau contingent, Kielmansegge's Hanoverians, and Ompteda's Germans. This gave him twenty-six battalions under his own control. In Charras's words, 'The right wing was bent back behind the centre.' A huge battery, reinforced with sandbags, stood at the very site now occupied by what we call 'the Waterloo Museum'. In addition, Wellington had Somerset's Dragoon Guards (fourteen hundred horse—the other half of the justly famous English cavalry) stationed in a dip in the ground. Ponsonby had been annihilated, Somerset remained.

The battery, if finished, might almost have been a redoubt. It was situated behind a very low garden wall, hastily augmented with sandbags and a broad bank of earth. But it wasn't finished; there hadn't been time to palisade it.

Wellington, worried but outwardly calm, stayed on horseback where he had been all day—slightly in front of the old Mont Saint-Jean mill (which is still in existence), under an elm tree subsequently bought, cut down, and carried away by a vandalous English zealot for two hundred francs. In that situation, Wellington was coolly heroic. Bullets kept raining down. Gordon, one of his aides-de-camp, fell at his side just before four p.m. Lord Hill pointed out a bursting shell and asked him: 'What are your instructions, my lord? What are your orders if you are killed?' 'Do what I'm doing', Wellington replied. 'Hang on here to the last man', he told Clinton laconically. Clearly the day was not going well. He called out to his old comrades, the men who had seen Talavera, Vitoria, and Salamanca,* 'Stand fast! We must not be beat—what will they say in England?'

About four o'clock, the English line was being driven back. Suddenly nothing could be seen on the crest of the plateau except the artillery and the sharpshooters; everyone else vanished. Under the impact of French shells and bullets, the regiments withdrew into a valley that is still crossed by the cowpath from Mont Saint-Jean farm. There was a backward drift; the English front was disintegrating, Wellington was forced to fall back. 'The retreat is starting!' exclaimed Napoleon.

vii. Napoleon in a Good Mood

The Emperor was a sick man, troubled on horseback by a local ailment; but he had never been in a better mood than he was that day. Ever since morning, his imperturbable countenance had worn a smile. On 18 June 1815 that deep-set and marble-masked soul was blindly radiant. The man who had been grim at Austerlitz was happy at Waterloo. Even the greatest Men of Destiny have such contradictions. Our joys are shadows. The last laugh is God's.

'When Caesar laughs, Pompey will weep', the soldiers of the

Thundering Legion* used to say. Pompey was not to weep on this occasion, but there's no doubt that Caesar laughed.

At one o'clock the previous night he had explored the hills around Rossomme on horseback with Bertrand during the thunderstorm, and had been pleased to see the long line of English fires lighting the horizon from Frischermont to Braine-l'Alleud. Ever since then, he had felt that Destiny, who had an appointment with him that day at Waterloo, was punctual. He had reined in his horse and stayed motionless for some time, watching the lightning and listening to the thunder; then, being a fatalist, he had been heard to utter these strange words in the darkness: 'We're in agreement.' Napoleon was mistaken. They were no longer in agreement.

He hadn't slept for a moment; every second of that night had brought him some new cause for happiness. He had been along the whole line of the vanguard, stopping here and there to talk to the sentries. At half past two, near the Hougoumont wood, he had heard the sound of a column marching; for a moment he imagined that Wellington was already retreating. 'That's the English rearguard stirring; they're going to get away', he told Bertrand. 'I'll capture the six thousand English who have just arrived at Ostend.' He chatted away warmly, with a renewal of the excitement he had shown during the landing on 1 March,* when he had exclaimed to the Grand Marshal, pointing out an enthusiastic peasant of Golfe Jouan: 'Well, well, Bertrand—a reinforcement already!' On the night of 17–18 June he made fun of Wellington. 'The little Englishman needs to be taught a lesson', he said. It rained more and more heavily; while the Emperor spoke, there was thunder.

At half past three in the morning he lost one of his illusions. Some officers sent out on reconnaissance told him that the enemy wasn't moving. Nothing was stirring; not a single campfire had been put out. The English army was asleep. There was a deep silence over the earth; the only noise was in the heavens. At four o'clock, a peasant was brought to him by the scouts. The fellow had acted as a guide for one of the English cavalry brigades—probably Vivian's, which was on the way to a position at the village of Ohain, on the extreme left wing. At five o'clock, two Belgian deserters who had just left their regiment told him that the English army was expecting a battle. 'So much the better!' Napoleon exclaimed. 'I'd much rather knock them down than chase them away.'

At sunrise he stepped down in the mud on the raised ground beside the turn of the road from Plancenoit. He ordered a kitchen table and country chair to be brought from Rossomme farm, sat down with a bundle of straw under his feet, spread out a map of the battlefield on the table, and said to Soult: 'Nice-looking chessboard!'

Because of the overnight rain, the convoys of provisions had bogged down in the soggy roads and failed to arrive at dawn; the soldiers hadn't slept and were wet and hungry; but Napoleon still cried out cheerily to Ney: 'We've got a nine-to-one chance.' Breakfast was brought to the Emperor at eight o'clock. He invited a number of generals to join him. During breakfast someone commented that Wellington had been at the Duchess of Richmond's ball* in Brussels two nights previously. Said Soult, that rough and ready soldier with the face of an archbishop: 'Today is the real ball.' Napoleon made fun of Ney for saying: 'Wellington won't be such an idiot as to wait for Your Majesty.' That was his way. 'He enjoyed a joke', says Fleury de Chaboulon. 'A lively sense of humour was the essence of his character', says Gourgaud. 'He was full of jokes, which tended to be outlandish rather than witty', says Benjamin Constant. This playful side of the Titan needs to be emphasized. 'Grumblers' was his name for his grenadiers; he used to pinch their ears or pull their moustaches. 'The Emperor always kept playing tricks on us', one of them declared. On 27 February, during his secret voyage back to France from the island of Elba, the French brig-of-war *Zéphir* encountered the brig *Inconstant* (in which Napoleon was concealed) out at sea. The *Zéphir* asked the *Inconstant* for news of Napoleon. The Emperor, still wearing the bee-embroidered hat with purple-and-white cockade that he had adopted on Elba, took the speaking trumpet himself and replied with a chuckle: 'The Emperor is getting along nicely.' Such laughter is the mark of a man at ease with everything that happens. Napoleon had a number of these jovial outbursts during his Waterloo breakfast. After breakfast he spent a quarter of an hour thinking; then two generals sat down on the bundle of straw, pen in hand and writing paper on knee, and the Emperor dictated the order of battle.

At nine o'clock the French army began to move off in five columns. The divisions were in two lines, with the artillery between the brigades; bands led the way with drumrolls and trumpet-blasts, beating time to the countryside; a powerful, vast, joyous ocean of helmets, sabres, and bayonets against the horizon. The Emperor, greatly moved, cried out twice: 'Magnificent! Magnificent!'

Incredible though it may seem, the whole army took up its position between nine and half past ten. It was arranged in six lines that formed, to quote the Emperor's phrase, 'six *V*s'. He had ordered three batteries of twelve-centimetre guns to be detached from the three corps of d'Erlon, Reille, and Lobau; they were to open the attack by bombarding Mont Saint-Jean at the point where the Nivelles and Genappe roads meet. When the battle line was in position—during the profound stillness that precedes a battle like a gathering storm—the Emperor stood watching these batteries file past. He tapped Haxo on the shoulder and said: 'Twenty-four pretty girls there, General!'

Sure of the outcome, he smiled encouragingly at the company of sappers from the First Corps as they passed before him; they had orders to occupy Mont Saint-Jean as soon as the village was taken. His serenity was varied only by one touch of contemptuous pity. When he saw the fine Scots Greys on their superb horses assembling to his left, in the region that is now a huge cemetery, he said: 'What a pity!'

Then he mounted his horse and went forward from Rossomme. He chose as his vantage point (his second during the battle) a narrow strip of grass on the right side of the road from Genappe to Brussels. His third station, which he adopted around seven o'clock in the evening, was a fearfully dangerous place between La Belle Alliance and La Haye Sainte: a relatively high mound, still in existence, behind which the Guard was massed in a hollow on the plain. Bullets ricocheted from the stones paving the road there and flew past Napoleon. As at Brienne, gunfire and cannon fire kept whistling around his head. Rusty old bullets, sabre blades, and misshapen shells have been found almost at the spot where his horse was standing. 'Flaky rust.'* A few years ago a sixty-centimetre shell was dug up there, still unexploded, with its fuse broken off at the casing. This final station was the place where the Emperor said to his guide Lacoste (a hostile frightened peasant tied to a hussar's saddle, flinching from every volley of gunfire and trying to hide behind him): 'You idiot, this is disgraceful! You'll get yourself shot in the back!' The writer of these lines did some personal digging in the loose sandy soil of the mound; he found part of the neck of a bomb, eroded by forty-six years of rust, and some bits of old iron that broke like alder twigs in his hands.

As everyone knows, the undulating plain where Napoleon met Wellington no longer slopes as it did on 18 June 1815. The fatal ground has been reused to make its own monument, and in the process, it has been robbed of its true contours. History looks at it in bewilderment, and no longer recognizes it. In order to glorify it, people disfigured it. 'What have they done to my battlefield!' was Wellington's exclamation when he revisited Waterloo two years later. Today, a great lion-topped pyramid of earth stands where there used to be a ridge that dropped toward the Nivelles road at a comfortable gradient but became almost a sheer escarpment on the Genappe side. The elevation of this scarp can still be judged from the height of the two great burial mounds flanking the road from Genappe to Brussels—the English mound on the left, the German on the right. There isn't any French burial mound; the whole plain is France's graveyard. Cartloads of earth were brought by the thousand, creating a knoll one hundred and fifty feet high and half a mile in circumference, and as a result, the Mont Saint-Jean plateau today is a gentle, easily accessible slope; on the day of the battle, however, its approaches were very steep and precipitous, especially on the La Haye Sainte side, which rose so sharply that the English artillery couldn't see the farm in the bottom of the valley below them, at the very centre of the conflict. On 18 June 1815, the rain had carved further gullies in this awkward ground. Mud made the ascent even more difficult; you didn't simply struggle, you bogged down.

Along the plateau's crest ran a kind of ditch that couldn't be seen from a distance. What was it? Let's explain. Braine-l'Alleud is one Belgian village; Ohain is another. The two villages, hidden from each other by the lie of the land, are linked by a four-mile road that often ploughs through the hills like a furrow, as it crosses the undulating terrain. At various points, therefore, it becomes a ravine. In 1815 its route cut across the Mont Saint-Jean plateau between the Genappe and Nivelles roads, just as it still does. But nowadays it's level with the plain; in those days it was a sunken road. Both of its embankments were taken away to make the memorial mound. Along most of its length, this road was, and still is, entrenched—entrenched, in some places, to a depth of twelve feet, with precipitous banks that crumble away here and there, especially in winter after storms.

Accidents have happened there. At the approach to Braine-l'Alleud the road became so narrow that one traveller was fatally run over by a cart, as shown by a stone cross standing near the cemetery and stating the name of the dead man, 'Monsieur Bernard Debrye, merchant, from Brussels', and the date of the accident, 'February 1637'.[1] On the Mont Saint-Jean plateau it became so deep that a peasant, Mathieu Nicaise, was crushed by a landslide there in 1783, as shown by another stone cross whose top disappeared during the alterations, though the overturned pedestal is still visible on the grassy slope to the left of the track between La Haye Sainte and Mont Saint-Jean farm.

On the day of battle there was no outward warning of this sunken road alongside the crest of the Mont Saint-Jean plateau—a trench at the highest point of the escarpment, a hidden ditch in the ground. It was invisible; in other words, terrible.

viii. The Emperor Asks his Guide Lacoste a Question

So, on the morning of Waterloo, Napoleon was quite content.

And with good reason. His battle plan was an excellent one, as we have seen.

Once the battle had begun, its many fluctuations scarcely altered the expression on his face. Resistance at Hougoumont. Even stronger resistance at La Haye Sainte. The death of Bauduin. The loss of Foy. The unforeseen wall that broke Soye's brigade. Guilleminot's fatal blunder: he had neither grenades nor gunpowder. The bogged batteries. The fifteen unescorted guns seized by Uxbridge in a sunken road. The projectiles that fell ineffectively on the English lines, simply burying themselves in the rain-drenched ground and raising nothing worse than volcanoes of mud, so that

---

[1] The inscription is as follows:
  MONSIEUR BERNARD
  DE BRYE MERCHANT
  FROM BRUSSELS
  WAS ACCIDENTALLY
  RUN OVER HERE
  BY A CART
  ON THE (*illegible*)
  OF FEBRUARY 1637
[*Hugo's note*].

gunshots were reduced to splashes. Piré's wasted show of force at Braine-l'Alleud: all that cavalry—fifteen squadrons—virtually wiped out. The English right wing hardly troubled, the left wing hardly disrupted. Ney's extraordinary mistake: instead of deploying the four divisions of the First Corps in echelon formation, he massed them together, so that a block two hundred men across and twenty-seven deep was exposed to gunfire and lacerated fearfully by cannon balls. The lack of coordination between attacking columns. The peripheral batteries suddenly uncovered on the flank. Bourgeois, Donzelot, and Durutte in danger. Quiot driven back. Lieutenant Vieux, that Hercules trained by the École polytechnique, wounded while he was chopping down La Haye Sainte's door under direct fire from the English barricade at the turn of the Genappe–Brussels road. Marcognet's division caught between infantry and cavalry—shot down at point-blank range in a wheatfield by Best and Pack, and sabred by Ponsonby. His battery of seven guns spiked. The Prince of Saxe-Weimar holding his ground, standing firm at Frischermont and Smohain despite the efforts of the Comte d'Erlon. The colours of the 105th taken. The colours of the 45th taken. The Prussian Black Hussar taken prisoner by scouts of the flying column of chasseurs (three hundred men scouring the countryside between Wavre and Plancenoit), and the disturbing news he brought. Grouchy's tardiness. The fifteen hundred men killed in less than an hour in the Hougoumont orchard. The eighteen hundred men laid low in an even shorter time at La Haye Sainte... All these storms swept like battle clouds before Napoleon without darkening the assurance in his imperial eyes. Staring war in the face was second nature to him. He never added up little columns of harrowing details; the individual figures mattered little to him, as long as the sum total was victory. If the early stages went badly, he wasn't at all perturbed, feeling that he was in absolute control of the outcome. He could afford to wait, since he believed he wasn't under threat. He eyed Destiny as an equal, and seemed to tell Fate: 'You wouldn't dare.'

Napoleon was half light and half darkness; he sensed that he was protected in his good moments and tolerated in his bad ones. Events connived, almost collaborated with him; like an ancient hero, he was invulnerable. Or so he believed.

Still, when you had the Berezina, Leipzig, and Fontainebleau* behind you, you might well have eyed Waterloo with some mistrust. A mysterious frown was starting to appear in the depths of the sky.

When Wellington began to draw back, Napoleon quivered with excitement. He saw the Mont Saint-Jean plain suddenly abandoned; the English front line vanished. It was rallying, but only under cover. The Emperor half rose in his stirrups. The gleam of victory flashed before his eyes.

If Wellington could be driven back into the Soignes forest and destroyed, England would be decisively crushed; France would have avenged Crécy, Poitiers, Malplaquet, and Ramillies. The man of Marengo was now wiping out Agincourt.*

Then, while he contemplated this fateful turn of events, the Emperor swept his spyglass across the whole battlefield one last time. His Guard, standing behind him with their weapons grounded, looked up at him with a kind of religious reverence. He was pondering, examining the hillsides, studying the slopes, scrutinizing the clump of trees here, the field of rye there, the path somewhere else; he seemed to be counting every single bush. He looked rather carefully at the English barricades on the two main roads, which consisted of huge tree trunks—one on the Genappe road above La Haye Sainte, armed with two cannon (the only English artillery able to fire on the lowest part of the battlefield), and one on the Nivelles road, where the Dutch bayonets of Chassé's brigade were catching the light. Close to that particular barricade he could see the old white-walled Chapel of Saint Nicholas at the crossroad leading to Braine-l'Alleud. He bent over and said something quietly to the guide, Lacoste. The guide shook his head in denial—probably deceitfully.

The Emperor straightened up and considered the situation.

Wellington had fallen back. Only one task now remained—to turn that withdrawal into a rout.

Napoleon swung round abruptly and sent a courier post-haste to Paris with the news that the battle was won.

Napoleon was the kind of genius who can command the thunder.

He had just found his thunderbolt.

He ordered Milhaud's cuirassiers to take the Mont Saint-Jean plateau.

ix. The Unexpected

There were three thousand five hundred of them. Their front line was a quarter of a league long. They were gigantic men riding colossal horses. There were twenty-six squadrons of them; and behind them, in support, were Lefebvre-Desnouettes's division (a hundred and six crack gendarmes), the Chasseurs of the Guard (eleven hundred and ninety-seven men), and the Lancers of the Guard (eight hundred and eighty). They wore plumeless helmets and wrought-iron breastplates; pistols were in their saddle holsters, and they carried long sabres. That morning, at nine o'clock, the whole army had watched in admiration as they moved up in a dense column with trumpets resounding and all the bands playing 'Veillons au salut de l'Empire'. One of their batteries was on their flank, the other in their centre. They had deployed in two rows between the Grenoble road and Frischermont, joining Napoleon's astutely positioned second line, where Kellermann's cuirassiers were on the extreme left and Milhaud's cuirassiers on the extreme right—two wings of iron, so to speak.

The aide-de-camp Bernard brought them the Emperor's order. Ney drew his sword and placed himself at their head. The immense squadrons began to move.

It was a formidable sight.

With the precision of a battering ram breaking open a door, that whole mass of cavalry, arrayed in columns, division by division, sabres raised, standards waving, and trumpets blaring, moved down the hillside of La Belle in a single sweep, as one man. It plunged into the fearsome hollow where so many men had already fallen, vanished in the smoke, then emerged from the shadows and reappeared on the valley's other side, still compact and orderly, cantering through a hail of gunfire up the muddy slope of the Mont Saint-Jean plateau. Its ascent was solemn, menacing, imperturbable; the mighty thunder of the hoofbeats could be heard between the gunshots and cannonades. Since there were two divisions, they rode in two columns, Wathier's division being on the right and Delord's on the left. From a distance they looked like two huge steel snakes slithering toward the crest of the plateau. Their movement across the battlefield seemed miraculous.

Nothing like it had been seen since the heavy cavalry assault that took the great Borodino redoubt. Murat* was missing now, but Ney was still there. The whole mass seemed to have become a monster with a single mind. The various squadrons coiled and spread out like the tentacles of an octopus. Now and then, through gaps in the heavy smoke, they could be glimpsed—jumbled helmets, shouts, sabres, horses' rumps bounding in frenzy through the cannonades and trumpet-sounds—a dreadful disciplined chaos clad in breastplates like dragons' scales.

Such tales seem to belong to another age. Similar scenes must have been evoked in the old Orphic epics* that told of ancient centaurs, man-horses, Titans with human faces and equine bodies, who scaled Olympus at a gallop, ghastly, invulnerable, glorious—gods, and yet brutes.

Twenty-six battalions stood ready to face these twenty-six squadrons—a curious numerical coincidence. Behind the crest of the plateau, under cover of the masked battery, waited the English infantry, calmly, silently, motionlessly, with muskets raised and levelled. They were drawn up in thirteen squares with two battalions in each. There were two lines of squares—seven in the first, six in the second. They couldn't see the cuirassiers, nor could the cuirassiers see them; but they could hear that tide of men rising. They could hear the ever-increasing noise of three thousand horses, the rhythmic beat of cantering hooves, the jingle of harness, the clatter of sabres, and a kind of immense savage breathing sound. There was a moment of dreadful silence, and then, all at once, a long line of uplifted arms brandishing sabres appeared on the crest, and helmets, and trumpets, and banners, and three thousand grey-moustached heads crying: 'Long live the Emperor!'—and the whole mass of cavalry surged onto the plateau like an earthquake beginning.

Suddenly disaster struck. On the English left—our right—the head of the cuirassiers' column reared up with a horrendous din. They reached the very edge of the crest at full tilt, furiously intent on wiping out the squares and cannon—and saw a ditch, a grave, between them and the English. It was the sunken road from Ohain.

That was an appalling moment. There, right at the horses' feet, lay the ravine, gaping and unexpected, four metres deep, with cliffs on either side. The second row pushed up against the first, the third row pushed up against the second; the horses reared, recoiled, fell backward, writhed with their feet in the air, piling up and throwing their riders. There was no way back; the whole column had become a single projectile. The impetus that had been gained to destroy the English destroyed the French. No escape from the ravine; it couldn't be conquered till it was full; riders and horses tumbled chaotically into it, crushing each other until the chasm was a single mass of flesh. Then, when the grave was full of living bodies, the rest rode over them and went on. Almost a third of Dubois's brigade fell into that abyss.

And that was how the defeat began.

A local tradition (clearly exaggerated) says that the sunken road from Ohain engulfed two thousand horses and fifteen thousand men. Presumably the figure would also include all the bodies thrown into the ravine next day, after the battle.

It's worth noting, incidentally, that this Dubois brigade—now put to the test with such fatal consequences—had, unaided, taken the colours of the Lunebourg battalion an hour earlier.

Before Napoleon ordered this charge by Milhaud's cuirassiers, he had surveyed the terrain carefully, but hadn't been able to see the sunken road—not even a wrinkle of it was visible on the surface of the plateau. Still, he'd been put on his guard by the little white chapel at the Nivelles crossroads, and he'd questioned the guide Lacoste—probably about the existence of some obstacle there. The guide had answered in the negative. You could almost say that Napoleon's downfall was caused by a peasant shaking his head.

Fate had still other things in store.

Was there any chance that Napoleon could have won this battle? I say no. Why not? Because of Wellington? Because of Blücher? No. Because of God.

A victorious Bonaparte at Waterloo wouldn't have been in keeping with the nineteenth-century pattern. A new chain of events was on the way, and it had no room for Napoleon. History had long been preparing to turn against him.

It was time for the great man to fall.

This one individual was upsetting the balance; he was carrying too much weight in the destiny of the human race. He alone amounted to more than all the rest of mankind. It would have killed civilization for the full flush of human vitality to be concentrated in one head, for the whole world to rush to the brain of one man—if it had lasted. The time had come for the Supreme Justice to deal with it; and He cannot be corrupted. I daresay formal complaints had been lodged by the principles and elements that determine the laws of gravity (which apply to morality no less than physics). Reeking bloodshed, overfilled graveyards, weeping mothers—those are very eloquent plaintiffs. When the earth is overburdened, mysterious groans can be heard in the dark, and the abyss will hear them.

Napoleon had been impeached in the limitless expanse, and his downfall had been decreed.

He was giving God trouble.

Waterloo wasn't a battle; it was a change in the structure of the universe.

x. The Mont Saint-Jean Plateau

At the moment when the ravine came out of hiding, so did the guns.

Sixty cannon and soldiers in thirteen squares blasted the cuirassiers at point-blank range. The brave General Delord greeted the English battery with a military salute.

The entire English light artillery galloped into position within their squares. The cuirassiers never wavered for an instant; the disaster at the sunken road had decimated but not disheartened them. They were the kind of men who grow stronger in spirit when they diminish in number.

The catastrophe had affected only Wathier's column. Ney almost seemed to have some premonition of the trap; he had sent Delord's column obliquely to the left, and it arrived unscathed.

The cuirassiers hurled themselves against the English squares.

Galloping at full stretch, reins loose, sabres between their teeth, pistols in their hands—so the attack began.

At times, in battle, a man's soul hardens so much that he turns from soldier to statue, from flesh to granite. The English battalions, though desperately assailed, didn't budge an inch.

The results were dreadful.

The English squares were attacked on all sides simultaneously; they were engulfed in a furious cyclone. Their infantry remained perfectly cool; they didn't show even a flicker of emotion. The first row knelt and met the cuirassiers with bayonets; the second row fired at them; behind the second row, gunners were loading their cannon. The front of the square would part to make way for a volley of grapeshot, and then close again. The cuirassiers retorted by crushing them; their huge horses reared up, trampled the ranks, leaped over the bayonets, and came down, gigantically, within those four living walls. Gunfire lacerated the cuirassiers, the cuirassiers lacerated the squares. Entire lines of men were crushed beneath the horses' hooves and disappeared. Bayonets, in turn, plunged into those centaurs' bellies. The injuries thus caused were terrible— nothing like them may ever have been seen in any other situation. Despite the ravages of this frenzied cavalry assault, the squares closed ranks again without wavering. They kept firing inexhaustibly into the midst of their attackers. It was a monstrous sight. The squares were no longer battalions of men; they were craters; and the cuirassiers were no longer a mass of cavalry; they were a hurricane. Every square was a volcano attacked by a thundercloud; lava was doing battle with lightning.

The square on the extreme right, being the most open to attack, was virtually annihilated in the very first assault. It consisted of the 75th Highland regiment. In the centre, while people were slaughtering each other all round him, the piper remained profoundly oblivious; he sat on a drum, held his bagpipe under his arm, and kept playing highland airs with his eyes fixed sadly on scenes of forest and lake. Those Scots died thinking of Ben Nevis, just as dying Greeks used to remember Argos.* A cuirassier's sabre finally struck down the pibroch and the arm that played it—stopping the music by killing the musician.

The cuirassiers' numbers were relatively small, having been reduced by the disaster in the ravine, and they were faced with practically the entire English army; but in practice they multiplied— each man counted for ten. Indeed, some Hanoverian regiments started to fall back, and Wellington, seeing this, thought of his own cavalry. If Napoleon, at the same time, had thought of his infantry, he would have won the battle. That oversight was his great and fatal error.

Suddenly the attacking cuirassiers found that they themselves were under attack. The English cavalry was behind them. The squares in front of them, Somerset at their rear; and 'Somerset' was fourteen hundred dragoons. On Somerset's right was Dornberg with the German light horse; on his left, Trip with the Belgian carabineers. Now the cuirassiers, attacked front, flank, and rear by both infantry and cavalry, had to face in all directions at once. What did they care? They were a whirlwind; their heroism was indescribable.

In addition, the artillery was constantly thundering away behind them. Nothing else could have wounded those men in the back. One of their cuirasses can now be seen in the Waterloo Museum collection, with a hole from a musket ball in the left shoulder plate.

Only such a band of Englishmen could have matched such a band of Frenchmen.

It was no longer a conflict, but a darkness, a fury, a dizzy whirl of souls and hearts, a tornado of flashing swords. In a moment the fourteen hundred dragoons were reduced to eight hundred; Fuller, their lieutenant-colonel, was among the dead. Ney hastily brought up Lefebvre-Desnouettes's lancers and chasseurs. The Mont Saint-Jean plateau was taken, retaken, and taken once again. The cuirassiers swung back and forth between cavalry and infantry; to put it more accurately, the whole dreadful mass of men grappled with each other and wouldn't let go. The squares still held firm. There were a dozen separate attacks. Ney had four horses killed under him. Half the cuirassiers fell on the plateau. The entire struggle lasted two hours.

The English army was profoundly shaken. If the initial assault hadn't been weakened by the disaster at the sunken road, the cuirassiers would clearly have broken the centre and won the day. Clinton, who had seen Talavera and Badajoz,* was still astounded by the power of that cavalry force. Wellington, though three-quarters beaten, admired the scene stoically. 'Splendid!' he murmured.[1]

The cuirassiers wiped out seven of the thirteen squares, captured or spiked sixty guns, and carried off six English regimental colours, which were brought to the Emperor outside the La Belle Alliance farm by three cuirassiers and three chasseurs of the Guard.

Wellington's situation had become distinctly worse. This strange battle was like a duel between two badly wounded savages, each continuing to fight on, neither willing to submit, yet both steadily losing blood. Which one would be the first to fall?

The struggle on the plateau continued.

[1] His very word [*Hugo's note*].

Just how far did the cuirassiers penetrate? No one can say. One thing is certain: the morning after the battle, a cuirassier and his horse were found dead in the weighing-shed at Mont Saint-Jean, at the very spot where the four roads (from Nivelles, Genappe, La Hulpe, and Brussels) meet. That rider had broken right through the English lines. One of the men who carried the body away is still living at Mont Saint-Jean. His name is Dehaze. At the time, he was eighteen years old.

Wellington could feel his own downfall coming. The crucial moment would soon arrive.

The cuirassiers hadn't succeeded, in the sense that the centre hadn't been broken. With everyone holding the plateau, nobody was holding it, and in effect it remained mainly in English hands. Wellington held the village and the height of the plain; Ney held only the crest and the slope. Both sides seemed to have taken root in this fateful soil.

Yet the English army seemed too weak to recover; it was bleeding away dreadfully. Kempt, on the left wing, called for reinforcements. 'There aren't any', Wellington replied; 'he'll simply have to fight to the death.'* At almost the same moment Ney sent to Napoleon for troops, and Napoleon exclaimed: 'Where does the fellow think I'm going to get any troops? Does he expect me to make them?' A striking coincidence, which shows how depleted the two armies had become.

Still, the English army was in the worse state. Its infantry had been crushed by frenzied onslaughts from the huge mass of iron- and steel-clad cuirassiers. A few men around a flag marked the place where a regiment had been; some battalions were now led by a mere captain or lieutenant; Alten's division, which had already suffered so much at La Haye Sainte, was now virtually wiped out; the brave Belgians of Van Kluze's brigade littered the ryefields all along the road from Nivelles; hardly anything was left of the Dutch grenadiers who had fought on our side against Wellington in Spain in 1811, and in 1815 had joined the English against Napoleon. There were heavy losses among the officers. Lord Uxbridge had a fractured knee; next day his leg was amputated and buried. On the French side, Delord, Lhéritier, Colbert, Dnop, Travers, and Blancard were put out of action during the cuirassiers' conflict; while on the English side, Alten was wounded, Barne was wounded, Delancey was killed, Van Merlen was killed, Ompteda was killed. Wellington's entire staff was decimated. Bloodshed was being weighed against bloodshed; and England was on the worse side of the scales. The 2nd regiment of Foot Guards had lost five lieutenant-colonels, four captains, and three lieutenants; the first battalion of the 30th infantry had lost twenty-four officers and a hundred and twelve men; of the 79th Highlanders, twenty-four officers were wounded, and eighteen officers and four hundred and fifty men were killed. Cumberland's Hanoverian hussars, an entire regiment under Colonel Hacke (subsequently court-martialled and cashiered), turned tail and fled from the fight into the Soignes forest, spreading panic as far as Brussels. When they saw the French gaining ground and drawing close to the forest, farm carts, ammunition wagons, baggage wagons, and cartloads of wounded soldiers fled; and some of the Dutch, cut to pieces by the French cavalry, cried havoc. According to eyewitnesses who are still alive, the roads were choked with fugitives for nearly two leagues in the direction of Brussels, from Vert-Coucou to Groenendael. The panic was so great that it spread as far as the Prince of Condé at Malines and Louis XVIII* at Ghent. Except for a small reserve force drawn up behind the field hospital in the Mont Saint-Jean farm, and Vivian's and Vandeleur's brigades on the left flank, Wellington had run out of cavalry. Many of the artillery units had been destroyed. Siborne admits these facts; Pringle goes so far as to say that the Anglo-Dutch army was reduced to thirty-four thousand men, but that exaggerates the extent of the disaster. The Iron Duke remained calm, but his lips were pale. The Austrian attaché Vincent and the Spanish attaché Alava, who were on the battlefield with the English staff, thought that the Duke's position was hopeless. At five o'clock Wellington took out his watch and was heard to murmur ominously: 'Night or the Prussians must come.'

About that time a distant line of bayonets could be seen glinting on the heights around Frischermont.

That was the turning point of the great drama.

xi. A Bad Guide for Napoleon, a Good One for Bülow

Everyone knows about Napoleon's terrible mistake. Grouchy was expected, Blücher came; instead of life, death.

Fate has such moments of transformation. He was looking for the throne of the whole world; what actually met his gaze was Saint Helena.*

If the little shepherd boy who acted as guide to Blücher's lieutenant Bülow had advised him to leave the forest above Frischermont, instead of below Placenoit, the whole shape of the nineteenth century might possibly have been different. Napoleon would have won the Battle of Waterloo. Any road other than the one below Placenoit would have led the Prussian army to a ravine that their artillery couldn't have crossed; and Bülow would not have reached the battlefield.

Another hour's delay, and Blücher wouldn't have found Wellington still fighting; 'the battle would have been lost', declares the Prussian General Müffling.

It was high time, then, for Bülow to arrive. He was already very late. He had bivouacked overnight at Dion-le-Mont and set out at dawn. But the roads were in no condition for use, and his divisions bogged down on them. The cannon sank up to their hubs. Furthermore, he had been forced to cross the river Dyle by the narrow bridge at Wavre. The street leading to the bridge had been set on fire by the French; the artillery and ammunition wagons were unable to pass between the rows of burning houses, and had been obliged to wait till the fire was put out. At midday, Bülow's vanguard was only just reaching Chapelle-Saint-Lambert.

Had the battle begun two hours earlier, it would have been finished by four o'clock, and Blücher would have stumbled into a battle already won by Napoleon. Happenings like these can have immense consequences—as immense as the infinite that lies beyond our grasp.

The Emperor, with his field glass, had been the first to notice something significant on the distant horizon. Already, at midday, he had said: 'I can see a little cloud over there; it looks to me like troops.' Then he had asked the Duc de Dalmatie: 'Tell me, Soult, what can you see over toward Chapelle-Saint-Lambert?' The marshal turned his own field glass in that direction and replied: 'Four or five thousand men, sire. Presumably Grouchy.' Yet the object remained motionless and hazy. The Emperor pointed out the 'little cloud' to his general staff, and all of them trained their glasses on it. Some of them said: 'It's stationary columns of men.' Most of them said:

'It's trees.' The fact remained that the cloud wasn't moving. The Emperor sent Domon's light cavalry on a reconnaissance mission to that indistinct site.

Bülow had indeed failed to move. His vanguard was too weak to do anything. He had to wait for the main body of his forces, and he had been ordered to regroup before entering the battle line; but at five o'clock, in view of the difficulty of Wellington's position, Blücher gave Bülow the order to attack, with these remarkable words: 'We'll have to give the English army a breather.'

Soon afterwards, Losthin's, Hiller's, Hacke's, and Ryssel's divisions deployed in front of Lobau's corps; Prince Wilhelm of Prussia's cavalry came out from the Bois de Paris; Plancenoit was in flames; and Prussian bullets began to rain down, even reaching the ranks of the Imperial Guard stationed in reserve behind Napoleon.

xii. The Imperial Guard

The rest of the story is familiar:* the third army arriving, the battle thrown out of joint, eighty-six guns suddenly thundering away, Pirch I meeting up with Bülow, Ziethen's cavalry led up by Blücher in person, the French driven back, Marcognet swept off the Ohain plateau, Durutte dislodged from Papelotte, Donzelot and Quiot retreating, Lobau attacked from the flank, our broken regiments faced at nightfall with a new battle to fight, the whole English line resuming the offensive and being driven forward, the decimation of the French ranks, the collaboration of English gunfire and Prussian gunfire. Wholesale slaughter; disaster on the front line, disaster on the flank; the Imperial Guard entering the battle line in the teeth of this terrible collapse.

They felt they were going to their death, and shouted: 'Long live the Emperor!'—a death rattle breaking into a cry of homage. There is nothing more poignant in recorded history.

All day the sky had been overcast, but suddenly, at that particular moment (about eight o'clock in the evening), the distant clouds parted and the grand sinister red light of the setting sun emerged through the elms on the Nivelles road. At Austerlitz, they had seen that sun rising.

During the final crisis every battalion of the Imperial Guard was commanded by a general. Friant, Michel, Roguet, Harlet, Mallet,

Poret de Morvan, were all there. When the grenadiers' tall helmets with their broad eagle badges appeared through the battle haze, symmetrical, orderly, calm, majestic, the enemy was conscious of the glory of France; they thought they could see twenty Victories flying onto the battefield with wings unfurled.* The conquerors thought they were being conquered, and drew back; but Wellington shouted: 'Up, Guards, and at 'em!' The scarlet lines of English Guards rose from their shelter behind the hedges; a hail of gunfire ripped through the tricolour fluttering alongside our eagles; everyone surged forward, and the final carnage began. In the gloom, the Imperial Guard could feel the army giving way around them and an immense flurry of headlong flight; the cries of 'Long live the Emperor!' were replaced by 'Every man for himself!' Nevertheless, despite the panic behind them, the Guard continued to press ahead, suffering more and more losses at every step. There were no cowards or waverers among them. In that band, the common soldier was as much a hero as the general. Not one man drew back from that act of suicide.

With all the heroism of a man accepting death, Ney threw himself frantically into the storm, risking his life at every onslaught. His fifth horse was killed under him. He poured with sweat, his eyes blazed, his mouth was foaming, his uniform had come unbuttoned, one epaulette had been half cut away by a Horse Guard's sabre stroke, his eagle badge had been pierced by a bullet. Bleeding, muddy, magnificent, with a broken sword in his hand, he cried out: 'Come and see how a marshal of France dies—on the battlefield!' But in vain; he didn't die. He was wretched and furious. 'Why haven't you got yourself killed?' he shouted at Drouet d'Erlon. While the whole barrage of artillery was crushing the last handful of men, he called out: 'Haven't you got anything for me? Shoot all those English bullets right into my belly, the whole lot of them!' But the luckless man was being reserved for different bullets—French ones.*

xiii. Disaster

Behind the Imperial Guard there was a woeful state of disarray.

The army fell back hurriedly on all sides—from Hougoumont, La Haye Sainte, Papelotte, Plancenoit. Cries of 'Treason!' were instantly followed by cries of 'Every man for himself!' An army falling apart is like an ice floe thawing. Everything is sagging, crumpling, cracking, drifting, floating, falling, smashing, rushing, dropping. Indescribable disintegration. Ney, hatless, scarfless, swordless, borrowed a horse, leapt on its back, and took up a position blocking the Brussels road against English and French alike. He kept trying to hold the soldiers back, calling them to order, hurling insults at them, clutching at them in their headlong flight. He was outflanked. The army fled from him, shouting 'Long live Marshal Ney!' as they did so. Two of Durutte's regiments zigzagged back and forth in terror, as if tossed like shuttlecocks between the Uhlans' sabres and the gunfire of Kempt's, Best's, Pack's, and Rylandt's regiments. Flight is the worst possible kind of turmoil; friends murder each other to escape; squadrons and battalions scatter and collide with one another—a kind of foam spread out across the battlefield. Even Lobau and Reille, on the furthest flanks, were swept away in the flood. Napoleon vainly tried to create a barrier with what Guard he had left; vainly he used up the squadrons at his own headquarters in one last effort. Quiot fell back before Vivian, Kellermann before Vandeleur, Lobau before Bülow, Morand before Pirch, Domon and Subervic before Prince Wilhelm of Prussia. Guyot, who had led the charge of the Emperor's squadrons, fell beneath the hooves of the English horse. Napoleon galloped among the fleeing multitudes, harangued them, urged them, threatened them, begged them. All the mouths that had been crying 'Long live the Emperor!' earlier in the day were now merely agape; people hardly gave any sign of recognizing him. The newly arrived Prussian cavalry sped onward, soaring, stabbing, slashing, hacking, killing, slaughtering. Teams of animals rushed hither and thither; the very cannon fled for their lives; artillerymen unhitched horses from the ammunition wagons and rode off on them; upturned service wagons lay with their wheels in the air, cluttering the road and causing further fatalities. People were crushing each other, trampling each other, treading on dead and living alike. Human limbs utterly gave way. A swirling multitude was filling the roads, paths, bridges, plains, hills, valleys, woods—all choked with forty thousand men in flight. Howls, groans, knapsacks, and muskets tossed into the long grass, passageways hacked out with the sword; no more comrades, no more officers, no more generals; terror beyond description. Ziethen could butcher France at his leisure. The lions had turned into lambs. That was the scene during this flight.

At Genappe there was one further attempt to return, form a line, and make a stand. Lobau managed to rally some three hundred men. They barricaded the entrance to the village; but at the very first volley of Prussian gunfire, everyone took flight again and Lobau was taken prisoner. You can still see the marks of that volley on the old gable of a ruined brick building to the right of the road, a few minutes before you reach the village. The Prussians, no doubt furious that they had so little to conquer, rushed into Genappe. The pursuit was a monstrous thing. Blücher gave orders to slaughter everyone. Roguet had already set the sorry example by threatening to kill any French grenadier who brought in a Prussian prisoner; but Blücher surpassed him. Duhesme, the general of the Young Guard, was caught at the door of a Genappe tavern; he surrendered his sword to a Death's Head hussar, who took it and killed him. Victory was crowned with the murder of the vanquished. We are History, so we should administer punishment: old Blücher was disgracing himself. This atrocity finished off the disaster. The frantic rout swept through Genappe, Quatre-Bras, Gosselies, Frasnes, Charleroi, Thuin, and never stopped till it reached the border. And who were the people fleeing like this? The Grand Army, alas!

Did this giddiness, this horror, this ruinous collapse of the finest and most amazing heroism in recorded history, happen for no reason? Far from it. Waterloo lay in the shadow of a great principle. The day belonged to destiny; a power beyond humanity was in control there. Hence all the heads bowing down in terror, all the noble minds surrendering their swords. Europe's conquerors fell headlong; there was nothing they could say or do; they could feel a dreadful Presence in the gloom. 'So it was fated.'* On that day the whole human landscape altered. Waterloo was the fulcrum of the nineteenth century. A great man had to pass away, so that a great age might arrive. The Unanswerable One saw to it. Thus the panic of all those heroes can be explained. What lay over the battle of Waterloo was more than a cloud, it was a meteor. God himself was passing by.

At nightfall, in a field near Genappe, Bernard and Bertrand took a distraught, pensive, gloomy man by the coat. He had been swept that far by the tide of the fleeing masses. Now he had dismounted, and, wild-eyed, leading his horse by the bridle, was making his way back toward Waterloo, alone. It was Napoleon, still trying to advance—the mighty sleepwalker of a shattered dream.

xiv. The Last Square

A few squares of the Imperial Guard, as immovable as rocks in a rushing stream despite the headlong flight that surged past them, held out till nightfall. Night was coming, and so was death; they waited for that twofold shadow, and, without wavering, allowed it to engulf them. Each regiment was cut off from its fellows and had no further ties to the now-shattered army; each was responsible for its own death. For this last stand some of them took up a position on the heights of Rossomme, others in the Mont Saint-Jean plain. There, abandoned, defeated, and terrible, those sombre squares suffered their mighty death agonies. Ulm, Wagram, Jena, Friedland* were dying with them.

By about nine o'clock in the evening twilight, at the foot of the Mont Saint-Jean plateau, only one such square remained. In the fateful valley, at the foot of the slope formerly scaled by the cuirassiers and now swamped by hordes of English, that square, faced with a terrifying intensity of concentrated artillery fire from the victorious enemy, fought on. It was commanded by a little-known officer named Cambronne.* At every volley the square diminished in numbers—and fought back. It answered artillery fire with gunfire, regrouping constantly as its walls were depleted. Distant escapees, briefly pausing for breath, could hear its dark thunder slowly dwindling in the shadows.

When the legion was finally reduced to a handful, when their flag was in tatters, when their rifles had run out of ammunition and could only be used as clubs, when the heaped dead outnumbered the assembled living, a kind of religious awe ran through the conquerors in the presence of those dying heroes. The English artillery paused to catch its breath, and fell silent. There was some sort of respite. The combatants seemed to be surrounded by a teeming swarm of ghosts, outlines of men on horseback, dark silhouettes of cannon, wheels, and cartridges with pale sky behind them. The gigantic skull always seen by courageous men in the smoke of battle was advancing toward them and staring them in the face. In the dusk they could hear the guns being reloaded; lighted matches surrounded them like nocturnal tigers' eyes—linstocks were being applied to all the cannon in the English battery. And then, touched by the situation, an English general—some say Colville, others Maitland—held back the moment of death that hung suspended above his enemies' heads, and called out to them: 'Brave Frenchmen, surrender!' Cambronne answered, *'Merde!'**

xv. Cambronne

Out of respect for the French reader, that word—perhaps the finest ever uttered by a Frenchman—can't be recorded. History isn't allowed to make use of the sublime.

At our own risk and peril, we're defying that prohibition.*

Among all those giants, then, there was one supreme Titan— Cambronne.

Say that word and then die—what could possibly be greater! (Someone who is willing to die *does* die; it wasn't the man's fault if he was shot and survived.)

The real winner on the Waterloo battlefield wasn't the Napoleon who was put to flight, or the Wellington who was in a dangerous position at four o'clock and a hopeless one at five, or the Blücher who never really fought at all; the real winner was Cambronne.

When you blast with such a word the very thunderbolt that is destroying you, you are indeed victorious.

When you give disaster such an answer—when you say such things to destiny—when you supply that kind of base for the future lion monument—when you hurl that reply at the overnight rain and Hougoumont's treacherous wall and Ohain's sunken road and Grouchy's delay and Blücher's arrival—when, in your very grave, you're the personification of irony—when you're felled to the ground and yet continue to stand tall—when you blow away the whole European coalition with a single breath—when you fling in the kings' faces the lavatories that they've always known so intimately (ever since the days of the Caesars)—when you turn the crudest utterance into the greatest one by investing it with the glory of France—when you bring down the curtain on Waterloo with an insolent Mardi Gras—when you cap Leonidas with Rabelais*—when you sum up the whole victory in one supreme word that can never be spoken—when you lose the field but make history—when you manage to have the laugh on your side after so much carnage—it's a magnificent thing.

It's an insult hurled at the lightning itself. It has the sublimity of Aeschylus.*

Cambronne's word is an explosion. It's a heart exploding with scorn; it's the excess energy of a death agony breaking out. Who, ultimately, was the winner? Wellington? No; he would have been lost without Blücher. Blücher? No; if Wellington hadn't started the job, he wouldn't have been able to finish it. Cambronne—that unknown soldier walking past at the last moment, that infinitesimal speck in the great war—could feel that there was something deceitful about the situation, something that was doubly bitter because its deceit lay embedded within a catastrophe; and, at the very moment when he was bursting with rage, people mocked him by offering him life! How could he possibly have avoided lashing out?

There they are, all the kings of Europe, the triumphant generals, the thundering Jupiters, with a hundred thousand victorious soldiers and a million more behind the hundred thousand; their guns are at the ready, their matches are lighted; the Imperial Guard and the Grand Army have been trodden beneath their feet; they have just destroyed Napoleon; and now only Cambronne remains—only that puny worm is left to utter a protest. He does utter a protest. He reaches for a word just as someone might reach for a sword. Spittle comes to his lips, and what he spits is the word. Faced with this prodigious and shabby victory, this victory with no victor, the despairing man draws himself up to his full height; he submits to its overwhelming immensity, but he knows that it's nothing at all. And he does more than spit on it. Crushed by the weight of numbers and brute force and physical power, he finds a spiritual means of expression—excrement. Let me repeat: to say that, to do that, to find that, was to be the victor.

At that fatal moment, the spirit of the glorious past descended on this unknown man. Cambronne found the word for Waterloo, as Rouget de l'Isle had found the 'Marseillaise', by inspiration from above. A breath of the divine whirlwind came down and passed through those men; they trembled, and one of them sang the supreme song, the other shouted the terrible cry. Cambronne didn't fling his expression of titanic scorn merely at Europe, in the name of the Empire—that would have been a little thing. He flung it at the past, in the name of the Revolution. You hear it, and you recognize that Cambronne had the spirit of the ancient giants. It sounds like the voice of Danton, or the roar of Kléber.*

When Cambronne uttered his word, the English voice replied:

'Fire!' The batteries flashed, the hillside shook; from all those bronze mouths came one last dreadful vomit of gunfire; a great cloud of smoke, faintly lit by the rising moon, drifted away, and when the smoke was gone, there was nothing left. The last formidable remnant had been annihilated; the Imperial Guard was dead. The four walls of the living fortress lay on the ground; hardly a flicker of movement could be glimpsed here and there among the corpses. And so the French legions—greater than the Roman legions—perished at Mont Saint-Jean on the rain-soaked bloodstained ground, among the dark crops, at the spot where Joseph goes past every morning nowadays at four o'clock, whistling and gaily whipping up his horse, with the mail from Nivelles.

xvi. How Much Does the General Weigh?*

The Battle of Waterloo is an enigma. The victors were as puzzled by it as the loser. To Napoleon, the explanation was panic;[1] Blücher saw it simply as a question of firepower; Wellington couldn't understand it at all. Look at the reports. The bulletins are confused, the commentaries hazy. The former stammer, the latter falter. Jomini finds four critical moments in the Battle of Waterloo; Müffling divides it into three phases. Charras alone (though we don't accept all of his views) has been sharp-eyed enough to see the crucial lines of this catastrophic episode, where human greatness was crushed by divine chance. All the other historians are blinded by its light to some extent, and grope around in their blindness. And indeed it was a day of lightning: the collapse of a military monarchy that had conquered all kingdoms (to the amazement of their kings); the downfall of armed force; the defeat of warfare.

Such an event bears the mark of something more than mere human cause and effect; man's share in it is nothing.

If you deny that Waterloo was due to Wellington and Blücher, are you taking anything away from England and Germany? Not at all. Neither England's reputation nor Germany's stature is affected by

---

[1] 'The end of a battle, the completion of a day, with various mistakes corrected and greater successes promised for tomorrow—all this was lost in a moment of sheer panic'—Napoleon, *Dictations at Saint Helena* [*Hugo's note*].

the puzzle of Waterloo. Thank heaven, the greatness of a nation doesn't depend on dismal attempts to use the sword. You can't contain either Germany or England or France in a scabbard. Nowadays, when Waterloo has become no more than a clash of sabres, Germany still has Goethe—who was greater than Blücher—and England still has Byron*—who was greater than Wellington. Our age is characterized by an immense sunrise of ideas; and England and Germany have contributed their special radiance to that dawn. They are majestic because they think. They have raised civilization to a higher plane, not by accident, but by their own intrinsic qualities. Their progress during the nineteenth century hasn't come from Waterloo. Only a barbarous nation makes any sudden advance after a victory, with the fleeting pride of a brook swollen by a thunderstorm. Civilized peoples—especially in modern times—are neither exalted nor humbled by the good fortune or ill fortune of some military commander. Their specific gravity within the human race is the result of something more than a battle. Thank God, their honour, their dignity, their enlightenment, their ability, aren't mere numbers to be tossed into the lottery of warfare by the gamblers known as heroes and conquerors. A battle lost is often an improvement gained. The less the glory, the more the liberty; only when the drum falls silent can the voice of reason be heard. Loser wins, in this game. Therefore, we should discuss both aspects of Waterloo dispassionately. Let us render to Chance the things that are Chance's, and to God the things that are God's. What was Waterloo—a victory? No; a lottery ticket that happened to win.

A lottery ticket won by Europe, and paid for by France.

It wasn't really worth going to the trouble of putting a lion there.

Actually, Waterloo was the strangest encounter in recorded history. Napoleon and Wellington. They're not enemies, they're opposites. God, who delights in antitheses, has never created a more striking contrast or a more remarkable confrontation. On one side precision, foresight, geometry, caution, provision for retreat, careful husbanding of reserves, inflexible composure, imperturbable methodicalness, strategies based on study of the terrain, tactics based on relative numbers of battalions, carnage measured by a plumbline, war directed by a stopwatch, nothing humanly possible left to chance, bravery of the old classic school, absolute correctitude; on the other side intuition, divination, military waywardness, superhuman instinct, a flashing glance, something that watches like an eagle and blasts like a thunderbolt, haughty impetuosity coupled with miraculous skill; all the mysteries of an unfathomable soul; kinship with Destiny; rivers, plains, forests, hills summoned and somehow forced to obey; despotism holding tyrannic sway even in the thick of battle; faith in a guiding star combined with a knowledge of strategy that enhanced yet interfered with it. Wellington was the Barrême of warfare, Napoleon was its Michelangelo,* and on this particular occasion, genius was defeated by calculus.

Both sides were waiting for someone. The one who got it right was the exact calculator. Napoleon was waiting for Grouchy; he didn't come. Wellington was waiting for Blücher; he did.

Wellington was the classic tradition of warfare getting its revenge. In his early days Bonaparte had faced that tradition in Italy and resoundingly defeated it. The old screech-owl had fled before the young vulture. Ancient notions of strategy had been not only crushed, but shocked. Who was this twenty-six-year-old Corsican? What did he amount to, this brilliant ignoramus who—with everything against him and nothing in his favour, with no provisions, no munitions, no guns, no men, and virtually no army—flung himself and his mere handful of soldiers against the massed and united forces of Europe, and snatched absurd victories from the jaws of impossibility? Where did he come from, this tempestuous madman who—with scarcely a pause for breath, and with the same band of warriors under his command—broke down the German emperor's five armies one after another, and piled Beaulieu on Alvinzi, Wurmser on Beaulieu, Melas on Wurmser, and Mack on Melas? Who was this upstart fighter with the effrontery of a blazing star? The academic school of warfare excommunicated him even as it fled before him. And so the old kind of imperialism developed an implacable hatred for the new kind, the orthodox sabre for the flashing sword, the rulebook for the genius. On 18 June 1815 that hatred had the final say; beneath Lodi, Montebello, Montenotte, Mantua, Marengo, and Arcola,* it wrote the word 'Waterloo'. Mediocrity triumphed—a pleasant sight for the majority! Fate allowed that touch of irony. In his declining years, Napoleon found another Wurmser before him—a younger one.

To turn Wellington into Wurmser, in fact, all you need to do is whiten his hair.

Waterloo was a major battle won by a minor general.

The really impressive thing at Waterloo was England—English determination, English tenacity, English blood. The finest thing England had on that battlefield was, if she doesn't mind my saying so, herself—her army, not her leader.

Wellington, in a curiously ungrateful letter to Lord Bathurst,* declared that his army—the army that fought on 18 June 1815—was detestable. What does the dark mass of bones buried in the fields of Waterloo think about that?

England has shown too much modesty in her view of Wellington. Aggrandize Wellington, and you belittle England. Wellington was only one hero among many. The Scots Greys, the dragoons, Maitland's and Mitchell's regiments, Pack's and Kempt's infantry, Ponsonby's and Somerset's cavalry, the Highlanders playing the bagpipe under fire, Rylandt's battalions, the raw recruits holding their own against veterans from Essling and Rivoli when they hardly knew how to handle a musket—now there's true greatness. Wellington was tenacious—that was his strong point, and I'm not under-estimating it—but the least of his foot-soldiers or horsemen had just as much stamina. An iron soldier is as good as an Iron Duke. For my part, my homage goes to the English soldier, the English army, the English people. If any trophies are to be handed out, they should be given to England. The Waterloo Column would have been more appropriate if it had raised to the heavens not a man's image but a whole nation's.

And yet this same mighty England will take offence at what I'm saying here. Even after our 1789 and her own 1688, she still cherishes her feudal illusions. She puts her faith in hierarchy and heredity. No one is mightier or more glorious, yet she prizes herself as a nation, not a group of people. As a group of people, she still willingly subjects herself and takes a lord for her leader. Her workers submit to sneers and her soldiers to lashes. At the Battle of Inkerman, as I remember, a sergeant who was said to have saved the army couldn't be mentioned in dispatches by Lord Raglan,* because the English military hierarchy wouldn't allow any man below the rank of a commissioned officer to be named in a report.

Above all things, in a clash like Waterloo, I marvel at the extra-ordinary skill of Chance. Overnight rain, the wall at Hougoumont, the Ohain sunken road, Grouchy's inability to hear the gunfire, the guide who misled Napoleon, the guide who led Bülow aright—the whole cataclysm was stage-managed amazingly well.

It must be said that Waterloo, overall, was less a battle than a massacre.

Waterloo was fought across a shorter front, in proportion to the numbers involved, than any other battle. Three-quarters of a league on Napoleon's side, half a league on Wellington's; and seventy-two thousand men on each side. The carnage was caused by that density.

According to estimates, at Austerlitz the French lost 14 per cent of their forces, the Russians 30 per cent, the Austrians 44 per cent. At Wagram the French lost 13 per cent, the Austrians 14 per cent. At Borodino the French lost 37 per cent, the Russians 44 per cent. At Bautzen,* the French lost 13 per cent, the Russians and Prussians 14 per cent. At Waterloo, the French lost 56 per cent, the Allies 31 per cent. Overall losses at Waterloo, 41 per cent of those involved. One hundred and forty-four thousand men fought; sixty thousand died.

Today the field of Waterloo has all the Earth's tranquillity and provides for mankind without emotion. It looks just like any other plain.

At night, however, a kind of visionary haze rises from it; and if a traveller wanders across it and looks and listens and dreams as Virgil once did on the plains of Philippi,* he becomes gripped by hallucinatory scenes of disaster. The dreadful 18 June comes back to life; the fake hill-monument vanishes, the commonplace lion disappears, the battlefield regains its reality; lines of infantry wind across the plain, frenzied gallopers charge across the horizon; the frightened dreamer can see sabres clashing, bayonets glinting, shells exploding, monstrous thunderbolts flying to and fro; he can hear the muffled noise of the ghostly conflict, like a death rattle coming from the depths of a tomb; those shadowy things are grenadiers, these luminous things are cuirassiers; this skeleton is Napoleon, that one is Wellington; though all these things have passed away, they keep on fighting and struggling; and the ravines turn crimson, and the very trees shudder, and fury echoes to the heavens, and, through the gloom, all those untamed heights—Mont Saint-Jean, Hougoumont, Frischermont, Papelotte, Plancenoit—seem to be indistinctly crowned with whirlwinds of wraiths slaughtering each other.

xvii. Should We Approve of Waterloo?

There's a very respectable liberal school of thought that thinks Waterloo wasn't such a bad thing. I don't subscribe to that view. To my mind, Waterloo was simply the date that unwittingly marked a liberation. It's most surprising to find such an egg hatching such an eagle.

If you take the broadest possible view of the subject, Waterloo was a victory of the counter-revolutionary spirit, at least in intention. It was Europe opposing France; it was Saint Petersburg, Berlin, and Vienna opposing Paris; it was the status quo opposing the spirit of innovation; it was 20 March 1815 attacking 14 July 1789; it was the forces of monarchy moving into action against the ever-defiant forces of French insurrection. Their aim was to extinguish, once and for all, a great nation that had been erupting continuously for twenty-six years. The Brunswicks, Nassaus, Romanovs, Hohenzollerns, and Habsburgs joined forces to support the Bourbon monarchy.* Waterloo was a horse ridden by the divine right of kings. Admittedly, the Empire had been despotic, and therefore the monarchy was bound to be a liberal one; the system that arose from Waterloo was (much to the regret of the victors) a grudgingly constitutional system. That was an understandable reaction. But the truth is that the Revolution couldn't really be conquered at all; it was ordained by Providence—it was absolutely fated to happen. Again and again it reappeared—before Waterloo, when Bonaparte overthrew the age-old thrones; after Waterloo, when Louis XVIII granted and submitted to the Charter. Bonaparte used inequality to assert equality; he put a coachboy on the throne of Naples and a sergeant* on the throne of Sweden. At Saint-Ouen, Louis XVIII endorsed the Declaration of the Rights of Man. The true nature of the Revolution is best expressed by the word 'progress'; and the true nature of progress is best expressed by the word 'tomorrow'. Tomorrow is inevitably doing its work, and it's already doing it today. In its own strange way, it invariably accomplishes what it plans. It uses Wellington to turn the mere soldier Foy into an orator; one moment Foy falls on the battlefield at Waterloo, next moment he stands up again on the floor in parliament. That's how progress acts. In its hands, no tool is a bad one. It doesn't mind making use of both the man who bestrode the Alps and Père Élisée's dear old doddering invalid* to produce its divine work. It employs the cripple as well as the conqueror—the conqueror in foreign affairs, the cripple in domestic ones. When Waterloo used the sword to stop Europe's thrones from being demolished, it simply helped to carry on the revolutionary work in a different way. Swordsmen were over and done with; now thinkers would have their turn. The century that Waterloo tried to stop has marched right over it and gone on its way. The ominous victory has been conquered by liberty.

In short, the spirit that triumphed at Waterloo—the spirit that stood behind Wellington and smiled—the spirit that brought him the baton of every marshal in Europe (including, we're told, the Marshal of France) and cheerily wheeled up barrows of bone-filled soil to erect the lion monument and smugly wrote the date '18 June 1815' on its pedestal and incited Blücher to slaughter the fleeing French and hovered over France on the Mont Saint-Jean plateau like a bird of prey and murmured the infamous word 'dis-memberment'—was, undeniably, the spirit of counter-revolution. Then, reaching Paris, it saw the volcano immediately ahead and realized that the lava would burn its feet; so it changed its mind. It started muttering about a charter instead.

We mustn't see anything more in Waterloo than there really is in Waterloo. A planned act of liberation? Nothing of the kind. The counter-revolution was unintentionally liberal, just as Napoleon, in the same way, was unintentionally revolutionary. The eighteenth of June 1815 threw Robespierre* from his horse.

xviii.   Return of the Divine Right of Kings

End of the dictatorship. A whole European system collapsed.

The Empire sank into a darkness like the darkness of the declining Roman empire. As in the days of the Barbarians, chaos was re-appearing. Except that the barbarism of 1815 (we should give it its individual name, counter-revolution) was short-winded, soon out of breath, and soon over. People—and heroes at that—mourned for the passing of the Empire. If a sword turned into a sceptre is glorious, then the Empire had been glory incarnate. It had illuminated the earth with all the light that tyranny can ever give—a sombre light. And, to go further, an obscure light. Compared to the true daylight, it's pitch darkness. And the disappearance of that darkness seemed like an eclipse.

Louis XVIII returned to Paris. The enthusiasm of 20 March was wiped away by the dancing in the streets on 8 July. The man from Corsica was counteracted by the man from Béarn. A white flag flew from the dome of the Tuileries. The exile was on the throne. The pine table from Hartwell was placed in front of Louis XIV's fleur-de-lised chair. Bouvines and Fontenoy were discussed as though they had happened only yesterday, while Austerlitz was relegated to antiquity. The altar and the throne solemnly fraternized. One of the nineteenth century's least criticized forms of social stability became established in France, and indeed across the entire continent. The whole of Europe adopted the white cockade. Trestaillon became famous. The motto 'superior to the many' reappeared in the stone sunburst on the façade of the Quai d'Orsay barracks. A red house appeared where there had once been an Imperial Guard. The Arc du Carrousel, with its display of embarrassing victories, felt out of place in the presence of these novelties (maybe, too, it was a bit ashamed of Marengo and Arcola), and saved face by erecting a statue of the Duc d'Angoulême. The Madeleine cemetery, the notorious common graveyard of 1793, shrouded itself in marble and jasper, since the bones of Louis XVI and Marie Antoinette lay somewhere in its dust. A memorial column rose within the precincts of Vincennes, to commemorate the fact that the Duc d'Enghien had died in the very month of Napoleon's coronation. Pope Pius VII had performed the aforesaid consecration (with the aforesaid corpse not far away); he now blessed the Emperor's downfall as coolly as he had blessed his rise. At Schönnbrunn there was a little four-year-old ghost whom it was seditious to call 'King of Rome'.* And all those things happened, and the kings returned to their thrones, and the master of Europe was caged up, and the *ancien régime* became the new regime, and all the darkness and light in the world changed places—all because, in a wood one summer afternoon, a shepherd boy had said to a Prussian: 'Go this way rather than that way'!

The year 1815 was a sort of dismal April. Old unhealthy pestilent realities changed their outward looks. Lies were married to 1789, the divine right of kings disguised itself behind a charter, fictions became constitutional truths, and, taking Article 14 to heart, prejudices, superstitions, and doubletalk got a gloss of liberalism. Snakes renewing their skin.

Napoleon had both elevated and humbled the human race. 'Ideal', during that reign of glorious materialism, was oddly renamed 'ideology'. A serious mistake for so great a man to ridicule the future. And yet the ordinary people kept their eyes on him; the cannon fodder loved the cannoneer. Where was he? What was he doing? 'Napoleon is dead', a visitor told a crippled veteran of Marengo and Waterloo. 'Dead?' the soldier exclaimed; 'how little you know him!' Imagination turned the fallen man into a god. After Waterloo, there was darkness in the heart of Europe; Napoleon's departure left an immense void for a long time.

Kings peered into that void and admired themselves there. Old Europe took advantage of it, and renewed itself. There was a Holy Alliance.* A 'Belle Alliance'—the fatal battlefield at Waterloo had already uttered the name.

In the presence of this renovation of ancient Europe—and in contrast to it—the outlines of a new France began to appear. The Emperor had mocked the future, but now the future made its entrance, with the star of Liberty on its brow. The eager eyes of the younger people turned towards it. Curiously, they were in love with the future—Liberty—and the past—Napoleon—at the same time. Defeat had magnified the defeated man; Bonaparte fallen seemed to be taller than Napoleon erect. The victors, in their triumph, were alarmed. England got Hudson Lowe to guard him; France got Montchénu to watch him. His folded arms were enough to frighten thrones. Alexander* called him 'the reason I can't sleep'. This fear was caused by his revolutionary component. That's the explanation of (and the excuse for) Bonapartist liberalism. Ghost though he was, he made the old world quake. Kings wore their crowns uneasily, with the rock of Saint Helena on the horizon.

While Napoleon lay dying at Longwood, the sixty thousand men who had fallen on the Waterloo battlefield rotted away in peace. Something of the same peace spread out over the whole world, enabling the Congress of Vienna to make the 1815 Treaty.* Europe called that 'the Restoration'.

So there you have Waterloo.

But what does it all matter to the Infinite? The whole stormy thundercloud known as war, and then the whole mass of darkness known as peace, could never disturb even for an instant the radiance of the immense Eye before whom a greenfly hopping from one blade of grass to the next equals an eagle flying from spire to spire until it reaches the turrets of Notre-Dame.*

Grandeur among the Middle Classes

i. Ninety Years and Thirty-Two Teeth

In the Rue Boucherat, Rue de Normandie, and Rue de Saintonge, there are still a few old denizens who remember a fellow named Monsieur Gillenormand and are glad to talk about him. He was already an old man when they were young. Even today, to those who feel a pang of regret when they look back at the teeming chaos of ghosts known as the past, his figure hasn't entirely vanished from the labyrinth of streets near the Temple—streets that were named after various French provinces in the days of Louis XIV, just as the streets of the new Tivoli quarter* have been named after various European capitals in our own day (a change that reveals an advance, incidentally).

In the year 1831 Monsieur Gillenormand was very much alive. He was one of those people who gain interest in an observer's eyes simply by living a long time, and who become odd because they once looked like everybody else and therefore now look like nobody else. He was a highly distinctive old man, definitely a man who belonged to a different era—a genuine one-hundred-per-cent eighteenth-century middle-class man, a bit of a snob, wearing his old-fashioned middle-class respectability with as much aplomb as a marquis wearing his title. He was over ninety years old, but he walked erect, talked without mumbling, saw clearly, drank hard, ate, slept, and snored. He had all his thirty-two teeth. He wore spectacles only for reading. Temperamentally he was a womanizer, but he declared that he had definitely and permanently given up girls ten years earlier. He couldn't attract them any more, he said—not because he was too old, but because he was too short of cash. 'If it weren't for the fact that I'm broke,' he would add, 'I'd—hee, hee, hee!' In fact the only money he had left was an income of about fifteen thousand francs a year. He dreamed of inheriting a fortune and having an income of a hundred thousand, so that he could keep mistresses. As you see, he was quite different from octogenarians of the aches-and-pains variety (Monsieur de Voltaire,* for instance), who have been dying all their life; his longevity wasn't the kind that is coming apart at the seams; he'd always been in good health, the sprightly old fellow. He was casual, hasty, easily annoyed. He'd blow up at the slightest provocation—especially when he was in the wrong. If people tried to contradict him, he'd raise his stick and give them a caning in the good old Louis XIV style. He had a daughter, who was over fifty and had never married; he didn't beat about the bush with her when he was angry, and he'd gladly have given her a thrashing. He treated her as though she were eight years old. He flogged his servants and called them 'sluts'. One of his favourite oaths was 'Odd's slippers!' The quirkiest things would please him. Every day he was shaved by a barber who was an ex-lunatic and hated him heartily; the barber's wife was pretty and flirtatious, and her husband eyed Monsieur Gillenormand with intense jealousy. Monsieur Gillenormand had a high opinion of his own judgement on any subject and considered himself very sagacious. One of his favourite sayings was: 'I'm pretty sharp, you know; when a flea bites me, I can always tell which girl I got it from.' His favourite words were 'good taste' and 'Nature'. The latter term, in his mouth, didn't have the far-reaching connotations it has nowadays. Instead, he'd put it in some cosy little fireside satiric context like this: 'The civilized world must have a little of everything, so Nature even supplies it with entertaining specimens of barbarism. Europe has small-scale replicas of Asia and Africa. The cat is a drawing-room tiger; the lizard is a pocket crocodile. The ballerinas at the Paris Opéra are rose-coloured cannibals. They're certainly man-eaters in their own way. Or rather, the little witches turn men into oysters and swallow them whole. The West Indians leave only the bones; they leave only the shell. Well, that's the way we live. We don't devour, we nibble; we don't kill, we scratch.'

ii. Like Householder, Like House

He lived at 6 Rue des Filles-du-Calvaire, in the Marais. The house was his own property. It has subsequently been pulled down and rebuilt; presumably its number has been changed too, during the various revolutions of numbering that have been imposed on the streets of Paris. He was housed in a spacious old apartment on the first floor, with the street on one side and gardens on the other; it was hung with big wall-length Gobelin and Beauvais tapestries full of shepherds and shepherdesses. The decorations on the armchairs echoed, in miniature, those on the wall-hangings and the ceilings. His bed was enclosed in a huge nine-panelled coromandel lacquer screen. Long flowing curtains fell in imposing, lavish pleats over the windows. The garden immediately below the windows could be reached by a flight of some twelve or fifteen steps set in a corner; the old fellow scampered up and down these at a remarkably lively pace. In addition to his bedroom (with adjoining library), he had a boudoir that he treasured—an elegant retreat swathed in opulent straw hangings patterned with flowers and fleurs-de-lis, which had been commissioned by Monsieur de Vivonne for his mistress and made by convicts in Louis XIV's jails. Monsieur Gillenormand had inherited them from a reclusive great-aunt who had been over the age of a hundred when she died. He had been married twice. His manners were halfway between those of a courtier (which he had never been) and a lawyer (which he might easily have been). He was cheery and, when he chose, affectionate. In his youth he'd been the type of man who is both a thoroughly disagreeable husband and a thoroughly charming lover—with the result that his wife is never faithful to him but his mistresses always are. He was a connoisseur of painting. In his bedroom he had a wonderful portrait by Jordaens of somebody or other, painted in broad, sweeping brushstrokes and crowded with details tossed down on the canvas chaotically without any apparent method. Monsieur Gillenormand's clothes weren't in Louis XV or even Louis XVI style; no, he dressed like a beau of the Directory period.* He had continued to regard himself as young till that time, and so had kept up with the fashion. He wore a coat of light cloth with broad lapels, long tails, and large steel buttons. Plus knee-breeches and buckled shoes. He always had his hands in his pockets. 'The French Revolution was a bunch of scoundrels', he'd declare emphatically.

iii. Luc-Esprit

One night at the Paris Opéra, when he was sixteen years old, he had
the honour of being noticed simultaneously by two beauties then
in their prime, whose praises were hymned in verse by Voltaire: La
Camargo and La Sallé. Caught between these two lines of fire, he
beat a heroic retreat in the direction of a little ballerina named
Nahenry, who was just sixteen like himself. She was as ordinary as
a tabby cat, and he fell in love with her. Later in life he was full of
memories. 'Ah yes,' he'd exclaim, 'La Guimard, that little darling—
what a pretty creature she was, the last time I saw her at Long-
champs—bedizened with generous sentiments, bejewelled with
turquoise allurements, robed in hues of novelty, and gloved in hues
of passion!' In his youth he'd worn a Nain-Londrin waistcoat, and
he was fond of talking about it. 'I was done up like a Turk from
the Oriental Orient', he'd say. When he was twenty, Madame de
Boufflers chanced to see him; she called him a 'charming rascal'. He
was scandalized by the surnames of the people now listed as being
in politics or in positions of power; he thought them vulgar, ill-
bred. He read the newspapers ('newsprints' or 'gazettes', he called
them) in fits of laughter. 'What kind of people are these!' he'd say.
'Corbière! Humann! Casimir Périer!* You call them politicians, do
you! I can just see the words "Monsieur Gillenormand, Member of
Parliament" in a newspaper! It'd be sheer farce—and yet they're
such idiots they wouldn't raise an eyebrow at it!' He never hesitated
to call anything by its proper (or improper) name, even when
there were ladies present. He uttered indelicacies, indecencies, and
obscenities with a coolness and lack of fluster that made them seem
elegant. That was the nonchalant way of his era. It's curious that the
age of circumlocution in verse should have been the age of crudity
in prose. His godfather had prophesied that he would be a man of
genius, and had given him the expressive names Luc-Esprit.*

iv. An Aspiring Centenarian

During his childhood he had won a number of school prizes in
Moulins, where he was born; and he had been crowned with a laurel
wreath by the Duc de Nivernais (whom he called the Duc de
Nevers). Neither the Convention, nor the death of Louis XVI, nor

Napoleon, nor the restoration of the Bourbon monarchy, could wipe away the memory of that coronation. To him, the 'Duc de Nevers' had been the great figure of the century. 'Such a charming nobleman', he'd say; 'and such an impressive sight, too, in his blue sash!' In Monsieur Gillenormand's eyes, Catherine the Great had atoned for the sin of dividing Poland when she bought the secret of Bestuzhev's gold elixir for three thousand roubles. On that subject he would wax eloquent. 'The elixir of gold,' he'd declare, 'Bestuzhev's yellow dye, General Lamotte's drops—in the eighteenth century they were the sovereign cure for the disasters of love, the panacea against the diseases of Venus. They cost one louis for a half-ounce bottle. Louis XV sent two hundred bottles to the Pope.' He'd have been very cross indeed—he'd have flown off the handle—if anyone had told him that the 'gold elixir' was merely ferric perchlorate. Monsieur Gillenormand worshipped the Bourbons and detested the year 1789. He was constantly describing how he'd managed to save his life during the Reign of Terror, and how his head would have been cut off if he hadn't been so high-spirited and quick-witted. If any young man dared to eulogize the Republic in his presence, he'd turn bright purple and lose his temper to the point of apoplexy. Sometimes he'd allude to his ninety years and say: 'I hope and pray that I'll never see '93* again.' But on other occasions he'd declare that he meant to live to the age of a hundred.

v. Basque and Nicolette

He had various pet theories. Here's one of them: 'If a man is a passionate lover of women, but he has a wife he doesn't much like— ugly, nagging, tyrannical, constantly asserting her rights, born and bred on the rule-book, and jealous whenever she gets the chance— there's only one way he can handle the problem and keep the peace, and that's by letting his wife control the purse strings. If he surrenders on that one point, he's free. It keeps the wife busy and gives her an interest in life—she handles money till her fingers turn green, she supervises the local tenantry and the farmers' produce, she assembles lawyers and lords it over notaries and harangues scriveners and hobnobs with the legal fraternity, she handles lawsuits, draws up leases, dictates contracts; she feels she's in control of everything—she buys and sells, settles and haggles, promises and compromises, contracts and cancels, cedes and concedes and retrocedes, arranges and disarranges, pinches and splurges; she does the silliest things, which keeps her happy as boss and as human being—and that's her revenge. Her husband may be neglecting her, but at least she has the satisfaction of ruining him.' Monsieur Gillenormand had applied this theory in practice; it had been the story of his life. His wife (the second one) had managed his affairs in such a way that one fine day, when Monsieur Gillenormand found he was a widower, he had just enough to provide himself with an income of fifteen thousand francs a year—if he put virtually all his capital into an annuity. Three-quarters of it would expire when he did. He hadn't hesitated to do this; he wasn't very concerned about leaving any money behind him. Besides, he'd seen unpredictable things happen to patrimonies—he'd seen them become 'national property', for instance; he'd witnessed the ups and downs of consolidated finance, and he didn't trust the death-duty regulations. 'That's all South Sea Bubble stuff', he used to say. As we said, the house in the Rue des Filles-du-Calvaire was his own property. He had two servants at a time, 'a male and a female'. Whenever they entered his service, he rechristened them. He named the men after their native province: Nîmois, Comtois, Poitevin, Picard. His last valet was a fat, wheezy, lethargic fifty-five-year-old, who couldn't run a distance of twenty paces; still, he'd been born in Bayonne, so Monsieur Gillenormand called him Basque. As for his female servants, he called them all Nicolette (even La Magnon, regarding whom see below). One day a proud woman of thoroughbred concierge blood, a cordon bleu cook, presented herself. 'What wages would you like?' Monsieur Gillenormand asked her.—'Thirty francs a month.'—'What's your name?'—'Olympie.'—'I'll give you fifty francs a month, and your name will be Nicolette.'

vi. In which we meet La Magnon and her two children

Grief, in Monsieur Gillenormand's case, manifested itself as anger—he was cross at being unhappy. He had prejudices of every kind and took liberties of every kind. As we've already noted, for the sake of external appearances and internal satisfaction he liked to adopt the pose of a dashing young blade; and he strove hard to present himself in that light. He called it 'regal notoriety'. His regal notoriety sometimes brought him strange blessings. One day, a basket—something like an oyster basket—was delivered to his house; it contained, carefully wrapped in swaddling clothes, a plump little newborn boy crying his head off, whose paternity a servant girl turned away six months earlier ascribed to Monsieur Gillenormand. He was all of eighty-four years old at the time. Indignation and outcry in the household. Just who did the shameless hussy think she was going to fool? The brazen impudence of it! A monstrous calumny! Monsieur Gillenormand himself, however, wasn't at all put out. He gazed at the bundle with the pleasant smile of a man flattered by slander, and announced to all and sundry: 'Well now, what's all this? What's the matter? What's all the fuss about? Here you are, all astounded—a fine display of imbecility, I must say! The Duc d'Angoulème was a bastard son of His Royal Highness Charles IX; and he married a girl of fifteen when he was eighty-five years old. Monsieur Virginal, the Marquis d'Alhuye, was a brother of Cardinal de Sourdis, Archbishop of Bordeaux; and *he* was eighty-three when he had a son by a chambermaid of Judge Jacquin's wife—a real lovechild, who became a Knight of Malta and a State Counsellor. One of the great men of the present age, Abbé Tabarand, was the son of a man eighty-seven years old. Such things happen all the time. Not to mention the Bible! Having said which, I must state that the little gentleman isn't my doing. But that isn't his fault. We'll have to take care of him.' This method of handling the situation showed a deft touch. Then, a year later, the creature—the La Magnon previously mentioned—sent him a second present. Again it was a boy. At that point Monsieur Gillenormand gave up the struggle. He returned the two brats to their mother and undertook to pay eighty francs a month for their keep—provided that the aforesaid mother didn't do it again. He added: 'I expect the mother to look after them properly. I shall come to see them from time to time.' Which he did. He had a brother, a priest, who was rector of the Poitiers Academy for thirty-three years and died at the age of seventy-nine. 'I lost him early in life', Monsieur Gillenormand used to say. Few memories of that brother remain; he was a staid, niggardly man who felt obliged to give alms to the poor who came his way, since he was a priest; but the coins he gave them were always small change long withdrawn from circulation—so that he was able to reach hell even from the road to paradise. The elder Monsieur Gillenormand, by contrast, gave alms gladly and generously, without stinting. He was kindly, gruff, and charitable; he might have made some magnificent gestures if he'd been rich. He wanted everything connected with him to be done on a grand scale, even dirty work. One day, when he'd been blatantly cheated out of an inheritance by some businessman, he exclaimed in all seriousness: 'Oh, that's a disgraceful thing to do! Petty tricks of that kind, quite frankly, embarrass me. Everything is going to the dogs nowadays—even the scoundrels. Dash it, that's no way to steal from a man like me. It's acting like a common high-wayman—and botching the job, at that. "Let the woods be worthy of a consul".' He'd been married twice, as we said; by the first marriage he had a daughter who never married, and by the second, another daughter. The latter died at the age of thirty or thereabouts, after marrying, for love or luck or some other reason, a soldier of fortune who had served in the Republican and Imperial armies, gaining a Cross of Honour at Austerlitz and a promotion to colonel at Waterloo.* 'The black sheep of the family', the old man called him. He took a great deal of snuff, and looked very graceful when he dusted down his lace jabot with the back of his hand. He had very little faith in God.

vii. Never receive visitors except in the evening

That was Monsieur Luc-Esprit Gillenormand. His hair—grey rather than white, and always combed in little ringlets—was as abundant as ever. All in all, and taking everything into consideration, a venerable figure.

He was a true child of the eighteenth century—frivolous and grand.

During the early years of the Restoration, Monsieur Gille-normand, who was still young (a mere seventy-four years of age in 1814), had lived in the Rue Servandoni near Saint-Sulpice, in the Faubourg Saint-Germain. He had retired to the Marais only when he withdrew from society, well after his eightieth birthday.

After leaving society, he became locked into various little habits. The main, and most inflexible, one was the rule that his door was shut all day, and never open to any visitor whatever, on any business whatever, till the evening. He dined at five, and after that his door was open. It had been the custom of his era, and he had no intention of relinquishing it. 'Daylight is plebeian', he'd say; 'it deserves nothing better than closed shutters. Any respectable person will light up his wits when the heavens light up their stars.' And he barricaded himself against everybody, including the king himself. The old-fashioned elegance of his epoch.

The House in the Rue Plumet

i. The Secret House

Some time in the middle of the eighteenth century, a periwigged judge of the Paris High Court, having a mistress and wanting to keep it quiet—for in those days the nobility paraded their mistresses and the middle classes kept theirs hidden—built himself a 'little house' in the lonely Rue Blomet (now the Rue Plumet), not far from the place then called the Combat des Animaux in the Faubourg Saint-Germain.

The house was a two-storey villa; two living rooms on the ground floor, two bedrooms above, a kitchen below, a boudoir above, an attic under the roof; in front of all these, a garden with a large iron gate opening onto the street. The garden covered about an acre. It was all that passers-by could see; but behind the villa there was a narrow courtyard, and, at the back of the courtyard, a little two-room-and-cellar cottage—an emergency precaution, intended to hide a nurse and child if the need should arise. From this cottage, a secret door at the rear led to a long narrow passage, paved and winding, flanked by two high walls and open to the heavens.* It was concealed with remarkable ingenuity; it seemed to disappear among the fenced gardens and fields as it followed their various twists and turns; but finally, through another secret door, it opened half a league away at the deserted end of the Rue de Babylone, in what was virtually a different quarter.

His lordship the Judge used to slip in through that entrance—so effectively that, even if people had watched and followed him and noticed that his lordship went on some mysterious journey every day, they would never have guessed that his visits to the Rue de Babylone were actually visits to the Rue Blomet. By crafty purchases of land, the ingenious magistrate had made the whole area his own property; as a result, he'd been able to construct this secret passage without arousing anyone's suspicions. After that, he sold off small lots adjacent to the passage as gardens and vegetable plots—and the new owners of those lots assumed that the wall they could see marked the boundary between their property and their neighbour's on the other side, never even suspecting that a long strand of footpath wound in and out between their flowerbeds and fruit trees. Only the birds had made that curious observation. Very likely the warblers and tits of last century indulged in a fair amount of gossip about his lordship.

The villa was built of stone in the style of Mansart, with wainscotting and furnishings in the style of Watteau,* all rococo inside and periwiggery outside, enclosed in a triple flowering hedge. There was something at once discreet, capricious, and solemn about it, which seemed to suit a flirtation within the legal profession.

The house and passage have now vanished; but they were still in existence fifteen years ago. In 1793 a metalworker bought the house, intending to demolish it; but he couldn't afford to do so, and was finally declared bankrupt. The house, therefore, demolished the metalworker. After that, it remained empty and slowly fell into ruin, as any house does when it's no longer kept alive by the presence of humanity. It still retained its old furnishings and was still offered for sale or lease; and the handful of people who walked down the Rue Plumet every year were notified of that fact by a yellow illegible sign that had hung on the garden gate ever since 1810.

iii. Of Leaves and Branches*

The garden thus left to its own devices for a good half-century had become a strange and delightful thing. The wayfarers of forty years ago would stop in the street and look at it, without guessing what secrets lay hidden behind its green and thriving shrubbery. More than one dreamer of the period allowed his eyes and thoughts to slip indiscreetly through the bars of the ancient twisted rickety padlocked gate that hung from a pair of green-covered moss-coated pillars and was grotesquely crowned with a pediment of intricate arabesques.

There were one or two heavily encrusted statues, a stone bench in one corner, some trellises dislodged by time and now rotting against the wall; no walks, no lawns; couch grass everywhere. Horticulture had left the place, and Nature had returned. Weeds were flourishing—a remarkable thing to happen in such a poor bit of soil. The wallflowers were living it up splendidly. All things have a God-given urge to live, and nothing in that garden opposed it; the sacred process of growth was thoroughly at home there. Trees bowed down toward brambles, brambles rose up toward trees; plants were climbing, branches were bending; creepers on the ground virtually met blossoms in the air; things blown about by the wind stooped toward things trailing in the moss; shoots, thorns, tree-trunks, boughs, leaves, twigs, tufts, tendrils were mingled and merged and mated and muddled; within that enclosure three hundred feet square, vegetation had celebrated and consummated in a close and penetrating embrace the sacred mystery of its kinship—a symbol of human kinship—under the satisfied gaze of its Creator. The garden was no longer a garden; it was one gigantic thicket, something as impenetrable as a forest, as populous as a town, as pulsating as a bird's nest, as dark as a cathedral, as fragrant as a bouquet, as solitary as a tomb, as alive as a crowd.

During the post-Revolutionary springtime, this enormous mass of shrubbery—within the freedom provided by its iron gate and four walls—entered the rutting season and silently began the universal labour of germination. It trembled in the early sunlight, almost like an animal that breathes the breath of cosmic love and feels the April sap rising and seething in its bloodstream. Then, tossing its mighty green mane in the breeze, it strewed stellar blossoms, pearls of dew, beauty, fertility, life, joy, and scent across the moist earth, across the crumbling statues, across the villa's disintegrating steps, even across the lonely street's footpath. By noon myriads of white butterflies were resorting to it—a marvellous sight, those living summertime snowflakes whirling among the shadows! There, within those gay dark verdant realms, hordes of innocent avian voices were whispering intimately; and what their chirpings left unsaid, the buzzing insects added. At dusk a dreamlike haze rose from the garden and enfolded it; a shroud of mist, a calm and celestial requiem, began to cover the scene; a ravishing fragrance of honeysuckle and convolvulus began to rise from its every cranny, like a delicate, subtle poison; you could hear the last calls of wagtail and woodpecker, as they fell asleep in the foliage. In that place you could sense a sacred harmony between bird and tree: by day the wings delighted the leaves, at night the leaves protected the wings.

In winter the undergrowth was dark, sodden, bristly, shivering, and the house could be glimpsed beyond it. Instead of flowers on the branches and dew on the flowers, you could see the long silver ribbons that snails had left on the thick cold carpet of yellow leaves. But in any situation, from any point of view, at any time of year—spring, winter, summer, autumn—the little enclosure gave off a scent of melancholy, contemplation, solitude, liberty, absence of humanity, presence of the Deity; and the old rusty gate seemed to be saying: 'This garden is mine!'

Yes, the streets of Paris were all round it, the classic stately mansions of the Rue de Varenne were only a couple of steps away, the dome of the Invalides was close at hand, the Chamber of Deputies wasn't far off; carriages from the Rue de Boulogne and the Rue Saint-Dominique rolled through the neighbourhood in all their pomp and circumstance; brown, yellow, white, red buses crossed and recrossed at the nearest intersection—but to no avail: the Rue Plumet remained a desert place; and the deaths of former owners, the passing of a revolution, the collapse of time-honoured fortunes, neglect, oblivion, forty years of abandonment and bereavement, had been quite enough to bring back into this favoured realm the ferns, mulleins, hemlocks, milfoils, foxgloves, long grass, huge crinkled weeds with pale broad leaves, lizards and scarab beetles and furtive quick-flying insects—to conjure up from the depths of the earth and display within these four walls an indescribable array of wild and savage grandeur. Nature scorns the petty contrivances of mankind, and always lavishes herself totally where she lavishes herself at all, whether among ants or eagles; in this shabby little Parisian garden she had eventually blossomed as wildly and majestically as in the virgin forests of the New World.

Nothing is really small; anyone who has looked into the very depths of Nature knows that. Philosophy may never reach any satisfying conclusion when it tries to define causes and distinguish effects, but a contemplative mind plunges into boundless depths of ecstatic meditation when faced with all these disintegrated forces that contribute to a unified whole. Everything is at work on everything else.

The principles of algebra apply even in the clouds; starlight does good to a rose; and what thoughtful person would confidently declare that scent from a hawthorn has no effect on the constellations? Who can predict where a molecule will go? How do we know that the fall of a sand grain may not lead to the creation of a whole world? Who can understand the reciprocal interaction of the infinitely great and the infinitely small, or the way a certain event may echo and re-echo across the cliffs of existence, or the avalanches that may happen within creation? Even the tiniest mite has its function. Little things are great, and great things are little; the laws of necessity hold everything in balance—a vision that terrifies the human mind. There is a miraculous bond between living and non-living things; and throughout this whole inexhaustible and ever-coherent realm, nothing, from a sun to a grub, can despise anything else; we need one another, all of us. Daylight knows perfectly well what it is doing, when it wafts earthly scents into the azure heavens; darkness bestows the very essence of stars on sleeping flowers. Every bird that flies is holding a strand of the infinite in its claws. Procreation may range from a swallow's beak breaking its eggshell to a meteor appearing; it may bring about the birth of an earthworm or the arrival of a Socrates. Where the telescope ends, the microscope takes over. Which of the two has the more far-reaching vision? You can take your pick. A speck of mould is a floral Pleiades;* a galaxy is a stellar anthill. A comparably close interrelationship exists, even more astonishingly, between mental and physical things. Elements and principles unite, combine, marry, and multiply with one another, so that ultimately the material realm and the moral realm stand in the same light. Everything we observe is constantly turning back on itself. During these vast cosmic transformations, universal life is coming and going in unknown quantities, swept along by some mysterious invisible tide; it puts everything to use, it never wastes a single dream of a single sleeper; it plants a micro-organism here, it crushes an immense star there; it winds and wavers; it turns light into a force and thought into an element; dispersed yet indivisible, it dissolves everything except that geometric point the self; it reduces everything to an atom—the soul; it makes everything blossom into God; it interweaves every act, from the lowliest to the loftiest, within some dark and dizzying mechanism; it links the flight of an insect to the motion of the earth; who knows? it may even subordinate the trajectory of a comet in the heavens to the whirl of a protozoan in a drop of water—if only by the fact that the same law applies in both cases. A machine that is made of mind. An immense clockwork appliance whose first moving part is the gnat and whose outermost wheel is the zodiac.

Leviathan's Intestine

i. The Earth Impoverished by the Sea

Every year Paris hurls twenty-five million francs into the sea. And that isn't metaphoric. How is it done? Night and day. What's the aim? There isn't any. What's the idea behind it? There isn't any. What is it meant to achieve? Nothing. What organ is doing it? The city's intestine. What is the city's intestine? Its sewer.

Twenty-five million francs is the lowest of the estimates given by technical scientific study.

Today, after long research, scientists know that the most fertile and effective type of manure is human manure. The Chinese, be it said to our shame, knew this before we did. No Chinese peasant (says Ekeberg)* goes to town without bringing back, on the ends of his bamboo pole, two buckets full of what we call waste. Thanks to human manure, the soil in China is still as fresh as it was in the days of Abraham. Chinese wheat brings forth a hundred and twenty times as much as is sown. No guano can compare in fertility to the detritus of a capital. A big city is the mightiest of all dungbeetles. If you used the city to manure the countryside, you'd be sure to succeed. Our gold may be filth, but on the other hand, our filth is gold.

What do we do with this gold filth? We sweep it into the abyss.

At great expense, we send out whole convoys of ships to collect the droppings of petrels and penguins from the South Pole;* and the incalculable wealth that we have right at hand, we dump in the ocean. The sum total of the human and animal manure that the world is losing, if returned to the earth instead of being thrown into the water, would be enough to nourish the world.

Those mounds of filth piled on the flagstones, those garbage carts lurching through the streets at night, those horrible barrels of rubbish, those fetid streams of subterranean muck that the pavement hides from you—do you realize what they are? They're flowering meadows, green grass, marjoram and thyme and sage, game animals and livestock, the contented lowing of well-grown cattle in the evening; they're fresh-smelling hay and golden wheat, bread on your table and warm blood in your veins; they're health and joy and life. Such is the intention of the mysterious creative force that is transformation on earth and transfiguration in heaven.

Put it in the great crucible, and out will come your abundance. Nourish the countryside, and you nourish humanity.

You have the power to lose that wealth—and laugh at me into the bargain. That would be the height of ignorance on your part.

According to statistics, France alone deposits half a billion francs every year in the Atlantic, through the mouths of her rivers. Note that, with those five hundred million francs, you could pay a quarter of the national budget. The human race is so smart that we prefer to get rid of the whole five hundred million in the gutter. The people's very substance is being carried away, sometimes drop by drop, sometimes in great torrents, when our sewers vomit wretchedly into the rivers and our rivers vomit wretchedly into the ocean. Every belch from our cloaca costs us a thousand francs. This has two consequences: the land is impoverished, and the water poisoned. Hunger comes out of the farmland, and sickness comes out of the river.

It's notorious, for instance, that the Thames is poisoning London at this very moment.

As for Paris, most of the sewer outlets have lately had to be shifted downstream beyond the last bridge.

An arrangement of twin channels, incoming and outgoing, with valves and sluices, a basic drainage system as simple as the human lung, is already operating efficiently in various regions of England. Such a system would adequately bring the pure water from the fields into our towns, and return the enriched water from the towns into our fields; and this straightforward exchange, the simplest thing in the world, would save us the five hundred million we're throwing away. But our minds are on other things.

The current procedure does harm by trying to do good. The intent is admirable, the result deplorable. We think we're cleansing the town, but we're sapping the people. A sewer is a mistake. When drainage (which works both ways, restoring what it removes) has replaced sewerage (which merely impoverishes), and when a new social economy is combined with it, then the earth's produce will be multiplied tenfold, and the problem of poverty will be substantially reduced. Add to that the eradication of parasites, and it will be solved.

In the meantime, the community's wealth runs away downstream, and leakage takes place. Leakage is the right word. In this way, Europe is wasting away to the point of ruin.

As for France, we've just given the statistics. Now, since Paris contains twenty-five per cent of the total French population, and since Parisian guano is the richest of the lot, an estimate of twenty-five million francs lost by Paris in the five hundred million discarded by France each year must be less than the truth. Those twenty-five million francs, used in welfare and public amenities, would double the splendour of Paris. The city is pouring them down its drains. We may say, then, that the really big extravagance of Paris, its amazing nightlife, its Beaujon-style prodigality,* its gold squandered with both hands, its opulence, its luxuriance, its magnificence, is its sewer.

By this means, thanks to the blindness of a bad system of political economy, the wellbeing of the whole population is drowned and left to float away downstream and go to perdition in the watery depths. We ought to have some Saint-Cloud netting* there to catch the public property.

Economically, the facts could be summed up thus: Paris is a basket with holes in it.

Paris, that model city—which every race tries to imitate; that patron saint of well-designed capitals; that metropolis of the Ideal; that glorious home of initiative, enterprise, and experimentation; that centre and dwelling-place of creators; that nation-city, that hive of the future, that marvellous compound of Babylon and Corinth,* would make a peasant of Fukien simply shrug his shoulders, from the point of view we've just been stating.

Imitate Paris and you'll ruin yourself.

Besides, Paris is itself an imitator—especially in this matter of senseless immemorial wastage.

There's nothing new about such extraordinary ineptitudes; the folly wasn't born yesterday. The ancient world acted as the modern world does. 'The cloacae of Rome', says Liebig, 'swallowed up all the wellbeing of the Roman peasantry.' When the Roman countryside had been ruined by the Roman sewer, Rome plundered Italy, and when she had tipped Italy down her cloaca, she poured down Sicily, and then Sardinia, and then Africa. The whole world was swallowed by Rome's sewer. The cloaca provided both city and world—*urbi et orbi*—with engulfment. An Eternal City*—and a bottomless sewer.

In those respects, as in others, Rome sets the example.

Paris is copying it—with all the stupidity that befits a clever city.

For the requirements of the operation we have just been describing, Paris has another Paris beneath it; a Paris of sewers; which has its streets, its crossroads, its squares, its dead ends, its main arteries, and its circulation—consisting of slime. Only the human presence is lacking.

After all, nothing, not even a great nation, should be flattered. A place that has everything will have ignominy alongside sublimity; and if Paris contains Athens, the city of light, Tyre, the city of power, Sparta, the city of virtue, and Nineveh, the city of extravagance, it also contains Lutetia,* the city of dirt.

Besides, the mark of her greatness is there too; Paris's titanic sinkhole is the realization among monuments of a strange ideal, realized among humanity by men like Machiavelli, Bacon, and Mirabeau:* the ideal of grandiose despicability.

If the eye could penetrate the surface, the subsoil of Paris would look like a gigantic madrepore. A sponge has hardly more holes and channels than the clod of earth, six leagues in circumference, on which the old city is laid. Setting aside the catacombs (which belong to a separate cellarage), setting aside the intricate lattice of gaspipes, and not counting the immense array of channels that distribute running water to the drinking-fountains, the sewers alone form a prodigious dark network on both sides of the river: a labyrinth with only its downward slope to mark the way.

There, in the damp gloom, appears the rat. That, it seems, is what Paris has given birth to.

ii. The Early History of the Sewer

If you imagine Paris lifted like the lid of a pot, the underground sewer network, in bird's-eye view, would form a kind of immense branch grafted onto the banks of the river. The main sewer on the right bank would be the trunk, the subsidiary channels would be the smaller branches, and the ends would be the twigs.

The comparison is apt only in part, because right angles, which are the usual angles in this kind of subterranean branchwork, occur very rarely in vegetation.

You'd have a more accurate image of this strange geometric design if you envisaged yourself looking straight down at some weird oriental alphabet scrawled chaotically on a dark background, with the misshapen letters linked either at their angles or at their ends in an apparently haphazard jumble.

Sinkholes and sewers played a major part in the Middle Ages, in the Byzantine Empire and the ancient Orient. Plagues were born there, tyrants died there. The masses regarded those beds of putrescence, those monstrous cradles of Death, with an almost religious fear. You would feel equally dizzy above the snake pit at Benares and the lions' den at Babylon. According to Rabbinic books, Tiglath-Pileser used to swear by the sinkhole of Nineveh. John of Leiden raised his false moon from the sewer of Münster, and his oriental twin al-Moqanna', the veiled prophet of Khorasan, raised his false sun from the sewage pit of Nakhsheb.*

The history of the human race is mirrored in the history of cloacae. Rome was summed up in the Gemonies. The sewer of Paris has been a fearsome old thing. It has been a sepulchre, it has been a sanctuary. Sin, sense, social protest, freedom of conscience, thoughts, thefts, anything that human laws can pursue or have pursued, is hidden inside this hole; Maillotins in the fourteenth century, Tire-Laines in the fifteenth, Huguenots in the sixteenth, Morin's Illuminati in the seventeenth, Chauffeurs in the eighteenth. A hundred years ago, nocturnal dagger thrusts emerged from it, pickpockets on the run slipped into it; forests had caves, Paris had the sewer. Vagrants, those Gallic gypsies, accepted the sewer as a branch of the Court of Miracles,* and at night, crafty and ferocious, they withdrew to the Maubuée vomitorium as if to a bedchamber.

It was only natural that those whose daily workplace was Pickpocket Lane or Cutthroat Street should have their nightly lodgings in the Chemin-Vert culvert or Hurepoix kennel. Hordes of well-remembered tales have arisen from that. All sorts of phantoms haunt those long solitary corridors; putrescence and miasma everywhere;

here and there a vent where Villon (inside) chats to Rabelais*
(outside).

The old Parisian sewer is the rendezvous of all the lost causes
and failed attempts. Political economy regards it as a detritus, social
philosophy as a residue.

The sewer is the city's conscience. All things converge there and
confront each other there. In that livid place, there are shadows, but
no more secrets. Everything appears in its true shape, or at least its
definitive shape. A garbage dump has this to be said for it: it doesn't
tell lies. Innocence has taken refuge in it. Basilio's mask will be found
there, but you can see its pasteboard and its strings, and the inside
as well as the outside; and it's tinted with good honest muck.
Scapin's false nose is next to it. Once they have lost their usefulness,
all the indecencies of civilization fall into this pit of truth where the
immense social downslide comes to an end. It swallows them up, but
it spreads them around too. This great chaos is a confession. No
more false appearances there, no possible whitewashing; filth strips
off its shirt, bares itself totally, illusions and mirages are put to flight,
nothing remains except what is—with the sinister look of what is
finished. Reality and disappearance. Over there, a broken bottle
confesses drunkenness, a basket handle speaks of domesticity; over
there, an apple core that used to have literary opinions returns to
being an apple core; the face on the big sou coin turns frankly into
verdigris, Caiaphas's spit meets Falstaff's vomit, the gold piece
tossed out of the gambling den collides with the nail holding the
suicide's rope, a livid foetus rolls past wrapped in the spangles
that danced last Mardi Gras at the Opéra, a wig that used to sit in
judgement on human beings wallows next to a mass of rottenness
that used to be Margoton's* skirt. This is more than fraternization;
it's personal intimacy. Everything that used to be painted with make-
up is now smeared with dirt. The last veil has been stripped away.
A sewer is a cynic. It says everything.

Personally, we like this sincerity of filthiness; it calms our soul.
When you have spent your time on earth enduring the grand poses
assumed by statecraft, clever diplomacy, human justice, professional
integrity, political promises, regrettable necessities, and incorruptible robes, it's soothing to walk into a sewer and see filth where it
ought to be.

It's educational, too. As we said a moment ago, history goes down a sewer. Bartholomew's Day Massacres are oozing there drop by drop, down through the paving stones. The great public assassinations, the political and religious butcheries, pass through this underside of civilization and push their corpses along it. A thinker can see all the historic murderers there, on their knees in the hideous shadow, with a fold of gravecloth for an apron, dismally sponging down their deeds. Louis XI is there with Tristan, François I with Duprat, Charles IX with his mother, Richelieu with Louis XIII, Louvois, Letellier, Hébert, and Maillard,* rubbing at the stones and trying to wipe out all trace of their activities. You can hear those ghosts' brooms echoing beneath the vaults. You can smell the mighty stench of national disasters there. You can see reddish glimmers reflected in the corners. Through that place runs a terrible fluid in which bloody hands have washed.

Anyone who studies society should enter those shadows. They're part of his laboratory. Philosophy is the microscope of thought; everything wants to escape it, but nothing can. Turning your back on it is futile. What side of yourself do you display when you turn your back? The shameful side. Philosophy looks at evil with an honest gaze, and doesn't allow it to slip away into the void. From the very fading of what disappears and shrinking of what vanishes, it can recognize the whole truth. It can reconstruct purple from mere threads and women from mere rags. Given a sewer, it can extrapolate the city; given a mass of slime, it can extrapolate the moral values. From a potsherd it can reconstruct an amphora or a pitcher. From the mark of a fingernail on a piece of parchment it can tell the difference between the Jewry of Judengasse and that of the Ghetto. In what remains it can rediscover what has been—good, evil, falsehood, truth; the bloodstain in the palace, the inkstain in the cavern, the sweatstain in the brothel; the trials that have been undergone; the temptations that have been gladly faced; the orgies that have been vomited up; the contortions that people have made by cringing low; the taints of prostitution in souls gross enough to be capable of it; and on the cloaks of Roman porters, the elbow-print of Messalina.*

iii. Bruneseau

In the Middle Ages, the sewer of Paris was already legendary. In the sixteenth century Henri II attempted a sounding, which failed. Less than a hundred years ago, according to Mercier's* testimony, the conduit was simply left to its own devices and became what it could become.

Such was the old Paris, devoted to squabbles and waverings and uncertain gropings. For a long time she was decidedly stupid. Later, the events of 1789 showed how intelligence can come to a city. But in the good old days, the capital didn't have much in the way of brains; she wasn't capable of managing her own affairs, either morally or materially, and she could sweep away garbage as little as injustice. Every last thing was an obstacle, every last thing raised questions. The sewer, for instance, obstructed progress at every step. People could no more find their way in its channels than they could come to an agreement in the city; the incomprehensible was above, the inextricable below. Beneath the confusion of tongues there was a confusion of caverns: Daedalus mirrored Babel.*

Now and then the Paris sewer got the urge to overflow, as if that neglected Nile had suddenly lost its temper. There were floods of sewage—a shameful thing. At times this stomach of civilization suffered indigestion; the cloaca flowed backwards into the city's throat, and Paris felt the aftertaste of its own filth. These remorse-like activities of the sewer had their good side: they were warnings (not very well received, admittedly); the city was angry that slime should have so much audacity, and couldn't abide the return of its waste. Get rid of the stuff more effectively.

The flood of 1802 is a living memory to eighty-year-old Parisians. In the Place des Victoires, where the statue of Louis XIV stands, the filth spread out in the shape of a cross; it entered the Rue Saint-Honoré through the two sewer inlets in the Champs-Élysées, the Rue Saint-Florentin through the Saint-Florentin sewer, the Rue Pierre-à-Poisson through the Sonnerie sewer, the Rue Papincourt through the Chemin-Vert sewer, the Rue de la Roquette through the Rue de Lappe sewer; it filled the gutters of the Rue des Champs-Élysées to a height of thirty-five centimetres; and at noon, as the Seine vomitorium was working in reverse, it penetrated Rue Mazarine, Rue de l'Échaude, and Rue des Marais, where it stopped at a distance of a hundred and nine metres, just a few steps from the house where Racine had lived—showing more respect for the seventeenth century's poet than for its king. It reached its maximum depth in the Rue Saint-Pierre, where it rose three feet above the stone waterspouts, and its maximum length in the Rue Saint-Sabin, where it stretched out for two hundred and thirty-eight metres.

At the beginning of this century, the Paris sewer was still a mysterious place. Filth has presumably never had a good reputation, but here it became so infamous that it was absolutely feared. Paris knew vaguely that it had a terrible cellar underneath it. People spoke of it as they spoke of the monstrous bog of Thebes, which swarmed with scolopendrae fifteen feet long and might have made an excellent bathtub for Behemoth. The sewermen's big boots never ventured beyond certain well-known points. This was still very close to the days when the scavengers' carts, from which Saint-Foix had fraternized with the Marquis de Crécy, emptied their contents straight into the sewer. As for cleansing, that was left to the thunderstorms, which blocked up more than they swept away. Rome still allowed her cloaca a whiff of poetry, and called it the Gemonies; Paris insulted hers, and called it the Stinkhole. Science and superstition were in agreement about its horribleness. The Stinkhole was just as revolting to hygiene as it was to legend. The Bogeyman had appeared under the fetid arch of the Mouffetard sewer; the corpses of the Marmousets had been thrown into the Barillerie sewer; Fagon had ascribed the dreadful malignant fever of 1685 to the great gap in the Marais sewer, which remained wide open in the Rue Saint-Louis, almost opposite the sign of the Jolly Messenger inn, till 1833. The sewer mouth in the Rue de la Mortellerie was renowned for the plagues that came out of it; with its grate of iron spikes resembling a row of teeth, it stood in that deadly street like a dragon's mouth breathing hellfire all over humanity. In popular imagination, that dark Parisian sinkhole was tainted with some unknown hideous concoction of the Infinite. The sewer was bottomless. The sewer was Barathrum.* Not even the police had any notion of exploring those leprous realms. To tempt the unknown, to drop a plumbline into the dark, to go on a voyage of discovery into the abyss—who would have dared such a thing? The very thought of it was terrifying. Nevertheless, someone did step forward. The cloaca had its Christopher Columbus.

One day, in 1805, during one of the Emperor's rare appearances in Paris, the Minister of the Interior—someone like Decrès or Crétet—attended his master's morning levee. The sabres of all the mighty Republic's and Empire's marvellous soldiers could be heard rattling in the Carrousel. Napoleon's door was positively clogged with heroes—men of the Rhine, the Scheldt, the Adige, and the Nile; comrades of Joubert, Desaix, Marceau, Hoche, and Kléber; Fleurus's balloonists, Mainz's grenadiers, Genoa's pontooneers; hussars who had been eyed by the pyramids, artillerymen who had been sprayed with Junot's bullets, cuirassiers who had taken the anchored fleet in the Zuiderzee by storm; some had followed Bonaparte on the bridge at Lodi, others had accompanied Murat in the trench at Mantua, others again had preceded Lannes in the sunken road at Montebello. There, in the Tuileries courtyard, was the entire army of the period, represented by a squad or a platoon, and guarding Napoleon's hours of rest; and this was during the glorious era when the Great Army had Marengo behind it and Austerlitz* ahead. 'Sire,' the Minister of the Interior said to Napoleon, 'yesterday I set eyes on the bravest man in your empire.' 'Who is the fellow,' asked the Emperor tersely, 'and what has he done?' 'It isn't what he's done, sire, it's what he wants to do.' 'What's that?' 'He wants to visit the sewers of Paris.'

There was indeed such a man, and his name was Bruneseau.*

iv. Unknown Details

The visit took place. It was a formidable campaign—a nocturnal battle against disease and asphyxia. It was a voyage of discovery, too. A few years ago, a survivor of the expedition, an intelligent workman who had been very young at the time, was still giving accounts of the interesting details that Bruneseau had felt obliged to omit from his report to the Prefect of Police, believing that they were beneath the dignity of administrative prose.* Methods of disinfection were very rudimentary in those days. Bruneseau had only just passed the first intersections in this subterranean network when eight of the twenty workers refused to go any further. The task was complex; the visit entailed cleaning; cleaning, therefore, had to be done—and measuring too: the points where fluid entered had to be noted, the grates and inlets had to be counted, the branches had to be recorded in detail, the current at the points of separation had to be indicated, the margins of the various basins had to be explored, the smaller sewers joining onto the main sewer had to be fathomed, the height of each conduit to its keystone had to be measured, and the breadth too, both at the origin of the arches and at floor level; finally, the exact survey coordinates of each fluid inlet had to be determined, either from the floor of the sewer or from the surface of the street. Progress was difficult. Not infrequently, the ladders sank into three feet of mire. Lanterns were at their last gasp in the stench. From time to time a sewerman fainted and was carried out. At some points there were sheer precipices. The floor had sunk, the paving had collapsed, the sewer had become a bottomless pit; no solid ground could be located any more; a man suddenly dropped from view, and they had great difficulty hauling him back. On Fourcroy's advice, large cages of resin-soaked oakum were lit at regular intervals in the places that were reasonably wholesome. Here and there the walls were covered with cancerous-looking shapeless masses of fungus; the very stone seemed diseased, in this unbreathable environment.

In his exploration, Bruneseau proceeded from source to outlet. At the junction of the two water conduits from the Grand-Hurleur, he made out the date 1550 on a projecting stone; that stone marked the point where Philibert Delorme had stopped when he was ordered by Henri II to visit the underground tunnels of Paris. That stone was the sixteenth century's imprint on the sewer. Bruneseau found the seventeenth century's handiwork in the Ponceau and Rue Vieille-du-Temple channels, roofed between 1600 and 1650, and the eighteenth century's handiwork in the west section of the collecting canal, lined and roofed in 1740. Those two vaults (especially the more recent, that done in 1740) were more cracked and decrepit than the masonry of the ring sewer, which dated from 1412—a time when the running stream of Ménilmontant was raised to the dignity of Paris's major sewer, a promotion comparable to that of the peasant who becomes the king's senior valet de chambre; something like Gros-Jean transformed into Le Bel.*

Here and there, especially below the Hall of Justice, they thought they recognized some former dungeon cells embedded in the sewer itself. A hideous *rest in peace*. An iron collar was hanging from one of them. They walled them all up. There were some bizarre discoveries, including the skeleton of an orang-utan that had vanished from the Paris Zoo in 1800, a disappearance probably related to the famous and undeniable appearance of the devil in the Rue des Bernardins during the final year of the eighteenth century. The poor devil had finally drowned itself in the sewer.

Within the long vaulted corridor that ends at the Arche-Marion, the connoisseurs marvelled at a ragpicker's basket in a perfect state of preservation. The slime, which the sewermen had learnt to handle fearlessly, abounded everywhere with precious things, gold and silver jewellery, gems, and coins. If a giant had sifted through this conduit, he would have had the wealth of the ages in his sieve. At the junction of the two branches from the Rue du Temple and the Rue Sainte-Avoye, they picked up a remarkable Huguenot* medallion made of copper, with a pig wearing a cardinal's hat on one side and a wolf capped by a papal tiara on the other.

The most startling discovery was at the entrance to the Main Sewer. This entrance had formerly been closed by a grate, though only its hinges now remained. From one of those hinges, there hung a kind of shapeless filthy rag, which drifted there in the gloom—no doubt it had been caught there on its way past—and was finally being worn to shreds. Bruneseau brought his lantern close to the rag and examined it. It was made of very fine cambric, and on a corner, less worn than the rest of the fabric, they could make out a heraldic crown embroidered above these seven letters: LAVBESP. The crown was a marquis's crown, and the seven letters meant *Laubespine*. They realized that they were looking at a piece of Marat's* shroud. Marat, in his youth, had been involved in a love affair with a certain noble lady. (In those days he was veterinary surgeon to the stables of the Comte d'Artois.) From that love affair, which is historically documented, he had retained this bedsheet. A bit of wreckage or a souvenir. When he died they buried him in it, since it was the only half-decent linen he had. Old women swaddled the tragic Friend of the People for his grave in the very material that had been a place of sensual pleasure.

Bruneseau moved on. They left that rag-end where it was; they didn't finish it off. Contempt or respect? Marat deserved both. And, after all, it was so steeped in destiny that they didn't care to touch it. Besides, things should be allowed the grave that they choose for themselves. In short, it was a curious relic. A marquise had slept in it; Marat had rotted in it; it had been through the Panthéon, and it met its end among the rats in the sewer. This scrap of bedlinen, whose folds Watteau would formerly have sketched with delight, had ultimately become worthy of the unwavering gaze of Dante.*

The entire investigation of Paris's filthy subterranean sewer network lasted for seven years, from 1805 to 1812. During his explorations, Bruneseau planned, supervised, and carried out some immense tasks; in 1808 he lowered the Ponceau floor; he added new lines everywhere, extending the sewer—in 1809, under the Rue Saint-Denis as far as the Fontaine des Innocents; in 1810, under the Rue Froidmarteau and the Salpêtrière; in 1811, under the Rue Neuve-des-Petits-Pères, the Rue du Mail, the Rue de l'Échappe, and the Place Royale; in 1812, under the Rue de la Paix and the Chaussée d'Antin. At the same time he had the whole network disinfected and sanitized. From the second year of work onwards, Bruneseau was assisted by his son-in-law Nargaud.

In that way, at the start of this century, the old civilization cleaned out its lower depths and dressed up its sewer. That much purification, at least, was done.

Tortuous, fissured, cracked and unpaved, riddled with quagmires, broken by fantastic twists and turns, rising and falling for no reason, fetid, untamed, uncivilized, steeped in darkness, with scars on its paving stones and slashes on its walls, a fearsome thing—such, seen in hindsight, was the old Parisian sewer. Ramifications in every direction, intersecting tunnels, forks, crows' feet, radiating shafts like those in mines, dead ends, culs-de-sac, saltpetred vaults, noxious cesspools, greasy encrustations on the side walls, droplets dripping from the ceilings, gloom—nothing could match the horror of that old exuvial crypt, that Babylonic digestive tract, cavern, cavity, chasm pierced by streets, that monstrous molehill in which the mind fancies it can see, crawling through the darkness, in the filth that had once been splendour, that enormous blind mole—the Past.

Such, we repeat, was the sewer of Olden Days.

v. Current Progress

Today the sewer is neat, cold, straight, and correct. It virtually attains the ideal summed up in England by the word 'respectable'. It's sedate and sober, drawn with a plumbline—neat as a pin, you might almost say. It's like a tradesman turned senator. You can almost see clearly in it. The filth behaves itself decently enough. At first glance, you could easily mistake it for one of those subterranean passages that used to be so common, which were so useful for fleeing princes or potentates in the good old days 'when people loved their kings'. Today's sewer is a handsome sewer, where the purest style is obligatory; the classic four-square alexandrine, driven out of poetry, seems to have taken refuge in architecture and merged into each stone of this long pallid gloomy vault; its every outlet is an arcade; the Rue de Rivoli is setting the fashion even in cloacal matters. Besides, if geometric lines have their place anywhere, surely that place is the faecal trenches of a great city. There, the shortest way should always be the deciding factor. Today the sewer has acquired a certain official look. The very police reports that are sometimes written on the subject now treat it with due respect. The words that are applied to it in administrative language are elevated, dignified words. What used to be called a wastepipe is now a gallery; what used to be called a sinkhole is now a clearing. Villon would no longer recognize his former emergency lodgings. Certainly, this network of cellars does still have its immemorial resident colony of rodents, more pullulant than ever; now and then some old Whiskerandos of a rat risks his neck at the sewer window and studies the Parisians; but even the vermin are getting tame nowadays, since they're so content with their subterranean palace. The cloaca has lost all its primitive ferocity. Rain, which formerly sullied the sewer, nowadays washes it. Don't be too confident, though. It's still the home of noxious fumes. It's hypocritical rather than irreproachable. The police force and the health commission can do what they like, but in spite of all their sanitary operations, it still exudes a vaguely suspect smell, like a Tartuffe* who has just been to confession.

All things considered, waste disposal is a tribute paid by sewers to civilization; and from that point of view, Tartuffe's conscience is indeed an advance on the Augean stables;* therefore, we can grant that Paris's sewer has certainly improved.

It's more than an advance; it's a transformation. Between the ancient sewer and the present-day sewer, there must have been a revolution. Who led that revolution?

The man whom everyone forgets, and whom we have named—Bruneseau.

vi. Future Progress

The excavation of the Paris sewer was no trivial matter. The last
ten centuries have toiled there without being able to finish it,
any more than they have been able to finish the city itself. The
sewer, in fact, has suffered repercussions from the expansion of
Paris at every stage. It's a kind of shadowy subterranean polyp with
myriad antennae, which has grown below in phase with the city
above. Every time the city puts out a street, the sewer sticks out an
arm. The old monarchy constructed a mere 23,300 metres of
sewer—that was the state of Paris on 1 January 1806. We shall return
to that time in a moment. Ever since then, the work has been
pursued strenuously and effectively; Napoleon (the figures are
remarkable) constructed 4,804 metres, Louis XVIII 5,709, Charles X
10,836, Louis-Philippe 89,020, the 1848 Republic 23,381, and
the current regime* 70,500; total, at the present day, 226,610
metres—sixty leagues—of sewers: the massive entrails of Paris.
A dim network of branches, always in progress; an unnoticed and
enormous job of construction.

As you can see, Paris's subterranean labyrinth is now more than
ten times as big as it was at the start of the century. It's hard
to imagine how much perseverance and effort have been needed
to bring it to its present state of relative perfection. The old
monarchical provostship, and, during the last ten years of the eighteenth century, the revolutionary mayoralty, had great difficulty
digging the five leagues of sewers that existed before 1806. Obstacles
of every kind hindered the task—some due to the nature of the soil,
others arising from the intrinsic prejudices of the Parisian workforce.
Paris is built on a site curiously resistant to pickaxe, hoe, drill, and
human management of any kind. Nothing is harder to pierce and
penetrate than the geological formation on which the marvellous
historical formation known as Paris has planted itself; whenever the
work gets underway and ventures, in any shape or form, into these
alluvial layers, it faces a host of subterranean hindrances. There are
fluid clays, running springs, hard rocks, deep soggy cavities of the
kind technically known as *moutardes*. The pick advances laboriously
through calcareous strata alternating with seams of very fine clay
and beds of schist encrusted with oyster shells dating from the pre-
adamite oceans. Sometimes a stream suddenly breaks through a

partly excavated vault and inundates the workers; or there's a landslide of marl that gives way and rushes down with the fury of a cataract, smashing the thickest roof-struts like glass. Just recently, at La Villette, when it became necessary to extend the collecting sewer under the Saint-Martin canal without emptying the canal or stopping the boat traffic, a fissure opened into the canal bed; instantly more water flooded into the underground construction site than all the pumps were able to drain; a diver had to be sent down to locate the fissure, which was in the neck of the great basin, and it was blocked only with difficulty. Elsewhere, near the Seine, and even at a fair distance from the river, at Belleville, for instance, at Grand-Rue and the Lunière arcade, there are quicksands where a man may sink and be dragged down in a moment. Add to that asphyxia by noxious fumes, burial by landslides, ground suddenly giving way. Add to that the typhus that the workers are slowly picking up. In our very own day, after excavating the Clichy gallery with a causeway to receive the water main from the Ourcq (a job carried out in a trench ten metres deep); after roofing the Bièvre from the Boulevard de l'Hôpital to the Seine (accompanied by mud-slides, assisted by struts and often putrid tunnels); after constructing a line of sewers from the Barrière Blanche to the Aubervilliers road (to rid Paris of the torrential runwaters from Montmartre and pro-vide an outlet for the nine-hectare fluvial lake that used to stagnate around the Barrière des Martyrs), after constructing that line, we repeat, in four months of work, day and night, at a depth of eleven metres; and after digging a sewer in the Rue Barre-du-Bec without a trench, in a subterranean tunnel six metres below ground level (an unheard-of procedure), a foreman named Monnot died. After roofing three thousand metres of sewers in every part of the city, from the Rue Traversière-Saint-Antoine to the Rue de Lourcine; after branching the Arbalète to drain the floods left by rainwater in the Censier-Mouffetard intersection; after constructing the Saint-Georges sewer on stone and concrete foundations in black ooze; and after directing the lowering of the Notre-Dame-de-Nazareth branch floor (a formidable task), an engineer named Duleau died. There are no bulletins to announce such deeds of heroism, even though they're more useful than the senseless carnage on battlefields.

In 1832 the Paris sewers were still far from being what they are today. Bruneseau had made a start, but it took cholera to motivate the vast reconstruction that has since taken place. It's amazing, for instance, that in 1821 a section of the ring sewer (known as the Grand Canal, like the one in Venice) was still stagnating in the open air in the Rue des Gourdes. Not until 1823 did the city of Paris find in its pockets the 266,080 francs 6 centimes necessary to cover that bit of turpitude. The three absorption pools—the Combat, the Cunette, and the Saint-Mandé, with their outlets, their machinery, their pits, and their purificatory branches—date only from 1836. Paris's intestinal canal has been renovated and, as we said, enlarged more than tenfold in the past quarter of a century.

Thirty years ago, at the time of the 5–6 June insurrection,* it was still the old sewer in many places. A great number of streets that are cambered today were sunken then. Very often you could see, at the lowest point in the gutter at the end of a street or an intersection, a big square grille whose thick iron bars, polished by countless human footsteps, were dangerous—slippery for carriages, lethal to horses. The official language of bridges and roadways gave these low points and grills the expressive name 'drops'. In 1832, the old Gothic cloaca still cynically showed its muzzle in a host of streets—Rue de l'Étoile, Rue Saint-Louis, Rue du Temple, Rue Vieille-du-Temple, Rue Notre-Dame-de-Nazareth, Rue Folie-Méricourt, Quai aux Fleurs, Rue du Petit-Musc, Rue de Normandie, Rue Pont-aux-Biches, Rue des Marais, Faubourg Saint-Martin, Rue Notre-Dame-des-Victoires, Faubourg Montmartre, Rue Grange-Batelière, the Champs-Élysées, Rue Jacob, and Rue de Tournon. They were immense lazy stone gaps, sometimes flanked, with monumental effrontery, by milestones.

In 1806 Paris still had virtually the amount of sewering specified in May 1663: 5,328 fathoms. On 1 January 1832, after Bruneseau it had 40,300 metres. From 1806 to 1831, on average, 750 metres had been added each year; since then, from 800 to as much as 1,000 metres of galleries have been constructed annually, in rubble masonry set in hydraulic cement on a concrete foundation. At two hundred francs per metre, present-day Paris's sixty leagues of sewering represent forty-eight million francs.

Apart from (as we noted at the outset) matters of economic progress, the great Parisian sewer question raises serious problems of hygiene.

Paris is situated between two layers—a layer of water and a layer of air. The water layer, lying a significant distance underground but already tapped by two bores, is located on the stratum of green sandstone between the Cretaceous chalk and the Jurassic* limestone; this bed could be pictured as a disc with a radius of twenty-five leagues; a host of rivers and streams filter into it; you can drink the Seine, the Marne, the Yonne, the Oise, the Aisne, the Cher, the Vienne, and the Loire in a glass of water from the Grenelle well. The layer of water is healthy—it comes first from the sky, then from the land; the layer of air is unhealthy—it comes from the sewer. All the noxious fumes of the cloaca are mingled with the exhalations of the city; hence its bad breath. A sample of air collected above a dunghill—this has been scientifically demonstrated—is purer than a sample of air collected above Paris. In a certain time, with the help of progress, as machinery becomes more perfect and new discoveries are made, the layer of water will be used to purify the layer of air— i.e. to clean the sewer. It will be appreciated that by 'cleaning the sewer' we mean returning the slime to the earth, putting dung back into the soil and manuring the fields. By this simple means the amount of suffering in the community as a whole will be reduced, and its health will be improved. At the present day, Paris's diseases spread out on a fifty-league radius from the Louvre, which may be taken as the hub of this plague-ridden wheel.

You could say that, for ten centuries, the cloaca has been the disease of Paris. The sewer is a vice that the city has in its blood-stream. Popular feeling about it has never been wrong. In former times the job of sewerman was almost as dangerous, and almost as repugnant to the people, as the job of slaughterman, which was held in such abhorrence that it was long left to the executioner. High wages were needed to persuade a stonemason to disappear into that fetid ooze; well-diggers hesitated to plunge their ladders into it; there was a popular saying: 'When you enter the sewer, you enter the grave'; and, as we have said, all kinds of hideous legends draped this colossal drain with horror—this dreadful sinkhole which bears the traces of the globe's revolutions no less than humanity's revolutions, and in which you can find relics of every cataclysm, from the Flood's fossil shells* to Marat's shroud.

from *The Toilers of the Sea*

A Turbulent Life and a Tranquil Conscience

Mess Lethierry, the famous man of St Sampson,* was a phenomenal sailor. He'd been on a good many voyages. He'd been cabin boy, sailmaker, able seaman, quartermaster, boatswain's mate, boatswain, pilot, and captain. Now he was a shipowner. No one knew the sea as he did. He was fearless when a ship was in distress. In heavy weather he used to roam the shore and watch the horizon. What's that out there? Someone in trouble. A Weymouth lugger, an Alderney cutter, a Courseulle biscayner, a nobleman's yacht, an Englishman, a Frenchman, a poor man, a rich man, the devil himself—never mind, he sprang into a boat, called up two or three brave men or, if necessary, did without them, threw off the moorings, grabbed the oar, pushed out to sea, pitched and tossed on the rolling waves, plunged into the storm, headed straight for the danger. You could see him far away in the thick of the squall, standing up in his craft, dripping with rain, swathed in lightning, with a lion's face and a mane of spray. Sometimes he spent the whole day out there in peril amid wave and wind and hailstorm, boarding some ship in distress, rescuing the men, rescuing the cargo, fighting the tempest. At night he'd return home and knit a pair of stockings.

He kept living that way for fifty years, from ten to sixty—as long as he was young. When he turned sixty, he found he could no longer lift the big anvil in the Varclin forge with one arm. (The said anvil weighed three hundred pounds.) Suddenly, too, he was crippled with rheumatism. So he had to give up the sea. He moved from being a hero to being a patriarch. He was no longer anything more than a good old fellow.

He became rheumatic and well-off at about the same time. Those two consequences of work often keep company. Just when you get rich, you're paralysed. A nice end to your life.

You tell yourself: 'From now on I'm going to have fun.'

On an island like Guernsey the population is composed of men who have spent their life doing the rounds of their field and men who have spent their life circumnavigating the globe. They're workers of two kinds—land workers and sea workers. Mess Lethierry was one of the latter. He did know the land, though. He'd led the hard life of a labourer. He'd travelled on the Continent. He'd been a ship's carpenter at Rochefort and Cette for a while. We've just been talking about circumnavigations; well, he'd circumnavigated France as a journeyman carpenter. He'd worked on the salt works in Franche-Comté. The fine fellow had led a life of adventure. In France he'd learnt to read and think and want. He'd done a bit of everything, and throughout it all he'd preserved his integrity. But he was a sailor at heart. Water was his element. 'The fish live in my house', he used to say. In fact, except for two or three years, his whole life had been devoted to the sea—'chucked into the sea' was his way of putting it. He'd sailed the wide oceans, the Atlantic and the Pacific, but he preferred the Channel. 'That's the roughest of 'em!' he used to declare fondly. That's where he'd been born, and that's where he wanted to die. Once he'd been around the world once or twice, and was in a position to pass judgement, he returned to Guernsey and never left it. Nowadays all his voyages were between Granville and Saint Malo.

Mess Lethierry was a Guernseyman—in other words, a Norman—in other words, an Englishman—in other words, a Frenchman. Within him lay this fourfold homeland, immersed and drowned, so to speak, in his greatest homeland—the ocean. All his life, wherever he went, he kept the habits of a Norman fisherman.

Which didn't stop him from opening some battered old tome and enjoying a book now and then, getting to know the names of a few thinkers and poets and having a go at languages of all kinds.

The Old Old Story of Utopia

In 182— a steamboat was quite a novelty in the waters of the Channel. For a long time the whole Norman coast was frightened of the thing. Nowadays ten or twelve steamers can pass to and fro in the same field of view and nobody bothers even to glance at them; at the very most, they may provide a moment's interest for some special expert who can tell from the colour of the smoke that Ship A is burning Welsh coal and Ship B Newcastle coal. They go past, and that's that. If they're arriving, welcome. If they're departing, *bon voyage*.

In the first quarter of our century, though, people were less comfortable with such inventions, and the Channel Islanders took a particularly dim view of the machines and their smoke. In this puritanical archipelago, where the Queen of England has been blamed for violating the Scriptures by giving birth under chloroform,[1]* the steamboat's first triumph was to be called 'the Devil's Boat'. Yes, these good fisherfolk—formerly Catholics, now Calvinists, and still bigots—regarded it as some kind of floating hell. A local preacher spoke on the question: 'Have we the right to make fire and water work together when God has separated them?'[2] Didn't this beast of fire and iron seem like Leviathan? Wasn't that just creating the primeval chaos all over again—to the extent that a mere human being could? (This isn't the only time that an advance has been described as a return to chaos.)*

'A crazy idea', 'a huge mistake', 'a silly notion'—that was the verdict of the Academy of Sciences, when Napoleon asked them about steamboats at the beginning of the century. In a question of science, we can pardon the fishermen of St Sampson for being on the same level as the mathematicians of Paris; and in a question of religion, a little island like Guernsey isn't necessarily going to be more enlightened than a whole continent like America. In 1807 Fulton's first steamboat made its first trip from New York to Albany, funded by Livingston, equipped with one of Watt's engines sent from England, and manned (apart from the ordinary crew) only by two Frenchmen, André Michaux* being one of them. This first steam voyage chanced to be on 17 August. In response to which, Methodism decided to make a speech, and in every pulpit preachers began anathematizing the machine, declaring that the number *seventeen* was the sum of the ten horns and seven heads of the beast in the Book of Revelation.* In America, the beast of the Apocalypse was called up to oppose steamboats; in Europe, the beast of Genesis was. That was the only difference.

The experts had rejected the steamboat as impossible; the clergy now rejected it as blasphemous. Science had condemned, religion

---

[1] Genesis 3: 16: 'In sorrow thou shalt bring forth children' [*Hugo's note*].
[2] Genesis 1: 4* [*Hugo's note*].

damned. Fulton was a kind of Lucifer.* The simple folk of shore and field supported this curse, because the new thing was upsetting them. Religion's view of the steamboat was as follows: 'Water and fire are in a state of divorce. This divorce has been ordained by God. What God hath joined together, let not man put asunder; what God hath put asunder, let not man join together.' The peasants' view was: 'It scares me.'

In those far-off days, it took nothing short of Mess Lethierry to dare run a steamboat between Guernsey and Saint Malo. He alone had the freedom of thought to conceive it and the seamanship to execute it. His French side got the idea, and his English side carried it out.

The Story of Utopia, Continued

As you'll of course appreciate, the thing started badly. Everyone who owned a cutter that ran between the island of Guernsey and the French coast began howling in protest. They denounced this attack on both Holy Scripture and their own monopoly. Sundry chapels fulminated against it. One religious gentleman, Elihu* by name, called the steamboat 'atheistic'. Only sailing ships were regarded as orthodox. People could plainly see the devil's horns on the heads of the cattle that the steamboat transported and landed.

The protest lasted for quite a while. However, little by little, they began to notice that the cattle arrived in a less worn-out condition and consequently fetched better prices, since their meat was better; that there were fewer dangers at sea for the crew as well; that the trip was faster, safer, and less costly; that the times of departure and arrival were more predictable; that fish was transported more quickly and in fresher condition—so that the surplus of the big catches common in Guernsey could now be offloaded in the French markets; that butter from Guernsey's excellent cows travelled more rapidly in 'the Devil's Boat' than in the sailing ships, and no longer deteriorated on the way—so that it was in demand at Dinan and Saint Brieuc and Rennes; and that, thanks to 'Lethierry's Galleyboat' (as it was called), there was at last a method of safe, prompt, easy, regular transport, which increased circulation, multiplied outlets, expanded commerce—with the result, in short, that they had to come to terms with this 'Devil's Boat' that violated the Scriptures and enriched the island. Some daring souls ventured to approve of it to a certain extent. Sieur Landoys, the clerk, acknowledged the worth of the boat. This, by the way, was very impartial of him, because he wasn't fond of Lethierry. For one thing, Lethierry was a *Mess* and he was only a *Sieur*. For another, although Landoys was clerk at St Peter Port,* he was a parishioner of St Sampson—and there were only two unprejudiced men in the parish, Lethierry and himself, so the least they could do was to hate each other. Being in the same boat drives people apart.

All the same, Sieur Landoys was honest enough to approve of the steamboat. Others followed him. The situation changed imperceptibly; such things are subject to tides. Time passed; the vessel's success continued and increased; it was obviously doing a service, there was clearly an improvement in everyone's welfare, and eventually everyone (apart from a few sages) was in favour of 'Lethierry's Galleyboat'.

People wouldn't be so much in favour of it now. A steamer of forty years ago would make today's shipbuilders smile. The marvel had its deformities, the prodigy its weaknesses.

There's no less of a gap between the fire-driven paddleboat in which Denis Papin plied the Fulde in 1707 and our present-day transatlantic ocean liners, than between the second-century Danish dromon now in the Flensburg Municipal Museum, which was found full of stone axes, bows, and war clubs in the salt marshes of Schleswig, and the three-decker *Montebello**—200 feet long, 50 feet wide, with a mainmast 115 feet long and a displacement of 3,000 tons, carrying 1,100 men, 120 cannon, 10,000 cannonballs, and 160 packets of grapeshot, belching 3,300 pounds of iron at each broadside when in action, and carrying 5,600 square metres of canvas before the wind when sailing.

Exactly a hundred years separate Papin's first boat (1707) from Fulton's (1807). 'Lethierry's Galleyboat' was no doubt a great advance on those two prototypes, but it was still a prototype itself. Yet it was a masterpiece all the same. Every scientific creation has those two aspects: it's a monstrosity in the womb, yet it's also a marvel in the process of development.

A Quirk of Lethierry's Character

Mess Lethierry had one fault—a big one. He hated a priest—not as a person, but as a thing. One day he was reading (yes, he did read) Voltaire* (yes, he did read Voltaire), and he came to these words: 'Priests are cats.' He dropped the book and was heard to mutter: 'It seems to me I'm a dog.'

You have to remember that the priests—Lutherans and Calvinists no less than Catholics—had strongly opposed and meekly persecuted him while he was building the local 'Devil's Boat'. It was damnably audacious to be a revolutionist in navigation and attempt to bring progress to the Norman archipelago and force the poor little island of Guernsey to be the guinea-pig for a new invention; we've made no attempt to conceal the fact. And therefore they did damn him a bit. (Oh, don't forget that we're talking about the clergy of old; today the clergy in nearly all the local churches are utterly different and tend to be quite liberal and progressive.) They obstructed Lethierry in dozens and dozens of ways; any obstacle that sermon and pulpit could possibly generate was used against him. The churchmen detested him, and he detested them. Their own hatred was some excuse for his.

We must say, though, that his dislike for priests was an idio-syncratic thing. There wasn't any need for him to hate them or be hated by them. As he said, he was a dog among cats. His way of thinking was opposed to theirs; and so were his instincts—which can't be modified so readily. He could feel their hidden claws, and so he bared his teeth at them. A bit wrongly and randomly, granted, and not always appropriately. It's a mistake not to make distinctions. Indiscriminate hatred is never a good thing. Not even the Savoyard Vicar* would have found favour in his eyes. I'm not sure that Mess Lethierry believed there *was* such a thing as a good priest. By virtue of being a thinker he lost a certain amount of wisdom. The tolerant can display intolerance, just as the moderate can display wrath. Still, Lethierry was too kindly to be a good hater. He repelled rather than attacked. He kept the churchmen at a distance. They'd done him harm, so he didn't wish them well; but that was the limit of it. There lay the difference between their hatred and his: theirs was animosity, his was antipathy.

The island of Guernsey, small though it is, has enough room for two religions: Catholic and Protestant. And, may I add, it doesn't squeeze the two religions into a single building. Each form of worship has its own church or chapel. In Germany, at Heidelberg for instance, they're not quite so fussy; they chop the church in half— one half for Saint Peter,* and the other for Calvin; between the two, a partition to prevent any punches on the nose; equal shares on both sides—the Catholics have three altars, the Protestants have three altars; the hours of worship are the same, so the one bell rings for both services at once, summoning everyone to God and the devil at the same time. Simple.

German unflappability can cope with such intimate juxta-positions. But at Guernsey every religion has its own home. There's the orthodox parish, and there's the heretic parish. You can choose whichever you like. Mess Lethierry's choice had been neither.

This sailor and thinker and upstart labourer looked very simple on the surface, but he was by no means simple underneath. He had his contradictions and his obstinacies. On the subject of priests, he couldn't be budged. He could have given points to Montlosier.*

He allowed himself some very disrespectful jokes. He said things that were idiosyncratic and odd-sounding, but carried a meaning. He called going to confession 'combing your conscience'. His small—very small—amount of literary knowledge, picked up in a quick glance between squalls now and then, was embellished with spelling mistakes. There were slips of the tongue too, and not always innocent ones. When Waterloo made peace between Louis XVIII's France and Wellington's England, Mess Lethierry wrote that Bourmont was the 'arbitraitor' between the two groups. On one occasion he spelled *pontifical* 'pontiffickle'.* Not that we think this was deliberate.

His opposition to the pope didn't reconcile him with the Anglicans. Far from it. The Protestant rectors loved him no better than the Catholic curés did. His irreligious tendencies would break out in the face of the most venerable doctrines; there seemed to be no stopping him. One day he happened to hear a sermon on hell by Reverend Jacquemin Hérode—a superb sermon, packed from end to end with sacred texts proving eternal anguish, torture, torment, damnation, unquenchable fire, inexorable punishment, inextinguishable malediction, divine vengeance, the wrath of the

Almighty, the fury of heaven—things absolutely beyond dispute. On the way out, he was heard to say *sotto voce* to one of the faithful, 'I've got a funny idea about God. I think he's good.'

This whiff of atheism came from his stay in France.

Even though he was a Guernseyman more or less pure-bred, the islanders called him 'the Frenchman' because of his 'improper' attitude. He was riddled with subversive notions, and never made any secret of it. His stubborn building of the steamboat, the 'Devil's Boat', had well and truly proved it. 'I was suckled on 1789',* he used to say. That isn't a good vintage of milk.

He was inconsistent, too. It's very hard to avoid that in a small country. In France the price of peace and quiet is 'keeping up appearances'; in England it's 'respectability'. 'Respectability' involves a host of little acts, from keeping Sunday properly sanctified to keeping your necktie properly tied. 'Don't get yourself pointed at' is another tremendous law. 'Getting pointed at' is a miniature version of excommunication. Small towns are hotbeds of gossip and excel at keeping their victims in solitary confinement—which is like an ecclesiastical malediction seen through the wrong end of the telescope. The most valiant souls flinch from that anathema. You may brave gunshot and hurricane, but you quail before Madame Pimbêche. Mess Lethierry was more stubborn than logical, but not even his obstinacy could hold out against that type of compulsion. He 'put a bit of water in his wine'—to use another expression rife with hidden (and not always mentionable) implications. He kept well away from the clergy, but he didn't absolutely shut his door to them. On official occasions, and at the customary times for pastoral visits, he welcomed now the Lutheran rector and now the Popish chaplain in a suitably courteous manner. Very occasionally he even accompanied his niece Déruchette to the Anglican parish church. As we remarked earlier, she herself went there only for the four major feasts of the ecclesiastical year.

When all is said and done, these compromises did cost him an effort and did bother him. Instead of drawing him closer to the churchfolk, they heightened his private estrangement. To absolve himself, he blasphemed all the more. That was the only acid tang in a temperament otherwise devoid of bitterness. No hope of curing it, though.

That was really and truly the way he was; you just had to accept it.

He didn't like clergy of any kind. He had the irreverence of the Revolutionary period. He drew no special distinctions between different forms of worship. He wasn't even impressed by disbelief in the real presence,* immense advance though that was. In such matters he was too shortsighted to see any difference between a minister and an abbé; he lumped reverend doctors and reverend fathers together. 'Wesley's no better than Loyola',* he used to say. When he saw a pastor out walking with his wife, he'd turn away in disgust. 'A married priest!' he'd say with the sarcastic intonation that those two words evoked in France at the time. He used to describe how he'd seen 'London's bishopess' on his last trip to England. He was so revolted by such unions that he'd become positively angry. 'One gown shouldn't marry another', he'd declare. Priesthood was a sex of its own, in his eyes; he'd certainly have said that priests are 'neither men nor women'. He spoke of Anglican and Popish clergy in equally derogatory terms, and with equal lack of taste; he swathed both kinds of cassock in the same phraseology; he applied the soldierly metaphors popular in those days to Catholic and Lutheran priests alike, without bothering to vary them. 'Marry whoever you like, as long as it isn't a padre', he'd tell Déruchette.

A Contradiction

Lethierry's character was as complex as the sea that had made him, and one of its contradictions is worth noting. Mess Lethierry never prayed.

Powerlessness is itself a kind of power. The human race is faced with two great blind things, fate and nature, and we have found our main support—prayer—in our very powerlessness.

Man's terror itself assists him; he turns to his fears for help; his anxiety tells him to kneel.

Prayer is a mighty force that belongs to the soul alone. It's cut from the same cloth as the Mystery. Prayer appeals to the magnanimity of the shadows; using the very eyes of the darkness, prayer gazes into the Mystery. Before the concentrated intensity of that suppliant gaze, you feel that even the Unknown may possibly be disarmed.

When you glimpse that possibility, you're already comforted.

But Lethierry didn't pray.

While he was happy, God existed for him—existed, you might say, as flesh and blood; Lethierry spoke to him, pledged his word to him, practically shook his hand now and then. But when he was unhappy, God was eclipsed. It's a common enough story. That's what happens when you invent a Dear Lord who is such a dear little fellow.*

from *Deeds and Words*

Emily de Putron

19 January 1865

Within the last few weeks, we have been concerned with two sisters: we have married one,* and now we are burying the other. There we have the perpetual oscillation of life. Dear brethren, let us bow our heads before the severity of fate.

Let us bow our heads hopefully. Our eyes are made to weep, but also to see; our hearts are made to suffer, but also to believe. Our faith in another life arises from our ability to love. In this troubled life that is soothed by love, we should not forget that faith comes from the heart. A son trusts that he will meet his father again; a mother cannot accept that her child is lost for ever. This rejection of non-existence is what makes humanity great.

The heart cannot go wrong. The flesh is a dream; it vanishes; if that disappearance were the end of humanity, our existence would have no value. We are not satisfied with the vapour that is matter; we need something certain. Anyone who loves knows and feels that humanity has no secure foundation on earth. To love is to live beyond life; without that belief, the heart could never give from its very depths. Love, which is humanity's goal, would be humanity's torment; that heaven would be hell. No! Let's say it aloud, a loving creature must be an immortal creature; a heart needs a soul.

There is a heart in this coffin, and that heart is alive. At this very moment, it can hear what I am saying.

Emily de Putron was the pride and joy of a respectable patriarchal family. Her friends and neighbours were enchanted by her grace and delighted by her smile. She was like a flower of happiness blossoming in the house. Affection of every kind had been lavished on her from her cradle; she had grown up happy; and because she received happiness, she gave it; because she was loved, she loved. Now she has departed!

Where has she gone? Into the dark? No.

We are the ones who are in the dark. She is in the dawn.

She is in the radiance, the truth, the reality, the reward. The grave gladly welcomes these dead girls who have done no harm on earth; their heads rise slowly from the pit toward a mysterious crown. Emily de Putron has gone to seek in heaven the ultimate serenity that completes an innocent life. She is youth on the way to eternity, beauty on the way to ideality, hope on the way to certainty, love on the way to infinity, a pearl on the way to the ocean, a spirit on the way to God.

Go onward, soul!

The marvel of the great celestial departure known as death is that those who depart do not go away. They are in a realm of light, but they witness and are moved by our realm of darkness. They are on high and yet at hand. If you have ever seen a loved one vanish in the grave, never believe that you have been deserted. That loved one is still there, beside you more than ever. The beauty of death is presence—the indescribable presence of loved souls smiling at our tears. The creature we mourn is vanished, but not gone. We can no longer see her lovely face; but we sense that we are under her wings. The dead are invisible, but not absent.

Let us give Death its due. We should not be ungrateful to it. It is not, as people say, a snare and a catastrophe. It would be a mistake to think that everything is lost in the gloom of this open grave. Everything is regained here. The grave is a place of restitution. Here the soul is satisfied with the infinite; here it retrieves its splendour; here it regains full possession of its mysterious nature; it is released from the body, released from the burden, released from necessity, released from fatality. Death is the greatest liberation of all, and also the greatest advance of all. In death, everything that has been alive ascends to a higher plane. A dazzling, sacred ascension. Everyone is enriched. Everything is transfigured in light and by means of light. One who has been merely worthy on earth becomes beautiful, one who has been merely beautiful becomes sublime, one who has been merely sublime becomes good.

And now, why am I speaking here? What can I bring to this grave? What right have I to speak to the dead? Who am I? Nothing. Wrong; I am something. I am an exile. Exiled by compulsion yesterday, exiled voluntarily today. Someone who is exiled is defeated, calumniated, persecuted, wounded by fate, disinherited of his homeland; he is innocent, yet he is crushed beneath a curse. Surely his blessing must have some value. I bless this tomb.

I bless the noble and gracious creature who is in this grave. In a desert we encounter oases, in exile we encounter souls. Emily de Putron was a lovely soul thus encountered. I have come to pay her the debt of a comforted exile. I bless her in the dark depths. In the name of the troubles she has gently and radiantly surmounted, in the name of the trials of fate—finished for her, continuing for us— in the name of everything she used to hope for and everything she has now obtained, in the name of everything she loved, I bless this dead creature; I bless her in her beauty, in her youth, in her gentleness, in her life, and in her death; I bless you, dear girl, in your white sepulchral robe, in the house that you have left desolate, in the coffin that your mother has filled with flowers and that the Lord will fill with stars.

from *Things Seen*

The Death of Madame Victor Hugo

25 August [1868]

Little Georges* is getting on very well. Now he's suckling both breasts. For a long time he wanted to suckle only the *left* breast. Democratic leanings.

About 3 p.m. today my wife suffered a stroke. Wheezing. Convulsions. Dr Crocq and Dr Jettrand were sent for. At midnight the convulsions subsided, but it became clear that she was hemiplegic. The right side was paralysed. Dr Jettrand telegraphed for Dr Émile Allix.

At 3 a.m. the convulsions stopped, fever had set in; pulse 110. Dr Jettrand applied leeches; the fever diminished; cold compresses on the forehead.

26 August [1868]

This morning we changed the bed; comatose.

The three leading doctors in Brussels consulted. Little hope, alas.

At noon I sent out for a nun to act as sick nurse. At two o'clock Dr Émile Allix arrived from Paris.—My wife opens her eyes when I speak to her, and squeezes my hand. Likewise with her sons.—This afternoon she moved her right arm. I do think she is better.

My wife is having fewer convulsions. Dr Allix sent Dr Axenfeld this telegram: 'Condition grave but hopeful.'

27 August [1868]

Died at 6.30 this morning.

I closed her eyes. Alas!

May God receive this kind and noble soul. I deliver her up to him. Bless her!

In accordance with her wishes, we'll send her coffin to Villequier, beside our dear departed daughter.*

I'll go with her as far as the border.

The French government's authorization is required before the coffin can enter France. Telegram to Paul Foucher to make the necessary arrangements.

Vacquerie has arrived. Laussedat has come. Paul Meurice* came at 10 p.m.

Ever since my daughter died, on 4 September 1843, I've always sealed my letters with black.

Our dear departed has been photographed.

28 August [1868]

Unbearable formalities all day. Exchange of telegrams to allow the coffin to cross the border.

At four o'clock, we put her in the coffin; oak coffin lined with lead and perfumed.

This evening we left with Her for Quiévrain, by the 7.12 train; then she will go on to Villequier; we'll return to Brussels.

Four p.m. The coffin is double, a lead coffin inside an oak coffin. She was placed inside it wrapped in a white shroud lined with muslin. Dr Allix covered her with spices, leaving the face bare. I took some flowers that happened to be there, and surrounded her head with them. Around her head I put a ring of white daisies, without hiding her face, after which I strewed flowers over her whole body and filled the coffin with them. Then I kissed her on the forehead and whispered: 'Bless you!'

And I stayed on my knees, close to her. Charles came forward, then Victor.* They wept and kissed her and remained standing behind me. Paul Meurice, Vacquerie, and Allix were weeping. I was praying. They bent down one by one and kissed her.

At five o'clock the lead coffin was soldered and the oak coffin was sealed. Before the lid was put on the oak coffin, I took a little key from my pocket and scratched on the lead, above her face, 'V.H.' Once the coffin was closed, I kissed it. There are *twenty-two* nails in the lid. I married her in 1822.

Before leaving, I put on the black that I shall wear for the rest of my life.

At six o'clock we left the house, 4 Place des Barricades, for the Gare du Midi. We were in three mourning carriages behind the hearse. Also Messieurs Laussedat, Gustave Frédérix, Gaston Bérardi, Coenaès, Albert Lacroix, and several others.—At seven o'clock, the coffin was placed in a special carriage and we set off. At nine we reached Quiévrain. There was a crowd around our carriage. We—Charles, Victor, and I—were in the same carriage with Auguste Vacquerie, Paul Meurice, Henri Rochefort, Émile Allix, and Camille Berru.* The crowd greeted me with obvious emotion when I got out. The stationmaster led me to the funerary carriage. It was opened. I climbed aboard. The coffin was in a kind of alcove hung with black on a platform, under a mourning sheet, between a pair of curtains strewn with tears, underneath a spray of green branches, ivy and laurel. I picked a few leaves and kissed the coffin. I whispered a few words to her, the crowd was respectfully looking into this tomb.

Then I got out again. When we were back on the ground, the carriage was shut. Vacquerie, Meurice, and Allix, who are going to take her to Villequier, got back into the train. I stayed there, watching the train go away into the darkness.

After a while, Charles touched me on the shoulder. A distinguished citizen of Quiévrain, Monsieur Pitot, invited us to his home. We moved toward the station exit. Rochefort offered me his arm. I said to him: 'You have just seen the vehicle in which I shall return to France.'

AFTER THE EXILE I: 1870–1878

from Things Seen

The Return to France

Yesterday, after the decisive battle had been lost, Louis Bonaparte surrendered his sword to the King of Prussia.* He had been taken prisoner at Sedan. Just a month ago, on 2 August, he was playing the game of war at Sarrebrück.

To save France now would be to save Europe.

Laussedat, Buichot, Amouroux* came to see me.

Newsboys are going past with enormous posters bearing the words: 'Napoleon III captured.'

5 o'clock. Charles* and our friends haven't come back yet.

Nine o'clock. Meeting of the exiles, 15 Grand'Place; I attend it with Charles (who came back at 5.30).

Aid for Marriat, ex.,* 17 Rue de ma Chaumière, 2nd floor, no. 11 opening onto Rue Verse: 5 fr.

Question: tricolour or red flag?*

Dear angel,* watch and pray. I put us all under your wings.

Today I taught Georges* his first prayer, in the following words, with his little hands folded together: 'Lord, watch over those who love me and those whom I love. Lord, blessed art thou.'

The emperor has been formally deposed. At one o'clock, meeting of the exiles at my home.

At three o'clock, received the following telegram from Paris: *'Bring the children immediately'* (signed Émile Allix), which means 'Come.'*

Week's expenses at the Hôtel de la Poste: 354–25

Peppermints: 1

Digestive tablets: 2

Monsieur Claretie and Monsieur Proust had dinner with us. During the meal, a telegram signed 'François Hugo' arrived, informing us of a 'provisional government Jules Favre, Gambetta, Thiers'.*

5 September [1870]

At 6 a.m. I receive a telegram signed 'Barbieux'* asking me what time I shall arrive in Paris. I send word by Charles that I'll arrive at 9 p.m.

We'll take the children.

We'll leave on the 2.35 train.

Paid for one of the exiles to go to Paris: 20

The provisional government (say the newspapers) includes all the deputies of Paris except Thiers.

Yesterday's expenses at the Hôtel de la Poste: 85–25

Carriage for the Gare du Midi: 2

Eight first-class to Paris: 272

(At noon, as I was about to leave Brussels for France, a young man, a Frenchman, stopped me on the Place de la Monnaie and said, 'Monsieur, I'm told you're Victor Hugo.' 'Yes.' 'Then please give me some information. I'd like to know whether it's wise to go to Paris at the moment.' I told him: 'It's most unwise, Monsieur, but we have to do it.')

We crossed the French border at 4 o'clock. Treated with great respect by the police superintendent at the frontier.

I was recognized at just about every station where the train stopped, and there were cries of 'Long live Victor Hugo!' At Tergnier, at 6.30, we dined on a piece of bread, a bit of cheese, a pear, and a glass of wine. Claretie insisted on paying, and told me, 'I'm determined to treat you to dinner on the day of your return to France.'

On the way I saw a camp of French soldiers—men and horses all together—in a wood. I called out to them 'Long live the army!' and wept. Constantly we kept coming across trainloads of soldiers on their way to Paris. Twenty-five separate troop convoys went past during the day. As one of them went past, we gave the soldiers all the provisions we had—bread and fruit and wine. There was bright sunshine, and after dark, bright moonlight. We arrived in Paris at 9.35. There was a huge crowd waiting for me. Indescribable welcome. I made four speeches. One from the balcony of a café, three from my carriage. The crowd escorted me to Paul Meurice's* home—

26 Rue de Laval, Avenue Frochot. As I left the people (they were still increasing in number) I told them: 'In one hour you've repaid me for twenty years of exile.'

(A battalion of soldiers went past on the boulevard. They stopped and presented arms to me. I told them: 'You are still the finest soldiers in the world. Never has the French army been more heroic. The whole of Europe feels for you and admires you. Prussia may have the victory in this dreadful war, but France has the glory.')

The 'Marseillaise' and the 'Chant du départ'* were sung. There were cries of 'Long live Victor Hugo!' Constantly you could hear lines from the *Châtiments* in the crowd. I must have shaken hands more than ten thousand times. The trip from the Gare du Nord to the Rue de Laval took two hours. They wanted to take me to the Hôtel de Ville.* I called out: 'No, citizens, I'm not here to overthrow the provisional government of the Republic, I'm here to support it.' They wanted to unharness my carriage, but I refused. A woman was holding one of the horses by the bridle the whole time. A man in shirtsleeves recited the lines about little Georges that are in my garden:*

> Come, little birds, acq.
> All the grain you req.
> From Little Georges, Esq.

He shouted 'Long live little Georges!' And the whole crowd shouted 'Long live little Georges!'

We arrived at Meurice's at midnight. I had supper with my travelling companions, plus Victor.* Madame Meurice has hired and furnished for me an apartment like her own. I went to bed at 2 a.m.

[6 September 1870]

At daybreak I was woken by a tremendous storm. Thunder and lightning.

I'll have lunch with Paul Meurice and we'll all have dinner together at the Hôtel Navarin, 8 Rue Navarin, where my family is staying.

Countless visits. Countless letters.

Bought a hat in the Rue des Martyrs: 16 fr.

Reimbursed Mariette* for carriage: 2 fr.

(Rey came and asked me whether I'd be prepared to take part in a triumvirate composed as follows: Victor Hugo, Ledru-Rollin, Schoelcher.* I refused. I told him, 'I'm almost impossible to amalgamate.')

A Prayer

9 August [1872]

Last night, two knockings.* The first around one o'clock; three raps. The second around four o'clock; again three raps.

I'm thinking about a poor ragged creature I met yesterday near Fort Regent.* She's very young and looks old. She was holding hands with a little girl (aged 7 or 8) less tattered than herself. I gave her some money and asked her how old she was. She replied: 'Seventeen.'* She prostitutes herself to the soldiers for two sous. It's dreadful.

O Lord, have mercy on everything that suffers, on everything that has stumbled or could stumble, on earth and beyond our earth; on all those who are fortunate, all those who are righteous, all those who are unfortunate; on my poor daughter Adèle, on my little darlings Georges and Jeanne, on all those who are innocent, on all those who are guilty, on all those who are unjust, on all those who are downcast, on Louis Bonaparte, on myself. Have mercy on my poor little Adèle. Have mercy. Release, forgive, redeem, transfigure! Have mercy on her and on me, and on my dear son Victor,* and on me, and on everyone, and on me. Have mercy!

from *La Légende des siècles*

La Ville disparue

Peuple, l'eau n'est jamais sans rien faire. Mille ans
Avant Adam, qui semble un spectre en cheveux blancs,
Notre aïeul, c'est du moins ainsi que tu le nommes,
Quand les géants étaient encor mêlés aux hommes,
Dans les temps dont jamais personne ne parla,   5
Une ville bâtie en briques était là
Où sont ces flots qu'agite un aquilon immense.
Et cette ville était un lieu plein de démence
Que parfois menaçait de loin un blême éclair.
On voyait une plaine où l'on voit une mer;   10
Alors c'étaient des chars qui passaient, non des barques;
Les ouragans ont pris la place des monarques;
Car pour faire un désert, Dieu, maître des vivants,
Commence par les rois et finit par les vents.
Ce peuple, voix, rumeurs, fourmillement de têtes,   15
Troupeau d'âmes, ému par les deuils et les fêtes,
Faisait le bruit que fait dans l'orage l'essaim,
Point inquiet d'avoir l'océan pour voisin.

Donc cette ville avait des rois; ces rois superbes
Avaient sous eux les fronts comme un faucheur les herbes. 20
Étaient-ils méchants? Non. Ils étaient rois. Un roi
C'est un homme trop grand que trouble un vague effroi,
Qui, faisant plus de mal pour avoir plus de joie,
Chez les bêtes de somme est la bête de proie;
Mais ce n'est pas sa faute, et le sage est clément.   25
Un roi serait meilleur s'il naissait autrement;
L'homme est l'homme toujours; les crimes du despote
Sont faits par sa puissance, ombre où son âme flotte,
Par la pourpre qu'il traîne et dont on le revêt,
Et l'esclave serait tyran s'il le pouvait.   30
Donc cette ville était tout bâtie en briques.
On y voyait des tours, des bazars, des fabriques,

from *The Legend of the Ages*

The Vanished City

Water is never idle.
In days of which no one has ever spoken,
When giants were still mingling among men,
A thousand years before
Adam,* the white-haired ghost we call our ancestor,
A brick-built city stood
Where mighty northerlies now lash the waves.
That city was a place riddled with lunacy;
At times, far away, pallid lightnings threatened it.
Where seas are visible now, a plain was visible
In those days; chariots, rather than ships, crossed it.
Today, typhoons have taken the place of tyrants;
To make a desert, God, Lord of the living,
Uses kings first, then hurricanes. Those people—
Swarming minds, voices, murmurs, flocking souls
Stirred up by feasts and funerals—
Made as much noise as bees do in a storm,
Untroubled that the ocean was their neighbour.

So the city had kings. Those fine kings trod
On faces as a reaper treads on grass.
Were they bad? No. They were just kings. A king
Is someone too great, who is faintly worried,
Who is a beast of prey among the beasts of burden,
And does more wrong because he wants more happiness.
Not that it is his fault—a wise man should be merciful.
Kings would be better if they were born otherwise;
Man is man everywhere; a despot's crimes
Are done by his authority—the shadow
In which his soul is drifting; by the purple
That trails behind him, in which people drape him.
A slave would be a tyrant if he could.
The city was all brick; bazaars, towers, textiles,

Des arcs, des palais pleins de luths mélodieux,
Et des monstres d'airain qu'on appelait les dieux.
Cette ville était gaie et barbare; ses places   35
Faisaient par leurs gibets rire les populaces;
On y chantait des chœurs pleins d'oubli, l'homme étant
L'ombre qui jette un souffle et qui dure un instant;
De claires eaux luisaient au fond des avenues;
Et les reines du roi se baignaient toutes nues   40
Dans les parcs où rôdaient des paons étoilés d'yeux;
Les marteaux, au dormeur nonchalant odieux,
Sonnaient, de l'aube au soir, sur les noires enclumes;
Les vautours se posaient, fouillant du bec leurs plumes,
Sur les temples, sans peur d'être chassés, sachant   45
Que l'idole féroce aime l'oiseaux méchant;
Le tigre est bien venu près de l'hydre; et les aigles
Sentent qu'ils n'ont jamais enfreint aucunes règles,
Quand le sang coule auprès des autels radieux,
En venant partager le meurtre avec les dieux.   50
L'autel du temple était d'or pur, que rien ne souille;
Le toit était en cèdre et, de peur de la rouille,
Au lieu de clous avait des chevilles de bois.
Jour et nuit les clairons, les cistres, les hautbois,
De crainte que le dieu farouche ne s'endorme,   55
Chantaient dans l'ombre. Ainsi vivait la ville énorme.
Les femmes y venaient pour s'y prostituer.
Mais un jour l'océan se mit à remuer;
Doucement, sans courroux, du côté de la ville
Il rongea les rochers et les dunes, tranquille,   60
Sans tumulte, sans chocs, sans efforts haletants,
Comme un grave ouvrier qui sait qu'il a le temps;
Et lentement, ainsi qu'un mineur solitaire,
L'eau jamais immobile avançait sous la terre;
C'est en vain que sur l'herbe un guetteur assidu   65
Eût collé son oreille, il n'eût rien entendu;
L'eau creusait sans rumeur comme sans violence,
Et la ville faisait son bruit sur ce silence.
Si bien qu'un soir, à l'heure où tout semble frémir,
A l'heure où, se levant comme un sinistre émir,   70
Sirius apparaît, et sur l'horizon sombre

Arches, palaces full of pretty lute-song,
And the bronze monsters known as gods, were seen there.
It was a gay, barbaric city; scaffolds
Amused the masses in its public squares.
They sang songs of forgetfulness—man is
A shadow, sheds a breath and lasts a moment.
The streets were lined with streams; the king's wives bathed
Naked in parks where spangled peacocks prowled;
Hammers, from dawn to dusk, rang on dark anvils,
Disturbing lazy sleepers; vultures perched
On shrines, preening their feathers with their beaks,
And had no fear of being driven off:
A savage idol loves an evil bird,
As dragons welcome tigers;
When blood flows from the radiant altars, eagles
Feel sure they never break the rules;
They come and share the murder with the gods.
The temple's altar was sheer gold, unsullied;
Its roof was cedar and had wooden pegs
Instead of nails—so that it never rusted.
Night and day, citherns, oboes, trumpets sounded
In the gloom, lest the savage god should sleep.
So the great town was living. Women came there
To prostitute themselves. One day, however,
The sea began to stir
Peacefully, gently, at the city's margin;
It swallowed reefs and dunes, quite calmly, without
Conflict, without convulsions, without struggles,
Like a grave workman who can take his time;
Gradually, like a solitary miner,
The wavering fluid undermined the land.
Even the most attentive watchman,
With ear pressed to the grass, would have heard nothing;
The water delved with neither sound nor strife.
The city made its noise above that silence;
And then, one evening—at the hour when all things
Appear to quake, when, like a sinister emir,
Sirius rises on the dark horizon

Donne un signal de marche aux étoiles sans nombre,
Les nuages qu'un vent l'un à l'autre rejoint
Et pousse, seuls oiseaux qui ne dormissent point,
La lune, le front blanc des monts, les pâles astres,　　　75
Virent soudain maisons, dômes, arceaux, pilastres,
Toute la ville, ainsi qu'un rêve, en un instant,
Peuple, armée, et le roi qui buvait en chantant
Et qui n'eut pas le temps de se lever de table,
Crouler dans on ne sait quelle ombre épouvantable;　　　80
Et pendant qu'à la fois, de la base au sommet,
Ce chaos de palais et de tours s'abîmait,
On entendit monter un murmure farouche,
Et l'on vit brusquement s'ouvrir comme une bouche
Un trou d'où jaillissait un jet d'écume amer,　　　85
Gouffre où la ville entrait et d'où sortait la mer.
Et tout s'évanouit; rien ne resta que l'onde.
Maintenant on ne voit au loin que l'eau profonde
Par les vents remuée et seule sous les cieux.
Tel est l'ébranlement des flots mystérieux.　　　90

Orphée

J'atteste Tanaïs, le noir fleuve aux six urnes,
Et Zeus qui fait traîner sur les grands chars nocturnes
Rhéa par des taureaux et Nyx par des chevaux,
Et les anciens géants et les hommes nouveaux,
Pluton qui nous dévore, Uranus qui nous crée,　　　5
Que j'adore une femme et qu'elle m'est sacrée.
Le monstre aux cheveux bleus, Poséidon, m'entend;
Qu'il m'exauce. Je suis l'âme humaine chantant,
Et j'aime. L'ombre immense est pleine de nuées,
La large pluie abonde aux feuilles remuées,　　　10
Borée émeut les bois, Zéphyre émeut les blés,
Ainsi nos cœurs profonds sont par l'amour troublés.
J'aimerai cette femme appelée Eurydice,
Toujours, partout! Sinon que le ciel me maudisse,
Et maudisse la fleur naissante et l'épi mûr!　　　15
Ne tracez pas de mots magiques sur le mur.

And summons all the countless stars to set out—
The only birds that never sleep, the clouds
Gathered and blown by wind,
The moon, the white-browed mountains, and the pale stars
Suddenly saw, like a dream, in a moment,
Domes, houses, arcades, and pilasters, the whole city,
Hordes, troops, and king—he was drinking and singing
And never had a chance to rise from dinner—
Collapse into some dreadful unknown darkness.
And, while the chaos, towers and palaces,
Summits and bases, sank into the chasm,
A savage murmur could be heard to rise,
And a hole could be seen, like a mouth gaping,
Shedding a spurt of bitter spray—a gulf
Which the town entered, and the sea came forth.
And all things vanished; just the surge remained.
Now only the deep wind-blown seas, alone
Beneath the skies, are visible in the distance.
Such is the impact of mysterious waves.

Orpheus

I swear, by Zeus, whose great nocturnal chariot pulls
    Nyx with stallions, and Rhea with bulls,
By Tanais, the black and six-urned waterway,
    By ancient Giants, and by men today,
Uranus our creator, Pluto our sepulchre,
    I love a woman, and I honour her.
O blue-haired dragon, O Poseidon, hear these things,
    Grant them! I am the human soul that sings;
I am in love. Rain teems among the fluttered leaves;
    Boreas stirs the woods, Zephyr* the sheaves;
Clouds fill the far-extended gloom in every part;
    Love, too, perturbs the depths within our heart.
Yes, I shall love this woman called Eurydice*
    Everywhere, always! Otherwise, on me,
On buds and standing grain,* let heaven's curses fall!
    Never trace magic words upon the wall.*

«Autrefois, j'ai connu Ferdousi dans Mysore . . .»

Autrefois, j'ai connu Ferdousi dans Mysore.
Il semblait avoir pris une flamme à l'aurore
Pour s'en faire une aigrette et se mettre au front;
Il ressemblait aux rois que n'atteint nul affront,
Portait le turban rouge où le rubis éclate,   5
Et traversait la ville habillé d'écarlate.

Je le revis dix ans après vêtu de noir.
Et je lui dis:

    —O toi qu'on venait jadis voir
Comme un homme de pourpre errer devant nos portes,
Toi, le seigneur vermeil, d'où vient donc que tu portes   10
Cet habit noir, qui semble avec de l'ombre teint?

—C'est, me répondit-il, que je me suis éteint.

Après les Fourches Caudines

Rome avait trop de gloire, ô dieux, vous la punîtes
Par le triomphe énorme et lâche des samnites;
Et nous vîmes ce deuil, nous qui vivons encor.
Cela n'empêche pas l'aurore aux rayons d'or
D'éclore et d'apparaître au-dessus des collines.   5
Un champ de course est près des tombes Esquilines,
Et parfois, quand la foule y fourmille en tous sens,
J'y vais, l'œil vaguement fixé sur les passants.
Ce champ mène aux logis de guerre où les cohortes
Vont et viennent ainsi que dans les villes fortes;   10
Avril sourit, l'oiseau chante, et, dans le lointain,
Derrière les coteaux où reluit le matin,
Où les roses des bois entr'ouvrent leurs pétales,
On entend murmurer les trompettes fatales;
Et je médite, ému. J'étais aujourd'hui là.   15

'I knew Firdausi in Mysore, long since . . .'

I knew Firdausi* in Mysore, long since.
He looked as if he'd caught the dawn's first rays,
Made them a plume, and set them on his head.
He seemed like some unsulliable prince
Turbaned in scarlet with a ruby's blaze;
He crossed the town adorned in brilliant red.

I met him ten years later dressed in black.
I said to him:

        'You used to go about
Like a vermilion man from room to room;
Sir Gules, why are you wearing on your back
A cloak so dark that it seems dyed in gloom?'

    'Because', he said, 'I've been put out.'

After the Caudine Forks

Rome was too glorious; the gods punished her
With the great shameful Samnite massacre.
We saw that tragedy—we who live on;
And still the gold-rayed sun has dawned and shone
Unhindered on the summits as before.
Near the Esquiline graves* a racecourse stands,
And sometimes, when the crowds drift to and fro,
I go and idly watch their wayward bands.
That racecourse leads to barracks where brigades
March round as in a town prepared for war.
Birds sing, and April smiles; in far-off glades
Behind the hills lit by the morning glow,
Where the wild roses just begin to bloom,
You can hear distant trumpet-calls of doom;
It makes me ponder. I was there today.

Je ne sais pas pourquoi le soleil se voila;
Les nuages parfois dans le ciel se resserrent.
Tout à coup, à cheval et lance au poing, passèrent
Des vétérans aux fronts hâlés, aux larges mains;
Ils avaient l'ancien air des grands soldats romains;   20
Et les petits enfants accouraient pour les suivre;
Trois cavaliers, soufflant dans des buccins de cuivre,
Marchaient en tête, et comme, au front de l'escadron,
Chacun d'eux embouchait à son tour le clairon,
Sans couper la fanfare ils reprenaient haleine.   25
Ces gens de guerre étaient superbes dans la plaine;
Ils marchaient de leur pas antique et souverain.
Leurs boucliers portaient des méduses d'airain,
Et l'on voyait sur eux Gorgone et tous ses masques;
Ils défilaient, dressant les cimiers de leurs casques,   30
Dignes d'être éclairés par des soleils levants,
Sous des crins de lion qui se tordaient aux vents.
Que ces hommes sont beaux! disaient les jeunes filles.
Tout souriait, les fleurs embaumaient les charmilles,
Le peuple était joyeux, le ciel était doré.   35
Et, songeant que c'étaient des vaincus, j'ai pleuré.

from *L'Art d'être grand-père*

A Georges

Mon doux Georges, viens voir une ménagerie
Quelconque, chez Buffon, au cirque, n'importe où;
Sans sortir de Lutèce allons en Assyrie,
Et sans quitter Paris partons pour Tombouctou.

Viens voir les léopards de Tyr, les gypaètes,   5
L'ours grondant, le boa formidable sans bruit,
Le zèbre, le chacal, l'once, et ces deux poëtes,
L'aigle ivre de soleil, le vautour plein de nuit.

Why the sun hid itself I cannot say;
Now and then banks of cloud do choke the sky.
Suddenly sunburnt veterans passed by
On horseback, with their huge fists gripping spears;
They looked like fine old Roman pioneers,
And small boys thronged behind. Three horsemen went
Ahead, in front of the whole regiment,
Blowing bronze trumpets; as they rode around,
Each in turn put the clarion to his lips
And then took breath, with no break in the sound.
Those warriors were glorious in the field;
They marched along with timeless, sovereign paces.
A bronze Medusa* was on every shield,
Displaying all three of the Gorgons' faces.
The men held their heads high; their helmet tips
Deserved to glitter in the dawn's first glare,
With plumes like lion manes tossed by the air.
'What handsome lads they are!' the young girls cried.
All things smiled; flowers scented the countryside,
The skies were gold, the people laughed and leapt.

     I thought of their defeat, and wept.

from *The Art of Being a Grandfather*

For Georges

Come with me, Georges* my friend; come, let's go down
To some menagerie, circus, or zoo;
Let's reach Assyria without leaving town,
And without leaving Paris, Timbuktu.*

Let's see the Tyrian leopard, the gruff bear,
The fearsome noiseless boa, the great kite,
Ounce, zebra, jackal, and that poet-pair
Eagle and vulture, steeped in day and night.

Viens contempler le lynx sagace, l'amphisbène
A qui Job comparait son faux ami Sepher,   10
Et l'obscur tigre noir, dont le masque d'ébène
A deux trous flamboyants par où l'on voit l'enfer.

Voir de près l'oiseau fauve et le frisson des ailes,
C'est charmant; nous aurons, sous de très sûrs abris,
Le spectacle des loups, des jaguars, des gazelles,   15
Et l'éblouissement divin des colibris.

Sortons du bruit humain. Viens au jardin des plantes.
Penchons-nous, à travers l'ombre où nous étouffons,
Sur les douleurs d'en bas, vaguement appelantes,
Et sur les pas confus des inconnus profonds.   20

L'animal, c'est de l'ombre errant dans les ténèbres;
On ne sait s'il écoute, on ne sait s'il entend;
Il a des cris hagards, il a des yeux funèbres;
Une affirmation sublime en sort pourtant.

Nous qui régnons, combien de choses inutiles   25
Nous disons, sans savoir le mal que nous faisons!
Quand la vérité vient, nous lui sommes hostiles,
Et contre la raison nous avons des raisons.

Corbière à la tribune et Frayssinous en chaire
Sont fort inférieurs à la bête des bois;   30
L'âme dans la forêt songe et se laisse faire;
Je doute dans un temple, et sur un mont je crois.

Dieu par les voix de l'ombre obscurément se nomme;
Nul Quirinal ne vaut le fauve Pélion;
Il est bon, quand on vient d'entendre parler l'homme,   35
D'aller entendre un peu rugir le grand lion.

Let's study the wise lynx; the amphisbaene*
To which Job likened Zophar* his false friend;
The tiger, in whose ebony face are seen
Two flaming tunnels with hell at the end.

At close range, fluttering wingbeats and wild birds
Are splendid; from secure retreats, we may
See panthers, wolves, gazelles in packs and herds,
And hummingbirds brilliantly on display.

Come to the zoo; leave human noise behind,
And look down through the gloom that stifles us
At lower cries for help of some strange kind
And rustling depths, obscure and dubious.

Those creatures are shades roaming a dark land;
They have distraught howls and funereal eyes;
Who can tell what they hear or understand?
Yet from them, glorious affirmations rise.

How many worthless things we masters say!
Who knows what harm we do in consequence?
Whenever the truth comes, we turn away;
We find sensible reasons to shun sense.

Set beside woodland animals, Corbière's
And Frayssinous'* speeches are so naïve;
Souls in the forest dream and shed all cares;
In church I doubt, on a peak I believe.

No Quirinal can match wild Pelion;*
In shadowy sounds God names himself; therefore,
When we have heard men talking on and on,
It's good to hear the mighty lion roar.

Encore l'Immaculée Conception

Attendez. Je regarde une petite fille.
Je ne la connais pas; mais cela chante et brille;
C'est du rire, du ciel, du jour, de la beauté,
Et je ne puis passer froidement à côté.
Elle n'a pas trois ans. C'est l'aube qu'on rencontre.   5
Peut-être elle devrait cacher ce qu'elle montre,
Mais elle n'en sait rien, et d'ailleurs c'est charmant.
Cela, certe, ressemble au divin firmament
Plus que la face auguste et jaune d'un évêque.
Le babil des marmots est ma bibliothèque;   10
J'ouvre chacun des mots qu'ils disent, comme on prend
Un livre, et j'y découvre un sens profond et grand,
Sévère quelquefois. Donc j'écoute cet ange;
Et ce gazouillement me rassure, me venge,
M'aide à rire du mal qu'on veut me faire, éteint   15
Ma colère, et vraiment m'empêche d'être atteint
Par l'ombre du hideux sombrero de Basile.
Cette enfant est un cœur, une fête, un asile,
Et Dieu met dans son souffle et Dieu mêle à sa voix
Toutes les fleurs des champs, tous les oiseaux des bois;   20
Ma Jeanne, qui pourrait être sa sœur jumelle,
Traînait, l'été dernier, un chariot comme elle,
L'emplissait, le vidait, riait d'un rire fou,
Courait. Tous les enfants ont le même joujou;
Tous les hommes aussi. C'est bien, va, sois ravie,   25
Et traîne ta charrette, en attendant la vie.

Louange à Dieu! Toujours un enfant m'apaisa.
Doux être! voyez-moi les mains que ça vous a!
Allons, remettez donc vos bas, mademoiselle.
Elle est pieds nus, elle est barbouillée, elle est belle;   30
Sa charrette est cassée, et, comme nous, ma foi,
Elle se fait un char avec n'importe quoi.
Tout est char de triomphe à l'enfant comme à l'homme.
L'enfant aussi veut être un peu bête de somme
Comme nous; il se fouette, il s'impose une loi;   35

The Immaculate Conception Revisited

Wait just a moment. I'm watching a little girl.
Don't know who the creature is, but she's singing and glittering,
She's laughter and heaven and daylight and beauty,
And I can't pass by coldly.
She isn't yet three. It's a meeting with dawn.
Should she be hiding what she is revealing? Possibly,
But she doesn't know that, and anyhow, it's a delight,
Surely there's more of the glorious firmament here
Than there is in the stern yellow face of a bishop.
The babble of mites is my library;
I open each word that they say, just as you pick up a
Book, and I find a deep and impressive meaning within it,
Sometimes a severe one. So I listen to this little angel;
Her chatter consoles me, avenges me,
Helps me to brush aside all the harm people want to do to me, stifles
My anger, and frankly prevents me from being tainted
With the shadow cast by Basilio's* grisly sombrero.
This child is a human soul, a carnival, a sanctuary,
God sets in her breath all the wildflowers and woodbirds,
God mingles them all with her speech;
My Jeanne,* who might be her twin sister,
Was towing last summer a trolley like hers,
Filling it, emptying it, laughing mad laughter,
Scampering. Yes, all children have the same plaything;
All adults too. Fine, off you go, have fun,
And, as practice for life, tow that cart.

Praise be to God! A child soothes my nerves, always.
Pretty thing! Look at the hands that it's got!
All right, on with your stockings again, young lady.
She's barefoot and muddied and beautiful;
Her cart has been broken, and (just like us—goodness!)
She's using whatever has come to hand as her chariot.
Children, like us, find triumphal cars everywhere.
Children, like adults, want to be beasts of burden
To some extent; they buffet themselves, impose laws on themselves,

Il traîne son hochet comme nous notre roi;
Seulement l'enfant brille où le peuple se vautre.
Bon, voici maintenant qu'on en amène une autre;
Une d'un an, sa sœur sans doute; un grand chapeau,
Une petite tête, et des yeux! une peau!   40
Un sourire! oh! qu'elle est tremblante et délicate!
Chef-d'œuvre, montrez-moi votre petite patte.
Elle allonge le pied et chante... c'est divin.
Quand je songe, et Veuillot n'a pu le dire en vain,
Qu'elles ont toutes deux la tache originelle!   45
La Chute est leur vrai nom. Chacune porte en elle
L'affreux venin d'Adam (bon style Patouillet);
Elles sont, sous le ciel qu'Ève jadis souillait,
D'horribles péchés, faits d'une façon charmante;
La beauté qui s'ajoute à la faute l'augmente;   50
Leur grâce est un remords de plus pour le pécheur,
Et leur mère apparaît, noire de leur blancheur;
Ces enfants que l'aube aime et que la fleur encense,
C'est la honte portant ce masque, l'innocence;
Dans ces yeux purs, Trublet l'affirme en son sermon,   55
Brille l'incognito sinistre du démon;
C'est le mal, c'est l'enfer, cela sort des abîmes!
Soit. Laissez-moi donner des gâteaux à ces crimes.

Jeanne endormi, iv

L'oiseau chante; je suis au fond des rêveries.

Rose, elle est là qui dort sous les branches fleuries,
Dans son berceau tremblant comme un nid d'alcyon,
Douce, les yeux fermés, sans faire attention
Au glissement de l'ombre et du soleil sur elle.   5
Elle est toute petite, elle est surnaturelle.
O suprême beauté de l'enfant innocent!
Moi je pense, elle rêve; et sur son front descend
Un entrelacement de visions sereines;
Des femmes de l'azur qu'on prendrait pour des reines,   10

They haul their toys around as we do our kings;
Except that children are radiant, whereas the populace wallows.
Right, now here's another one being brought in;
Just a year old, her sister presumably; big bonnet,
Little head, eyes! and skin!
And a smile! Oh! she's so trembling and delicate!
Show me your little paw, masterpiece.
She sticks out one of her feet and sings... it's divine.
When I reflect, and Veuillot* can't have said this in vain,
That both of them carry the stains of original sin!
The Fall* is their middle name. They both are infected
With Adam's vile venom (the proper Patouillet* jargon);
Beneath the heavens that Eve once sullied, they both
Are horrible sins in an exquisite package;
Beauty makes evil much worse;
Their charm is simply one extra pang for the sinner.
And now their mother appears, blackened, you see, with their
     whiteness;
These children, fondled by sunrise and scented by flowers,
Are infamy wearing the mask of innocence;
Within those pure eyes—Trublet* in his sermons affirms it—
There blazes the devil's sinister incognito;
It's evil, it's hell, it's come out of the bottomless pit!
Fine. Let me give lollies to crimes of this kind.

Jeanne Asleep, iv

A bird sings; I am deep in reveries.

She—sleeping rose underneath flowering trees—
Lies in her trembling nest-like cradle, eyes
Tenderly closed; nor does she realize
How shade plays over her, or sunbeams fall.
So supernatural she is; so small:
Innocent children have such loveliness!
She dreams, I ponder; through her brows progress
Sequential visions, interlaced, serene:
Some woman from the azure, like a queen—

Des anges, des lions ayant des airs bénins,
De pauvres bons géants protégés par des nains,
Des triomphes de fleurs dans les bois, des trophées
D'arbres célestes, pleins de la lueur des fées,
Un nuage où l'éden apparaît à demi,   15
Voilà ce qui s'abat sur l'enfant endormi.
Le berceau des enfants est le palais des songes;
Dieu se met à leur faire un tas de doux mensonges;
De là leur frais sourire et leur profonde paix.
Plus d'un dira plus tard: Bon Dieu, tu me trompais.   20

Mais le bon Dieu répond dans la profondeur sombre:
—Non. Ton rêve est le ciel. Je t'en ai donné l'ombre.
Mais le ciel, tu l'auras. Attends l'autre berceau;
La tombe.—

       Ainsi je songe. O printemps! Chante, oiseau!

from *Toute la lyre*

Lettre

La Champagne est fort laide où je suis; mais qu'importe,
J'ai de l'air, un peu d'herbe, une vigne à ma porte;
D'ailleurs, je ne suis pas ici pour bien longtemps.
N'ayant pas mes petits près de moi, je prétends
Avoir droit à la fuite, et j'y songe à toute heure,   5
Et tous les jours je veux partir, et je demeure.
L'homme est ainsi.

       Parfois tout s'efface à mes yeux
Sous la mauvaise humeur du nuage ennuyeux;
Il pleut. Triste pays. Moins de blé que d'ivraie.
Bientôt j'irai chercher la solitude vraie,   10
Où sont les fiers écueils, sombres, jamais vaincus,

An angel—lions, somewhat frolicsome—
Poor, gentle giants sheltered by Tom Thumb—
In the woods, floral triumphs, trophies borne
By heavenly trees, lit by the fairies' dawn—
Eden half visible between high-piled
Cloud-masses—all come to this sleeping child.
Cradles are palaces of lovely dreams;
God heaps on children such deceitful schemes:
Hence their fresh smiles, hence their deep harmony.
'God,' they'll cry later, 'you were tricking me!'

But God declares, from the celestial host:
'Your dream is heaven; I gave you its mere ghost;
Yet you shall have it, in your following
Cradle—the tomb.'

                              I dream so. Springtime! Yes, bird: sing!

from *The Whole Lyre*

Letter

Dreadfully ugly country, this Champagne;* but no matter,
        I have some air, a bit of grass, a vine nearby;
And anyhow, I shan't be here much longer.
        Since the children aren't with me, I maintain
I can escape—I dream about that constantly,
        Daily I want to leave, and I remain.
Man is like that.

                        From time to time everything vanishes
        Before some bothersome bad-tempered cloud;
Rain comes down; wretched scene. Chaff-fields rather than
    wheatfields.
        Soon I'll go out and look for the true solitude,
Where the proud reefs are, sombre, never vanquished—

La mer. En attendant, comme Horace à Fuscus,
Je t'envoie, ami cher, les paroles civiles
Que doit l'hôte des champs à l'habitant des villes;
Tu songes au milieu des tumultes hagards;   15
Et je salue, avec toutes sortes d'égards,
Moi qui vois les fourmis, toi qui vois les pygmées.

Parce que vous avez la forge aux renommées,
Aux vacarmes, aux faits tapageurs et soudains,
Ne croyez pas qu'à Bray-sur-Marne, ô citadins,   20
On soit des paysans au point d'être des brutes;
Non, on danse, on se cherche au bois, on fait des chutes,
On s'aime; on est toujours Estelle et Némorin;
Simone et Gros Thomas sautent au tambourin;
Et les grands vieux parents grondent quand, le dimanche,   25
Les filles vont tirer les garçons par le manche.
Le presbytère est là qui garde le troupeau.
Parfois j'entre à l'église et j'ôte mon chapeau
Quand monsieur le curé foudroie en pleine chaire
L'idylle d'un bouvier avec une vachère.   30

Mais je suis indulgent plus que lui; le ciel bleu,
Diable! et le doux printemps, tout cela trouble un peu;
Et les petits oiseaux, quel détestable exemple!
Le jeune mois de mai, c'est toujours le vieux temple
Où, doucement raillés par les merles siffleurs,   35
Les gens qui s'aiment vont s'adorer dans les fleurs;
Jadis c'était Phyllis, aujourd'hui c'est Javotte;
Mais c'est toujours la femme au mois de mai dévote.

Moi, je suis spectateur, et je pardonne; ayant
L'âme très débonnaire et l'air très effrayant.   40
Car j'inquiète fort le village. On me nomme
Le sorcier; on m'évite; ils disent: C'est un homme
Qu'on entend parler haut dans sa chambre, le soir;
Or on ne parle seul qu'avec quelqu'un de noir.—
C'est pourquoi je fais peur.

The sea. Meanwhile, dear friend, I'm sending you,
Horace-to-Fuscus* style, the polite words that a guest of the country
    Should send back to a dweller in the town;
While you ponder amid those wild and tumultuous regions
    I offer you my very best respects,
I who look on the ants, to you who look on the pygmies.

Just because town folk have the forge that makes
All the big noise, the fame, the brash and rowdy doings,
    Don't think the denizens of Bray-sur-Marne*
Are such absolute peasants that they're merely brutes;
    Oh no, they dance, meet in the woods, slip up,
Make love, are Juliets and Romeos basically;
    While the tambourine plays, Jack hoofs with Jill,
And all the Aged Parents grumble every Sunday
    When the girls go out flirting with the boys.
The flock is shepherded by its presbyters; sometimes
    I go to church and doff my hat and hear
The local Reverend blasting from his public pulpit
    This farmhand's and that milkmaid's dalliance.

Still, I'm more tolerant than he is; the fair springtime
    And blue skies do cause trouble now and then,
Not to mention the little birds—what a shocking example!
    May, the young month, is always the old shrine
Where lovers, gently teased by chirpy blackbirds,
    Adore each other while the flowers bloom.
Nowadays she's Javotte, in the olden days she was Phyllis,*
    But always she's a girl and worships May.

Well, I'm a forgiving chap, merely a spectator
    With easygoing soul and fearsome look—
I scare the village awfully, they shun me, call me
    Sorcerer; 'he's the kind of man', they say,
'That talks to himself out loud at night in his bedroom.
    If you talk alone, it must be with someone black.'
That's what's so frightening.

                        La maison que j'habite,   45
Grotte dont j'ai fait choix pour être cénobite,
C'est l'auberge; on y boit dans la salle d'en bas;
Les filles du pays viennent, ôtent leurs bas,
Et salissent leurs pieds dans la mare voisine.
La soupe aux choux, c'est là toute notre cuisine;   50
Un lit et quatre murs, c'est là tout mon logis.

Je vis; les champs le soir sont largement rougis;
L'espace est, le matin, confusément sonore;
L'angélus se répand dans le ciel dès l'aurore,
Et j'ai le bercement des cloches en dormant.   55
Poésie: un roulier avec un jurement;
Des poules becquetant un vieux mur en décembre;
De lointains aboiements dialoguant dans l'ombre;
Parfois un vol d'oiseaux sauvages émigrant.
C'est petit, car c'est laid, et le beau seul est grand.   60
Cette campagne où l'aube à regret semble naître,
M'offre à perte de vue au loin sous ma fenêtre
Rien, la route, un sol âpre, usé, morne, inclément.
Quelques arbres sont là; j'écoute vaguement
Les conversations du vent avec les branches.   65
La plaine brune alterne avec les plaines blanches;
Pas un coteau, des prés maigres, peu de gazon;
Et j'ai pour tout plaisir de voir à l'horizon
Un groupe de toits bas d'où sort une fumée,
Le paysage étant plat comme Mérimée.   70

Effets de réveil

On ouvre les yeux; rien ne remue; on entend
Au chevet de son lit la montre palpitant;
La fenêtre livide aux spectres est pareille;
On est gisant ainsi qu'un mort. On se réveille.
Pourquoi? parce qu'on s'est la veille réveillé   5
Au même instant. Ainsi qu'un rouage rouillé
Et vieilli, mais exact, l'âme a ses habitudes.

                    I live as a hermit,
My chosen dwelling is a lonely cave—
The village inn; people have a drink downstairs;
     The local girls come along and strip off
Their stockings to muddy their feet in the nearest quagmire.
     Our entire menu here is cabbage soup;
My entire lodgings are a bed and four walls.

I live. At dusk the fields turn rather red,
At dawn the whole place is chaotically resonant;
     When the sun rises church bells fill the air,
And I have tolling knells to lull my slumbers.
     Poetry here: a travelling carter's curse,
Faraway woofs conversing in the darkness,
     A few hens pecking on a ruined wall,
Sometimes a flight of wild birds emigrating.
     It's ugly, so it's small; beauty alone
Is big. The sun seems sorry to get up here;
     My window gives me far-flung vistas of
Nothing—the road, rough ground, glum, worn, recalcitrant.
     There are a few trees; I can faintly hear
The wind holding discussions with the branches;
     Dusky plains alternate with lighter plains;
No hillocks, not much grass, some scrawny meadows;
     My sole delight is to see, far away,
A clump of lowly roofs emitting wisps of smoke,
     The landscape being flat as Mérimée.*

Waking Impressions

You open your eyes. Nothing stirs. You hear
Your watch throbbing beside the bed. The clear
Window appears quite ghostly. There you lie
Like a dead body. Ah! You're waking. Why?
Because that's when you woke up yesterday.
The soul's like clockwork: old and worn away,
It still keeps time—it's so habitual.

Oh! la nuit, c'est la plus sombre des solitudes!
L'heure apparaît, entrant, sortant comme un passeur
D'ombres, et notre esprit voit tout dans la noirceur;   10
Des pas sans but, des deuils sans fin, des maux sans nombre.
Le rêve qu'on avait et qui tremblait dans l'ombre
S'ajuste à la pensée indistincte qu'on a.
Tous les gouffres au bord desquels nous amena
Ce fantôme appelé le hasard, reparaissent;   15
Les mêmes visions redoutables s'y dressent;
Ici le précipice, ici l'écroulement,
Ici la chute, ici ce qui fuit, ce qui ment,
Ce qui tue, et là-bas, dans l'âpre transparence,
Les vagues bras levés de la pâle espérance.   20
Comme on est triste! on sent l'inexprimable effroi,
On croit avoir le mur du tombeau devant soi;
On médite, effaré par les choses possibles;
Toute rive s'efface; on voit les invisibles,
Les absents, les manquants, cette morte, ce mort;   25
On leur tend les mains: ombre et songe! On se rendort.

Homme, debout! voici le jour, l'aube ravie,
L'azur; et qu'est-ce donc qui rentre? C'est la vie,
C'est le cri du travail, c'est le chant des oiseaux,
C'est le rayonnement des champs, des airs, des eaux;   30
La nuit traîne un linceul, l'aurore agite un lange;
Tout ce qu'on vient de voir spectre, on le revoit ange;
Du père qu'on vit mort on voit l'enfant vivant;
Le monde reparaît, clair comme auparavant;
On ne reconnaît plus son âme; elle était noire,   35
Elle est blanche; elle espère et se remet à croire,
A sourire, à vouloir; on a devant les yeux
Un éblouissement doré, chantant, joyeux,
On ne sait quel fouillis charmant de lueurs roses;
Et tout l'homme est changé parce qu'on voit les choses,   40
Les hommes, Dieu, les cœurs, les amours, le destin,
A travers le vitrail splendide du matin.

Night is the darkest solitude of all.
Hours arrive, leave, like someone wandering
The shadows. And the mind sees everything
Black: pointless steps, endless grief, boundless doom.
The dreams you dreamed, which quivered in the gloom,
Dissolve into the thoughts you dimly think.
Once more all the vast chasms—to whose brink
That ghost Chance led you—gape before your eyes;
Once more the same terrible scenes arise:
Precipices nearby, catastrophes,
Downfalls, whatever lies, whatever flees
Or kills—and, through the acrid mists down there,
Pallid hope lifting her faint hands in prayer.
How sad you are! You feel a nameless dread,
You sense that the tomb's verge is just ahead;
Frightened by what might be or might have been
You ponder; boundaries fade; you can see the unseen,
The departed, the lost, dead women and dead men;
You reach for them—wisps, dreams! You fall asleep again.

Mortal, get up! It's day, rapt dawn, blue sky;
And what is coming back now? Life; the cry
Of work, the song of birds, the radiance
Of fields and streams and seas and the expanse.
Night dragged a shroud, dawn flourishes swaddling bands;
Where a wraith lately stood, an angel stands;
You see, alive, the child of the corpse you saw;
The world comes back again, bright as before;
Its spirit is transfigured: it *was* black,
It *is* white; its beliefs and hopes are back,
Its smiles and wishes; golden gleaming rays,
All singing and rejoicing, meet your gaze—
Some pretty muddle of pink glimmerings;
You're utterly changed, now that you see things,
Man, Fate, God, passions sacred and profane,
Through morning's glorious stained-glass window pane.

Ave, dea; moriturus te salutat

La mort et la beauté sont deux choses profondes
Qui contiennent tant d'ombre et d'azur qu'on dirait
Deux sœurs également terribles et fécondes
Ayant la même énigme et le même secret.

O femmes, voix, regards, cheveux noirs, tresses blondes, 5
Brillez, je meurs! ayez l'éclat, l'amour, l'attrait,
O perles que la mer mêle à ses grandes ondes,
O lumineux oiseaux de la sombre forêt!

Judith, nos deux destins sont plus près l'un de l'autre
Qu'on ne croirait, à voir mon visage et le vôtre; 10
Tout le divin abîme apparaît dans vos yeux,

Et moi, je sens le gouffre étoilé dans mon âme;
Nous sommes tous les deux voisins du ciel, madame,
Puisque vous êtes belle et puisque je suis vieux.

from *Religions et religion*

«Dante écrit deux vers ...»

Dante écrit deux vers, puis il sort; et les deux vers 1535
Se parlent. Le premier dit:—Les cieux sont ouverts!
Cieux! je suis immortel.—Moi, je suis périssable,
Dit l'autre.—Je suis l'astre.—Et moi le grain de sable.
—Quoi! tu doutes étant fils d'un enfant du ciel!
—Je me sens mort.—Et moi, je me sens éternel.— 1540
Quelqu'un rentre et relit ces vers, Dante lui-même;
Il garde le premier et barre le deuxième.
La rature est la haute et fatale cloison.
L'un meurt, et l'autre vit. Tous deux avait raison.

Hail, Goddess, Hail from One about to Die

Beauty and death: they go so deep, those two;
They seem so azure and so shadowy—
Sisters equally secret and taboo,
With matching terror and fertility.

Girls, voices, glances, blonde hair, black hair—glow,
Gleam; I am dying! dazzle, ravish, bloom,
You pearls tossed by the mighty ocean's flow,
You radiant birds within the forest's gloom!

Our fates are more alike than men might hold
When, Judith, they compare my face with yours;
The whole divine abyss is in your eyes,

And in my soul the starry chasm lies;
Madame, both of us are on heaven's shores,
For you are beautiful and I am old.

from *Religions and Religion*

'Dante wrote two lines . . .'

Dante* wrote two lines; then he left. The lines
Talked to each other. Said one: 'Heaven shines!
I am immortal.' Said the next: 'I'm not.'
'I am a star.' 'I'm a mere sand-grain.' 'What!
Made by a son of God—yet you're unsure?'
'I feel dead.' 'I feel life for evermore.'
Someone—Dante—came back; reread his text;
He kept the first line, but crossed out the next,
Drawing a fatal wall between the two.
One lived, one perished. Both views had been true.

from *History of a Crime*

The Rue Tiquetonne

Bancel and Versigny* had rejoined me.

Just as I was leaving the boulevard and moving back toward the centre of Paris—swept away in the whirl of the terrified crowd, without really knowing where I was going—a voice suddenly whispered in my ear, 'There's something you ought to see.' It was E.P.'s* voice.

E.P. is a dramatist, a gifted man; in the days of Louis-Philippe I'd helped him to get an exemption from military service. I hadn't seen him for four or five years, and now I met him again in this tumult. He talked to me as if we'd seen each other the day before. Crises are like that. You don't have time for rulebook greetings. You talk as though everything is on the run.

'Oh, it's you!' I said. 'What can I do for you?'

'I'm living in a house over there', he replied.

Then he added, 'Come with me.'

He led me into a dark street. You could hear shooting; at the end of the street there was the remains of a barricade. Versigny and Bancel, as I've just said, were with me. E.P. turned toward them.

'These gentlemen can come too', he said.

I asked him, 'What's this street?'

'Rue Tiquetonne. Come along.'

We followed him.

I've described this tragic episode elsewhere (in *Châtiments*).*

E.P. stopped in front of a tall, dark house. He pushed open the front door (it wasn't shut), and then another door. We reached a small room lit by one lamp. It was absolutely quiet.

The room seemed to be next to a shop. At the back you could see two beds side by side—one large, and one small. Over the small bed hung a woman's portrait, and over the portrait a holy palm-branch.

The lamp was over the fireplace, where a little fire was burning.

Near the lamp, on a chair, was an old woman. She was bent forward, hunched, folded over as if broken in half, above something shadowy that she was holding in her arms. I moved closer. What she had in her arms was a dead child.

The poor woman was sobbing quietly.

E.P., who was living in the same house, touched her on the shoulder and said:

'Let's see it.'

The old woman raised her head; on her knees I could see a pale, pretty little boy, half undressed, with two red holes in his forehead.

The old woman gazed at me but evidently didn't see me; she murmured to herself:

'And to think he was calling me "Granny" only this morning!'

E.P. picked up the child's hand. It fell back again.

'Seven years old', he told me.

There was a basin on the ground. They had been washing the child's face; trickles of blood were running down from the two holes.

A woman was standing at the back of the room, near a half-open clothes-press with some linen in it. She was about forty, serious, poor, neatly dressed, and rather pretty.

'One of the neighbours', E.P. told me.

He told me that a doctor was living in the house. The doctor had come down and said: 'Nothing to be done.' The child had been hit in the head by two bullets while he was crossing the street to 'get out of the way'. They had brought him back to his grandmother. 'He was all she had left.'

The portrait of his dead mother was hanging over the little bed.

The boy's eyes were half open; he had that indescribable look of the dead, where the sight of reality is replaced by the vision of the infinite. Now and then, in between her sobs, his grandmother said: 'Lord in heaven, is it possible! Who would ever have imagined! Bandits, that's what they are!'

She cried out, 'So that's the government, is it?'

'Yes', I said.

We finished undressing the child. He had a top in his pocket. His head slipped back and forth from one shoulder to the other; I held it and kissed his brow. Versigny and Bancel took off his stockings. Suddenly the grandmother gave a start.

'Don't hurt him!' she said.

She took the two little icy white feet in her hands and tried to warm them.

When the poor little body was naked, we began to lay it out. We took a sheet from the clothes-press.

Then the grandmother burst into bitter tears.

'I want him back!' she cried.

She drew herself up and stared at us, and began to talk wildly, jumbling together Bonaparte and God and her little boy and his school and her lost daughter, and abusing us too. She was pale and haggard, as if she could see a vision in front of her; she was more of a ghost than the dead child.

Then she buried her face in her hands again, folded the boy in her arms, and began sobbing afresh.

The woman who was there came up to me and wiped my mouth with a handkerchief, without saying a word. There was blood on my lips.

Ah, but what could we do? We went away, feeling shattered.

It was quite dark. Bancel and Versigny left me.

from *Things Seen*

The Emperor of Brazil

22 May [1877]

9 a.m. Visit from the Emperor of Brazil. Long conversation. Very noble mind. He saw *The Art of Being a Grandfather** on a table. I offered it to him and picked up a pen. He said, 'What are you going to write?' I replied, 'Two names—yours and mine.' He said, 'Nothing else. That's exactly what I was going to ask you.' I wrote:

To Don Pedro de Alcantara

VICTOR HUGO

'What about the date?' he asked me.

I added:

22 May 1877

He said, 'I'd like to have one of your drawings.' I had with me a drawing I had made of the chateau at Vianden. I presented it to him. He asked me, 'What time do you have dinner?' I replied, 'Eight o'clock.' He said, 'One of these days I'll come and ask you for a dinner invitation.' I replied, 'Any day that suits you. You'd be welcome.'

He showered kisses on Georges and Jeanne. On the way in, he said to me, 'Please give me some reassurance. I'm a bit nervous.'

He referred to kings and emperors as 'my colleagues'. At one point he said 'my rights...'. Then he corrected himself. 'I don't have any rights. I have only an authority bestowed on me for no reason. I need to use it for good. Progress and freedom!'

When Jeanne came in, he said to me, 'I have one ambition. Please introduce me to Mademoiselle Jeanne.'

I said to Jeanne, 'Jeanne, let me introduce you to the Emperor of Brazil.'

Jeanne confined herself to the *sotto voce* observation, 'He hasn't any costume.' The emperor said to her, 'Come and kiss me, Mademoiselle.' She presented her cheek. He said, 'No, Jeanne, give me a hug.'

She held him in her little arms. He asked me for their photograph and mine, and promised me his.* He left me at eleven o'clock. He had talked with me so sensibly and seriously that, as we parted, I told him, 'Sire, you are a great citizen.'

Another detail. When I introduced Georges to him, I said, 'Sire, let me introduce my grandson to Your Majesty.' He said to Georges, 'My boy, there is only one majesty here, and that's Victor Hugo.'

from *Deeds and Words*

The Hernani *Dinner*

9 December 1877

[*On 9 December 1877, in response to the press's unanimous acclaim for the revival of* Hernani, *Victor Hugo gave a dinner at the Grand-Hôtel for journalists and also for the actors who were performing the play.*]*

Let me ask my guests for permission to drink their health.

I am in debt to everyone here, and I wish to begin with a few words of thanks. I wish to thank the gifted and generous writers and notable celebrities around me for their presence, their attendance, and their kind support. I wish to thank the personnel, as represented by the director, of the magnificent national theatre* that is linked with the beginning and end of half a century of my life. I wish to thank my dear and devoted helpers, the excellent artists who are showered with applause every night by the public. [*Cries of 'Bravo!'*]

I shan't mention any specific names, because I'd have to name every one of them. However [*Victor Hugo turns toward Mademoiselle Sarah Bernhardt**], allow me, Madame, to make one exception—an exception that is permitted, indeed demanded, by your sex.

You have just shown yourself to be not only the rival, but the equal of three great actresses—Mademoiselle Mars, Madame Dorval, and Mademoiselle Favart*—who have preceded you in the role of Doña Sol.

Let me go further. I have the right to say this, because I, alas, saw the production in 1830. [*Laughter in approval.*] You have surpassed and eclipsed Mademoiselle Mars. That is indeed a glorious thing. You are a queen twice over—a queen of beauty, and a queen of talent. [*Victor Hugo bends over and kisses Mademoiselle Sarah Bernhardt's hand, with the following words.*] Madame, I thank you! [*Enthusiastic applause.*]

Ladies and gentlemen, what is this gathering? It's a simple banquet, entirely friendly and entirely literary. Gatherings of such a kind have always been welcome, even—and especially—in stormy and difficult times.

No word will be said here that could refer to an enthusiasm for anything other than the ideal and the absolute—which we all share.

We're in a realm of peace. We're meeting on the serene plateau of pure spirits. There are storms around us; there are none among us. [*Applause.*]

It's a good thing for the literary world to shed its bright, cloudless light on the political world. It's a good thing for our realm of peace to offer the realms of conflict a great example—the example of harmony—and an admirable sight—the sight of brotherhood. [*Triple volley of applause.*]

I was going to stop there, but your applause encourages me to keep going; let me therefore say a few words more.

People of my age, ladies and gentlemen, generally have—generally end up having—some fixed idea. A fixed idea is like a fixed star: the darker the night may be, the more brilliantly the star shines. [*Reaction.*]

It's the same with an idea. My idea seems to me all the more dazzling in times of greater gloom. I'll tell you what this fixed idea is. It's peace.

All my life, from my youthful beginnings to these final days of old age, I've always tried to bring peace—peace for the mind, peace for the soul, peace for the heart. I've hoped for the abolition of war, the abolition of hatred; the nations engaged only in work, industry, welfare, progress, and prosperity by peaceful means. [*Reaction. Applause.*]

I still retain that hope—in spite of all past or future trials—and until my very last breath I'll never weary of striving to make it a reality.

When Corneille, the aged Corneille, the great Corneille, felt himself close to death, he emitted a magnificent desire for glory, a final great outcry, in the words: 'As I face death, I am striving to shine bright.'*

Well, ladies and gentlemen, if anyone had the right to speak after Corneille, and if I myself were allowed to express my own ultimate desire, I'd say: 'As I face death, I am striving to bring peace.' [*Prolonged applause, intense emotion.*]

That, ladies and gentlemen, is the significance, the meaning, the goal of this meeting, this brotherly love-feast. It has no hidden implications or misunderstandings—nothing but what is great, and good, and generous. [*Volley of applause. 'Hear, hear!'*]

All of us here—poets, thinkers, writers, artists—have two home-lands: one is France, the other is art. [*Intense applause.*]

Yes, art is a homeland; it's a city with these eternal radiant citizens: Homer, Aeschylus, Sophocles, Aristophanes, Theocritus, Plautus, Lucretius, Virgil, Horace, Juvenal, Dante, Shakespeare, Rabelais, Molière, Corneille, Voltaire...* [*Unanimous shout: '... Victor Hugo!'*]

And another city—less populous, but equally great—is what we might call our national history, with its equally great citizens: Charlemagne, Roland, Du Guesclin, Bayard, Turenne, Condé, Villars, Vauban, Hoche, Marceau, Kléber, Mirabeau.* [*Renewed applause.*]

Well, dear colleagues, dear guests, we belong to those two cities. Let's be proud of them; and allow me to say, when I drink your health, that I'm drinking the health of our two homelands: the mighty realm of France, and the mighty realm of art!

AFTER THE EXILE II: 1878–1885

«Soudain La Porte S'ouvre . . .»

Soudain la porte s'ouvre et les danses, les pas,
L'orchestre, les chansons, les rires, tout s'arrête.
Et la mort dit: Je viens, quoique l'on ne m'ait pas
     Invitée à la fête.

Dernières Volontés

Je donne cinquante mille francs aux pauvres.

Je désire être porté au cimetière dans leur corbillard.

Je refuse l'oraison de tous les églises; je demande une prière à toutes les âmes.

Je crois en Dieu.

Dernier Vers

C'est ici le combat du jour et de la nuit.

'Suddenly the door opened . . .'

Suddenly the door opened; the gavotte,
The song, the music, and the laughter ceased.
And Death said: 'Here I am, though I was not
        Invited to the feast.'

Last Wishes

I give fifty thousand francs to the poor.
I wish to be borne to the grave in a pauper's hearse.
I reject the rites of all the churches; I request a prayer from
every soul.
I believe in God.

Last Line

This is the struggle between day and night.

APPENDIX

THE STRUCTURE OF THE *CONTEMPLATIONS*, *THE LEGEND OF THE AGES*, AND *GOD*

'One of the characteristics of the present age', wrote Hugo's colleague Michelet in a letter dated 12 December 1857, 'is a desire for what is alive. And however brilliant it may be, nothing is alive unless it is organic—in other words, interlinked, or if possible, strongly unified . . . *Organic unity* alone brings success nowadays.'

Hugo strove to give his poetry collections that kind of 'organic unity'. Though the individual poems can be understood and enjoyed separately, they are 'interlinked' and 'unified' by being arranged in a certain sequence. This applies particularly to his three largest verse projects, *Contemplations*, *The Legend of the Ages*, and *God*.

The present Appendix summarizes the contents of those collections, and lists the poems from each that have been translated in the following bilingual volumes:

C   Victor Hugo, *Contemplations, Lyrics, and Dramatic Monologues*, ed. E. H. and A. M. Blackmore (North Charleston, SC: Imprint Books, 2002).

E   Victor Hugo, *The Major Epics of Victor Hugo*, ed. E. H. and A. M. Blackmore, 2 vols. (Lewiston, NY: Edwin Mellen Press, 2002).

N   *Six French Poets of the Nineteenth Century*, ed. E. H. and A. M. Blackmore (Oxford: Oxford University Press, 2000).

S   Victor Hugo, *Selected Poems of Victor Hugo*, ed. E. H. and A. M. Blackmore (Chicago: University of Chicago Press, 2001).

Poems included in the present volume are asterisked. Page numbers are added for the convenience of those who wish to read the poems in sequence; 'N57', for example, is p. 57 in *Six French Poets of the Nineteenth Century*.

from *Contemplations*

In its final form, *Contemplations* is divided into six books. Books I to III form the first volume, 'Then' ('Autrefois'), and are concerned with the narrator's life before the death of his daughter: his adolescence and early literary struggles (Book I), his private life and love during early adulthood (Book II), and his public life in society (Book III). Books IV to VI form the second volume, 'Now' ('Aujourd'hui'), and trace the narrator's life after the death of the daughter: his private sufferings in response to the bereavement (Book IV), his continuing public life and concern with social problems (Book V), and his meditations on the underlying philosophical issues (Book VI).

from *The Legend of the Ages*

In its final form, *The Legend of the Ages* contains four main blocks of material. Parts I to IV survey what Hugo called, in an 1877 manuscript note, 'the world of the gods'—the negative forces of priestcraft and false religion, their impact on human history, and the struggle against them. Parts V to XXXIV study the analogous 'world of the kings', from the despots of earliest prehistory to those of the poet's own day; parts XXXV to LVIII then reread the same story, noting the counterbalancing 'world of the people'—the love and personal integrity seen by Hugo as underlying humanity's perennial resistance to its tyrants. Finally, Parts LIX to LXI contemplate 'the world of God'.

God

In its final form, *God*, like the *Contemplations* and *The Legend of the Ages*, consists of an unnumbered prologue followed by a sequence of numbered parts. In the prologue ('The Threshold of the Abyss'), the narrator sets out in search of God but is impeded by various voices warning him of the difficulties that lie ahead. He is told that death will answer his question— but when he dies (in the prologue's final section), he finds himself still infinitely distant from his goal; he sees ahead an endless succession of winged creatures, proclaiming successive approximations to the truth about God. The speeches of the first eight creatures form Parts I to VIII of the poem; just as the ninth begins to speak, the poem breaks off— indicating that the series could be extended for ever. 'God is the infinite', Hugo wrote on his manuscript. 'He recedes endlessly—no transformation of life catches up with him—One merely goes forward in the light.'

The material listed below reconstructs and translates the full extant text of the poem, as Hugo left it at his death; the author's last surviving instructions regarding presentation and arrangement of each section have been followed. This reconstruction differs from previously printed texts in two major respects. All previous editions expanded 'The Threshold of the Abyss' with material that Hugo either never intended to include in the poem or else ultimately decided to omit from it (as his note on MS 106/82a and his marginal annotations to the poem indicate). Moreover, all previous editions either misplaced the death episode or made no attempt to insert it (overlaps on Hugo's manuscripts demonstrate that he intended to place it at the end of the prologue). The evidence for our reconstruction is summarized in *Six French Poets of the Nineteenth Century*, ed. E. H. and A. M. Blackmore (Oxford, 2000), 301–2, 305.

God is nowadays perhaps more highly regarded than any other single Hugo poem. John Porter Houston, in his classic introductory survey, calls it 'to my mind Hugo's most enthralling book' (*Victor Hugo*, 2nd edn. (Boston, 1988), 151); the standard English-language bibliography not only finds 'Hugo's poetic masterpiece' here, but also says that it 'contains probably the highest poetry written in French' (David Bagueley (ed.), *A Critical Bibliography of French Literature, v. The Nineteenth Century* (Syracuse, NY, 1994), 212). It is therefore appropriate that it should be the first volume of Hugo's nondramatic poetry to be fully available in English.

EXPLANATORY NOTES

Technical terms, proper names, and other obscurities are annotated only on their first appearance in each extract. The specified date of writing is generally that when the passage was completed; if Hugo worked for a long time on a piece before completing it, or if he later made substantial changes to it, these points are also noted.

The Song of the Circus

Written January 1824. Ode XIII in *New Odes* (1824); Ode IV. xi in the 1828 and subsequent editions of *Odes and Ballads*.

3 *Augustus*: Roman emperor (died 14 CE), who overthrew the republic and permanently established the imperial system of government in Rome.

Hail . . . from those about to die!: the gladiators' customary greeting to the emperor when they entered the arena.

Hyrcanian tigers and Hibernian brutes: tigers from Hyrcania, in northern Persia; human captives from northern Europe, on the war-torn fringe of the Roman empire.

Aediles: ancient Roman magistrates.

5 *Vestals*: virgin priestesses serving the Roman goddess of domesticity.

Praetorian soldiers . . . Gangeans: the Roman emperor's official guard; people born near the Ganges River in India, at the extreme eastern border of the Roman empire.

Cybele: major goddess of ancient Phrygia (now in Turkey).

Irminsul . . . Mani: a wooden pillar worshipped by the ancient Saxons, and a Persian religious leader of the third century CE (the founder of Manichaeism).

Consul: an annually elected magistrate; one of the supreme officials in ancient Rome.

Gauls: the ancestors of the modern French.

To a Traveller

Written 22 October 1825. Ballad X in *Odes and Ballads* (1826 and all subsequent editions); in the first edition, it was the collection's final poem.

7 *Mad Song*: the epigraph is Hugo's own composition; he reused it a year or two later in his play *Cromwell*, IV. i (1827).

Zara Bathing

Written July 1828; poem XIX in *Orientalia* (1829).

9 *Illysus*: a stream near Athens; site of a temple sacred to the Muses in ancient times.

13 *griffins*: mythical creatures, half eagle and half lion.

Preface to *Cromwell*

Written 30 September–27 October 1827; published 4 December 1827, as the preface to Hugo's drama *Cromwell*. The play itself attracted comparatively little attention; the preface was widely attacked (especially by those who resented its advocacy of Shakespeare in preference to Racine), and perhaps no one other than its author accepted every detail of it, but even its most vehement opponents generally conceded the literary skill with which the train of thought was developed.

16 *an official censorship ban ... an infallible theatre committee*: censorship (usually applied on political grounds) had been re-established by law in June 1827; the committee of France's leading theatre, the Comédie-Française, tended to reject unconventional or innovative plays.

solus, pauper, nudus: Hugo is recalling the description of the church at Laodicea (Revelation 3: 17) in the Latin Vulgate translation.

driven critics to attack him: the preface to Hugo's *New Odes* (1824) had provoked a long controversy in the journals; the dispute revived after the publication of his *Odes and Ballads* (1826, with a new preface).

17 *Che sera, sera*: 'What will be, shall be' (Italian proverb, less familiar in France than in the English-speaking world).

Académie: the Académie française, France's leading literary body, a traditional court of appeal in aesthetic debates.

the Spanish storyteller: Tomás de Iriarte, in his *Fabulas literarias* (1782).

Goliaths: an allusion to the boy David's defeat of the Philistine giant Goliath using a slingshot (1 Samuel 17).

18 *poetry woke with him*: compare the opening section of 'The Consecration of Woman', *The Legend of the Ages*, II. i (p. 295).

the Book of Genesis: the first part of the Law of Moses in the Hebrew Scriptures, dealing with the creation of the world and the early history of the human race; Hugo consistently regards it as dating essentially from the time of Moses (perhaps fifteenth century BCE). Though usually set as prose in modern editions, much of it is written in an irregular rhythmic form not readily categorized as either prose or verse (indeed, Claus Westermann, *Genesis 1–11* (London, 1984), 90, speaks of 'a fusion of poetry and prose' in its opening chapter); Hugo is therefore able to assimilate it to the ode, the most metrically irregular type of poetry recognized by traditional literary criticism.

19 *Homer*: here and elsewhere, Hugo accepts the traditional view that the two major Greek epics of the eighth century BCE, the *Iliad* and *Odyssey*, were written by a single author named Homer.

Pindar ... Herodotus: though conventionally classified as 'lyric' because they were sung with lyre accompaniment, the works of the archaic Greek poet Pindar are characterized by a grandeur and sublimity recalling those of the Homeric epics; both he and the pioneer historian Herodotus lived during the fifth century BCE.

rhapsodists: specialist reciters of epic poetry in ancient Greece.

20 *Prometheus . . . The Phoenician Women*: Hugo's first two examples are drawn from the tragedies *Prometheus Bound* by Aeschylus (mid-fifth century BCE) and *The Phoenician Women* by Euripides (late fifth century BCE).

Achilles . . . Troy: in the *Iliad*, xxii. 395ff., the body of the Trojan hero Hector is tied behind the chariot of his slayer, the Greek Achilles, and dragged around in front of the walls of Troy.

Virgil: the Latin epic poet Publius Vergilius Maro (died 19 BCE), whose *Aeneid* is consciously modelled on the *Iliad* and *Odyssey*.

A spiritual religion: the religion of Christ.

21 *Pythagoras . . . Plato*: familiar names evoking the successive ages of Greek philosophy and its sporadic anticipations of the teachings of Christ: Pythagoras (sixth century BCE), Socrates (fifth century BCE), Plato (fourth century BCE), and Epicurus (third century BCE).

theogony: family of gods.

Its gods required a cloud . . . its heaven was a mountain: in the world of the ancient epics, the king of the gods, Zeus, wraps himself and his consort Hera in a cloud when they copulate, so that no one will see them (*Iliad*, xiv. 342–5); Ares, the god of war, is wounded by the mortal Diomedes (*Iliad*, v. 855–63); Hephaistos, the blacksmith god, is thrown from heaven by Zeus and permanently lamed by his fall (*Iliad*, i. 590–4); thunderbolts are made of 'three streaks of hail twisted together' (Hugo quotes *Aeneid*, viii. 429); the world is suspended by a golden chain from the hand of Zeus; the sun-god Helios travels across the sky in a chariot; the underworld can be entered from the crater of Lake Avernus (*Aeneid*, vi. 235–63); the gods dwell in bliss on Mount Olympus.

Ajax . . . Mars: the Greek hero Ajax defies the gods in *Odyssey*, iv. 499–505. In the Homeric poems, the warrior Achilles is nowhere specifically compared to the god of war Mars (Ares); Hugo means simply that the former seems as imposing as the latter.

22 *Cato*: the Stoic statesman Marcus Porcius Cato (died 46 BCE), who committed suicide when his political opponent Julius Caesar was victorious.

23 *Longinus . . . Augustine*: the unknown author of the famous critical work *On the Sublime* (first century CE, formerly attributed to the third-century philosopher Longinus); Augustine of Hippo (died 430), Latin theologian noted for his insistence on the universality of original sin and the predestined damnation of the wicked.

24 *less precise . . . words*: Hugo repeatedly stressed that the words 'Romantic' and 'Classical' have no precise meaning; the point is made particularly in the preface to *New Odes* (1824), to which he refers below.

24 [*Note*] *a famous foreign writer*: unidentified.

[*Note*] *Callot . . . David*: Jacques Callot (1592–1635), French engraver and etcher noted for the squalor and realism of his later works; Benvenuto Cellini (1500–71), flamboyant Italian sculptor; and three painters whose intensely emotional pictures have sometimes been seen as precursors of Romantic art: the Italians Salvator Rosa (1615–73) and Bonifacio Veronese (Bonifacio de' Pitati, died 1553 or 1557), and the Spaniard Bartolomé Estéban Murillo (1617–82). Hugo contrasts them with the neoclassical French painter Jacques-Louis David (1748–1825), whose works have often been criticized as cold and academic.

[*Note*] *Job . . . Campistron*: the suffering heroes of the Hebrew Book of Job and Sophocles' tragedy *Philoctetes* (409 BCE) are set against the decorous characters favoured by the minor French dramatist Jean Galbert de Campistron (1656–1723).

25 *Aristotle . . . La Harpe*: two influential literary critics—the Greek philosopher Aristotle (fourth century BCE) and the French poet Nicolas Boileau (1636–1711)—deflated by association with a decidedly less illustrious third: the conservative French critic Jean François de La Harpe (1739–1803).

Thersites . . . Silenus: the cowardly Greek soldier Thersites of the *Iliad* and the lame blacksmith god Hephaistos (identified with the Roman Vulcan); two celebrated comic scenes in Euripides' tragedies *Helen*, 434–82 and *Orestes*, 1506–30 (Hugo cites the traditional Renaissance act-divisions, not generally supplied in modern editions); various minor deities of Classical mythology: the Tritons (sea-gods), Satyrs (rural deities, half human and half goat), Cyclopes (one-eyed giant blacksmiths toiling in forges underneath volcanoes), Sirens (female monsters whose singing lured men to destruction), Furies (female avengers sent by the gods to torment the guilty), Fates (goddesses who determined the life and death of all mortals), and Harpies (cruel and vindictive monsters, half woman and half bird); Polyphemus, the brutish giant who kills the nymph Galatea's lover in Ovid, *Metamorphoses*, xiii. 738–897; Silenus, a drunken gluttonous attendant of Bacchus, who feasts with the comparably ignoble Phrygian king Midas in *Metamorphoses*, xi. 90–9.

Eumenides: as Hugo notes in the Conclusion to *Napoleon the Little* (p. 221), the name is an attempt to appease the Furies by flattering them.

26 *the Olympians . . . Plautus*: the Olympians (the gods dwelling on Mount Olympus) are contrasted with Thespis (the legendary inventor of drama), and the Greek tragic dramatists Aeschylus, Sophocles, and Euripides (all fifth century BCE) with the comic dramatists Aristophanes of Greece (fifth century BCE) and Plautus of Rome (died 184 BCE).

Hercules . . . in his lionskin: Philostratus, *Imagines*, ii. 22, tells the story that the Greek hero Hercules was attacked in his sleep by Egyptian pygmies, but simply caught them in his lionskin and carried them to Eurystheus.

horns and cloven hoofs and the wings of a bat: attributes first assigned to Satan in Roman Catholic tradition during the early centuries CE.

Dante . . . Faust: the poets Dante Alighieri (1265–1321) and John Milton (1608–74) depicted hell in their *Inferno* and *Paradise Lost* respectively. Michelangelo Buonarotti (1475–1564), as one of the most majestic Renaissance artists, provides a natural contrast to Callot (whom Hugo has already discussed). Scaramouche, Crispino, and Harlequin are characters of the Italian *commedia dell'arte*, popular in Renaissance times and later. Sganarelle is the boorish servant of the sceptical Juan in Molière's *Dom Juan* (1665), and Mephistopheles is the demonic attendant of the sceptical protagonist in all versions of the Faust story.

[*Note*] *Diogenes . . . the Scipios*: Hugo draws an analogy between Aristophanes and the famous Cynic philosopher Diogenes (fourth century BCE), preferring such uncouth personalities to Publius Terentius Afer (died 159 BCE), the most restrained and inoffensive of ancient comic dramatists (his works were long regarded as ideal school texts). Scipio the Elder (died 183 BCE) and the Younger (died 129 BCE) stand here as distinguished patricians in the social milieu courted by Terence.

27 *Lernaean hydra . . . Pluto*: in Classical mythology, the Lernaean hydra was a seven-headed dragon slain by Hercules in the second of his twelve famous labours; Pluto was the Roman god of the underworld. *Graouilli*, *chairsallée*, *drée*, and *tarasco* were dialectal French names for dragon-like creatures.

Rubens: Peter Paul Rubens (1577–1640), prolific and imaginative Flemish painter, the favourite court artist of his day.

28 *Tartarus . . . aspioles*: in Classical mythology, Tartarus was the underworld (or the lowest part of it); Naiads were water-nymphs, Tritons were sea-gods, and Zephyrs were wind-gods. In Dante's *Inferno*, Francesca da Rimini is the adulteress poignantly glimpsed in v. 73–142, and Count Ugolino is seen (xxxii. 125–xxxiii. 90) gnawing the brain of the archbishop who starved him to death in the Tower of Famine, while Beatrice is the poet's heavenly guide in his *Paradiso*. Hugo's list of graveyard-haunting creatures ('vampires, ogres', etc.) derives from Charles Nodier's much-loved *Smarra* (1821); the *aspioles*, indeed, seem to have been invented by Nodier.

Goujon: Jean Goujon (1510–69), French sculptor.

Juliet . . . Figaro: characters from plays by Shakespeare (Juliet from *Romeo and Juliet*, Desdemona and Iago from *Othello*, Ophelia and Polonius from *Hamlet*, Falstaff from the *Henry IV* plays and *The Merry Wives of Windsor*), Molière (Harpagon from *L'Avare*, and the title characters of *Tartuffe* and *Les Fourberies de Scapin*), and Beaumarchais (Basilio, Bartolo, and Figaro from *Le Barbier de Séville* and *Le Mariage de Figaro*).

28 [*Note*] *Erlking*: Goethe's 'Erlkönig' (1782).

29 *Persius . . . Apuleius*: four Latin satirists of the first and second centuries CE: Persius and Juvenal in verse, and Petronius (author of the *Satyricon*) and Apuleius (author of the *Golden Ass*) in prose.

romanceros . . . they could possibly find: the *romanceros* are collections of medieval Spanish ballads; the quotation is taken from lines 10357–8 (by Jean de Meung) of the thirteenth-century French allegorical poem *Le Roman de la rose*.

30 *Scarron . . . Rabelais*: Paul Scarron (1610–60), scurrilous French satirist, a husband of Madame de Maintenon (later the mistress of Louis XIV); Ludovico Ariosto (1474–1533), Italian epic poet, author of the *Orlando furioso*; Miguel de Cervantes (1547–1616), Spanish novelist, author of *Don Quixote*; François Rabelais (died 1553), French prose writer, author of *Gargantua* and *Pantagruel*. Hugo's footnote pays graceful tribute to the influence of his friend Charles Nodier (1780–1844), remembered as a writer of short stories.

Beauty and the Beast: fairy tale whose definitive form was established in 1757 by Madame Leprince de Beaumont.

Veronese: Paolo Veronese (1528–88), influential Italian Renaissance painter. In the next clause, the Rubens painting is clearly, from Hugo's description, the so-called *Small Last Judgement* in Munich (Antwerp is the home of the equally well-known *Descent from the Cross*).

as Dante says of Homer: in *Inferno*, iv. 88.

31 *Adam . . . Othello*: the first three characters come from Genesis; Achilles from the *Iliad;* Atreus and Orestes from Aeschylus' *Oresteia* and plays on the same subject by Sophocles and Euripides; and the last three characters from Shakespeare's tragedies.

Malherbe . . . Job: François de Malherbe (1555–1628), influential lyric poet; Jean Chapelain (1595–1674), author of a now-forgotten epic, *La Pucelle*; Pierre Corneille (1606–84), outstanding dramatist. Orpheus, according to Greek legend, was the first poet. The Hebrew Books of Kings are traditionally placed later than Genesis and earlier than Job in printed Bibles, but of course this need not reflect the order of composition (elsewhere, e.g. in *William Shakespeare*, I. ii. ii, Hugo dates Job even earlier than Genesis; their relative dates are still disputed).

32 *'what does it prove?'*: according to an oft-repeated eighteenth-century joke, a mathematician once went to a performance of Racine's tragedy *Phèdre* and came away asking 'What does it prove?'

'the French have no head for epics': from the 1732 French version of Voltaire's *Essai sur la poésie épique*, where the remark is attributed to the mathematician Nicolas de Malézieu (1650–1727).

Athalie . . . Revelation: Athalie is Jean Racine's last tragedy, first performed privately in 1691 (when it attracted little notice) and not staged in public until 1716; Ariel and Caliban are characters in Shakespeare's comedy *The Tempest*; the Revelation of Jesus Christ to John, prophesying (among other things) the doom of the wicked, is the final book of the Scriptures.

33 *in dramatic terms*: Milton's epic poem *Paradise Lost* (1667) was first planned, over a quarter of a century earlier, as a drama.

34 *The Lilliput Militia . . . its slightest movement will break them*: an allusion to the opening chapter of Jonathan Swift's *Gulliver's Travels* (1726).

Pourceaugnac: the protagonist of Molière's comedy *Monsieur de Pourceaugnac* (1669).

35 *says the judge . . . afraid of falling*: for 'Put him to death, and now let's go to dinner!' see Voltaire's *Socrate* (1759), III. i (and the 1761 footnote); for Domitian's turbot, Juvenal, *Satires*, iv. 37–143; for Socrates' incongruous remark about Aesculapius, Plato, *Phaedo*, 118a; and for Elizabeth I's cursing and Latin, Robert Cecil's report of her confrontation on 25 July 1597 with the Polish ambassador Paul Dzialynski: ' "God's death, my lords" (for that was her oath ever in anger), "I have been enforced this day to scour up my old Latin, that hath lain long in rusting!" ' Armand Jean du Plessis, Cardinal Richelieu (1585–1640), the most powerful man in France, was profoundly influenced by his secretary François Leclerc du Tremblay (Père Joseph, 1577–1638), the famous 'Grey Eminence'; Louis XI (1423–83) was similarly influenced by his barber Olivier le Daim (died 1484; on this subject, Hugo would expect his readers to be familiar with Walter Scott's 1823 novel *Quentin Durward*). The anecdotes about Cromwell come from Abel-François Villemain, *Histoire de Cromwell* (1819), i. 144, 215–16. According to Suetonius, *Julius Caesar*, xxxvii, Caesar nearly fell from his chariot during the triumphal procession after his conquest of Gaul. Napoleon's utterance is reported by Dominique de Pradt, *Histoire de l'ambassade dans le grand-duché de Varsovie* (1815), 215.

Heraclitus . . . Democritus: two contrasting Greek philosophers of the fifth century BCE, respectively a sombre mystic and a cheerful sceptic.

36 *Dandin . . . Don Juan*: characters from plays by Shakespeare (the nurse and Mercutio from *Romeo and Juliet*, the title character of *Richard III*, Osric from *Hamlet*), Pierre Corneille (Prusias from *Nicomède*), Molière (Trissotin from *Les Femmes savantes*, the title characters of *Tartuffe* and *Dom Juan*), Racine (Dandin from *Les Plaideurs*), Beaumarchais (Brid'oison from *Le Mariage de Figaro*, Bégears from *La Mère coupable*, Figaro from both), and Goethe (Mephistopheles from *Faust*).

law of the two unities: the law of the three unities, which derived from Renaissance commentaries on Aristotle's *Poetics*, demanded that a play should depict a single action occurring in a single place during the span of a single day; Boileau gives the classic statement of it in his *Art poétique*, iii. 45–6. Observance of the law was obligatory in French tragedy between the 1630s and the 1820s; the topic was therefore very much a live issue at the time when Hugo's preface was published.

36 *the Muses love alternation*: a quotation from Virgil, *Eclogues*, iii. 59.

37 *Melpomene*: in Classical mythology, the Muse of tragedy.

Rizzio . . . the Tuileries: in 1566, David Rizzio, the favourite of Mary Queen of Scots, was murdered in her bedroom by order of her husband Lord Darnley. Henri IV of France was assassinated in the public street in 1610. Joan of Arc was burnt at the stake in 1431, at Rouen (Hugo would expect his readers to think of Schiller's 1801 play *Die Jungfrau von Orleans*, in which Joan dies on the battlefield). The powerful Henri, Duc de Guise, was assassinated in 1588 at Blois, where his supporters seemed to be outnumbering the king's. Charles I of England and Louis XVI of France were beheaded at Whitehall in 1649 and at the Place de la Révolution (near the royal palace, the Tuileries) in 1793 respectively.

40 *Cid . . . Nicomède*: Hugo reviews the controversy aroused by Corneille's brilliant tragicomedy *Le Cid* (1637), which was accused of breaking the law of the three unities. The main accusers were Corneille's less successful literary rivals—Hugo names Jean Mairet (1604–86), Jean Claveret (died 1666), François, Abbé d'Aubignac (1604–76), and Georges de Scudéry (1601–67)—and, with Richelieu's support, they succeeded in having the play formally condemned by the Académie française. Hugo quotes from Corneille's *Lettre apologétique . . . contenant sa réponse aux Observations faites par le Sieur Scudéry* and from Scudéry's *Lettre . . . à l'illustre Académie* and *Preuve des passages allégués dans les Observations sur le Cid*; originally he cited the passages in modern spelling, but in revision he restored the period spelling to underline the archaic nature of the dispute. Scudéry invokes a flurry of illustrious names, including particularly those of the scholars Julius Caesar Scaliger (1484–1558) and Daniel Heinsius (1580–1655) and the poets Torquato Tasso (1544–95) and Battista Guarini (1538–1612, the author of the once-famous pastoral play *Il pastor fido*). Hugo compares *Le Cid* with Corneille's earlier comedies (*Mélite*, 1629–30; *La Galerie du palais*, 1631–4) and later Roman tragedies (among which he most admires *Nicomède*, 1651); he also recalls the *Edinburgh Review*'s celebrated negative judgement on Byron's first volume, *Hours of Idleness* (1807).

41 *Racine . . . the cup of reconciliation*: Racine's short lyrical play *Esther*, like his *Athalie*, was first performed privately (in 1689) and attracted little notice; for reasons of dramatic propriety, his tragedy *Britannicus* (1669) leaves the poisoner Locusta offstage (she is merely mentioned, IV. iv. 1409) and narrates rather than depicts the poisoning of Britannicus (v. v. 1638–64).

the Hebrew giant: Samson (Judges 16: 3).

Voltaire . . . wouldn't accept Shakespeare: his main criticisms are given in his *Lettre à l'Académie sur Shakespeare* (1776).

42 *'The Greeks . . . in the days of Shakespeare'*: the quotation, from Voltaire's *Discours sur la tragédie* (1731), alludes to Euripides' *Hippolytus*,

Sophocles' *Philoctetes* and *Oedipus Rex*, and Aeschylus' *Choephori*, *Prometheus Bound*, and *Eumenides*.

43 *Richelet*: César Pierre Richelet (1631–98), French grammarian and critic.

Lope de Vega: the quotation is from his *Arte nuevo de hacer comedias* (1609), 40–1.

Sosie: in Molière's comedy *Amphitryon*, the god Mercury disguises himself as the servant Sosie.

[*Note*] *Scott . . . Deschamps*: the novels of Walter Scott (1771–1832) were immensely popular in nineteenth-century Europe and were frequently turned into plays and operas. Amable Tastu (1798–1885) was a poet and children's writer; the translation of *Romeo and Juliet* by Émile Deschamps (1791–1871) was completed in 1829 and is still partly familiar, as it provided the text for Berlioz's symphony.

45 *Vaugelas and Richelet*: the grammarian Claude Favre de Vaugelas (1585–1650), author of *Remarques sur la langue française* (1647), long regarded as an authority on matters of taste; Richelet, already mentioned, appears here as the author of *La Versification française* (1671).

[*Note*] *Goethe . . . Faust*: the quotation is from an 1820 review of Manzoni's tragedy *Il conte di Carmagnola* (Goethe, *Sämtliche Werke*, vol. 13.1. *Die Jahre 1820–1826*, ed. Gisela Henckmann and Irmela Schneider (Munich, 1992), 356). In reply, Hugo alludes to the title characters of Goethe's play *Faust* (the first part, 1808; the second part was of course still unpublished) and his novel *Die Leiden des jungen Werthers* (1774).

47 *Delille . . . Homeric catalogue*: the prolific but notoriously mediocre poet Jacques Delille (1738–1813); the much-imitated catalogue of ships in *Iliad*, ii. 484–877.

48 '*chicken in the pot*' . . . '*a purple rag is sewn on*': in Jean-Baptiste Legouvé's tragedy *La Mort de Henri IV* (1806), the king's celebrated remark 'I want the poorest peasant in my kingdom to have a chicken in the pot on Sunday' was reduced to a statement about 'The type of nutriment reserved for ease'. The quotation about the purple robe is from Horace, *Ars poetica*, 15–16.

A herd of men . . . in Agrippina's bed: the references are to Corneille's *Cinna*, IV. i. 1493, *Le Cid*, III. iv. 987, *Nicomède*, I. i. 22 and II. iii. 564, and *Horace*, III. v. 1009; and to Racine's *Athalie*, II. v. 506 and *Britannicus*, IV. ii. 1137.

'*sbodikins*: *ventre-saint-gris*, a favourite oath of Henri IV.

'*fountain of waters*': an aptly scriptural phrase; in particular, Hugo is recalling Jeremiah 2: 13 and/or 17: 13 ('they have forsaken the Lord, the fountain of living waters').

50 *caesuras*: natural pauses within lines of verse. In seventeenth- and eighteenth-century French verse, there was generally a distinct pause after the sixth syllable of a standard twelve-syllable line; Hugo and his contemporaries advocated greater variety in the placement of caesuras.

50 *Proteus*: in Classical mythology, a sea-god who had the ability to change his shape.

[*Note*] *Talma*: François Joseph Talma (1763–1826), reputed the leading French actor of his day.

52 *Lhomond ... Pascal*: two influential grammarians, Charles François Lhomond (1727–94) and Pierre Restaut (1696–1764); four successive major prose writers, François Rabelais (died 1553), Michel de Montaigne (1533–92), Blaise Pascal (1623–62), and Charles de Montesquieu (1689–1755).

Joshuas: Joshua, who had led the Israelites into the Promised Land, commanded the sun to stop (Joshua 10: 12–14).

Iriarte: Hugo cited Iriarte earlier in the Preface; but we have not traced this particular phrase in his works.

53 *'Systems ... can't fit through a couple of others'*: a quotation from the article 'Barbe' in Voltaire's *Dictionnaire philosophique* (1764).

It's theory, not poetry: the closing paragraphs of the Preface deal exclusively with Hugo's play *Cromwell*, and are therefore not included in this selection.

Joanny

Written 7 March 1830; the title was supplied by Hugo's literary executors. Hugo's drama *Hernani* was first performed by France's leading dramatic company, the Comédie-Française, on 25 (not 28) February 1830. It created a furore, and the performances became a public battleground between supporters and opponents of Romanticism.

53 *Théâtre français*: theatre where the Comédie-Française usually performs.

54 *Mademoiselle Mars ... Joanny*: Mademoiselle Mars (Anne Boutet, 1779–1847) played Doña Sol in the original production of *Hernani*; Pierre-Marie Michelot (1786–1856) played Hernani; Joanny (Jean-Baptiste Brissabarre, 1778–1849) played Ruy Gomez.

Madame Dorval's husband, Monsieur Merle: the actress Marie Dorval (1798–1849) was (and is) much more famous than her journalist husband.

Don Diego ... Corneille: Don Diego is the white-haired father of the protagonist in Pierre Corneille's celebrated tragicomedy *Le Cid* (1637); the original performer of the part is indeed 'now forgotten', but may possibly have been André Baron. Joanny's parallel is a remarkably deft one: *Le Cid* also provoked intense controversy and marked the arrival of a new fashion in French drama.

from *Journal of the Ideas and Opinions of a Revolutionary of 1830*

Written 1830–4; published in *A Blend of Literature and Philosophy* (1834). The diary-like arrangement of the maxims is purely a literary strategy, and does not always reflect the dates of composition.

54 *July 1830*: in July 1830 a revolution overthrew the absolute monarchy of the House of Bourbon, and replaced it with a constitutional monarchy under Louis-Philippe.

55 *Louis XIV*: his reign (1643–1715) marked the zenith of absolute royal power in France.

'divine right' . . . *'grace of God'*: the hereditary kings of France claimed that they had been given authority to rule by the grace of God; any challenge to their authority was thus seen as an act of disobedience to God.

1688 . . . *1789*: the revolution in England that replaced James II with William III and Mary II (often regarded in liberal circles as a milestone in establishing the people's right to choose their own rulers), and the revolution in France that ultimately replaced the monarchy with a republic.

56 *the Bourbon monarchy*: the absolute monarchy overthrown in July 1830.

the July Revolution: the revolution of July 1830.

Benjamin Constant: Benjamin Constant de Rebecque (1767–1830), French politician and writer, whose advocacy of moderate liberalism during the 1820s may have been one of the factors that made the July Revolution possible.

57 *Goethe . . . Pius VIII*: Johann Wilhelm von Goethe (1749–1832; the widespread rumours of his death in 1830 were false), German writer, whose work Hugo never greatly admired; Pius VIII (1761–1830), who had been pope for only twenty months but had seemed to approve of France's July Revolution. Hugo would probably have considered that all three 'popes' had made mild contributions to human progress, but that the real work still remained to be done.

Final Pages (Undated): these pages were published on 19 September 1833. 'Undated' is Hugo's own designation.

a king: Nebuchadnezzar of Babylon (Daniel 4).

a senate that made gods, a conclave that makes saints: the ancient Roman senate voted to bestow divine honours on deceased emperors; the modern Roman Catholic conclave elects popes.

Mirabeau . . . Napoleon . . . Robespierre: the statesman Honoré-Gabriel, Comte de Mirabeau (1749–91), an advocate of constitutional monarchy, played a crucial part in the early stages of the French Revolution and was elected president of the Constituent Assembly on 30 January 1791, but died soon after. Napoleon Bonaparte (1759–1821) first rose to prominence as a result of his spectacular military successes in Italy during 1796. The most influential political figure of the intervening period was Maximilien Robespierre (1758–94), who was largely responsible for the Reign of Terror.

58 *Shakespeare . . . Napoleon*: the dramatists William Shakespeare (1564–1616) and Molière (Jean-Baptiste Poquelin, 1622–73) were vilified by

some of their contemporaries; Christopher Columbus (1451–1506) was imprisoned in 1500 and disgraced as a result of conflict with those under his command; Bernard of Clairvaux (1090–1153) became involved in profound theological controversy with Abelard and others; Napoleon Bonaparte (1769–1821) was opposed, even at the height of his success, by numerous conspirators (Hugo's godfather Victor Lahorie was among them).

Notre-Dame

Written 17 October 1830; chapter III. i of *Notre-Dame de Paris* (1831). Hugo's major sources for the novel included Pierre Matthieu, *Histoire de Louys XI* (1628), Philippe de Commines, *Mémoires* (1706–14 edn.), Jacques Du Breul, *Le Théâtre des antiquités de Paris* (1612), and Henri Sauval, *Histoire et recherche des antiquités de la ville de Paris* (1724); some of these are cited by him in the text.

Although many English translations have entitled the novel *The Hunchback of Notre-Dame*, Hugo saw the cathedral itself as the book's real protagonist. In some ways, therefore, the present chapter is the true heart of the work and contains the most searching exploration of several of its most central concerns: the passage of time; the advance and regression of human civilization; the oppression of humanity and art by tyranny and convention, and the ability of humanity and art to survive and triumph over such oppression. The chapter exerted a profound influence on public attitudes to the preservation of historic monuments in France.

58 *Charlemagne . . . Philippe Auguste*: the French kings Charles the Great (died 814) and Philippe II (1165–1223). The existing cathedral of Notre-Dame was begun in 1163, and the high altar was dedicated in 1189; but major additions were still being made in the fourteenth century.

Tempus edax, homo edacior: 'Time the devourer, humanity the greater devourer'. The first phrase is from Ovid, *Metamorphoses*, xv. 234; the second is Hugo's addition.

ogive: the characteristically Gothic pointed arch. An ogive doorway is a doorway capped by such an arch.

59 *the Iliad and the romanceros*: the ancient Greek epic, and the printed collections of medieval Spanish ballads on epic and historical themes.

its chroniclers: the quotation is drawn from Du Breul, *Théâtre*, 6.

Childebert: Childebert I (died 558), king of the Franks.

Biscornette . . . Louis XV: the former (twelfth century) was responsible for the ironwork of Notre-Dame's doors; the latter reigned from 1715 to 1774.

60 *Hercandus . . . Louis XIII*: Hercandus was bishop of Paris in the ninth century; the repair of the altar, vowed by Louis XIII in 1638, was accomplished under Louis XIV in 1699.

its Constable: Charles de Bourbon (1490–1527), whose treason consisted of supporting the Holy Roman Emperor Charles V against the French in 1523.

Sauval: the quotation comes from Sauval, *Histoire des antiquités*, ii. 209.

61 *Catherine de Médicis . . . Madame du Barry*: the former (1519–89) was the wife of Henri II; the latter (1741–93) was a mistress of Louis XV—as Hugo's image reminds us, she died not with the stoicism of most aristocrats who faced the guillotine, but shrieking and pleading frantically for mercy.

Luther . . . Vignola: Martin Luther (1583–1646), German religious reformer; Honoré-Gabriel, Comte de Mirabeau (1749–91), French revolutionary leader; Marcus Vitruvius Pollio (first century BCE), and Giacomo da Vignola (1507–73), influential Classical or Classicizing writers on architecture.

the Parthenon: fifth century BCE building at Athens, dedicated to Athena Parthenos; a model, or an excuse, for many generations of architects.

62 *Cenalis . . . Herostratus*: Robert Céneau (Cenalis, 1483–1560), French bishop and historian. The temple of Artemis (identified with the Roman goddess Diana) at Ephesus, one of the seven wonders of the ancient world, was burned down in the fourth century BCE—according to legend, by a certain Herostratus, who did it simply because he wanted to become famous (Strabo, xiv. 640). The quotation comes from Du Breul, *Théâtre*, 10.

the Abbey of Tournus . . . Bourges Cathedral: the Benedictine Abbey of Saint-Philibert at Tournus, built in the late eleventh century, and the Cathedral of Saint-Étienne at Bourges, built around 1200.

63 *abbey of Saint-Germain-des-Prés . . . Saint-Jacques-de-la-Boucherie*: the former was founded by Childebert I and consecrated about 558, though it was subsequently rebuilt several times; the latter was founded in the tenth century, expanded during the next few centuries, and destroyed (except for its sixteenth-century tower) in 1797—hence Hugo's past tense.

Gregory VII . . . Flamel: Pope Gregory VII (died 1085) proclaimed the supremacy of the pope over earthly rulers and thus marks the culmination of papal power, which Luther was to challenge several centuries later; the French scholar Nicholas Flamel (1330–1418) was reputed to be an alchemist and magician.

Cyclopean ruins: Mycenaean ruins; due to the huge size of their component stones, they were believed in Classical times to have been the work of the legendary Cyclopes.

64 *'the works are broken off in suspense'*: a quotation from Virgil, *Aeneid*, iv. 88.

[Note] Tho' various features . . . in ev'ry face: Ovid, *Metamorphoses*, ii. 13–14 (Addison's translation).

65 *Jumièges Abbey ... Rouen Cathedral*: most of Hugo's examples are familiar architectural showpieces: the Abbey of Saint-Philibert at Jumièges, begun in 1040; Rheims Cathedral, begun in 1210; the Cathedral of Sainte-Croix at Orleans, begun in 1610 (not completed till 1829, and despite its dates, more Gothic than Renaissance); the Tour Guinette at Étampes and the Basilica at Saint-Denis, both built in the mid-twelfth century; the Abbey of Saint-Georges at Boscherville, begun in 1113; Rouen Cathedral, begun in 1200, though its Tour de Beurre dates from the early sixteenth century.

An Impartial Peep at the Magistrates of Old

Written 29 September 1830; chapter VI. i of *Notre-Dame de Paris* (1831). For Hugo's sources, see the note to the preceding selection.

66 *the comet*: Halley's comet; on its appearance in 1456 (not 1465), Pope Callistus III instructed all Catholics to pray for deliverance from 'the Devil, the Turk, and the Comet'. In the same year, Callistus appointed his nephew Rodrigo Borgia (the future Pope Alexander VI) a cardinal.

'a dignity ... with many rights and prerogatives': the quotation comes from Sauval, *Histoire des antiquités*, iii. 230.

d'Estouteville ... Tristan l'Hermite: the historical Robert d'Estouteville died in 1479. Louis XI married Charlotte de Savoie in 1451, but the marriage was not consummated till her arrival in Paris on 14 February 1457. His daughter Jeanne married Admiral Louis de Bourbon on 7 November 1465; the League of Public Welfare was formed by French and Burgundian noblemen opposed to Louis XI in 1464. Tristan l'Hermite (1406–90) was Louis XI's most influential adviser.

67 *at Montlhéry*: in 1465, when the royal army was defeated by the League of Public Welfare.

'that little cell ... eleven feet in heighth': the quotation comes from Sauval, *Histoire des antiquités*, iii. 261.

Nemours ... the Constable: Jacques d'Armagnac, Duc de Nemours (executed 1476), and the Constable Louis de Luxembourg, Comte de Saint-Pol (executed 1475); Les Halles and the Grève were places of public execution in medieval Paris.

68 *Charles VIII*: the story is set during the final year of Louis XI's reign; he was succeeded in 1483 by his son Charles VIII (1470–98).

69 *the Marché-Neuf*: a well-known haunt of prostitutes.

The letter of the law is cruel: Hugo's adaptation of *lex horrendi carminis* (Livy, i. 26).

74 *Saint Eustachius*: mythical second-century martyr, traditionally invoked in difficult situations.

Baillet ... Barme: Thibaut Baillet (died 1585), president of the High Court of Paris; Roger Barme, the author of *De regulis juris* (1498).

Heard on the Mountain

Written 27 July 1829; poem V in *Autumn Leaves* (1831).

  77 *the Sound*: the strait between Denmark and Sweden.

  79 *Zion*: Jerusalem.

      Daniel: Hebrew prophet who survived, unharmed, in a den of lions (Daniel 6).

  81 *the Eternal*: in French, the Hebrew name of God (YHWH) is customarily rendered *l'Éternel*.

'Sometimes, beneath the clouds' deceptive twists . . .'

Written September 1828; poem XXXV. v in *Autumn Leaves* (1831).

  81 *Babel*: where people attempted to build 'a tower whose top may reach unto heaven' (Genesis 11: 4).

A Ball at the Hôtel de Ville

Written May 1833; poem VI in *Songs of the Half-Light* (1835). The Hôtel de Ville was for centuries a centre of much social and political activity in Paris.

  83 *Isis*: Egyptian goddess, depicted in Roman times as a veiled figure embodying secret wisdom.

'O that I could fill your deep reverie . . .'

Written 19 September 1834; poem XXIV in *Songs of the Half-Light* (1835). As with many of Hugo's other love poems of the 1830s, the subject is Hugo's daily meetings with Juliette Drouet in the valley of the Bièvre during September 1834, at the height of their romance.

'The rest of them drift any way at all . . .'

Written 17 October 1834; poem XXXV in *Songs of the Half-Light* (1835). The most complex of the poems in the final section of that collection, which are addressed to the poet's wife; its strengths have been analysed in detail by Pierre Albouy in the Pléiade edition of Hugo's *Œuvres poétiques I* (Paris, 1964), 1411–13.

A Popular Man

Written 10 April 1839; poem VI in *Sunlight and Shadows* (1840).

'Indian caverns! tombs! monumental arrays . . .'

Written 14 April 1839; poem XIII in *Sunlight and Shadows* (1840).

  91 *Babel . . . Piranesi*: Babel, the ancient city where people attempted to build 'a tower whose top may reach unto heaven' (Genesis 11: 4); Giovanni Battista Piranesi (1720–78), Italian artist, noted for his prints of bizarre architectural fantasies.

The Shadow

Written March 1839; poem XXXIII in *Sunlight and Shadows* (1840). Compare 'Uttered in the Shadows' in *Contemplations* (p. 181).

Thérèse's Party

Written 16 February 1840; poem I. xxii in *Contemplations* (1856). This famous poem was a major inspiration for Verlaine's *Fêtes galantes* (1869) and, like that volume, offers a fictional reconstruction of the pleasures of the pre-Revolutionary French aristocracy; its narrator is thus even further than usual from being simply Hugo himself. The poet had recently been reading the section of Molière's collected works containing *Le Mariage forcé* and *La Princesse d'Élide*, which would naturally lead him to reflect on the type of *divertissement* at which the latter work had first been staged ('The Pleasures of the Enchanted Isle', offered in 1664 to entertain Louis XIV's current mistress Louise de la Vallière). Watteauesque fantasies of the kind were common subjects for poetry in the nineteenth century; Gautier and Musset, among others, had already written in this genre. Most of the theatrical figures mentioned in 'Thérèse's Party' are stock characters of the Italian *commedia dell'arte* and its descendants, which were extremely popular in eighteenth-century France.

97 *Cupid*: the god of love.

all of Paris: an allusion to the old French folk song praised by Alceste in Molière's comedy *Le Misanthrope* (1666), i. ii.

Amintas … Leonoras: the names evoke the romantic shepherd of Torquato Tasso's influential play *Aminta* (1573) and the stereotypic heroines of many post-Renaissance Italian and French comedies.

Plautus: Roman comic dramatist (died 184 BCE).

99 *Venus*: the Roman goddess of love, born from the sea foam, and carried to land on a cockleshell.

Alcantor … Arbates: secondary characters in Molière's successive comedies *Le Mariage forcé* and *La Princesse d'Élide* (both 1664); the unexpectedly serious adjectives recall the eighteenth century's sentimental view of Molière's plays.

For Dust Thou Art

Written 3 February 1843; poem III. v in *Contemplations* (1856). The title cites God's decree to Adam: 'For dust thou art, and unto dust shalt thou return' (Genesis 3: 19).

Written on the Plinth of an Ancient Bas-Relief

Written 8 June 1839; poem III. xxi in *Contemplations* (1856). The poem was dedicated to the composer Louise Bertin (1805–77), who had collaborated with Hugo on the opera *Esmeralda* (1836).

'The child saw Grandma busy spinning . . .'

Written 25 August 1843; poem III. xxv in *Contemplations* (1856).

'Life, dear sir, is a comedy . . .'

Written 2 November 1842; MS 79/121, published in *Last Gleanings* (1902). A draft of a speech for a play.

107 *Olympian*: majestic.

Near Avranches

Written May 1843; poem III. vi in *The Four Winds of the Spirit* (1881).

107 *Saint-Michel*: Mont-Saint-Michel, conical islet off the coast of north-western France, crowned by a medieval abbey; during the nineteenth century it was used as a political prison.

Cheops: fourth-dynasty Egyptian king (twenty-seventh century BCE), the builder of the Great Pyramid at Giza; here, as often in Hugo, his name stands for the pyramid itself.

Talleyrand

Written 19 May 1838; the title was supplied by Hugo's literary executors. The French statesman Charles-Maurice de Talleyrand-Périgord (1754–1838) rose to prominence after the French Revolution; during a long and extraordinary career, he was instrumental in effecting Napoleon's seizure of consular power in 1799, the restoration of the Bourbon monarchy in 1814–15, and the appointment of Louis-Philippe as constitutional monarch in 1830.

110 *Machiavelli . . . Voltaire*: Niccolò Machiavelli (1469–1527), Italian statesman famous for his defence of amoral power politics in *The Prince*; Jean-François de Gondi, Cardinal de Retz (1614–79), political agitator, one of the instigators of the Fronde; Joseph Fouché (1759–1820), who abandoned his Oratorian upbringing to become an unscrupulous revolutionary; Voltaire (François-Marie Arouet, 1694–1778), French writer noted for his wit and irreverence.

the July Revolution: the revolution of July 1830, which overthrew the absolute monarchy of the House of Bourbon and set up the constitutional monarchy of the House of Orléans.

111 *Mirabeau . . . Thiers*: the statesmen Honoré-Gabriel, Comte de Mirabeau (1749–91, one of the early leaders of the French Revolution), and Adolphe Thiers (1797–1877, one of France's leading politicians during the 1830s).

Sieyès . . . Louis-Philippe: a glittering swarm indeed: Emmanuel Sieyès (1748–1836), French statesman influential during the Revolutionary and early Napoleonic eras; Madame de Staël (Germaine Necker, 1766–1817), literary and cultural critic, an early advocate of Romanticism in France; Benjamin Constant de Rebecque (1767–1830), French liberal politician (and author of the now-celebrated novel *Adolphe*, though Hugo would probably not have been thinking of that); the three leaders of the Holy

Alliance after Napoleon's defeat in 1815: Tsar Alexander I of Russia (1777–1825), Kaiser Friedrich Wilhelm III of Prussia (1770–1840), and Emperor Francis I of Austria (1768–1835); Louis XVIII (1755–1824), who became king of France after the fall of Napoleon in 1814–15, and Louis-Philippe (1773–1850), who became king after the July Revolution of 1830.

Bayonne

An extract from Hugo's diary of his 1843 journey to the Pyrenees, which was evidently intended as a companion volume to his 1842 travel book on the Rhineland, but which was broken off unfinished when he received news of his daughter Léopoldine's death. The incomplete diary was ultimately published in 1890, as part of the volume *Alps and Pyrenees*. It contains perhaps the finest non-fiction prose he had yet written; as in verse, his art was perceptibly gaining depth and brilliance.

The town of Bayonne, situated on the Adour 789 kilometres south-west of Paris, had a population of about 20,000 in the early nineteenth century. Hugo first visited it in 1811, when his mother was travelling to Spain with her children to join her husband.

112 *the great wars . . . El Empecinado*: the wars under Emperor Napoleon I; the guerilla Juan Martín Díaz (El Empecinado, 1775–1825), a major leader of Spanish resistance to Napoleonic rule.

Comtesse d'Escarbagnas . . . The Ruins of Babylon: one-act comedy (1671) by Molière; three-act melodrama (1810) by Guilbert de Pixérécourt, set in the days of Caliph Harun al-Raschid of Arabian *Nights* fame.

114 *Lahorie*: General Victor Fanneau de Lahorie (1766–1812) was executed on 29 October 1812 after a failed conspiracy against Napoleon.

Amaryllis or Galatea: country girls praised in Virgil's *Eclogues*; Hugo is thinking particularly of iii. 64–5, 'Galatea . . . flees toward the willows— and hopes to be seen before she reaches them.'

Sobrino . . . Cormon: Francisco Sobrino, *Nouvelle Grammaire espagnolle et françoise* (1703, frequently reissued); J. L. Barthélemy Cormon, *Dictionnaire . . . espagnol-français et français-espagnol* (1800). Hugo's older brothers are studying the language of the country to which they are travelling.

King Louis-Philippe

Written August 1844; the title was supplied by Hugo's literary executors. During the 1840s, Hugo was fairly close to the French royal family; his diaries of the period contain many interesting glimpses of the lives of King Louis-Philippe and his relatives. The writer's retrospective appraisal of the king, in a famous chapter of *Les Misérables* (IV. i. iii), derives much of its strength from the inside knowledge he acquired during these years.

117 *Duc d'Orléans*: Ferdinand-Philippe, Duc d'Orléans (1810–42), was the oldest son of Louis-Philippe and therefore, after the 1830 revolution, the

heir apparent to the French throne. He died in a carriage accident on 13 July 1842.

Duc de Penthièvre ... Comte de Beaujolais: Louis, Duc de Penthièvre (1725–93), Louis-Philippe's maternal grandfather; Louis-Charles, Comte de Beaujolais (1779–1808), his brother.

Villemain

Written 3 December 1845; the title was supplied by Hugo's literary executors. Abel-François Villemain (1790–1870) taught French literature at the Sorbonne from 1816 to 1830; many people regarded him as the most brilliant lecturer of his era. He was elected to the Académie française in 1821 and profoundly influenced its policies for almost half a century, becoming its permanent secretary in 1832. He also played an important role in politics. As Hugo's vivid account shows, he suffered a severe psychotic depressive episode during the mid-1840s and resigned most of his official duties. He recovered fully, and remained active for many years afterwards.

117 *Dictated by me*: Hugo dictated the passage to Juliette Drouet.

118 *the Institute*: the organization of which the Académie française is part.

the current Moniteur: the political newspaper *Le Moniteur universel* (1789–1901), the official journal of all successive French governments between 1799 and 1869.

History of the Consulate and the Empire: Charles Lacretelle's *Histoire du Consulat et de l'Empire*, 6 vols. (post-dated 1846 by its publisher).

121 *Guizot ... Lamartine*: three of the country's leading statesmen at the time: François Guizot (1787–1874), Adolphe Thiers (1797–1877), and Alphonse de Lamartine (1790–1869, better known nowadays as a poet).

123 *'I'll see you soon, won't I?'*: Hugo remained in close contact with Villemain, though his diaries do not systematically record the later meetings.

A Righteous Man

Written late November 1845; chapters I. i. i–ii of *Les Misérables* (1862). The 1845 draft of the novel began with Jean Tréjean's arrival at Digne (chapter I. ii. i in Hugo's final numbering), continued with the description of Monsieur Myriel ('A Righteous Man', I. i), and then returned to Jean Tréjean (I. ii. ii and following). The order of the chapters was transposed, and the name Tréjean changed to Valjean, when Hugo revised his work in 1860–1.

123 *Digne*: Digne-les-Bains, at the foot of the Alps ('Digne is in the mountains', I. ii. i) 750 kilometres south-east of Paris, at an altitude of 608 metres; its population in 1815 would have been about 4,000. Here and elsewhere, the original edition (1862) gave the name of the town simply as D——; it was first printed in full, at Hugo's request, in the 1881 *ne varietur* edition.

124 *the tragic events of 1793*: the Reign of Terror, when over forty thousand people were executed.

124 *Napoleon's coronation*: 2 December 1804.

Cardinal Fesch: Joseph Fesch (1763–1839), Napoleon's maternal uncle, who was instrumental in arranging for the coronation to be blessed by Pope Pius VII.

126 *Pujet . . . Senez*: the Henri de Pujet of history was bishop of Digne from 1708 to 1728. The list of guests at his dinner is designed to demonstrate the exalted social realms in which he (unlike Myriel) moved: Prince Charles III Brulant de Genlis of Embrun (died 1714), Grand Prior of the Order of Malta Philippe de Vendôme (1655–1725), and the controversial Jansenist Jean Soanen of Senez (1647–1740) were particularly illustrious figures.

128 *fifteen hundred francs a year*: Leviticus 27: 32 and other passages required the ancient Israelites to give one-tenth of their earnings to God. Myriel does the reverse: he gives away nine-tenths and retains one-tenth.

129 *Napoleon's seizure of power in 1799*: on 9 November 1799, Napoleon Bonaparte, previously army leader, seized absolute power in a *coup d'état*.

(Relations with Rome were a little strained at the time.): the leaders of the French Revolution were profoundly hostile to Roman Catholicism; the church was not officially re-established in France until the Concordat of 1801 between Napoleon and Pope Pius VII.

130 *I do say that it's a reasonable likeness*: the portrait is partly modelled, even in some of its most extraordinary features, on the character of Charles-François Bienvenu de Miollis (1753–1843), bishop of Digne from 1806 to 1838.

The Fall

Written intermittently between 17 November 1845 and 24 November 1846; chapters I. II. i–vii, ix–xii of *Les Misérables* (1862). (Chapter I. II. viii was added only toward the end of 1861, after the novel proper had been completed.) In ordinary usage 'the Fall', without further qualification, would be the fall of Adam and Eve when they were tempted by Satan in the garden of Eden; a similar drama is now enacted in a different garden.

131 *forty-six to forty-eight*: in fact he is 46 (I. II. iii)—the same age as Napoleon.

Napoleon . . . from Cannes to Paris: in February 1815, Napoleon escaped from exile on the island of Elba. He landed at the Golfe Jouan (about 5 kilometres east of Cannes in the French Riviera) on 1 March and marched to Paris, receiving an enthusiastic welcome from crowds on the way. Jean Valjean's reception will be somewhat different.

132 *Drouot*: the French general Antoine Drouot (1774–1847), who had followed Napoleon to Elba and returned with him.

140 *the Wars of Religion*: during the sixteenth-century civil wars between Catholic and Huguenot factions in France, Digne was taken and retaken five times.

142 *four of them ... the Letter to the Corinthians*: the relevant Scripture
passages read, in part: duties toward God, 'seek ye first the kingdom of
God, and his righteousness'; duties toward oneself, 'if thy right eye
offend thee, pluck it out'; duties toward one's neighbour, 'all things what-
soever ye would that men should do to you, do ye even so to them'; duties
toward the created world, 'take no thought for your life, what ye shall eat,
or what ye shall drink; nor yet for your body, what ye shall put on'; duties
for rulers and their subjects, 'let every soul be subject unto the higher
powers: for there is no power but of God'; duties for magistrates, etc.,
'submit yourselves therefore ... unto governors, as unto them that are
sent ... for the punishment of evildoers, and for the praise of them that
do well; ... likewise, ye wives, be in subjection to your own husbands';
duties for husbands, etc., 'husbands, love your wives; ... children, obey
your parents in the Lord; ... fathers, provoke not your children to wrath;
... servants, be obedient to them that are your masters'; duties for
believers, 'let us hold fast the profession of our faith without wavering';
duties for virgins, 'it is good for them to abide even as I: but if they
cannot contain, let them marry'. The references therefore act somewhat
like Bunyan's marginal notes to *The Pilgrim's Progress*: they tempt the
novel's more inquisitive readers to explore beyond its printed pages and,
in so doing, to gain some additional insights into the matter under consideration (in this case, the character of Monsieur Myriel). Significantly,
Myriel's own book will remain uncompleted; he is too busy living a life of
this kind to write about it.

in 1806: Mademoiselle Baptistine last bought new clothes after her
brother was appointed bishop; since then she, like he, has been living too
frugally to afford luxuries.

145 *Unquestioning Obedience*: when Napoleon III seized power on 2 December 1851, one of his first official pronouncements was a message to the
army declaring that 'unquestioning obedience [*obéissance passive*] to
orders is the strict duty of every military man, from general to private'.
The same phrase had been used in a message from his Minister of
War, sent on 28 October 1851 and designed to smooth the way for the
coup: 'we all know, generals, that there can be no discipline in an army
where unquestioning obedience is replaced by a right to examine
orders critically'. Hugo sardonically takes up the catchphrase (as he had
already done in *Châtiments*, II. vii), but he gives it a significance which its
inventors can never have envisaged.

yellow ticket-of-leave: released convicts were given a yellow ticket-of-
leave, which they were legally obliged to display in all the towns they
visited.

148 *the Medusa raft*: the ship *Medusa* was wrecked off the coast of West Africa
on 2 July 1816. For twelve days the survivors drifted on a raft 20 metres
by 7 metres in size; 119 people began the journey, only fifteen were left at
the end. The incident is best known from Géricault's painting *Le Radeau
de la Méduse* (1819).

149 *the Pontarlier Cheese Industry*: Hugo's information about this subject comes from a book by his brother Abel Hugo, *La France pittoresque* (1835).

her childhood friend: the translators have introduced these clarifying words from a parallel episode in I. i. ix, which has not been included in this selection.

154 *Voilà Jean*: 'There's Jean'.

milk fever: infection following childbirth; a common cause of death in those days, especially among the poor.

Nobody ... ever knew him to have a 'girlfriend': Hugolian heroes are characteristically endowed with the chastity traditionally assigned to fictional heroines (Marius in *Les Misérables* and Gilliatt in *The Toilers of the Sea* are other conspicuous examples of this); their sexual energies are sublimated in other fields. In Hugo there is no double standard: the principles of conduct, positive or negative, are the same for males and females alike.

156 *the penal code*: established in 1791.

Montenotte ... Year IV: the battle of Montenotte (12 April 1796) was one of Napoleon's earliest triumphs; once again his career provides an antithesis to Jean Valjean's. The dating system is that of the French Revolutionary calendar, in use between 1792 and 1805; Hugo is quietly reminding his readers that things were done differently in those days.

158 *Gueux*: Claude Gueux (1804–32), thief and murderer; protagonist of an 1834 story by Hugo.

161 *God made man good*: 'God saw every thing that he had made, and, behold, it was very good' (Genesis 1: 31); 'God made man upright: but they have sought out many devices' (Ecclesiastes 7: 29).

162 *Dante at the gates of hell*: the inscription over the gate of Dante's hell ends with the words 'Abandon hope, all ye who enter here' (*Inferno*, iii. 9).

163 *caryatids*: massive sculptured figures supporting the columns of the Portrail des Atlantes (1656–8) at Toulon, by Pierre Puget (1620–94).

173 *Les Guillons*: a hamlet in the Jura mountains; no doubt there is some sly private allusion here, but no fully convincing explanation of it has yet been offered.

The Living Pictures

Written late 1846; the title is supplied by the present editors. One of Hugo's richest prose explorations of the ambivalent social significance of female nudity; it invites comparison with 'Zara Bathing' (p. 9) and 'The Consecration of Woman' (p. 295).

176 *the Porte-Saint-Martin*: a leading Paris theatre of the time (destroyed in 1871); many of Hugo's plays were staged there.

Madame Rey . . . Ruy Blas: Madame Jourdain Rey, who played Maria de Neubourg, Queen of Spain, in the 1841 revival of Hugo's drama *Ruy Blas* (1838).

The Princes

Written 1847; the title was supplied by Hugo's literary executors. The Duc de Nemours (1814–96), the Duc d'Aumale (1822–97), and the Duc de Montpensier (1824–90) were respectively the second, fourth, and fifth sons of King Louis-Philippe.

177 *Neuilly*: the Château de Neuilly, on the outskirts of Paris, had been a residence of Louis-Philippe and his family since 1818.

178 *the Infanta*: Marie-Louise de Bourbon, the sister of Queen Isabella of Spain, had married the Duc de Montpensier in October 1846. The couple ultimately had six children, and the Duc became very closely allied with his wife's family, exerting a major influence on Spanish politics during the later nineteenth century.

the Tuileries: fifteenth-century palace at Paris; a traditional residence of the kings of France.

Uttered in the Shadows

Written 3 November 1846; poem II. xv in *Contemplations* (1856). Compare 'The Shadow' in *Sunlight and Shadows* (page 95).

While Looking at the Heavens One Evening

Written 26 January 1846; poem II. xxviii in *Contemplations* (1856)..

'At first, oh! I was like a maniac . . .'

Written November 1846; poem IV. iv in *Contemplations* (1856).

187 *wept bitterly*: the phrase, an obvious reminiscence of the apostle Peter's tears after his denial of Christ, gives the poem's situation startling resonances.

'While mariners, who estimate and doubt . . .'

Written 8 April 1847; poem IV. x in *Contemplations* (1856).

Veni, Vidi, Vixi

Written 11 April 1848; poem IV. xiii in *Contemplations* (1856). The Latin title puns on Julius Caesar's familiar *veni, vidi, vici* ('I came, I saw, I conquered'); Hugo has altered the last word to *vixi* ('I lived'), a term commonly used on funerary inscriptions and implying that the speaker's life is now over.

191 *the gates of night*: the image is derived from Job 38: 17.

'Tomorrow, when the fields grow light . . .'

Written 4 October 1847; poem IV. xiv in *Contemplations* (1856). The poem describes a walk from Le Havre (where Hugo was then living) to Léopoldine's grave at Villequier.

At the Académie française

The title was supplied by Hugo's literary executors. The Académie française, France's leading literary institution, was founded by Richelieu in 1635 for the standardization of the French language and the maintenance of literary standards. It contains a maximum of forty members, who are elected by their peers and serve for life. Applicants traditionally visit the existing members in the hope of enlisting their support (a practice contrary to the rules of the organization, as Hugo notes). Admission to the Académie is keenly contested, and the conventional writers of any era find the path much smoother than innovators like Balzac do (as the third note below will illustrate). Hugo himself was elected at his fourth attempt, in 1841.

192 *Dupin senior*: André-Marie Dupin (1783–1865), lawyer and politician, noted for his caustic wit.

Balzac: the French novelist Honoré de Balzac (1799–1850). His work was not widely appreciated by his contemporaries; but Hugo's own opinion will be evident from the diary entries and funeral speech that follow.

Flourens . . . Brifaut: the men who had entered the Académie at their first attempt were Pierre Flourens (1794–1867), physiologist, elected in 1840 (in preference to Hugo, who was making his third attempt at the time); Henri-Joseph-Guillaume Patin (1793–1876), Classical scholar, elected in 1842; Saint-Marc Girardin (1801–73), conservative literary critic, elected in 1844; Mathieu Molé (1781–1855), prominent royalist politician, elected in 1840; and Charles Brifaut (1781–1857), conservative poet and dramatist, elected in 1826.

Vigny: the poet Alfred de Vigny (1797–1863), one of Hugo's earliest literary friends; he was elected to the Académie française on 8 May 1845, but was not well received by some of the established members.

Empis . . . Leclerc: Adolphe Empis (1795–1868), dramatist and librettist (usually in collaboration); Victor Leclerc (1789–1865), conservative literary scholar.

Deschamps . . . Béranger: Émile Deschamps (1791–1871), Romantic poet and critic; Félicité-Robert de Lamennais (1782–1854), socialist and liberal theologian; Alfred de Musset (1810–57), Romantic poet and dramatist; Pierre-Jean de Béranger (1780–1857), anti-authoritarian popular songwriter. The last three of these are now much more famous than either Empis or Leclerc.

Chateaubriand's successor: the prose writer and royalist politician François-René de Chateaubriand (1768–1848), the leading French author of the post-Revolutionary era, had died on 4 July 1848.

193 *22, 23, and 24 February*: the three days of street fighting during the 1848 revolution that overthrew the Orléanist monarchy and inaugurated the Second Republic.

the Institute: the Institut de France, organized in 1795, and including the Académie française as well as two scientific academies.

Cousin . . . Dupaty: Hugo's keen eye for incongruity glances sardonically from a distinctly ill-assorted threesome—Victor Cousin (1792–1867), philosopher and friend of Hugo; Prosper Mérimée (1803–70), short-story writer and enemy of Hugo; and Charles-François de Rémusat (1797–1875), liberal politician—to a marriage of natural allies—the royalist politicians Étienne Pasquier (1767–1862) and Mathieu Molé (1781–1855). Emmanuel Dupaty (1775–1851) was an idiosyncratic dramatist and librettist; his poetry is usually felt to suffer from artifice and preciosity.

La Fontaine: Hugo means simply that the word *gages* ('remuneration') is characteristic of the literary era epitomized by Jean de La Fontaine (1621–95); it occurs in his *Fables*, x. x. 70 and XII. xv. 9.

194 *Sainte-Aulaire . . . Villemain*: The royalist politician Frédéric Albert Falloux (1811–86) aimed to impose Roman Catholic education on all French children (the result would be the notorious *loi Falloux* of 15 March 1850); it must have been fascinating to hear that policy criticized by Charles-Marie de Feletz (1767–1850), a Catholic priest who had suffered for his beliefs during the Reign of Terror. The other academicians mentioned in this paragraph are Louis-Clair de Sainte-Aulaire (1778–1854), diplomat and historian; Prosper-Claude de Barante (1782–1866), historian; Sanson de Pongerville (1792–1870), a mere translator; and Abel-François Villemain (1790–1870), literary critic and permanent secretary of the Académie (see also page 117).

Vatout . . . Lamartine: Jean Vatout (1792–1848), librarian and committed supporter of the House of Orléans (he followed Louis-Philippe into exile and died shortly afterwards); François Guizot (1787–1874), leading politician under Louis-Philippe (he too fled into exile after the February 1848 revolution, but returned a year later); Alphonse de Lamartine (1790–1869), poet and statesman, who was France's virtual head of government between February and June 1848 but lost power as the year progressed.

Ségur . . . Ancelot: the academicians not previously mentioned are Philippe-Paul Ségur (1780–1873), historian; Jean-Jacques Ampère (1800–64), literary historian and travel writer (the son of the famous scientist); Ludovic Vitet (1802–73), art critic and politician; Pierre Baour-Lormain (1770–1854), poet and critic; Pierre-François Tissot (1768–1854), historian and Classical scholar; Eugène Scribe (1791–1861), dramatist and opera librettist; Pierre-Antoine Lebrun (1785–1873), poet and dramatist; Auguste Mignet (1796–1884), historian; Henri-Joseph-Guillaume Patin (1793–1876), Classical scholar; Alexis de Tocqueville (1805–59), political writer; Adolphe Thiers (1797–1877), politician and historian; Jean-Pons-Guillaume Viennet (1779–1868), poet; and Jacques-Arsène Ancelot (1794–1854), dramatist. Hugo inadvertently lists Mérimée twice: an interesting Freudian slip.

Noailles: Paul, Duc de Noailles (1802–85), parliamentary speaker and friend of Chateaubriand; his publications had been few and undistinguished, and his election to the Académie provoked widespread protests in the newspapers and elsewhere.

194 *when Monsieur Hugo was nominated by Monsieur Nodier*: in 1839. At the time, Hugo had vainly urged Balzac not to withdraw his candidature. Hugo himself was not elected until 1841.

195 *Berryer*: Pierre-Antoine Berryer (1790–1868), a brilliant lawyer and a royalist politician noted for his personal integrity.

Salvandy: Narcisse-Achille, Comte de Salvandy (1795–1856), politician and historian.

196 *Madame de Staël*: Germaine Necker (1766–1817), literary and cultural critic, an early advocate of Romanticism in France.

the Dictionary: one of the Académie's traditional functions is the preparation and revision of the standard dictionary of the French language.

The Death of Balzac

Written August 1850; the title was supplied by Hugo's literary executors. Balzac returned to Paris, seriously ill with heart failure, on or around 20 May 1850 and died there shortly before midnight on 18 August.

196 *Madame de Balzac*: the Polish countess Eveline Hanska (1801–82), who began to correspond with Balzac in 1832; they married on 14 March 1850.

February Revolution: the revolution of February 1848, which overthrew the Orléanist monarchy and set up a republic.

197 *Soulié*: Frédéric Soulié (1800–47), prolific novelist and dramatist; Hugo had delivered his funeral oration.

Louis Hugo: (1777–1853), a Napoleonic officer; the protagonist of his nephew's poem 'The Cemetery at Eylau' (*Legend of the Ages*, XLIX. vi).

Beaujon: Nicolas Beaujon (1708–86), immensely wealthy French business-man; the opulence and extravagance of his Paris home were legendary.

David: David d'Angers (Pierre-Jean David, 1788–1856), who also sculpted Hugo himself.

198 *Pourbus and Holbein*: the painters Frans Pourbus the Younger (1569–1622), who makes a memorable fictional appearance in Balzac's 1831 short story 'Le Chef-d'œuvre inconnu', and Hans Holbein the Younger (died 1543).

199 *Peer of France*: Hugo had been made a Peer of France by King Louis-Philippe in April 1845. In February 1848, when the monarchy was replaced by a republic (a move which Hugo supported, but which the royalist Balzac did not), such titles were abolished.

Riza . . . Arrivabene: Hasan Riza Pasa (1809–59), Ottoman statesman; Ramón de Navarrete y Fernández y Landa (1818–97), Spanish dramatist; Giovanni Arrivabene (1787–1881), Italian patriot and politician (in exile 1848–59).

the erstwhile farmer-general: Beaujon; the office of farmer-general was important and lucrative in eighteenth-century France.

Giraud: Eugène Giraud (1806–81), French painter and engraver.

200 *Baroche*: Pierre-Jules Baroche (1802–70), lawyer and politician; a staunch supporter of Louis-Napoléon, and not disposed to view either the royalist Balzac or the republican Hugo with favour.

Dumas: Alexandre Dumas *père* (1803–70), the distinguished novelist. The other two pallbearers were Baroche and Balzac's bitter enemy the literary critic Sainte-Beuve—an irony which the deceased himself might have relished.

Nodier . . . Delavigne: two authors whom Hugo respected: Charles Nodier (1780–1844), writer of short stories; Casimir Delavigne (1773–1843), poet.

Balzac's Funeral

Written 20 August 1850. Perhaps the most frequently cited of Hugo's many funeral orations; it is particularly remarkable for its pioneering recognition of the subversive undercurrents underlying Balzac's apparent conservatism.

201 *after Richelieu*: Armand Jean du Plessis, Cardinal Richelieu (1585–1640), the leading political figure of his age; in alluding to a 'famous seventeenth-century constellation' Hugo would have been thinking particularly of Pierre Corneille (1606–84), Jean Rotrou (1609–50), Jean de La Fontaine (1621–95), Molière (1622–73), and Jean Racine (1639–99).

Tacitus . . . Rabelais: the grave Roman historian Cornelius Tacitus and the gossipy Roman biographer Gaius Suetonius Tranquillus (both first–second centuries CE), the lightly subversive French dramatist Beaumarchais (Pierre-Augustin Caron, 1732–99), and the flamboyantly subversive French prose writer François Rabelais (died 1553).

Molière . . . Rousseau: the nineteenth centry found dark undercurrents in several major comedies by Molière (Jean-Baptiste Poquelin, 1622–73), including *Dom Juan*, *Tartuffe*, and *Le Misanthrope*; Jean-Jacques Rousseau (1712–78) maintained the innate goodness of humanity, yet he was personally mistrustful and quarrelled with many of his own friends.

Pius IX and Louis Bonaparte

Written April 1850; the title is supplied by the present editors. At the time, Louis-Napoleon Bonaparte (1808–73) was president of the French Republic; Pius IX (Giovanni Mastai-Ferretti, 1792–1878) had been pope since 1846. Both had appeared sympathetic to liberal ideas before gaining power, but had since become increasingly represssive and anti-democratic, joining forces to oppose the rising nationalist movement in Italy.

203 *Charles X . . . Antonelli*: Charles X (1757–1836), the last Bourbon king of France, whose reactionary policies and failure to win the trust of the public instigated the 1830 revolution; Cardinal Giacomo

Antonelli (1808–76), papal secretary of state, Pius IX's main political assistant.

203 *the Immaculate Conception*: in Roman Catholicism, the doctrine that Mary, uniquely, inherited no original sin when she was conceived; after centuries of dispute, it was officially proclaimed by Pius IX in 1854. For Hugo's attitude, see 'The Immaculate Conception Revisited' (page 443).

the Bois de Boulogne: a famous park in Paris; at the time, a fashionable place for clandestine assignations.

Miss Howard: Elizabeth Haryett, later Comtesse de Beauregard (1822–65), Louis-Napoléon's mistress.

204 *the Élysée*: Louis-Napoléon's official residence.

Lady Douglas . . . the Marquise de Contades: Princess Marie de Bade (Lady Douglas, later Duchess of Hamilton; 1817–88) and Princess Mathilde Bonaparte (1820–1904) were Louis-Napoléon's cousins; Émilie, Marquise de Contades, was the wife of his chamberlain.

Proposed Grant to Monsieur Bonaparte

The italicized prefatory and concluding paragraphs were added by Hugo when he reprinted the speech in 1853, two years after it had been delivered. On 18 January 1851 the National Assembly passed a motion of no confidence in its president, Louis-Napoléon Bonaparte, who had just dismissed his leading right-wing opponent General Nicolas Changarnier (1793–1877) from command of the army—a move that was widely interpreted as preparing the way for a possible *coup d'état*. Louis-Napoléon's subsequent application to the Assembly for funds therefore aroused considerable debate. Hugo's speech was delivered during the preliminary committee discussions, on 6 February 1851; the final vote occurred on 10 February.

204 *Léon Faucher . . . Bineau*: Léon Faucher (1803–54), royalist politician; Michel de Bourges (Louis-Chrysostom Michel, 1797–1853), republican politician; Pierre-Henri Sainte-Beuve (1819–55), Louis Combarel de Leyval (1808–69), and Jean-Martial Bineau (1805–55), members of the Assembly's finance committee.

205 *the first grant*: in June 1850, the Assembly had voted Louis-Napoléon a grant of 2,160,000 francs.

Satory . . . Praetorian attempts: at Satory (a military camp near Versailles), in September 1850, army troops paraded past Louis-Napoléon with shouts of 'Long live the Emperor!'—behaviour denounced by Changarnier as 'Praetorian' (the Praetorians, in ancient Rome, were the emperor's personal guard; they were regarded as eminently corruptible). The Tenth of December Society was formed by militant partisans of Louis-Napoléon after his election as president of the Republic on 10 December 1848; it was noted for its use of violence to secure its objectives.

206 *a political prison . . . in support of the underprivileged classes*: Louis-Napoléon was imprisoned at Ham between 1840 and 1846, after an

abortive attempt to seize power; he seemed to advocate democratic and socialist policies in *The Abolition of Poverty* (1844) and a number of earlier publications.

Postscript

Written October 1851. First published, posthumously, as poem V. ii in the 1893 edition of *The Whole Lyre*; it is poem V. xii in the 1897 edition, and poem V. xvi in the 1935 Imprimerie Nationale edition. The title was supplied by Hugo's literary executors.

209 *Misères*: one of Hugo's early titles for *Les Misérables*, which he had laid aside in order to devote himself more fully to politics after the February 1848 revolution.

Monsieur Bonaparte . . . Jesuits, Rome, Faucher or Molé: crucial political issues of the time: the unreliability of Louis-Napoléon Bonaparte (1808–73), then president of the Republic; the subversive influence of the Jesuits; the failure of attempts to set up a republic in Rome; and the right-wing political activities of Léon Faucher (1803–54) and Mathieu Molé (1781–1855).

some Nosy Parker: the French text names the royalist General Nicolas Changarnier (1793–1877), whom Hugo once described as an 'epauletted Jesuit'.

Paris Sleeps; the Doorbell Rings

Written late December 1851; chapter I. ii of *The History of a Crime* (1877–8).

211 *Versigny*: the lawyer Claude-Marie Versigny (1818–1910).

Bastiat: the economist Claude Frédéric Bastiat (1801–50), an advocate of free trade.

Michel de Bourges and Théodore Bac: two republican lawyers; the former (Louis-Chrysostom Michel, 1797–1853) was a major influence on the thinking of George Sand, and the latter (1808–65) was a friend of Louis Blanc.

Baune: Eugène Baune (1799–1880), noted for his personal integrity and commitment to social reform; he was actively assisted by his equally remarkable wife Julie (1807–71) and their daughter Françoise, whom Hugo mentions below. After his arrest Eugène was exiled without a trial; like Hugo, the Baunes never revisited France as long as Napoleon III remained in power.

Mauguin: on 27 December 1850 a member of the Assembly, François Mauguin, had been imprisoned for debt (despite the laws guaranteeing parliamentary inviolability); troops had been sent to free him.

Lefranc: Pierre Lefranc (1814–78), writer of vaudevilles and founder of *Le Chaire catholique*.

212 *Laissac*: Gustav Laissac (1809–58), left-wing politician.

Yvan: Melchior Yvan (1803–73), physician and socialist.

How Dark the Crime Was

Written late December 1851 or shortly thereafter; chapter I. v, paragraphs 1–23 of *The History of a Crime* (1877–8).

213 *The law of 31 May . . . Changarnier*: on 31 May 1850 the French government passed a law restricting the power to vote, in ways that tended to exclude political radicals and the unemployed; Hugo was one of the minority who had opposed this. Louis-Napoléon felt that he could obtain much support from the unemployed, and he intended to imprison or exile the leading radicals; thus he decided to rescind the law. Nicolas Changarnier (1793–1877), former army leader and committed royalist, was potentially one of the most serious threats to Louis-Napoléon's coup.

Carini . . . Mieroslawski: the Italian patriot Giacinto Carini (1821–80) later served with distinction (and great personal heroism) under Garibaldi; Ladislaw Mieroslawski (1814–78) led an unsuccessful revolt against the Bourbons at Palermo in March–April 1849.

Biography

Written May–June 1852; chapter I. v of *Napoleon the Little* (1852).

214 *Hortense . . . Louis-Philippe*: in 1802, Napoleon I arranged a marriage between his stepdaughter Hortense de Beauharnais (1783–1837) and his brother Louis Bonaparte (1778–1846), King of Holland 1806–10. The marriage was disastrous from the start, and the paternity of Louis-Napoléon, born to Hortense in 1808, has always been doubted; hence Hugo's careful wording specifies his mother, but not his father. Louis-Philippe (1773–1850) ruled France from 1830 to 1848; during this time, as Hugo notes, Louis-Napoléon made two attempts to start a revolution, at Strasbourg in 1836 and at Boulogne in 1840, but both attempts elicited very little support.

215 *the famous landing at Cannes*: Napoleon I landed near Cannes on 1 March 1815 after his escape from Elba; Louis-Napoléon's landing at Boulogne in 1840 was planned as an imitation of that event.

Ham: a fortress on the Somme in northern France.

some books: published between 1833 and 1844, before and during his imprisonment at Ham.

the February Revolution of 1848: the revolution of 24 February 1848, which replaced the monarchy of Louis-Philippe with a republic.

216 *the Roman Republic . . . the 'Gold Ingot Lottery'*: on 8 February 1849, a republic was proclaimed in Rome; in April, Louis-Napoléon sent French troops to suppress it and to strengthen the power of the papacy. He inaugurated the Gold Ingot Lottery in December 1850; the proceeds financed the deportation of his political opponents and, probably, some of the costs of his 1851 coup.

the inviolable Representatives: by law, members of the National Assembly could not be arrested.

5 April 1852

Written June–July 1852; chapter VII. v of *Napoleon the Little* (1852).

216 *the Tuileries*: fifteenth-century palace in Paris; one of Napoleon III's official residences.

217 *Troplong*: the lawyer Raymond-Théodore Troplong (1795–1865), president of the Supreme Court of Appeal; one of Louis-Napoléon's most trusted associates.

Abbatucci: Jacques-Pierre-Charles Abbatucci (1792–1857), magistrate and politician; a staunch supporter of Napoleon III.

218 *Nicole*: Pierre Nicole (1625–95), influential advocate of Jansenism (one of the most rigorously devout and least orthodox French religious movements, noted for its refusal to accept that kings and popes had absolute authority; a Jansenist would not be expected to submit to rulers as readily as an orthodox Roman Catholic might do).

The Littleness of the Master

Written June–July 1852; part I. i of the Conclusion to *Napoleon the Little* (1852).

221 *Tacitus . . . Philip II*: the distinguished historian Cornelius Tacitus (first–second centuries CE) was highly critical of most of the ten Roman emperors (from Tiberius to Domitian) whose reigns he chronicled. Hugo's list of early tyrants includes the powerful ancient Mesopotamian ruler Nimrod (Genesis 10: 8–10), the legendary Egyptian pharaoh Busiris, the Sicilian dictator Phalaris (sixth century BCE), who is said to have executed his enemies by roasting them alive in a bronze bull, so that the animal might seem to bellow as they cried out (Hugo is recalling Ovid, *Ars amatoria*, i. 647–54, where Busiris and Phalaris are mentioned in succession), and the brutal Seleucid king Antiochus Epiphanes (second century BCE), who is said to have flayed seven brothers (often, though inaccurately, termed 'Maccabees') and burned them alive. By an understandable slip of the pen, Hugo accidentally writes 'Ahasuerus' (Xerxes) instead of 'Antiochus' ('All tyrants, fundamentally, are one', he remarks in 'The Infanta's Rose', *Legend of the Ages*, XXVI. 220). Among the Roman emperors, he names Nero (died 68 CE), who persecuted the Christians and either caused or encouraged the great fire of Rome in 64 CE; Tiberius (died 37 CE), who used his island retreat on Capri for acts of sexual licence and cruelty; Domitian (died 96), Caracalla (died 277), Heliogabalus (died 222), and Commodus (died 192; ironically the son of the philosopher Marcus Aurelius), all of whom have acquired lasting reputations for corruption and oppression. The 'Borgia tiger' is the notorious pope Alexander VI (Rodrigo Borgia, 1431–1503). The medieval and later rulers on the list are Philip 'the Good' of Burgundy (1396–1467), Richard III of England (1452–85), Henry VIII of England (1491–1547), Christian II of Denmark (1481–1559), and Philip II of

Spain (1527–98). The Furies of Greek mythology were called Eumenides ('Kindly Ones') in order to flatter and appease them, for fear of the harm they could do if they heard themselves described accurately.

221 *Claudius ... Ferdinand II*: the proverbially weak and foolish Roman emperor Claudius (died 54 CE); Ferdinand VII of Spain (1784–1833), whose disastrous reign left an aftermath of civil war; Ferdinand II of Naples (1469–96), whose one-year reign began with flight to escape the army of Charles VIII of France.

Pedro the Cruel ... Siwas: Pedro IV of Aragon (died 1387), notorious for his vindictiveness; Tamerlane (Timur, 1336–1405), the famous Mongol conqueror who brutally massacred the inhabitants of Siwas (Sivas in Turkey) in 1400, and whose empire included Harat in Afghanistan, Sabzawar in Iran, Takrit and Baghdad in Iraq, and Aleppo in Syria.

222 *Magnan ... Clichy*: in response to suspicions that he had been involved in the 1840 Boulogne episode, the French general Bernard-Pierre Magnan (1791–1865) publicly dissociated himself from Louis-Napoléon; a major Parisian debtors' prison was located in the Rue de Clichy.

Caligula ... Charles IX: Caligula (died 41 CE), notoriously corrupt Roman emperor; Philip III (1578–1621), king of Spain who expelled all Moors (including even converts to Roman Catholicism) from the country; Tomás de Torquemada (1420–98), Spanish grand inquisitor responsible for the execution of thousands of Jews and other heretics; Khayr ad-Din (Barbarossa, died 1546), powerful Turkish pirate and admiral; Ezzelino III (1194–1259), ruthless and tyrannical Ghibelline ruler of north-eastern Italy; Michel Le Tellier (1603–85), Roman Catholic priest and statesman, who advocated vigorous persecution of non-Catholics; Ludovico Sforza (1452–1508), unscrupulous duke of Milan; Charles IX (1550–74), king of France responsible for the Bartholomew's Day massacre.

Writing to France

Written 17 March 1853; the title is supplied by the present editors. During the years immediately following Louis-Napoléon's 1851 coup, Hugo's letters to France were carefully examined by the French authorities and sometimes censored. Thus he resorted to various subterfuges when he wanted politically sensitive material to reach France. In 1853, a letter from England to the future novelist Gustave Flaubert (1821–80), then merely an obscure middle-class invalid living in relative isolation on a country estate at Croisset, would be unlikely to arouse the suspicions of the authorities. There would be nothing unusual about a letter from Flaubert to the novelist Louise Colet (1810–76), his most regular correspondent; or about a letter from the Parisian author Colet to the Parisian editor and journalist Jules Janin (1804–74). Janin was an outspoken supporter of the exiled Hugo.

Charles II

Written 29 May 1853; the title is supplied by the present editors. Hugo was perennially intrigued by a nation's capacity for remaining content with—and even admiring—rulers of the worst possible kind. Here he surveys some major points in the career of Charles II (1630–85): his summary executions of his enemies, his secret concessions to Louis XIV in exchange for much-needed funds, his disastrous naval defeat by the Dutch in 1667, his conflict with (and eventual rule without) Parliament, and his personal promiscuity and callousness.

223   *29 May 1651*: in history, the Battle of Worcester took place on 3 September 1651. Hugo was relatively familiar with this period of English history; it had formed the setting of his play *Cromwell* (1827).

     Louis XIII . . . Louis XI: Louis XIII (1607–43) was dominated by his ministers, especially Richelieu; Louis XV (1710–74) was notorious for his promiscuity (particularly his sexual exploitation of the daughters of the poor); Louis XI (1423–83) gained a reputation for treachery and brutality.

'When, France, you are mere prostrate slaves . . .'

Written 30 March 1853; poem I. i in *The Empire in the Pillory* (1853).

'Night—dark night, deep, and full of drowsy things . . .'

Written 28 October 1852; poem I. xiv in *The Empire in the Pillory* (1853).

227   *Maupas . . . Saint-Arnaud*: Charlemagne-Émile de Maupas (1818–88) and Leroy de Saint-Arnaud (1798–1854), prominent supporters of Louis-Napoléon; Hugo is addressing them by the titles they have earned under the new regime.

Apotheosis

Written 31 January 1853; poem III. i in *The Empire in the Pillory* (1853). The poem sardonically traces Louis-Napoléon's progress from debt-ridden poverty to resplendent glory beside the world's great emperors.

227   *1815*: the date when Napoleon's family was officially exiled from France, after the battle of Waterloo.

     Garat: Martin Garat (1748–1830), first director of the Banque de France; long after his death, his signature continued to be printed on many French banknotes.

229   *Romieu*: the journalist Auguste Romieu (1800–55), whose fanatically anti-republican pamphlets during 1851 attempted to stir up fears that bloodthirsty socialists were on the point of starting a new Reign of Terror in the land.

     long live our king Joe Blow!: a quotation from Molière's 1655 comedy *L'Étourdi*, II. viii.

     the Seine . . . freezes over: the Seine froze in January 1852, a phenomenon seen by many writers of the time as Nature's response to the new regime. The reference to the Neva (the river on which Saint Petersburg is situated) echoes the Russian term 'ukases' in the previous line.

229 *the Medici ghost*: the Tuileries palace, one of Napoleon III's official residences, was said to be haunted by the ghost of Marie de Médicis (1573–1642), the wife of Henri IV.

Alexander the Sixth: Rodrigo Borgia (1431–1503), one of the most notoriously corrupt popes.

Carrara! Paros! Attic marbles!: the marble for Classical sculptures was quarried from Carrara in Tuscany, the Greek island of Paros, and Mount Pentelicus in Attica.

231 *Pericles and Scipio*: both the Athenian statesman Pericles (fifth century BCE) and the Roman general Scipio Africanus the Elder (died 183 BCE) faced public disgrace and prosecution after making major contributions to the welfare of their homeland.

Trajan ... Augustus: Marcus Ulpius Trajanus (died 117) and Caesar Augustus (died 14), among the most powerful and highly regarded Roman emperors.

Sweeney Todd: in the original, the villainous name is that of Robert Macaire, the central character in *L'Auberge des Adrets* (1823) and various subsequent popular melodramas.

The Man Has Laughed

Written 30 October 1852; poem III. ii in *The Empire in the Pillory* (1853). The epigraph is taken from the journal *La Patrie*; 'Elysian newspapers' is an ironic allusion to the Élysée, one of Louis-Napoléon's official residences.

The Joint Commissions

Written 7 May 1853; poem IV. iii in *The Empire in the Pillory* (1853). The Joint Commissions, composed of military, legal, and political officials, were set up by Louis-Napoléon in February 1852 to deal with opponents of his *coup d'état* more speedily than the existing courts could do. The Commissions sentenced about ten thousand people to deportation.

233 *foreign hulks and holes*: the French text names Cayenne in French Guiana and Bone in Algeria, two of the major prison colonies to which Louis-Napoléon's political opponents were deported.

The Black Hunter

Written 22 October 1852; poem VII. iii in *The Empire in the Pillory* (1853). The Black Hunter is a familiar figure (almost always maleficent) in Teutonic legend.

235 *Saint Anthony*: Egyptian ascetic hermit (fourth century CE), famous for his visions of numerous diabolic temptations.

'I was in Brussels; it was June . . .'

Written 20 May 1853; poem VII. v in *The Empire in the Pillory* (1853).

239   *Charlet . . . Cirasse . . . Cuisinier*: murderers guillotined in June and July
       1852. Only Jacques Charlet was a known republican; but in Hugo's eyes,
       capital punishment was never excusable, whatever the victim's guilt or
       political persuasion.

       his plebiscite: a national plebiscite on 20–1 December 1851 endorsed
       Louis-Napoléon's *coup d'état* by a majority of almost seven million votes.

The Last Word

Written 14 December 1852; poem VII. xiv in the 1853 edition of *The Empire in
the Pillory*, and VII. xvii in the 1870 and subsequent editions.

239   *the Potter's Field . . . Sibour*: a burial ground in Jerusalem, bought with
       the silver paid to Judas Iscariot for betraying Jesus; Auguste Sibour
       (1792–1857), Archbishop of Paris, who held a *Te Deum* at Notre-Dame
       cathedral on 1 January 1852 to celebrate Louis-Napoléon's coup.

241   *Charlemagne . . . Bill Sikes*: in the original French, the illustrious
       Charlemagne (Charles the Great, king of the Franks; died 814) is set
       against the celebrated bandit and murderer Louis Mandrin (1724–55).

243   *the Hun*: the original French specifies the Roman dictator Lucius
       Cornelius Sulla (died 78 BCE), a notorious tyrant.

The Birds

Written 14 October 1854; poem I. xviii in *Contemplations* (1856).

Unity

Written 2 July 1853; poem I. xxv in *Contemplations* (1856). The last line recalls
Correggio's reputed exclamation on first seeing the paintings of Raphael,
'Then I am a painter too!'; but Hugo's adaptation gives it new, and remarkably
complex, resonances.

Wayside Pause

Written 7 May 1855; poem I. xxix in *Contemplations* (1856).

249   *an old saint*: the sign of the inn; but Hugo is also starting to prepare for
       the deepening and darkening of mood in the poem's second half.

       a Christ being buffeted: a picture on the bedroom wall, depicting the
       opponents of Christ buffeting him during his trial.

251   *The Gemonies*: the Stairs of Mourning at ancient Rome, where the bodies
       of common criminals were exposed after their execution.

       Dante . . . Scipio: representative opponents of tyranny, all of whom,
       according to history or legend, were killed, exiled, or disgraced by their
       enemies: Dante Alighieri (1265–1321), Italian poet, author of the *Divine
       Comedy*; Aeschylus (fifth century BCE), Greek dramatist, author of
       Prometheus Bound; Socrates (fifth century BCE), Greek philosopher; John

Milton (1608–74), English poet; Thomas More (1478–1535), English statesman; Scipio Africanus the Elder (died 183 BCE), Roman general.

251 *Aristides . . . John Huss*: Aristides the Just (fifth century BCE), Athenian statesman, exiled because of his opposition to Themistocles; John Huss (died 1415), Bohemian religious reformer, burnt at the stake because of his opposition to the doctrines of the Roman Catholic Church.

253 *Caiaphas*: Jewish high priest, one of the leading instigators of Christ's arrest and crucifixion.

'I was reading. Reading what? The timeless poem . . .'

Written 24 January 1855; poem III. viii in *Contemplations* (1856). Léon Cellier, in his edition of *Les Contemplations* (Paris, 1969), 578, regards 'this remarkable poem, in which Hugo's "symbolist" stance is presented with equal subtlety and intensity', as comparable in both character and quality with Baudelaire's sonnet 'Correspondances'. It is interesting in other ways too. A profound sense of personal guilt is often implicit in Hugo's middle-period work, but it rarely surfaces as strikingly as it does at the end of this piece.

253 *God's flowers*: the narrator learns the word of God (which one person might read in the Bible and another in the world's major writers) from the created universe.

The Beggar

Written 20 October 1854 (though much of it had already been composed by 1846); poem V. ix in *Contemplations* (1856). A remarkably rich and complex poem; note, among other things, the slight hints of religious terminology ('retreat', 'the cloth'), which present the beggar as a kind of idiosyncratic hermit.

Lowing of Oxen

Written 26 July 1855; poem V. xvii in *Contemplations* (1856).

257 *Virgil*: Publius Vergilius Maro (died 19 BCE), Latin poet; a phrase from his *Georgics*, ii. 470 forms the title of Hugo's poem.

259 *At the hour when . . . smoke is rising*: a reminiscence of Virgil, *Eclogues*, i. 82–3.

Apparition

Written 23 August 1855; poem V. xviii in *Contemplations* (1856).

261 *it was female*: in French, the noun *ange* ('angel') is masculine; but this angel is assimilated to the dead Léopoldine and to Death itself (*la mort*, feminine). Hence the speaker's terror: his visitor has come from the realm beyond the grave.

Cerigo

Written 11 June 1855; poem V. xx in *Contemplations* (1856). The poem was evidently suggested by Baudelaire's 'Un Voyage à Cythère' ('A Voyage to

Cythera'), published in the *Revue des deux mondes* on 1 June 1855. The Greek island of Cythera (later known as Cerigo) was sacred in ancient times to the goddess of love, Aphrodite (identified with the Roman Venus). Baudelaire's imaginary visit finds that the island is actually a barren and desolate place, where wild beasts and birds of prey devour a decaying human corpse. Hugo, a great admirer of Baudelaire's writings, fully agrees—but he suggests that the true place to look for Venus is in the heavens, not on earth. His poem thus draws on the traditional distinction between sacred and profane love, reflecting the discussion in Plato's *Symposium* and embodied, for instance, in Titian's famous painting on the subject.

261 *The Cyprian's sacred shell*: in Classical mythology, Venus was born from the sea foam and carried on a cockleshell to the island of Cyprus, one of the major centres of her worship (hence her title 'the Cyprian').

star: the goddess ('soul') Venus was identified in ancient times with the planet; Hugo is preparing for the second part of his poem.

263 *siren*: in Classical mythology, a female monster whose singing lured sailors to destruction.

Lemnos . . . Lepanto: the Greek island of Lemnos was a major centre of the worship of Aphrodite ('the Lemnian Venus') in ancient times; the town of Lepanto, on the Gulf of Corinth, existed in ancient times (as Naupactus) but is for ever associated with a later event: the defeat of the Turkish navy in 1571, one of the first steps in the struggle that limited Ottoman power in the Mediterranean and ultimately resulted in Greek independence. Even while it speaks of ancient times, Hugo's line therefore recalls the changes that shaped the modern world.

The nymphs and the Olympians: in Classical mythology, female and male deities (dwellers on Mount Olympus).

Cupid, Mars, and Psyche: in Roman mythology, respectively god of love, god of war, and goddess of the soul (symbolically wedded to Cupid in later myths).

doves: sacred to Venus in Classical mythology.

When the Lord God laid her bare: Classical mythology gives way to Scripture; Hugo is recalling the creation of the stars in Genesis 1: 16, while stressing (*dévoila*, 'laid her bare') that God's creation was naked and unashamed. Contrast the nakedness of the worldly Venus, which ought to be veiled (line 18), and compare 'The Consecration of Woman' (page 295).

265 *halcyon*: in Classical mythology, a sea-dwelling bird of good omen.

the morning star and evening star: the planet Venus, when visible at dawn and dusk respectively.

'The poet's verse-form used to pillage April's basket . . .'

Written 4 November 1854; poem V. xxv in *Contemplations* (1856). In Classical mythology, Persephone (Proserpina), the daughter of the earth-goddess Ceres, was abducted while she was gathering flowers in the meadows; she became the consort of her abductor—Pluto, god of the underworld. Hugo's remarkable reinterpretation of the myth is his own invention.

The Weather Clears

Written 4 July 1855; poem VI. x in *Contemplations* (1856).

267 *the sacred sap*: these lines are reworking Virgil, *Georgics*, ii. 325–7.

'The soul dives in the chasm . . .'

Written in the first three months of 1854; poem VI. xiv in *Contemplations* (1856).

Storm

Written about 1854; poem III. xxxii in *The Four Winds of the Spirit* (1881).

from *The Threshold of the Abyss*

'The Threshold of the Abyss', written during the first half of 1856, is the prologue of Hugo's epic poem *God* (published 1891). Searching for God, the poem's protagonist hears a succession of voices warning him of the difficulties that lie ahead. (In the original draft, these voices arose from 'the Human Spirit', the perennial spirit of compromise and mediocrity; but Hugo later decided to make their origin more mysterious and less specific.)

273 *Oh! so your plummet wants to sound*: the sixth of the preliminary voices (numbered 'Voix V' in the edition of *Dieu: Le Seuil du gouffre* by René Journet and Guy Robert (Paris, 1961)). The passage surveys the sheer immensity and diversity of human metaphysical and religious enquiries— and their inconclusiveness. Its torrent of proper names is therefore a strategy designed to evoke immense vistas of historical philosophers and theologians, receding in all directions from the well known (Plato, Jerome, Pascal) through the half known (Zeno, Pelagius, Lyra) to the little known (Nicomachus, Theotechnus, Cardano) and even the totally unknown (John Catechumenus, invented by Hugo himself). In many instances, the specific beliefs of these thinkers are less relevant to the poem than the simple fact that they existed and disagreed with each other—though in some cases Hugo's juxtapositions will be relished all the more by readers who appreciate what strange bedfellows the poet has coupled together.

The bibles borne on sphinxes' breasts: the hieroglyphic inscriptions between the paws of Egyptian sphinxes.

theogonies: tales of the origin of gods; Hesiod's Greek *Theogony* is the most familiar example.

John Climacus or John Catechumenus: the former was a famous Sinaitic hermit of the fifth century; the latter is Hugo's invention, modelled on 'catechumen' (a new convert) and John Cantacuzene (Byzantine emperor, 1347–54).

Astarte . . . Horus: the Phoenician goddess of love, and a major Egyptian sky-god.

Irminsul: an ancient Saxon deity, usually embodied in a wooden pillar, but here envisaged as dwelling on or in a stone pillar (a menhir).

275 *Olympius*: fourth-century dedicatee of Gregory of Nyssa's treatise *On Perfection*.

Theophilus: Theophilus of Caesarea (second century), who convened a synod to determine the much-contested date of Easter.

Ammon: a major Egyptian god, whose temple in Libya was visited by many pilgrims, the most famous being Alexander the Great; 'the pug-nosed colossi' are sphinxes.

Caesarius . . . Bellarmine: Caesarius of Nazianzus (fourth century), physician who became a monk late in life; Robert Bellarmine (1542–1621), precocious Roman Catholic theologian.

Denis . . . Boethius: the patron saint of France (third century) and the celebrated pagan philosopher (died 524), both of whom were reportedly beheaded.

Pythagoras . . . Glareanus of Basle: Pythagoras (sixth century BCE), Greek mystic; Ado of Vienne (died 875), French bishop; Onufrio Panvini(o) (1530–68), Italian monk and historian; Glareanus (Heinrich Lorit, 1488–1563), Swiss philosopher.

druid, fakir, bonze: religious devotees of the Celtic, Muslim (or Hindu), and Buddhist faiths respectively.

Doric entablature: the oldest style of Greek temple architecture.

Volta . . . Augustine grace: a representative list of human scientific and religious thinkers (its disorganization and semi-obscurity are part of its point): Alessandro Volta (1745–1827), Italian scientist, not otherwise known as an opponent of the French mathematician Alexis Clairaut (1713–65); Cyril of Jerusalem (died 387), who claimed to see an enormous cross of light in the sky above Golgotha (the hill where Jesus was crucified); John Calvin (1509–64), French Protestant theologian, whose doctrines were opposed by the Roman Catholic orator Jacques-Bénigne Bossuet (1627–1704); Mani (third century CE), Persian religious leader and founder of Manichaeism, who was opposed by Bishop Archelaus of Cascar and others; Pope Gregory VII (Hildebrand, died 1085), who asserted the absolute authority of the papacy over all secular rulers; Martin Luther (1483–1546), German Protestant theologian, whose *Wider die himmlischen Propheten* (1524–5) describes the people as *Herr omnes* ('Mr Everyone'); two contrasting French philosophers, the believer Blaise Pascal (1623–62) and the sceptic Denis Diderot (1713–84); Johann Reuchlin (1455–1522), German scholar; Voltaire (François-Marie Arouet, 1694–1778), French writer and sceptic, whose article 'Épiphanie' in his *Dictionnaire philosophique* (1764) questions the origin of the Magi (the so-called 'three kings'), and who repeatedly attacked the orthodox Roman Catholicism of Dom Augustin Calmet (1672–1757); Philippus Aureolus Paracelsus (died 1541), German scientist and religious writer (his 'three blazing Pegasi', or winged horses, appear to be Hugo's invention); Solomon (tenth century BCE), king of Israel, who built the temple at Jerusalem; John Huss (died 1415), Bohemian religious reformer, who opposed orthodox Roman Catholic doctrine; Pelagius (fourth–fifth centuries), British monk who advocated salvation by faith and works; Augustine of Hippo (354–430), North African theologian, who vehemently opposed Pelagius and advocated salvation by faith alone.

275 *Epicurus with Ezekiel*: the Greek sceptic of the third century BCE with the Hebrew prophet of the sixth century BCE.

277 *Alcuin, Gorgias Leontinus, and Aquinas*: the ancient sophist Gorgias of Leontini (fifth century BCE) incongruously joins two orthodox Roman Catholic theologians, the English Alcuin (735–804) and the Italian Thomas Aquinas (1225–74).

menologies: collections of saints' lives.

Thebes with a hundred gates and Thebes with seven: Thebes in Egypt and Thebes in Greece; both cities were major religious centres in ancient times.

Sadolet or Bembo: Cardinals Jacques Sadolet (1477–1547), the opponent of Calvin, and Pietro Bembo (1470–1547), the influential scholar; the title 'cardinal' is derived from the Latin *cardo*, 'hinge'.

John: the prophet John the Baptist (first century CE), who lived in the wilderness on a diet of 'locusts and wild honey'.

Halcyons: in Classical mythology, sea-dwelling birds of good omen.

Novatus . . . Parsees: representatives of contrasting religious doctrines: a Montanist, Novatus of Carthage (third century CE); two Arians, Eustathius of Antioch (fourth century) and Arius himself (died 336); an anti-Arian schismatic, Meletius of Lycopolis (died 326); the Rabbis of Judaism; and the Parsees of Zoroastrianism.

morphastic dances: ancient Greek dances imitating the movements of animals (Athenaeus, *Deipnosophistae*, xiv. 629).

Sirius . . . Perseus . . . Septentrion: the brightest star, and two constellations near the north celestial pole ('Septentrion' refers to the seven major stars of the Great Bear).

Domnus . . . Tornielli: Domnus (third century CE), orthodox Catholic elected as bishop of Antioch in 268 to replace the heretic Paul of Samosata; Joseph Justus Scaliger (1540–1609), distinguished French Classical scholar; John Cassian (died 435), an opponent of Augustinianism; Agostino Tornielli (1543–1622), Italian monk and religious historian. Their advice would be bewilderingly varied!

haruspices: ancient Roman soothsayers.

279 *Lipsius . . . Gerbert*: Justus Lipsius (1547–1606), German scholar, who bequeathed his silver pen to a convent at Hainaut; Zeno of Citium (third

century BCE), Greek philosopher, founder of Stoicism; Pope Sylvester II (Gerbert, died 1003), French scholar reputed to be in league with the devil.

centiaires: square metres.

cap that Cheops with a pyramidion: cap that pyramid (Cheops was the fourth-dynasty Egyptian king who erected the Great Pyramid at Giza) with its pyramidal apex.

Spiridion: Spiridion of Trimithus (fourth century), who is said to have converted a sceptical philosopher during a dispute about the Trinity.

the resounding cock . . . Lenore's ghastly horse: the former crowed when the apostle Peter denied Christ; the latter, in Gottfried August Bürger's famous ballad 'Lenore' (1773), carried a dead rider.

Wycliffe . . . Theotechnus: John Wycliffe (died 1384), English religious reformer; Gottfried Wilhelm Leibnitz (1646–1716), German philosopher; Ambrose of Alexandria (third century CE), the friend of Origen; Basilides of Alexandria (second century) and Emanuel Swedenborg (1688–1772), leaders of idiosyncratic religious sects; Nicolas of Lyra (died 1340) and Rupert of Deutz (died 1129), influential medieval theologians; Geronimo Cardano (1501–76), Italian astrologer; Alcidamas of Elea (fifth century BCE), Greek sophist; Eusebius of Caesarea (fourth century CE), distinguished church historian and theologian; Photinus (fourth century), eccentric religious theorist; Magnus Aurelius Cassiodorus (sixth century), Roman statesman and monk; Potamon of Heraclea (fourth century), zealous Trinitarian; Paphnutius of Thebes (fourth century), opponent of universal priestly celibacy; Sophronius of Jerusalem (seventh century), opponent of Monothelitism; Theotechnus of Caesarea (third century), follower of Origen.

Epidaurus: an ancient Greek city, noted particularly for its temple to Aesculapius.

impetrating prayer: in theology, a prayer of request or entreaty.

Saint-Maur . . . Trent: the Maurists were a reform group of Benedictine monks, active between 1621 and 1792; the twenty-five sessions of the Roman Catholic Council of Trent were held between 1545 and 1563.

Sibylline Leaves: the Sibyl of Cumae was said to write her prophecies on leaves (Virgil, *Aeneid*, iii. 441–6); Hugo may also be thinking of the so-called Sibylline Oracles, oracular Greek verses written by adherents of Jewish and allied cults between approximately the second century BCE and the second century CE.

281 *Jerome . . . Origen*: some of the most illustrious thinkers in human history: the theologians Jerome (fourth–fifth centuries) and Origen (third century); John the seer of the Book of Revelation (first century CE), 'roaming the shores' of the Greek island of Patmos; the poet Dante Alighieri (1265–1321); the scientists Isaac Newton (1643–1727) and Leonhard Euler (1707–83); and the philosopher Plato (fourth century BCE).

281 *Delphi, Idumaea*: the former was the site of a famous Greek oracle; the latter was a proverbial home of wise men (Jeremiah 49: 7), situated east of Israel.

'*Zeus*', '*Mithra*', '*Vishnu*': major gods of Greek, Persian, and Hindu religions respectively.

Dendera: a town in Egypt; its Ptolemaic temple of Hathor contained a famous representation of the zodiac.

Nicomachus . . . Thales: ancient philosophers of the first century CE and the sixth century BCE respectively.

Have you seen thinkers set off for the heavens?: the eleventh of the preliminary voices (numbered 'Voix X' in the Journet and Robert edition).

Elijah . . . Paul: the prophet Elijah (eighth century BCE) was carried off to heaven in a fiery chariot; the apostle Paul (first century CE) 'was caught up to paradise, and heard unspeakable words'.

283 *Old are the mountains*: The twelfth and last of the preliminary voices (numbered 'Voix XI' in the Journet and Robert edition), and the only one to offer the poem's narrator any encouragement, however equivocally it may be expressed. (Indeed, in the margin of his manuscript, at this point, Hugo jotted the summary: 'I, nevertheless, encourage you.')

from *The Eagle*

The body of Hugo's *God* (published 1891) consists of nine numbered sections, in which nine successive winged creatures utter their different conceptions of God. In Section V, an eagle declares that there is one God—a God of vengeance. The chosen extract is a later addition to the eagle's speech, written mainly in the early months of 1856, and is fundamentally modelled on the challenges uttered by Elihu and the Lord in Job 37 and 38. As in those passages, the cumulative questions are designed to expose the listener's (and reader's) ignorance. How can someone so limited hope to comprehend the mysteries of the universe?

The line numbers against the French text conform to those in *Dieu: Le Seuil du gouffre*, ed. René Journet and Guy Robert (Paris, 1960). The title 'The Eagle' was supplied by Hugo's literary executors.

285 *When it thunders*: 'God thundereth marvellously with his voice: great things doeth he, which we cannot comprehend' (Job 37: 5).

Jebel . . . Jungfrau: Jebel Musa in the Sinai Peninsula, traditionally supposed to be the peak where Moses received the law from God; the Atlas Mountains in Morocco and Algeria; the Jungfrau ('the Virgin') in the Swiss Alps.

287 *still the waves!*: 'Who shut up the sea . . . and said, Hitherto shalt thou come, but no further: and here shall thy proud waves be stayed?' (Job 38: 7–11).

where God cast him: in Jewish pseudepigraphical literature, Satan was originally an angel, and was cast out of heaven because of his sin;

this legend is retold in the opening section of Hugo's epic *The End of Satan*.

Cassandra . . . Ajax . . . Aegisthus: in Greek legend, the Trojan princess Cassandra foresaw the fall of Troy, her own rape by the Greek invader Ajax, and the murder of the Greek leader Agamemnon by his wife's lover Aegisthus.

thrice-greatest: Trismegistus, an attribute of Hermes the Egyptian, legendary author of 'hermetic' religious literature.

289 *the double spirit of Elijah*: which his disciple, the prophet Elisha, prayed successfully to inherit.

Endor's and Baalbek's black diviners: King Saul of Israel consulted a female necromancer at Endor; Baalbek was an ancient city in Lebanon, devoted to the worship of Baal.

'What do you think of death, you vain philosopher? . . .'

Written 1856; MS 106/278b; poem III. xliv in the 1897 edition of *The Whole Lyre*, and III. lxii in the 1935 Imprimerie nationale edition. *Reliquat* ('remainder' or 'residue') was Hugo's name for the material left over when a literary project had been completed. This passage and the next one were drafted for the epic *God* (perhaps as utterances for the preliminary voices heard in 'The Threshold of the Abyss'), but were not finally used in that poem; in Hugo's terminology, they therefore belong to the *reliquat* of *God*.

'The depths of the I AM are swathed in cloud . . .'

Written 1856; MS 106/518b; published in the 1911 Imprimerie nationale edition of *God*. The passage was greatly admired by Jean Massin, who remarked, 'The relationship between psychological fantasy and politico-religious mythology has perhaps never been better expressed' (Victor Hugo, *Œuvres complètes*, ed. Jean Massin (Paris: 1967–71), x. 83).

293 *Jupiter . . . Cybele*: representative deities of human invention. Jupiter, Molech, Mithra, Brahma, and Odin, were major gods in ancient Roman, Ammonite, Persian, Indian, and Norse religion respectively; Venus, Isis, and Cybele were well-known goddesses of the Romans, Egyptians, and Phrygians; sphinxes were revered in Egypt (Thebes was one of the country's capital cities).

The Consecration of Woman

Written 17 October 1858; poem I. i in the first series (1859) of *The Legend of the Ages*, and II. i in the September 1883 collected edition. The poem depicts sexual activity and pregnancy as occurring in the sinless conditions of primeval Eden. Its fundamental source is Genesis 2, especially the statement that 'they were both naked, the man and his wife, and were not ashamed' (2: 25); but the concept of sexual activity in Eden derives from one of Hugo's favourite poems, Milton's *Paradise Lost* (1667). Hugo is thus defying both the common nineteenth-century belief that all sexuality contains something inherently sinful, and the Roman Catholic doctrine of the Immaculate Conception (first proclaimed by Pope Pius IX in 1854), which teaches that Mary the mother of Jesus was unique among humans in being conceived without original sin. *All* conceptions are immaculate, Hugo insists; compare 'The Immaculate Conception Revisited', in *The Art of Being a Grandfather* (p. 443).

295 *halcyon*: in Classical mythology, a sea-dwelling bird of good omen.

297 *One in All*: 'I am no pantheist', Hugo wrote in a letter of 31 July 1867; 'the pantheist says "all is God", but I say "God is all." '

299 *primal forms*: the dinosaurs and other strange fossil creatures discovered by nineteenth-century geology; Hugo frequently stressed the prodigious element in divine (and artistic) creation.

307 *something in her womb that stirred*: 'And Adam knew Eve his wife, and she conceived and bare Cain' (Genesis 4: 1; the Scriptures do not say whether the conception occurred in Eden). The product of the pregnancy will be the world's first murderer (as the very next poem in *The Legend of the Ages*, 'Conscience', may remind us), but this does not affect the purity of the act.

Boaz Asleep

Written 1 May 1859; poem I. vi in the first series (1859) of *The Legend of the Ages*, and II. vi in the September 1883 collected edition. The poem's primary source is the Book of Ruth (especially 3: 1–8).

307 *gleaning*: as Ruth herself did (Ruth 2: 3–7, 15–16).

309 *A judge was leader*: because 'in those days there was no king in Israel' (Judges 21: 25)—a thematically important point in *The Legend of the Ages*, where monarchs are associated with tyranny and oppression (see e.g. 'The Vanished City', p. 431).

Jacob ... Judith: Jacob's dream of angels ascending and descending (Genesis 28: 12) is a source of Boaz's dream in this poem; Judith is presumably added merely for the sonority.

a king ... a god: David the psalmist, great-grandson of Ruth and Boaz, and Jesus Christ, David's remote descendant. The nocturnal meeting of wealthy Israelite and impoverished Moabite will have momentous consequences.

311 *a Moabite*: elsewhere in *The Legend of the Ages* (as in the Scriptures) Moabites are enemies of Israel and worshippers of false gods; the present poem depicts, among much else, a process by which customary barriers and prejudices may be transcended.

Gilgal: in this context, presumably the pre-Israelite kings' city of Joshua 12: 23 (the passage in which Hugo found the name Jerimoth).

313 *Ur and Jerimadeth*: the east and the west: the pre-Israelite kings' cities of Ur in Chaldaea, almost due east of Bethlehem, and Jerimoth (Jarmuth) in

Judah, almost due west (the intrusive *-d-* in the latter name arose by a characteristically Hugolian process of contamination from 'Judith', the word that most recently came into the poet's head when he needed a name for a rhyme). It has also been argued that *Jérimadeth* embodies a pun on *j'ai rime à -dait* ('I must rhyme to *-dait*'), though that would seem neither thematically relevant here nor particularly plausible (Hugo's puns, though frequent, belong to a few relatively predictable types, and this one is not within his repertoire).

Christ's First Encounter with the Tomb

Written 23 October 1852; poem I. viii in the first series (1859) of *The Legend of the Ages*, and II. viii in the September 1883 collected edition. The poem was originally written for *The Empire in the Pillory*, in which context it would have stressed mainly on the perennial tendency of religious orthodoxy to support the political establishment; its final home gives it much more extensive implications. It is woven largely from phrases of Scripture, principally the narratives of the life of Christ.

313 *Job and Elijah*: representing the ancient patriarchs and prophets respectively.

315 *with tripled strength*: incorporating a reminiscence of Isaiah 40: 30–1, 'Even the youths shall faint and be weary . . . but they that wait for the Lord shall renew their strength'.

Solomon: king of Israel in the tenth century BCE, and builder of the temple at Jerusalem to house the Ark of the Covenant.

three days' journey off from Bethany: a mistake that crept into the poem while Hugo was revising his manuscript. Bethany was only 15 stadia from Jerusalem (probably about 2–3 kilometres); but Hugo always tended to overestimate distances when they were expressed in stadia.

Thomas: the disciple who would—at first—doubt Christ's resurrection.

Connubial Bliss

Written 5 October 1859; poem I. II. v in *Songs of Street and Wood* (1865).

319 *the Graces*: in post-Hesiodic mythology, three beautiful daughters of Venus.

Flora and Faun: the Roman goddess of flowers and a goatish rural deity, startlingly and incongruously coupled here in a parody of the stock phrase 'flora and fauna'.

Goliath . . . Delilah: the French original has simply masculine Philistine and feminine Philistine. To overcome the lack of gender inflections in English, our translation ventures to supply the most famous specimen of each type; the resultant pairing seems quite in the spirit of Hugo's poem.

Cupid: the Classical god of love, usually depicted as a mischievous boy.

'Nature? she's amorous everywhere . . .'

Written 1859; poem I. III. iv in *Songs of Street and Wood* (1865). 'Jeanne', in this volume, stands for Juliette Drouet, as Hugo's handwritten dedication of the copy presented to her makes clear.

321 *the stooge . . . the soubrette*: in the original French they are given the stock names Orgon and Angélique, familiar from seventeenth- and eighteenth-century comedies (e.g. Molière's *Tartuffe* and *Le Malade imaginaire*).

From Woman to Heaven

Written 31 May 1859; poem II. I. i in *Songs of Street and Wood* (1865). The poem marks the transition from Book I of the volume, 'Jeunesse' ('Youth'), which is concerned with earthly love (the realm of the heart), and Book II, 'Sagesse' ('Truth'), which is concerned with heavenly love (the realm of the soul). In the tradition of the Scriptures and Plato's *Symposium*, the earthly is seen as preparation for the heavenly.

An Alcove in the Sunrise

Written 3 July 1859; poem II. II. ii in *Songs of Street and Wood* (1865).

During an Illness

Written 3 October 1859; poem II. IV. ii in *Songs of Street and Wood* (1865).

327 *Epicurus*: Greek philosopher (third century BCE), a religious sceptic.

   Spinoza: Baruch Spinoza (1632–77), Dutch philosopher, a pantheist.

Waterloo

Written 21 December 1861; chapters II. I. i–xviii of *Les Misérables* (1862). Hugo tells the story of Waterloo dramatically, starting at a tangent and then plunging straight into the conflict; his early readers would not have required any background explanations, and would already have been familiar with the names of most of the leading participants, especially those on the French side. The following paragraphs contain only information directly relevant to Hugo's narrative.

   Napoleon escaped from captivity on the island of Elba in February 1815, landed at the Golfe Jouan on 1 March, and marched toward Paris. Louis XVIII instructed the army leader Michel Ney (1769–1815) to meet him and stop him. Instead, Ney joined forces with Napoleon and placed the army at his disposal. Louis XVIII fled to Ghent. English and Dutch troops under the command of Arthur Wellesley, Duke of Wellington (1769–1852), and Prussian troops under the command of Gebhard von Blücher (1742–1819), were sent to oppose Napoleon. The main confrontation took place on 18 June 1815, at Waterloo in Belgium.

   Among the French officers mentioned by Hugo were Marshal Jean de Dieu Soult, Duc de Dalmatie (1769–1851; the army's chief of staff), Jean-Baptiste Drouet d'Erlon (1765–1844), Charles-Claude Jacquinot (1772–1848), Honoré, Comte Reille (1775–1860), Gilbert Bachelu (1777–1849), Prince

Jérôme Bonaparte (1784–1860; Napoleon's brother), Maximilien Foy (1775–1825; in later years a well-known politician), Armand-Charles Guilleminot (1774–1840), Pierre François Bauduin (1768–1815, killed at Waterloo), Jean-Louis Soye (1774–1832), Georges, Comte Lobau (1770–1838), François Kellermann (1735–1820), Jean-Baptiste Milhaud (1766–1833), Antoine Drouot (1774–1847; Hugo has already planted a brief but telling glimpse of him in the very earliest pages of *Les Misérables*, on p. 132 above), François-Nicolas Haxo (1774–1838), and Philibert-Guillaume Duhesme (1766–1815, died in the custody of the Prussians to whom he surrendered after the battle). Thirty thousand further soldiers under Emmanuel de Grouchy (1766–1847) failed to arrive—which, in Napoleon's later opinion, was the main cause of the French defeat.

Wellington's officers included Prince William of Orange (1792–1849), Rowland Hill (1772–1842), George Cooke (1769–1837), Charles von Alten (1764–1840), Hendrik George de Perponcher-Sedlnitzky (1771–1856), David Henry Chassé (1765–1849), Henry Clinton (1771–1829), and Charles Colville (1770–1843), Christian von Ompteda (1765–1815, killed at Waterloo), James Kempt (1764–1854), Thomas Picton (1758–1815, killed at Waterloo), Henry Paget, Earl of Uxbridge (1768–1854), Lord Edward Somerset (1776–1842), William Ponsonby (1772–1815, killed at Waterloo), and Jean Alphonse de Collaert (1763–1830).

Blücher's Prussian troops reached the field late in the day and took part in the final stages of the battle. Hugo mentions three of the four corps leaders—Hans Ernst Zieten (1770–1848), Georg Ludwig von Pirch (1763–1838; known as 'Pirch I' to distinguish him from his brother, whom Hugo does not discuss), and Friedrich Wilhelm Bülow (1755–1816)—and also the cavalry commander Prince Wilhelm of Prussia (1797–1888; the future Kaiser Wilhelm I of Germany). Bülow's corps was the first to arrive.

The conflict was close and hard-fought, and its outcome remained in doubt for much of the day. As usual with complex and chaotic military encounters, eyewitness accounts vary considerably. Moreover, as Wellington wrote on 8 August 1815, even if 'some individuals may recollect all the little events of which the great result is the battle won or lost', still 'no individual can recollect the order in which, or the exact moments at which, they occurred, which makes all the difference to their value and importance'. Some (though not all) modern historians doubt whether either the arrival of Blücher or the non-arrival of Grouchy had any significant effect on the outcome, whether anything really happened at the 'sunken road from Ohain', whether Cambronne really uttered his famous word, and so on. Hugo's Waterloo, like Shakespeare's Agincourt, offers us the truth of parable rather than the truth of historical reconstruction. 'Here I am in the vicinity of Waterloo', he wrote in a letter on 20 May 1861. 'I'll have only a few words to say about it in my story, but I want those words to be right. So I've come here to study the episode on the spot and compare the legend with the reality. I'll tell the truth. No doubt it will be merely my own personal truth. But you can supply only the reality that you yourself possess.' And in the text of the episode itself he says, 'History isn't our concern' (II. i. iii).

Hugo names some of his sources in the text: Jean-Baptiste Charras, *Histoire de la campagne de 1815: Waterloo* (1857); Pierre-Alexandre Fleury de Chaboulon, *Mémoires pour servir à l'histoire . . . de Napoléon en 1815* (1815); Gaspard Gourgaud, *Mémoires pour servir à l'histoire de France sous Napoléon* (1823); Benjamin Constant, *Mémoires sur les Cent-Jours* (1820–2); Friedrich von Müffling, *Aus meinem Leben* (1851). The book by his political ally and fellow exile Charras influenced him most. He would not have expected his readers to be familiar with the Waterloo section of Stendhal's *La Chartreuse de Parme* (1839); that novel was still virtually unknown in the 1860s.

330 *the author of this story*: Hugo arrived at Mont Saint-Jean on 7 May 1861.

331 *a lion*: in 1823–6 a monument in the form of a 28-ton cast-iron lion on top of a mound 45 metres high was erected at Waterloo, allegedly over the place where the Prince of Orange had been wounded during the battle.

336 *Le Nôtre*: André Le Nôtre (1613–1700), Classical French architect and landscape designer, responsible for formal gardens at Versailles and Fontainebleau.

337 *the revocation of the Edict of Nantes*: the Edict of Nantes (1598) provided at least partial protection for French Protestants in a predominantly Roman Catholic country. It was revoked by Louis XIV in 1685 and extensive persecutions followed. Many Protestant families left the country.

Austerlitz: one of Napoleon's most important victories, against Austrian and Russian forces on 2 December 1805.

Abu Qir: Napoleonic victory over Turkish forces in Egypt, on 25 July 1799.

338 *Dante . . . Hannibal*: the Italian poet Dante Alighieri (1265–1321) wrote the *Divine Comedy* during the last fifteen years of his life; the Italian artist Michelangelo Buonarotti (1475–1564) painted the *Last Judgement* after the age of 60 and was working on the Rondanini *Pietà* shortly before his death. By contrast, the Carthaginian military leader Hannibal (died 183 BCE) seemed invincible early in his career but was repeatedly defeated in later life.

339 *Scott . . . Thiers*: the original edition of *Les Misérables* (1862) mentioned only the work by Charras; for the *ne varietur* edition (1881) Hugo broadened the tribute to include books by some of the other colleagues he most admired: Walter Scott's *Life of Napoleon Buonaparte* (1827), Alphonse de Lamartine's *Histoire de la restauration* (1851), Achille de Vaulabelle's *Campagne et bataille de Waterloo* (1845), and two books that appeared shortly after his own account had been written: Edgar Quinet's *Histoire de la campagne de 1815* (1862) and the Waterloo volume (1862) of Adolph Thiers's *Histoire du Consulat et de l'Empire* (1843–69). Lamartine had been severely critical of *Les Misérables*, so the addition of his name is a generous gesture.

an unwitting symbol: the lion was consciously intended as a symbol of Belgium.

340 *Marengo*: decisive Napoleonic victory over Austrian forces on 14 June 1800.

341 *Babylon ... Titus*: Babylon was captured in 330 BCE by Alexander the Great, who intended to rebuild it radically as his own capital (Hugo's description may also recall Alexander's notorious burning of Persepolis); Julius Caesar 'enslaved' Rome when he became its dictator in 49 BCE; Jerusalem was sacked and destroyed in 70 CE by Roman forces under the command of the future emperor Titus.

Quid Obscurum: the phrase is completed later in the chapter: *quid obscurum, quid divinum* ('something dark, something divine').

343 *Rosa ... Gribeauval*: Salvator Rosa (1615–73), Italian painter of picturesque and intensely dramatic landscapes; Jean-Baptiste de Gribeauval (1715–89), French artillery general.

Rembrandt ... Polybius: the painters Rembrandt van Rijn (1606–69) and Adam Frans van der Meulin (1632–90; noted for his battle scenes); the Greek military writer Polybius (second century BCE) and his French commentator Jean François Folard (1669–1752).

346 *Talavera ... Salamanca*: major English victories during the Peninsular War against France: Talavera de la Reina (1809), Salamanca (1812), Vitoria (1813).

347 *Caesar ... the Thundering Legion*: the rival Roman rulers Julius Caesar and Pompey the Great fought for control of the Mediterranean world until the latter's murder in 48 BCE. The so-called Thundering Legion (*Fulminata*, either 'hurled like a thunderbolt' or 'marked by [Jupiter's] thunderbolt'), formed by Augustus late in the first century BCE, was a typical Roman military body.

the landing on 1 March: Napoleon's landing at the Golfe Jouan on his return from Elba.

348 *the Duchess of Richmond's ball*: on 15 June 1815; Hugo would have expected his readers to be familiar with Byron's frequently quoted stanzas about it, *Childe Harold's Pilgrimage*, III. xxi–xxii ('On with the dance! let joy be unconfined').

349 *'Flaky rust'*: a quotation from Virgil, *Georgics*, i. 495: some future farmer, ploughing the earth at Philippi (where, in 42 BCE, Antony and Octavius had finally defeated the Republican forces led by Brutus and Cassius), 'shall find old spears eaten away with flaky rust' (trans. C. Day Lewis).

352 *the Berezina ... Fontainebleau*: more than ten thousand French soldiers had died between 26 and 29 November 1812 while crossing the Berezina river, during Napoleon's retreat from Moscow; during the Battle of Leipzig (16–19 October 1813), Napoleon had been decisively defeated by allied Austrian, Prussian, Russian, and Swedish forces; at Fontainebleau, on 11 April 1814, Napoleon had signed his decree of abdication.

353 *Crécy ... Agincourt*: famous English victories over the French, during the Hundred Years War (Crécy in 1346, Poitiers in 1356, Agincourt in

1415) and the War of the Spanish Succession (Ramillies in 1706, Malplaquet in 1709).

355 *Murat*: Joachim Murat (1767–1815), king of Naples, whose personal bravery and military skill had contributed to various Napoleonic victories, including that at Borodino (7 September 1812, against Russia; often reckoned the bloodiest battle of its era). When the Emperor returned from Elba, in 1815, Murat offered his services but was rejected because he had been negotiating with the Allies. Napoleon later regretted this decision, and felt that Murat's support at Waterloo might have made a difference to the outcome.

Orphic epics: in Greek legend, Orpheus was the first poet; Hugo here imagines him as an author of now-lost pre-Homeric epics on mythological themes.

358 *Ben Nevis . . . Argos*: the former is the highest mountain in Scotland; the latter was reputedly the most ancient city in Greece.

359 *Badajoz*: another English victory over Napoleonic forces in Spain, on 5 April 1812.

360 *'There aren't any . . . he'll simply have to fight to the death'*: evidently a paraphrase of Wellington's reply when Halkett requested some relief ('Impossible') and his instructions to Pack, 'They must hold their ground to the last man.'

361 *the Prince de Condé . . . Louis XVIII*: Louis-Joseph, Prince de Condé (1736–1818), a lifelong opponent of Napoleon; Louis XVIII (1755–1824), who had become king of France on Napoleon's abdication in 1814 but had fled to Belgium when the Emperor returned from Elba.

362 *Saint Helena*: the Atlantic island to which Napoleon was exiled after Waterloo.

363 *The rest of the story is familiar*: Hugo had already told much of it in verse in 'The Expiation', *Châtiments*, V. xiii. 69–156.

364 *Victories . . . with wings unfurled*: the Greek goddess Nike (Victory) was usually depicted with wings.

different bullets—French ones: after the defeat of Napoleon, Ney was tried by his peers and convicted of high treason. He was executed by firing squad on 7 December 1815.

366 *'So it was fated'*: Hugo is adapting the phrase *hoc erat in votis* ('so it was vowed'), Horace, *Satires*, II. vi. 1.

367 *Ulm . . . Friedland*: famous Napoleonic victories: Ulm, 17 October 1805, and Wagram, 6 July 1809 (both against Austria); Jena, 14 October 1806 (against Prussia); Friedland, 14 June 1807 (against Russia).

Cambronne: General Pierre-Jacques-Étienne Cambronne (1770–1842).

368 *'Merde!'*: no English expletive has anything like the resonances identified by Hugo in this celebrated outburst, an expression of both the utmost defiance and the utmost frustration; the closest social parallels, either

historical or fictitious (Wellington's 'Publish and be damned', Eliza Doolittle's 'Not bloody likely'), serve only to emphasize the immense differences between the two languages and cultures. Whether Cambronne uttered it has been much disputed (in later life he had a reputation for propriety), but ever since the publication of *Les Misérables* it has been known as *le mot de Cambronne* ('Cambronne's word').

we're defying that prohibition: at first, Hugo intended merely to allude to Cambronne's word, without actually printing it; his earliest manuscript draft reads: 'Cambronne answered—we shall not quote his word; apparently there's a prohibition against the inclusion of the sublime in history' (Hugo, *Chantiers*, ed. René Journet (Paris, 1990), 898). In 1862 there was no precedent for printing the word in full in a work of respectable literature, and as late as 1896 the utterance of something like it onstage in Alfred Jarry's play *Ubu roi* provoked a furore. Its inclusion in *Les Misérables* has thematic relevance. 'It has every right to enter my book,' Hugo wrote when challenged; 'it's the *misérable* among words.'

Leonidas with Rabelais: the king of Sparta who died heroically at Thermopylae in 480 BCE and the sixteenth-century French satirist famous for his disrespectful stance and earthy language.

Aeschylus: the grandest and most majestic of the Greek tragic dramatists (fifth century BCE).

369 *Rouget de l'Isle . . . Kléber*: three people closely associated with the spirit of the French Revolution: the political leader Georges Jacques Danton (1759–94), the military leader Jean-Baptiste Kléber (1753–1800), and Claude-Joseph Rouget de l'Isle (1760–1836), who composed the 'Marseillaise'.

370 *How Much Does the General Weigh?*: a quotation from Juvenal, *Satires*, x. 417 (meditating on the ashes of the Carthaginian military leader Hannibal).

371 *Goethe . . . Byron*: Johann Wolfgang von Goethe (1749–1832), German poet; George Gordon, Lord Byron (1788–1824), English poet.

372 *Barrême . . . Michelangelo*: François Barrême (died 1703), French arithmetician, whose ready reckoners were long famous; Michelangelo Buonarotti (1475–1564), Italian painter and sculptor.

Beaulieu . . . Arcola: early opponents of Napoleon, the veteran Austrian generals Johann von Beaulieu (1725–1819), Joseph Alvinzi (1726–1810), Dagobert-Sigismond de Wurmser (1724–97), Michael Melas (1729–1806), and Karl von Mack (1752–1828); Napoleonic victories against them: Lodi, 10 May 1798, Montenotte, 12 April 1796, Mantua, 2 February 1797, and Arcola, 17 November 1796; and Jean Lannes's later victory against Austria at Montebello, 9 June 1800. Wurmser was aged 72 when he faced Napoleon; Wellington was 43 at the time of Waterloo.

373 *Wellington . . . to Lord Bathurst*: in his Waterloo despatch to Lord Bathurst (19 June 1815), Wellington wrote that 'the army never, upon

any occasion, conducted itself better. . . . There is no officer nor description of troops that did not behave well' (*The Despatches of Field Marshal the Duke of Wellington*, ed. John Gurwood, 12 vols. (London, 1858–64), xii. 484). Nevertheless, many of those who had served under him felt that the curt phrase 'description of troops' was a deliberate slight. Wellington himself is said to have later admitted, 'I should have given more praise.'

373	*Inkerman . . . Raglan*: James Henry Somerset, Lord Raglan (1788–1855), commanded British forces during the Crimean war; the Battle of Inkerman was fought on 5 November 1854.

374	*Bautzen*: a hard-fought Napoleonic victory against combined Russian and Prussian forces on 20 May 1813. Hugo's statistics are drawn from an article that appeared in *L'Étoile belge* on 6 June 1861.

	Virgil . . . Philippi: a further reminiscence of Virgil's beautiful meditation on the battlefield of Philippi (*Georgics* i. 489–97), already cited on page 349.

375	*20 March 1815 . . . the Bourbon monarchy*: Napoleon had returned to Paris from Elba on 20 March 1815; the French Revolution had begun with the storming of the Bastille on 14 July 1789. The dukes of Nassau had been ruling their homeland since the tenth century, and the dukes of Brunswick since 1235; Habsburg rule in Austria dated back to 1282, Romanov rule in Russia to 1613, Hohenzollern rule in Prussia to 1618, and Bourbon rule in France to 1589.

	a coachboy . . . a sergeant: Joachim Murat (1767–1815), the son of an innkeeper, married Napoleon's sister Caroline and was eventually (in 1808) proclaimed king of Naples; one of Napoleon's army officers, Jean-Baptiste Bernadotte (1763–1844), became crown prince of Sweden in 1810 and King Charles XIV John in 1818.

376	*Saint-Ouen . . . doddering invalid*: in a declaration at Saint-Ouen on 2 May 1814, the new king Louis XVIII promised that he would give the people a 'liberal constitution'; this was a significant compromise with the democratic Declaration of the Rights of Man (issued by the French Revolutionary government on 26 August 1789) and a significant departure from the absolutist policies of earlier French kings. The eccentric surgeon 'Père Élisée' (Marie-Vincent Talochon, 1753–1817), who had a colourful and startling career, was favoured by Louis XVIII (the 'dear old doddering invalid').

	Robespierre: the radical French Revolutionary leader Maximilien Robespierre (1758–94), who was largely responsible for the Reign of Terror.

377	*20 March . . . 'King of Rome'*: Napoleon returned to Paris from Elba on 20 March 1815; Louis XVIII returned to Paris on 8 July 1815. Under his rule, the ancient white flag of the kings of France flew from the royal palace (the Tuileries), the ancient motto of Louis XIV (actually *nec pluribus impar*) was revived. Official propaganda exploited the popularity of his ancestor Henri IV (1553–1610; born in Béarn) to counteract the popularity of Napoleon (born in Corsica), and publicized such royalist victories as Bouvines (27 July 1214) and Fontenoy (11 May 1745) to counterbalance such Napoleonic victories as Austerlitz. Trestaillon (Jacques Dupont) was one of the White Terrorists, fanatical Catholic royalists at Nîmes who assaulted and murdered their political and religious enemies during 1815–16. The deaths of Louis XVI and Marie Antoinette in 1793 and of Louis-Antoine-Henri, Duc d'Enghien (1772–1804), on 21 March 1804 (at the orders of Napoleon), were regarded as martyrdoms. Pope Pius VII (1742–1823) had consecrated Napoleon as emperor on 2 December 1804; after Napoleon's downfall, the pope reversed many of his previous pro-Napoleonic edicts. At his birth, Napoleon's son (sometimes known as 'Napoleon II'; 1811–32) had been designated king of Rome by his father; he was now a hostage in Austria.

378 *a Holy Alliance*: the Holy Alliance, designed to secure international peace in matters of politics and religion, was signed by the rulers of Russia, Austria, and Prussia on 26 September 1815; all European sovereigns subsequently added their signatures except for the Pope, the Sultan of Turkey, and the English Prince Regent.

Hudson Lowe . . . Alexander: Hudson Lowe (1769–1844), English general appointed to guard Napoleon on Saint Helena; Henri, Marquis de Montchénu (1757–1831), France's official representative on the island (he was a committed royalist and bitterly antagonistic to Napoleon); Alexander I (1777–1825), tsar of Russia.

Longwood . . . the 1815 Treaty: the converted farmhouse Longwood was Napoleon's residence on the island of Saint Helena until his death in 1821. The Congress of Vienna (1814–15) determined European territorial boundaries after the fall of Napoleon, and thus helped to prevent major wars for several decades.

379 *an eagle flying . . . until it reaches the turrets of Notre-Dame*: an allusion to Napoleon's proclamation of 22 February 1815, on his escape from Elba: 'The Eagle, bearing the national colours, will fly from spire to spire until it reaches the turrets of Notre-Dame.'

Grandeur among the Middle Classes

Drafted about November 1847, but radically revised and expanded about September 1860; chapters III. ii. i–vii of *Les Misérables* (1862).

379 *in the days of Louis XIV . . . the new Tivoli quarter*: Louis XIV reigned from 1643 to 1715. Under Napoleon III the crooked alleys and dance-halls of Paris's Tivoli quarter were replaced by rectilinear streets and high-rise buildings.

380 *Voltaire*: the French writer François-Marie Arouet (1694–1778), famous for his alertness and activity in old age.

381 *Gobelin . . . the Directory period*: the Gobelins and Beauvais tapestry workshops opened in 1662 and 1664 respectively, and remained active throughout the eighteenth century. The Flemish painter Jacob Jordaens

(1595–1678), a pupil of Rubens, was noted for his vibrant, almost slap-dash style—and for his productivity. The Directory governed France from 1795 to 1799, between the Reign of Terror and Napoleon's seizure of absolute power; the fashionable young men of the period were noted for their ultra-conservative Royalist views.

382 *La Camargo ... Périer*: Camargo (Marie Anne de Cupis, 1710–70) and Marie Sallé (1707–56), celebrated rival dancers in eighteenth-century Paris; Jacques, Comte de Corbière (1767–1853), Jean-Georges Humann (1780–1842), and Casimir Périer (1777–1832), leading statesmen of post-Napoleonic France.

Luc-Esprit: Luke, after the 'beloved physician' who accompanied the apostle Paul; Esprit, French for '[the Holy] Spirit', 'intelligence', or 'wit'. The names turn out to have a kind of appropriateness—but not in the way Gillenormand's godfather intended.

383 *Nivernais ... '93*: Louis-Jules Mancini-Mazarini, Duc de Nivernais (1716–98), refined and witty diplomat and writer of fables and light verse; 'Duc de Nevers' had been the older form of the title, borne by his father and grandfather. The National Convention governed France during the Reign of Terror—the '93 dreaded by Gillenormand; the Bourbon monarchy was restored when Louis XVIII came to the throne in 1814. Alexius Petrovich Bestuzhev-Ryumin (1693–1768), grand chancellor of Russia, invented his famous elixir by the 1720s; it was taken to France by a brigadier called Lamotte, who marketed it as his own. The Russian empress Catherine the Great (Sophie von Anhalt-Zerbst, 1729–96) annexed large tracts of Polish territory during three partitions of that country (1772–95). Her sexual promiscuity made her a logical client for Bestuzhev's remedy, and the same may be said of Louis XV; but we hope the latter was mistaken in assuming that the pope would also be interested.

386 *'Let the woods be worthy of a consul' ... Waterloo*: the quotation deftly misapplies Virgil, *Eclogues*, iv. 3. Austerlitz (2 December 1805) and Waterloo (18 June 1815) were fought by the upstart usurper Napoleon; distinguished service at such encounters would not impress the royalist Gillenormand.

The House in the Rue Plumet

Written about December 1847, but with major revisions and additions during 1860–1; chapters IV. III. i, paragraphs 1–5, and IV. III. iii of *Les Misérables* (1862).

387 *open to the heavens*: 'the eye of the adulterer observeth darkness, saying: No eye shall see me; ... but [God's] eyes are upon his ways' (Job 24: 15–24).

388 *Mansart ... Watteau*: two extremely famous and fashionable French artists: the architect Jules Hardouin Mansart (died 1708), responsible (among other things) for much of Louis XIV's palace at Versailles, and the painter Antoine Watteau (1684–1721).

Of Leaves and Branches: a quotation from Lucretius, *De rerum natura*, v. 971.

391 *Socrates . . . Pleiades*: the former was a celebrated Greek philosopher (fifth century BCE); the latter is a spectacular cluster of bluish-white stars in the constellation of Taurus.

Leviathan's Intestine

Written late 1860 and early 1861; chapters V. II. i–vi of *Les Misérables* (1862). Leviathan is the mighty and fearsome monster of Job 41: 1–34 ('he is king over all the children of pride'); Hugo studies the great creature from its less presentable end.

392 *Ekeberg*: Carl Gustave Ekeberg (1716–84), Swedish explorer.

the South Pole: in the mid-nineteenth century, guano (the dried droppings of seabirds, used as fertilizer) was collected mainly from islands off the Pacific coast of South America.

394 *Beaujon-style prodigality*: the Folie Beaujon (destroyed in 1865) was an extravagant Parisian resort built by the wealthy businessman Nicolas Beaujon (1708–86).

Saint-Cloud netting: nets were hung at this point in the River Seine to retrieve the bodies of suicides who had drowned themselves further upstream.

Babylon and Corinth: the analogies are hardly complimentary; in the ancient world, both cities were regarded as centres of decadence and (especially) sexual licence. Fukien (Fujian) is a province of south-eastern China.

395 *Liebig . . . Eternal City*: Justus von Liebig (1803–73), the famous German agricultural chemist. Papal messages are traditionally addressed *urbi et orbi* ('to the city and to the world'); Rome is traditionally known as the Eternal City.

Athens . . . Lutetia: Athens, home of major Greek philosophers (Socrates, Plato, Aristotle); Tyre, leading city of ancient Phoenicia, long a dominant trading power in the Mediterranean world (Ezekiel 27); Sparta, ancient Greek city-state known for the simplicity and unpretentiousness of its customs; Nineveh, opulent capital of the Assyrian empire; Lutetia, the ancient name of the city of Paris, popularly derived from the Latin *lutum* ('dirt').

Machiavelli, Bacon, and Mirabeau: three influential statesmen often criticized for meanness of spirit or baseness of character: the Italian Niccolò Machiavelli (1469–1527), author of *The Prince*; the Englishman Francis Bacon (1561–1626), whose *Essays* are classics of worldly wisdom; and the Frenchman Honoré-Gabriel, Comte de Mirabeau (1749–91), active in the early stages of the French Revolution.

396 *Benares . . . Nakhsheb*: Benares (Varanasi), sacred city in northern India; Babylon, ancient Mesopotamian city where Daniel was cast into the

lions' den (Daniel 6); Tiglath-Pileser III (eighth century BCE), powerful
ruler of Assyria (Nineveh being his capital city), the leading character in
many later legends; John of Leiden (Jan Berkelson, 1509–36), self-styled
prophet who ruled the German city of Münster during 1534–5;
al-Moqanna' ('the Veiled One', died 779), self-styled incarnation of God
who led a rebellion in Khorasan and was said to have raised a mysterious
light from a pit near Nakhsheb. The last two would have been familiar to
Hugo's readers from Meyerbeer's opera *Le Prophète* (1849) and Thomas
Moore's poem *Lalla Rookh* (1817) respectively. All editions examined by
us (including the 1862 original and the 1881 *ne varietur*) print the nonsensical *Kekhscheb* for *Nekhscheb* (Hugo's usual spelling of 'Nakhsheb');
this evidently arose as a misreading of handwriting at some stage in the
preparation of the text (capital *N* can easily be misread as capital *K* in
either Hugo's hand or his copyist Juliette Drouet's).

396   *the Gemonies . . . the Court of Miracles*: in ancient Rome the corpses of
executed criminals were thrown on the Gemonies (Stairs of Mourning)
near the main sewer, the Cloaca Maxima (Suetonius, *Tiberius*, liii, lxi;
Tacitus, *Histories*, III. xciv). In Paris, the Maillotins rebelled in 1382–3 in
response to the imposition of new taxes; the ringleaders were executed.
Tire-laines ('cloak-snatchers') is an archaic (mainly seventeenth-century)
term for robbers; the Huguenots were the French Protestants, many of
whom perished during the sixteenth-century Wars of Religion (Hugo
would be thinking particularly of the Bartholomew's Day Massacre in
1572); the Illuminati were followers of Simon Morin (1623–63), who
was burned alive for teaching that he was an incarnation of Christ and
that the spiritually enlightened were incapable of sin; the Chauffeurs
('Heaters') were brigands active around 1800, so named because they
tortured their victims by burning their feet. The Court of Miracles was
an area of Paris inhabited by beggars and thieves during the Middle
Ages; it features prominently in Hugo's *Notre-Dame de Paris*.

397   *Villon . . . Rabelais*: François Villon (born 1431), medieval French poet;
François Rabelais (died 1553), Renaissance French prose writer. Both
had a reputation for scurrility and unrespectability, but the convicted
murderer Villon lived in much closer contact with the sewers than the
priest Rabelais.

Basilio . . . Margoton: the paragraph contains a miniature rogues' gallery:
Basilio, the hypocritical slanderer in Beaumarchais's comedies *Le Barbier
de Séville* (1775) and *Le Mariage de Figaro* (1784); Scapin, the deceitful
servant in Molière's comedy *Les Fourberies de Scapin* (1671); Caiaphas,
the high priest responsible for securing the arrest and crucifixion of
Jesus; Falstaff, the disreputable knight of Shakespeare's *Henry IV* plays
and *The Merry Wives of Windsor*. Margoton is a stock name for a
lower-class woman, evoking the other end of the social scale from the
periwigged judge.

398   *Bartholomew's Day . . . Maillard*: on Bartholomew's Day, 24 August

1572, a massacre of Protestants was carried out in Paris. Tristan L'Hermite (1406–90) was the powerful adviser of Louis XI, Antoine Duprat (1463–1535) of François I, Catherine de Médicis (1519–89) of her son Charles IX, and Armand Jean du Plessis, Cardinal Richelieu (1585–1640), of Louis XIII; all had a sinister reputation. François, Marquis de Louvois (1641–91) and Michel Le Tellier (1603–85) were instrumental in revoking the Edict of Nantes and renewing the persecution of French Protestants (1685); Jacques-René Hébert (1757–94) and Stanislas-Marie Maillard (1763–94) were radical leaders during the French Revolution.

Messalina: the wife (died 48 CE) of the Roman emperor Claudius; she was said to be promiscuously adulterous with strangers of all social classes (Juvenal, vi. 114–32).

399 *Henri II . . . Mercier*: the former reigned from 1547 to 1559; the latter (Louis-Sébastien Mercier) wrote a massive *Tableau de Paris* (1781–8).

Daedalus mirrored Babel: the subterranean maze (in Classical mythology, Daedalus devised an elaborate maze for the tyrannic King Minos of Crete, in which the monstrous Minotaur was concealed) mirrored the chaotic high-rise buildings (in Genesis 11: 1–9, Babel was the place where 'the Lord confounded the language' of the city-dwellers who were trying to build 'a tower whose top may reach unto heaven').

400 *scolopendrae . . . Barathrum*: scolopendrae are millipedes, polychaete worms, or similar-looking creatures; Behemoth is the mighty animal described in Job 40: 15–24 ('he drinketh up a river, and hasteth not'); Barathrum was originally a valley near Athens where the bodies of executed criminals were dumped. The writer Germain-François Poullain de Saint-Foix (1698–1776) collected popular myths and anecdotes about Paris, and therefore represents the era that produced Ferdinand-Denis, Comte de Crécy (1744–1810), who, unlike most members of his social class, actively supported the Revolution. The Marmousets were aristocratic conspirators against Cardinal Fleury in 1730. Guy-Crescent Fagon (1638–1710), one of the leading French doctors of his day, was ultimately appointed principal physician to Louis XIV.

401 *Decrès . . . Austerlitz*: the paragraph recalls some of the most heroic (by conventional standards) episodes of the previous decade: the battles at Fleurus (15 June 1794, when observers tethered in a balloon above the battlefield directed the French troops), Mainz (29 October 1795), Lodi (10 May 1798—though the bridge incident occurred at Arcola, on 17 November 1796), Mantua (2 February 1797, after a siege during which the young Joachim Murat played a prominent part), the Zuiderzee (where the icebound Dutch fleet surrendered to the French in January 1795, an incident freely exaggerated by popular folklore), Genoa (besieged April–June 1800), and Montebello (9 June 1800, won by French forces led by Jean Lannes), with Austerlitz (2 December 1805) soon to come; and the military leaders Barthelémy Joubert (1769–99), Louis

Desaix de Veygoux (1768–1800), François Marceau (1769–96), Lazare Hoche (1768–97), Jean-Baptiste Kléber (1753–1800), and Andoche Junot (1771–1813; noted for his erratic temperament). The ministers mentioned are Denis Decrès (1763–1820), Minister of the Navy and the Colonies 1801–15, and Emmanuel Crétet (1747–1809), Minister of the Interior 1807–9.

401 *Bruneseau*: the engineer Pierre-Emmanuel Bruneseau (1751–1819).

a survivor . . . beneath the dignity of administrative prose: the survivor is of course fictitious, enabling the novelist to invent whatever 'unknown details' may suit his own confessedly undignified prose.

402 *Gros-Jean . . . Le Bel*: Gros-Jean, a stock eighteenth-century name for a peasant (compare 'Hodge' in English); Dominique Guillaume Le Bel (died 1768), Louis XV's senior valet de chambre (in popular report, no one had any hope of approaching the king without gaining Le Bel's approval).

403 *Huguenot*: French Protestant. The medallion is satirizing the Roman Catholic hierarchy.

Marat: the radical French revolutionary leader Jean-Paul Marat (1743–93), whose influential newspaper *L'Ami du peuple* (*The Friend of the People*, begun in 1789) advocated extreme measures and helped to turn public opinion against more moderate political groups. In 1777 he had been appointed physician to the Comte d'Artois (the future Charles X), though his medical competence was much disputed; while in that position, he had treated the Marquise de Laubespine for tuberculosis. His assassination was regarded by some as a martyrdom, by others as a deserved punishment.

404 *Watteau . . . Dante*: Antoine Watteau (1684–1721), decorative rococo painter; Dante Alighieri (1265–1321), author of the *Inferno*.

405 *the classic four-square alexandrine . . . Tartuffe*: the alexandrine was the twelve-syllable line of traditional French verse; Hugo and many of his contemporaries saw its rigid metrical rules as literary equivalents of the old political regime, and deliberately set out to break them. In the Rue de Rivoli region of Paris, the old tangle of crooked little streets had recently (since 1853) been replaced by a long straight road displaying the latest fashions in architecture; it was politically useful as visible evidence of the advantages Paris was gaining from Napoleon III's dictatorship. The title character of Molière's comedy *Tartuffe* (1664–9) is the quintessence of religious hypocrisy. The whole paragraph is thus a sly criticism of France's new government and its policies.

the Augean stables: in Classical mythology, the stables of King Augeus of Elis housed thousands of oxen in a state of constant filth; they were finally cleansed by Hercules, in the fifth of his celebrated labours.

406 *Napoleon . . . the current regime*: Napoleon reigned until 1815, Louis XVIII until 1824, Charles X until 1830, Louis-Philippe until 1848, and

the subsequent Republic until 1851. Hugo does not deign to name 'the current regime' (Napoleon III's).

408 *the 5–6 June insurrection*: on 5 June 1832, republicans and other people dissatisfied with Louis-Philippe's government rioted in Paris; next day the insurrection was suppressed, and on 7 June a state of siege was proclaimed. The latter stages of *Les Misérables* contain a fictional depiction of these events.

409 *Cretaceous . . . Jurassic*: nineteenth-century geologists used the term *la craie* ('the Chalk') to refer specifically to the chalk of a particular geological period, the Cretaceous. Hugo's subsequent reference to the Jurassic (the period immediately preceding the Cretaceous) shows that this is the sense intended here.

the Flood's fossil shells: nineteenth-century geologists commonly interpreted marine fossils as traces left by the Flood in the days of Noah.

A Turbulent Life and a Tranquil Conscience

Written 15 June 1864; chapter I. II. i of *The Toilers of the Sea* (1866).

410 *Mess . . . St Sampson*: on nineteenth-century Guernsey, a *Mess* was a man one step below a *Monsieur* (gentleman) in the social hierarchy. The town of St Sampson, 5 kilometres north of St Peter Port on the island of Guernsey, would have had a population of about 600 in the 1820s ('little more than a village', Hugo says in III. I. i); the earliest surviving census (1831, during a period of rapid maritime growth) gives the population of the whole parish as 1019.

The Old Old Story of Utopia

Written late June 1864; chapter I. III. ii, paragraphs 1–5 of *The Toilers of the Sea* (1866).

412 *chloroform*: first used as an anaesthetic by James Young Simpson, in 1847; controversially, Queen Victoria accepted it during the birth of her last two children, Prince Leopold (1853) and Princess Beatrice (1857). In some circles the practice was opposed as a violation of Genesis 3: 16; Simpson himself replied (from the Scriptures) in *An Answer to the Religious Objections Advanced Against the Employment of Anaesthetic Agents* (1847), which is the direct or (probably) indirect source of Hugo's information here.

Leviathan . . . a return to chaos: Leviathan is the mighty seagoing creature described in Job 41: 1 ff. Hugo was much criticized in his early years for disregarding the traditional rules of artistic order and propriety; in reply he often stressed the chaotic element in God's creation, and the importance of mirroring that in art.

Fulton . . . Michaux: the steamship inventor Robert Fulton (1765–1815) made his famous first voyage on 17 August 1807; Robert R. Livingston (1746–1813) was his financial backer, and the French botanist François-André Michaux (1770–1855) was on board. The Scottish inventor James

Watt (1736–1819) had retired from the manufacture of steam engines in 1800, but his company continued to issue them.

412 *the beast in the Book of Revelation*: in Revelation (the Apocalypse) 13: 1, John sees 'a beast rise up out of the sea, having seven heads and ten horns'; needless to say, the book's own explanation (17: 9–14) is rather different from those offered by Fulton's opponents!

[*Note*] *Genesis 1: 4*: 'God divided the light from the darkness' (the latter 'was upon the face of the deep', 1: 2).

413 *Lucifer*: 'light-bringer', Latin rendering of a title assigned to the king of Babylon in Isaiah 14: 12 and applied (inaccurately) to Satan in later tradition.

The Story of Utopia, Continued

Written late June 1864; chapter I. III. iv of *The Toilers of the Sea* (1866).

413 *Elihu*: 'He is my God', the name of the young man whose 'wrath was kindled . . . against Job' and whose denunciations of Job are recorded in Job 32–6.

414 *a Sieur . . . St Peter Port*: a *Sieur* was a man one step below a *Mess* in the social hierarchy. St Peter Port is the capital of Guernsey; its population in 1821 was 11,173.

Papin . . . Montebello: Denis Papin (born 1647), French physicist and inventor; his paddleboat seems to have been human-powered, but he did also devise a steam engine. 'Dromon' is Hugo's favourite word for any large ancient ship; a warship now dated to the fourth century was excavated in 1863 from a bog near Nydam in Schleswig (territory claimed by Denmark until 13 October 1864). The warship *Montebello* was launched in 1812.

A Quirk of Lethierry's Character

Written late June 1864; chapter I. III. xii of *The Toilers of the Sea* (1866).

415 *Voltaire*: François-Marie Arouet (1694–1778), French writer noted for his anticlericalism.

the Savoyard Vicar: a character in Rousseau's novel *Émile* (1762), who expounds a rationalistic natural theology remote from orthodox Roman Catholicism.

416 *Saint Peter*: an allusion to the Roman Catholic claim that the apostle Peter was the first pope.

Montlosier: François-Dominique, Comte de Montlosier (1755–1838), anticlerical journalist of the Restoration era.

Bourmont . . . 'pontiffickle': the Napoleonic general Louis-Auguste-Victor, Comte de Bourmont (1773–1846) changed sides four days before Waterloo. In the French, Lethierry's lapses are *traître d'union* ('connecting traitor') for *trait d'union* ('hyphen') and *pape ôté* ('pope gone away') for *papauté* ('papacy').

417 *'I was suckled on 1789'*: he 'had the irreverence of the Revolutionary period', as Hugo remarks a couple of paragraphs later.

418 *the real presence*: the doctrine that the bread and wine of the Lord's Supper are transformed into the real body and blood of Christ—a view accepted by orthodox Roman Catholics, but denied by many Protestants.

   Wesley ... Loyola: the Protestant reformer John Wesley (1703–91), founder of the Methodists, is paired with the Roman Catholic counter-reformer Ignatius of Loyola (1491–1556), founder of the Jesuits.

A Contradiction

Written 30 March 1865; chapter III. i. i, paragraphs 12–18 of *The Toilers of the Sea* (1866). The title is supplied by the present editors. Prayer was an important part of Hugo's own life ('I never go four consecutive hours without praying', he remarked in January 1867); the subject is studied by Henri Guillemin, 'La Prière de Hugo', in Hugo, *Œuvres complètes*, ed. Jean Massin, vol. xii (Paris, 1969), pp. i–xvii.

419 *a dear little fellow*: the thought is similar to that of *Religions and Religion* and the prologue to *God*. Lethierry has constructed a god to suit his own convenience; the true God is both less comfortable and less limited.

Emily de Putron

Written mid-January 1865. Emily de Putron (1834–65) was the fiancée of Hugo's son (François-)Victor and contributed substantially to his classic translation of Shakespeare. She died of tuberculosis on 14 January 1865; François-Victor was already suffering from the same disease, which would cause his own death eight years later. In his diary Hugo noted: 'At three o'clock, at the Foulon cemetery, Miss de Putron was buried. Lovely winter sunshine. Crowd. Tears. I spoke. I sent Victor the manuscript from which I read. You always need to write down what you have to say at funerals; no lightly spoken word is possible in such a situation.' The oration, one of Hugo's finest, naturally identifies affianced daughter-in-law with married daughter, Emily with Léopoldine.

419 *we have married one*: Emily's sister Mary had married Charles Guérin in November 1864.

The Death of Madame Victor Hugo

The title was supplied by Hugo's literary executors. Hugo's wife Adèle suffered a cerebrovascular stroke on 25 August 1868 and died on the morning of 27 August, at Brussels. The loss prompted him to write his most extended and most emotionally intense diary-entries of the 1860s; the psychological forces at work here are very different from those unleashed by the death of his daughter Léopoldine a quarter of a century earlier, and he deals with them in a much more controlled way, but on close examination their roots may possibly be found to go just as deep. Often his writings are designed to generate or release emotion; in these pages, all his literary skills are working to restrain it.

Juliette Drouet's responses to the situation were equally fascinating. On 10 October, for instance, she wrote to Hugo: 'Now I love you with the magnanimous heart of your dear departed, as well as with my own. I ask that glorious witness of your earthly life to bear witness also to mine, before God's throne. I ask her permission to love you as long as I live, both in this world and in the next. I also ask her for some little part of the divine gift she had—the gift of making you happy—and I hope that she will grant me this, because she can see the very depths of my heart. May all people on earth always bless and honour her memory as I do.'

421 *Georges*: Hugo's grandson, 9 days old at the time.

422 *our dear departed daughter*: Léopoldine, buried at Villequier.

Foucher . . . Meurice: Madame Hugo's brother Paul Foucher (1810–75), a prolific dramatist and journalist; the physician and republican politician Louis Laussedat (1809–79), who, like Hugo, was exiled by Napoleon III and lived in Brussels from 1851 to 1876; the writers Auguste Vacquerie (1819–95) and Paul Meurice (1820–1905), Hugo's closest professional associates and, subsequently, his literary executors.

423 *Charles . . . Victor*: Hugo's two sons, Charles and (François-)Victor.

Frédérix . . . Berru: the Belgian publisher Albert Lacroix (1834–1903) made his name by issuing editions of Hugo's works; the other people mentioned are left-wing French or Belgian journalists: Gustave Frédérix (1834–94), Gaston Bérardi (born 1849), Henri Rochefort (1831–1913), and Camille Berru (who had been closely associated with Hugo's 1848–51 periodical *L'Évènement*).

The Return to France

Written 3–6 September 1870; the title was supplied by Hugo's literary executors. During mid-August 1870, Hugo's diary-entries became fuller and more urgent, in response to the developing political crisis in France. On 10 August he began 'to sort out my manuscripts and pack them, in case developments should force me to leave suddenly for France'. On 15 August he left Guernsey for London, and two days later he arrived in Belgium, where he could easily cross the border into France if necessary. His diary-entries reveal a mood of sustained tension and excitement but comparatively little joy, in spite of the downfall of his old enemy (the 3 September entry is pitying rather than jubilant) and his enthusiastic reception in Paris.

425 *the decisive battle . . . the King of Prussia*: on 2 September 1870, the French army suffered a crushing defeat at Sedan. Napoleon III himself was taken prisoner and surrendered to Kaiser Wilhelm I of Prussia.

Laussedat, Buichot, Amouroux: Louis Laussedat (1809–79) and Charles Amouroux (1843–85) were exiled French politicians; Buichot may be the wealthy Belgian tobacconist of that name (who was certainly known to Hugo's family, but would not be expected in the present context).

Charles: Hugo's son.

ex.: the manuscript's *pros.* could be interpreted as an abbreviation for either *proscrit* ('exile') or *prostituée* ('prostitute'). In the absence of external information, it is obviously impossible to choose between these options; dogmatism would be foolish, but we have adopted the translation 'ex[ile]' because the immediate context shows that the aid was given during or after a 'meeting of the exiles'. (Compare the entry a few paragraphs later, 'Paid for one of the exiles to go to Paris', where the word *proscrits* is not abbreviated and the sense is consequently not in doubt.)

tricolour or red flag: the French Revolutionary flag, or the socialist flag.

Dear angel: Hugo's daughter Léopoldine.

Georges: Hugo's grandson, currently aged 24 months.

'Come': on 20 August, Hugo and his friends in Paris had arranged a simple code for use in telegrams. 'Don't bring the children' would mean 'Wait'; 'Bring the children' would mean 'Come'.

426 *Claretie ... Thiers*: in the precarious political situation, Hugo's son Victor (often known as 'François-Victor') was signing his telegrams cautiously; one of them even bore the signature 'François Foucher' (Foucher being his mother's maiden name). The radical politician Léon Gambetta (1838–82), a great admirer of Hugo, was instrumental in the proclamation of the Third Republic; Adolphe Thiers (1797–1877) was to be its first president, and Jules Favre (1809–80) its first vice-president. Jules Claretie (1840–1913) was a liberal journalist and historian; Antonin Proust (1832–1905) was a close political associate of Gambetta.

Barbieux: Charles Barbieux, the managing editor of the journal *Le Rappel*, which had been set up in 1869 to promulgate Hugo's views in Napoleon III's France.

Meurice: Paul Meurice (1820–1905), dramatist; he and his wife Palmyre (died 1874) were long-term friends of Hugo.

427 *the 'Chant du départ'*: famous French Revolutionary song, written 1794; music by Méhul, words by Marie-Joseph Chénier.

the Hôtel de Ville: the temporary seat of government in Paris.

the lines about little Georges that are in my garden: on 22 May 1870, Hugo had written in a letter to his son Charles and daughter-in-law Alice: 'On my own balcony I've put a bowl of breadcrumbs with a board on which I've written' the lines in question; 'so now the invitations have been sent out.' Thus the little stanza might well have been the most recent snippet of Hugolian verse to reach Paris. The abbreviations (*acq. . . . req. . . . Esq.*) have been supplied by the translators, in an attempt to suggest something of the playful tone of the original.

Victor: Hugo's son (François-)Victor, now appearing by his usual name.

Mariette: Hugo's maid, a trusted member of the household.

428 *Rey ... Schoelcher*: Alexandre Rey (born 1812), left-wing journalist and politician; Ledru-Rollin (Alexandre Auguste Ledru, 1807–74), lawyer

and politician; Victor Schoelcher (1804–93), republican politician whose outstanding achievement was perhaps the abolition of slavery in all French colonies (1848). All three members of the proposed triumvirate had been in exile since 1851.

A Prayer

Written 9 August 1872; the title is supplied by the present editors. Jean Massin has drawn particular attention to this passage. 'Is there any need to stress its value? It presents us with a rare glimpse of one of Hugo's private prayers—in an unedited transcript, as the repetition of "and on me" clearly shows' (Victor Hugo, *Œuvres complètes*, ed. Jean Massin (Paris, 1967–71), xv–xvi/2. 789). The repetition of the prayer for Adèle is equally significant. Few of Hugo's writings take us as far into his innermost self.

428 *two knockings*: in his diary Hugo always noted any strange nocturnal noises, sometimes deleting the passage later when their explanation became evident.

Fort Regent: a fort built in 1815, to the south-east of Saint Helier on Jersey. In Hugo's day it was garrisoned by English troops and was out of bounds to the general public, but there was nothing to stop prostitutes from plying their trade just outside.

'*Seventeen*': in English in the original. Hugo adds parenthetically the French translation *seize ans* ('sixteen years old'): even after twenty years in the Channel Islands, his knowledge of English remained fallible.

Adèle . . . Victor: Hugo specifically mentions his two surviving children Adèle (now permanently psychotic) and (François-)Victor, his two grandchildren Georges and Jeanne, and his great enemy Napoleon III. 'Her' is, of course, the ever-faithful Juliette Drouet.

The Vanished City

Written 14 August 1874; poem IV in the second series (1877) of *The Legend of the Ages*, and V in the September 1883 collected edition.

431 *before Adam:* many distinguished nineteenth-century palaeontologists theorized that fossil human bones were the remains of races who had lived and died before the time of Adam and Eve.

Orpheus

Written 3 February 1877; poem XVIII. i in the second series (1877) of *The Legend of the Ages*, and XXXVI. i in the September 1883 collected edition. Orpheus, in Greek mythology, was a poet and sage whose song had magical powers; a mystic cult grew up around his legend, and arcane poetic texts (the Orphic writings, which Hugo read in Leconte de Lisle's translation) were ascribed to him.

435 *Zeus . . . Zephyr*: names from Classical mythology, mainly suggesting the supernatural realm behind the visible world: Zeus, king of the gods; Nyx and Rhea, goddesses associated respectively with the primordial darkness

and the ancient Golden Age; Tanais, the river Don; the Giants, sons of Earth who rebelled against the gods (in *The Legend of the Ages* Hugo depicts their rebellion as an emblem of the constant struggle against tyranny and oppression); Uranus, god of the sky, the most ancient of the gods (and therefore the ultimate source of all creation); Pluto, god of the underworld and the dead; Poseidon, god of the sea ('blue-haired' derives from Leconte de Lisle); Boreas, the harsh north wind; Zephyr, the gentle west wind.

Eurydice: in Classical mythology, the wife of Orpheus; her death was the cause of his journey to the underworld.

On buds and standing grain: the imagery is drawn from Hosea 8: 7 ('it hath no standing grain; the bud shall yield no meal').

Never trace magic words upon the wall: the curious power of this final line depends on its mysteriousness, which therefore should not be dispelled by 'explanation'. Among other things, it draws on the age-old view that words contain a power beyond human comprehension (recalled in Hugo's famous 'Reply to a Bill of Indictment' and its 'Continuation', *Contemplations*, I. vi–vii), on the obscurity to modern eyes of ancient inscriptions (see e.g. the LAVBESP on page 403 above—one of a number of arcane or fragmentary texts contemplated at various points in *Les Misérables*), on the 'magic words' used in the Orphic cult and other mystic religions, and on the writing on the wall that foretold the death of Belshazzar (Daniel 6).

'I knew Firdausi in Mysore, long since . . .'

Written 12 January 1871; poem IX. iii in the June 1883 supplementary volume of *The Legend of the Ages*, and XXXVIII. iii in the September 1883 collected edition. One of André Breton's favourite Hugo poems.

437   *Firdausi*: Abdul Qasim Mansur (tenth–eleventh centuries CE), Persian epic poet; favoured at first by Sultan Mahmud of Ghazni, he was subsequently neglected and fled into exile. He is not elsewhere associated with the city of Mysore in India.

After the Caudine Forks

Written in the early 1870s; poem XXI. xii in the second series (1877) of *The Legend of the Ages*, and XLIX. xv in the September 1883 collected edition. At the Caudine Forks, in 231 BCE, the Samnites (an ancient Italian tribe) inflicted a crushing defeat on the Romans. Within *The Legend of the Ages*, Hugo placed this poem in the section concerned with the defeat of France in 1870.

437   *the Esquiline graves*: a burial site for common criminals in ancient Rome.

439   *Medusa*: in Classical mythology, one of the three Gorgons—female monsters with the power to turn onlookers to stone.

For Georges

Written 15 January 1876; poem IV. iv in *The Art of Being a Grandfather* (1877).

439 *Georges*: Hugo's grandson, aged 7 at the time when the poem was written.

Assyria . . . Timbuktu: exotic civilizations of ancient Mesopotamia and sixteenth-century West Africa respectively; fertile sources of fantasy and legend.

441 *amphisbaene*: a reptile (usually a mythical serpent with a head at each end).

Zophar: one of the unhelpful friends in the Hebrew book of Job. Job repeatedly compares his critics to animals (see e.g. Job 30: 1 and, in many translations, 30: 12)—though of course his speeches contain no exact equivalent for Hugo's 'amphisbaene'.

Corbière . . . Frayssinous: Jacques, Comte de Corbière (1767–1853), prominent right-wing politician of the 1820s; Denis-Luc Frayssinous (1765–1841), Roman Catholic preacher.

Quirinal . . . Pelion: the sixteenth-century royal palace at Rome is contrasted with the mountain in Thessaly (particularly associated with the legend of the Giants' rebellion against the gods of Olympus, frequently used by Hugo as a symbol of opposition to unjust tyranny).

The Immaculate Conception Revisited

Written 22 August 1875; poem XV. vii in *The Art of Being a Grandfather* (1877). The Immaculate Conception, in Roman Catholicism, is the doctrine that Mary, uniquely, inherited no original sin when she was conceived; it was officially proclaimed (after centuries of debate) by Pope Pius IX in 1854. Hugo, by contrast, regards all conceptions as immaculate and denies that sin is ever inherited (it is acquired after birth, though the roots may begin very early in childhood).

443 *Basilio*: the scheming and corrupt abbé in Beaumarchais's comedies *Le Barbier de Séville* (1775) and *Le Mariage de Figaro* (1784).

Jeanne: Hugo's granddaughter, aged 5 when the poem was written.

445 *Veuillot*: the journalist Louis Veuillot (1813–83), a fanatical supporter of the papacy.

The Fall: the sin of Adam and Eve, which caused them to be cast out of Eden; in orthodox Roman Catholic theology, all human beings are supposed to have inherited this sin.

Patouillet: Louis Patouillet (1699–1779), orthodox Jesuit writer, a severe critic of Jean-Jacques Rousseau and the Jansenists.

Trublet: Nicolas Trublet (1687–1770), a fashionable preacher and Academician satirized by Voltaire.

Jeanne Asleep, iv

Written 31 May, year unspecified (early 1870s); poem XVII in *The Art of Being a Grandfather* (1877). The last of four meditations on Hugo's sleeping granddaughter, which punctuate the *Grandfather* volume at irregular intervals.

Letter

Written 1874; poem II. iii in the 1888, 1897, and 1935 editions of *The Whole Lyre*.

447   *Champagne*: a flat, relatively arid region of north-eastern France.

449   *Horace . . . Fuscus*: Quintus Horatius Flaccus (died 8 BCE), Latin poet; Hugo is thinking particularly of *Epistles*, I. x (on the joys of simple country life), addressed to the scholar Aristius Fuscus.

      Bray-sur-Marne: Hugo's invention, modelled on the little town of Bray-sur-Seine in the Department of Seine-et-Marne (population in Hugo's day 1622).

      Javotte . . . Phyllis: the former was a popular nineteenth-century woman's name, especially in rural areas, and passed into common use as a term for a gossip or chatterer; the latter was the name of a country girl in Virgil (*Eclogues*, iii, v, vii, and x) and hence became a stock heroine's name in eighteenth-century pastoral convention.

451   *Mérimée*: Prosper Mérimée (1803–70), French short-story writer and staunch supporter of Napoleon III.

Waking Impressions

Written 14 September 1872; poem III. i in the 1888, 1897, and 1935 editions of *The Whole Lyre*.

Hail, Goddess, Hail from One about to Die

Written 12 July 1872; poem V. xix in the 1888 edition of *The Whole Lyre*, V. xxvi in the 1897 edition, and V. xxxiv in the 1935 Imprimerie nationale edition. This, the most famous of Hugo's few sonnets, was addressed to the novelist and poet Judith Gautier (1845–1917), the daughter of Hugo's friend and fellow poet Théophile Gautier. She had a dog who was trained to sit up at the words 'Victor Hugo' and go to sleep at the word 'Ponsard' (the name of the Classicizing poet whose play had been preferred to Hugo's *Les Burgraves* by 1843 audiences); this will sufficiently indicate the spirit of the family. The sonnet's title parodies the Roman gladiators' customary greeting to their emperor, 'Hail, Caesar, hail from those about to die', which Hugo had used in his 1824 'Song of the Circus' (page 3).

'Dante wrote two lines . . .'

Written early 1876; lines 1535–44 of *Religions and Religion* (1880), which mark the crucial shift from the sceptical 'Voices' of the poem's preceding sections to the resoundingly affirmative 'Conclusion'. This little parable had long been taking shape in Hugo's mind; its genesis has been studied in detail by Jean-Claude Frizaine, 'Quelques remarques sur le manuscrit de *Religions et religion*', in *Hugo de l'écrit au livre*, ed. Béatrice Didier and Jacques Neefs (Paris, 1987), 77–95.

The line numbers against the French text conform to those in Hugo, *Œuvres poétiques complètes*, ed. Francis Bouvet (Paris, 1961).

455 *Dante*: Dante Alighieri (1265–1321), Italian poet, author of the *Divine Comedy*.

The Rue Tiquetonne

Written late 1877; chapter IV. i, paragraphs 7–52 of *The History of a Crime* (1877–8). Hugo is recalling the events of 4 December 1851, when Louis-Napoléon's troops fired at random on bystanders in various Parisian streets. In the official casualty records the dead boy is identified only by his surname, Boursier.

456 *Bancel and Versigny*: the republican lawyers François-Désiré Bancel (1822–71) and Claude-Marie Versigny (1818–1910).

E.P.: Édouard Plouvier (1821–76), a former manual labourer who gained fame as a poet and librettist (for Offenbach and others).

in Châtiments: Hugo had already described the incident in 'The Night of the Fourth: A Recollection' (*Châtiments*, II. iii). The prose account, written almost a quarter of a century later, is less impassioned and more complex in tone. In the poem, the picture over the bed is not described (from the context, commentators usually assume it to be a religious scene; here it becomes simply a portrait of the child's mother. In the poem, the grandmother complains about 'Monsieur Bonaparte'; here she also abuses Hugo and his colleagues. The poem rises to a brilliantly sardonic climax in which the narrator 'defends' Louis-Napoléon's behaviour; the prose piece ends in darkness and silence. And the extraordinary many-sided gesture of solidarity in suffering, when the neighbour quietly wipes the blood from Hugo's lips, has no counterpart in the poem.

The Emperor of Brazil

Written 22 May 1877; the title is supplied by the present editors. Pedro II (1825–91), emperor of Brazil 1831–89, had intrigued Hugo for a long time; on 28 August 1846 the poet wrote in his diary: 'The current emperor of Brazil is a young man twenty-two years of age, kindly, sincere, and peaceful. He speaks French well. He also knows English, Italian, and German. He is very interested in astronomy. The tutor who taught him was a Frenchman.' The admiration was mutual. One of the main reasons for the emperor's visit to Europe was to meet Hugo, whose writings had been a major influence on his thinking.

458 *The Art of Being a Grandfather*: published ten days earlier. At the time, Hugo's grandchildren Georges and Jeanne were aged 7 and 6 respectively.

459 *and promised me his*: subsequent diary entries record the exchange of photographs and the dinner. Hugo addressed his photograph 'to the descendant of Marcus Aurelius' (the second-century philosopher-emperor of Rome). The Emperor of Brazil signed his 'Pedro d'Alcantara, 29 May 1877'.

The *Hernani* Dinner

Hugo's play *Hernani* (first staged in 1830) was revived by the Comédie-Française on 25 November 1877; the new production was an immense success. The author's speech at the 9 December 1877 commemorative dinner is characteristically masterful, particularly in its handling of his public image and his relationship with his listeners.

459 *[On 9 December ... performing the play]*: this opening paragraph is excerpted from the introductory material added by Hugo's associates Paul Meurice and Auguste Vacquerie when the speech was published.

460 *national theatre*: the Comédie-Française, France's leading theatre company (formed in 1680 by the union of Molière's former players with the Hôtel de Bourgogne troop), which had given the first performances of *Hernani* in 1830.

Bernhardt: Sarah Bernhardt (1844–1923) played the leading female role, Doña Sol, in the 1877 revival of *Hernani*.

Mars ... Favart: Doña Sol was played in the original production by Mademoiselle Mars (Anne Boutet, 1779–1847), and in early revivals by Marie Dorval (1798–1847) and Maria Favart (1833–1908).

461 *I am striving to shine bright*: Hugo adapts lines 36–7 of the 1676 poem 'Au Roi' ('Est-il vrai, grand Monarque ...') by the 70-year-old Pierre Corneille.

Homer ... Voltaire: Homer, supposed author of the Greek *Iliad* and *Odyssey* (eighth century BCE); the Greek dramatists Aeschylus, Sophocles, and Aristophanes (fifth century BCE); the Latin dramatist Plautus (died 184 BCE); the Latin poets Lucretius (first century BCE), Virgil (died 19 BCE), Horace (died 8 BCE), and Juvenal (first–second centuries CE); the Italian poet Dante Alighieri (1265–1321); the English dramatist William Shakespeare (1564–1616); and the French writers François Rabelais (died 1553), Molière (1622–73), Pierre Corneille (1606–84), and Voltaire (1694–1778).

Charlemagne ... Mirabeau: Charles the Great (died 814), emperor of the Franks, is the only monarch on Hugo's list. Nearly all the other 'great citizens' mentioned are soldiers: Roland (ninth century), hero of the *Chanson de Roland*; Bertrand du Guesclin (died 1380), who consolidated France during the reign of Charles V; Pierre, Seigneur de Bayard (died 1524), renowned for his chivalry; Henri, Vicomte de Turenne (1611–75), the victor at Nördlingen in 1645; Louis II, Prince de Condé (1621–86), who opposed Louis XIV during the Fronde and its aftermath; Claude, Comte de Villars (1653–1734), victorious at Denain in 1712 during the crucial last stages of the War of the Spanish Succession; Sébastien le Prestre de Vauban (1633–1707), victorious against the League of Augsburg; Lazare-Louis Hoche (1768–97), François Marceau (1769–96), and Jean-Baptiste Kléber (1753–1800), each of whom successfully opposed foreign and royalist forces during the Revolutionary wars.

Honoré-Gabriel, Comte de Mirabeau (1749–91), leader of the moderate party during the early stages of the French Revolution, marks the transition to a new social and political order.

'Suddenly the door opened . . .'

Probably written 1879–80; MS 92/160; published in *Poésie IV*, gen. ed. Jacques Seebacher and Guy Rosa (1986).

Last Wishes

Written 2 August 1883; published in May 1885 and collected in the post-humous edition of *Acts et paroles III: Depuis l'exil* (1889), where Hugo's literary executors prefaced it with this explanation: 'On the 2 August 1883 Victor Hugo handed over to Auguste Vacquerie, in an unsealed envelope, the following testamentary lines, which contained his last wishes for the period after his death.' The document is thus the final codicil to Hugo's will. The title has been supplied by the present editors from the executors' words.

Last Line

Reportedly uttered on 20 May 1885, during Hugo's final illness; published in Richard Lesclide, *Propos de table de Victor Hugo* (Paris, 1885), 344, and numerous other contemporary accounts. The title has been supplied by the present editors.

   The authenticity of the line has been much debated. Those who accept it point out that anyone who writes large quantities of verse will tend to generate verse automatically in states of reduced consciousness, such as sleep or delirium. Hugo himself had frequently done so; in his notebooks he had often jotted down some line or passage that had come to him while he was asleep. Other poets in the same culture experienced the same phenomenon (see e.g. Verlaine's 'Sites urbains'), as do present-day verse-writers (and even verse-translators). Moreover, the line reported by the deathbed witnesses is perfectly plausible Hugolian verse. It is exactly in his style. Its themes and images are ones that had preoccupied him all his life: in the preface to *Cromwell*, for instance, he had described sunset as 'a struggle between day and night, life and death' (p. 32).

   Those who deny the authenticity of the line observe that it derives solely from the testimony of witnesses; and if any alleged act or utterance by Hugo rests solely on such testimony, there must always be some doubt about its veracity. His career was a particularly fertile source of legend; both friends and foes often told highly coloured and implausible stories about him, and even the most punctilious biographer is rarely able to determine which of those stories are factual and which are not.

   Hugo himself would not have been greatly concerned. 'People have denied the Abbé Edgeworth's remark to Louis XVI; people have denied Cambronne's remark at Waterloo', he wrote in one of his diaries. 'Let history have its glorious lies; don't challenge them. The lies that history may tell are just as valuable as the truths that we create.' The disputed line may therefore still be 'valuable' if it comes from the indeterminate borderland between 'truths' and 'lies'. It marks the transition from the Hugo of history to the Hugo of legend; and it reminds us that we may not always be able to tell precisely where the former ends and the latter begins.